The dBASE Reports Book

Creating Reports and Labels in dBASE Plus

Ken Mayer

Second Edition

The dBASE Reports Book

Creating Reports and Labels in dBASE Plus

Second Edition

by Ken Mayer

ISBN: 978-0-9892875-8-6 (soft cover printed)
978-0-9892875-9-3 (electronic pdf file)

First Printing, 2007
Second Printing, 2016
Printed in the United States of America

Cover: Word Cloud created by using: http://www.tagxedo.com; layout done in Microsoft Publisher.

Table of Contents

About the Author

Ken Mayer has used dBASE both as a hobbyist and as a professional coder for many years, starting with dBASE III+ and working up to dBASE PLUS.

Ken worked for Borland, Intl. for two years as a Senior Quality Assurance Engineer on the Intrabuilder and dBASE products (Intrabuilder 1.0, Visual dBASE 7.0 and 7.01), and also worked for five years for dBASE Inc. as a Senior Quality Assurance Engineer, also working on dBASE (Visual dBASE 7.5, dB2K and dBASE PLUS, as well as dQuery). Ken was a contributing editor to dBASE Advisor magazine for the one and a half years or so it was in publication.

He served on Borland's TeamB (volunteer technical support) when Borland owned dBASE, and has helped many in the dBASE developer community. He was a member of the dBVIPS for dataBased Intelligence, Inc. (now dBASE, LLC), doing the same things he did with TeamB. He authored a good portion of the Knowledgebase articles that are available online for dBASE PLUS, and authored the original dBASE PLUS tutorial. Some of the material in this book will look suspiciously familiar to anyone who has used the Knowledgebase.

Ken has also been the librarian of a freeware library of code made available to all dBASE developers called the dBASE Users' Function Library Project (dUFLP) for so long he's lost count. He has been a speaker at Borland and other conferences on dBASE, speaking about coding techniques.

Ken is the author of The dBASE Book, The dBASE Reports Book and The dBASE Book Plus.

At the time the book is being published Ken is looking for full-time work – the school he was working at for 8 years shut down suddenly due to a variety of issues we don't need to get into here *(let's not open those wounds again)*.

When not working, Ken is very active in the Society for Creative Anachronism, Inc. (http://www.sca.org), and enjoys cooking, movies, games, and reading.

Ken lives in Walnut Creek, CA with his wife Carolyn Eaton.

(Photograph of the author is by Sandra Linehan, December, 2012)

Introduction

dBASE Plus has a fairly complex and robust Reporting Engine, and with that a Report Designer. Between the two of these tools, a developer can create a lot of really good looking reports and labels.

However, in order to get the data into a report, the developer needs to understand how the engine works, how the tools work, and try to find the best way of using their time. As many developers have found, the Report Designer can be a bit daunting and sometimes confusing tool to use.

This book is an attempt at helping a developer come up with some good habits when designing reports *(using custom reports and classes)*. More than The dBASE Book, this book is a tutorial – it is meant to be used as a tutorial, meaning that many of the exercises in later chapters rely on the reader having completed the exercises in earlier chapters. To that end, it behooves you to take the time to start at the beginning, even if some of the early exercises seem awfully basic, so that when you do get to material you would like to learn more about you won't get frustrated because you don't have some file or report to build on. Of course, the source code is downloadable so you can avoid some of that frustration that way.

Ultimately the goal is for the reader to be more comfortable with designing and creating reports that present the data in an application in a clear and meaningful way.

A Second Edition?

The last time I worked on The dBASE Reports Book was shortly after the first edition of The dBASE Book. I have decided to add some missing information and go back over it, updating the appearance, and any changes in the way reports work, as well as enhancing some of the information – adding some new techniques, etc. There are rumors that the developers may be looking at adding some more report abilities into dBASE Plus 11, but I cannot verify anything beyond that.

I had some complaints that the first edition of this book, being laid out more as a tutorial, is not as useful as a reference as The dBASE Book is. To that end I have expanded this edition with a chapter toward the beginning meant to provide that level of detail, noting all of the properties, events and methods of the various report objects all referenced in the index of the book.

I have gone over the errata (errors) from the first printing and corrected those as well. The formatting has changed a bit, but that's pretty minor as these things go. The index is better than the first edition. Word makes it much easier than WordPerfect combined with PageMaker did. This whole book is being created completely in Word.

I have also spent time on the wording in some places (hopefully making it more clear), breaking down larger paragraphs of text into smaller ones, and have added arrows on some of the screen captures to show a specific "thing" that is being discussed in the chapter at that point. If you are familiar with the first edition of this book, you will find this one more robust, with more screen shots, more code examples, and some interesting ideas to make your reports better.

Acknowledgments and Thanks

I would like to thank the people who have helped make this book possible. While I cannot thank by name every single person who may have contributed indirectly to the writing of this book, I would like to thank the following specifically.

The dBASE Community

Thanks to the dBASE community for the encouragement which helped me to decide that writing this book was a good idea. I cannot possibly name everyone who sent me "Please do this!" messages, either in private email or in the newsgroups, but my thanks to you all.

In addition, when I posted messages asking for ideas or specific information in the dBASE newsgroups many people came forward with their thoughts, advice, and assistance, sometimes providing code samples. Some of these folk are mentioned by name in the book, where I have referenced posts by them in the dBASE newsgroups, code I am using of theirs, etc. Again, thanks to you all.

Quite helpful were the attempts to explain Cross-Tab reports. Between the many messages I printed, and the looking I did on the internet, I found some good explanations that helped me understand this concept, and write a chapter that I hope will help *you* understand it.

Contributors

Unlike my previous book (The dBASE Book), I really had one major contributor to this one: Michael Nuwer, who gave me permission to use examples and materials, and even text describing how and why to do things from his dBASE Reports Tutorial available from his website. Michael's approach was very different from mine in the overall scheme of things, but his tutorial helped me find ways of explaining concepts, and his examples were often used as a starting point for my own. For the second edition, Mervyn Bick helped out with a few issues as well.

At dBASE, LLC

Michael Rozlig, CEO of dBASE, Inc. Michael has ensured I was part of the Beta team, meaning I had access to current versions of the software, and was able to stay on top of things.

Marty Kay, head of R&D has always been pretty straightforward, although quite politic, when dealing with issues. I worked with Marty when the company was dBASE, Inc., all those years ago. The interesting thing is that I have never met him. Suffice it to say that when I bring an issue to his attention he is usually very fast to turn things around, even it if it means telling me I forgot something or made a stupid error in my own code.

Kathy Kolosky, a woman of many talents. Again I have never met Kathy, but she's always tried her best to be helpful, whether in a Tech Support position, QA (my old job), or working on the Project Explorer and trying to provide as much help as she can. She has tried hard to provide assistance as I stumbled through aspects of this edition of the book.

My Wife

Last, but far from the least, I need to thank my wife of twenty-two years *(as of the time this version of the book becomes available)*, Carolyn Eaton, for being supportive of pretty much everything I do. When I wrote the 1st and 2nd Editions of the The dBASE Book, it was a tough time financially. However, she supported this effort despite the difficulties with nary a complaint. All the time I worked on the book I was also looking for work, and trying to pick up some paying contracts. Now she puts up with me muttering and mumbling while I work on the text, and sometimes cursing and swearing when a code example doesn't work.

And of course, I am now looking for full-time employment again and she's supporting me again *(sigh)*. She has always been supportive – how can you ask for more? There are simply not enough words to thank her ... except to say "I love you!"

Part I: The Basics

This first section of the book is the reference part – it goes into all the basics of reports, and then discusses (in the second chapter) the report objects in more detail, the properties, events and methods of those objects, and so on.

However, the term "The Basics" also includes the early part of the Tutorial. Starting with Chapter 3, which is all about setting up folders and files, and all that, and moving forward from there, if you follow along with the exercises in this book you will rapidly become an expert at creating reports in dBASE Plus.

Chapter 1: Report Basics

One of the primary reasons for a database application is to be able to generate useful reports from the data. This is an old axiom I learned years ago when I was first learning about databases. This chapter is lifted from The dBASE Book, and modified just enough to be useful in this book.

The Report Designer

When you are using the Report Designer, you will see a very busy screen, which can be a bit confusing at first – although if you've used the Form Designer you may be used to it, to an extent.

There are the palettes you've used in the Form Designer:

- The Inspector – used to inspect and change properties and events;
- The Component Palette – used to place specific controls onto your report;
- The Field Palette – one method of placing fields (columns from the rowset(s)) onto the report;
- The Format Toolbar – used to insert HTML formatting into your text controls.

By default these windows are "docked" to the sides of the dBASE *frame window* – I always detach them (click on the titlebar and drag them away from the frame), which allows me to move them around as needed.

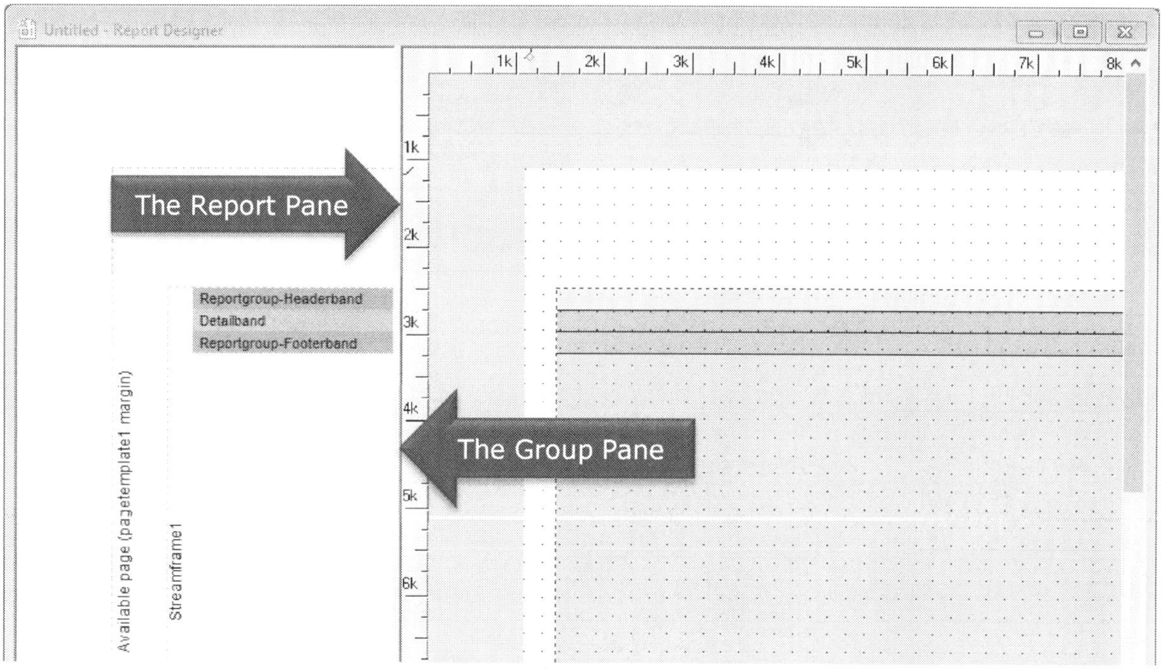

Figure 1-1

In addition, there is the report designer itself – this actually has two parts, although the default is to show just the report. These are called *panes* (it's a window) – the pane on the left is called the Group Pane and the pane on the right is the Report Pane. When you first open the Report Designer, there is a vertical bar on the left of the Report pane – if you drag this bar to the right, you will see the Group pane.

The Group Pane shows the hierarchy of objects in the report down to the bands (it does not show controls). The Report Pane shows the report appearance with the corresponding structures shown in the Group Pane – this uses live data. The Report Pane is where you will be working. The Group Pane has some use to show you what groups and bands you are working with, but it is not interactive and is not where you will do most of your work. I tend to leave this pane closed when working on reports, opening it only if I am confused with what part of a complex report I am working on.

Metrics

The default metrics for the report designer are *twips*. There are 1440 twips to the inch (a twip is a "twentieth of a point"; there are 72 *points* to the inch). This, for people used to thinking in inches, (or centimeters, or ...) can be a bit mind-boggling and trying to determine the width of a page, or how far from the left margin you wish to set an object can be difficult at best. However, like the Form Designer, you can change the metrics for your reports.

If you think in inches, then by all means, change the metrics for your reports to inches. Metric is found in the Inspector as a property of the "form" object – if you are designing a report, the *form* is the report – and if you click on *metric* in the Inspector, you will see a combobox with several options: Chars; Twips (default); Points; Inches; Centimeters; Millimeters; Pixels. Most people don't think too clearly in anything but Inches, Centimeters or perhaps Millimeters – so you may want to get used to setting the *metric* property as soon as you start designing a report (just as with the Form Designer and forms, you could use a custom report that set this and any other properties you commonly change from the defaults for you – we will discuss this in the next chapter). Throughout this book the examples use "inches" as the *metric* setting.

Report Designer Settings

The Report Designer has some basic settings that you should be familiar with. To see them, open the Report Designer by going to the Navigator window and double-clicking the icon "[New Report]".

Right click on the design surface (the white area – the *pageTemplate* – is usually safe). You will see a popup menu with some options, including the listing of the tool windows that are used with the Designer. They should all be checked – if not, you should check them.

Next go to the bottom of this menu and select "Report Designer Properties". You should see:

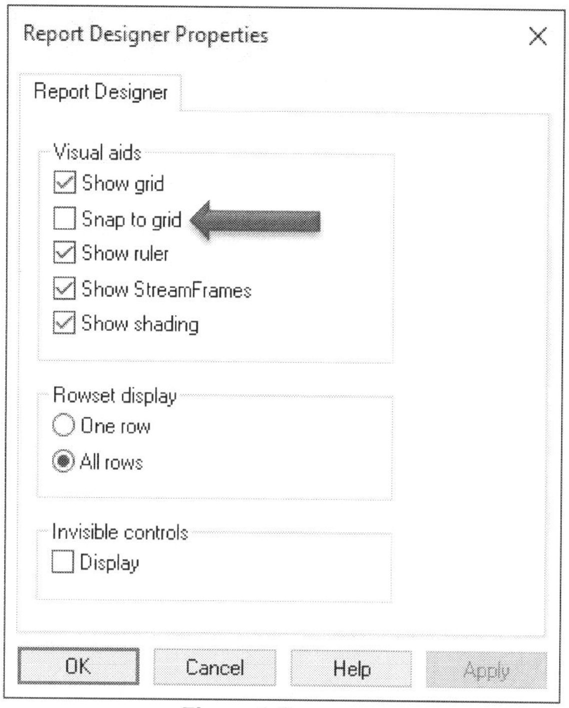

Figure 1-2

By default "Snap to grid" is checked – notice that in the dialog above (Figure 1-3), I have unchecked it. I find this setting makes me a little crazy as when I move controls around they jump around on the page "snapping to the grid", and sometimes other controls move when I didn't want them to. Unchecking this avoids that issue. For the most part all of the rest should be left as shown *(for now)*.

Creating a Simple Report

Setup

In a later chapter we will get into more setup for the tutorial aspects of this book, but it is a good idea to set a working area *just* for this book. I recommend using either the dBASE Navigator (click the folder button to the right of "Look in:") or Windows/File Explorer that you create a folder structure something like:

```
C:\dBASEReports
```

And then create a folder for each individual chapter – either now or as we go. Most chapters of this book will end up with code in them that you can then come back to and examine later. For example, you might want to create a Chapter 1 folder:

```
C:\dBASEReports\Chapter 1
```

In the dBASE Navigator, make sure that this is the current folder. This can be done by noting at the top of the Navigator window, that there is a "Look in:" area, with a drop-down list (or combobox – the "correct" term), and a folder button to the right. Click the folder button, find the correct folder, and "Select" it in the dialog. When you do this, the "Look in:" section will show the folder you are working in.

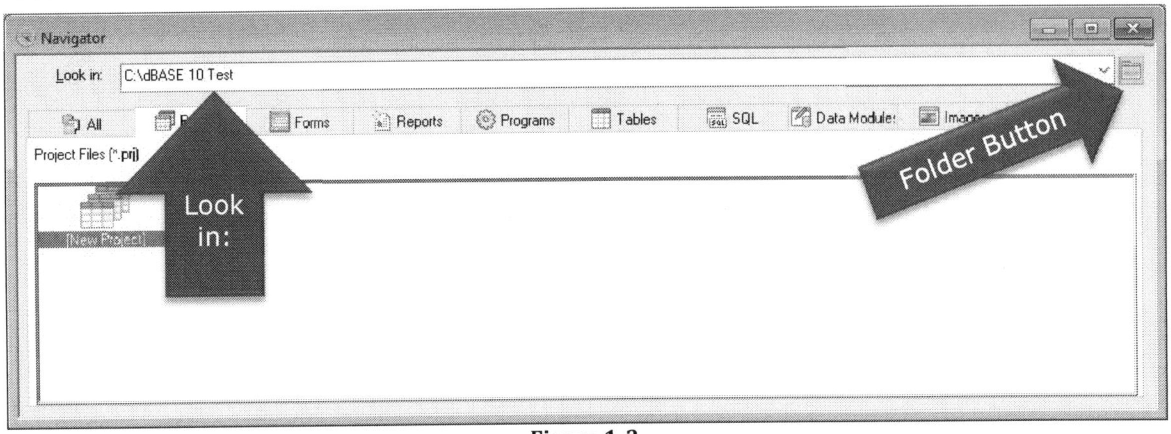

Figure 1-3

Figure 1-3 (above) shows the standard Navigator pane in dBASE.

Start a Report

Before we get into all the details of each report object *(in the next chapter)* – let's take a look at creating a simple report.

If you have not done so, start a new report in the Report Designer. There are several methods of starting a new report, most of the time in this book I will use the first:

1. Go to the "Reports" tab in the Navigator window, then double-click on the "[New Report]" icon
2. Go to the "Reports" tab in the Navigator window, then right click on the "[New Report]" icon, selecting "New Report"
3. Press Shift+F2
4. In the Command Window type:
   `create report`

The last one has an optional parameter "wizard" which would bring up the optional report wizard. This is a tool I never use and it is not discussed in this book. You will also find that by default dBASE by default will ask if you wish to use the report wizard, something you can turn off by using the menu in dBASE, selecting "Properties", then "Desktop Properties". On the dialog click the "Application" tab, and uncheck the items under "Prompt for Wizards".

The Report Designer should come up and look very much like Figure 1-4.

There are a couple of settings I suggest you look at right away that are specific to the report itself.

In the Inspector window (if it is not open, right click on the design surface and select "Inspector" or press the F11 key) find the report's *autoSort* property. We will discuss this in more detail later, but for the moment, make sure it is set to *false (this is the default setting and should automatically be set, but be sure)*.

The other is the report's *metric* property, which is discussed in depth earlier in this chapter. While you have the option to use pixels for the metrics (discussed in my other books for forms), I suggest using a metric your brain can wrap itself around, such as *(if you are an American)* inches. Select the appropriate metric, and we'll move on. Throughout this book, it is assumed the metric is "inches", but please use what works best for you.

A Quick Look at the Design Surface

When you look at the report design surface you will see that you have a white area – this represents the printable area of the page – inside your margins – this is called the *pageTemplate*. You will see the yellow area – this represents the *streamFrame*, which is where the details from your data will be displayed/printed. You will see a pink or coral colored section, this is the *detailBand*, which is where the detail for your report goes. By default, you will see also a light green section, which represents the *reportGroup.headerBand* and a light purple or purplish-blue colored band which represents the *reportGroup.footerBand*.

For this report, we will not be using these last two bands. Select the *reportGroup.headerBand*, look in the Inspector and you will see that it has a *height* (if your report's *metric* is set to inches) of 0.17. If you change that to zero (0), the band will disappear. Do the same for the *reportGroup.footerBand*. Note that I said "disappear" – these bands are still there, but at a height of zero you do not see them.

> **NOTE**
> The *reportGroup.headerBand* and *reportGroup.footerBand* default height may change in later versions of dBASE. R&D is examining options – this is a change that was made in dBASE PLUS release 2.5, to give a default *height* to all band objects on a report. While this can be useful, it has caused a lot of developers to have to modify their reports so that the *height* is zero for these and sometimes other bands. While the *height* property is still set in release 10.3, if nothing is on these bands, they will not render. This means you do not **have** to change the *height* property.

The Report Design main window should look something like:

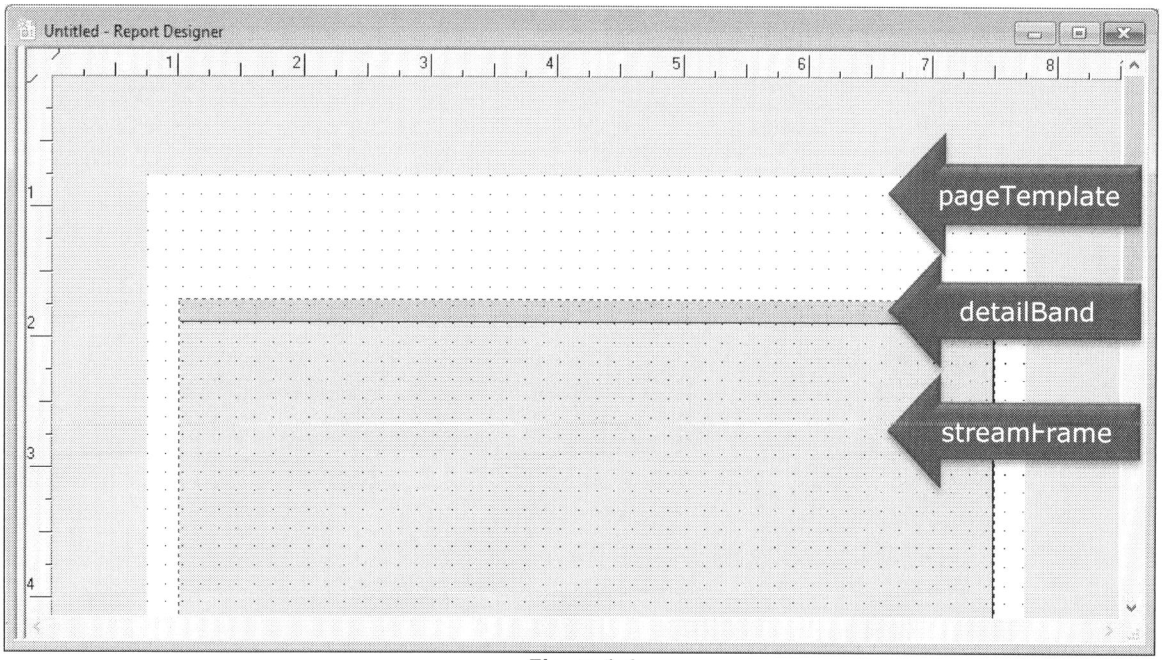

Figure 1-4

Report Headings

Before we get to placing controls on the *streamFrame* or *detailBand*, we should consider what we want to appear where. By definition, any control that is placed on the *pageTemplate* will appear on each page of the report. Therefore you should, as a general rule, never place fields from a table on the *pageTemplate*. This actually can confuse the report engine in dBASE and you may get some odd results.

However, you *can* place controls, text, images, etc., on the *pageTemplate*. This is a good place to put a report title, the date the report was printed, a page number if you want one, because any control on the *pageTemplate* will appear on all pages of the report.

Go to the Component Palette (if this window is not open, right click on the design surface, select "Component Palette") and on the "Standard" tab you will see the Text control. Drag this to the white area *(the pageTemplate)* at the top of the page. For some reason, when you drop a control onto the design surface, dBASE takes focus away from the control and moves it to the parent, so click on the text control if necessary.

> **NOTE**
> If your controls jump around as you move them, then it is likely the setting for reports "Snap to Grid" is turned on. Personally I find this setting really annoying, and typically turn it off. To do this, right-click on the Report Design surface, click on "Report Designer Properties", and uncheck the box for "Snap to Grid". This will save you a lot of frustration as you try to line up controls on your reports.
>
> This is, like many things, a personal preference issue – you may find you like this feature, in which case by all means, leave it turned on.

Widen the text control by dragging the right side (click on the small square or *handle* in the middle of the right border and drag it to the right) – make it a couple of inches (or something roughly equivalent) for the moment – it can be resized as needed.

Click on the text control so that you are in "edit" mode – you will see a blinking vertical line – the cursor), delete "Text1" and type "My Fish Report". Go to the Inspector and find the *fontSize* property, change the value to 14. Change the *name* property to "MainTitle".

You should save this report, do so by pressing Ctrl+S (or using the toolbar, etc.) and give it a name of "MyFishReport".

Move this control toward the very top of the *pageTemplate (this is the printable area of the report, so you can go to the edge – it's not the edge of the paper – we will discuss this in a later chapter).* It is a good idea to center the text. This is actually very easy – you make sure that the text control is selected, then choose the "Layout" menu, "Align" and "Center Horizontally in Window". This will center your text control within the margins of the *pageTemplate*. If you wish to be absolutely certain your text will be centered, you should also set the text control's *alignHorizontal* property to "1 - Center" – this will center the text inside the control's "frame".

It is useful to have a date on reports so you can reference the date it was printed. Place another text control on the *pageTemplate,* and change the control's *name* property to "DateText". Make this control an inch or two wide. Find the *text* property in the

Inspector and click on the "Type" button (the letter "T"). Select "Codeblock" from the combobox. Notice that the text changes to:

```
{||"Text1"}
```

Click on the tool button. This will bring up a dialog. Change the text:

```
"Text1"
```

to read:

```
"Date: "+date()
```

and click the "OK" button. This has told dBASE that each time this codeblock is seen, to re-evaluate it so that the date function is called, and the current date is displayed after the word "Date: " *(note there is a space inside the quotes after the colon)*.

Resize the text control a little, then center it on the page ("Layout" menu, etc. like we did with the title and again you may want to set the text control's *alignHorizontal* property to "1 - Center").

Adding a Page Number

When creating reports it is also a good idea to have a page number appear, because even if the report is only one page long *now*, at some point, it is likely to get larger. Having page numbers is often useful *(if the report is dropped, re-collating it will be difficult at best)*.

By default dBASE loads a custom text control that handles page numbering. I suggest that first you scroll down to the bottom of the page in the Report Designer, so that you can place this at the bottom, on the *pageTemplate*, under the *streamFrame* (not on it!).

If you move through the tabs of the Component Palette, you *should* see a tab that says "Paging". If you do not, you can get this to appear by going to the Command Window, then typing:

```
set procedure to :ReportControls:Report.cc
```

Clicking back on the Report Design surface and then on the Component Palette, you should now find the "Paging" tab.

This will have a single control, which will appear pretty obvious as the icon will be a number "1" with the name of the control next to it. Drag this to the bottom of the page.

When I did this in dBASE Plus 10.3, the *top* property was set too high and it appears off the bottom of the report. In the inspector, set the *top* property to something like 9.08 *(that would be inches)* and it will appear. You may need to adjust the height and width of the control as well, as this appears to be not very wide and too tall because the text is wrapping inside the control. Set the *alignHorizontal* property to "1 – Center" then tell the Report Designer to center it in the window as we did with the title text controls ("Layout" menu, etc.). You may want to move the control so the bottom of the frame is at the bottom of the *pageTemplate*.

> **BUG**
> The issue with the *width* of the pageNumber control is actually a bug in dBASE, possibly from when the base code for dBASE itself was converted to a more Windows-friendly codebase (dBASE Plus 8 and later). Custom controls seem to always be set to a specific width (despite any *width* property settings or *metric* settings) and always end up below and to the right of where you place them. This can be disconcerting. We will discuss it again when we get to using custom controls.

Index for Sample Table

For some reason the developers at dBASE removed the index tags from the sample table we are going to use *(they used to be in the dBASE Plus 2.62 and earlier versions, but in later versions the table was modified a little and the index tags are gone)*, so we need to create the index.

You can do the following with the Report Designer open. You may want to save your work first, though (Ctrl+S).

In the Navigator, click on "Tables", then select "DBASESAMPLES" as the database (from the combobox). Right click on the "Fish" table in the Navigator, select "Design Table".

In the table designer, change the index for "Name" to "Ascend", save and close the table (Ctrl+W).

Add a Table to the Report

We to put the table on the report so it knows what table to use. The simplest way to do this is to go to the Navigator, and click on the "Tables" tab. Select the "Look in:" combobox, and find the "DBASESAMPLES" database alias. Drag the "Fish" table from the Navigator window to the design surface.

You should see something *like (the icons will be on top of each other – I tend to move them off the pageTemplate and rearrange them to make it easier to see what I am working with)*:

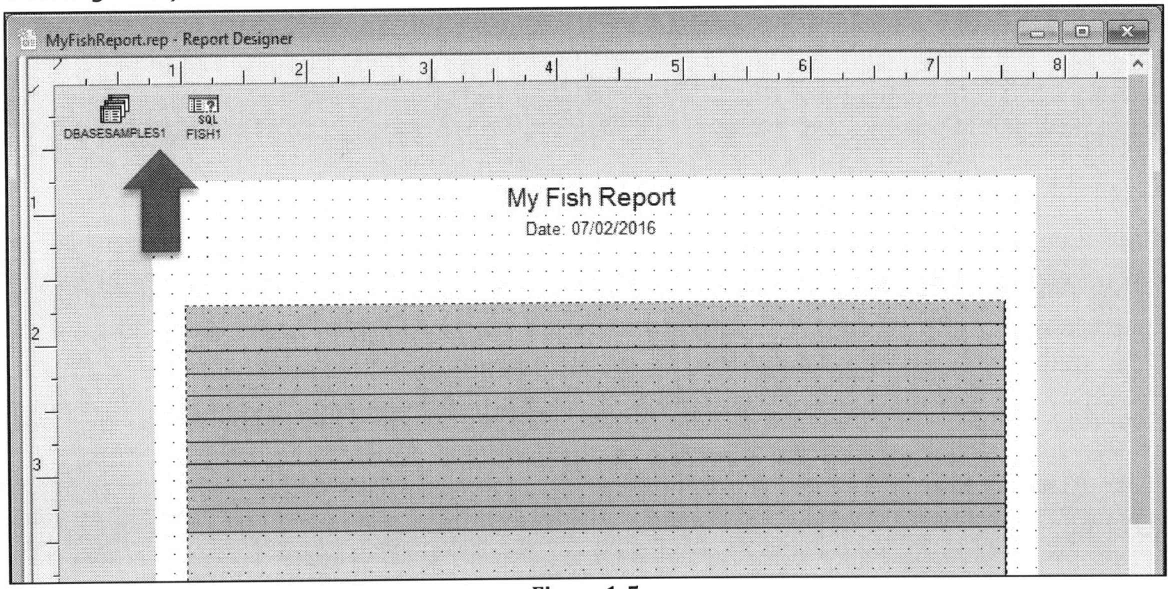

Figure 1-5

Notice that the Field Palette now shows the fields in the table. Also notice that there are individual "bands" – these are the individual *detailBands* – one for each record or row in the table. As we add text to the bands you will see that the text controls will reflect the data from the different rows.

If you know you have an index you want to use for a report, a good time to set it is after you have dragged the table to the report design surface.

Click on the icon for the query object ("FISH1") so that it has focus, then in the Inspector find the *rowset* property of the query object. Click on the Inspect button ("I") which will drill down to the rowset for this table. Find the *indexName* property, and in the combobox for this property, select "NAME". That is all that is necessary to display the data in the correct sequence *(you won't see a difference at this time)*.

Place Fields on the Report

The next thing that we need to do is to tell dBASE to place fields from the table on the report surface. These will go in the *detailBand* of the report. For the time being we are going to use the Field Palette to place fields on the design surface.

If the Field Palette is not displayed, right click over the main report, and then select it in the list. If you don't see it, you may want to move some windows around. If you look at the Field Palette, you should see a listing of the fields in your table. Click on the "Name" field and drag it to the first band on the report (the first pink band), see what happens.

By default, dBASE places a heading control above the field! In dBASE Plus 10.3, this shows for each row – we will look at changing that, because we really only need it at the top of the report. This can be useful, but it can also be a little disconcerting if you aren't expecting it.

> **NOTE**
> If you are not seeing this behavior, perhaps you (or someone) modified the default settings – they should be reset for this exercise. To change this, move the mouse over the Field Palette, right click. Select "Customize Tool Windows ...". In the dialog, click the tab for "Field Palette", and click the radiobutton for "Add field label", that says "Above field". Click "OK", click on the text you just added and press the "Del" key. Try the step given above.

We want to examine a couple of things here. The first is the title text that was placed on the report for you. Click on this, in the Inspector note that the *suppressIfBlank* property has been set to *true* (the default is *false*) and that there is code assigned to the event handler for the *canRender* event:

```
{||this.parent.firstOnFrame}
```

This is a way of telling dBASE that if the *detailBand* (or other band) is being rendered for the first time on the current *streamFrame*, to display this text. To evaluate this a step further, the *canRender* event is an event handler that must return a logical value of *true* or *false*. If there is an event handler associated with this event, which returns a value of *true*, then the control will be displayed. If the code returns a value of *false*, then the text control will not be displayed (or **rendered**).

The *suppressIfBlank* property tells dBASE that if the *text* property is blank, or if the control is not rendered, to not reserve room for it on the band. You can see this if you look at the other bands of the report – notice that the name field appears at the top of the band! That's because dBASE was told to "suppress" this if it's blank. No room is being reserved for it if there is nothing to print.

> **BUG**
> The Report Designer *sometimes* evaluates the *canRender* event handler, and sometimes does not. The screen captures here show that most of the time it does not. The headings should only appear once. When the report is rendered (when you "run" the report), the report code handles this fine. Sometimes when you close the report in and reopen it the designer, the designer will then recognize this code. However, trust that it will work properly when you actually render the report.

I suggest moving this so that the *top* and *left* properties are zero. You can do this either by moving the control yourself, or by going to the Inspector, finding these properties and set the values there.

Next, select the name text control in the first *detailBand*, set the *left* property to zero and adjust it so it is just below the title. If you are using "Inches" for your metric, set the *top* property to 0.21 inches.

You should see something close to:

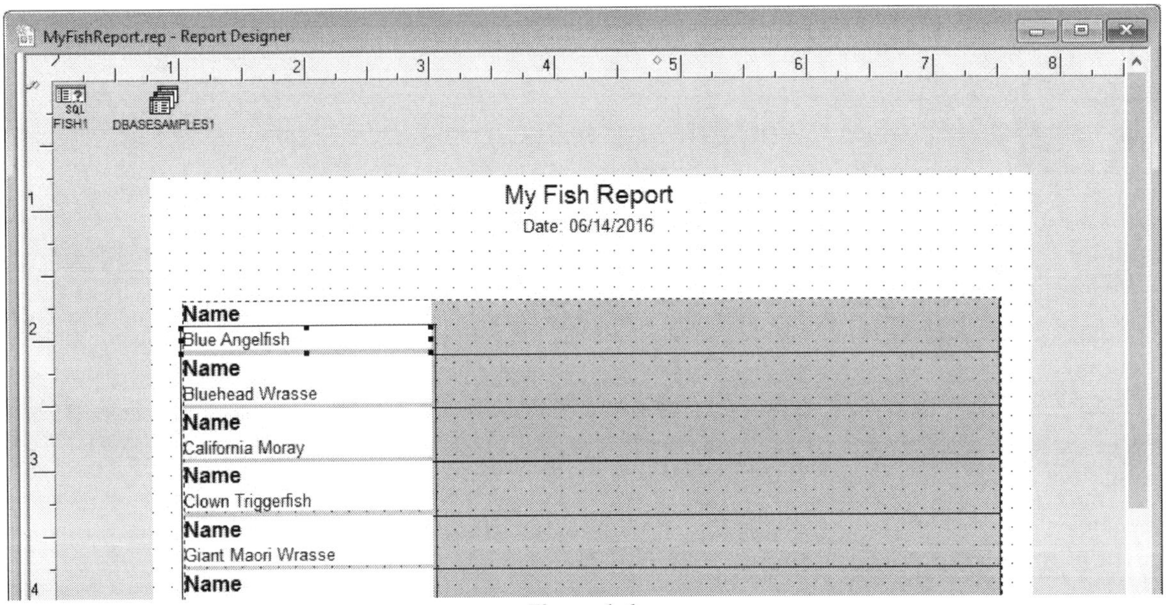

Figure 1-6

Repeat the process for the other two fields we are going to place on the report:

- Select "Species" from the Field Palette and drag it to the right of the Name field
- Select "Length CM" from the Field Palette and drag it to the right of the Species field

That pretty much uses all of the space on the report!

Next, line up the controls vertically and horizontally. You can do this using a combination of the Inspector (set the *top* and/or *left* properties of the controls) and the align toolbar at the top of the screen.

Note that these three fields take up a good portion of the detailBand. How would you add more fields? You can modify the *pageTemplate* margin properties, you can then widen the *streamFrame* so it fills the entire width of the *pageTemplate* and you can reduce the width of some of the columns you are displaying. If you change the *fontSize* property of individual text controls, you can reduce the widths further. Any combination of these will add more room for your report. All of these will be discussed in later chapters of this book.

However, for the moment, let's leave it as it is. This is just our first report and we're looking at the basics.

Save the report (Ctrl+S). At this point, you should have a report that looks something like:

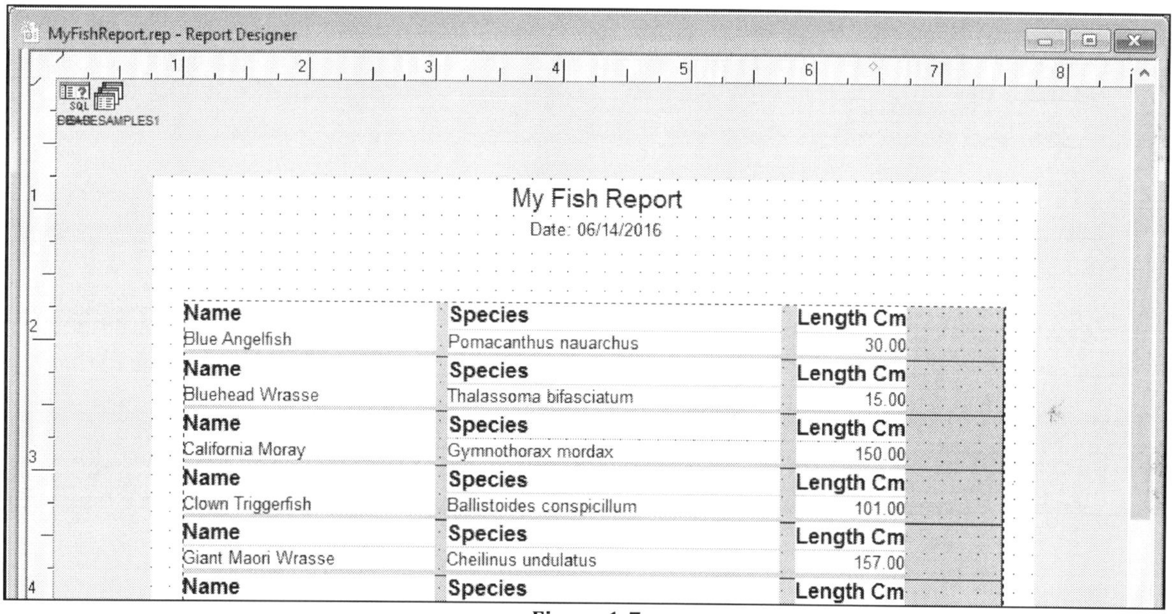

Figure 1-7

Of course, this is not really what it is going to look like once it is rendered. For example, the colors used on the design surface to show the bands and the *streamFrame* will not appear in the displayed or printed version of the report, and the *canRender* event for the headings will be respected.

To get an idea what this report will look like when printed, you can run it from here. Use the "Run Report" toolbutton in the toolbar (the one with the lightning bolt on it). You should see a preview window:

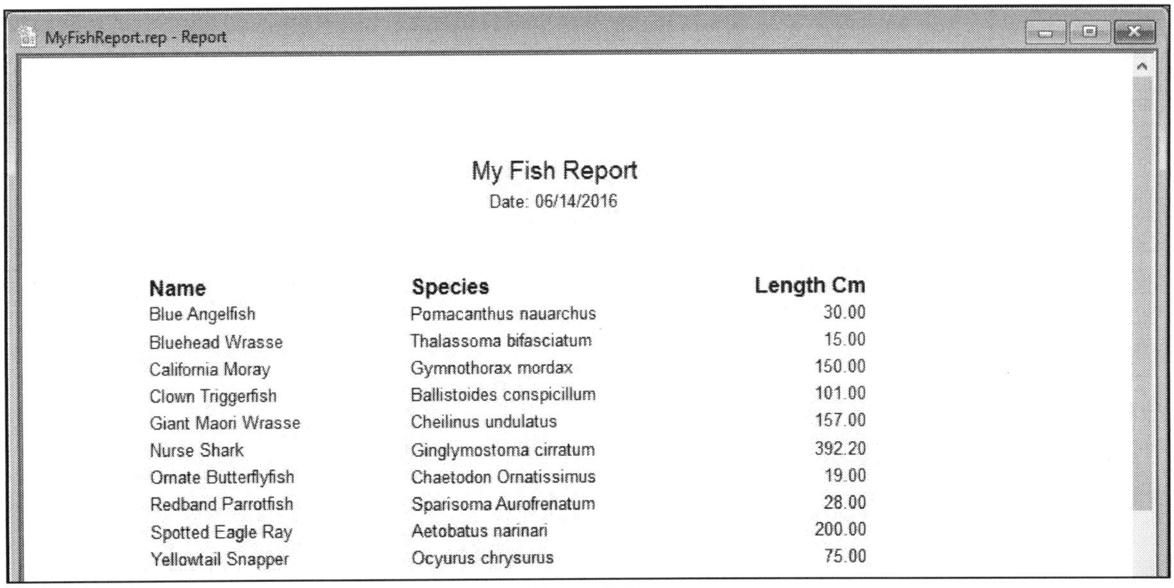

Name	Species	Length Cm
Blue Angelfish	Pomacanthus nauarchus	30.00
Bluehead Wrasse	Thalassoma bifasciatum	15.00
California Moray	Gymnothorax mordax	150.00
Clown Triggerfish	Ballistoides conspicillum	101.00
Giant Maori Wrasse	Cheilinus undulatus	157.00
Nurse Shark	Ginglymostoma cirratum	392.20
Ornate Butterflyfish	Chaetodon Ornatissimus	19.00
Redband Parrotfish	Sparisoma Aurofrenatum	28.00
Spotted Eagle Ray	Aetobatus narinari	200.00
Yellowtail Snapper	Ocyurus chrysurus	75.00

Figure 1-8

The default setting for dBASE is to output a report to a preview window, which is useful as you will not waste a lot of paper while working on a report.

Close the preview window once you are done examining your work.

Printing the Report

Once you have your report as you want it, the question then becomes "How do I print it?" As noted above, the default for a report is to output to a preview window. There are multiple ways to print a report, and we will revisit this in a later chapter. The big trick is the report's *output* property.

Find this report in the Navigator, right-click on it, and open it in the Report Designer. Find the Inspector window, and the *output* property. Notice that it is set to "3 – Default". If you click the down arrow for the combobox, you will see several options. Select "1 – Printer". If you were to save the report right now, the next time you run it, it will print to the *default* printer in Windows. This may not be optimal, however. I suggest leaving the *output* property as "3 – Default" – change it back.

Only do the following if you actually wish to print the report!

From the Command Window (you can do the same from a program) you can do more and have better control – you could do something like the following:

```
set procedure to MyFishReport.rep
r = new MyFishReportReport()
r.output := 1
r.printer.choosePrinter()
r.render()
```

Note that this opens the report as a procedure file, assigns a memory variable to an instance of the report, sets the *output* property to "1 – Printer", then allows you to choose the printer to send the report to – we will discuss this option later – and finally renders the report by calling the report's *render()* method.

The Report Wizard

I want to briefly discuss the Report Wizard. This is a tool that ships with dBASE to help create reports. However, it is fairly limited in scope.

By default dBASE assumes that you may want to be asked about using the Wizards when you develop applications. You can turn this on or off, I personally recommend turning it off. This is done by going to the "Properties" menu in dBASE, select "Desktop Properties". You should see:

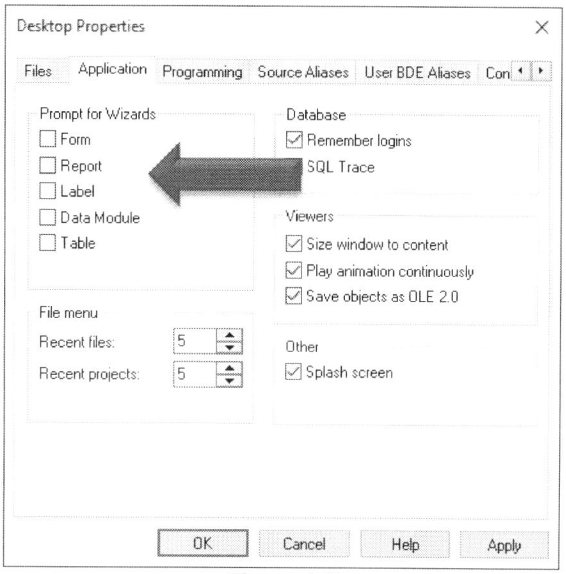

Figure 1-9

If these options are checked, when you start creating a new report (or form, etc.), you will be asked about using the Wizard. By unchecking them the question is never asked.

You can still *use* the Wizard, if you wish to. Type the following in the Command Window:

```
create report wizard
```

When you type this, you will see the first of seven screens:

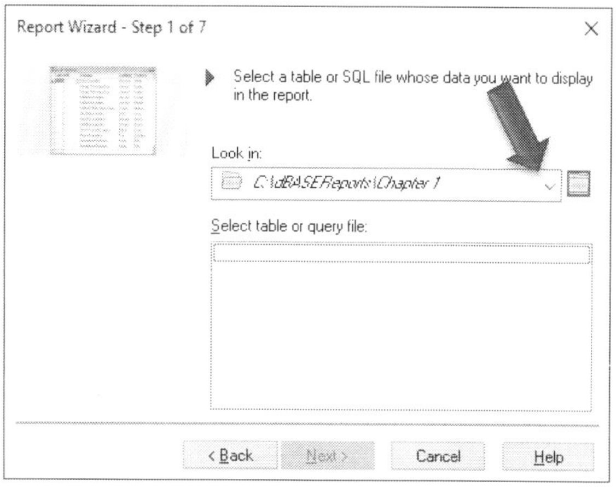

Figure 1-10

Use the down arrow of the combobox "Look in:", and select "DBASESAMPLES". The "Select table or query file:" list will be populated. Click on the "Fish" table, and then "Next >".

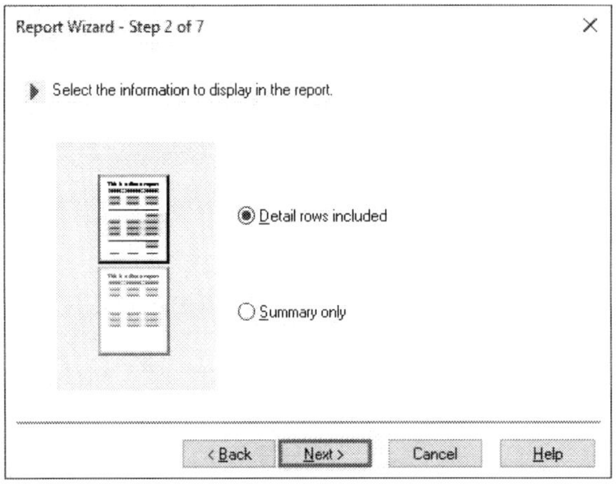

Figure 1-11

Leave the default here as "Detail rows included", and click "Next >".

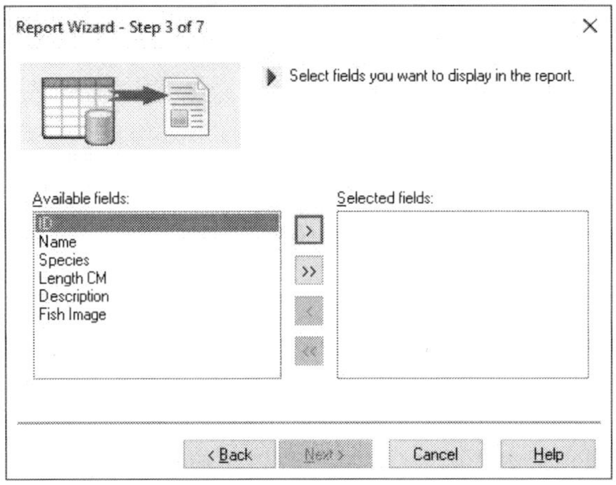

Figure 1-12

Select the Name, Species, Length CM, and Description fields, by clicking on them, and clicking the ">" button. This will move them to the "Selected fields:" box on the right. This should look like Figure 1-13:

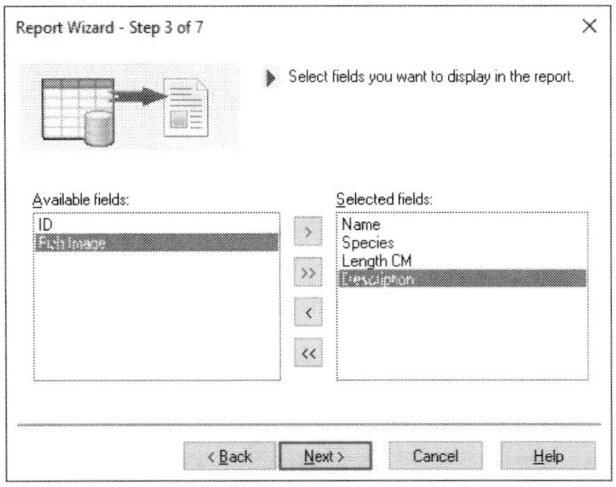

Figure 1-13

Once you have this, click "Next >".

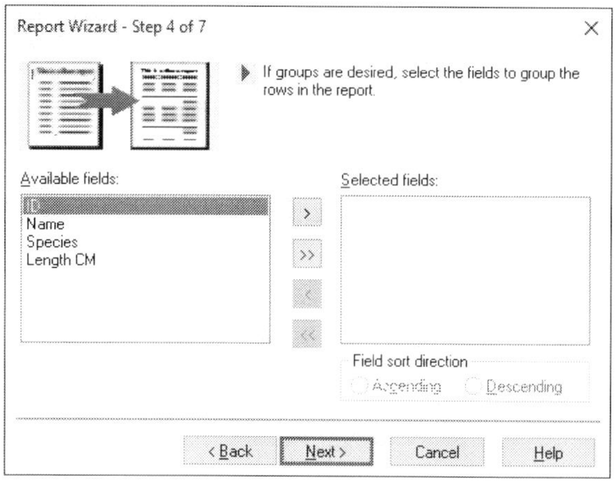

Figure 1-14

We're not going to work with groups, so click "Next >", and you should see:

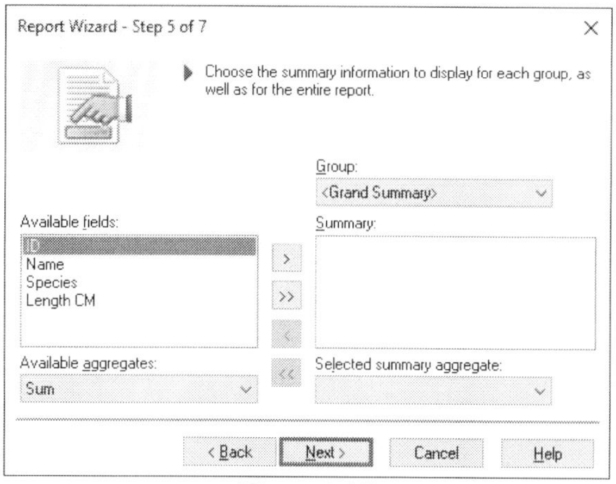

Figure 1-15

Again, we're not going to worry about summaries, so click "Next >".

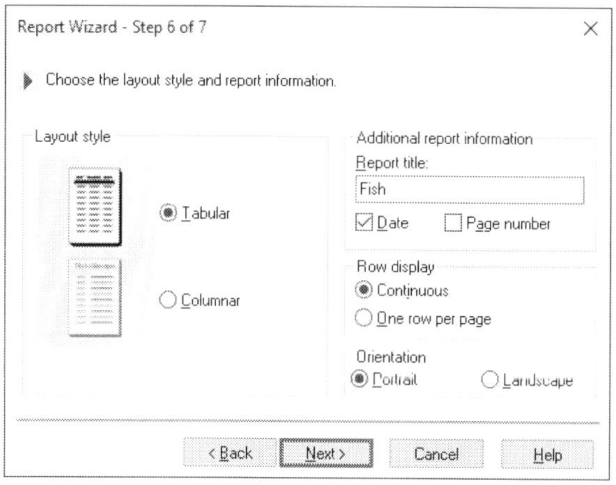

Figure 1-16

We're going to use all the default settings for this report, so click "Next >". You will see the final screen of the Wizard:

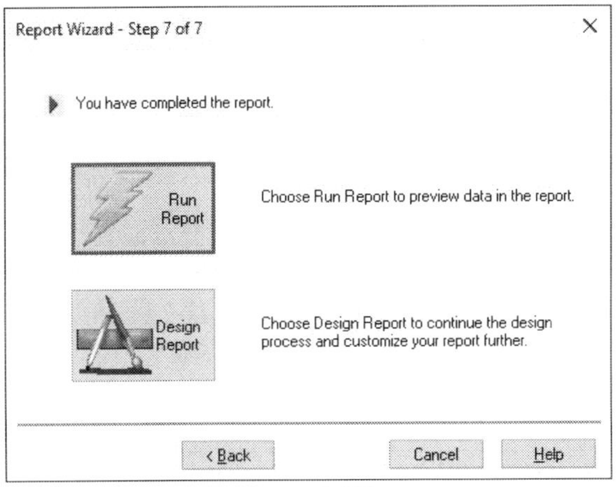

Figure 1-17

Click "Run Report". When asked for the filename, enter "MyFishReport2", and click "Save". You should now see:

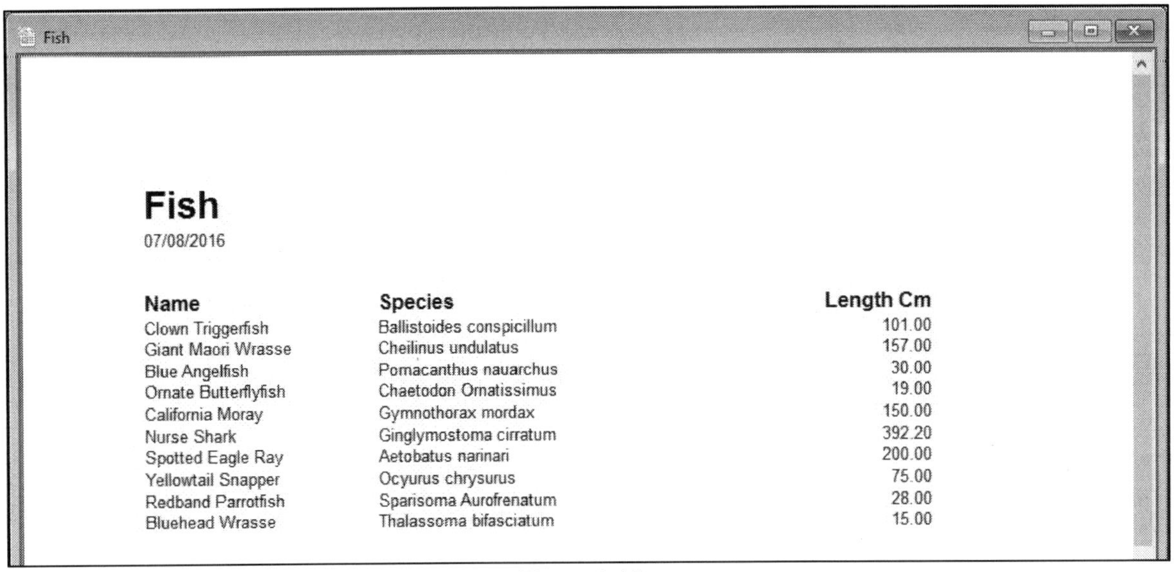

Figure 1-18

Interestingly the Description field does not appear to be output to this report at all, despite clearly having selected it. What has happened, really, is that it is off the *pageTemplate* to the right of the report. If you were to open this in the Report Designer, you can find the control "description1" in the Inspector – you will see that it's there, but in a location that doesn't allow you to see it. It won't print, and in the default viewer you cannot scroll to the right to see the field.

As you can see, this report is not all that interesting, but it could be a starting point if you really needed one. You could open this in the Report Designer and work on it, and move the Description field to a more useful location, and so on.

Notice that there was no option to use an index (allowing you to sort the data), or anything of that sort. The Wizard is pretty limited in its capabilities, which is why this book exists, and why from now on we will ignore the Report Wizard.

Cleanup

For every chapter of this book that has "follow-along" instructions, there will a "Cleanup" section at the end, to ensure that you don't cause yourself some frustration if you take a break from the book and go work on your own applications.

You should close the database that was used this chapter.

This is done simply by typing in the Command Window:

```
close databases
```

(And press the Enter key after.)

Source Code

The following is a listing of the sample code in the folders we have been working with. If you downloaded the files from my website the structure will be different (see below). You may use the code contained in these folders for your own applications if you desire, with the caveat that credit be given appropriately.

From working on this chapter:

```
C:\dBASEReports\Chapter 1\MyFishReport.rep
C:\dBASEReports\Chapter 1\MyFishReport2.rep
```

Downloaded version – same files but with this path:

```
C:\ReportsBookSourceCode\Chapter01\filename
```

Summary

This chapter was aimed at getting you started working with the Report Designer.

As you can see, the Report Designer in dBASE is a powerful tool and you can do a lot with it. This is good, because as you work more and more with application development, you will find that being able to do a *lot* with the report tool will be handy.

The next chapter is going to be all reference material – discussion in detail of the various report objects and how they relate to each other.

Chapter 2: Report Objects

In the first chapter we did a high-level look at the various objects that are used with a report. In this chapter we are going to go into depth, discussing the objects and their properties, events and methods.

Before we jump in – I want to make sure this is clear, and we'll discuss it in later chapters: Reports and Labels are the *same thing* as far as dBASE is concerned. The only difference is the size of some of the objects on the report and how they're streamed out, but that is really it. The source code for a report and a label file will look very similar. All of the same objects and properties, etc. are available in both.

It should be noted that this chapter is not a "tutorial" chapter – in that there is no "follow-along" aspect to it. It is meant to be a reference chapter, with a vast amount of detail about the report objects themselves.

An Overview

Before we get into the mechanics and details of the Report Designer and building reports, let's take a look at things from a "lower level".

The report engine in dBASE is what is called a "banded report" engine, in that the processing of your data occurs through "bands". The bands are processed (when the report is rendered) in a specific sequence, as are the other controls of the report.

It should be noted that the dBASE Report Engine is specifically designed to work with dBASE's OODML *(Object-Oriented Database Manipulation Language)*, and **will not** work with the older XDML *(XBase Database Manipulation Language)* that many coders are more comfortable with.

In addition the report engine is what is called a "Single-Pass" engine – this means that in order to process the report it makes *one pass* through all objects (and in the process, through the rowset/data), rather than making multiple passes through the data and controls *(which is what would be needed to, say, generate a "Page 1 of x" type output – this can be done, but is more complex than what is covered here ...)*. Very few report engines do a "multiple pass" automatically, as the amount of processing involved is horrendous and time consuming!

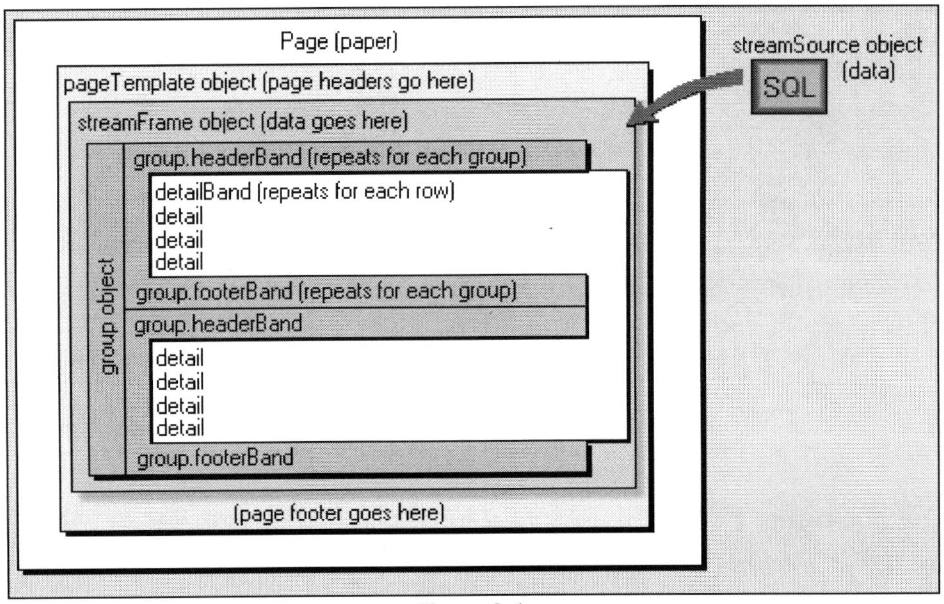

Figure 2-1
(Image by Gary White, used with his permission)

This image (Figure 2-1) was created for the Knowledgebase for dBASE at my request, to show the layout of the objects for a report. It leaves out the report *headerBand* and report *footerBand*, which we will examine as well.

The Bands

There are three primary "bands" in a report – the *detailBand*, and attached to a *group* there are the *headerBand* and the *footerBand*.

The *detailBand* is where the details of your report will go. For a simple report, this is where all of the data from each row of a table is actually *rendered* (generated or printed). Your details are shown by placing what I call *"Visible Controls"* (Text, Image, etc.) onto the *detailBand*.

The *group* object is designed to help you group your data in a way that makes sense. A very simple example is perhaps with a customer table – you might want all the customers in each state grouped together. The *group* is how you do that. At the beginning of each group, you might want to note which state is being currently displayed – this would be done with the group's *headerBand*. If you wanted to display a count of all the detail records that were displayed for that state, you would most likely do that in the group's *footerBand*. *(If you need to do a parent/child table report, the group's headerBand and/or footerBand would normally be used to display data from the parent table's rows, and the detailBand would be used to display the child table's rows.)* In order to show the fields, you would also use "Visible Controls".

The report engine will automatically handle a lot of the processing for you – if you have only a *detailBand* in the report, it will loop through your table and generate one *detailBand* for each row or record in the table. The report is done rendering when the last row is processed.

If you have a *group* or groups on the report, the report engine will examine each row in the *detailBand* and determine if it belongs in the current group, or if it belongs the next group. It handles the necessary processing to perform the group "break".

Stepping Up a Level – *streamFrame* and *streamSource*

In order to accomplish the above, the *detailBand* and group's *headerBand* and *footerBands* must be controlled in some fashion. There are two objects involved here – the first is the visible one – this is called a *streamFrame*. The *streamFrame* appears as a container on the report, and is used to control the layout of the report. Your *detailBand* and other bands are placed on a *streamFrame* (which is placed on a *pageTemplate* – see below).

However, more importantly, in the background there is a *streamSource* object which is linked to your table(s). The *streamSource* is what actually controls the output – this is what looks at the data, loops through it row by row, and tells the report engine what to print.

Stepping Up Yet Another Level - *pageTemplate*

When we step back a bit and look at the larger picture, there is the *pageTemplate* – which is used to lay out the report's page design.

By this I mean that you can set your report's margins, you can determine what you wish to print on each page of the report *(commonly called headers and footers, although there are no such objects directly in this engine -- this is done using the "Visual Controls")*, and so on.

The *pageTemplate* is exactly what it sounds like – it is a template. When we get to examining the properties of the *pageTemplate* later in this chapter, we will see more.

The *pageTemplate* is also the object that visually holds (or contains) the *streamFrame*, which in turn visually holds (or contains) the *detailBand* and group header and *footerBands*.

Up to the Top Level - *report*

Finally, stepping all the way back and looking at the big picture, we have the *report* object itself. This object is what is used to control things like where the report is being sent to, what pages of the report to print through the printer object (attached to the report object), whether the report is portrait or landscape, and all of that.

How The Report is Rendered (Generated)

Without getting into *all* of the details, the following is an explanation of how a report is rendered. The term "rendered" is really just another term for "generated", but I am using it here because the method of the report object that actually does the generation is called *render*.

A report gets rendered (or generated) by calling the report's *render* method. The sequence of this generation is along these lines:

- The report's *firstPageTemplate* property is looked at to determine which *pageTemplate* (if there are multiple) is the first to be rendered (or generated).
- In the process of rendering the *pageTemplate*, all controls that are defined for that *pageTemplate* are rendered, in the order they are defined in the source code (this is also called the z-order). The important thing to note in this process is that it doesn't matter what order these controls appear on the report surface, but the order in which these controls appear in the source code.

- The *streamSource* is controlled by the data – your query (or queries), or more specifically, the rowset generated by the query (or queries). Most reports have only one *streamSource*, and the rowset for that *streamSource* controls the report.
- The *streamSource* controls how a *streamFrame* is rendered and for every row in the rowset referred to by the *streamSource* a *detailBand* is rendered inside the *streamFrame*. As with the *pageTemplate*, the z-order controls the order in which controls on the *detailBand* are processed. This is an important concept and can really change the appearance of a report.
- When a *streamFrame* is filled up, if there are still more rows to be rendered they will be rendered in other *streamFrames* on the same *pageTemplate* – if any exist. *(What this means is that you can have multiple streamFrames on a page – which is how labels are generated, as well as columnar reports – this topic will be discussed in much more detail in later chapters.)*
- If the current *streamFrame* is the last one on the *pageTemplate* (or the only one) and there are still more rows in the rowset to be rendered, then the *pageTemplate* looks at its *nextPageTemplate* property to determine where to go next. At that point a new *pageTemplate* gets scheduled, and the report's *onPage* event fires.
- The report will continue rendering until all rows in the rowset have been rendered.

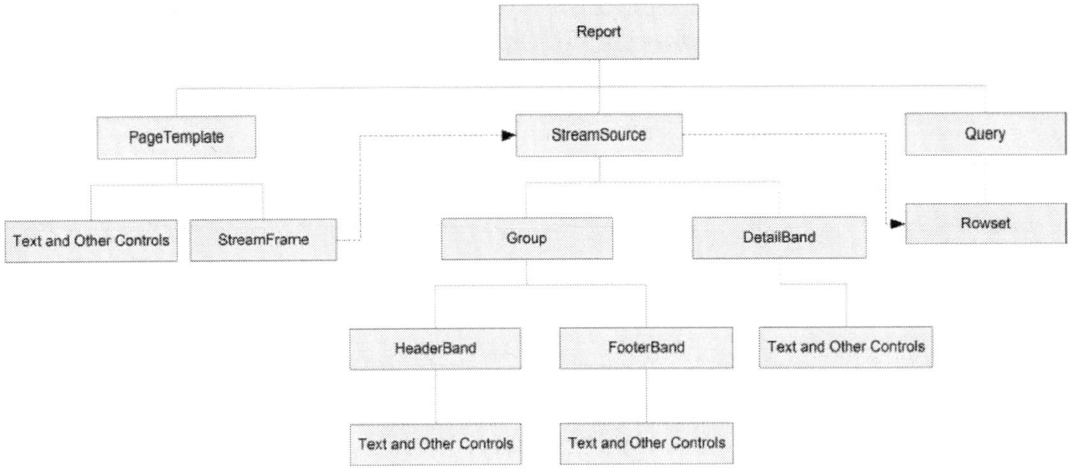

Figure 2-2
Based on a chart by Charles Overbeck

The Report Objects

This section of the chapter will cover each of the report objects, discussing their relationship a bit with the other objects, and will go over the main properties, events and methods of each.

Note that we are going in pretty much the opposite sequence from the first section of this chapter – we are starting at the outside and working our way down to the fine details.

The report Object

As you might expect, the first object you need to be aware of is the report object itself. The report object is the "big container" for everything. It is very similar to the form object in that sense, but it has different properties, events and methods.

While from one aspect the report object contains the "whole report", when you start looking at how everything works, it really only can contain six types of objects (some of these will be discussed in great detail later):

1. The *printer* object
2. An *elements array*
3. A *reportGroup* object
4. The *streamSource* (there *can* be multiple streamSources) – these will be discussed in detail as a separate object.
5. The *pageTemplate* (there can be multiple pageTemplates) – these will be discussed in detail as a separate object.
6. The database objects (Query, Datamodule ...)

Any other controls on a report are contained by the *pageTemplate*, *streamSource*, and other objects.

The following *report* properties, events and methods are ones you should be aware of:

The *autoSort* property is designed to automatically set the appropriate sort sequence (ORDER BY) in the SQL of the controlling rowset for the report. The problem is, it does this without asking you, and may override a sequence you need. The default setting for this is *false*, as the developers were requested to change it at dBASE some years ago.

The *baseClassName* property is always "REPORT", for the report object. This is very important when creating reports, as the *className* may be something else, but the *baseClassName* is always "report". Every object in dBASE has a *baseClassName*.

The *className* property is the name of the report class. When you create a report and name it, dBASE streams out a statement that gives a name to the report, this is what the *className* property reflects. Every object in dBASE has a *className*.

The *elements* property is an object reference to an array that contains all of the elements on the report object.

The *endPage* property defaults to negative one (-1) which means that there is no "end page". The point of this and the *startPage* property (below) is to allow you to print only the pages you want to print. If the value is -1, it means print everything, if it is any other value, the report engine, when rendering the report, will check the current page number (*reportPage*) and if the *reportPage* property and the *endPage* property are equal, stop printing when the current page is complete.

The *firstPageTemplate* property is normally set automatically for you if you are using the designer. This property tells the report engine which *pageTemplate* is the one to start with when rendering the report. This will be covered in more detail when we get to the *pageTemplate* object.

The *inDesign* property is a logical property that can be tested to see if you are in the designer, or running the report. This might be useful when designing custom classes.

The *mdi* property is a logical property used to determine if the preview window is an MDI or non-MDI form when running the report (DO reportname.rep or double-clicking the report in the Navigator, etc.).

The *metric* property is the "metrics" used when designing a report. The big problem is that the metrics default to twips. A twip is a "Twentieth of a point". A point is a very small value (there are 72 *points* to the inch), and a twip is even smaller (there are 1440 *twips* to the inch). The human brain doesn't normally think that way *(although there are some developers that prefer using twips)*. There are a variety of options for metrics, I suggest you use Inches, Millimeters or Centimeters. It will make it easier to determine how big things are.

Metric	***Description***
0	Chars
1	Twips *(default)*
2	Points
3	Inches
4	Centimeters
5	Millimeters
6	Pixels

There may be situations where using the metric setting of "chars" is useful – specifically when using monospaced fonts. This can allow you some very precise alignment of your text controls.

The *output* property determines where your report is going to go. The default is to a window *(reportViewer)*. You can output to a file, but the output is *not* ASCII (or ANSI) as you might expect, but rather is a printer file – it contains all the formatting codes necessary to generate the report *for the printer defined in the printer driver*. There is no option to output directly to a text file, unless you set up the "Generic/Text" driver that comes with Windows, and output your report to that driver *(this will be discussed in a later chapter)*. You can output to an HTML file, which is a really spiffy ability. You can, of course, output to a printer. Note that option 5 is *only* useful for web applications which are not discussed in this book.

Output	***Location***
0	Window
1	Printer
2	PrinterFile
3	Default *(default)*
4	HTMLFile
5	CGI response

The *outputFilename* property is necessary if you are outputting to a file *(set the* output *property to 2 or 4)* – otherwise any value you set is ignored.

The *printer* property is a pointer to the printer object, which will be discussed shortly.

The *reportGroup* property is another object pointer – to the report's group. This will be discussed after the *printer* object below.

The *reportPage* property is the current page of the report as it is being displayed, or rendered. This is a read-only property – you cannot change it. You can, however, query it *(obtain the value)*.

The *reportViewer* property is the name of the *reportViewer* object that is being used to view this report. This is a way to reference the *reportViewer* object from the report and check/modify properties. Note that this property itself is read-only.

The *scaleFontBold* property determines whether the font used for the character *metric* is boldfaced or not. *(See online help for more details.)*

The *scaleFontName* property is the base font used for the character *metric*. *(See online help for more details.)*

The *scaleFontSize* property is the size of the base font used for the character *metric*. *(See online help for more details.)*

The *startPage* property can be used to set a different starting page for the report than page 1. The default value for this is 1.

The *title* property displays a report title at the top of the preview window. This has the added use for generating output to software such as PDF995 – the value of the *title* property will be used as the name of the PDF file generated.

The *usePrintingDialog* property determines if, when the report is rendered, the default dBASE printing dialog appears *(showing the page count as it is sent to the printer)*. This property is logical, and defaults to *true*. This is new to dBASE Plus in one of the more recent versions – if you do not see it in the Inspector, you can't work with it.

The *beforeRelease* event fires if a call is made to the *release* method of the report. It allows you to perform any cleanup you might wish, before the report is released from memory.

The *onDesignOpen* event fires when the report is opened in the designer. The purpose is to allow you to perform some tasks that will only occur in the designer (perhaps filling some text controls with "dummy" information, or other purposes ...).

The *onPage* event fires when a report page has been rendered, just before we start to render the next page. This allows you to program code that you may wish to execute before rendering the next page *(such as setting page totals to zero)*.

The *close* method closes the report, but does not release it.

The *isLastPage* method returns a logical value based on whether we are on the last page of the report.

The *render* method is what actually causes the report to render (render is like the form.open()and form.readModal() methods for forms). When we get to the text and other controls, you will see different events: *canRender, preRender* and *onRender* – these are related to the *render* method of the report.

The *release* method will release the report from memory. This method is particularly important when you run a report programmatically, creating your own instance of the report and so on.

It is possible to programmatically control all or access of the above, and to use some of them in special code to test for specific conditions (such as *isLastPage*).

The printer Object

The *printer* property of the *report* object is actually a pointer to an object associated with the report. This object has a bunch of settings you may find useful, such as *orientation* which allows you to set your report to landscape or portrait, and so on. Note that making settings in *reportname.printer* should never affect the global *_app.printer* settings. However, *_app.printer* settings will be the defaults unless you make changes in your report.

The *printer* object has a call to *choosePrinter()*, which allows you to set the printer for the *current* report only. *(If you use* _app.choosePrinter()*, you affect your whole application. If you use* reportname.printer.choosePrinter() *you only affect the current report.)* As a developer, you could call the *report.printer*'s *choosePrinter()* method, and after the user has interacted with that, then you could render the report *(this would be very useful in a networked office, where there might be several printers available to any individual user ... they could select the printer that they want the report to go to).*

The *printer* object has the following properties and methods you should be aware of:

The *color* property determines whether the default output should be color/greyscale *(if you do not have a color printer attached, colors will be evaluated and printed to a greyscale)*, plain monochrome *(black and white and very little grey if any)*, or "default" *(which is the printer driver default).* dBASE will use what Windows tells it is the default here.

Color	***Option***
0	Default
1	Monochrome
2	Color

The *copies* property lets you set the number of copies to print. Note that there is no "Collate" option, which means you would get the number of copies of page 1 of the report, and then the same number of copies of page 2, etc.

The *duplex* property is used to determine whether to print in duplex mode for a printer that supports this ability. Obviously this is going to be printer specific.

Duplex	***Option***
0	None
1	Vertical
2	Horizontal

The *orientation* property is used to determine whether a report should print in *portrait* mode or *landscape* mode. It should be noted that to print in *landscape* mode there are other changes that should be made to your report - discussed in detail in a later chapter.

Orientation	***Option***
0	Default
1	Portrait *(default)*
2	Landscape

The *paperSize* property allows you to set the *paperSize* for the report. This uses a numeric scheme that varies based on the printer driver *(some printers support paper sizes that are not supported in other printers)*.

The *paperSource* property allows you to determine which tray or bin the paper will come from, if you are using a printer that allows this kind of selection. *(You should be able to change the* paperSource *on the fly – this might be useful if you have a company letterhead you wanted to use on a cover page for a report, and then print the rest of the report on plain paper.)*

The *printerName* property stores the name of the printer. This is blank by default, which means that your default printer for your Windows setup will be used. In most circumstances you should NOT set this *(among other things, the* printerName *will be saved in the report's source code, which might cause problems when you attempt to render the report on a computer that does* ***not*** *have that printer available)*.

The *printerSource* property refers to which *printerName* to use – the chances are you don't want to set this either. Instead, use the *choosePrinter()* method.

printerSource	***Option***
0	dBASE PLUS Default *(default)*
1	Windows Default
2	Specific

The *resolution* property allows you to set the resolution for your report's output. For the most part you should probably leave this alone, unless you use a dot-matrix printer. The default is "4 – High" for most printers.

Resolution	***Option***
0	Default *(default)*
1	Draft
2	Low
3	Medium
4	High

The *trueTypeFonts* property can be used to determine how the printer will handle TrueType™ fonts. It is probably safest to leave this alone.

trueTypeFonts	***Option***
0	Default *(default)*
1	Bitmap
2	Download
3	Substitute
4	Outline

The *choosePrinter* method can be used to ask the user how to print for *this* report *(using the choosePrinter dialog from the current report will not affect all reports generated from an application, which would happen if you used _app.Printer.choosePrinter())*

The reportGroup Object

The *reportGroup* property of the *report* object is another object pointer – to the report's *group*. This is used to handle aggregate calculations for the whole report, and to set a report header using the *headerBand* (prints at the beginning of the report *only*) and/or a report footer using the *footerBand* (prints at the end of the report *only*). The *headerBand* and *footerBands* for the *reportGroup* object have the same properties as their counterparts of the standard *group* object.

The *reportGroup* object has the same properties, events and methods of the *group* object (see the discussion of this later in this chapter), but the parent of the *reportGroup* is the *report* itself, rather than the *streamSource*.

The *reportGroup*'s *groupBy* property should be empty, and while you can try to place something there it will be ignored.

Interestingly, there is a *headerEveryFrame* property for the *reportGroup*, which does nothing, nor does the *headerBand's beginNewFrame* property, as placing a *reportgroup's headerBand* onto a report forces the *detailBand* to start on the next *streamFrame* (or page if there is only one *streamFrame*).

On the other hand, the *footerBand's beginNewFrame* property will ensure that the *footerBand* ends up on its own *streamFrame* (page if there is only one *streamFrame*), if this property is set to *true*.

The pageTemplate Object

The *pageTemplate* object is what is used to define the layout of the report's page. This includes your margins (top, left, right, bottom), and any controls you wish to print as "headers" or "footers" for each page of the report. For example, you might wish to always print a page number at the bottom of each page of the report – if you place the text control for this under the *streamFrame*, it will print for every page *at the same location* each time.

The *pageTemplate* is a container for the following controls:

1. Any visual controls you wish to display (as noted above)
2. The *streamFrame* or *streamFrames*.

The *pageTemplate* is aptly named, since it is literally what defines the layout of the page, or is the template for the page.

It is possible to use multiple pageTemplates, for example you may wish to design a cover page that only prints once, or you may wish to have one *pageTemplate* for even numbered pages and another for odd numbered pages.

> **NOTE**
> The *pageTemplate must* be named "pageTemplate1" if it is the only *pageTemplate* in the report, and if there are multiple pageTemplates, the second *must* be named "pageTemplate2". Even though you change the name property, it will be reset back to what is required by the designer.

The *pageTemplate* object has the following properties that you should be aware of:

The *backGround* property is used to specify a background image – this is very much the same as the *background* property used on a form. This is for HTML output and may not print if you set it and just print the report to a regular printer.

The *colorNormal* property is the color of the *pageTemplate*. When streaming a report to HTML, it will set the BGCOLOR of the BODY tag to this color. When printing to a color printer this will print the background of the report in this color *(but only to the edge of the* pageTemplate *itself – any margins to the edge of the page will remain the paper color)*. The default is "WHITE". Be warned, this will use vast quantities of ink or toner in your printer if you use anything other than "WHITE". I suggest not doing much with this for most reports.

The *gridLineWidth* property defaults to zero, and is used to determine the width of lines around elements in the report if it is greater than zero. This puts a border around each element in the report, much like you might see in a table in HTML. If you have blank fields this may appear a bit odd as no lines appear around the blank fields. If you output your report to HTML, this translates to the table BORDER attribute.

The *marginBottom*, *marginLeft*, *marginRight*, and *marginTop* properties are used to set the margins *(these are based on the report's metrics property – if you use the default metrics of twips, you will see really large values for these)*. These margins are from the edge of the paper – they default to approx. 3/4".

> **SUGGESTION**
> Set the margin properties here to use as much of the paper as you need to. The streamFrame's *left* and *width* properties should be set to go out to the edge of the *pageTemplate* (unless you are using multiple streamFrames).

The margin properties can be set programmatically, which may be useful if you are concerned with binding offsets and such *(this topic will be discussed in a later chapter of this book)*.

The *name* property is the name of the current object. At this time, changing this is not a good idea. There are several places where changing the name of the object may cause problems, and changing the name of the *pageTemplate* is one of them.

The *nextPageTemplate* property is an object reference to the next *pageTemplate* to be rendered when the current one is done. The default for this is to point back to the first *pageTemplate* (the report designer assumes you have only one *pageTemplate*). The only time this needs to be changed is if you are using multiple pageTemplates. This will be discussed in a later chapter of this book.

The *streamFrame1* property is an object reference to the default *streamFrame* (there is always a minimum of one *streamFrame*). The *streamFrame* (detailed later) is how the *streamSource* controls the *detailBand* and the group *headerBand* and *footerBand*.

The *width* property is the width of the *pageTemplate*.

The *streamSource Object*

The *streamSource* is the conduit between the *rowset* object (in the case of a multiple-table report, the controlling or master/primary rowset) and the *detailBand* on the *streamFrame*. The *streamSource* therefore controls the output to the *streamFrame*.

Each *streamFrame* is assigned to a *streamSource*, and multiple *streamFrames* (if used) can be *(and typically are)* assigned to the same *streamSource* (this is the default behavior). The data in the *streamSource* is rendered to all *streamFrame* objects linked to the *streamSource*.

If your report is using groups they will also be assigned to the *streamSource*, and you will see, in the Inspector, entries for each group object (it is possible to "nest" groups).

NOTE: The *streamSource must* be named "streamSource1" if it is the only *streamSource* in the report, and if there are multiple streamSources, the second must be named "streamSource2". Even if you change the *name* property, it will be reset back to what is required.

The *streamSource* is a container for:

- *detailBand*
- *group*(s)

If you examine all the code generated by the report designer, it might appear that the *streamSource* is also the container for the *rowset* object – this is not quite true – it holds a *reference* to the *rowset* object, but is not the container (the container of the *rowset* is the *query* object).

The following properties and methods are available to the *streamSource*:

The *detailBand* is the primary output stream for the report – this is where the detail for your rowset will be displayed or printed. This property is a pointer to the actual *detailBand* object. More detail on this control is discussed later.

The *maxRows* property is used to set a maximum number of rows that can be printed in each streamFrame or page of the report.

The *rowset* property is a pointer to the rowset *(and through the rowset to the standard rowset or ADORowset properties, events and methods, as well as the individual fields)*.

The *beginNewFrame* method is used to force the report to start the NEXT row of the rowset on a new *streamFrame*. *(This will be discussed in a later chapter.)*

> **NOTE**
> While the text here makes it *sound* like you can work with multiple *streamSource* objects on a report, it is a bad idea to try to do this. dBASE gets confused easily when you do this - I have not found a reliable way to make multiple *streamSources* work. Basically there must be *one* controlling *streamSource*. We will discuss working with multiple tables in several places throughout this book.

The *streamFrame Object*

The *streamFrame* object is what is used to define the actual output of your report. The *streamFrame* is controlled by the *streamSource* object (noted above), but it is not contained by it. The parent object of the *streamFrame* is the *pageTemplate*.

It is possible to have multiple *streamFrame*s on a report. This gives you the option to do reports with "multiple columns", and is actually how labels are designed using the label designer (one *streamFrame* per label).

If you have multiple *streamFrames*, the default is that each *streamFrame* uses the same *streamSource*. Because of this you only have to design the layout for the first *streamFrame* – after that, if you have more than one *streamFrame*, all you have to do is set the *streamSource* pointer (see below) to the *streamSource* that you need, and you are set.

The *streamFrame* appears (in the designer) to be the container of the *detailBand* and *group* (and group *headerBand* and *footerBand*) objects, but these are really contained (and more importantly, controlled) by the *streamSource*. Visually, the *streamFrame* is sort of a container for these, as they cannot exist outside of the *streamFrame*, but the actual parent or container of these controls is the *streamSource*. This can be a little confusing when trying to determine the *parent* of an object. *(Discussed later in this chapter.)*

The *streamFrame* object has the following properties, and events that you should be aware of:

The *borderStyle* property is used to set a border around the *streamFrame* itself. This can be very useful when using multiple *streamFrames*, as it gives you a clear visual representation of where the edges of each *streamFrame* are. Suggest not using anything except "Single" or "Double" as the others give some odd results when printing.

borderStyle	***Option***
0	Default *(none)*
1	Raised
2	Lowered
3	None
4	Single
5	Double
6	Drop Shadow
7	Client
8	Modal
9	Etched In
10	Etched Out

The *expandable* property allows you to determine if the *streamFrame* itself should be expandable (change height as needed). This defaults to *false*, and frankly I cannot see, for the *streamFrame*, a reason to set this otherwise except perhaps if you are outputting your report to HTML.

The *form* property allows you to refer to the *report* object in code without having to go through the object tree structure.

The *marginHorizontal* and *marginVertical* properties are used to set margins *inside* the *streamFrame*. I recommend leaving these at zero and simply placing your controls in the bands appropriately.

The *streamSource* property is a pointer to the *streamSource* that controls the *streamFrame*. (The default is *streamSource1*.)

The *top* property is the top of the *streamFrame* in the *pageTemplate* (measured from the top of the *pageTemplate*).

The *width* property is the *width* of the *streamFrame*.

The *canRender* event is used to determine if this *streamFrame* should be rendered at all. You can write code that checks this based on a variety of factors, such as the page number, or what have you. This event MUST return a value of *true* or *false*.

The *onRender* event fires once the current *streamFrame* has rendered. It can be used to do such things as clear out totals that you may be accumulating for each *streamFrame* (and with some thought you can probably determine other purposes as well).

> **SUGGESTION**
> If you are using one *streamFrame* (the default for most reports), set the *streamFrame's left* and *width* properties so that they go to the edge of the *pageTemplate*. The *pageTemplate* has already set the margins for you, and if you have your *streamFrame* smaller inside the *pageTemplate*, then you are setting up even more white space around the edge of your report.

The *detailBand* Object

This is one of the most important parts of the report, as it is where you place the controls you want to print (or display) for each row in your detail *rowset*. See the section below on Visual Controls regarding the actual controls you can use for this.

The *detailBand* is really a subclass of the band object (if you look at this in online help you will find the actual details in the band object's definition).

The *detailBand* has the following properties, events and methods that you should be aware of:

The *beginNewFrame* property can be used to determine if you want each row to print in a new *streamFrame* (new page, etc.). *(Do not confuse this with the* streamSource*'s beginNewFrame method.)* This is used in labels to ensure that only one row will print in each *streamFrame*.

The *context* property is used as a property of the BAND object, but in *detailBand*s it is always set to 0 (normal) and is read-only. This is used for *drillDown* (HTML) reports. For more details on this property see online help.

The *expandable* property is used for those reports where you are laying out your data in other than a set of columns – it allows the *detailBand* to expand (or not) depending on the amount of data being printed/displayed. The default for this property is *true*. Only set this to *false* if you want to force your *detailBand* to <u>always</u> be the same size.

The *firstOnFrame* property is used to determine if the band is being rendered for the first time in the current *streamFrame (this can be useful to print something only once on a page and is used with column headings a lot)*.

The *height* property defaults to zero – if used in conjunction with the *expandable* property it will allow the *detailBand* to be just as big as necessary for each individual row *(but only if the height is zero at the time the report is rendered)*. If you need the *detailBand* to be a specific height all the time, make sure you set the *expandable* property to *false*.

The *renderOffset* property is the location of the <u>*bottom*</u> of the current *detailBand* from the top of the current *streamFrame* using the current report *metric*. This can be used to determine if there is enough room (using the *onRender* event, for example) for the *next* row (*detailBand*) to display, and if not, you could then use the streamSource's *beginNextFrame* method to force the next row to the next *streamFrame*. There is an example of this in the suggestion box below and in a later chapter of this book there will be an example.

The *streamFrame* property is a pointer to the *streamFrame* that is the *(apparent)* parent of the *detailBand* (the "real" parent is the *streamSource*).

The *visible* property can be used to determine if this band is visible. *(If you need to do a summary report that only prints the group header/footerbands, then setting the* detailBand*'s* visible *to* false *would be all that was necessary.)*

The *onRender* event fires after the *detailBand* has been rendered.

The *preRender* event fires before the *detailBand* is rendered. This is similar to the *canRender* event, but does not require a return value, and cannot be used to tell dBASE to not display this band (unless you set the *visible* property *false*).

> **SUGGESTION**
> Using a combination of the *onRender* event, and the *renderOffSet* property and *streamSource's beginNewFrame* method, you can determine if there is enough room to display or print the next *detailBand* (or row of the table) after the current *detailBand* (or row) in the *streamFrame*. If not, call the *streamSource's beginNewFrame* to force the next row to the next *streamFrame* (or page). There will be code examples of this later in this book.

The *group* Object

The *group* object is how you tell the report engine to change the processing when a specific field (or fields) change value. This is useful in a lot of reports, from single table to multi-table *(it is practically required for multi-table reporting)*. Example: If you are printing a listing of customers from your customer table, and you wish all of the customers in one state to be grouped together with a heading for each state, and possibly some totals, you would use a group.

The *group* object includes a group *headerBand* and a *footerBand* – the *headerBand* prints at the top of the *detailBand*, and the *footerBand* prints at the bottom of it. These two objects have the same properties/events as the *detailBand*, which is derived from the *band* class.

Note that there is a difference between the *reportGroup* and a "normal" *group*. The *reportGroup* affects the whole report, and is really designed to specifically give you the *headerBand* and *footerBand* (which as described elsewhere in this chapter appear *only* once in the report). The "normal" group object is used in the regular processing of your data to handle grouping the data itself.

It is possible to have multiple groups on a single report, a *group* within a *group*.

Groups have the following properties:

The *drillDown* property allows you to specify that a grouped report is done as a "drill down" report – the group header/footer is displayed for each group and then the detail bands. This property determines if the header and footerBands are repeated with the detailBands. This is *only* useful if you wish to generate an HTML report. *(This will be discussed in a later chapter.)*

drilldown	**Option**
0	None *(default)*
1	Drilldown
2	Drilldown, repeat header
3	Drilldown, repeat footer
4	Drilldown, repeat header and footer

The *footerBand* is an object that is subclassed from the *band* object. It has properties very much like the *detailBand*. The *footerBand* prints at the end of the last *detailBand* that matches the current group and before the *headerBand* of the next group. The *footerBand* defaults to being empty.

The *groupBy* property is a string that is used to denote which field is used to group the report. If you wish to group by multiple fields, then you must create a calculated field in the fields array of the rowset object. There are many examples of the use of this property throughout this book. **NOTE:** For your group to work at all, this property is required.

The *headerBand* is much like the *footerBand*, but it displays at the top of the group. The Report Designer automatically adds a default text control on a *group headerBand*. You can use that text control, or remove it and place your own. In most grouped reports you will want a *headerBand*, and you may want (or need) a *footerBand*, particularly if doing aggregate calculations (see below).

The *headerEveryFrame* property states whether or not you want the group's *headerBand* to print at the top of each *streamFrame*. This is useful for those reports where the group gets broken up when printing. Typically when a group starts printing at bottom of the *streamFrame* (or page) there may not be room for all the detailBands necessary. When the data continues rendering on the next *streamFrame* (or page) the *headerBand* for the group does not get rendered. If you set this property to *true* it is rendered, making the report easier to understand.

Aggregate Functions:

The report engine allows you to perform the following calculations in your groups. You can place references to these methods in your group *footerBand*, with the name of the field you wish to calculate on, and the calculation is performed for you. Better, the calculation is automatically reset when the group break occurs. Online help delves into these in some good detail ("aggregate calculation (reports)").

- The *agAverage* method is used to average a numeric field.
- The *agCount* method can be used to count the number of rows in the group.
- The *agMax* method will return the largest value of any row for a specific field.
- The *agMin* method is the opposite of the *agMax* method (smallest value).
- The *agStdDeviation* method performs a standard deviation on the values in the group.
- The *agSum* method returns the total of a field in the group.
- The *agVariance* method returns the variance on the values in the group.

NOTE

You can use these same calculations in the report's *footerBand*. To place these onto the *group*'s *footerBand* manually (rather than using the menus to do it), use a text control, and set the codeblock for the text control to:

```
{||this.parent.parent.agCount({||this.parent.rowset.fields["
State ID"].value})}
```

Make sure that you put the correct fieldname in the brackets.

It is possible to "nest" groups in a report if you are doing a more complicated report. You may, for example, wish to group your report on the parent record in a parent/child relationship, and then in the child data, have another grouping of data. Placing two groups into your report will automatically "nest" them one inside the other. It is not possible to have multiple groups that are not nested.

> **NOTE**
> When you design a *group*, the *groupBy* property is required. However, as noted back toward the beginning of this chapter, the report's *autoSort* property may mess you up unless you set it to *false*. If it is set to *true*, it may add to the query's *sql* property an additional "ORDER BY" clause, which if unexpected will change the sorting sequence of the data in your report (ignoring the *indexName* property you may have set for your *rowset*).

Visual Controls

When designing a report, there are a small quantity of stock controls that you can use for your report.

Here are details about the visual controls that may be placed on a report, either on the *pageTemplate* or on a band (*detailBand*, *headerBand* or *footerBand*).

Most visual controls have *frames*, which define the outer edge of the control. When designing these controls, they have *handles* which can be used with the mouse to resize the control. The *handles* appear as small squares on the line defining the frame. If you set a border the control will use the frame as the outside edge of the border.

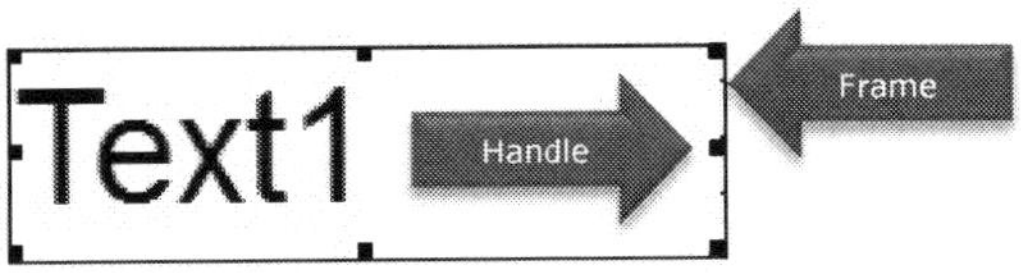

Figure 2-3

The text control shown in Figure 2-3 is larger than usual so you can see the detail discussed.

You can move visual controls around by clicking *once* on the control, and holding the mouse over the frame (not the handles!), click and drag the control. You can work with multiple controls in a similar fashion, by using the Ctrl key with the mouse to select multiple controls. Using the mouse to move controls around is great for big movements, but for fine-tuning you can use a technique called "nudging" – with the control (or controls) having focus, use the arrow keys on your keyboard to move the controls up, down, left or right.

With text controls – you can enter the text in the Inspector (by changing the *text* property) or you can change directly on the control. You click on it once to get focus (you will see the frame and handles), then another click (this is *not* a double-click – it is two separate mouse clicks) will place you in "edit" mode – you will see a flashing vertical cursor – you can delete the default text, change the text, edit what is there. Interestingly, with a *textLabel* control you have to use the Inspector to change the text.

There are quite a few properties, events and methods for these controls. They are not all discussed here. There are many that are discussed in The dBASE Book and the online help for dBASE. However, there are some properties that have special significance in the report engine, and we will examine those here.

Text

The *text* control is the most commonly used control on reports. This control is how you display the contents of most fields, calculations, text displayed for report headings, dates, page numbers, and so on. The text control is able to handle some standard HTML tags, which is useful when generating a report – keep in mind that HTML has progressed a long way since these controls were created – many features will not work here. If, however, you don't need some of the functionality of the text control, see below for a description of the *textLabel* control, which works in reports as well.

The *text* property is used to display the contents of fields (or whatever other text you may need to display). If you drag a field from the field palette to the surface of the report, you will see a *codeblock* along the lines of:

```
{||this.form.test1.rowset.fields["test"].value}
```

This *codeblock* is evaluated each time the band is rendered (see *detailBand* and *group* above), and will return the value of the field.

This is important to note. There is a section later on calculated fields that will cover some of this in more detail.

The following properties and methods are specific to text controls when used on reports:

The *alignHorizontal* property allows you to define within the frame of the text control how the text lines up side-to-side. The last option is only useful for larger text if you want it right justified *(see also trackJustifyThreshold below)*:

alignHorizontal	***Option***
0	Left (default)
1	Center
2	Right
3	Justify

The *align* property is a combination of the settings for *alignHorizontal* and *alignVertical*:

Align	***Option***
0	Top Left
1	Top Center
2	Top Right
3	Center Left
4	Center
5	Center Right
6	Bottom Left
7	Bottom Center
8	Bottom Right
9	Wrap Left
10	Wrap Center
11	Wrap Right

The *alignVertical* property is useful if your text control is tall – you can specify how the text lines up vertically. I would use this with column headings to ensure that all the headings lined up at the bottom of the frames. Justify is an odd one for vertical, but if you use it, also see *verticalJustifyLimit* below.

alignVertical	**Option**
0	Top (Default)
1	Middle
2	Bottom
3	Justify

The *border* property is a logical value. It defaults to *false*, setting it to *true* should set the *borderStyle* to "4 – Single", and setting the *borderStyle* property to anything other than either 0 or 3 should set this to *true*.

The *borderStyle* property allows you to set a border on a text control, but except for the option "4 – Single", you may find the border ends up making the text itself difficult to read. If you use a *borderStyle* on a text control, you would want to make the control larger (taller/wider) in most cases, and work with the *marginHorizontal* and *marginVertical* properties to move the text further from the text control's *frame*, which is the outside edge of the control itself.

borderStyle	**Option**
0	Default *(none)*
1	Raised
2	Lowered
3	None
4	Single
5	Double
6	Drop Shadow
7	Client
8	Modal
9	Etched In
10	Etched Out

The *colorNormal* property is used to set the foreground and background colors of a text control. The default is "BtnText/BtnFace" which is effectively black text on a white background, unless your Windows color definitions are different. You can always use "black/white" for this property.

The *fixed* property determines whether the text object's position is fixed, vertically, if other text controls are empty, or not displayed. If you set a text control at a specific position and always want it to display at that position (this may be very useful for pre-printed forms, for example), set this property to *true* (it defaults to *false*).

The *leading* property is the distance between consecutive lines in an object (if the text wraps inside the control). The default of '0' means to use the font's default line space.

The *marginHorizontal* and *marginVertical* properties refer to the distance between the text and its frame (if you set a border, this uses the frame for its dimensions).

The *rotate* property allows you to rotate the text in one of four directions – in degrees:

Rotate	**Option**
0	Normal (default)
1	90 degrees
2	180 degrees
3	270 degrees

The *suppressIfBlank* property is useful in that it allows the report engine to compress the band if a *text* object is empty. See tips section of this chapter regarding blank lines.

The *suppressIfDuplicate* property will not display a value if it is a duplicate from the previous row. This can be useful for those reports where you have columns of data *(for example dates, where the report is grouped by dates -- you may only wish to print the first time a specific date appears, and then blank it out until the date changes – rather than writing a bunch of code, this property will handle it for you).*

The *text* property defines the text that is displayed. You can hard-code specific text (useful for labeling data, column headings, etc.), or you can use codeblocks to specify the text displayed *(this is the most common way of obtaining the value of a field and displaying it)*. The text is always kept inside the frame of the control, so if you cannot see all the text you would need to change the *width* of the control, or the *height* of the control (or both), or other properties such as *fontSize*, *fontName*, and so on. The *text* property has a "Type" button you can use to modify the type of the text displayed, using the Inspector:

Type
Boolean
Numeric
Date
Integer
Character *(default)*
Object
Null
Time
DateTime
Codeblock

The *tracking* property is the space between characters. If the default of '0' is used, the font's spacing is used.

The *transparent* property is used when you place text on top of other objects – if set to transparent, there is no apparent background and the objects "beneath" the text should show through. This is a logical value and defaults to *false*.

The *trackJustifyThreshold* property is the maximum amount of space added between words on a fully justified line. *(Fully justified means that both the left and right margins line up.)* The default of '0' (zero) means "no limit."

The *variableHeight* property allows you to specify if a text control can have a variable amount of height based on the content from one row to another in the table. This is particularly useful for memos or long character fields.

The *verticalJustifyLimit* property is the vertical version of the *trackJustifyThreshhold* property.

The *canRender* event can be used for a wide variety of things, including calculating exactly what you wish to print for the current text control. Note that this event **must** return a logical value of *true* or *false*, and can be used to suppress printing of the current text control.

The *onRender* event fires when the text control has rendered.

textLabel

The textLabel control is a less complex version of the text control, and it does not have the ability to rotate, or use HTML. Other properties and events are pretty much the same as the text control, except that the *textLabel* does not have some of them, such as *canRender* and *onRender*, *suppressIfBlank*, etc. These should only be used for controls that you want to always print.

Line

The line object is just what it says – a line. The line, by default is horizontal, but you can place a vertical line between two columns, if desired. We will take a look at this later in the book. For *horizontal* lines it is important for the *top* and *bottom* properties to be the same if you want a "straight" line. For *horizontal* lines, the *left* and *right* properties should be the same for a "straight" line.

The line object has the following properties, and has the *canRender* and *onRender* events:

The *bottom, left, right,* and *top* properties are used for positioning the line. If you are using a horizontal line, the *top* and *bottom* should be the same, if you are using a vertical line, the *left* and *right* properties should be the same.

The *colorNormal* property defines the color of the line itself. The default is "WindowText", which in most cases is black.

The *fixed* property ensures that the line does not move if the controls around it do (this is useful for a form – if you have some text controls with *suppressIfBlank* set to true and they collapse, the line would not shift even though some of the other controls might). This is a logical value, and defaults to *false*.

The *pen* property is used to define the type of line used based on the following:

Pen	Option
0	Solid
1	Dash
2	Dot
3	DashDot
4	DashDotDot

The *width* property is the width of the line. It is measured in *pixels*, and defaults to a value of 1.

Image

The image control is used to display images on reports.

The image control has the following properties, and has the *canRender* and *onRender* events:

The *alignment* property is used to define how the image is lined up inside the frame (defined by the *height* and *width* properties below) of the image.

Alignment	**Option**
0	Stretch *(default)*
1	Top left
2	Center
3	Keep Aspect Stretch
4	True Size

The *borderStyle* property defines the appearance of the border of the image control. Some of the options might require making the frame of the image larger so you do not change the appearance of the image itself. See the *text* control's *borderStyle* property for a listing of the options – they are identical.

The *dataSource* property is used to define where the image displayed comes from — a resource file, an image file, or from a field in a table.

The *fixed* property is the same as the one for the *line* object above.

The *height* and *width* properties are used to define the size of the image control.

The *left* and *top* properties are used to define the position of the image control on the band (or pageTemplate) that it is placed on.

The *transparent* property of the image control is useful if your image uses background transparency (not all images do). In cases like that, the background (the object(s) under the image) will display as the background of the image.

Shape

The Shape control is a flexible control that allows you to do some rudimentary graphics on a report, creating circles, rectangles, etc.

The shape control has the following properties as well as the *canRender* and *onRender* events:

The *colorNormal* property defines the colors used for the shape. What is unusual about this property is that it uses both foreground and background colors (the default is "WindowText/Window"), but there is no text. The foreground color defines the border of the shape, and the background color defines the inside color of the shape. If you do not want a different border, you would use the same color for both (example: "red/red" would give a red shape with no apparent border).

The *drawMode* property of the shape control is an unusual one and deals with how the inside of the shape appears. See the online Help for more details on this one – it is hard to describe *(or you could just experiment with the options)*.

The *height* and *width* properties are used to define the size of the shape control.

The *left* and *top* properties are used to define the position of the shape control on the band (or pageTemplate) that it is placed on.

The *penStyle* property matches that of the *image* control above.

The *penWidth* property specifies the width of the border in pixels (much like the *width* of a *line* object).

The *shapeStyle* property of the shape control is one of the most important, as it defines the actual shape you wish to draw.

shapeStyle	***Option***
0	Rounded Rectangle
1	Rectangle
2	Ellipse
3	Circle (*default*)
4	Round Square
5	Square

Container

Containers have one interesting (but slightly annoying) property in reports – they cannot be used in the *detailBand* (or group bands) because of their nature. They are a subclass of the window object, and cannot repeat the way other objects can *(I got this information directly from one of the developers of the report classes)*.

Rectangle

Rectangles cannot be changed to circles or other shapes, and default to having text. This can be used in a "form report" to layout sections of the report to great effect.

The rectangle object has the following properties, but does *not* have the *canRender* or *onRender* events:

The *border* property determines if a border will be displayed. For a rectangle object this seems like a moot point – the purpose of the object is to display the border of the rectangle. That said, the default for this property is *true*.

The *borderStyle* property is the type of border displayed. See the *text* control above, as the options for this are identical. The default is a single line.

The *colorNormal* property works on a rectangle much like it does on a shape control – the foreground is the border and text color, and the background is the color of the rectangle control.

The font properties (*fontBold, fontItalic, fontName, fontSize, fontStrikeout,* and *fontUnderline*) all affect the text of the rectangle only – the text that appears at the top left, if you decide to use it. It has no effect on any text placed *on* the rectangle.

The *patternStyle* property defines any pattern used on the inside of the rectangle. The purpose is to add cross-hatching to the background of the control. The color of the lines in the cross-hatching will match the color of the border. This property only has an effect if the *systemTheme* property is set to *false*.

patternStyle	**Option**
0	Solid *(default)*
1	BDiagonal
2	Cross
3	Diagcross
4	FDiagonal
5	Horizontal
6	Vertical

The text assigned to the *text* property of a rectangle is placed on the top border to the left. If you delete the default text ("Rectangle1"), there will be no text displayed on the rectangle.

ActiveX

These are special. The author has no experience using these in reports, however, you should be able to. You may want to, for example, chart some values and place them in the report's *footerBand* using a charting ActiveX control.

Database Objects

Database Objects are how dBASE's OODML (Object Oriented Database Manipulation Language) interacts with the data. I wanted to add just a small amount of information here, although this topic is covered in much more detail in my other books. As noted in the discussion about the *streamSource*, this is the connection between the report and your *rowset*.

Database/ADODatabase

The *database* and *ADODatabase* objects are used to connect to the database itself. In this book I use both the DBASESAMPLES and DBASEREPORTS databases, which refer to local (DBF) tables. However, if you work with a SQL Server, you can either use the standard dBASE database object, or if you are working with ADO, you can use the ADODatabase object. In either case these objects work fine with the dBASE report engine. While I would not call them interchangeable, they work pretty much the same for all intents and purposes.

Query/ADOQuery

The query object is used to connect with a table (or tables). If you are using the ADODatabase object to connect to a database, you should be using the ADOQuery object instead.

Rowset/ADORowset

A *rowset* object is automatically created when you set the *query* object's *active* property to *true*. This is a reference to the rows of data in a table (or tables if you use a join in the SQL statement). There is a single rowset for each query. If you are using ADO to connect with your database, you will automatically be using the *ADORowset* instead of a standard *rowset*.

Field/ADOField

As with the *rowset* class, the *field* object is automatically created, as is the *fieldArray* object. And again, if you are using ADO, then you will find that you are working with the *ADOField* and *ADOFieldArray* objects.

More on ADO

If you need more information on working with ADO, I recommend The dBASE Book Plus, and of course using the online help with dBASE (which is not really complete in this area, but it is a starting point).

ADO and the Report Designer/Report Engine

While I have not spent a lot of time working with ADO and reports, the effort I put in in the aforementioned The dBASE Book Plus, there were no issues – everything worked as if I had been working with the standard dBASE database objects. You should not have a lot of problems here.

A Few Notes

The rest of this chapter contains a few notes that will be detailed later in the book, but are kind of an overview of things you should be aware of.

Rendering a Report

When you wish to render (generate) a report, there are several methods that can be used in dBASE.

The simplest is to double-click on the report icon in the navigator.

Another is to call the report in your code with:

```
DO MYREPORT.REP
```

The first two are lacking a bit in developer control. Another method is to load the report into memory, and then create an instance of the report:

```
set procedure to myreport.rep additive
r = new myreportReport()
r.render()
```

This has the advantage that you can, as the developer, add code that can modify the report's *output* property (which is used to determine where the report will "go" when rendered), and a *lot* more – some of which will be discussed throughout the book.

The last is to use a *reportViewer* control on a form. This allows the developer to set up a way for the user to preview a report before printing, and allows you to let the user decide if they want to print it (among other things). A working PREVIEW form can be found in the dBASE Users' Function Library Project (dUFLP) – details on where to find it will be in the appendix of this book as well as the next chapter, and there will be at least a few examples of the use of this in various chapters in this book.

Working with the Report Designer

Here are some suggestions for working in the designer to make your life easier. The developers at dBASE know that there are some issues involved with the designer surface *(it's not quite as friendly as we, the developer community, would like; and it's not as stable as we would like)* and have committed to fixing this in a future release of the software, indeed, some of the stability issues have been resolved.

Snap to Grid

The first time you go into the designer, I seriously recommend that you turn the "snap to grid" feature off. This causes a lot of frustration with dropping controls onto the surface of the report – the symptoms are basically when you drag a new control onto the surface (particularly onto the *streamFrame*), other controls in the same band (*detailBand*, *headerBand*, etc.) shift on their own – sometimes quite radically. *(This is caused usually, although not always, by controls overlapping, and the snap-to-grid feature is trying to keep that from happening.)*

You can turn this feature off by right clicking on the report designer surface, select "Report Designer Properties". In the top set of checkboxes, you will see "Snap to Grid" – make sure it is unchecked, and then click "OK".

You won't have to set this off each time, as this is a system-wide setting.

Metric

Set the report metrics to a useful setting. TWIPS is a metric setting that is hard for most folk to get their minds around. There are 1440 twips to the inch *(a twip is a "twentieth of a point"; there are 72 points per inch)*. The values that appear in the designer are hard to understand. If you are used to working in inches, set the metrics to inches. If you are used to working in centimeters or millimeters, by all means, use those settings.

AutoSort

Set *autoSort* to *false*. This property defaults to being set to *false,* however, **if** it is set to *true*, it is a good idea to set it back. There is a discussion of why you should do this way back at the beginning of this chapter in the discussion about the *report* object. Suffice it to say that you will probably be a lot happier if you set this to *false*, especially if you work with grouped reports.

These three items by themselves will solve a multitude of problems that people have when they first get started working with the report designer.

You should consider using custom reports which handle the above, and perhaps some basic other settings (such as *pageTemplate* margins, *streamFrame* height, left and width properties). By using a custom report to make these settings, you can save yourself the trouble of remembering to make them each time you start a new report.

> **NOTE**
> When setting your *streamFrame* to the size you need, be sure to leave room at the top and/or bottom of the *pageTemplate* for any report headers and footers you want to print.

Who Is the Parent of Who?

As you work with controls and work with designing reports, you will find that at various points you need to reference other controls, either going to the report object itself, or to one of the various contained objects. The problem is that the syntax gets quite confusing.

If you examine a typical codeblock for a text control that is placed onto a report, you will see something like:

```
{|| this.form.test1.rowset.fields["test"].value}
```

If you get confused working with the dot syntax in the form designer, this is going to get really messy in the report designer where you have no choice but to use the built-in containers.

I find that the confusing part for me is when I am using the *canRender* event of a control to set up my calculations for the control's output, and cannot remember exactly how to get to the *streamSource*, or to another control somewhere in the report.

What I have found works really well for me is to add in the *canRender* event handler, while I am working on that particular bit of code:

```
? this.className
? this.baseClassname
? this.parent.className
? this.parent.baseClassName
```

In order to get to the *streamSource* from an object on the *detailBand*, the full path might be:

```
? this.parent.parent.className
```

So what I find helps is if the current "parent" is not the one I need, I add another ".parent" (note the leading dot) into the statement.

Another way to find the relationship is to use the inspector object. In the combobox at the top of the inspector you will see a tree listing which can be used to find the correct number of "parents".

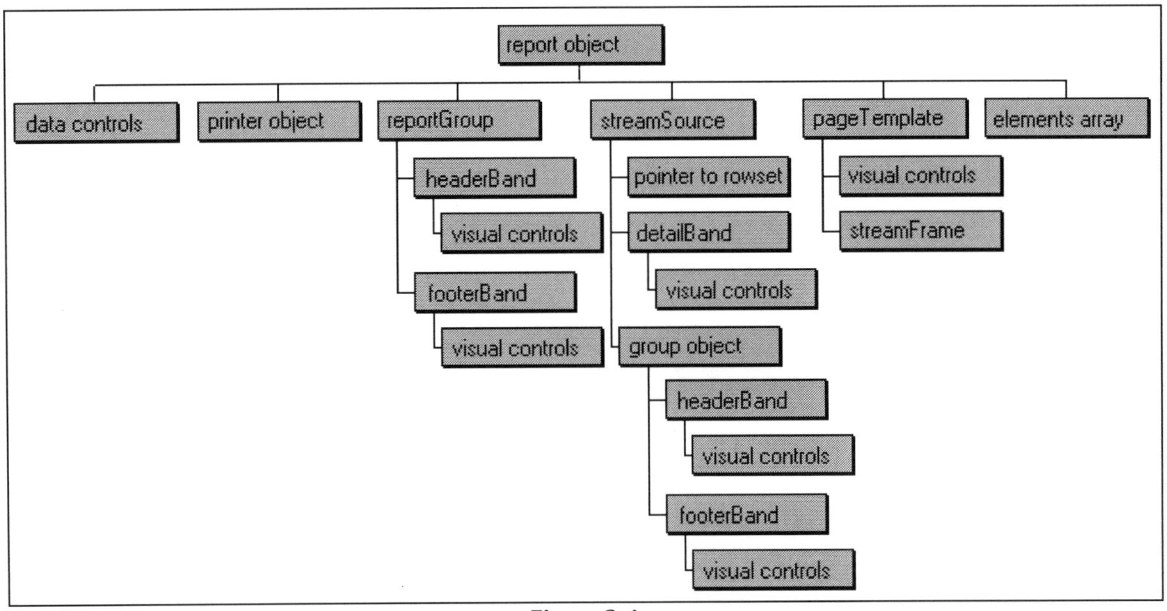

Figure 2-4
This image was created by Gary White, and is used with his permission

This chart may be useful in helping determine where to reference an object in your code.

Alignment Tools

When you are working in the design surface, getting your controls to line up can be bothersome. You can do it the hard way – going to the inspector for one control, looking at the values, and then setting the same properties for other controls; or you can use the alignment tools.

When you are in the report designer, in the toolbar are a set of toolbuttons designed to help you line up controls *(see Figure 2-5)*. To use this, select two or more controls that you wish to line up (use the Ctrl key and the mouse to select them), and then you can line them up on the left, the right, top or bottom. *(You can also make your controls the same size – height and/or width.)*

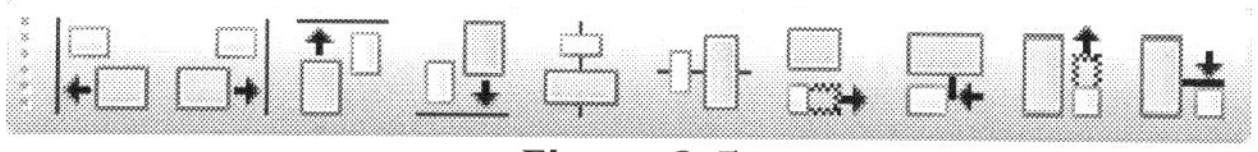

Figure 2-5

I do want to note however that this will get you *close* for alignment, often the Designer does not set the *top* or *left* properties exactly. You might try to align two controls to another that is set with a *top* (or *left*) of 0.00, and your other two controls will end up at 0.01. This may not seem like a lot of difference, but you may want to double-check. It can look off when you view the report.

You can also center controls horizontally in the band you are working in (or the *pageTemplate*) by clicking on them and going to the Layout menu, and selecting "Align" and then "Center Horizontally in Window". *(In most cases you probably don't want to "Center Vertically in Window".)*

Lines

If you want to place a line between *detailBands* experimentation has shown that your best bet is to place the line at the top of the *detailBand*, not at the bottom, or in the group *headerBand* or *footerBand* (if you are using groups). This way, you always have the line at the top of the *detailBand* for each row that prints. We'll look at this in a later chapter.

Navigating in the Report Designer

If you are dealing with a large report, it is helpful to view data on various pages. In the designer, you can see the next page by pressing the PgDn key on the keyboard, and to see the previous page, you can press the PgUp key.

Displaying Numeric Values

Sometimes getting numeric values to display just the way you want them can be a bit tricky. You should consider using the picture clause or the *transform()* function to make sure that your numeric values line up just right in your report.

One simple method of lining your numbers up on the right is to set the text control's *alignHorizontal* property to Right.

For example, if you have data that must display two digits on the right of the decimal, but in one calculation or field you have a value that has zeros for the digits to the right, you may end up seeing an integer value appear.

If you set a picture clause, you can get the value to always display two digits on the right of the decimal (999.99, for example).

In addition, in some cases, you may want to display percent symbols and such – you may want to use *transform()* (see online help for details) to get everything to line up.

Summary

This chapter was aimed at giving a reference point for the various objects in reports, giving you some details, some concepts, and even some ideas for working with some of them in a more efficient manner.

If you have used the Knowledgebase for dBASE you will recognize a lot of what is in this chapter from the document I wrote in 2004 titled "Beginning Reports". This has been updated for the current release of dBASE Plus (10.3.1), with a lot more detail in some parts.

Moving forward, the next chapter will begin the "tutorial" part of the book, which is frankly most of the rest of it. We will start out by setting up the folders, and source code for this book so you have a starting point.

Chapter 3: Preparing to Follow Along with the Book / Tutorial

A good portion of the rest of this book is designed to be, rather than a reference source, a tutorial. To follow along, it is a good idea if you do some basic setup, and download the sample tables and source code. This chapter is about getting ready for the rest of the book.

Setting Up for the Exercises in This Book

The purpose of this book is to make report development easier. At the beginning we'll take time to create the resources needed to fully take advantage of the power of dBASE's Report Engine.

Custom Reports and Controls

Throughout this book we are going to use custom reports and custom report controls some of which are included in the dBASE Users' Function Library Project (dUFLP). If you have not downloaded this free library of code, you should take advantage of it. We will take a look at a few classes and other code in the dUFLP in later chapters.

The dBASE Users' Function Library Project

In order to get you set up for some of what we're doing in the book, download the dBASE Users' Function Library Project (dUFLP), which can be gotten at *(note that the URL is case-sensitive "duflp" needs to be typed as shown)*:

```
http://www.goldenstag.net/dbase/index.htm#duflp
```

This is a freeware library of code that is probably the largest open-source project for dBASE currently out there. Details on this can be found both on the website, and also in the library. You should download the current version.

Using unzip software, or Windows itself (right click the downloaded file), unzip to a folder such as: "C:\dUFLP".

Start dBASE, and once you are in dBASE, use the file folder button at the top of the Navigator window to navigate to the folder you unzipped the dUFLP library into. Once you have done that, run the following program (double-click it):

```
Setup.prg
```

This will, when done, exit dBASE and restart it *(depending on which version of the dUFLP, the message that displays may be misleading in that it may tell you to exit and restart dBASE when you don't need to).*

This program will set up information in a special table to help us organize the visual components in the dUFLP more easily, making it possible to find things easier when we get to that point.

If you already have the dUFLP installed, you may want to check and see if you have the most current version, as this code is updated every so often *(depending on factors such as time available to the librarian, and the amount of updates/changes/new code donated to the library, and in some cases the dBASE R&D Team finishing a new release of dBASE itself).*

Folders to Place Your Work In

I suggest that you set up a folder to place your exercises in *(if you did this in Chapter 1, you can ignore this instruction here)*, such as:

```
C:\dBASEReports
```

In that folder, you should create another, called:

```
C:\dBASEReports\Tables
```

We'll come back to this folder shortly.

You should create folders for the various chapters as we go, and when working, make sure you navigate to the correct folder. For example, this is Chapter 3, so you should add a folder:

```
C:\dBASEReports\Chapter 3
```

Make sure you navigate *to* this in the Navigator using the "File Folder" button to the right side of the "Look in:" combobox. *(You can create the folder from the dialog that appears.)*

Tables

Next we will need some tables. We will use the ones that Michael Nuwer has built in his excellent tutorials and a few others. In later chapters we will create one or two other tables as needed. In addition we will use for a few exercises in the book some of the tables provide with dBASE in the "DBASESAMPLES" database. The ones specific to this book need to be downloaded from my website at:

```
http://www.goldenstag.net/dbase/Books/dBASEReportsBook.htm
```

(Scroll down the page, click the link for "Source Code", and download the file "dBASEReportsTables.zip".)

Unzip the tables to the folder:

```
C:\dBASEReports\Tables
```

There are several tables:

- Dogs – contains data for something like 7,000 animals, including their registration numbers, names and sex, and more
- Litters – contains about 2,700 litters
- Dams – contains data for about 350 female dogs
- Household – for a household budget, with over 100 entries

- LogicalField – used to show how to use a specific custom control in a later chapter – a small table ...
- ReportTemplate – used in one chapter as a reusable report table

In addition, there is a file "Invoice.dmd" that will be used in Chapter 11.

Report Designer Settings

In Chapter 1 we discussed Report Designer Settings. Please go back to that chapter and go over them. The "Snap to Grid" setting in particular should be turned off.

Database Alias

Next you need to create a database alias that points to the folder that the tables are in. If you are unfamiliar with the concept of database aliases, I refer you back to early chapters of The dBASE Book, which explains in some detail why this is a good thing to do.

If you are working with versions of dBASE older than dBASE Plus 8, (2.62, dB2K, etc.), you will need to do this the hard way *(skip to the heading "Using the BDE Administrator to Create a Database Alias")*. If you are using more recent versions of dBASE, you can use a different and simpler means of setting up an alias.

Creating a User BDE Alias

Note that this will only work for dBASE Plus 8 and later, but is a very useful tool. The instructions here work for the IDE (Integrated Developer Environment), see The dBASE Book (3rd Edition or later, Volume I) for details on setting this up in a .INI file, or in source code if you need your User BDE Alias for a deployed application.

With dBASE Plus open, click on the "Properties" menu, select "Desktop Properties", and you should see the appropriate dialog. Use the arrow buttons on the Notebook of the dialog so that you see "User BDE Aliases".

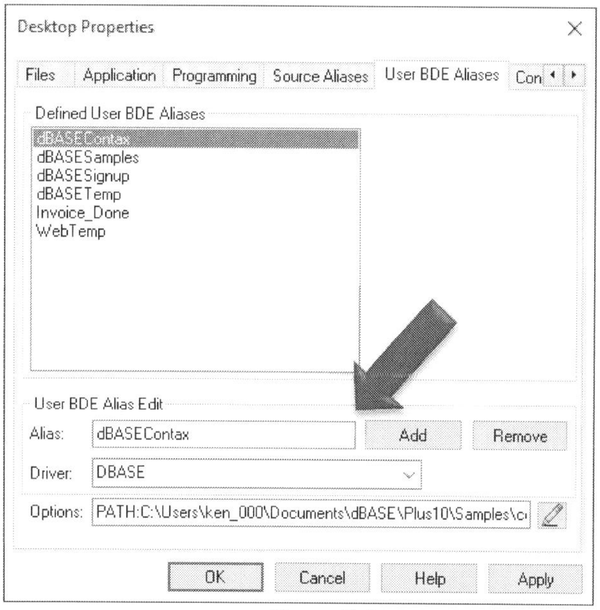

Figure 3-1

The list of defined aliases showing will vary depending on what is set up on your computer already.

Change the name of the Alias to: "dBASEReports", and then click the button with the pencil to select the path to your folder.

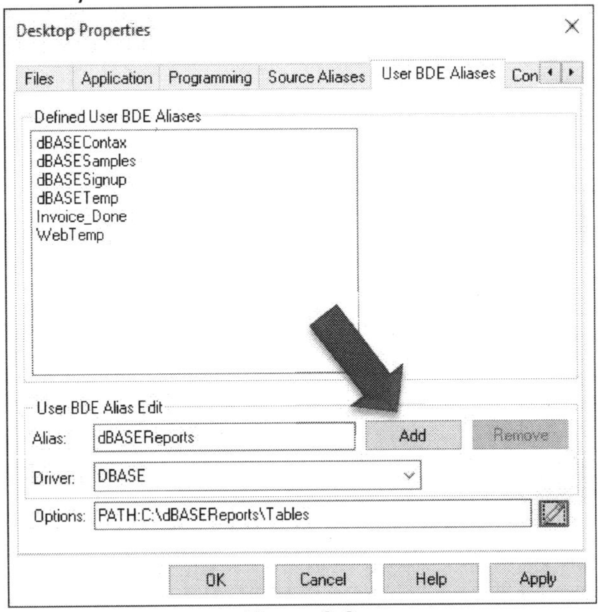

Figure 3-2

Click the "Add" button, the alias will appear in the list, click "OK", the dialog will close. You could of course add more User BDE Aliases if you needed to, but for our needs, this is good enough. You are now set.

To see the tables, assuming you have downloaded them and put them into the correct folder, in the Navigator click on the "Tables" tab, in the dropdown list, select "dBASEReports" and you should now see something like:

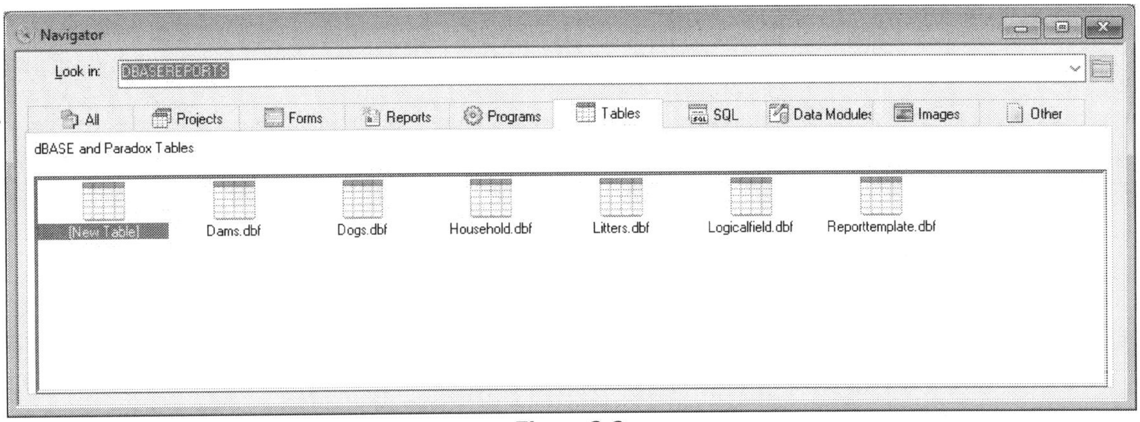

Figure 3-3

Using the BDE Administrator to Create a Database Alias

If you are using versions of dBASE older than dBASE Plus 8, you need to follow these instructions:

If dBASE or any dBASE application is open, be sure to close it before starting.

To do this you will need to start the Borland Database Engine (BDE) Administrator. This was installed when you installed dBASE Plus, and an icon for it should be in the dBASE Plus folder – note that a shortcut is not provided for dBASE Plus 9 or 10 for the BDE Administrator. You will want to use Windows explorer and find it here (run this program):

```
C:\Program Files (x86)\Common Files\Borland\BDE\bdeadmin.exe
```

Or you can use the "search the web" option in the taskbar and type "BDEAdmin.exe".

When you run this, you will most likely be asked about allowing this application to modify Windows, click the "Yes" button.

Step 1: Create a new alias

When you open the BDE Administrator, make sure that the "Databases" tab has focus:

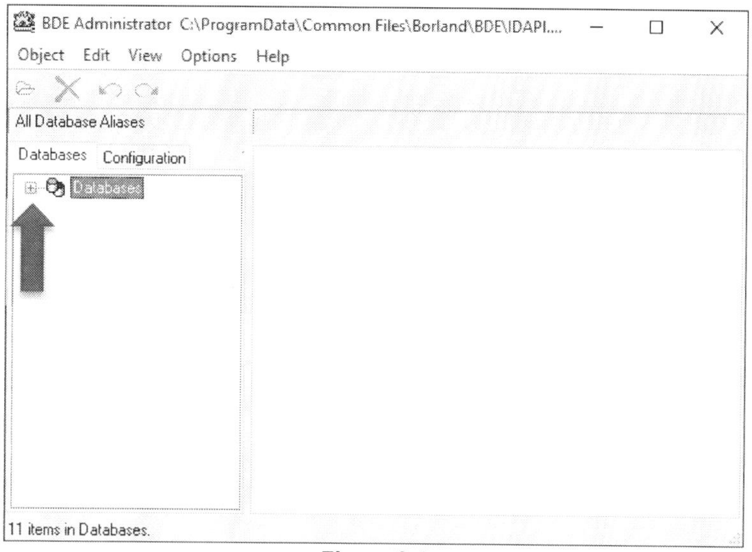

Figure 3-4

You may wish to open the list (the "+" sign next to "Databases"), but it isn't necessary. Next, press: Ctrl+N or select the "Object" menu and "New ....".

You will see a dialog that looks like:

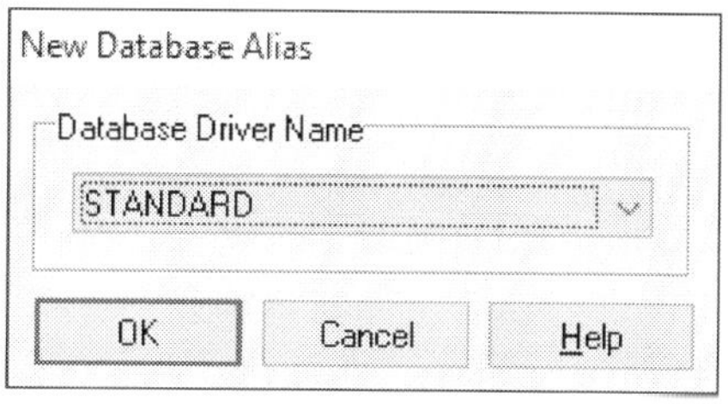

Figure 3-5

Click the "OK" button.

Step 2: Change the name of the alias

The default name for an alias is "STANDARD1". Click on this so that it has focus and change the name to "dBASEReports" (without quotes or a space). Press the enter key. You should see something like:

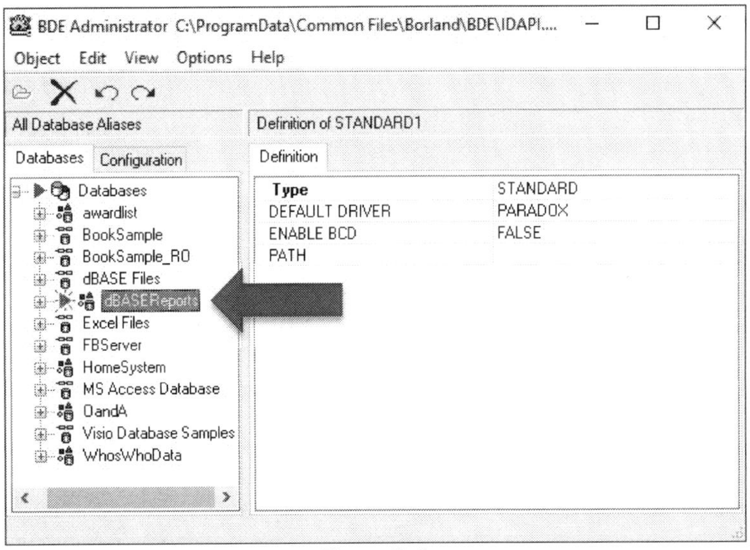

Figure 3-6

Step 3: Set properties

The alias now exists, with the name we gave it, but we have to tell the Administrator the path to where the tables are, and it is a good idea to tell dBASE the default driver is "dBASE", not "Paradox". Click on the dropdown/combobox for "DEFAULT DRIVER", click the down-arrow and select "dBASE".

Click the entryfield for "PATH", and then click the button "..." that appears. This will bring up a dialog to find the folder. Find the folder you created called "C:\dBASEReports", double-click on that, and you should see the folder under it named "Tables". Double click on that so it is open, and click "OK".

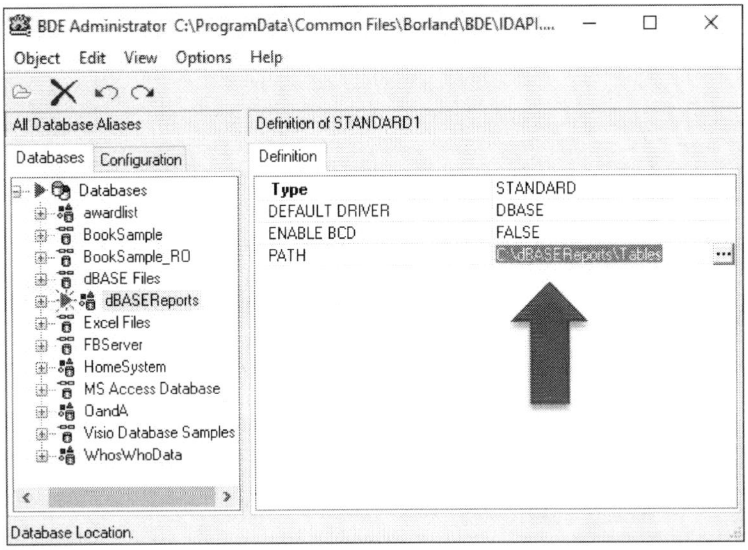

Figure 3-7

Save the new alias with "Ctrl+A" (or use the "Object" menu, and "Apply"), and close the BDE Administrator.

Open dBASE, click the "Tables" tab of the Navigator, select the combobox at the top, and find the dBASEReports database alias – click it, and you should see the same list of tables shown in Figure 3-3 above.

Data Module

We are going to create a basic data module for the reports used in this book for starters. Note that you are not required to use a data module to create reports – the report designer allows you to use tables without the use of a data module – many examples in this book do this. The primary advantage to using a data module is that once you have your data structure designed (parent/child table relationships and so on), you have code that you do not have to recreate each time you need to do something new, whether it be a new form or a new report – if the data module has the data design you need, why do it again?

Look at the Navigator window. If you are not currently pointing to the folder you created earlier for this book (C:\dBASEReports), please do so now. This can be done by clicking on the "Folder" button to the far right of the "Look in:" part of the Navigator. This will bring up a dialog box that allows you to select a folder:

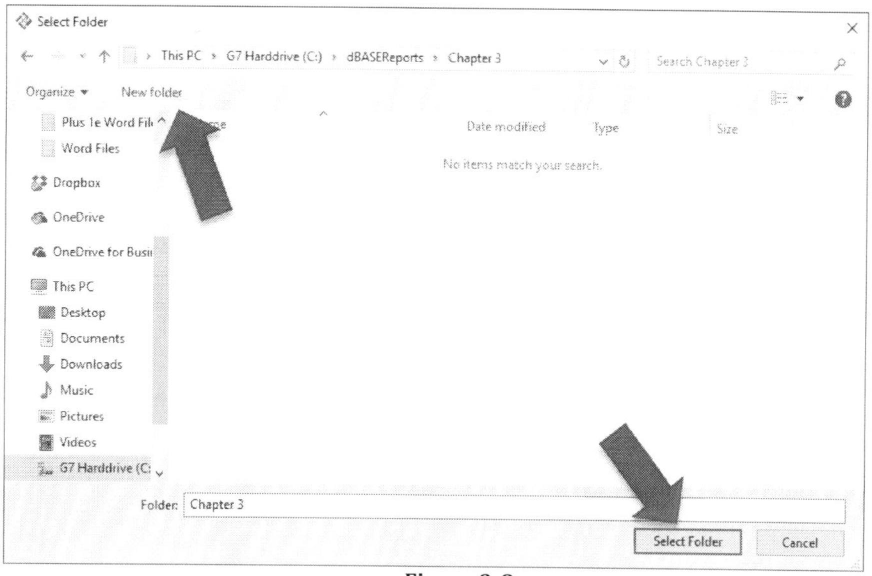

Figure 3-8

You need to create a "Chapter 3" folder if you did not do that earlier *(since that is the chapter we are working on)* – click "New folder" and create the "Chapter 3" folder (click "OK"). Click on it, and then Click "Select Folder".

Now that we know we are pointing to the correct folder, let's create our first data module.

In older versions of dBASE we had dQuery, in the more current versions we have a very simple Data Module Designer.

In the Navigator pane, click "Data Modules", you should see something like:

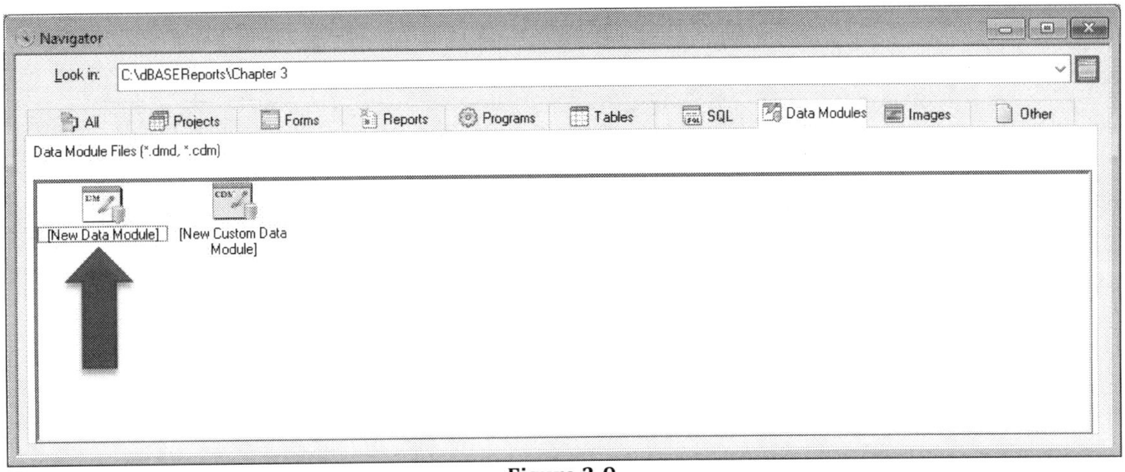

Figure 3-9

To create a new data module, double click the icon "[New Data Module]". This will start the Data Module Designer.

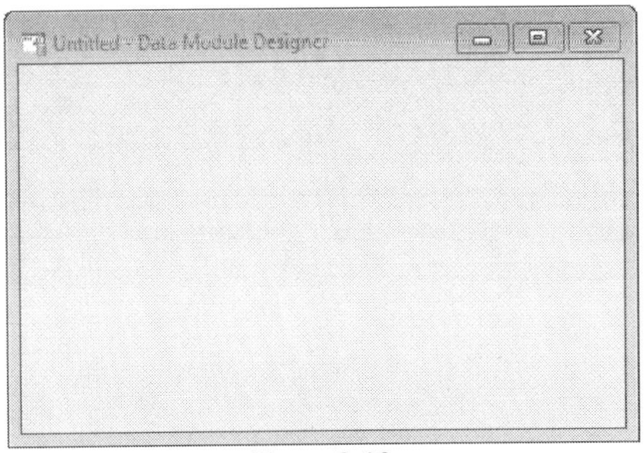

Figure 3-10

This is what the designer looks like to start. It's pretty basic. You should also see a couple of tool windows – the Inspector and the Component Palette. On my screen I move them off to the side.

Move this window down so it is under the Navigator (or move it to the side of it), so we can see both the Navigator and the designer. Find the table "Dams" in the Navigator (click on the "Tables" tab), and drag it to the designer. Note that you get two objects here, one is the database; the second is the query for the table. Because the first table was dragged onto the design surface and no database object was set, the designer was smart enough to know that you would need the database object. However, it does tend to overlap them, I would move them around a bit so that they are not on top of each other.

Then select the "Dogs" table and drag it to the design surface. Note that there is not a second database object on the surface. Again, you might want to move the icon around a bit, to show relationships and such (we haven't set any – that's the next step).

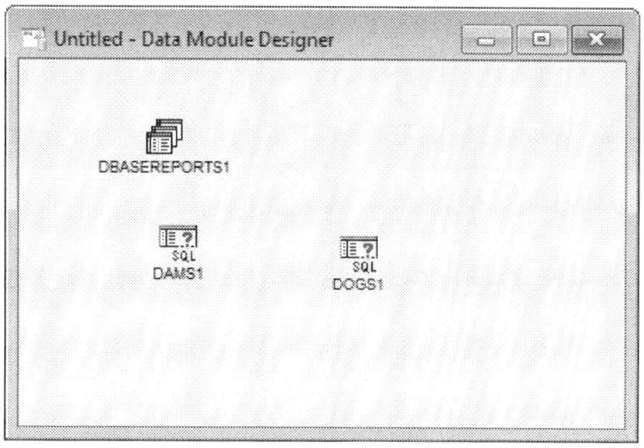

Figure 3-11

The next thing to do is to set indexes on the tables, and then set up the relationship between the two tables.

Click on "DAMS1" and go to the Inspector window. Click the *rowset* property, then the "I" (Inspect) button. Click *indexName* and then the down-arrow that appears. Select "NAME".

Click on "DOGS1" and go to the Inspector window. Click the *rowset* property, then the "I" button. Click *indexName*, and select "DAM".

To make the connection between the tables, we need to then change two more properties: *masterRowset* needs to be set to "DAMS1" (click on the property, and then the down-arrow and select "DAMS1"); and we need to tell dBASE what field to link on. Click on *masterFields* and select "DAM" from the list of fields.

Unfortunately this designer does not draw lines to show relationships between tables, but it does create the necessary code. Save the file (Ctrl+S) as "DamsParentChild.dmd".

Close the Designer (use the "X" on the title bar), and you should see this file under the "Data Modules" tab in the Navigator.

We will use this data module in later chapters as we work on the tutorial part of the book. You will be asked to copy it to new folders for the various chapters, and perhaps even make some changes as we go.

Download the Source Code

This is optional, but it is possible to download the source code for all the chapters of the book. It might be handy for some of the places where there is a *lot* of code, or if you just want to look it over. You can download the Source Code from the same location as the tables (see earlier in this chapter). There will be a link, and it will note the edition of the book *(as the code has changed a little since the first edition)*. I recommend unzipping it to a different location than the "working" folders we created for the tutorial aspect of the book.

Cleanup

Close the database that was used for this chapter. This is done simply by typing in the Command Window:

```
close databases
```

(And press the Enter key after.)

Summary

This chapter is really just aimed at getting you set up and ready to go for the tutorial parts of the book. Having the folder structure started, the tables and database alias set up, and a starting Data Module will make it easier for further chapters.

If you have the first edition of this book, there were a large set of caveats about the designer crashing and more. I don't want to scare off readers, but there are still issues with the software crashing at odd times. The best solution I can give is to simply get used to saving whatever work you are doing *(Ctrl+S is your friend)* whenever you grab a cup of water, answer the phone, talk to the cat, etc. That way, if the software decides to crash, you don't have to start over.

Moving forward, the next chapter will begin the "tutorial" part of the book, which is frankly most of the rest of it. We will start out building some custom classes and custom reports. These will be the building blocks of a library for creating your own reports. I cannot emphasize enough how important custom classes can be.

Chapter 4: Custom Reports and Custom Controls

We are going to be looking at Custom Reports and Custom Controls before we get into all the other aspects of creating reports, because it is a good idea to use both of these. This is a vital chapter, as most of the reports you will be doing in this book *(if you follow along)* will be based on these custom reports and custom classes.

A Place for Our Work

As we work through the chapter we will be needing a place for the files we create, so please create a folder for this chapter:

```
C:\dBASEReports\Chapter 4
```

And in the Navigator, be sure to navigate to this folder.

Source Code Aliases

You should set up a couple of folders, one for custom reports, and the other for report controls, and then source code aliases for them. Source Code Aliases are useful in that you don't need to know the full path for where these files are when you use them. You can simply reference the Source Code Alias.

You need to create these folders, using Windows File Explorer or the Navigator in dBASE:

```
C:\dBASEReports\ReportControls
C:\dBASEReports\Reports
```

To create the Source Code Aliases, following these instructions:

1. Select "Properties" from the menu and then "Desktop Properties"
2. Click on the "Source Aliases" tab if it is not selected
3. Click the "Add" button
4. Enter "MyReportControls" for the Alias
5. Select the folder for the alias using the tool button by the Path entryfield
6. Click the "Add" button – this will add the new alias to the list
7. Click the "Add" button – to start a new source alias
8. Enter "MyReports" for the Alias
9. Select the folder for the alias using the tool button by the Path entryfield
10. Click the "Add" button
11. Click "OK" to save and close the dialog

Custom Reports

The use of custom reports allows for standardized settings for all of your reports, the ability to make a single change that affects all of your reports, and so on. While a bit of initial effort is required, these can make your life as a developer easier in the long run, especially in a situation where your application, client, etc. requires a lot of reports.

You should create a "base" custom report, and then perhaps for each project or application you would create yet another custom report that was derived from your base report. All of the reports for a specific project would be based on the project-specific custom report, any changes made to the custom report for that project would filter down through any reports derived from it.

To create a custom report, go to the Navigator and find the report icon that says "[New Custom Report]" and double-click on it (or use other means of opening a new custom report).

When you do this, you will be placed in the Report Designer as in Chapter 1, but unless you tell it otherwise, dBASE will assume that this report is going to be a Custom report when you save it.

The first thing to do is set the report *metric* to whatever metric you are comfortable working with. It is important to note that once you start creating reports based on this one, it is a really bad idea to change the *metric* property of the custom report. If you do, it will most likely have some pretty bad, if not "disastrous" effects on the appearance of any report derived from it! For the purposes of this book, I will assume you are using a *metric* of "3 - Inches", but if you are more comfortable with another setting, please use it.

If the *autoSort* property is showing as *true*, it is a good idea to set this to *false* as discussed in the earlier chapters of this book.

Next, as with the previous reports we created, the *reportGroup headerBand* and *reportGroup footerBand* both have their respective *height* properties set to a value. It is a good idea to set this property for both of these bands to zero. This means that all reports that are derived from this report will automatically have this set! So, click on the *reportGroup headerBand* (the green band) and in the Inspector change the *height* property to 0. Then do the same for the *reportGroup footerBand* (the blue band).

Other Things to Consider

I usually suggest setting the margins to a value that makes sense to you. I like to use as much of the page as I can for generating reports, because many of the reports I create have a lot of information to get out there – to that end, let's go to the Inspector and look at the report's margins.

In America, the default piece of paper for most printers is 8 ½" wide by 11" tall. This will be important for the demonstration, because of course you may be using different dimensions for your own paper/reports.

Click on "form" in the Inspector (which is the top-level object in the Designer), note that there are no margin properties. How do you change the margins? The *pageTemplate* object is what defines what the paper looks like. To see the properties needed, examine the *pageTemplate* object, which appears as *pageTemplate1* in the Inspector. You should now see in the Inspector properties of *marginBottom*, *marginLeft*, *marginRight*, and *marginTop*. If your *metric* is Inches, you will see a value of "0.75" for each, which is 3/4 of an inch. I usually use a ½" margin, so set these properties to "0.50" for each of them.

Now when you did this, notice that the *streamFrame* shifted left, and if you scroll to the right you will see that there is more room to the right of the *streamFrame*. This is where we will be printing the data from our table, so why not use all the space available from left to right?

> **NOTE**
> It should be noted that all of this is suggestion, and you do *not* have to use the exact same design, layout, etc. as shown here. Indeed, you could take advantage of the ability to change the size of the *streamFrame*, and place a logo or graphic down the side of the page, if you so desired! Let the ideas flow, and use them when you want/need to. For the purposes of this book you might want to just follow-along, but for your own reports, use your imagination or the needs of your business/client.

To get the most out of the printed page set the *streamFrame* to cover the *pageTemplate* from left to right.

This is done by setting the *streamFrame's left* property to 0, and the *streamFrame's width* property to the appropriate width (8.5" minus .5" on each side, or 7.5" wide). If you set the properties correctly, the *streamFrame* should now cover the *pageTemplate* completely from left to right.

You could have dragged the *streamFrame* to the left of the *pageTemplate*, and then using the mouse widened the *streamFrame* to the width of the *pageTemplate*, but I find that for precision, sometimes it is easier to use the Inspector.

Now we don't usually want the *streamFrame* to cover the *pageTemplate* from top to bottom, but if you scroll toward the bottom of the report using the scrollbar on the right, you will see that we could easily be using more space toward the bottom than we are now. Set the *streamFrame's top* property at 1", which *should* give room for what needs to go above it on the *pageTemplate*. Then change the *height* property to a much larger value than we are using now. What you might want to do is use the mouse (click on the *streamFrame* – the yellow part of the design surface) and drag the bottom down to what appears to be about the right amount of room. You should end up with a *height* close to 8.65" (if you look at it in the Inspector).

Should you place any controls on this report? For the most part you shouldn't. For each application that you create you should create a new custom report that is *based* on this one (or derived from it), and any special text (including page numbers) can be handled on that custom report. This one should only be for the absolute basics.

So, we are pretty much done. If you press Ctrl+S to save this report, where should you save it? You should use the folder you created earlier for storing custom reports:

```
C:\dBASEReports\Reports
```

When the dialog comes up use the pushbuttons to find the appropriate folder, and then name this file "Base" – dBASE will assign a file extension of ".crp" for "Custom RePort". Close the designer for the moment.

Using a Custom Report Class

Now that you have the "base" report class, we need to learn how to work with it.

To see how this works, we need to create a standard report, so double-click on "[New Report]" icon in the Navigator on the "Reports" tab. You will see the usual start-up of the Report Designer.

To tell dBASE we want to use a Custom Report, we need to select the "File" menu, and "Set Custom Report Class ...". This brings up a dialog that looks like:

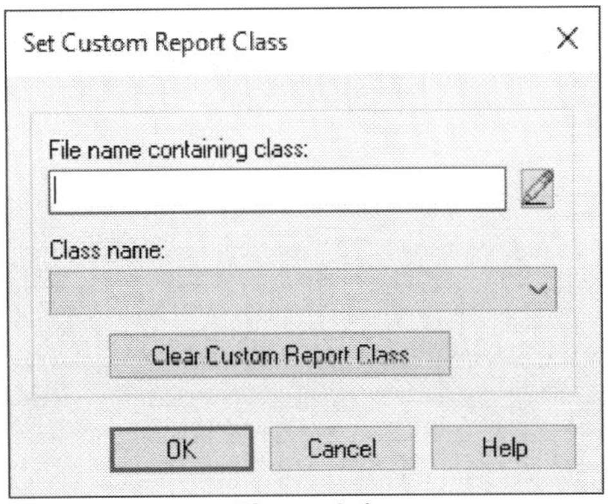

Figure 4-1

Click the tool button (with the pencil) next to the first entryfield, and find the folder that we created to store our custom reports ("C:\dBASEReports\Reports"). You will find the file "Base.crp" there, select that file, and click "Open". Note that the "Class name:" combobox now displays the name of the custom report class. When you click the "OK" button on the original dialog, you will see your report has changed appearance a little – to match the base custom report.

> **NOTE**
> It is possible to store multiple custom reports in one .CRP file. I mention this here, because the "Class name:" combobox in the dialog in figure 4-1, would have a list of multiple custom reports if you did this. When the first versions of dBASE Plus (called Visual dBASE 7.0 and 7.01) were released, I thought this was a nifty idea. I worked with it and found it was a bit confusing. Largely the problems deal with any comments you might place in the .CRP file to explain which custom report is which – if you bring one of these into the Report Designer, the comments are not moved with them when the report code is put back into the .CRP file, and I spent more time trying to deal with maintaining the comments than anything else. From personal experience, I recommend just putting one custom report in a .CRP file.

The *metric* property is set, and other properties of various report objects have been set, such as the *pageTemplate* object's margin properties, the *streamFrame's* size properties, and so on.

What this means is that as a developer if you use custom reports, you do not have to remember to set all of these properties each time!

Everything else about a report derived from a Custom Report will work the same. You can drag tables to the design surface, drag fields to the *detailBand*, and so on.

A Custom Report Derived from a Custom Report

We are going to take this custom layer one level deeper. You have a base custom class, but you might want to have more than one custom report. In this book you will end up with several custom reports, all of them derived from "Base.crp". The term "derived" here means that the custom report is based on another custom report, and all of the properties and settings in the first custom report will be part of the new custom report.

With the basic settings in our "Base" report, we could easily create new custom reports based on this one.

If you've been following along, close the current report without saving it.

Go to the Navigator and double-click the "[New Custom Report]" icon under the Reports tab. This will tell dBASE to create a Custom Report in the Report Designer. Because we are doing a Custom Report, dBASE does *not* assume that we want to base this on "Base.crp".

Select the "File" menu, and "Set Custom Report Class ...". Notice that the dialog shows the last selected Custom Report. Click "OK", and now the Custom Report we are working on has the properties of the "Base" report.

Since this report is going to be the main custom report for a company, we might want to place a title at the top of the page that will be on all of our reports, that shows the company name.

Add Page Titles

Select a text control from the Component Palette – place it on the *pageTemplate*. You will need to click on the control again to give it focus. Make the control fairly wide (approximately two inches) by dragging the right edge to the right. Set the *fontSize* property to 20 points. As soon as you do that, notice that the *height* of the text control will need to be changed – the simple way is to drag the bottom of the control down a bit with your mouse *(or hold the Ctrl key and use the down arrow)*.

Click on the text (or use the Inspector and change the *text* property), and type "My Company Name" (without the quotes) – if typing on the text control directly, do NOT press Enter when done, or you will add a hard return at the end of the line. *(If necessary, readjust the height of the control so the text is all on one line.)*

Click on the design surface to take focus off the control for the moment. Now click once on the text control to give it focus again. We should change a few more properties:

alignHorizontal	1 - Center
name	MainTitleText
fontItalic	true
top	0

> **NOTE**
> The topic of font sizes is important, but not really discussed in many places in the database application world. When you get to reports, however, you should understand the basics. Font sizes are based on *points*, there are 72 points to an inch. When we set a *fontSize* to 20 points, we are talking about 20/72 of an inch. However, fonts are not quite that straight forward in the real world. Fonts designed to work in Windows have to take into account ascenders (the tops of letters that go above the base characters such as the top of a "t"), and descenders (ex: the bottom of the letter "g"). In addition most fonts have some padding above and below, as well as between characters. You should try to be aware of these things when designing your controls – a bit of carelessness or lack of observation and you can truncate the tops or bottoms of the letters in the text.

You could get *really* fancy and place a border around the text (set the *borderStyle* property), play with the *colorNormal* property, and so on. We'll come back to these options in a later chapter of this book.

We do, however, want this completely centered on the report. To do that, use the "Layout" menu, and select "Align", and "Center Horizontally in Window".

We are going to add a secondary title – select a *text* control from the Component Palette and drag it to the *pageTemplate*, placing the top of the control very close to the bottom of the MainTitleText control we just created. This might be used to give define the reason for the report. Set the following properties:

fontSize	16
alignHorizontal	1 - Center
name	SecondaryTitleText
text	Purpose of Report

Also select the "Layout" menu, "Align" and "Center Horizontally in Window" option.

Finally, let's place one more control on the report – one that displays the date in a format that easy to read and is not ambiguous. We did a simple version of this in the first chapter using the default date format in dBASE ("mm/dd/yyyy" if you are set to American date formats).

We're going to create a text control that shows the text for the month, the day of the month, and the year ("July 5, 2016", for example).

Place one more text control on the *pageTemplate* below the secondary title that we just created. Widen it a bit. Go to the Inspector and find the *text* property. Click on the type button ("T"), and select "Codeblock".

Click on the tool button and in the "Build Codeblock" dialog, type:

```
cmonth(date())+" "+day(date())+", "+year(date())
```

(" " has a space between the quotes, ", " has a comma and a space after it between the quotes)

Click "OK" and you should see a date formatted along the lines of:

```
June 15, 2016
```

NOTE
You could use the undocumented function *DTOJ()*, which produces a similar date layout as that discussed here, but also includes the day of the week and inserts a leading zero for the day if needed:

```
Tuesday, March 01, 2005
```

Set these properties:

fontSize	12
alignHorizontal	1 - Center
name	DateText

And once again, select the "Layout" menu and center this in the window, as we did with the other controls.

This should look something like:

Figure 4-2

Custom Control Classes for Reports

This date text class is rather useful, don't you think? Wouldn't it be useful to make it available without having to re-create it each time for all of our reports? How about the other controls? What about a situation where within a company, the CEO decides he wants the font to be a different font for the main title? If you have a bunch of reports, this can take time to change. OR you can turn these into custom classes, and if the CEO wants a different font, you only have to change it in the custom class definition!

We can do that easily enough. Hold the Ctrl key and click on all three of the controls we have created.

Select the "File" menu. Select "Save as Custom", and in the dialog click on the tool button next to the "Custom Component Filename". Select the folder we created earlier in this chapter for Report Controls ("C:\dBASEReports\ReportControls"), and then enter the name of the class file ("MyReportControls.cc").

Click "Save", and then in the dialog, uncheck the box "Place in Component Palette" (so that we don't automatically load this control each time we go into the report designer). The dialog should look something like:

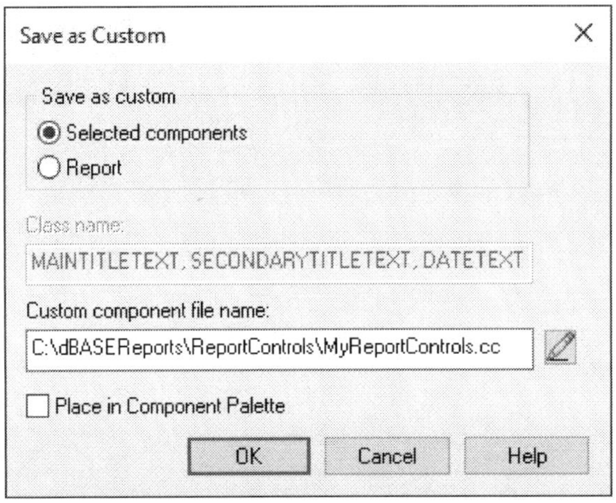

Figure 4-3

Click "OK". This will have saved our *DateText* class, and the other two classes we selected, out so that we can reuse them if we want to for other custom (or other) reports.

We can do this for other controls of course. If we had a company logo we might want to do the same sort of thing. Note that this is just one method of creating a custom class – the other is to create the class in the Source Code Editor directly. The drawback to the second method is that you do not get the visual aspect of designing the class – sometimes it is helpful to be able to see what the class looks like before saving it. There are advantages to either method, and like a lot of things in dBASE, you, as a developer will need to find the method that works best for you. I tend to use both depending on the situation I am in.

Save the custom report by pressing Ctrl+S. In the dialog, remember we want this to go in the folder with our custom reports, so use the tool button and find the folder ("C:\dBASEReports\Reports"), and name this "MyCompanyReport.crp".

At this point, we are going to exit the Report Designer and go examine the custom classes we created. While we *could* leave the Report Designer open and do this, it is sometimes confusing. Save and exit (Ctrl+W) the Report Designer.

If you have read The dBASE Book, you will know that there can be a problem with the Report Designer and the default means of streaming out custom controls to a .CC file. This problem deals with how an object is named when it is placed on a form or report. The solution is to remove one of the parameters that is automatically added. To do this, open the custom class file in the Source Code Editor:

```
modify command :MyReportControls:MyReportControls.cc
```

You will see all of three of the controls we defined streamed out in this file, the problem is in the first line for each (underlined in the example below):

```
class MAINTITLETEXT(parentObj, name) of TEXT(parentObj, name) custom
```

The second parameter "name" is the issue. If we remove that and the comma in front of it, we can avoid problems with the Report Designer streaming these out with confusing names. To do this, press Ctrl+R (Replace dialog) and in the dialog that appears, enter ", name" (that is a comma, a space, and the word "name" without the quotes) in the "Find what" entryfield. In the "Replace with" entryfield, do not put anything. This should look like:

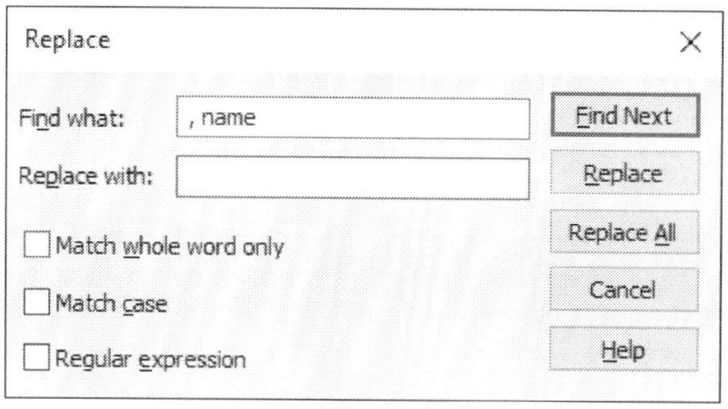

Figure 4-4

Click the "Replace All" button, and this will be done. Close the dialog (click on the .Close. button). The line should now look like:

```
class MAINTITLETEXT(parentObj) of TEXT(parentObj) custom
```

Press Ctrl+W to save this and exit the Source Code Editor. We will take a look at modifying fonts or other properties in the custom class file later.

Back to Our Custom Report

Bring the Custom Report back up in the Report Designer by either right clicking on it in the Navigator window and selecting "Design Report", or by pressing Shift+F2, or by clicking on the "Open in Designer" tool button at the top of the dBASE frame window.

We want to do one more thing – place a page number at the bottom of the report. As noted before this is done easily as dBASE ships with a custom class for this purpose. Using the scrollbar on the right side of the report, scroll down, so we see the very bottom of the page. There should be a small amount of white space there.

On the Component Palette find the "Paging" tab, and drag the *Pagenumber* control to the *pageTemplate* at the bottom. Widen the control, then move it around, and adjust as necessary, so that you can actually see a page number. Select the "Layout" menu, and center this on the page.

Save the report and close the Report Designer (Ctrl+W).

NOTE

If the "Paging" tab is not available on the Component Palette, then this custom class is not set up to be used in dBASE. There are several ways to add this, the one I recommend, because this is something that might be useful in many reports, is:

- Click on the Component Palette to give it focus
- Right click
- Select "Set Up Custom Components ..."
- Click the "Add" button, and find the folder that holds the REPORT.CC class in the dBASE folders (by default in English, this is

```
C:\ProgramData\dBASE\Plus10\dBLClasses\ReportControls
```

- Select "REPORT.CC" and click "Open"

This will make sure that every time you open the Report Designer, this custom class is available and on the "Paging" tab of the Component Palette.

We have now created a custom report that we can use to base all reports for our company on. This is very useful, because if the company name changes, we can change it in *one place* – the custom report. If some decision is made by the manager of the company that the page margins have to change, then again all reports that are derived from this report don't have to be changed – just the custom report. And so on.

After all that work, there is a bit more we want to do to make the custom classes we created work properly. The problem is that while we saved the text controls to the custom class file, they were also streamed out in their entirety to the custom report file "MyCompanyReport.crp". We need to modify the report's source code and remove some properties, so that if we change them in the custom class file they will affect this report *(and any reports derived from it)*.

To do this, open the file in the Source Code Editor by typing the following in the Command Window:

```
modify command :MyReports:MyCompanyReport.crp
```

Scroll down to the constructor code for "MainTitleText", which should look like:

```
this.PAGETEMPLATE1.MAINTITLETEXT = new TEXT(this.PAGETEMPLATE1)
   with (this.PAGETEMPLATE1.MAINTITLETEXT)
      height = 0.3646
      left = 2.2083
      top = 0.0
      width = 3.0833
      prefixEnable = false
      alignHorizontal = 1  // Center
      fontSize = 20.0
      fontItalic = true
      text = "My Company Name"
      form.MAINTITLETEXT = form.pagetemplate1.maintitletext
   endwith
```

The first thing that needs to be changed is the first line needs to show the control as being subclassed from the custom class:

```
this.PAGETEMPLATE1.MAINTITLETEXT1 = new MAINTITLETEXT(this.PAGETEMPLATE1)
```

Make the changes shown in boldface (add the number 1 to the end of the first "MainTitleText", and add the word "MAINTITLE" to the word "TEXT" after the word "new" ...).

Next change the following line by adding the "1" after "MAINTITLETEXT":

```
with (this.PAGETEMPLATE1.MAINTITLETEXT1)
```

And change the references inside the with/endwith structure for "maintitletext" to "maintitletext1" (add the number 1 to the end of each).

After this, we need to remove properties that we might want to change in the custom class file or are defined in that file that shouldn't need to be here in the report. Basically all that needs to be here is what shows below:

```
this.PAGETEMPLATE1.MAINTITLETEXT1 = new MAINTITLETTEXT(this.PAGETEMPLATE1)
with (this.PAGETEMPLATE1.MAINTITLETEXT1)
   left = 2.2083
   top = 0.0
   form.MAINTITLETEXT1 = form.pagetemplate1.maintitletext1
endwith
```

We left the properties *left* and *top* here because they are specific to this report. The other properties are ones that we might want to change in the custom class file, and if they are in the custom report, the report will ignore the properties in the .cc file.

We need to do the same for the other two text controls, make them look like the following (make sure to add the number 1 in places that require it as shown below):

```
this.PAGETEMPLATE1.SECONDARYTITLETEXT1 = new SECONDARYTITLETEXT(this.PAGETEMPLATE1)
with (this.PAGETEMPLATE1.SECONDARYTITLETEXT1)
   left = 2.5833
   top = 0.3854
   form.SECONDARYTITLETEXT1 = form.pagetemplate1.secondarytitletext1
endwith

this.PAGETEMPLATE1.DATETEXT1 = new DATETEXT(this.PAGETEMPLATE1)
with (this.PAGETEMPLATE1.DATETEXT1)
   left = 2.6979
   top = 0.6771
   form.DATETEXT1 = form.pagetemplate1.datetext1
endwith
```

Finally, go to the top of the report, and look at these lines:

```
class MyCompanyReportCReport of BASECREPORT custom from :MyReports:Base.crp
   set procedure to :ReportControls:REPORT.CC
```

In the statement above, dBASE *may* have streamed out the full path to this, something like (this would be on a single statement in the editor):

```
    set procedure to
C:\Users\username\Documents\dBASE\Plus10\dBLClasses\ReportControls\REPO
RT.CC
```

It is a good idea to change this to use the Source Code alias "ReportControls" as shown above. *("username" would be your username in Windows ...)*

Note that there is no reference to the "MyReportControls.cc" class file. This needs to be here. Add the following line of code right after the "class" statement:

```
    set procedure to :MyReportControls:MyReportControls.cc
```

The constructor for the report should now start with:

```
class MyCompanyReportCReport of BASECREPORT custom from :MyReports:Base.crp
    set procedure to :MyReportControls:MyReportControls.cc
    set procedure to :ReportControls:REPORT.CC
```

> **NOTE**
> The sequence of the SET PROCEDURE statements shown here is not important. If they are in a different sequence that's okay and will not harm your report(s) in any way.

If you see the word "additive", it is not necessary in these statements *(that is now the default behavior of dBASE)*, and should not be being streamed out in these statements – you can remove the word "additive" from those statements with no ill effects.

Save this and exit the Source Code Editor by pressing Ctrl+W. *(Note that if we had created the custom text controls outside of the designer, and then used them in this report in a different fashion, this would not have been as complicated a process ...)*

You should try opening the Custom Report (double-click it in the Navigator) and make sure it opens. If you get any errors, check for typos *(while working on this chapter, I found I had left out a number '1' in one of the places the name of a control was used, for example – it took a while to find it)*.

Even More Custom Classes

We need to have a couple more custom controls to use with our reports –the text associated with a field, and the text heading. We could create these the way we did earlier, but it is a good idea to get used to doing this sort of thing by hand as well – understanding how the code works is vital to really creating good reports in dBASE.

A custom class contains constructor code, and as we will see in later chapters, you can add code (methods) that executes as needed, and more. For reports most of the custom classes you will need are text controls, and that is what we will start with.

To create new custom classes for our reports, let's open the MyReportControls.cc file in the Source Code Editor:

```
modify command :MyReportControls:MyReportControls.cc
```

Go to the bottom of the file, after the last class currently there.

The first part of the custom control defines what it is subclassed from. If we wanted to create a standard text control to use in our reports for text that is linked to a field in a table, we might define it as:

```
class DATATEXT(parentObj) of TEXT(parentObj) custom
```

To go with the CLASS statement, we must have an ENDCLASS statement, which we will add later.

We could use the with/endwith structure that the classes already in the file use, or we could just simply add properties with "this.*somepropertyname*". The with/endwith option is useful because it means we don't need the "this." reference for each property. We are going to assign values to the properties *fontSize*, *fontName*, and a basic *text* property which we can use in later reports. There isn't a lot that needs to be done here. Your finished class should look like:

```
class DataText(parentObj) of TEXT(parentObj) custom
   with (this)
      fontName = "Arial"
      fontSize = 10
      text = "DataText"
   endwith
endclass
```

We can also add a text control for headings, which would be the same as this one, but with the *fontBold* property set, and the text modified:

```
class DATAHEADINGTEXT(parentObj) of DATATEXT(parentObj) custom
   with (this)
      fontBold = true
      text = "DataHeadingText"
   endwith
endclass
```

Notice that what we did here is to subclass the "DATAHEADINGTEXT" class from the "DATATEXT" class – this means that any changes made to "DATATEXT" will affect "DATAHEADINGTEXT", except the *fontBold* property. Save and exit (Ctrl+W), we will use these in most of the reports in this book.

Using a Custom Report

The steps for this process will seem very similar to what we have done so far. If you have not closed the Report Designer or the Source Code Editor you should do so.

In the Navigator window, double-click the "[New Report]" icon, and bring up the Report Designer again.

Notice that currently this is using the "Base.crp" file – this was the last custom report we used. Instead, we want to use the new custom report we just created. Go to the "File" menu, and select "Set Custom Report Class ...". In that dialog, click on the tool button by the first entryfield, and select "MyCompanyReport.crp". Click "OK".

Now all new reports – until we either change the class, or use the "Clear Custom Report Class" button *(on the dialog we just closed)* – will use "MyCompanyReport.crp" as the custom class that they are derived from.

Your new report will now have the text controls we placed on the *pageTemplate* of the custom report. We're going to do a very simple report, basically similar to the report we did in the first chapter, except that we will also be using the custom classes we just created.

Click on the "SecondaryTitle" control (the one that says "Purpose of Report"). Click once again (do this slowly – the first click gets focus, the second click puts us in edit mode), and change the text to say "Some Dogs" (without the quotes). Click back on the *pageTemplate*, and notice that the text automatically centers and adjusts for the width of the text.

Next, find the Navigator window, and select the "Tables" tab. Click the combobox down-arrow button and select the "DBASEREPORTS" database if necessary, and then select the "Dogs" table, dragging it to the Report surface.

You will now see a *detailBand* for each row in the table (that could fit on this *streamFrame*). Click on the "DOGS1" query object and find the *rowset* object in the Inspector, click on the Inspect button ("I"), and on the rowset, find the *indexName* property. Select "Name".

Now that the data is sorted the way we might want it to be, we should start using the custom classes to put the body of our report together.

If we went by how we had done things in the past, we might go to the Field Palette and drag the fields off the palette to the *detailBand*. However, to use our custom classes, we have to do this differently. While the amount of work involved is a bit more complex, the results will be that since we are using custom classes global changes to these reports will be easier.

Go to the Component Palette, select the "Custom" tab, and drag an instance of "DataHeadingText" to the *detailBand*. If necessary drag it to the top of the *detailBand*, and move it to the left. You may need to widen it as well. You should see something like:

Figure 4-5

BUG

There is a bug in current version of dBASE that affects custom controls and reports – placing a custom control onto a report will:

- Remove focus from the control, placing it on the parent (detailBand, or pageTemplate ...)
- Place it lower than it should be (you will have to move it up or change the *top* property in the inspector), often it is closer to center than it ought to be or sometimes very far to the right (move it left or right, or modify the *left* property),
- The width seems to be some specific (small) setting, you will need to modify the *width* property as well.

To deal with this, find the control in the Inspector's combobox. Example: you placed the "DataHeadingText" control on the *detailBand*, so look for "detailBand" and then under that "dataheadingtext1". Once you have given it focus, you can, in the Inspector, change the *top* and/or *left* properties so it is on the *detailBand (if the right property looks too big, make it smaller)*, move it to where it needs to go using the mouse, widen it, and then work with it like normal.

After you do this a few times it will become second nature.

With this control the text may not appear as boldfaced, even though the *fontBold* property was set. This is due to a minor bug in the report designer. For the moment, don't worry about that. Click on the control (since it already has focus, this should put it into edit mode) and change the *text* to "Name". (Don't type the quotes.)

Now go to the Component Palette and drag an instance of "DataText" (don't confuse this with "DateText"!) to the *detailBand*. Note that the only place to put it is to the right of the heading. That's okay. Once you place it on the *detailBand (see note above about a bug with custom controls)*, try moving it down below the first text control – notice that the *detailBand's height* automatically adjusts to make room for this control. Again you will need to widen it and work with the positioning a bit.

Your report should now *something* look like:

Figure 4-6

Next you will want to widen the "DataText" control so it covers about half the width of the *detailBand* (long enough for the names that will be displayed). To do that, click on the right edge and drag the right edge over to about half the width of the report.

The next thing is the tricky part of what we need to do, because we need the codeblock that will be used by dBASE to get the value of the field and display it. If we had just dragged this control off the Field Palette the Report Designer would have automatically placed the codeblock into the *text* property of this control. However, to use custom classes in reports requires a bit more work. What we need to do is work out the object hierarchy for the control.

this = the text control
form = the report
dogs1 = the query object used to reference the table
rowset = the rowset of the query
fields = the fields array

So, with that in mind, we need to create a codeblock for this text control. The way to do this is to go to the Inspector and find the *text* property. When you click on this, you will see two buttons on the right. The first is a wrench (don't click it yet – we will in a moment), the other has the letter "T" (for Type). Click this and look for "Codeblock". Select this. Notice that the text property has changed in the Inspector to:

```
{||"DataText"}
```

Now that the Report Designer knows this will be a codeblock, click on the tool button (the "screwdriver?"), which will bring up a dialog:

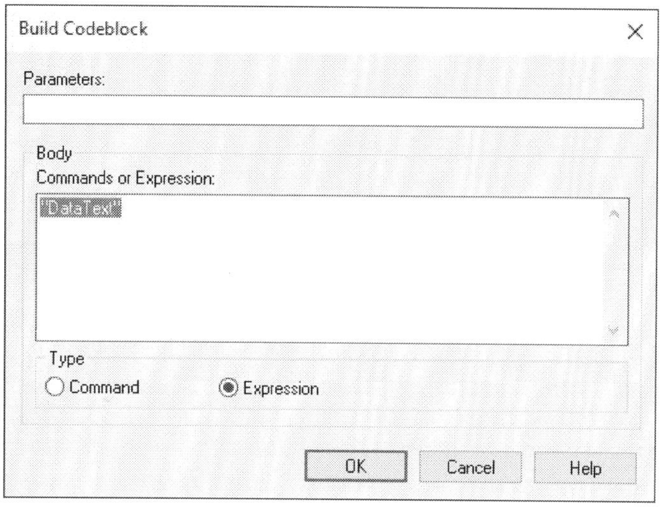

Figure 4-7

We need to change the text "DataText" to:

```
this.form.dogs1.rowset.fields["name"].value
```

When you change the text, and click "OK" your report should now look something like:

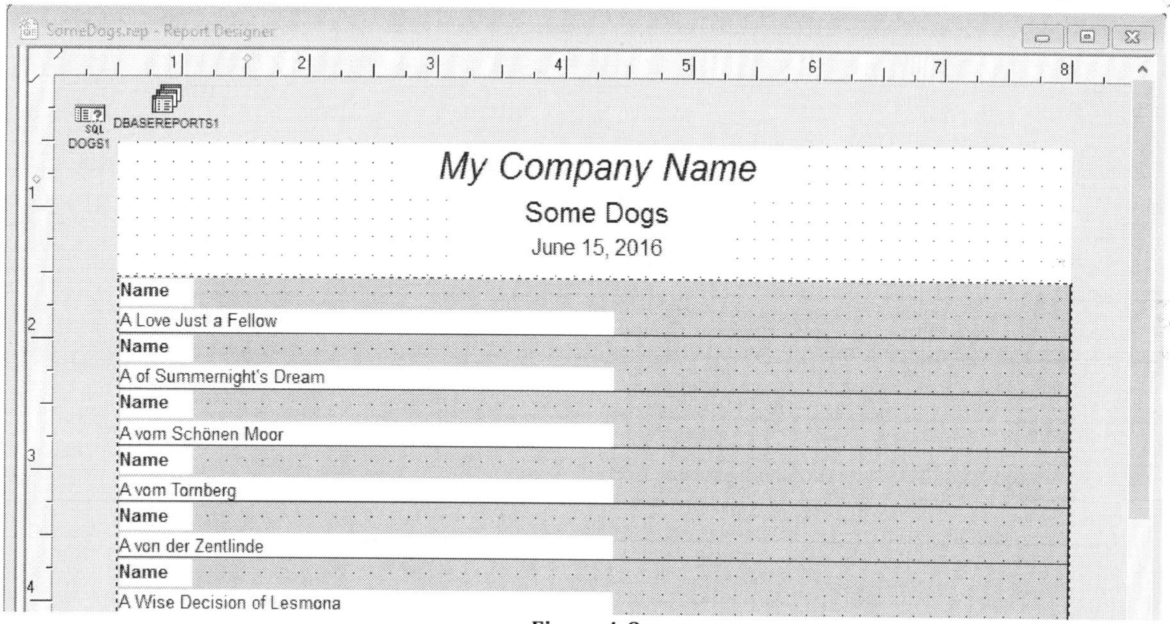

Figure 4-8

As we are keeping this simple, this is all we want to do for this report. Press Ctrl+S to save this report, make sure the folder is "Chapter 4" and name the report "SomeDogs.rep".

The one problem is that the heading appears on each record or *detailBand*. How do we suppress this, so that it only appears once – at the top of the page? We need to set a property and an event handler for an event.

To do this, click on the text that says "Name", and change this property in the Inspector:

suppressIfBlank true

Next, click on the "Events" tab in the Inspector, and find the *canRender* event. Click on it, set the Type (use the "T" button) to Codeblock, and then click on the Tool button (the screwdriver?), and type:

```
this.parent.firstOnFrame
```

The report should now only show the "Name" heading at the top of the column, rather than for each *detailBand*. We will examine this technique in more detail in later chapters, but it is a good one to know.

Indeed, we could set the property and event handler in the custom class, but since we might want to use this control for different types of *detailBand* layout, we will leave it for now – we'll come back to this. It should also be noted that this property will cause the text to appear on *each page* at the top of the *detailBand* (this is because by default the Report Engine sees a page as a new *streamFrame*, and we're checking for the first time on the frame).

If you run this report (click the "Lightning" button in the toolbar), you should see something like:

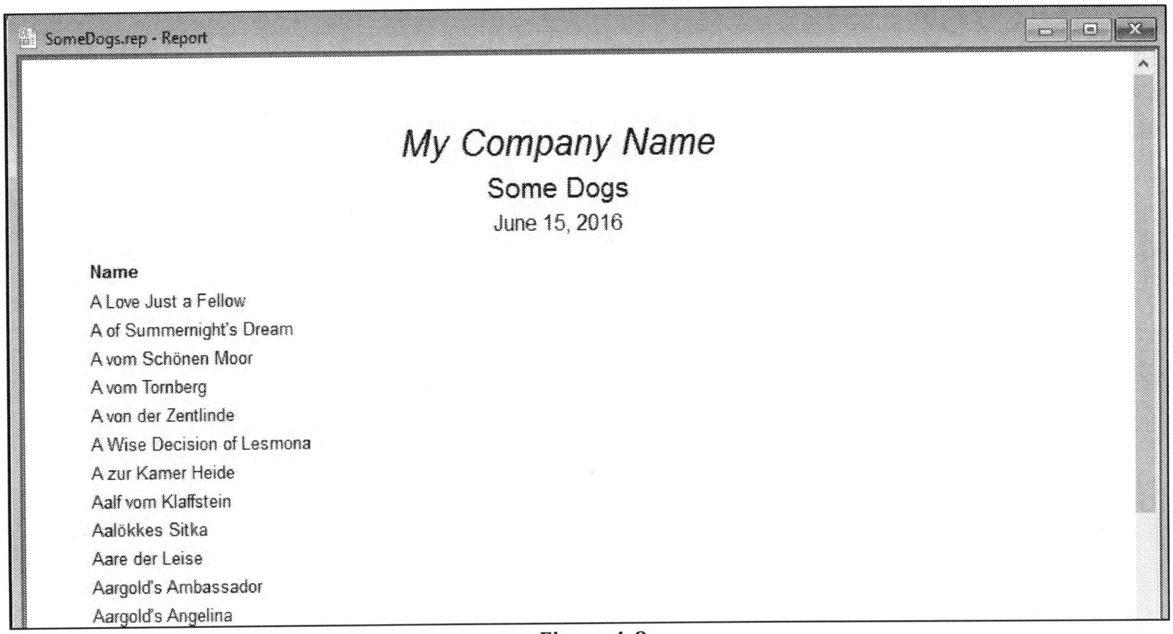

Figure 4-9

As noted, this is pretty basic.

The one thing to note is that the changes we made to the "DataHeadingText" control to only display at the top of the page on this report will only affect this report. What does that mean for you, as a developer? It means that basically if you left things as they are, every report in which you used the "DataHeadingText" control would require that you make the same two changes we just did for the heading to be useful. This means that frankly, this custom class is not all that handy. You can instead create a *new* custom class and add those two changes into the class, and any reports that use the new class will automatically inherit those properties.

To do this, close the report, and in the Command Window type:

```
modify command :MyReportControls:MyReportControls.cc
```

Find the code for the DataHeadingText class, and copy the code down to the endclass statement:

- Use the mouse and select from *class* to *endclass*
- Press Ctrl+C
- Move the mouse after the *endclass* statement
- Press Ctrl+V to paste it

and make the changes shown (in bold):

```
class DATACOLHEADINGTEXT(parentObj) of DATAHEADINGTEXT(parentObj) custom
   with(this)
      text = "ColumnHeadingText"
      suppressIfBlank = true
      canRender = {||this.parent.firstOnFrame}
   endwith
endclass
```

Note that the *canRender* statement shown above uses a codeblock. After the curly brace ({) we use two vertical bars (or pipes) – "|". This is the proper syntax. Also note that this custom class is subclassed from the DataHeadingText custom class – what this means is that it inherits the properties defined by the DataHeadingText class, such as the *fontName* and *fontBold* properties.

Save and exit the Source Code Editor by pressing Ctrl+W, and from now we have two different controls that can be used for the headings in reports, one for Tabular reports (more on this term in a later chapter), and one for Form reports (also in a later chapter).

Now that we've created the new custom class, we should examine the source code for this report.

Report Source Code

As noted elsewhere in this book, all of the designers in dBASE generate or create dBL source code. By studying the code generated from the designers, you can learn a lot about how these objects work.

In the Command Window, type:

```
modify command SomeDogs.rep
```

You should see the following at the beginning of the constructor code:

```
class SomeDogsReport of MYCOMPANYREPORTCREPORT from :MyReports:MyCompanyReport.crp
   set procedure to :MyReportControls:MyReportControls.cc
   set procedure to :ReportControls:REPORT.CC
```

The first line tells dBASE that this report is derived from "MYCOMPANYREPORT" – the report we created earlier in this chapter, which is in the source code file ":MyReports:MyCompanyReport.crp". Notice that dBASE should have automatically substituted the Source Code Alias that we created for the path. If we did not use a Source Code Alias, dBASE would have placed the path in there (i.e., "C:\dBASEReports\Reports").

The first SET PROCEDURE statement ensures that the report can find the classes in the MyReportControls.cc class. The second SET PROCEDURE statement makes sure we are using the report class for page numbering.

You can spend time examining the other source code if you wish, but for the purpose of this book, let's move on. Close this without making any changes. Now in the Command Window, type:

```
modify command :MyReports:MyCompanyReport.crp
```

As you work with dBASE reports, never hesitate to spend some time examining the source code. Sometimes you may want to modify something, at others, it is just useful to know what is there.

Close the Source Code Editor for now (Ctrl+W).

Modifying Custom Classes

One of the nicest aspects of using custom classes is that you can change a property once, and have it affect all instances of that class, without having to change each report that uses that class. To see how this works, let's make a minor modification to the MainTitleText class we created earlier. In order to do this, we need to open the source code for the MyReportClasses file:

```
modify command :MyReportControls:MyReportControls.cc
```

With that open, the MainTitleText class should look like:

```
class MAINTITLETEXT(parentObj) of TEXT(parentObj) custom
   with (this)
      height = 0.3646
      left = 2.2083
      top = 0.0
      width = 3.0833
      metric = 3     // Inches
      prefixEnable = false
      alignHorizontal = 1  // Center
      fontSize = 20.0
      fontItalic = true
      text = "My Company Name"
   endwith
endclass
```

If we change things so that we comment out the *fontItalic* line, and add a line with the *fontName* (the default font in dBASE is "Arial") property pointing to a different font than the default, such as (you may need to see what fonts are available on your computer):

```
// fontItalic = true
fontName = "Calligraphic"
```

> **NOTE**
> If you do not know what fonts are available in Windows, or what the name of a specific font is, try bringing up the Command Window, and typing:
>
> ```
> ? getFont()
> ```
>
> This will display a dialog showing the fonts available and what they look like. Select a font. When you click "OK" the dialog will close and the name of the font chosen will appear in the Output Pane of the Command Window. You can then copy that into the class for this exercise.

Save and exit this file (Ctrl+W), and double-click on the "SomeDogs" report in the Navigator window, you should see something like:

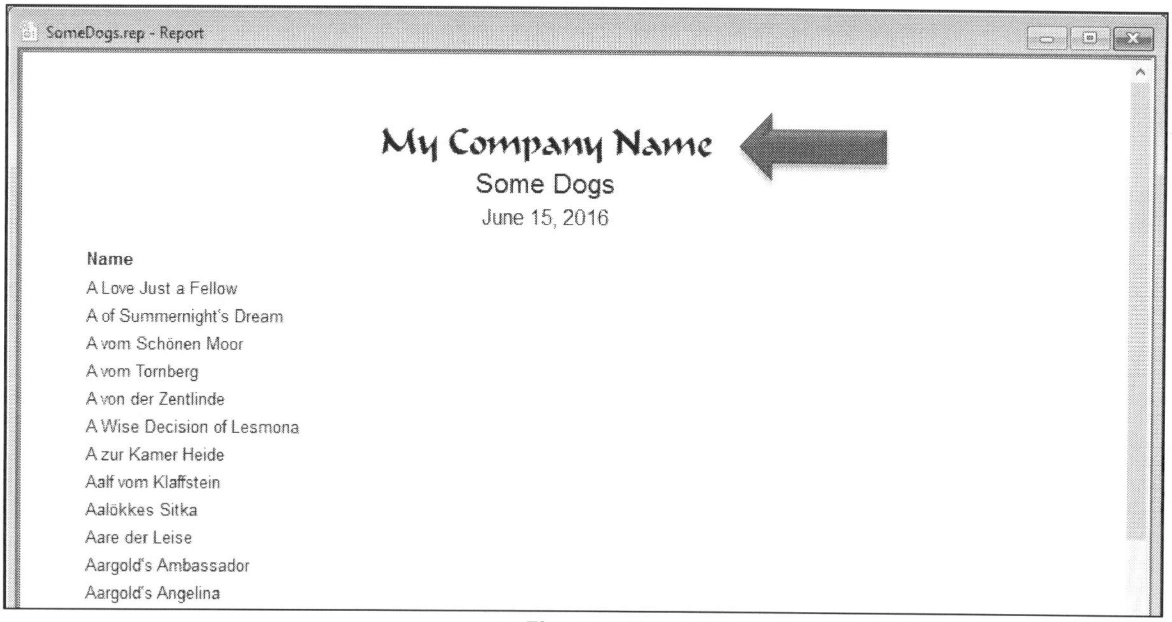

Figure 4-10

For the rest of the tutorial, it's probably a good idea to reset this, so open the file again:

```
modify command :MyReportControls:MyReportControls.cc
```

And change these two lines:

```
// fontItalic = true
fontName = "Calligraphic"
```

by removing the "//" before the *fontItalic* line, and removing the *fontName* line (or putting the comment marker in front of it). Save and exit (Ctrl+W) and the next time you run the report it will look like it did previously.

This shows how easy it is to modify all reports in an application by simply changing the custom classes used by the report.

Clearing Custom Reports

Once you have set a custom report to be used for your application, dBASE remembers this, and every report you create will be derived from that custom report. You can however clear these out, and it is a good idea to do so after you have completed a chapter of this book, or before you go on to working on your own applications.

Follow along:

- Start a new report by double-clicking the [New Report] icon in the Navigator
- Select the "File" menu
- Select the "Set Custom Report Class ..." menu option
- Click the "Clear Custom Report Class" button
- Click "OK"
- Close the Report Designer without saving the report

Cleanup

You should close the database that was used to create these reports as well as clearing the custom report. This is done simply by typing in the Command Window:

```
close databases
```

(And press the Enter key after.)

Source Code

The following is a listing of the sample code in the folders we have been working with. If you downloaded the files from my website the structure will be different (see below). You may use the code contained in these folders for your own applications if you desire, with the caveat that credit be given appropriately.

From working on this chapter:

```
C:\dBASEReports\Chapter 4\SomeDogs.rep
C:\dBASEReports\ReportControls\MyReportControls.cc
C:\dBASEReports\Reports\base.crp
C:\dBASEReports\Reports\MyCompanyReport.crp
```

Downloaded version – same files but with this path:

```
C:\ReportsBookSourceCode\Chapter04\filename
C:\ReportsBookSourceCode\ReportControls\filename
C:\ReportsBookSourceCode\Reports\filenames
```

Summary

This chapter discussed very specifically the use of Custom Reports, and a little with Custom Classes. We will come back to more custom classes as we go. If you are familiar with Chapters 17 and 18 of The dBASE Book (3rd Edition), you know that there is more to this topic than was discussed in this chapter. This is because we will be covering those topics in other chapters. Some of the topics discussed in those chapters are fairly advanced, and we're starting small and working up to them here.

The next chapter of this book will spend a bit of time on the Event Model for reports – how the various events affect each other, and so on. The concepts in that chapter are very important to being a more effective developer when it comes to working with reports.

NOTES:

Chapter 5: The Report Event Model

dBASE uses an object-oriented programming (OOP) language called dBL in the Report Designer and Reporting Engine (the program that runs reports). What this means is that the report is an object, which contains other objects, and each object has properties, events and methods. These objects can interact with each other by referencing the objects, and so on. The various report objects were discussed in detail in Chapter 2. This chapter is designed to help you learn more about how the event model works, and to help you learn to use it to your advantage.

A Place for Our Work

As we work through the chapter we will be needing a place for the files we create, so please create a folder for this chapter:

```
C:\dBASEReports\Chapter 5
```

And in the Navigator, be sure to navigate to this folder.

Understanding the Event Model

Object-oriented programming is, among other things, event driven. dBASE provides a series of events that the programmer can use to create event handlers *(user defined code that is run when the event occurs)*. Our code executes in response to events that fire within the dBASE reporting engine. It is therefore useful to understand the behavior of the event model in order to know where to place code to get the end effect that you desire.

The following describes three of those events:

canRender

Nearly all visual components on a report, like text objects, images, rectangles, and shapes, as well as the *streamFrame* have the *canRender* event. The event fires just before the component is rendered and the return value determines whether the component is displayed. It fires every time the object is rendered which means that for a component in a *detailBand*, it fires for every row in the rowset. This event requires that a logical value (*true* or *false*) be returned.

preRender

Report bands (*detailBand*, *groupHeaderBand*, *groupFooterBand*, etc.) do not have a *canRender* event. Instead, they fire the *preRender* event. Like the *canRender* event, this event fires before the band begins rendering. Unlike the *canRender* event, however, you cannot prevent the band from rendering in the *preRender* event handler using a returned value.

onRender

All visual components, the *streamFrame*, and all the bands have the *onRender* event. The *onRender* event fires after the component is rendered and it is fired every time the object is rendered. This event fires for the bands after all the objects in that band have been rendered. For *streamFrame* objects, the event fires after that *streamFrame* has been rendered.

Event Sequences

To clearly understand the sequence in which these events fire, and how they relate to each other, we are going to create a report that uses these events, that when executed shows them firing in the Command Window. By seeing these events fire in sequence, we should then get a better understanding of how and when they may be useful.

Before starting you will want to copy the data module (DamsParentChild.dmd) we created in Chapter 3 to the folder for Chapter 5 (which you hopefully created at the beginning of the chapter). Navigate to the new Chapter 5 folder if you haven't already. In the Command Window, type the following:

```
copy file "..\Chapter 3\DamsParentChild.dmd" to DamsParentChild.dmd
```

Create the Report

To start, we need to bring up the dBASE Plus Report Designer (double click on the "[New Report]" icon in the Navigator ...). Normally for our exercises in this book we will use a custom report, but we are not going to do that now. We are going to simply create the parts of the report, using each of the objects and events as noted.

Since we are not using a custom report, we need to set some properties of the report:

metric	3 (Inches) – or whatever measurement you prefer
autoSort	false *(if it is not set to false – it should be by default)*

The next thing needed is the data that will be used for the report. We will work with the datamodule ("DamsParentChild.dmd") because it will give us a grouped report – we will discuss groups in detail in a later chapter, but this will help us get set up. To use this, go to the Navigator, click on the "Data Modules" tab, and drag it to the report surface. I tend to place data objects in the upper left corner of a report, off the *pageTemplate*, so I can find them. We will take a look at this in a moment.

Next we need to set some controls on the *pageTemplate*. However, dBASE doesn't automatically load them when we design a report, because we told it not to earlier when we created them. Go to the Command Window and type:

```
set procedure to :MyReportControls:MyReportControls.cc
```

This will make them available on the Component Palette. You can check this by clicking on the Component Pallet, and then on the "Custom" tab. You should see:

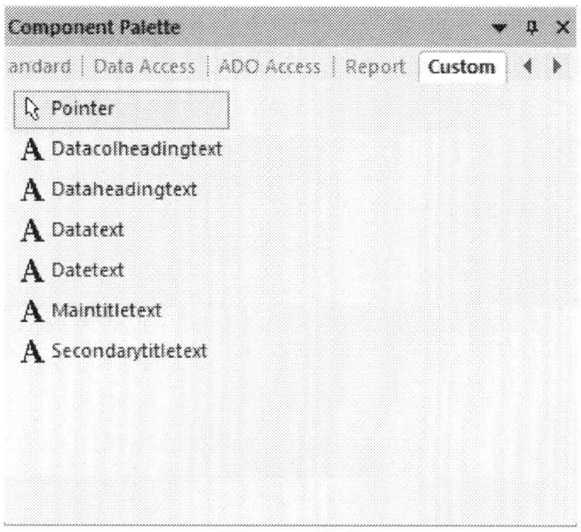

Figure 5-1

Let's drag two of them to the *pageTemplate*, namely "SecondaryTitleText" and "DateText". Place the first near the top of the *pageTemplate*, and the second (DateText) under that *(when you place them on the report they may not appear where you expect them to – move them appropriately)*. Note you will need to widen both controls so the text displays properly. Next – hold the Ctrl key and with the mouse and select both of them. Select the "Layout" menu, and "Align", then "Center Horizontally in Window". This will line them up nicely. Click on the *pageTemplate* to take focus off the text controls.

Click on the "SecondaryTitleText" control once to give it focus, and another to put it into edit mode (do this with a pause between clicks – a double-click will not have the desired effect - often doing nothing more than a single-click would), and change the text to "Show Events Report". If necessary, widen the control, and re-align it so it is centered on the report.

Save the report by pressing Ctrl+S, and typing "ShowEventsReport" when asked for a report name.

Next we need to add data to the report. To do that, we are going to go for simple (meaning we won't be using Custom Controls for this report), and so click on the Field Palette and click on the tab "Dogs1".

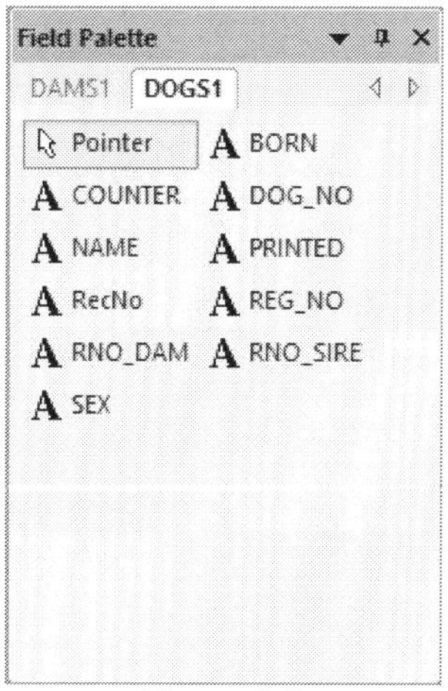

Figure 5-2

Click on the "Name" field and drag it to the Coral (pinkish) *detailBand* on the report. This gives us something on the *detailBand*. Delete the text control with the field name

("Name") – click once on it (it will look like all the text is selected unless you look carefully) and press delete. Then move the text control with the name field ("textname1") up to the top of the *detailBand* (in the Inspector you can also set the *top* property to 0 – sometimes that's easier).

Now we want to create a *group*. There are multiple ways to do this. Let's do this the simple way by going to the Component Palette. Click on this, and then click on the "Report" tab, and find "Group". Drag this to the report. You should see something like:

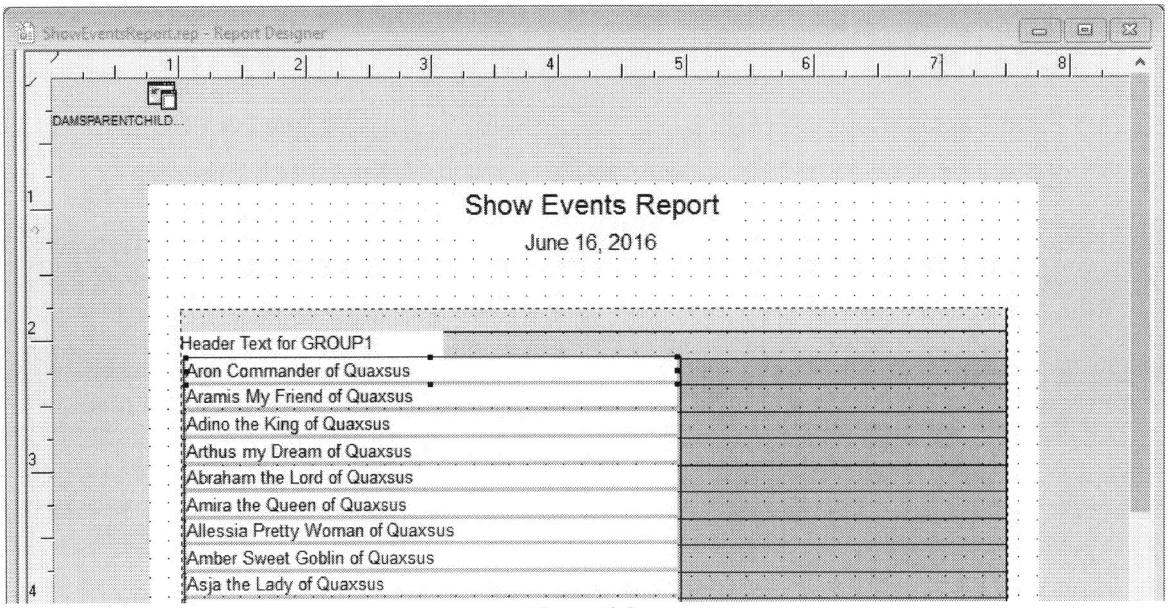

Figure 5-3

The text "Header Text for Group1" was added automatically for us. Go to the Field Palette and click on the "Dams1" tab. Drag the "Name" field to the right of the "Header Text for Group1" text object. Click twice (slowly) on the first text object, and change the text to: "Dam:". In the Inspector for this object, find the *fontBold* property and set it to *true*. Change the width so that this takes less space, and drag the Name of the Dam to the left. You may want to work with other properties a bit (*left*, *height*, etc.) to get the text to look decent. I will leave that as an exercise for you. *(We will spend more time on appearance of reports in later chapters.)*

Click on the name field in the *detailBand*, and move it to the right a little.

> **NOTE**
> A very useful tip here is that you can move controls on the design surfaces in dBASE with the arrow keys on your keyboard. This is called "nudging" them. I find it useful for fine-tuning where a control is. To move something quickly over a large part of a design surface I use the mouse to drag it, then when it is close to where I need it to be, I use the arrow keys and nudge it into place.

You should now see something like:

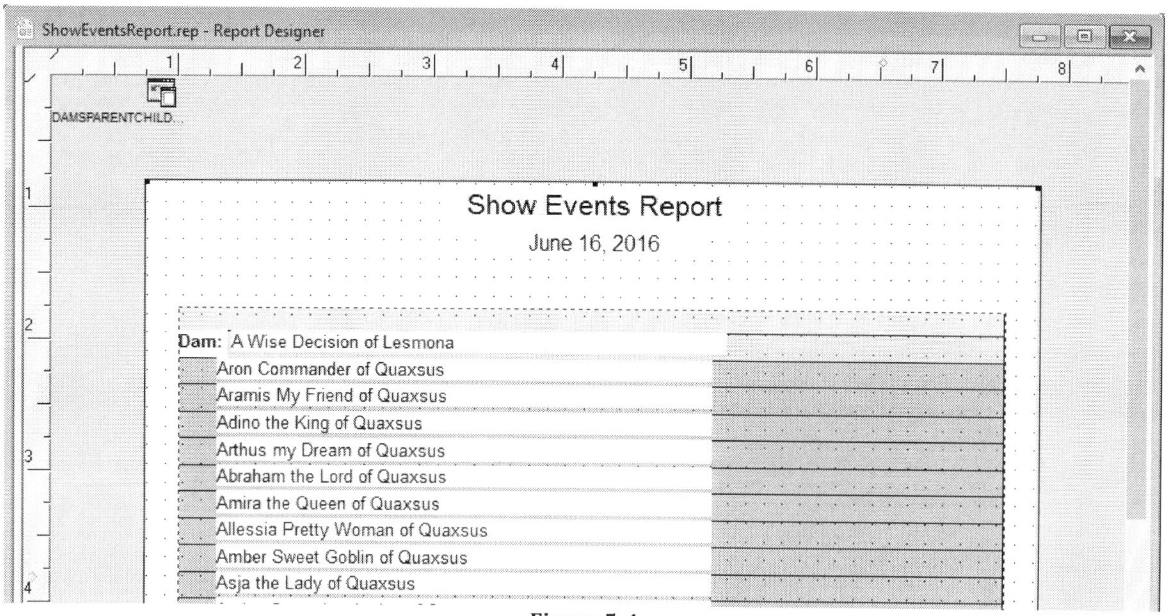

Figure 5-4

Go to the Inspector and find: "group1" and select it (be sure you do NOT select "reportgroup"). Find the *groupBy* property, and click on it. Select in the list of fields "DAM".

You should see the data is now broken up by Dams, with each of their offspring listed below them. There may not be a large difference in the appearance of the report.

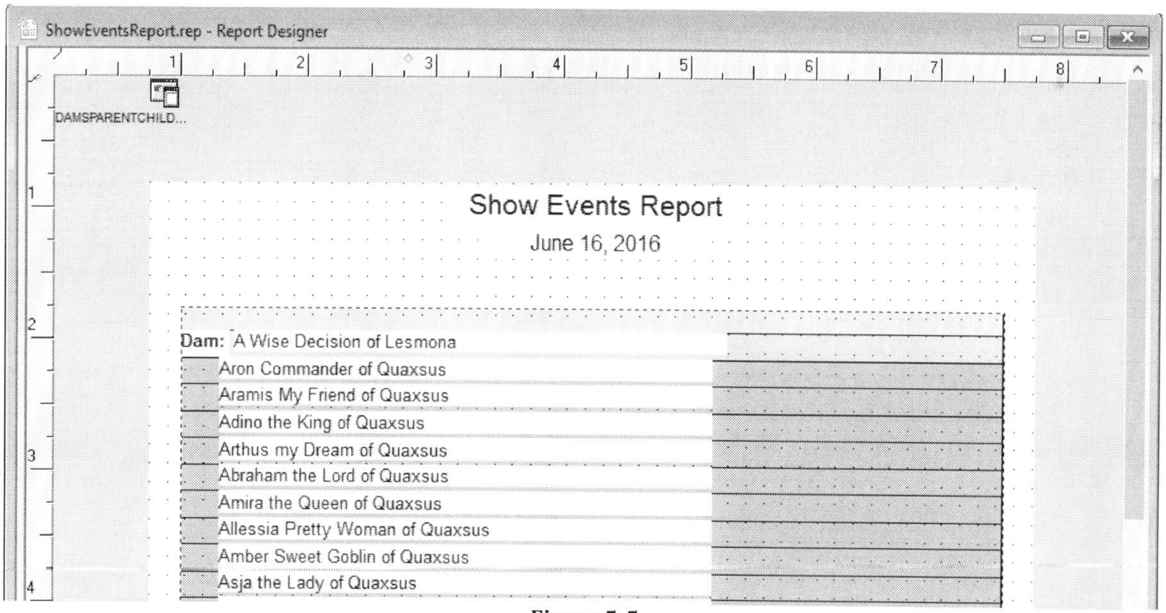

Figure 5-5

We are going to do a couple of other things really briefly, and then start working with the events. First, let's put an aggregate function in the group *footerBand*. This aggregate function will count the number of offspring and display it.

Go to the Inspector. It should still show the group object, if not, find "form.streamSource1.group1" and select it in the combobox. Then find the *footerBand* in the Inspector. Click on that and the "I" button. Now you should see the properties of the *footerBand* object. Set the *height* property to ".5" for the moment (this is ½ inch). You should see a purplish blue band appear. Select the "Layout" menu and "Add Groups and Summaries..." option. A dialog should appear. Quickly walking through this:

- Click the "Summaries" tab
- In "Available Fields" find "Dam" and click on it
- In "Available aggregates" find "Count" and select it
- Click the right arrow button, and you should see something like:

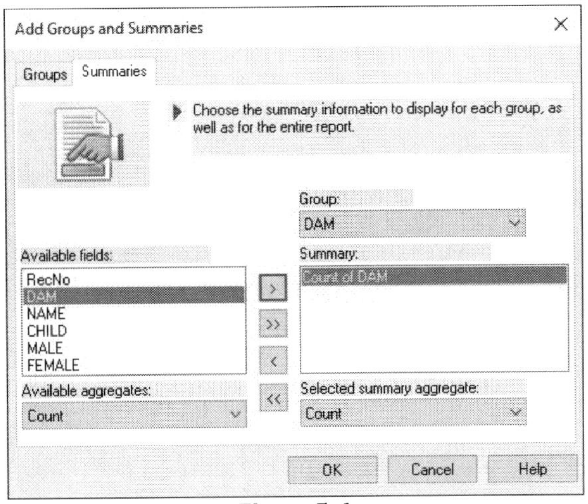

Figure 5-6

Click "OK". In the Inspector set the *height* property back to zero.

The report now has text for the group's *headerBand* and *footerBand*, and we also have text on the *detailBand*.

At the very top of the report, above the group *headerBand*, we have a green band, this is the report's (or *reportGroup*'s) *headerBand* – this prints at the beginning of the report (we'll look at this in more detail in a later chapter). Drag a text control from the Component Palette (you may have to click on the "Standard" tab first). Widen it a little and change the text to say "Report Header", and leave it at that.

We could do the same for the report's *footerBand*, but it's not really necessary. Suffice it to say the report's *footerBand* is the last part of the report and prints at the end. We will discuss this in more detail in a later chapter of the book.

Work With Events

Now we need to start looking at events. To do this, click on the "Inspector", and the "Events" tab. In the combobox, select "form" – this is the report. You should see three events:

beforeRelease
onDesignOpen
onPage

For now let's ignore the *beforeRelease* and *onDesignOpen* events, but for the *onPage* event let's add a line of code to the event handler. To do this, click on the event, and then the tool button. Make the code look like:

```
function form_onPage()
   ? "**** Report onPage -- a new page begins here ****"
return
```

Leave the Source Code Editor open – we'll keep coming back to it.

The events we are specifically interested in right now are the *preRender*, *canRender* and *onRender* events, and the report object does not have any of these.

In the Inspector select "form.pagetemplate1.secondarytitletext1" and you will see something like:

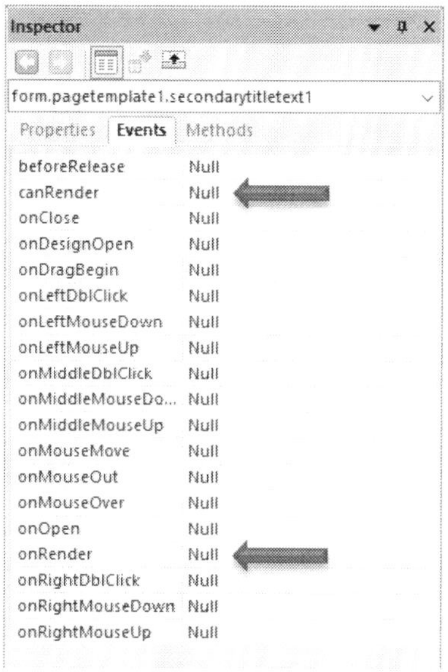

Figure 5-7

The two events we are interested in are the *canRender* and *onRender* events. Some of these are not really useful in reports (such as the *onDragBegin*, or *on...Mouse...* events ...) as dBASE reports are not interactive in that fashion.

Click on the *canRender* event, and then the "tool" button that appears. In the Source Code Editor, make the code look like:

```
function SECONDARYTITLETEXT1_canRender()
   ? "Secondary Title Text - canRender event"
return true
```

Note that the "return true" statement was added for you – the default value for this event is to return a "true" – if it returns "false", then the Report Engine will not display this control. We will discuss this in depth in a later chapter of this book.

We need to do something similar for the *onRender* event (click on it, then the tool button):

```
function SECONDARYTITLETEXT1_onRender()
   ? "Secondary Title Text - onRender event"
return
```

Next, in the Inspector select in the combobox at the top "form.pagetemplate1.streamframe1". You will see only two events here, *canRender* and *onRender*. We need to do the same sort of thing for both of these events:

```
function STREAMFRAME1_canRender()
   ? "StreamFrame1 - canRender event"
return true

function STREAMFRAME1_onRender()
   ? "StreamFrame1 - onRender event"
return
```

Next we need to add event handlers for the different bands and the controls on the bands. If a band has more than one control, we will not add event handlers for each of them, but just a single control.

Start with "form.reportGroup.headerBand" in the Inspector. You will see two events – *onRender* and *preRender*. Enter code similar to what was done above. Once you have done that, do the same for the text control on the ReportGroup Header band (the one that says "Report Header") for the *canRender* and *onRender* events. You should have added to the report:

```
function HEADERBAND_onRender()
   ? "ReportGroup Header Band - onRender event"
return

function HEADERBAND_preRender()
   ? "ReportGroup Header Band - preRender event"
return

function TEXT1_canRender()
   ? "ReportGroup Header Band -- text 1 - canRender event"
return true

function TEXT1_onRender()
   ? "ReportGroup Header Band -- text 1 - onRender event"
return
```

We need to do the same for the following objects and events:

- form.streamSource1.group1.headerBand
  - onRender
  - preRender
- form.streamSource1.group1.headerBand.text1
  - canRender
  - onRender
- form.streamSource1.detailBand
  - onRender
  - preRender
- form.streamSource1.detailBand.textName1
  - canRender

  - onRender
- form.streamSource1.group1.footerBand
  - onRender
  - preRender
- form.streamSource1.group1.footerBand.text1
  - canRender
  - onRender

That's a lot of code, and normally for a report not all of these events will be assigned event handlers. This is a special report.

One last set of code needs to be added for the navigation of the rows in the tables. This is important to show how rowset navigation effects the various bands in the report.

Click on the datamodule object on the Report Designer surface (most likely in the upper left corner of your report, it will have text under it like: "DAMSPARENT...". In the Inspector click on the "Properties" tab and you will see under the "User Defined" heading three objects: "DAMS1", "DBASE_REPORTS1" and "DOGS1". - "DBASE_REPORTS1" is the database object, and we don't have to worry about that. Click on "Dams1", and click on the "I" (for Inspect) button. Follow these steps:

- Click on the "rowset" object
- Click on the "I" button
- Click on the "Events" tab
- Click on the *onNavigate* event
- Click on the "Tool Button"

If you get an error about the event not existing, click "OK". You should see, in the Source Code Editor:

```
function rowset_onNavigate(type, nRows)
return
```

Between these two statements, add:

```
function rowset_onNavigate(type, nRows)
   ? "   Dams Rowset -- onNavigate event"
return
```

(There are three spaces before "Dams" - this just makes the line stand out a bit - it breaks up the output for readability.)

We will repeat the steps above, but for the Dogs rowset. Use the Left Arrow button at the top of the Inspector twice, and you should find yourself back on the Datamodule in the Inspector. Click on the "Properties" tab, and go to the "Dogs1" object, click the "I" button, and:

- Click on the "rowset" object
- Click on the "I" button
- Click on the "Events" tab
- Click on the *onNavigate* event
- Click on the "Tool Button"

If you get an error about the event not existing, click "OK". You should see, in the Source Code Editor:

```
function rowset_onNavigate1(type, nRows)
return
```

Between these two statements, add:

```
function rowset_onNavigate1(type, nRows)
   ? "   Dogs Rowset -- onNavigate event"
return
```

Now you should save your work (Press Ctrl+S).

We could just leave it like this, but what will end up happening is that we have enough output that the Command Window's Output Pane cannot hold it all. So we want to have the report write this information to a text file that we can then look at when we run the report.

To do this, we need to save the report and exit the Report Designer (Ctrl+W – you may need to do this twice, once to close the Source Code Editor and the second the designer). Open the report in the Source Code Editor:

```
modify command ShowEventsReport.rep
```

In the beginning of the report, before the "** END HEADER -- do not remove this line" comments and code at the beginning, add the following:

```
set safety off
set alternate to ShowEvents.txt
set alternate on
local r
r = new ShowEventsReport()
r.render()
close alternate
set alternate off
set safety on
return
```

What this will do is to open a file that the output will be placed in as the report is run, then close that file when the report is done rendering. The "set safety" command simply stops dBASE from asking if you want to overwrite the file. Once you have done that, save and exit the Source Code Editor (Ctrl+W), and we want to run the report.

Go to the Navigator and find the "Reports" tab, find this report ("ShowEventsReport.rep") and double-click it – the report will run. You can scroll through the report, and all that. As you do, output is created in the file. When you close the Report Viewer, we can then view the events and the sequence in which they fired:

```
modify command ShowEvents.txt
```

The output should look similar to:

```
   Dams Rowset -- onNavigate event
   Dogs Rowset -- onNavigate event
StreamFrame1 - canRender event
ReportGroup Header Band - preRender event
ReportGroup Header Band -- text 1 - canRender event
ReportGroup Header Band -- text 1 - onRender event
```

```
ReportGroup Header Band - onRender event
Group1 headerBand - preRender event
Group1 headerBand -- text1 - canRender event
Group1 headerBand -- text1 - canRender event
Group1 headerBand - onRender event
detailBand - preRender event
detailBand - textName1 - canRender event
detailBand - textName1 - onRender event
detailBand - onRender event
   Dogs Rowset -- onNavigate event
detailBand - preRender event
detailBand - textName1 - canRender event
detailBand - textName1 - onRender event
detailBand - onRender event
   Dogs Rowset -- onNavigate event
detailBand - preRender event
detailBand - textName1 - canRender event
detailBand - textName1 - onRender event
detailBand - onRender event
   Dogs Rowset -- onNavigate event
```

This is not all of it, by any stretch, but if you scroll through the file, you will see the sequence all of these events fired in. Once you understand the sequence these events fire in, you can have much more control over how your report works, and when we get to the chapters on calculated fields, counting and accumulating, and programmatic control of reports, this will be very useful information.

Close the file (Ctrl+W) and we're done.

Source Code

The following is a listing of the sample code in the folders we have been working with. If you downloaded the files from my website the structure will be different (see below). You may use the code contained in these folders for your own applications if you desire, with the caveat that credit be given appropriately.

From working on this chapter:

```
C:\dBASEReports\Chapter 5\DamsParentChild.dmd
C:\dBASEReports\Chapter 5\ShowEventsReport.rep
C:\dBASEReports\Chapter 5\ShowEvents.txt
```

Downloaded version – same files but with this path:

```
C:\ReportsBookSourceCode\Chapter 05\filenames
```

Summary

Many of the report examples used in this book rely on an understanding of the report engine's event model. We will use the *preRender* and *canRender* events to set values before printing, and the *onRender* events to reset values after printing. Moreover, we will be able to move a row pointer to some desired location, evaluate a field value, and move the row pointer back. We can do all this because we have a clearer understanding of the event model.

The next chapter will discuss and provide examples of different types of report layouts, using standard terms so that if someone asks you to create a specific type of report, you have a better idea what they're talking about!

Chapter 6: Report Layout

When looking at reports, there are many ways to lay them out. So far we have focused on the default layout in dBASE reports, which is to lay the data out in columns, one next to the other. This is a good, straightforward way of doing reports, because of course the data is stored in columns and rows. However, there are other ways to do reports.

A Place for Our Work

As we work through the chapter we will be needing a place for the files we create, so please create a folder for this chapter:

```
C:\dBASEReports\Chapter 6
```

And in the Navigator, be sure to navigate to this folder.

Types of Reports

For the purposes of this book, we are going to define these different types of reports in two ways. There are probably many terms and ways to define reports, I went with what seemed like fairly obvious descriptions.

Tabular Reports

A report like the ones we have done so far, with the data laid out in columns, we will call *tabular*. Why *tabular*? The Webster's Dictionary defines *tabular* as "relating to, or arranged in a table specifically set up in rows and columns". (Definition 2a) This definition fits what we are doing in these reports – the data appears in rows and columns. Each *detailBand* is a row (relating to the row in the table), and each column matches the columns or fields in a table. We'll work with these some more in later chapters of this book.

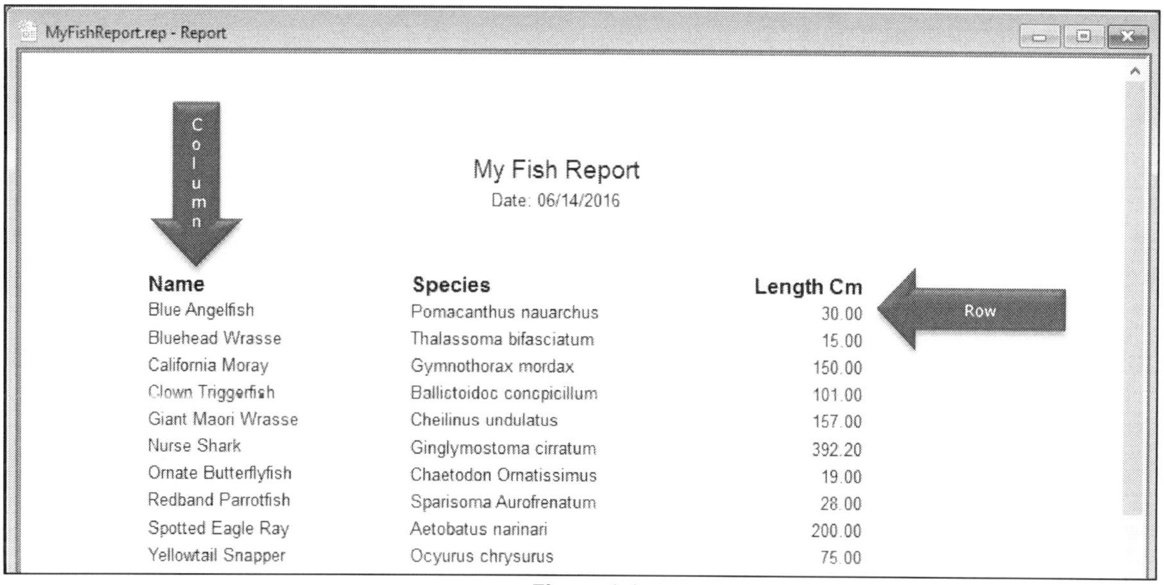

Figure 6-1

Form Reports

A *form* report is more free-form. Data does not have to be in columns, and can be laid out in a wide variety of ways. This is more flexible, as you might imagine, because you can put your text wherever you need it to be and you can display data wherever you need it to be. You could even combine some of the design concepts of *tabular* reports with *form* reports, if that suits the needs of your report.

There are many reasons you might need to use a *form* style report, including when a tabular report doesn't have enough room for all the data, even if you go to a landscape (sideways) print, and/or larger paper. Other reasons to use a *form* report might include printing something on pre-printed forms, creating your own special output (for example, you might want to create your own Invoice forms with your own special layout), and so on.

A *form* report might have a *detailBand* with a flexible *height*, which is less common in a *tabular* report, or a *form* report may have a fixed *height* for the *detailBand*. We will look at this capability.

The *form* report is where we start to see some of the real flexibility of the dBASE Report Designer and Report Engine. In this chapter we will create a couple of relatively simple *form* reports, just so that you get an understanding of what can be done. In later chapters we will do more with this.

Example Reports

We have already been doing some work with *tabular* style reports in earlier chapters of this book. However, we have not dealt with the concepts of a *form* style report. We will start with something fairly simple, using the FISH table from the dBASE Samples.

Make sure you are using the Chapter 6 folder (in the Navigator).

Create a new report in the Report Designer by double-clicking on the "[New Report]" icon in the Navigator.

In order to use the settings in your custom report, then you need to set this:

- Select the "File" menu
- Select "Set Custom Report Class"
- Select the "tool" button next to the "File name containing class:" entryfield and find the file "MyCompanyReport.crp".
- Select the custom report, and click "Open"
- Click "OK"

Now we will have the options set for the report without having to set them again.

Click on the "SecondaryTitle" text control (the one that says "Purpose of Report") and then click on it again, which will put you in "edit" mode – allowing you to change the text. Type:

    A Form Report

And then click on the *pageTemplate* (or anywhere on the report that is not this text object).

Save the report (so we don't forget later) by pressing Ctrl+S and when the dialog comes up, enter "FormReport1" as the name of the report file.

Go to the Navigator window, and click on the "Tables" tab. Find the database "DBASESAMPLES" in the combobox, and select that. You should see "Fish" and some other tables in the Navigator window. Click on "Fish" and drag it to the report design surface.

In order to work on/create a *form* style report, we will most likely want to set the *height* of the *detailBand*, at least temporarily, so that we have room to work. To do this, click on the first *detailBand* in the report, and in the Inspector find the *height* property. Type "1" and press the Enter key – this will set the *detailBand* to 1 inch tall for each row in the table, even though there is nothing there. *(As always, if you are working with a different metric, use something appropriate.)*

We could drag fields from the Field Palette, but then we would not be using the custom controls that we should be using for our reports. To use those, click on the "Custom" tab of the Component Palette. You should see six text controls and their names to the right of them.

Find the custom class called "DataHeadingText", and drag this to the *detailBand*. Move it up to the top and left, and widen it as necessary. Click on it once to change the text and change the text to read "Name:".

Next we need a "DataText" control, but rather than placing this *under* the heading, place it to the right of it. Don't worry if the two controls don't line up exactly just yet – we will fix that in a bit.

Go to the Inspector, find the *text* property, and click on the "T" button (for "Type"). Select "Codeblock". Notice that the text changes. Next click on the tool button *(the one with the screwdriver on it)*, and in the dialog enter the following:

```
this.form.fish1.rowset.fields["name"].value
```

Click the "OK" button, and notice that the text control now displays the value of the field. You will want to work with the *width* property to get the text control wide enough to display the text from the field.

A TRICK
Since we are working with the Report Designer, we can get it to help us with things like the *width* property of a control that is displaying the value of a field. We want our custom control to be the width necessary to display the field properly, correct? One way to do this is to place an instance of the text control that would be placed on the report if we used the Field Palette, and use that to help us set the width property. Go to the Field Palette, select the "Name" field and drag it to the *detailBand* anywhere *(if placed on the right of the existing controls it makes it easier to work with)* – we will delete it when done. Now click on the text control we need to modify, and hold the Control key down and click on the new control we just placed on the form. In the alignment toolbar at the top of the screen find the toolbutton that shows a screentip that says "Grow to Largest Width". Click on this. Now the custom control should be the same width. Click on the *detailBand* to take focus off the two controls, then click on the new control you just placed on the report, and delete it by pressing the Delete key. This is a nifty trick to get the Report Designer and your custom controls to be appropriate widths for fields. *(Hint: you can use this trick in the Form Designer too ...)*

It should be noted here, that while this trick is useful, it is not perfect – dBASE performs calculations to attempt to determine the proper width for the control when it is placed on the report, but often it is not wide enough for some data. You need to experiment sometimes with the data, and try combinations, perhaps add some test records that fill each field to the largest possible value.

Next you will want to line the two controls up. One way of doing this is to select both controls, then go to the alignment toolbar at the top of the screen, and use the toolbutton that says "Align Top" when you hold your mouse over it. You can also manually move the controls around by clicking on them and dragging, or clicking on them and using the keyboard arrow keys ("nudging" them up, down, etc.). Note that you don't need these at the very top of the detailBand – in my example, the *top* property is at "0.04", which gives a little bit of visible space at the top of the *detailBand*.

It should be noted that the alignment tools will get your controls close, but sometimes you still need to use the ability to "nudge" them (use the arrow keys on the keyboard), the mouse, or the Inspector to get them "just right".

To show the *form* report properly, we're going to place more fields on the report, using the same techniques as shown above. Use the steps above to place controls on the report for the Species and Length CM fields *under* the Name field.

You may want to work with lining the controls up a bit at this point, such as lining the heading text up on the right (click on the first, hold the Ctrl key and click on the other two – then go to the toolbar and click the "Align Right" button), so that you have something similar to the image shown here:

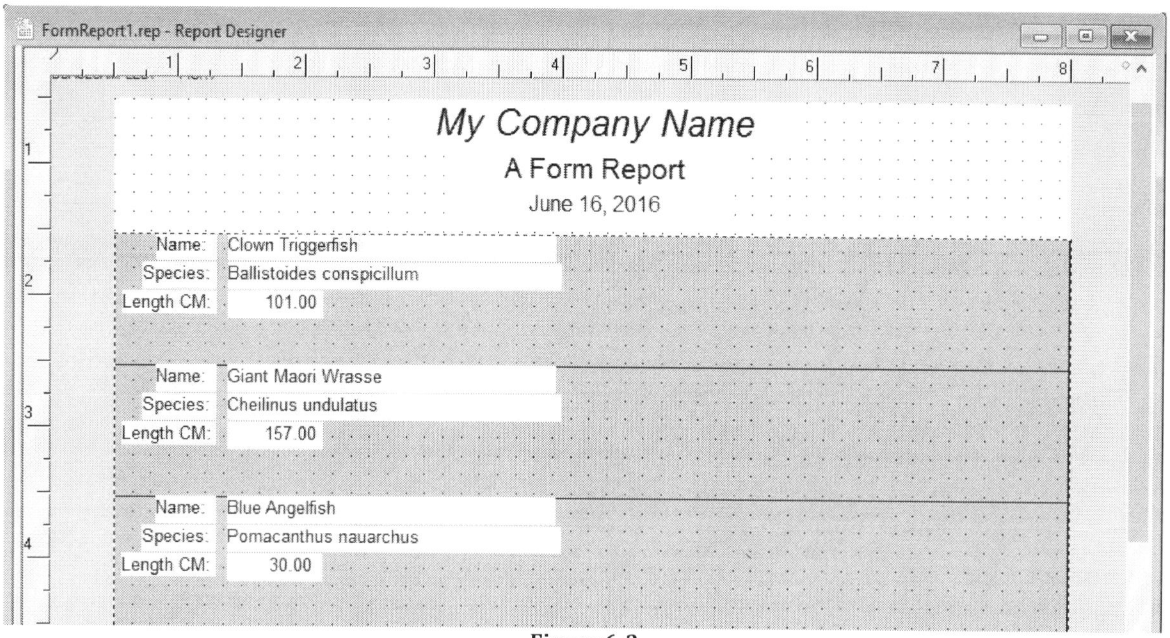

Figure 6-2

Now that we have these fields, let us move on to the last two that we want to display – the image ("Fish Image"), and the memo ("Description") fields. We could display the ID field, but there is no real point for this report.

Go to the Component Palette and click on the "Standard" tab. Drag an instance of the Image object to the *detailBand,* to the right of the text controls that are there. Using the Inspector, set the *alignment* property to "3 - Keep Aspect Stretch". What this means is that the image will not be distorted as we resize the object.

> **BUG**
> There appears to be a bug with the way image controls are placed onto the *detailBand* in current versions of dBASE. An outline will appear, but if you click off the control it looks like it was deleted or is just gone. It is still there. To get it back go to the Inspector, click on the combobox and find the control in the list (typical name will be "image1" if it is the first image, etc.). The outline of the control will reappear. Once you have assigned a *dataSource* for the control this does not seem to be a problem.

Click on the *dataSource* property in the Inspector, and then the tool button. In the new dialog select "Binary" for the "Location" combobox, and click on the tool button (pencil) for the "Image" entryfield. A new dialog appears and shows any fields that might be useful, in this case there is only one. Click "OK", and then "OK" on the first dialog. Now the image object shows the fish image field. You may want to widen the image object a little and perhaps make it taller (see image of completed report).

Put a DataHeadingText control (go back to the "Custom" tab of the Component Palette) on the *detailBand*, under the existing text controls on the left, and change the text to "Description:". You will need to widen the control a little.

Next place a DataText control to the right of the heading control. Set the *text* property as we have done for the other text controls (Codeblock, etc.). Notice that you only get one line of the text. The solution is to use the *variableHeight* property. Notice that this defaults to *false*. If we set this to *true* in the Inspector, the text will adjust to the height needed to display all of the text in the field.

Also notice that the *detailBand* will adjust its height automatically as well!

If you adjust the width of the text a bit, and then move the image and perhaps adjust its height and/or width a bit, you will end up with something like:

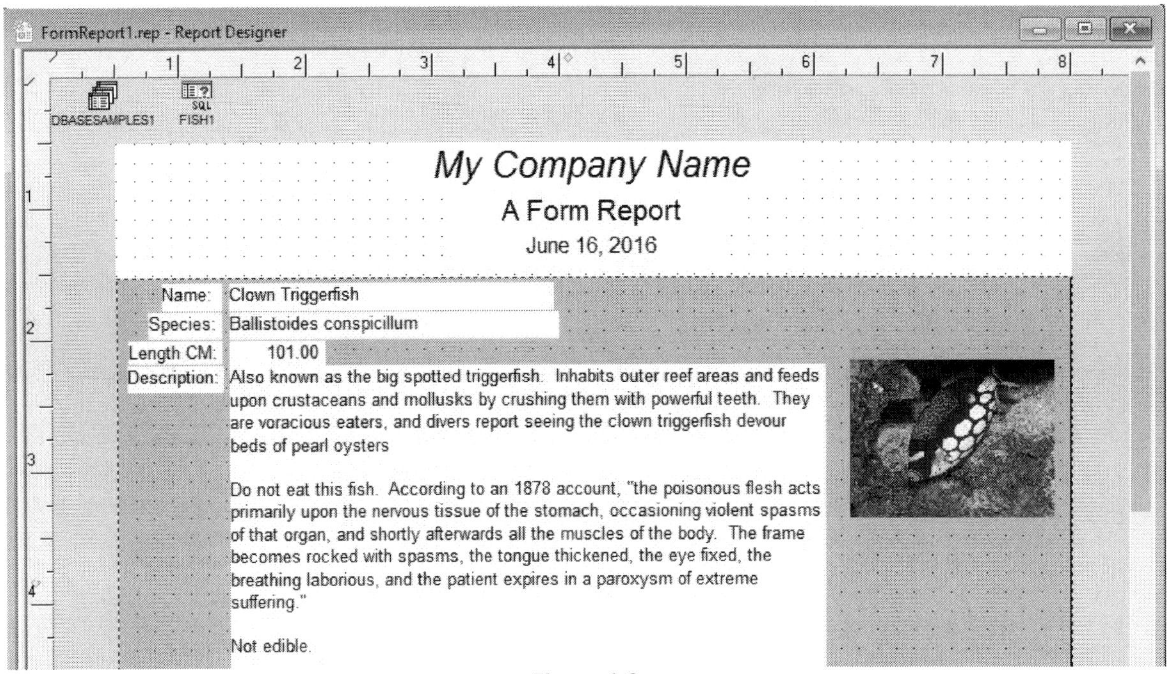

Figure 6-3

If you save this report (Ctrl+S) and then run it, you should see:

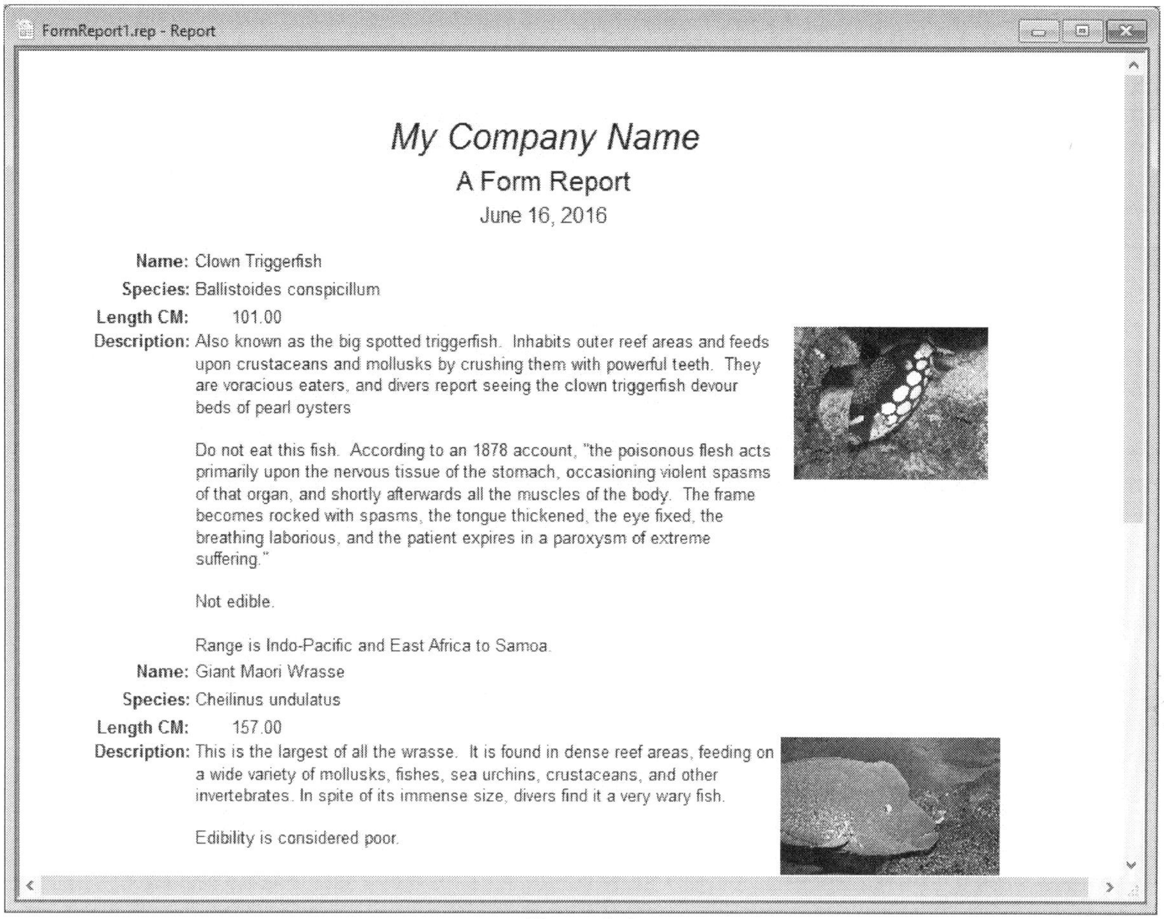

Figure 6-4

There are more things we could do, but this is a pretty good start. As you can see, your report looks nothing like the way it might if you were viewing the data in a grid (which is the concept behind a *tabular* report). That was the major point to this exercise.

Some Notes

When working with this type of report, the *detailBand* as we defined it was 1 inch tall. However, it expanded as necessary to show the contents of the memo field "Description". What if that field is empty or does not have enough data to fill an inch or greater? What if that leaves the *detailBand* with a bunch of empty space at the bottom? (In this example this is not an issue, this is a "what if?" exercise.)

The solution to a situation like this would be to set the *detailBand's height* property to zero (0). This tells dBASE to use as much room as is needed.

Why did we add the Description field after we added the image? This is a bit trickier, and has to deal with the concept of z-order, and the sequence in which the Report Engine executes the code for the controls on the report. In this case, because the *height* of the memo field varies from one row to another, the memo needed to be the last control defined on the *detailBand*. If we had placed the image on the *detailBand* first, and then placed the Description field on the *detailBand*, there could have been some odd effects dealing with the placement of the image, and possibly with the way the Report Engine defined the height of the memo field. This is just one example of the sequence the controls are defined *in the source code* affects the way the report is rendered. We will come back and discuss this in more depth later.

For a report like this, sometimes it's nice to have a line between *detailBands* so that the items do not all run together. We could have done that by placing a line object in the *detailBand* above the "Name" text, and extending it to the width of the *streamFrame*. We will look at enhancing reports in a later chapter of this book.

Cleanup

Close the report viewer, and then create a new report (in the Navigator, click on the "Reports" tab, double-click on the "[New Report]" icon). Select the "File" menu, select "Set Custom Report Class", and in the dialog, click the "Clear Custom Report" button, then click "OK". This clears out the custom report setting in the Plus.ini file, so that the next report you create is not based on this one. Close that report without making any changes.

Make sure the database is closed by going to the Command Window and typing:

```
close databases
```

This will also ensure that you don't end up creating tables in the wrong location, etc.

Source Code

The following is a listing of the sample code in the folders we have been working with. If you downloaded the files from my website the structure will be different (see below). You may use the code contained in these folders for your own applications if you desire, with the caveat that credit be given appropriately.

From working on this chapter:

```
C:\dBASEReports\Chapter 6\FormReport1.rep
```

Downloaded version – same files but with this path:

```
C:\ReportsBookSourceCode\Chapter 06\filename
```

Summary

The main point of this chapter was simply to give you an idea of the differences in the types of reports that you can create, and to give a basic overview, without going into every single possible permutation of what you might want or need to do. Hopefully the example you created (if you followed along with the exercise) will help you get some ideas for what you can do with reports. You are certainly not limited to just the design given here – a *form* style report can be as complex or as simple as you want or need it to be. You are really only limited by your imagination. We will come back to this in a later chapter.

Looking ahead, the next chapter is going to focus on calculated and lookup fields. These are topics that are covered in The dBASE Book, but it doesn't hurt to go over them here. They work the same in forms and programs as they do in reports.

Chapter 7: Calculated and Lookup Fields

This chapter is going to look at two different types of field that can be added or modified for your reports to enhance them, in some cases making life easier (less coding), and handling some things (like lookups) automatically. In this chapter we will look at the basics of calculated fields, and will get into more complicated calculations in other chapters.

A Place for Our Work

As we work through the chapter we will be needing a place for the files we create, so please create a folder for this chapter:

```
C:\dBASEReports\Chapter 7
```

And in the Navigator, be sure to navigate to this folder.

Calculated Fields

A calculated field is a field where the value that appears is calculated "on-the-fly" — in other words, it is not part of the table. You might think of it as a "virtual" field, and a couple of the methods we will discuss are quite literally that.

Methods to Create Calculated Fields

There are at least four methods for creating a calculated field in a report.

Using the SQL Select statement of a query to create a calculated field as part of a fields list. The drawback to this is that you must specify all the fields you wish to appear in your SQL select statement. The effects of this are that you have added a field similar to the way you can in the discussion of "Using the Query".

Using Codeblocks – A text control on a report can display a calculation by evaluating a codeblock. The codeblock is evaluated for each row as the report renders and you can concatenate strings or perform arithmetic in this codeblock. We have used this to get the value of a field in previous chapters, but you can do a lot more with codeblocks than just getting a field from the table.

Using the Text Object's *canRender* Event – When the calculations are a bit more complex, and the codeblock cannot handle them easily, you can use the *canRender* event handler for an individual text control. The *canRender* event fires before the text object prints. You can therefore do a calculation and assign the result to the *text* property of the object. For more complex calculated fields this is a good way to go, but of course it is not the only way to do this.

Using the Query – Finally, you can use a query object to create a calculated field object. In this case you would create a new field in the query, and it would contain the results of some calculation. This is done using the *onOpen* event of the query object. With this ability you can create some fairly complex calculated fields.

Sample Reports

The first report we will create for this chapter is a fairly simple tabular report, the second will be a tabular report that is grouped on a field so that we can use the aggregate calculations built into dBASE.

We will base some of these reports off the datamodule created in Chapter 3 "DamsParentChild.dmd". Copy this file to the folder being used for this chapter by typing the following in the Command Window:

```
copy file "..\Chapter 3\DamsParentChild.dmd" to DamsParentChild.dmd
```

Simple Tabular Report

As we've done before, we will need to create a report based on our Custom report. Start by creating a new report (go to the Navigator window in dBASE, click on the "Reports" tab, and double-click the "[New Report]" icon).

Select the "File" menu, select "Set Custom Report Class", and using the tool button find the file "MyCompanyReport.crp", and click "OK", then click "OK" again. As usual, the report will now inherit the settings and objects of the custom report.

Save this now so that we get a name. Press Ctrl+S, and name this "BaseTabular.rep".

Change the secondary title text (click on it once to give focus, then click on it again to put it into "edit" mode). Highlight the text and change it to "Calculated Fields" (without the quotes), then click on the *pageTemplate* surface to take focus off the text. Widen the control and re-center it if necessary.

Go to the Navigator window, and click on the "Tables" tab. Select the "DBASEREPORTS" database from the list, and drag the "Dogs" table to the report surface. Click on the "DOGS1" query object, and in the Inspector, find the *rowset* object. Click the Inspect button. We want to set the *indexName* property so that the data is sorted by names – select the "NAME" index tag.

Go to the Component Palette, and select the "DataColHeadingText" object and put an instance onto the *detailBand* of the report. Change the text to "Name" (without the quotes), and do other modifications (widen, move, etc.) as necessary.

Next place a "DataText" control in the *detailBand* below the heading. Set the "Type" to "Codeblock", click on the tool button and in the dialog enter:

```
this.form.dogs1.rowset.fields["name"].value
```

Click "OK".

At this point you will want to widen this field so that you can see all of the name.

Following the instructions given above, put the "BORN" field on the report, with both a heading text, and the data text.

Spend a few minutes getting the columns and rows lined up, and you should end up with something that looks similar to:

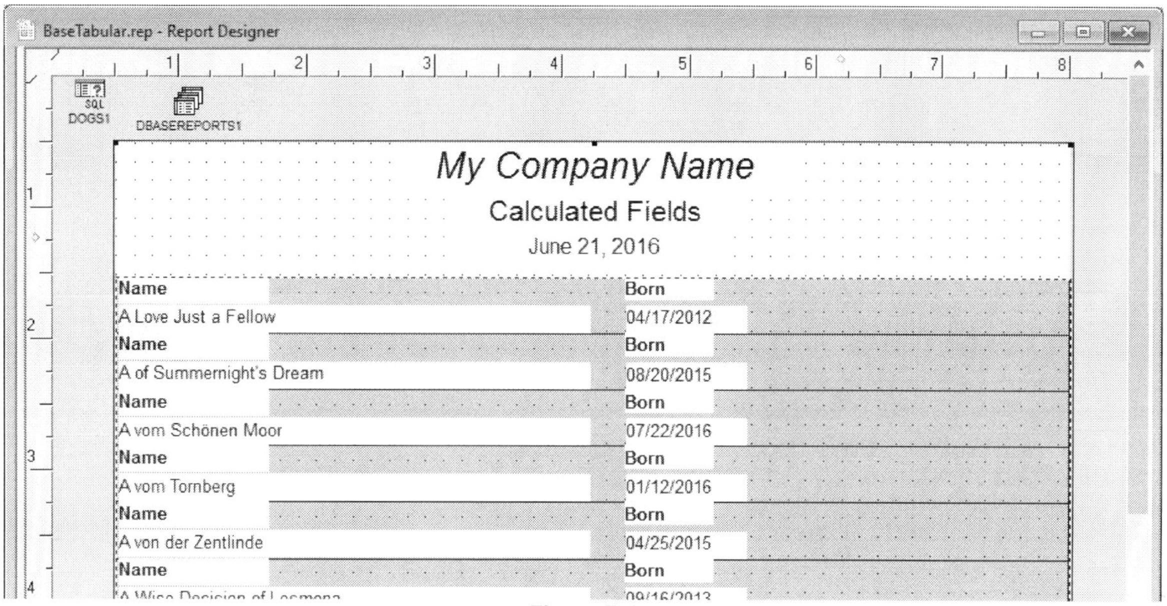

Figure 7-1

Note the one date on the first page shows a set of asterisks (or "stars") – this means the field is blank. Nothing will display when you run the report.

Save this, and exit the Report Designer, so we can create the next report.

Grouped Report

This report will use the data module, so we can group the data on a parent/child relationship. Go to the "Reports" tab of the Navigator, and double-click on the "[New Report"] icon.

Change the secondary title to read "Calculated Fields – Groups" (without the quotes). You may need to widen the text object a little to see the word "Groups". If that is the case, after widening this, you may want to also choose the "Layout" menu, and select "Align" and "Center Horizontally in Window", so that it is properly centered on the report.

Save this (Ctrl+S), and call it "BaseGroup.rep".

Next you will want to go to the Navigator, select the "Data Modules" tab, and drag the "DamsParentChild" data module to the Report Designer surface.

Go to the Component Palette, and select the "DataColHeadingText" object and put an instance onto the *detailBand* of the report. Change the text to "Name" (without the quotes), and readjust the control as necessary, moving it to the top left of the *detailBand*, and so on.

Next place a "DataText" control in the *detailBand* below the heading. Set the "Type" to "Codeblock", and then use the tool button, and place this in the dialog:

```
this.form.damsparentchilddatamodule1.dogs1.rowset.fields["name"].value
```

At this point you will want to widen this field so that you can see all of the name(s).

Following the instructions above, put the "BORN" field on the report, with both a heading text, and the data text.

Spend a few minutes getting the columns and rows lined up. I suggest you move everything to the right a little, as we will be adding a *group*, and it helps for readability.

On the Component Palette click on the "Report" tab, and select "Group". Drag this to the report surface. The *group headerBand* is automatically added to the report.

Go to the combobox at the top of the Inspector and find "group1" – select this. Click on the properties tab if this does not currently have focus. Select the *groupBy* property, and in the combobox list, select "Dams". You should now see the group *headerBand* repeat and the data will be broken up by the Dams.

We want to continue using custom controls, however if you just delete the text that says "Header Text for Group 1", the group *headerBand* will seem to disappear (the *height* is set to zero (0) and if there are no controls on this band, it will reduce to that height). Drag an instance of the "DataHeadingText" control to the group *headerBand*. Now delete the text that was automatically placed on the report. Move the "DataHeadingText" object all the way to the left, and the top of the band, and change the *text* to read "Dam: " without the quotes.

Place a "DataText" control on the group *headerBand* next to the heading text, set the *text* property type to "Codeblock", click the Tool button, and enter this:

```
this.form.damsparentchilddatamodule1.dams1.rowset.fields["name"].value
```

Widen this text control so that you can see the full name.

With a bit of effort, your report should now look similar to:

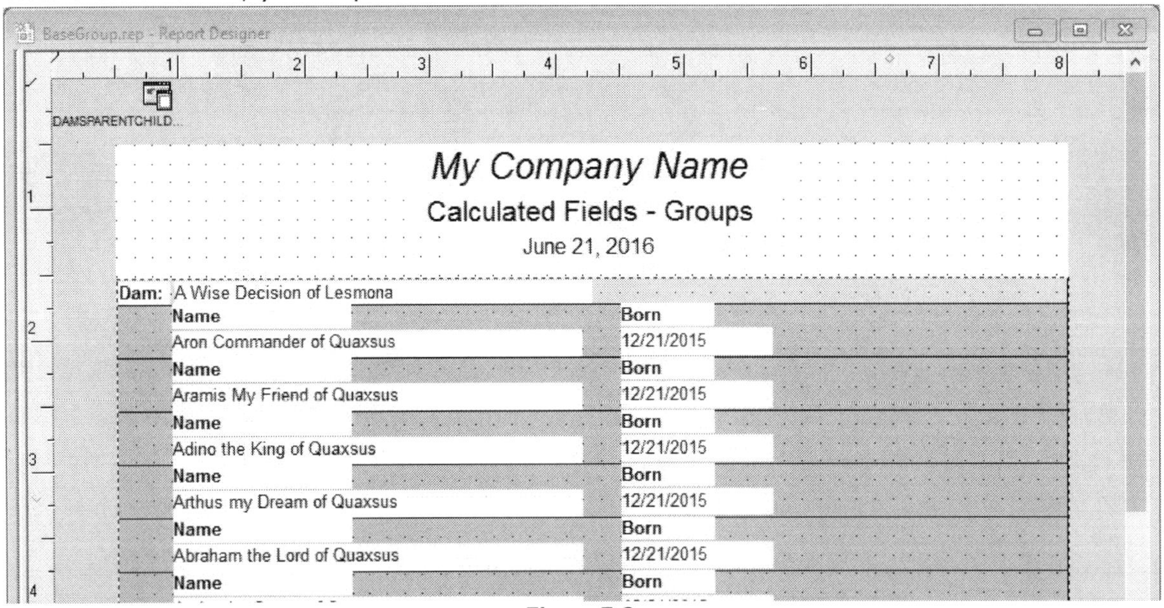

Figure 7-2

When done, save this, and exit the Report Designer (Ctrl+W).

We are now ready to start working with copies of these reports, and seeing how different types of calculated fields can be created.

Reports with Calculated Fields

As noted at the beginning of this chapter, there are several ways to create calculated fields for a report. We will look at each of these as we go through most of the rest of this chapter.

Codeblocks

We have already worked with codeblocks for our reports. Basically we modify the *text* property of a *text* (or *textLabel*) control, setting the Type to "Codeblock", and then either enter the codeblock or go to the codeblock editor allowing us to create the expression.

So far, all we have done is to tell the Report Engine to pull the value of a field each time the text control is rendered and to display it on the report. However, we could do a lot more with that.

For example, if we wanted to calculate the age of a dog based on the date the report was generated *(using the "Born" field)* we could do that. Age is not as simple a calculation as it might first appear, however there are plenty of examples of calculations that will give us a fairly accurate age value.

Before we do start, we want to copy the first report we did for this chapter. There are several ways to do this. The one we will use will ensure that dBASE does not confuse the original report with the one we need to modify. (There are explanations for this issue in The dBASE Book.) Before starting the Report Designer, go to the Command Window, and type:

```
copy file BaseTabular.rep to Tabular_CB.rep
```

"CB" stands for "Codeblock" – this way we know which report we are working with. You should see a new .rep file in the Navigator window. Click this file with your mouse and then right-click. Select "Open in Source Editor".

In the beginning of the report are two places we need to change the name of the report class. The easiest thing to do is to use the Replace dialog in the Source Code Editor. Press Ctrl+R, and a dialog will appear allowing you to tell dBASE what to find and what to replace it with. In the "Find what" entryfield enter "BaseTabular" (without the quotes), and in the "Replace with" entryfield enter "Tabular_CB". Click the "Replace All" button, and then click "Close". This will have replaced the two instances with exactly the same thing, and we can save the report and close the Source Code Editor (Ctrl+W will do both). If you were to run this report it would look identical to what we had before – for now.

Next you will want to open this report in the Report Designer. Right click and select "Design Report".

In the Report Designer the first thing we will want to do is change the "SecondaryTitle" text, which currently says "Calculated Fields". Click on this once to give it focus, and again to place it into edit mode. Change the text to "Age – Codeblock", so that when viewing the report at a later date you will know what its purpose is. Click on the *pageTemplate* to take focus off the text control.

Click on the "Custom" tab of the Component Palette, and place a "DataColHeadingText" control on the *detailBand* to the right of the existing text, and line it up with the other headings. Change the *text* to read "Age".

Place a "DataText" object on the *detailBand* under the heading you just placed there. This next part will take a little work, so follow along carefully. First go to the *text* property in the Inspector. Set the "Type" to "Codeblock" (click on the "T" button ...). Now you want to click on the tool button, which will bring up a dialog for creating and editing codeblocks.

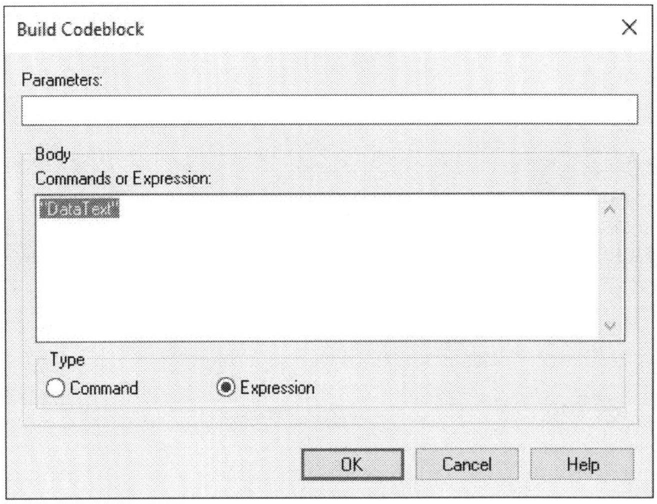

Figure 7-3

Enter the following codeblock *(enter as a single line -- do not press the Enter key to wrap it – it will wrap inside the window on its own)*:

```
int ( floor( val( dtos( date() ) ) - val( dtos(
form.dogs1.rowset.fields["BORN"].value ) ) ) / 10000 )
```

The important thing is to get all of the parentheses in the correct places. Count them carefully. Note that it uses the value returned by the *date()* function, as well as the value of the BORN field from the table. Basically this function is taking the values of the dates, subtracting them, rounding down to the nearest integer value, and then dividing that value by 10,000. This is hard to explain in more detail, but it does work.

> **NOTE**
> Dates in Windows, and therefore in dBASE, are simply numbers. Date math works because of this – you can add a day to a date by using date+1. Dates are calculated based on the integer value of a date value – values to the left of the decimal are days from a starting point determined by Windows (January 1, 1970), values to the right of the decimal are time (milliseconds after midnight). The date class in dBASE works with milliseconds since January 1, 1970 (from the online help for dBASE). dBASE allows you to do a lot of manipulation of dates through both the date object, and just basic dates themselves. The dUFLP has a custom class file called "DateEX.cc" which contains many methods for manipulating dates.

You should adjust your report, moving the text controls so everything lines up. Since the value returned is an integer, click on the text control, and go to the Inspector, set a *picture* of "99" (without the quotes). Then you could make the width a bit smaller, and do more cleaning up of the report to get things to line up just the way that looks right to you.

If you run the report, you should see something like:

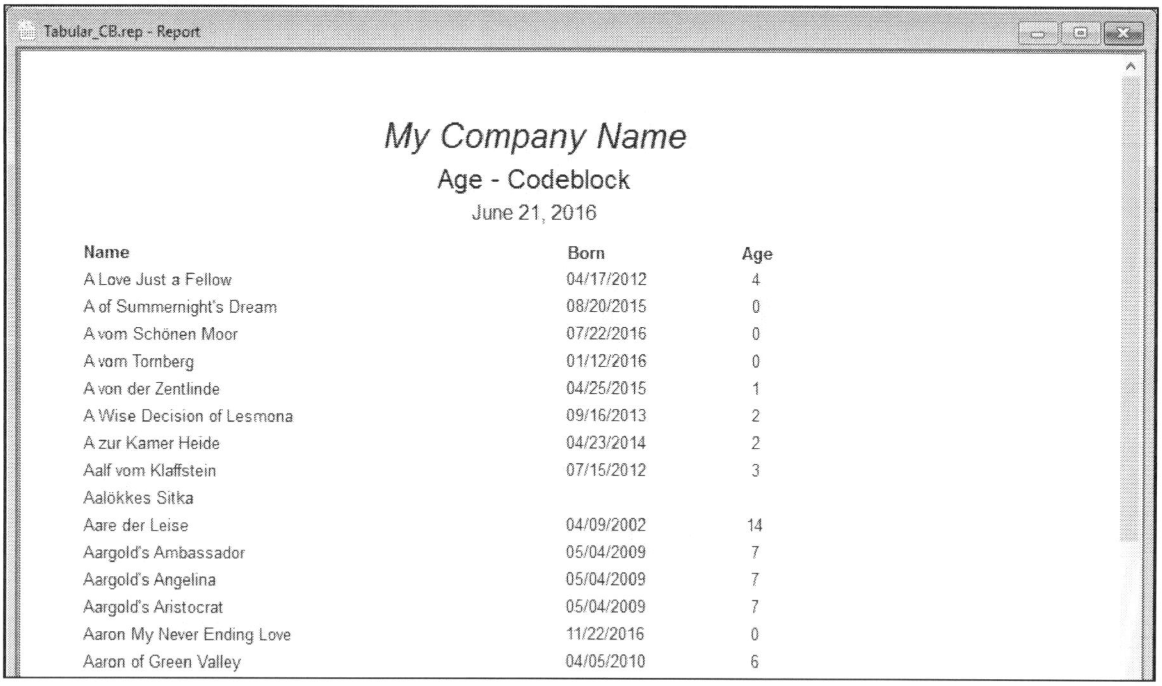

Figure 7-4

If you think about it, an age of "zero" means that the dog would be less than one year old. You could work out a way to display something like "<1", but this would complicate things quite a bit.

This should give you some idea of what can be done in a report using codeblocks for calculated fields. The one difficulty is that a codeblock can get hard to read. In addition, if you have conditions for a calculation (IF or CASE statements), you might find that it is easier to do this in another way.

The Text Object's *canRender* Event

We have worked a little with the *canRender* event, mostly for the column headings for tabular style reports. What we did there was to check to see if the *detailBand* was the first one on the *streamFrame* (this.parent.firstOnFrame). If the *firstOnFrame* property of the *detailBand* evaluated to *true* we rendered the heading control, if it was *false*, we didn't. If the *canRender* event RETURNs a value of *true*, the text control is rendered for the current row, if it RETURNs a value of *false* the control will not be rendered for the current row. The event is evaluated each time the Report Engine is told to render the text object.

However, you can do a lot more with it than just decide if a text control should be rendered. This event fires before the control is rendered by the Report Engine. What this means is that if you assign an event handler to this event, you can write code that can range from very simple to quite complex and you can change the text property of the control based on your calculuations. For now we are really looking at doing *a simple example* just so that you can get a feel for what can be done.

Morphing a Field

One way of using this event is to *morph* a field – change what it looks like when rendering it. If you have read The dBASE Book there are some examples of this sort of thing there. We are going to use this to do a simple morph using the "sex" field in the DOGS table. The value contained is a single letter, "M" for Male, and "F" for Female. Rather than displaying "M" we could display "Male", and the same for "Female". In some cases the field is empty *(and conceivably might contain some other value)*, so we might want to note "Unknown".

To start this example, we will copy the BaseTabular.rep file to a new file (type the following in the Command Window):

```
copy file BaseTabular.rep to Tabular_canRender.rep
```

Open the file in the Source Code Editor (right click on the new file in the Navigator, and select the "Open in Source Editor" option), and let's do a Find and Replace (Ctrl+R), to change the name of the report class internally. In the Find and Replace dialog, in the "Find what:" entryfield, enter "basetabular", and in the "Replace with:" entryfield enter "Tabular_canRender". Then click "Replace All". When done (this is quick), click the "Close" button. Press Ctrl+W to save and exit the Source Code Editor, so we can bring the new report into the Report Designer.

Right click on the file in the Navigator, and select "Design Report".

Change the secondary heading text control by clicking on it once to give focus, and again to place it in edit mode, and add " -- canRender" to the end of the text. You will need to widen this control so you can see the text. Then select the "Layout" menu, selecting "Align" and "Center Horizontally in Window".

Next, place a "DataColHeadingText" object on the *detailBand* to the right of the existing controls. Rearrange it (move it as necessary, widen, etc.) Change the text (click once to give focus, and once again to put it into edit mode) to simply "Sex".

Place a "DataText" control on the *detailBand* under this heading. Set the *text* property to a type of Codeblock, and click the tool button, and place this text in the dialog:

```
this.form.dogs1.rowset.fields["sex"].value
```

You should see either "M", "F" or maybe a "*" for an empty field, although the first page of the report does not show any empty values for this field.

This is the value that we need to morph so that it reads more clearly than it does now. We are going to create an event handler for this text control. This will allow us to modify the value displayed by the Text control, based on the value in the rowset, each time the text control is rendered.

Go to the "Events" tab of the Inspector, and click on the tool button next to *canRender*. This will bring up the Source Code Editor, and automatically insert some code:

```
function DATATEXT3_canRender()
   return true
```

The last statement is important, because it tells dBASE to render the text. If we did not wish the text rendered, we could change it to return a value of *false*, instead. The next thing we want to do is get the current value of the field, so we are going to insert some program statements between the "function" and "return" statements.

When working with fields in a report, I find it simpler to use a dBASE shortcut which is a variable that references a longer object structure. In this case we are going to point to the fields array of the rowset we are using for the report. The first statement we will add is:

```
f = form.streamSource1.rowset.fields
```

This provides a simple way to reference the fields array, less typing if you are doing something more complex than our code (referencing multiple fields, for example). Next we need to determine if the value in the field is "M", "F" or something else. The code below will do the trick. Enter it as shown:

```
function DATATEXT3_canRender
   f = form.streamSource1.rowset.fields
   if f["Sex"].value == "M"
      this.text := "Male"
   elseif f["Sex"].value == "F"
      this.text := "Female"
   else
      this.text := "Unknown"
   endif
return true
```

When you click on the design surface, this is not being rendered the way you might expect! It is instead showing the same values it did before – why is that? Because the values have already been evaluated, and the Report Engine does not re-evaluate them after adding the code. When you run the report it will work, and the next time you bring the report into the Report Designer it will evaluate this control as well. Save your changes and run the report. You should see something like:

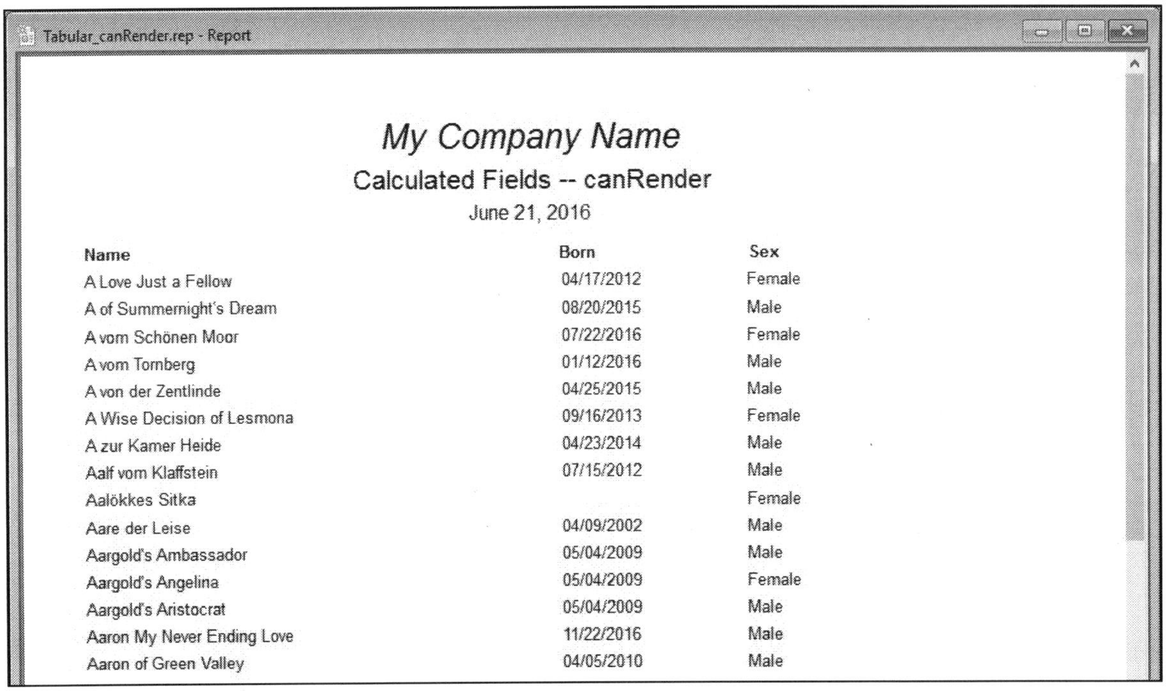

Figure 7-5

There is one other way to get this kind of calculation, or indeed, the codeblock we used in the previous report to get the age, and that is to create a virtual field for our table.

Create a New Field

There are two ways to create a virtual field for a table, one is using the SQL SELECT statement for the query object, and creating the calculated field that way. This has the disadvantage that to use it you have to make your SELECT statement fairly long and complex *(we will do something with this in a later chapter)*. The other way is one I prefer, and is what we will examine here – this is to create a virtual field by using the query object's *onOpen* event, and adding a field object to the fields array.

To do this we will want to do similar starting steps to what we did before – making a copy of the report, and so on. Follow along:

Copy the BaseTabular.rep file (type the following in the Command Window):

```
copy file BaseTabular.rep to Tabular_NewField.rep
```

Open the file in the Source Code Editor (right click on the new file in the Navigator, and select the "Open in Source Editor" option), and let's do a Find and Replace (Ctrl+R), to change the name of the report class internally. In the Find and Replace dialog, in the "Find what:" entryfield, enter "basetabular", and in the "Replace with:" entryfield enter "Tabular_NewField". Then click "Replace All". When done (this is quick), click the "Close" button.

Press Ctrl+W to save and exit the Source Code Editor, so we can bring this into the Report Designer.

Right click on the file in the Navigator, and select "Design Report".

When this report opens in the Report Designer, change the secondary heading text control by clicking on it once to give focus, and again to place it in edit mode, and add "-- New Field" to the end of the text. You will need to widen this control, then select the "Layout" menu, selecting "Align" and "Center Horizontally in Window".

This is where things really diverge in our steps. We need to tell dBASE to create a new field when the query object for the table is opened. The interesting thing is that this creates what might be called a "virtual field" because it is not really a part of the table. When the report is done the field will no longer be there. We are not actually adding a field to the table as it is stored on disk, just in the version that is in memory as we generate the report.

To get this process started, click on the "DOGS1" query (if you cannot select this, which sometimes happens depending on where the object is on the screen, you can find "DOGS1" in the Inspector's combobox at the top – select the control there). Click on the Inspector, and select the "Events" tab. You will see only five events. Find *onOpen*. Click the tool button, and you will find the Source Code Editor has appeared, and the following has been inserted into the report's source code:

```
function DOGS1_onOpen()
   return
```

We are going to insert some code between those two statements.

```
function DOGS1_onOpen()
   f = new field()
   f.fieldName := "SexText"
   this.rowset.fields.add( f )
   f.beforeGetValue := {||iif(this.parent["Sex"].value=="M", "Male",
iif( this.parent["Sex"].value=="F", "Female", "Unknown"))}
return
```

The long statement (begins with "f.beforeGetValue") that wraps in the example above needs to be a single line in the code. This is a complex statement that really does the same thing that we did in the *canRender* example earlier. It checks to see if the value of the "Sex" field is "M", and if so, it returns the word "Male", otherwise, it checks to see if the value of the "Sex" field is "F" and if it is, it returns the word "Female", otherwise it returns "Unknown". This is nesting the *iif()* function one inside the other.

> **NOTE**
> iif() stands for "Immediate IF" – which means to evaluate the condition, and return a value depending on whether the condition returns *true* or *false*. It is very handy for simple calculations, however, if you need to do something more complex, you may want to consider creating an event handler for the *beforeGetValue* event of the field object. The example here shows a nested iif() statement.

If we needed to, we could add several new field objects to the table at this point – once you have told dBASE what to do with the first field, you could add a second, third, and so on. It is a good idea to make sure that you have everything finished for each field before moving on to another.

With this new field in our query we can now treat it as any other field in a table for the purpose of the report.

In order for the Report Designer to "see" the new field, save the report and exit the Designer, and then immediately open the report back into the Report Designer. This is done by following these steps: Press Ctrl+W (save and exit), then right click on this report in the Navigator, and select "Design Report".

Click on the design surface of the Report Designer, and add a column heading ("DataColHeadingText"), setting the *text* to "Sex".

Place a "DataText" object on the *detailBand* under the heading, and set the *text* property to a codeblock, click the tool button, and enter:

```
this.form.dogs1.rowset.fields["SexText"].value
```

When you click "OK", notice that the value displays the way it would for any other field. Spend a moment and line up the controls, then save the report and exit the Report Designer (Ctrl+W).

Grouping on Part of a Field

Another use of a calculated field is for generating groups in a report, which will give you more flexibility as to how you can group your data. You can, for example, create a calculated field based on two or more fields and use it to create a group in your report. An example might be where we want to group a report by both the Dam and Sire. A Dam can have more than one litter with the same Sire and can have litters with more than one Sire.

Here we will create a report group based on a substring of a field. The registration number is 16 characters long, with the last 13 of those being unique values, but the first three characters of the registration are not unique, and can be used to group the data.

To start, we need to create a brand new report, because the "BaseGroup" report we created earlier isn't grouped the way we need it to be, we need to set the report up differently.

Create a new report by double-clicking the "[New Report]" icon in the Reports tab of the Navigator. This should base the report on the custom report we have been using.

Change the SecondaryTitle text control to read:

> Calculated Fields - Groups - Partial Field

You will want to widen this text control, and then re-center it (use the "Layout" menu, "Align", "Center Horizontally in Window").

Save the report (Ctrl+S) and name it "Group_PartialField.rep".

Next go to the Navigator window, find the "Tables" tab, and drag an instance of the "Dogs" table to the report's design surface.

With the "Dogs1" query having focus, click on the Properties tab of the Inspector, find the *rowset* object, and click the "I" button. This will change the Inspector's focus to the *rowset*, and find the *indexName* property – select "reg_no" from the combobox.

Place an instance of the "DataColHeadingText" control on the *detailBand*, and change the text to "Name". Next, place an instance of the "DataText" control under this on the detailBand (move things to make it work), set the *text* property "Type" to Codeblock, click the tool button, and enter in the dialog:

```
this.form.dogs1.rowset.fields["name"].value
```

When you click "OK", you will now see the names of the dogs. You should probably indent these controls a little on the *detailBand*, and spend a moment getting them to line up, like we did in the first Group report at the beginning of this chapter.

Go to the Report tab of the Component Palette, and drag an instance of the Group object to the design surface. Notice that the *group headerBand* is automatically added with a text control on it. Go to the Inspector, and if necessary select "group1" from the combobox at the top. Set the *groupBy* property to "REG_NO".

Note that now the data is grouped, but each dog has its own group. This is not quite as useful as we'd like. As noted earlier each registration number is unique, which is why the report is grouped this way.

We would like to be able to group the dogs by the first three letters of their registration number. To do this we need to add a calculated field to the *onOpen* event of the query.

Click on the "DOGS1" query object to give it focus. In the Inspector, click on the "Events" tab, and click the tool button by the *onOpen* event. As has happened before, dBASE inserted the basics for this event handler, but we need to add the details. Change this new code to look like:

```
function dogs1_onOpen()
   f = new field()
   f.fieldName := "LeftRegNo"
   this.rowset.fields.add( f )
   f.beforeGetValue := {||left(this.parent["Reg_No"].value, 3) }
return
```

The only other thing we need to do is to reset the *groupBy* property for the group. This report already has a "group1" object, so we will use the Inspector to locate the "group1" object, and set the *groupBy* property to the calculated field. However if you look, there is no field "LeftRegNo" listed. That is because the *canOpen* event of the Query object has not been executed since we added an event handler to it.

The simplest way to force it to fire is to save the report and exit the designer, and then immediately open the report back into the Report Designer. Press Ctrl+W (save and exit), then right click on this report in the Navigator, and select "Design Report". Now when you go to the "group1" object in the Inspector, you will find in the combobox, at the bottom, "LeftRegNo". Select this. The data will immediately "regroup"!

Place a "DataHeadingText" control onto the group's *headerBand*. You can now delete the text control placed there by the Report Designer as a place holder. Change the text of this control to "Reg No:".

Now place a "DataText" control onto the *headerBand*. Set the *text* property to a Codeblock and click the tool button, enter this in the dialog:

```
this.form.dogs1.rowset.fields["LeftRegNo"].value
```

Click "OK", and now the report should be complete. If you run this, and page through it you should find the dogs grouped by the first three letters of the registration number appropriately.

If you page through the data, you will see that a large group will have to break over multiple pages. How do you know what the group is? The heading is only displayed at the beginning of the group! Well, there is a setting that can be made to tell dBASE that when the report is rendered, it should display the group header at the top of each *streamFrame*.

Close the preview window and open the report back in the designer, find "group1", then set the *headerEveryFrame* property to *true*, you won't see an immediate effect, but the next time you run the report and page through it, you should see the header for the group at the top of each page, even if it is not a new group.

When you run the report, you should see something like:

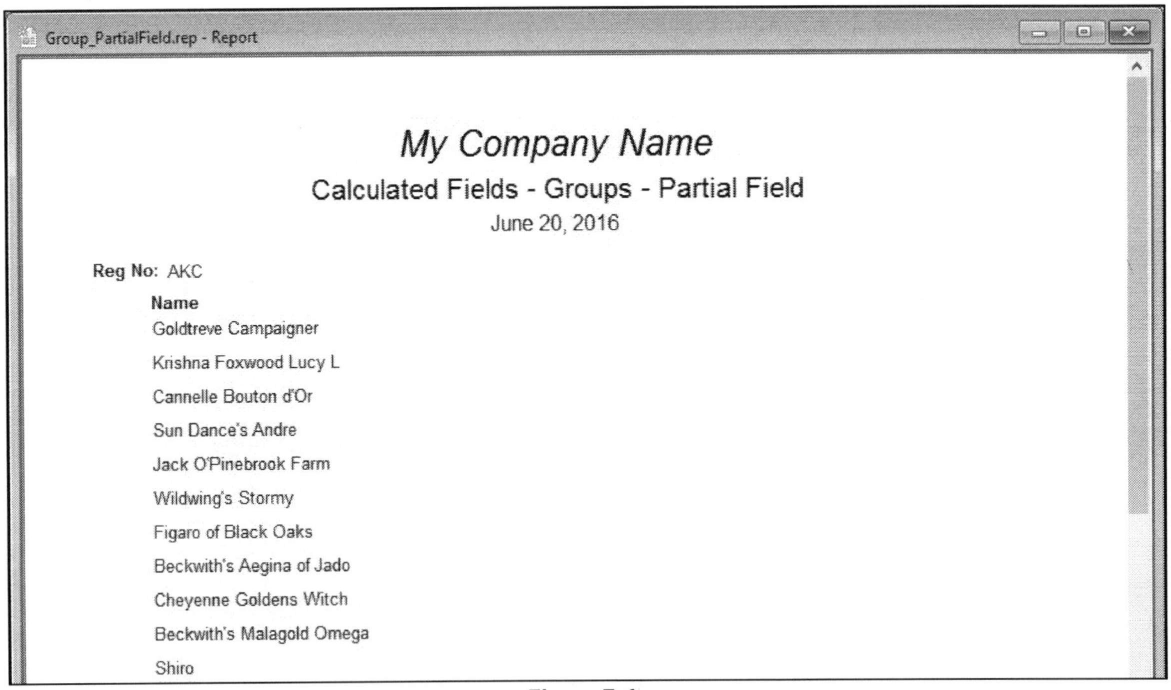

Figure 7-6

If you look at this, you will see other things, like the fact that you might want to sort the data by the "reg_no" *and* the "name", but that's a fairly simple exercise (modify the table in the Table Designer, add a new index tag, and then use that index for the report.).

lookupSQL and *lookupRowset*

Lookup fields can be used in reports just as they are used in forms. In fact, in reports lookups can be very useful because a report is generally only reading data from tables. In this example we are going to create two lookups and use them in a report. Moreover, we will see that the *lookupRowset* can contain calculated fields that will display in the report.

In order to do this, we will use the Data Module Designer to create a data module. As noted elsewhere, the advantages to using a data module include reusable code – in other words, we could use the same data module in a form, or multiple reports, without having to re-create the specific details (in this example, some lookups).

In addition, as a reminder, a data module is not really required, but it is considered good practice to use them. We have not used data modules for some of the reports earlier in this chapter, although we could have. The Report Designer can work with your tables whether using data modules or not.

Before we start, let's look at why we want the lookups in the first place.

In the Navigator window, click the "Tables" tab, and double-click the "Litters" table. Notice that for both "Dams" and "Sire" we have a bunch of codes:

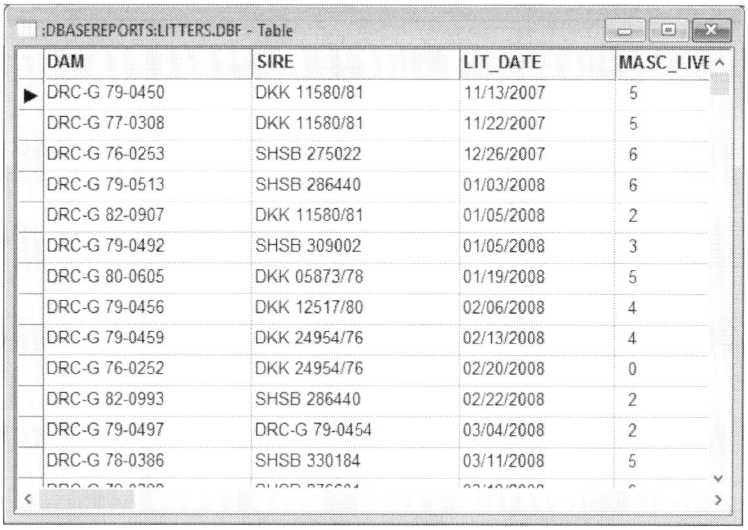

DAM	SIRE	LIT_DATE	MASC_LIVE
DRC-G 79-0450	DKK 11580/81	11/13/2007	5
DRC-G 77-0308	DKK 11580/81	11/22/2007	5
DRC-G 76-0253	SHSB 275022	12/26/2007	6
DRC-G 79-0513	SHSB 286440	01/03/2008	6
DRC-G 82-0907	DKK 11580/81	01/05/2008	2
DRC-G 79-0492	SHSB 309002	01/05/2008	3
DRC-G 80-0605	DKK 05873/78	01/19/2008	5
DRC-G 79-0456	DKK 12517/80	02/06/2008	4
DRC-G 79-0459	DKK 24954/76	02/13/2008	4
DRC-G 76-0252	DKK 24954/76	02/20/2008	0
DRC-G 82-0993	SHSB 286440	02/22/2008	2
DRC-G 79-0497	DRC-G 79-0454	03/04/2008	2
DRC-G 78-0386	SHSB 330184	03/11/2008	5

Figure 7-7

It would be useful to be able to see, instead of codes, the names of the Dam and/or Sire.

Close this window, and if you have any reports open, you should close them.

Go to the Data Modules tab of the Navigator window, and double click on the "[New Data Module]" icon. Move the design surface to the side of the screen, and select the "Tables" tab of the Navigator. Drag the "Litters" table to the design surface. This will place a Database object on the surface as well as a Query. The Database object will point to the "dBASEReports" database alias, and the query will use the "Litters" table.

For the Dams we will use a *lookupSQL*. This method finds a match on a key field, and returns a field from the table. This is useful in cases where we only really want to pull a single field. To do anything more complex, it is probably a better idea to use a *lookupRowset*, which we will do shortly.

Click on the "Litters1" query on the design surface, click on the "rowset" property in the Inspector window, click the "I" button, click "Fields", click the "I" button, select "Dam", click the "I" button. Click on *lookupSQL*, and then the tool button. Enter the following:

```
select reg_no, name from dogs
```

We are selecting only the two fields we need – the first should match the field we are connecting the data to, the second is the "return" value – if we find a match this is the text we want to display.

Click "OK". You will not see any immediate change here, that's fine. This will be more useful when we go to create the report.

For the Sires we will use the other method, a *lookupRowset*. The *lookupRowset* is useful in that it allows us to use more than a single field from the table we are performing the lookup on, and we can also do things such as creating a calculated field.

In order to use *lookupRowset*, a query for the table we are looking in must be available. So for this case, drag an instance of the "Dogs" table to the design surface.

In the Inspector, with the "Dogs1" query having focus, find the *sql* property and replace the existing text with the following:

```
select reg_no, name||" ("||reg_no||")" as CalcName from dogs order by reg_no
```

Let's break this down:

```
select reg_no,
```

This part of the statement is pretty straight forward. We are selecting the reg_no field, however, the next gets more complex.

```
name||" ("||reg_no||")" as CalcName
```

We are taking the *name* field, and concatenating – using the SQL "concatenate" operator which is two vertical bars (or pipes) "||" – with a space and an open parenthesis, then we are concatenating the *reg_no* field, and then concatenating to *that* a close parenthesis.

We follow it with "as CalcName" which is a way of naming this calculated field so we can reference it.

Hopefully the rest of the statement makes sense. Note that we are sorting the data (order by) on the reg_no field, which is required for the lookup to work properly.

Next we need to set the *lookupRowset* property of the Sires field in the "Litters" table to point to this rowset. Click on the "Litters1" query, find the *rowset* property and click the "I" button, find *fields* and the "I" button, the "Sire" field and the "I" button, find the *lookupRowset* property and select "dogs1" – this references the "dogs1" query's rowset.

Press Ctrl+S to save the Data Module as "Litters.dmd", then close the Data Module Designer (we could also have pressed "Ctrl+W").

At this point, we are now ready to create a report that uses this data module and the lookups contained in it. It should be noted that what we have done is fairly simple. With the *lookupRowset* we could have done a lot more, returning other data such as the birthdate of the Sire.

Start a new report by going to the Navigator tab, and selecting "Reports". Double-click on the "[New Report]" icon, and when the report opens in the designer *(it should be using the custom reports we've been working with)*.

Change the text of the Secondary Title to "Calculated Fields -- Lookups". Widen the control as necessary, and reset the alignment as we've done before (Center Horizontally in Window).

Go back to the Navigator Window, click on the "Data Modules" tab, and select the "Litters.dmd" file. Drag that to the report design surface. We are going to place the names of the Dams and Sires, as well as the Litter Date in this report.

Go to the Component Palette and select the "Custom" tab. Drag an instance of the "DataColHeadingText" object to the *detailBand*, and change the text to "Dam". Repeat this for "Sire" and "Litter Date" (changing the text, width and lining them up ...).

Next place a "DataText" object under the heading for "Dam". Set the *text* property type to "Codeblock", click the tool button, entering this in the dialog:

```
this.form.littersdatamodule1.litters1.rowset.fields["dam"].value
```

Place another DataText object under the heading for "Sire", and set the *text* property type to "Codeblock", click the tool button, entering this in the dialog:

```
this.form.littersdatamodule1.litters1.rowset.fields["sire"].value
```

Finally, place one more DataText object under the heading for "Litter Date", set the *text* property type to "Codeblock", click the tool button, entering this in the dialog:

```
this.form.littersdatamodule1.litters1.rowset.fields["lit_date"].value
```

Put a little effort into lining up the text controls, and widening the "Dam" and "Sire" data so that you can see all of each name. You should end up with something like that below. Save this (Ctrl+S) and name it "Lookups.rep".

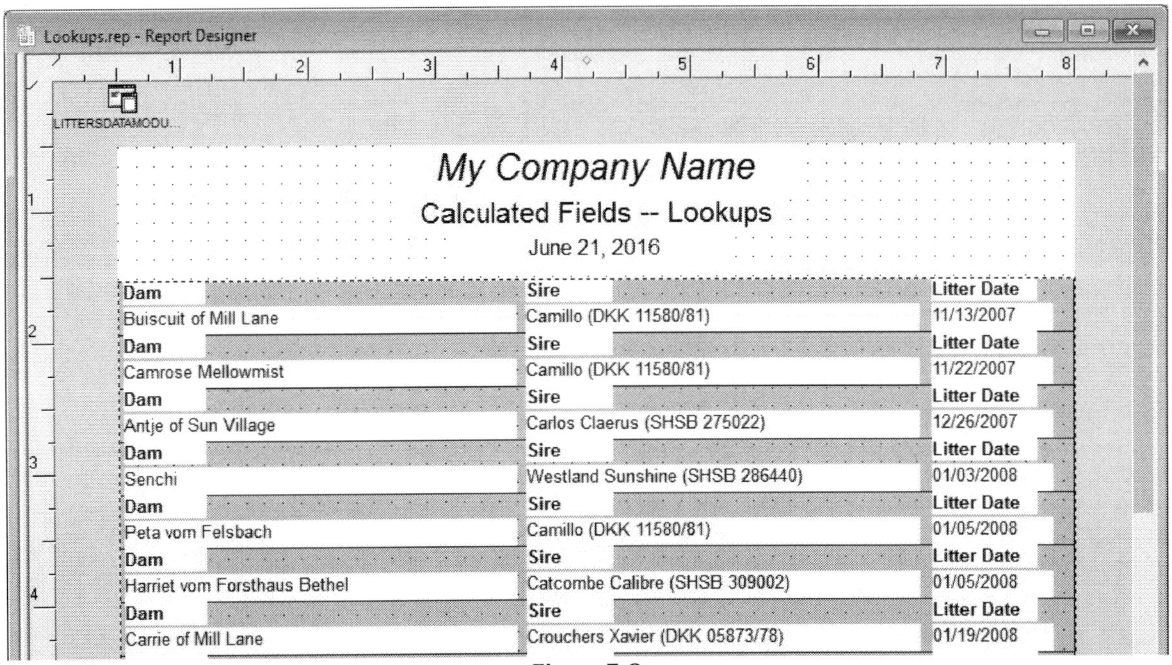

Figure 7-8

And when run, it should look like:

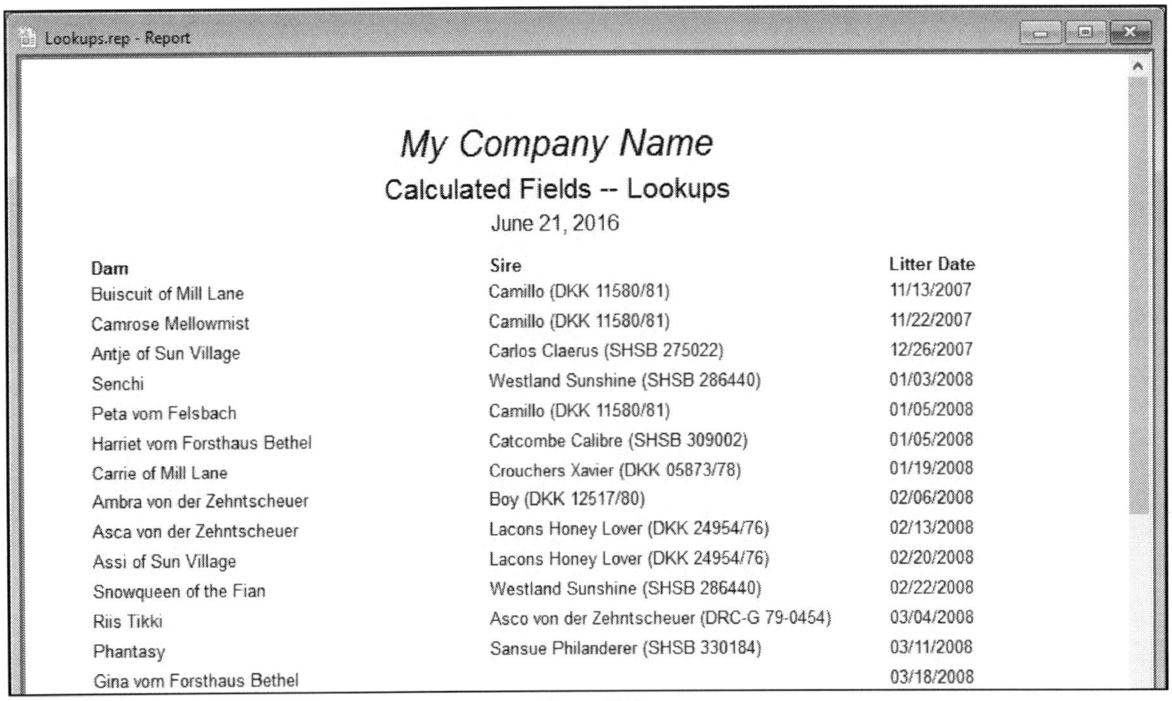

Figure 7-9

You should close the report once you are done looking at your handiwork.

The nice thing about using lookups in the way we have is that you don't have to do all the work necessary to find the appropriate data. Having written lookup code in earlier versions of dBASE *(prior to the 32-bit version, which has this ability)*, it is a lot of work. This is much simpler.

Cleanup

Create a new report (in the Navigator, click on the "Reports" tab, double-click on the "[New Report]" icon). Select the "File" menu, select "Set Custom Report Class", and in the dialog, click the "Clear Custom Report" button, then click "OK". This clears out the custom report setting in the Plus.ini file, so that the next report you create is not based on this one. Close that report without making any changes.

Make sure the database is closed by going to the Command Window and typing:

```
close databases
```

This will also ensure that you don't end up creating tables in the wrong location, etc.

Source Code

The following is a listing of the sample code in the folders we have been working with. If you downloaded the files from my website the structure will be different (see below). You may use the code contained in these folders for your own applications if you desire, with the caveat that credit be given appropriately.

From working on this chapter:

```
C:\dBASEReports\Chapter 7\BaseGroup.rep
C:\dBASEReports\Chapter 7\BaseTabular.rep
C:\dBASEReports\Chapter 7\DamsParentChild.dmd
C:\dBASEReports\Chapter 7\Group_PartialField.rep
C:\dBASEReports\Chapter 7\Litters.dmd
C:\dBASEReports\Chapter 7\Lookups.rep
C:\dBASEReports\Chapter 7\Tabular_CanRender.rep
C:\dBASEReports\Chapter 7\Tabular_CB.rep
C:\dBASEReports\Chapter 7\Tabular_NewField.rep
```

Downloaded version – same files but with this path:

```
C:\ReportsBookSourceCode\Chapter 07\filenames
```

Summary

There's a lot you can do with these calculated fields, isn't there? Believe it or not, we've just scratched the surface. As we move through later chapters in this book you will start seeing more and more things you can do, and perhaps even start to get ideas for improving some reports you've already been working on, or just start getting ideas for future projects. Lookups add an extra dimension, whether you use *lookupRowset* or *lookupSQL*, allowing a quick lookup in another table, or a more complex retrieval of appropriate data.

As you can see, this report tool is pretty powerful once you get under the hood and start tinkering.

The next chapter will take a look at everything that needs to be modified to generate a landscape report.

Chapter 8: Landscape Reports

In an ideal world, you could simply make one change to an existing report and print it landscape. However, there are other factors that must be accounted for besides the orientation of the paper when a report prints. If a report was set as *portrait* and you change the definition to *landscape*, the report will still attempt to print information off the bottom of the page and will not take advantage of the new *width* of the page.

This chapter will take a look at what is necessary to turn a report sideways and print it in landscape mode. We will also take a look at creating a Custom Report that has the necessary settings, so that you do not have to re-create them each time.

For this chapter we are not creating any files that need to be in a special folder.

Landscape vs. Portrait

There are two paper orientations when creating reports. Portrait is pretty standard – it is when the width of the paper is shorter than the length of the paper – in other words, looking at this book, you will see it was printed in Portrait orientation. Landscape turns the page sideways so that the top of the printed page is along the widest edge of the paper.

In America the standard "letter" size page is 8.5 by 11 inches. If you turned this to landscape, the report would be 11 by 8.5 inches. If you are using A4 or perhaps "Legal" paper in America, the sizes of the paper will vary.

For the purpose of this chapter, we will assume standard 8.5 x 11 letter paper. I have done some reports for a client that used legal size paper which is longer but not wider than letter – and making the page landscape the paper went to 14 by 8.5 inches.

The advantage to Landscape printing is that if you are creating tabular reports you can fit more columns of data onto the page *(a topic that will be examined in a later chapter)*.

What Must Change?

When you change a report from Portrait to Landscape, you have to make several changes in the report.

1. The first change is to tell the *printer* object that the *orientation* is landscape. Once you have done this, you will most likely see *no* apparent changes in your report.
2. You must set the pageTemplate's *height* and *width* properties to the correct height and width (in this case using American letter sized paper, the height becomes 8.5 and the width becomes 11 inches).
3. You must set the streamFrame's *height* and *width* for the new settings.

Only when all three of these are done will your report really print properly.

Creating a Custom Landscape Report

To see this, we will create a new Custom Report that we will use for the rest of this chapter.

Select the "Reports" tab on the Navigator, and double-click the "[New Custom Report]" icon. Notice that by default this does not inherit the settings of our Custom main custom report. Go to the "File" menu, and select "Set Custom Report Class", and select the report we've been using "MyCompanyReport.crp". When you click "OK", you will see this custom report inherit all of the settings and text controls of the main custom report.

Let's go through the three items that we must change:

First we need to tell the *printer* object that the page orientation is landscape. To do this, go to the Inspector, and find the *printer* object. Click the Inspect ("I") button. Find the *orientation* property, and select "2 – Landscape". That's it for that part of this process.

You should save this Custom Report. Press Ctrl+S and save this to the "C:\MyCompany\Reports" folder, with the filename of "MyCompanyReportLandscape.crp".

Second – we want to modify the pageTemplate's *height* and *width* properties. In the Inspector, find the *pageTemplate* object, and change the *height* to 8.5 and the *width* to 11. You should see the white area expand to the right in the Report Designer.

Third -- we need to modify the streamFrame's *height* and *width* properties. The *width* is easy – we know we have a page of 11 inches wide, and our margins in the *pageTemplate* are 0.5 inches each, so the *width* is 10 for the *streamFrame*.

The *height* is more complex. Previously it was 8.65 inches. However, that is now taller than the page. We need to reduce the *height* – try setting it to 6.2 inches in the Inspector. This will give room for the page number control at the bottom of the page. Scroll down to the bottom of the report using the scrollbar on the right.

Where's the page number control? The *top* property for this was set to a value that is way down off the bottom of the page! In the Inspector, find "pagenumber1" – this is the object that displays the page number on our reports. Set the *top* property to 7.25. NOW it appears where you expect to find it at the bottom of the page.

The last thing to do is re-center the text controls on the *pageTemplate* – currently if printed, they will be offset to the left side of the report. Why is that? They were centered for a report that is in Portrait orientation, and all the changes we just made have not changed the *left* property of these controls.

Click on the "pagenumber1" control at the bottom of the report, then using the scrollbar scroll back up to the top of the report. When there, hold the Ctrl key, and click on each of the other three controls at the top of the report. Select the "Layout" menu, "Align", and "Center Horizontally in Window". This will shift the controls to where they now need to be.

Save and exit the Report Designer (Ctrl+W).

Using the Custom Landscape Report

Once you have your Custom Landscape Report created, it is just as easy to use as with any other custom report. To see this, double-click on the "[New Report]" icon in the Navigator. Note that the report is derived from the usual "MyCompanyReport" custom report, which is in Portrait orientation. To change this, go to the "File" menu, and select "Set Custom Report Class". Select "MyCompanyReportLandscape.crp", and click "OK". Now your report will use the settings for the landscape custom report we just created.

There is no real need to go through the steps of creating a report to test this at this time *(we will use this for a report later in this book)*. This will allow you to work with landscape or portrait reports with ease. And if you use the custom reports as shown in this book, one change in the "MyCompanyReport" will drill down through any reports derived from that, including your landscape reports. For example, if you changed the font used for the main title, it would automatically appear in all reports as before.

Notes

If your applications only use landscape reports infrequently you may not wish to bother creating a custom landscape report. Instead you can just create a report using your main custom report, and set the settings as shown in the section of this chapter titled "Creating a Custom Landscape Report", moving the controls as needed, etc. That single report will print landscape, and work as expected.

Cleanup

Create a new report (in the Navigator, click on the "Reports" tab, double-click on the "[New Report]" icon). Select the "File" menu, select "Set Custom Report Class", and in the dialog, click the "Clear Custom Report" button, then click "OK". This clears out the custom report setting in the Plus.ini file, so that the next report you create is not based on this one. Close that report without making any changes.

Make sure the database is closed by going to the Command Window and typing:

```
close databases
```

This will also ensure that you don't end up creating tables in the wrong location, etc.

Source Code

The following is a listing of the sample code in the folders we have been working with. If you downloaded the files from my website the structure will be different (see below). You may use the code contained in these folders for your own applications if you desire, with the caveat that credit be given appropriately.

From working on this chapter:

```
C:\dBASEReports\Reports\MyCompanyReportLandscape.crp
```

Downloaded version – same files but with this path:

```
C:\ReportsBookSourceCode\Reports\filename
```

Summary

As you can see, landscape reports are not that hard to do. Indeed, they are really no more difficult than any other report, the main thing is to do the three sets of changes mentioned at the beginning of the chapter. Once that is done, create the report as you normally do, and you're set. When you print the report, it will print in landscape orientation.

The next chapter will take a look at working with labels.

Chapter 9: Labels

Mailing labels and labels of other sorts are important to many developers and users of applications. The most common use of labels is for mailing, but the Label Designer *(which is really the Report Designer)* in dBASE can handle just about any label type you wish.

By default dBASE uses mostly labels by Avery, a company that specializes in this type of product. Many other companies create labels that match the same sizes and specifications as those used by Avery. However (and we will examine this later in this chapter) you can add your own label definitions to those used by dBASE.

The interesting thing about working with labels in dBASE is that the Report Designer automatically does something that for us to do manually would take a lot of work – it creates a *streamFrame* for each label in a sheet. So if your sheet of labels has 30 labels on it, there should be 30 streamFrames in the *pageTemplate* in the designer. dBASE keeps track of which *streamFrame* is next, and works through it all automatically. This is a technique that we will look at in a later part of this book, because it can be useful for reports as well as labels.

Probably the best thing to do when discussing this topic is to jump right in and take a look at it.

A Place for Our Work

As we work through the chapter we will be needing a place for the files we create, so please create a folder for this chapter:

```
C:\dBASEReports\Chapter 9
```

And in the Navigator, be sure to navigate to this folder.

A First Set of Labels

Go to the Navigator Window in dBASE Plus, and click on the "Reports" tab. The third icon is for labels "[New Labels]". If you double-click this, dBASE will bring up a default label definition. Note that there is no "[New Custom Labels]" icon.

However, you can easily change this by selecting the "Layout" menu, and "Set Label Type ...". This shows a dialog that looks like:

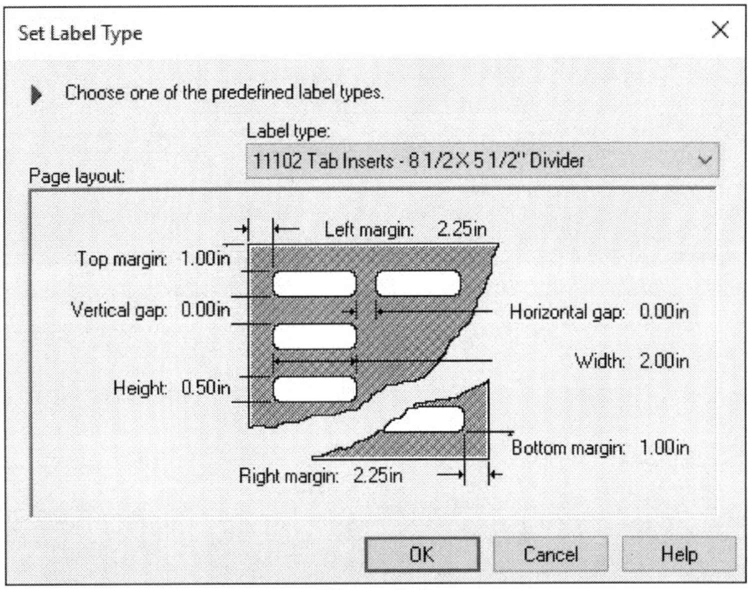

Figure 9-1

The "Label type:" combobox if you examine it will show a very large selection of label types. If you know the label types you wish to use, select them from the list. Avery works off a numeric value followed by a text description.

If the label type you need is not in the list, you *can* add it to the list, a topic we will discuss in a later part of this chapter. The dialog shown in Figure 9-1 (above) shows all of the various settings you would need to know for creating your own custom labels – these are described in a later part of this chapter in some detail.

For our purposes right now, use the "5260 Address" label as shown below *(Figure 9-2)*. This label is pretty standard in America, it comes in sheets of 30 labels (10 down and three across). Click "OK".

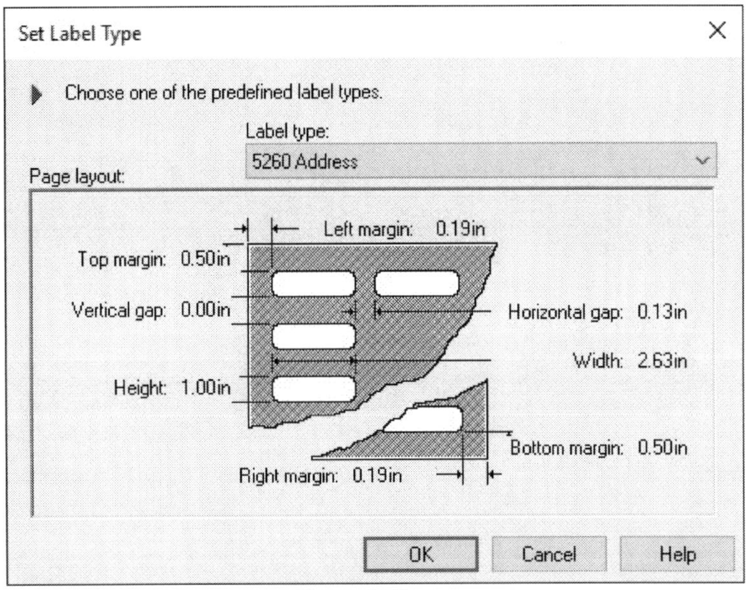

Figure 9-2

Note that values of the settings on the dialog have changed to match the currently selected labels.

In the designer you should see something like:

Figure 9-3

For this set of labels, we will use the Customer table in the "dBASESamples" database (which ships with dBASE).

To make it easier to manipulate everything, set the *metric* property to the appropriate value for the "form" using the Inspector. (I would select "3 – Inches" based on my own preferences.)

Go to the Navigator window, select the "Tables" tab and select the "dBASESamples" database using the "Look In:" combobox. Drag the "Customers" table to the design surface.

Save the file (Ctrl+S) as "Customers" in the Chapter 9 folder.

We could use the custom controls that we've been using in earlier chapters, but for now let us do this the easy way, and pull controls from the Field Palette.

Click on the "Company" field and place it on the first label in the upper left. This is the working area, as it were. Move the control so that it's at the top of the label and to the left. You may want to resize it so it doesn't go off the right side.

Next select the "FirstName" field, and drag it to the label. We will use some of what we've learned before to combine this and the "LastName" field. Widen this so it is about as wide as the Company field. Go to the Inspector, and click on the "Events" tab. Select the *canRender* event, and click on the tool button. In the Source Code Editor, type:

```
function TEXTFIRSTNAME1_canRender
   f = form.streamSource1.rowset.fields
   this.text := f["FirstName"].value.rightTrim()+;
   " "+;
   f["LastName"].value.rightTrim()
return true
```

This will trim the first name of extra spaces, add a single space, then add the last name to it (also trimming it), creating a single text control for the name.

> **BUG**
> This bug was mentioned in an earlier chapter, but I wanted to remind you – the designer does not always run the *canRender* event – so while we put the name together here, you may not see it until we actually render the labels or exit the designer and reopen the file back in the designer.

It should be noted here that if you are using a *metric* of inches, the default *height* for a text control is 0.21 inches tall. If you multiply that by 5, you get 1.05 inches, which would place text in the last control printing off the bottom of the label (which is 1 inch tall) – this is obviously not very desirable. You might want to consider changing the height of each of the text controls. I have found that 0.18 inches works well for a text control with a *fontName* of "Arial" and a *fontSize* of 10. You may need to experiment to find the *height* that works best for your situation.

Next drag the "Address1" field to the first label under the name. We need to set the height as noted above – find the *height* property in the Inspector and set it to .18 (or an appropriate height for your *metric*).

Drag the "Address2" field to the first label. Set the *height* property appropriately. The problem that may occur is that typically some companies use the second address field, but not all. If you see a set of asterisks ("******") in the text it means that the field is empty for that row. The problem is that if you just leave this as it is, your labels will have a blank line for those customers that do not use a second address field. The next line will have the city and such – and having a blank line between them looks unprofessional.

We will look at this again in later chapters of this book, but for this to work, we need to suppress this text control if the value is empty. The way we handle this is to go to the Inspector and set the *suppressIfBlank* property to *true* (it defaults to *false*). We'll come back to this in a moment.

Next we need to add the last row to the label, the one containing the City, State and Zip (or Postal Code ...). Drag the "City" field to the first label, and widen it so it takes up most of the width of the label. Set the *height* as with the other controls. Go to the Inspector, select the *canRender* event, and click on the tool button. Enter the following, which will combine the City, State and Zip in a meaningful way, creating a single text control displaying all three fields:

```
function TEXTCITY1_canRender()
   f = form.streamSource1.rowset.fields
   this.text := f["City"].value.rightTrim()
   this.text += ", "
   this.text += f["State"].value.rightTrim()
   this.text += " "
   this.text += f["Zip"].value
return true
```

As with the previous calculated field, this most likely is not showing the results of the calculation.

For the moment, let's just work on lining everything up. You want a small amount of room on the left, right, top and bottom of the labels, because 9 times out of 10 things will not line up 100% perfectly when printing. Giving the extra room will prevent some of these difficulties.

Save this as "Customers.lab", and try running it. It should look something like:

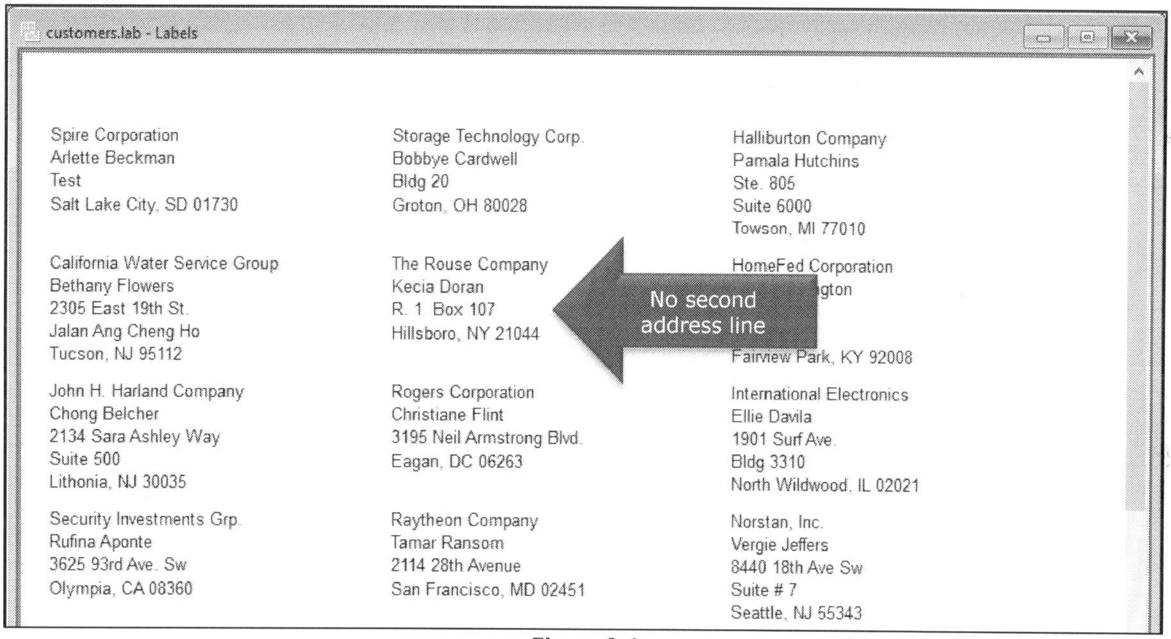

Figure 9-4

Testing Your Labels

If you have the actual labels handy you could test this by running the labels and printing the first page to a plain sheet of paper. Why would you want to do that? Labels can get expensive, and printing a bunch of tests to make sure everything lines up properly could be a problem. By printing to a blank sheet of paper you can then hold a sheet of labels up behind the printed sheet and hold this to a light to compare to make sure everything lines up (and nothing prints off the labels). If all is well, you are set and can then print the labels.

Sorting the Labels

Can you sort the labels? Of course you can. This would be done with the query object like always. You can either set the *indexName* property for the rowset if an index tag exists that is useful, or use an ORDER BY clause in the SQL statement of the query itself.

For example, you might want to sort the labels by the company name, or perhaps the Zip code (if you are doing bulk mailing in the US for example, the Post Office requires the items mailed be sorted by zip codes and broken down into appropriate "packages").

Other Types of Labels

As mentioned earlier in this chapter you might want to do other types of labels. Labels don't have to be mailing labels, and indeed don't really have to be labels at all. For example, Avery produces some card stock that is used for name badges for conventions and such. We will take a look at doing something along these lines, again using the Customers table, as it is handy. We might assume that every customer listed is showing up at a convention, and we need name badges for each of them.

The first thing to do is to start a new set of labels (in the Navigator double-click the "[New Labels]" icon). Notice that the Label/Report Designer remembers the last label style you used. This can be handy if you use that type of labels a lot.

Go to the "Layout" menu, and select "Set Label Type ...". In the "Label type" combobox, find the labels that are named "5384 Name Badge Inserts - 3" x 4"" and select it. Click the "OK" button. The designer should now show a sheet of 6 labels, two across, and three down.

Change the form's *metric* property to "3 – Inches".

Let's start these by putting some text on them that will print on every label. Since we do not have a *pageTemplate* to work with, we will simply place the control directly on the label.

Select a *text* object and place it on the first label. Change the *text* to read "My Convention" (without the quotes). Next, go to the inspector, and set the *fontSize* to 26, and set the *fontItalic* property to *true*. Make the *height* as tall as necessary to see the text (either through the inspector, or by dragging the controls on the text control). Finally set the *alignHorizontal* property to "1 – Center". Change the *fontName* property if you wish, but this is not necessary *(and may require more adjustment to various properties to make it look correct)*.

Next place a *line* object on the first label under the text. Set the *width* property to 3. We will discuss this object in more detail in a later chapter, but this can be useful for enhancing the appearance of any report or label. Widen the control (drag it right) to make it wider, and make sure (using the inspector) that the *top* and *bottom* properties are the same when done. Move it up or down if needed.

Unfortunately the option we have used before to center controls on a page horizontally will not work with labels, so you may want to spend some time trying to get these close to centered on the first label – this is called "eyeballing" it – using your eyes to line things up.

We should save our work, so press Ctrl+S and give a filename of "ConventionBadges.lab".

Next we want to put information about the individual customer on the badge. This is so that each person at the convention can quickly read someone else's badge and know some things that might be useful.

To do that, we need to put get the data. Go to the Navigator, and click on the "Tables" tab. If you do not see the "Customers" table, make sure that the "Look in:" combobox is showing the "dBASESamples" database. Drag the "Customers" table to the design surface.

When you drag the table to the designer, suddenly the text and line created earlier is on each of the labels on the page. This is because until now there was no data, so the designer didn't know how many rows there were *(very much like the detailBand on a report)*.

Drag the "FirstName" field from the Field Palette to the first label, and widen it. Next go to the Inspector, and click on the "Events" tab, selecting the *canRender* event. We are going to do what we did earlier and combine the first and last names. Click on the tool button, and change the code so it looks like:

```
function TEXTFIRSTNAME1_canRender
   f = form.streamSource1.rowset.fields
   this.text := f["FirstName"].value.rightTrim()
   this.text += " "
   this.text += f["LastName"].value.rightTrim()
return true
```

Change the *fontSize* property to 14. This will make it larger, and easier to read. Also set the *alignHorizontal* property to "1 - Center". Readjust the position so it is fairly centered both left and right, and vertically on the label.

Drag the "Company" field to a location below the name.

Next drag the "City" field to under that. For the City field, we will combine the City and the State, but we don't need the zip (or postal) code. This is really just to give other people an idea where someone is from without giving all the specific details. Click on the tool button for the *canRender* event of the City field. Change the code to read:

```
function TEXTCITY1_canRender
   f = form.streamSource1.rowset.fields
   this.text := f["City"].value.rightTrim()
   this.text += ", "
   this.text += f["State"].value
return true
```

This will show just the city and state, separated by a comma and a space.

You should set the *alignHorizontal* property for these two fields to "1 - Center".

Save your work. Now of course, we could add more detail to this. Each badge might have a logo (using an image object), or a date, or other information. But you get the idea, I hope. Try running this. You should see something like:

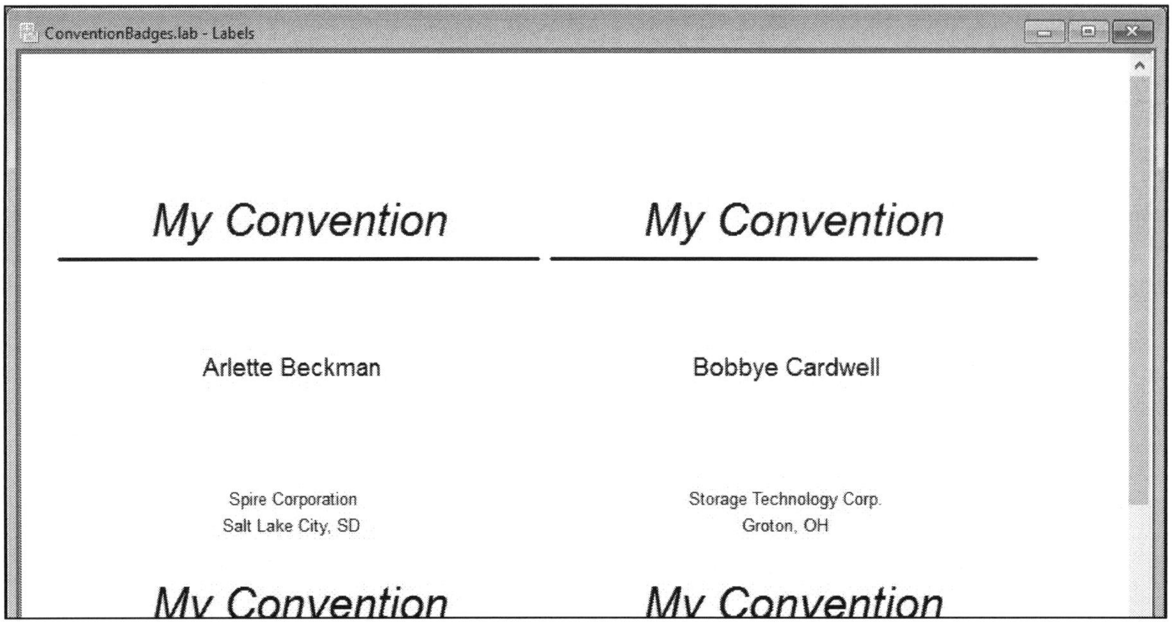

Figure 9-5

Label Type Not In List (Custom Labels)

An important consideration to creating labels is if your label type is not in the list, or you are using something very non-standard, possibly your own design, or whatever.

In cases like this, you can add your own label information, but there is a lot of information you need to know to do so. For starters, you need to know where dBASE gets this information from, and then you need to know the purpose of each of the fields in the table.

To begin, the table that needs to be used is stored in a very special location. When dBASE is installed, this table is stored in a subfolder. dBASE stores things differently in versions prior to dBASE Plus 8 to the current version. In dBASE Plus 10.3.1 the tables used by the label designer are here:

```
C:\ProgramData\dBASE\Plus10\Designer\label
```

There are several Paradox tables in this folder, the one we will examine is the table called "labe0009.db". You can attempt to modify data in this table but you will find that dBASE does not handle Paradox numeric values well in the default browse mode. So if you were to do something like type the following in the Command Window:

```
use "C:\ProgramData\dBASE\PLUS10\Designer\label\labe0009.db"
browse
```

and you tried to modify a number you would find that anything to the right of the decimal would not be accepted into the table.

Don't change the values in the table for existing data – you could mess up something you might need!

There is another way to do this. If you opened the table, you should close it – close the Browse window if it is open, and type "use" in the Command Window without the quotes, and press the Enter key *(this closes the open table)*.

In the dUFLP, which you installed in Chapter 3, there is a form that allows you to modify the table, either changing an existing record (although that's not really a good idea), or adding your own custom label (a better idea).

This form gives some information that is useful about each field as well, and I will explain each of the options in more detail in the text after the screen capture (Figure 9-6).

In the Command Window of dBASE, type:

```
do :dUFLP:CustLabl.wfm
```

This form should appear:

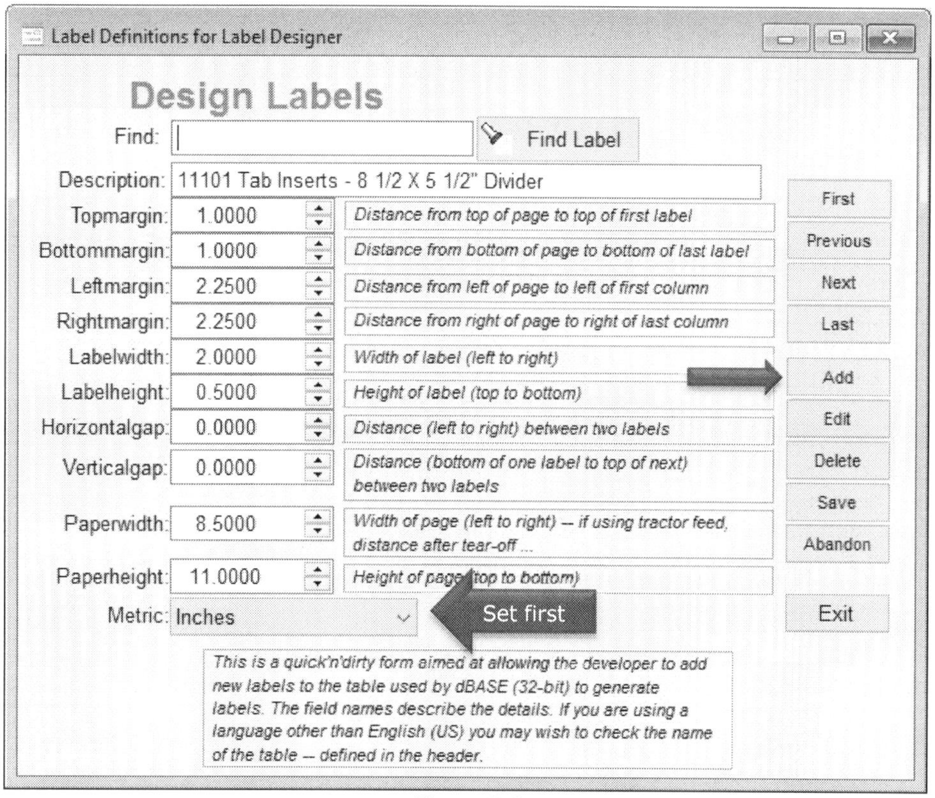

Figure 9-6

This will allow you to add your own label definitions to the table used by the Label Designer. There are things you need to know. Much of this can be gotten from the package of labels if the package is well designed. However, you can also get this information by using a ruler. The (text) labels on the left are the names of the fields in the table.

The only field that doesn't show you the actual value stored in the table is **Metric**. This matches what is used in the designer. For example, the first label here shows "Inches". If you create a form or report, the value stored for the *metric* property is numeric, and

"Inches" is really the number 3. However, for the purposes of making this form useful, some morphing is done to show the text rather than the numeric value.

The **Description** is where you would put the title that displays in the Label Designer when you select the option to set the label type. If you were creating your own (by clicking the "Add" button), you might enter something like "My Labels for The Customer Database".

The **Topmargin** field is the distance from the top of the page to the top of the first label on the sheet. This should be entered in the same metric that you selected at the bottom. So if you are using Inches for metrics, make sure you measure your labels in inches.

The **Bottommargin** field is the distance from the bottom of the page to the bottom of the last label.

The **Leftmargin** field is the distance from the left of the page to the left edge of the first label. This is crucial information, because it determines where the label will start printing.

The **Rightmargin** field is the distance from the right edge of the page to the right edge of the last label or column. If you have three labels across, this is the distance between the right edge of the third label to the right edge of the paper.

Labelwidth is the width of each label (left to right). This should not change from label to label, so you only have to enter this information once. Each label is the same size on a standard sheet of labels.

Labelheight is the height of each label, top to bottom. As with Labelwidth, this is the same for all labels in a sheet.

Horizontalgap is the distance from left to right *between* two labels. You must measure this carefully.

Verticalgap is the distance from top to bottom *between* two labels – from the bottom of one label to the top of the next.

Paperwidth is the width of the page from left to right. If you are using a tractor feed (for a dot matrix printer, for example), this is the distance between the tear-off parts.

Paperheight is the height of the page from top to bottom.

Using this form you can modify existing labels, although this is generally a bad idea, you *can* add your own. The problem? If you upgrade the version of dBASE this table may be overwritten, and if you have to change computers (for whatever reason), you will need to re-enter this information. You should write down the descriptions of any custom labels, so that if you need to, you can re-create this information. If this is a "one-time" thing, then you probably don't have to worry about it.

Note that if you need to change the table used in this form because English is not the language you use for your development language, you would need to open the form in the Source Code Editor *(it is a bad idea to open this form in the Form Designer, as it will rewrite some of the code and make it harder to use ...)*:

```
modify command :dUFLP:CustLabl.wfm
```

Find the following statement and change the name of the table:

```
// If using a language other than American English, check
// to see if this is the correct table name ...:
#define TABLENAME  "labe0009.db"
```

> **NOTE**
> This is a quick reference list for the different language versions of the label definition table:
>
> labe000A is Spanish
> labe000C is French
> labe0007 is German
> labe0009 is English
> labe0010 is Italian
> labe0011 is Japanese

Once you have added your own labels, they should appear when you go to create a new set of labels in the designer, and dBASE will set the streamFrames the correct sizes and at the correct intervals to work for your labels.

> **NOTE**
> As I am working on finishing this book, there is discussion in the "beta" newsgroups of setting something up with the CustLabl form shown in this chapter to allow you to add custom labels to a new table, and then have the option to append them to the table used by the Label Designer. This would avoid some of the issues mentioned above, where if you add custom labels to the table used by the Designer, and you upgrade dBASE, the tables are overwritten in the install and your custom label definitions are gone.

The Sequence Labels are Generated In

The Report Designer assumes when you have labels that are more than one column on a sheet that you want to generate them across the columns, before going down a row. What I mean by this is that if you were creating a series of address labels with three columns of labels across the width of the page and 10 rows of columns down, the Report Designer will generate code that specifies that the labels are generated row by row. The first label would be the one in the first row on the page, in the left-most column. The second label would be printed on the first row, but in the center column; the third label would be printed in the first row, third column. The fourth label would go back to the first column, but in the second row, and so on until all the labels are generated.

But what if you wanted your labels to "snake" – go down the first column until they hit the last label at the bottom of the column and then come back up to the second column, and so on?

This could be done by modifying the source code of the label file. If you examine the source code for your label (.lab) file, you will find the following:

```
this.PAGETEMPLATE1.STREAMFRAME1 = new STREAMFRAME(this.PAGETEMPLATE1)
   with (this.PAGETEMPLATE1.STREAMFRAME1)
      height = 1440.0
      left = 0.0
      top = 0.0
      width = 3780.0
      form.STREAMFRAME1 = form.pagetemplate1.streamframe1
   endwith

this.PAGETEMPLATE1.STREAMFRAME2 = new STREAMFRAME(this.PAGETEMPLATE1)
   with (this.PAGETEMPLATE1.STREAMFRAME2)
      height = 1440.0
      left = 3960.0
      top = 0.0
      width = 3780.0
      form.STREAMFRAME2 = form.pagetemplate1.streamframe2
   endwith

this.PAGETEMPLATE1.STREAMFRAME3 = new STREAMFRAME(this.PAGETEMPLATE1)
   with (this.PAGETEMPLATE1.STREAMFRAME3)
      height = 1440.0
      left = 7920.0
      top = 0.0
      width = 3780.0
      form.STREAMFRAME3 = form.pagetemplate1.streamframe3
   endwith
```

and so on down to StreamFrame30. If you really look at these, you can figure out that the first three have a *top* of 0.0, which puts them in the first row, and StreamFrame4 has a *top* of 1440.0 *(these are using the default metric of twips)*. This puts it in the second row. The columns these are in are defined by the *left* property.

Rearranging the Z-Order, or the sequence these controls are in the label file would cause these to be rendered in a new sequence, but it would have to be done *very* carefully:

```
this.PAGETEMPLATE1.STREAMFRAME1 = new STREAMFRAME(this.PAGETEMPLATE1)
   with (this.PAGETEMPLATE1.STREAMFRAME1)
      height = 1440.0
      left = 0.0
      top = 0.0
      width = 3780.0
      form.STREAMFRAME1 = form.pagetemplate1.streamframe1
   endwith

this.PAGETEMPLATE1.STREAMFRAME4 = new STREAMFRAME(this.PAGETEMPLATE1)
   with (this.PAGETEMPLATE1.STREAMFRAME4)
      height = 1440.0
      left = 0.0
      top = 1440.0
      width = 3780.0
      form.STREAMFRAME4 = form.pagetemplate1.streamframe4
   endwith
```

```
this.PAGETEMPLATE1.STREAMFRAME7 = new STREAMFRAME(this.PAGETEMPLATE1)
   with (this.PAGETEMPLATE1.STREAMFRAME7)
      height = 1440.0
      left = 0.0
      top = 2880.0
      width = 3780.0
      form.STREAMFRAME7 = form.pagetemplate1.streamframe7
   endwith

// moving streamframes 10, 13, 16, 19, 22, 25, and 28 here
this.PAGETEMPLATE1.STREAMFRAME2 = new STREAMFRAME(this.PAGETEMPLATE1)
   with (this.PAGETEMPLATE1.STREAMFRAME2)
      height = 1440.0
      left = 3960.0
      top = 0.0
      width = 3780.0
      form.STREAMFRAME2 = form.pagetemplate1.streamframe2
   endwith

this.PAGETEMPLATE1.STREAMFRAME5 = new STREAMFRAME(this.PAGETEMPLATE1)
   with (this.PAGETEMPLATE1.STREAMFRAME5)
      height = 1440.0
      left = 3960.0
      top = 1440.0
      width = 3780.0
      form.STREAMFRAME5 = form.pagetemplate1.streamframe5
   endwith

// moving streamFrames 8, 14, 17, 20, 23, 26, 29 here
this.PAGETEMPLATE1.STREAMFRAME3 = new STREAMFRAME(this.PAGETEMPLATE1)
   with (this.PAGETEMPLATE1.STREAMFRAME3)
      height = 1440.0
      left = 7920.0
      top = 0.0
      width = 3780.0
      form.STREAMFRAME3 = form.pagetemplate1.streamframe3
   endwith

this.PAGETEMPLATE1.STREAMFRAME6 = new STREAMFRAME(this.PAGETEMPLATE1)
   with (this.PAGETEMPLATE1.STREAMFRAME6)
      height = 1440.0
      left = 7920.0
      top = 1440.0
      width = 3780.0
      form.STREAMFRAME6 = form.pagetemplate1.streamframe6
   endwith

// moving streamFrames 9, 15, 18, 21, 24, 27, 30 here
```

This would get very tedious to do, very quickly. It would be nice if the Label Designer gave us the option to set the labels to go across or to go down in a snaking fashion, but currently that option is not available.

Glenn Fausel posted the following in the dBASE newsgroups – by creating a special index for the table you can get the labels to snake the way you want – use the following index expression – it assumes you have a field that is numeric called "LabelNum", which is the sequence you want the labels generated in (in other words, the first label you want printed would have a LabelNum of 1, the second would have a LabelNum of 2, etc. – you would need to write some code to fill that in, which I will leave as an exercise for you to work out):

```
str(int((labelnum-1)/30)) + str(mod(labelnum-1,10))
```

The value 30 is the number of labels on the page, and the value 10 is the number of rows on the page (if you wish to try this with different label designs).

Add this to your table as an index, and make sure when creating the labels in the designer that you have this index tag set (in the Inspector find the rowset for the report/labels, find the *indexName* property ...), and your labels should "snake" properly. This was tested by Glenn on 1200 records, and appears to work fine. *(Author note: I have not tried this, cannot verify it ...)*

Using a Label Printer

I had the opportunity for one of my clients to create some simple mailing labels for one of his customers using a label printer – a printer designed *just* to print labels. These act a little differently from a standard printer in that they are designed to print a single label at a time, where with a normal printer, labels tend to be generated in sheets.

As it turns it, these are pretty easy to work with. The client I did the work for sent me a printer with labels, so it was ready to go. I plugged it into a USB port on my computer, and dealt with setting up the printer driver.

Creating the actual labels went like this:

Create a new label file
Measure the labels being used by the client
Set the *metric* property to 1 for the labels (form)
Dragged an instance of the table to the design surface
Set these properties for the *printer* object:

orientation	2 - landscape

Set these properties for the *pageTemplate (based on the measurements of the labels)*:

marginBottom	0
marginLeft	0
marginRight	0
marginTop	0
height	1.15
width	3.5

Set these properties for the *streamFrame (based on the measurements of the labels)*:

height	1.15
left	0
top	0
width	3.5

From here I placed the elements on the label that I wanted to print, dealt with the address fields possibly being blank *(canRender* event, and *suppressIfBlank* property), and so on. I lined everything up so it looked good on the screen.

The last bit is actually based on some slightly more advanced topics that are covered in later chapters. I created an overridden *render* method for the label file that required that the programmer set a unique value (in this case the customer number):

```
function form_render
   // overridden method:
   if type( "form.CustNumber" ) == "U"
      msgbox("Programmer didn't pass Customer Number!",;
      "Programmer Error!", 16 )
      return
   endif
   // one record only!
   form.AddressL1.rowset.setRange( form.CustNumber )
return CustomerLabels::render()
```

If I had set an actual range, say from a starting CustNumber to an ending CustNumber, this would have generated as many labels as needed for that range of customers. The code for the labels was set up to pass the customer number (CUSTNUMBER) field to the label file, and to call the *choosePrinter()* dialog, allowing the user to select the label printer before printing the label (we will discuss some of these techniques in more detail in later chapters of this book).

From there I had to do a bunch of testing to get the text controls where they needed to be. Apparently the printer in question has some non-printing areas on the labels, so I had to print a label, check the way things printed, move the text controls a little, and try again. Ultimately this worked out quite well. I was pleasantly surprised. When done I mailed the printer back to the client, and that was that.

Cleanup

We didn't use any custom reports, so we don't have clear those out.

Make sure the database is closed by going to the Command Window and typing:

```
close databases
```

This will also ensure that you don't end up creating tables in the wrong location, etc.

Source Code

The following is a listing of the sample code in the folders we have been working with. If you downloaded the files from my website the structure will be different (see below). You may use the code contained in these folders for your own applications if you desire, with the caveat that credit be given appropriately.

From working on this chapter:

```
C:\dBASEReports\Chapter 9\ConventionBadges.lab
C:\dBASEReports\Chapter 9\Customers.lab
```

Downloaded version – same files but with this path:

```
C:\ReportsBookSourceCode\Chapter 09\filename
```

Summary

Labels can be a very useful tool for the developer, and for the developer's clients. By understanding how these work you can add a new dimension to what you can offer your clients, enhancing any software you design for them. They are flexible, and powerful, and you can do more than just print mailing labels, as we have seen.

Thanks to Kathy Kolosky at dBASE for helping me document the languages used for the different label definition tables.

The next chapter will take a look at working with a report viewer form – both creating your own, and using a pre-designed one that is in the dUFLP (that has a lot of functionality built in).

Chapter 10: Using a *reportViewer*

A *reportViewer* is a useful tool, as it allows the user to view a report before printing, which can sometimes allow them to modify something in their data, or perhaps (depending how the *reportViewer* is used) change parameters used to generate the report, and so on. Strictly speaking, the *reportViewer* object is a form control, and is not a report control, but its purpose is as the name of it implies, to allow a user to view a report.

In the dUFLP is a popular report preview form called Preview.wfm. We will come back and look at using this later, but before we do, let's take a look at the ability to add a report preview to any form you might want to use it with.

This is done using the *reportViewer* object in dBASE (which is what Preview.wfm uses as well). We will begin with creating our own form with a *reportViewer* object, the form will also contain some controls to filter the data that is printed in the report. This is a useful way to see how the *reportViewer* object works.

It is common for a user to want to be able to enter parameters that affect the output of a report, such as a date range, or a sort order for the report. In later chapters of this book we will spend some time looking at programmatically selecting specific data and printing it as well, but let's start here.

A Place for Our Work

As we work through the chapter we will be needing a place for the files we create, so please create a folder for this chapter:

```
C:\dBASEReports\Chapter 10
```

And in the Navigator, be sure to navigate to this folder.

Creating a Form with a *reportViewer* Object

A form that is able to display a report will need to have a certain amount of flexibility. Follow along a bit at a time, and hopefully it will all make sense as we go.

First we need to create a form. Using the Navigator in dBASE Plus, navigate to the Chapter 10 folder if you have not done so already. Click on the "Forms" tab, and double-click the "[New Form]" icon. This will start a new form in the Form Designer. Let's set the form's *metric* property to "6 – Pixels" before doing anything else, so we are using a common metric. (Use the Inspector as we have done for previous chapters of this book.)

Save the form (Ctrl+S) and call it ReportViewer.wfm.

Next we are going to add a container at the top of the form. This will be for some specific controls. Go to the Component Palette and on the "Standard" tab, find the Container object. Place one on the form. Find the *anchor* property for this container in the Inspector, and set this to "2 – Top". By setting the *anchor* property, this control will resize when the form size changes, which is useful. The control will also always be at the top of the form. Change the *name* property to "Buttons".

Add a second container. This container will have the *anchor* property set to "1 – Bottom". Change the *name* property to "Filters".

Set the *height* of the top container to 44, and the *height* of the bottom container to 66. These containers will have controls placed on them shortly (these are just starting heights and can be modified as needed).

Next we want to add a *reportViewer* object between the containers. Set the *anchor* property of this control to "6 – Container". This will allow the control to resize as well, not just horizontally, but also vertically. We placed these controls on the form in this sequence intentionally. If we had placed the *reportViewer* control on the form before one of the others, it would size differently than it does by being placed where it is now. *(This is related to the z-order issues that have been discussed in reports ...)*

Place four pushbuttons on the top container, grouping the first three together and placing the fourth a bit further to the right. Then after you have them placed, go to each pushbutton and set properties as shown below:

Pushbutton 1

text	Open Report
name	PBOpen

Pushbutton 2

text	Previous Page
name	PBPrevPage

Pushbutton 3

text	Next Page
name	PBNextPage

Pushbutton 4

text	Print
name	PBPrint

Notice that we have not added code for these pushbuttons yet. That's okay. We'll come back to that. Spend some time lining these up so they look good. We'll also come back to the container at the bottom of the form. Your form should look something like:

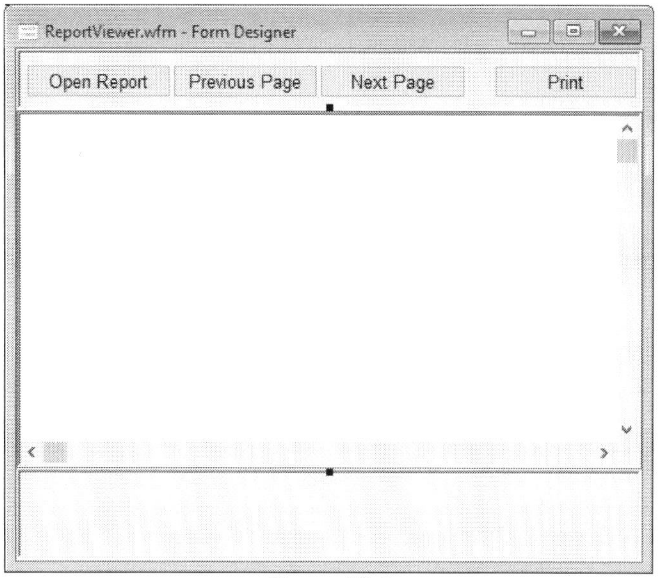

Figure 10-1

Before we do much else, we need to have a report that we will use for testing with this. This is going to be a special purpose report, because the last part of this form is going to have controls that will allow us to change the way the data is displayed. Press Ctrl+W to save the form and exit the designer. We will come back to this form shortly.

A Sample Report

Go to the Navigator, and select the "Reports" tab. Double-click the "[New Report]" icon. If your report comes up with no controls on it, then select the "File" menu and "Set Custom Report Class". You will need to open the "C:\dBASEReports\Reports\MyCompanyReport.crp" file, and then click "OK". Now your report has the settings we need.

Click on the SecondaryTitle control and change the *text* to "Report Viewer Sample". Save the report (Ctrl+S) and name it "ViewerSample.rep".

Next go to the "Tables" tab of the Navigator, and if you do not see the "dBASEReports" database, select it in the "Look in" combobox. Drag an instance of the "Dogs" table to the report design surface.

We will go through the steps of creating a report quickly, as by now you're pretty used to setting up a report using the custom controls we created earlier. This is going to be a simple tabular report, with four fields from the table on it.

Place four instances of the "DataColHeadingText" control on the report in the *detailBand*, and space them out a bit so they don't overlap each other. (Note that it is important that you place these on the *detailBand*, and not the *pageTemplate* – it's easy to accidentally place the top of one of these on the *pageTemplate*, and the Report Designer will believe it belongs to the *pageTemplate* and not the *detailBand*!)

Set the *text* property for them in this sequence:

Reg. Num.
Sex
Name
Birth

Now place a "DataText" control under the first column heading. Set the control's *text* property Type to "Codeblock" (use the "T" button in the Inspector), and then set the codeblock to (using the tool button and the dialog that comes with it):

```
this.form.dogs1.rowset.fields["reg_no"].value
```

Do the same for the others, setting the type of the *text* property to "Codeblock", and then set the codeblocks (using the tool button/dialog) for the other three to:

```
this.form.dogs1.rowset.fields["sex"].value
this.form.dogs1.rowset.fields["name"].value
this.form.dogs1.rowset.fields["born"].value
```

Spend a few minutes lining things up, and getting the data and the titles to look good. Then save the report, and exit the Report Designer (Ctrl+W).

Back to the *reportViewer* Form

Now that we have a report that we can use, let's go back to the *reportViewer* form. Click on the "Forms" tab on the Navigator, and right-click on the file "ReportViewer.wfm", selecting "Design Form". Before doing much else, make the form larger. For the example shown here, I am using a *height* of 563 (pixels) and a *width* of 813. This was just done by quickly dragging the bottom right corner of the form to make it larger.

The first thing we need is to add code for the first pushbutton's *onClick* event. This code will open the report we just created, setting that report as the one used by the report viewer on the form. *(We could make this more flexible, but then the options in the second container might not be useful ...)*

Click on the "Open Report" button, and in the Inspector find the *onClick* event. Click the tool button, and in the Source Code Editor, add the following code:

```
function PBOPEN_onClick
   form.ReportViewer1.filename = "ViewerSample.rep"
return
```

The *filename* property tells the *reportViewer* object which report to open. The report will become visible as soon as the *filename* property has been assigned a value.

Test your code now by running the form, and clicking on this button. When you do, the report should appear.

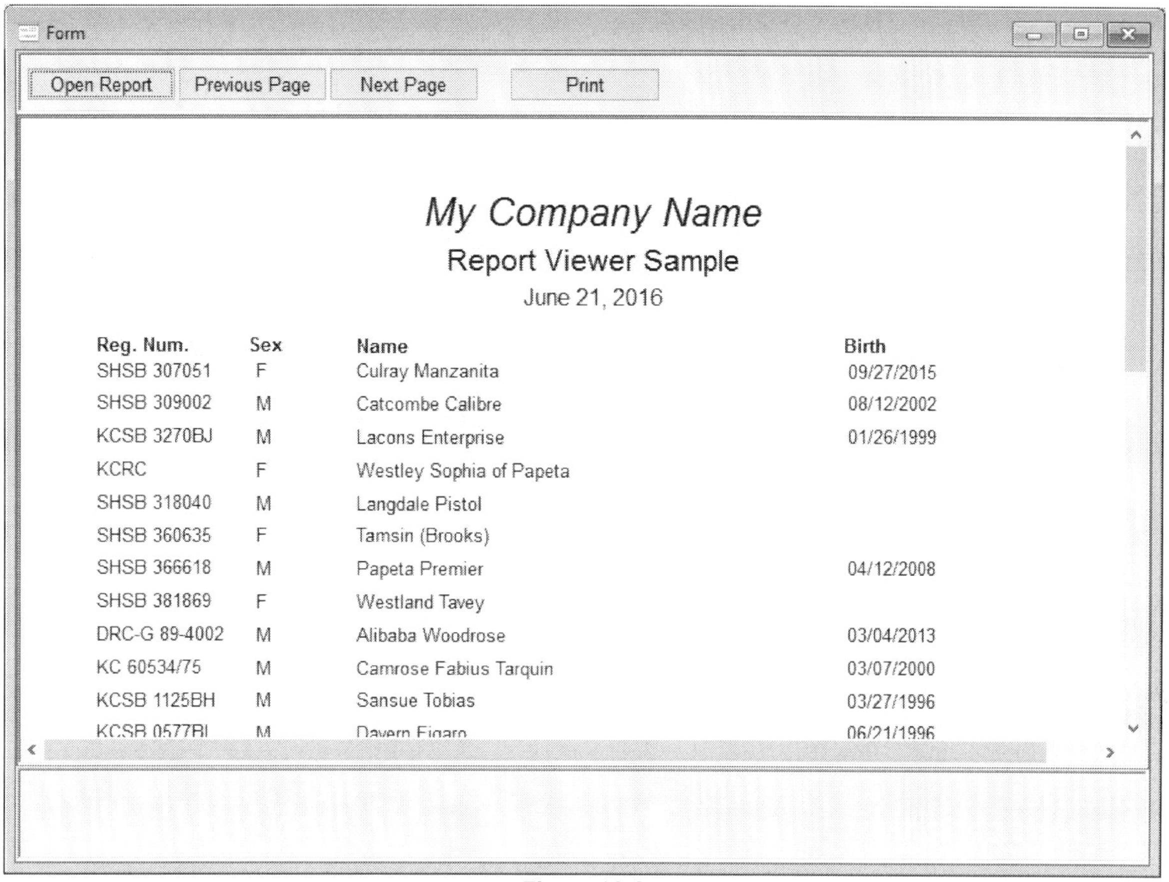

Figure 10-2

Once you have done this, we need to return back to the Form Designer.

The *reportViewer* object stores a live reference to the report object in the *ref* property. This is very useful, because it allows us to reference the actual report from within the form's code. You can read or set any of the report's properties via the *ref* property of the *reportViewer* object. (Indeed, in current versions of dBASE you can set the *ref* property directly, which we will discuss later in this chapter ...)

To see how this works let's use the *ref* property to increment and decrement the report's page number. This will let us see different pages in the report.

Click on the "Next Page" button (the third one) in the Form Designer, and in the Inspector find the *onClick* event, click the tool button, and in the Source Code Editor enter the following code:

```
function PBNEXTPAGE_onClick
   local oViewer
   oViewer = form.ReportViewer1
   if not oViewer.ref.isLastPage()
      oViewer.ref.startPage++ // increment
      oViewer.ref.render()
   endif
return
```

The code creates a shortcut to the ReportViewer1 object, checks that the report is not at the last page, then increments the *startPage* property in the report object. The next line re-renders the report – without that, the change to the *startPage* property would mean nothing.

The "Previous Page" button's event handler code is very similar to the "Next Page", except that we have to check to make sure we're not on the first page of the report, and we decrement the *startPage* property instead of incrementing it. Click on the second button, and in the Inspector find the *onClick* event, click on the tool button, and enter this code:

```
function PBPREVPAGE_onClick
   local oViewer
   oViewer = form.ReportViewer1
   if not oViewer.ref.startPage == 1
      oViewer.ref.startPage-- // decrement
      oViewer.ref.render()
   endif
return
```

Save the form and let's test it again. Run the form, click the "Open Report" button, then use the "Next Page" and "Previous Page" buttons to navigate through the report.

Bring the form back into the Form Designer, and let's continue. The "Print" button requires some special code to ask the user for the printer to print to, and then send the report to the printer. Click on the button in the Form Designer, find the *onClick* event in the Inspector, click the tool button and enter this code:

```
function PBPRINT_onClick
   local oViewer, bPrinter
   oViewer = form.ReportViewer1
   bPrinter = oViewer.ref.printer.choosePrinter()
   if bPrinter
      oViewer.ref.startPage := 1
      oViewer.ref.output := 1 // printer
      oViewer.ref.render()
      oViewer.ref.output := 3 // default
   endif
return
```

The code starts by calling the *choosePrinter* method of the report's *printer* object. This gives the user the option of choosing an installed printer. If the user selects a printer (bPrinter will evaluate to *true*), the code sets the reportViewer's *ref* object's *startPage* to 1 (so the report starts at the top); sets the *output* property to go to a printer; and it renders the report. After the report is rendered, it sets the *output* property back to the default setting, which in this case, is the *reportViewer* object. One might close the form after the report prints (by adding code: form.close()), but that is an option that might be dependent on the user, the application, etc.

> **NOTE**
> If you move the vertical scrollbar down a page to view the page in a reportViewer, and you then navigate to another page, it will retain the position on the new page, which may be confusing to your users. This is the default behavior and is "as designed". A solution was found by Roger Sauer after I published the first edition of this book. It uses the Windows API (Application Programmer Interface) to set this. An example of its use is in the file "Preview.wfm" in the dUFLP, which will be discussed later in this chapter. If you want to incorporate it in your own form, look for *(in that file)* the function "ScrollHome()".

It is common for a reporting system to give users the ability to select parameters that customize a report. These often include values that are used to filter the data and/or change the sort order. We will use the second container at the bottom of this form to allow the user to set some filter conditions and set them in the report.

First we want to allow the user to filter the report by the date of birth of the dogs, giving an option of a range. If they want to use the option they enter a value for a start date, and optionally an end date; if not, it is left blank. We need to allow for all 3 possible choices. This will make the code to create the filter a bit complex, but it is doable.

Place two *textLabel* controls on the bottom container (from the "Standard" tab of the Component Palette). Using the Inspector set the *text* for the first control to "Start Date:" and for the second to "End Date:". Place these so that the first is above the second.

Now we need to add two entryfields. Set the *name* property of the first to "StartDateEntryfield", the *value* to nothing (delete what is there), and set the type of the *value* to "Date". For the second entryfield set the *name* to "EndDateEntryfield", and the *value* to nothing, and the type of the *value* to "Date".

Next we also want to allow the user to filter the data by sex, selecting nothing (all), or "M" for "Male", "F" for "Female". To do this easily, we will simply use a combobox object which will allow us to limit the options. First place a *textLabel* control to the right of the entryfields, and change the *text* to read "Sex".

Place a combobox control under that. Change the *name* property to "SexCombobox", change the *style* property to "2 – DropDownList". Then go to the *dataSource* property, and click on the tool button. In the dialog that appears, make sure "Array" is selected in the combobox on the left, and click the tool button on the right. This opens yet another dialog (the Array Builder). Click the first "Add" button (in the "String" part of the dialog) to give us a blank entry, then type "M" in the entryfield, and click the same "Add" button, type "F" in the entryfield and click the same "Add" button. Click "OK" and then "OK" again, closing the dialogs.

Place a pushbutton on the form to the right, and set the *name* to "PBFILTER", the *text* to "Set Filter". Find the *onClick* event in the Inspector, and enter the following code, carefully. Notice there are comments embedded in the code, to help explain what it is doing.

```
function PBFILTER_onClick
   local oViewer, cFilter, oC
   cFilter = ""
   oC = this.parent // container object shortcut
   // If we have a value for the start date:
   if not empty( oC.StartDateEntryfield.value )
      // set the filter string to include the start date
      cFilter += [Born => ']+oC.StartDateEntryfield.value+[']
   endif
   // If we have a value for the end date:
   if not empty( oC.EndDateEntryfield.value )
      // Does the filter have a value? If so we need an AND
      // condition:
      if not empty( cFilter )
         cFilter += [ and ]
      endif
      cFilter += [Born <= ']+oC.EndDateEntryfield.value+[']
   endif

   // do we have a value for the Sex?
   if not empty( oC.SexCombobox.value )
      // does the filter have anything in it?
      if not empty( cFilter )
         cFilter += [ and ]
      endif
      cFilter += [Sex = ']+oC.SexCombobox.value.rightTrim()+[']
   endif

   // store the filter string in the params array of
   // the ReportViewer:
   form.ReportViewer1.params["filter"] = cFilter

   // let's re-execute the report:
   if form.ReportViewer1.ref # null // if we have a report
      form.ReportViewer1.ReExecute()
   endif
return
```

When this code runs, the *reportViewer* object will contain an associative array with a single element called "filter". This sample code works for this specific situation, but of course, you may find that there are other ways to do what you need that are more appropriate for you.

This is only one part of what needs to be done, however. The other is to tell the report itself what to do with the *params* array. There are again multiple ways to do this, but for this example we will create our own *bootstrap code* for the report. When we examine the Preview.wfm form later, we will use the report's *render* method.

Close the form (Ctrl+W), and go to the Navigator window. Click on "Reports", and open the report "ViewerSample.rep" in the Source Code Editor (right-click, select "Open in Source Editor"). At the top of the report you will see the original "bootstrap" code, which is created by the Report Designer:

```
** END HEADER -- do not remove this line
//
// Generated on 06/20/2016
//
local r
r = new ViewerSampleReport()
r.render()
```

You should never modify this code, because the designer will simply recreate it. However, you can place code before the comments that begin "** END HEADER". By doing so, the Report Designer will ignore that code, and you can add whatever you need to. One trap, however, is that if you do not add the statement:

```
return
```

at the end of your bootstrap code, dBASE will finish your code, and then go on to the default bootstrap, and depending on what your code does, may render the report more than once.

Add the following code before the comments:

```
// add our own bootstrap code:
if argcount() >= 1
   local r, cFilter
   r = new ViewerSampleReport( )
   // look for the "filter" in the params
   // array [warning, the assocarray is
   // case sensitive]:
   if r.ReportViewer.params.isKey( "filter" )
      cFilter = r.ReportViewer.params["filter"]
   else
      cFilter = ""
   endif
   // Set the report filter
   r.streamSource1.rowset.filter := cFilter
   // render the report
   r.render( )
   // return, so we don't render the report again:
   return
endif
```

This code looks to see if the *params* array exists at all. If it does, it checks for a value called "filter". If this exists, it sets the rowset's *filter* before rendering the report. When the filter pushbutton is clicked on the ReportViewer form after entering conditions for the filter, these are added to the associative array called *params*, open the report file which runs the custom bootstrap code, and the sets the filter in the report and renders it.

Run the ReportViewer form, and try it out. Open the report, then change the filter options and click the pushbutton. You should see the data change to match those conditions. When done, close the form.

Change the Sort Order of the Report

We can make this even more robust by changing the sort order of the report as well. This simply takes a bit more work, modifying what we've done so far.

Open the ReportViewer form in the Form Designer (right click on it in the Navigator, and select "Design Form"). Move the Set Filter button further to the right, and we will add two more controls.

Place a new *textLabel* control on the bottom container, and change the *text* property to: "Order Report By:" (don't use the quotes). Place a combobox under that, and change the *name* property to "SortCombobox", change the *style* property to "2 - DropDownList", and then set the *dataSource* by clicking on the tool button in the Inspector for this property. Click the toolbutton to the right on this dialog as well. In the "String" option, click the "Add" button once so we have a blank entry, then in the entryfield enter "Reg_No" and click "Add", and finally enter "Name" and click "Add". This will give us three options. Click "OK" and on the previous dialog click "OK".

Click on the "Set Filter" button, and change the text to "Set Filter/Order". Next, go to the Inspector, and click the tool button for the *onClick* event. We will be changing the code just a little, as we need to add code to deal with setting a new option for the *params* array of the ReportViewer object which will handle changing the index used for the report.

Change this line:

```
local oViewer, cFilter, oC
```

to:

```
local oViewer, cFilter, cIndex, oC
```

(Add "cIndex,". to the statement as shown.)

Next, go to the comment:

```
// let's re-execute the report:
```

and add code just above it:

```
// deal with report order:
cOrder = oC.SortCombobox.value.rightTrim()
form.ReportViewer1.params["index"] = cOrder
```

This code places the value contained in the combobox into a new element of the *params* array called "index".

We need to modify the report to handle this as well. Save the form and exit the Form Designer (Ctrl+W).

Open the report in the Source Code Editor by going to the "Reports" tab of the Navigator, right click on the report and selecting "Open in Source Editor".

Change this line:

```
local r, cFilter
```

to:

```
local r, cFilter, cIndex
```

And modify the code by adding what is in **bold** below:

```
// look for the "index" in the params array:
if r.ReportViewer.params.isKey( "index" )
   cIndex = r.ReportViewer.params["index"]
else
   cIndex = ""
endif

// Set the report filter
r.streamSource1.rowset.filter := cFilter

// Set the report index
r.streamSource1.rowset.indexName := cIndex
```

This code will check for the index element in the *params* array, and if it exists, it will set the *indexName* property of the rowset appropriately (setting it to blank clears out any existing index, and the report will appear in "natural" order).

Save the report, and exit the Source Code Editor (Ctrl+W), and test the changes by running the ReportViewer form. Click the "Open" button to open the report, and then select one of the indexes, clicking the pushbutton.

You should see the report change sequence. You can also add filter options at the same time – this should look something like:

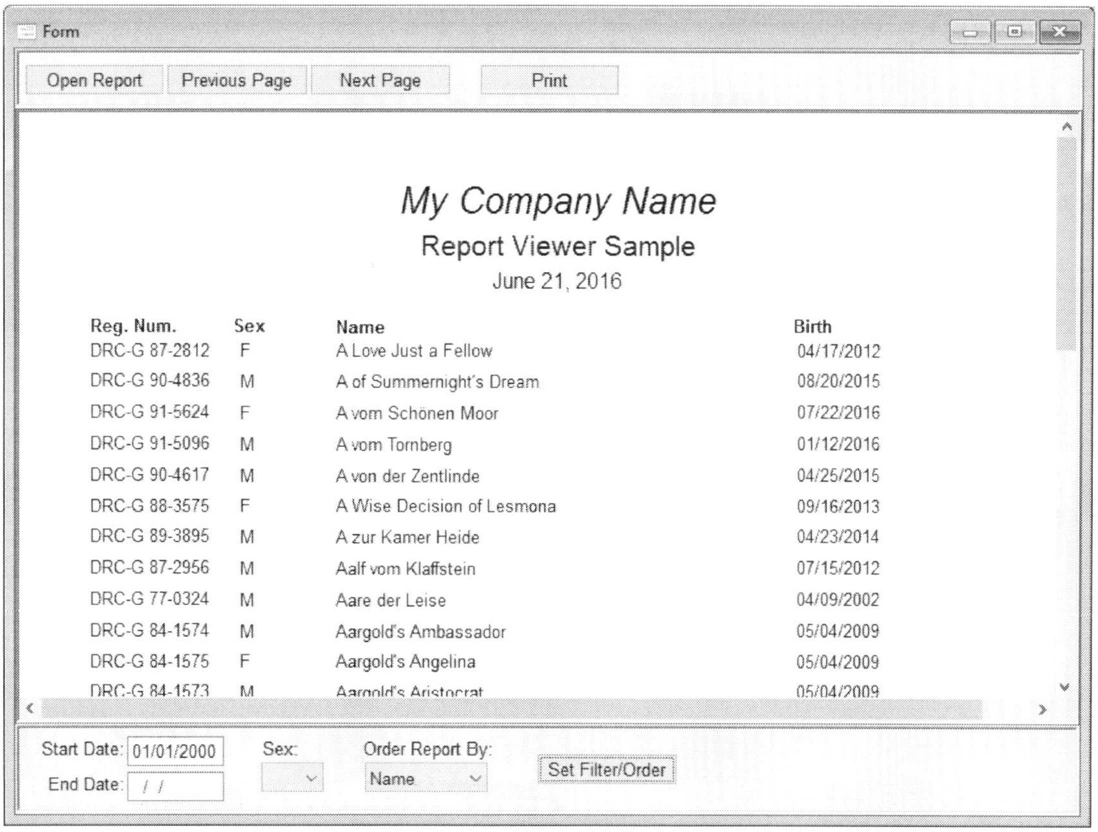

Figure 10-3

As noted earlier, this really is designed around a very specific report, and is really only useful for this report. There are other ways to do this sort of thing, but hopefully this has given you a good understanding of how code can interact with a *reportViewer*, and the report itself.

> **NOTE**
> The real difficulty with this form is that it is specific to the one report. You could remove all the filtering options (the whole bottom container), and change the code for the "Open Report" button – this would allow you to view different reports by selecting the one you want. However, you would then need a different method of passing the filtering or index information to the report. This is shown as an example of what *can* be done, not necessarily the most optimal method of doing it.

The Preview.wfm Form from the dUFLP

This is a more robust preview form for reports. This form was written in the early days of Visual dBASE 7.0, when I still worked at Borland as a QA Engineer. Over the years it has been modified both by myself and by other developers and is able to handle just about anything that can be thrown at it. The current version, which is what we will be looking at in this chapter, was almost completely re-written by Todd Kreuter to simplify most of the code and to allow a developer to take advantage of some new functionality in dBASE Plus. More recently Mervyn Bick came along and modified it so that some of the processing was faster.

We will look at two ways of using this report viewer form, one is fairly complex, the other is fairly simple – both will accomplish the same tasks. The reason for the first version is that you may not be using a version of dBASE Plus that allows for the simpler functionality, and it also allows you to see how to override the report's *render* method.

The Preview form in the dUFLP can be used in many ways. At its most simple, it can be called with a single command:

```
do :dUFLP:preview.wfm with "ViewerSample.rep"
```

Or to get the same results programmatically:

```
set procedure to :dUFLP:preview.wfm additive
oPreview = new PreviewForm()
oPreview.viewer.fileName := "ViewerSample.rep"
oPreview.open()
```

Either of these two options would open the preview form with the report we've worked with so far, called "ViewerSample.rep". It should look something like:

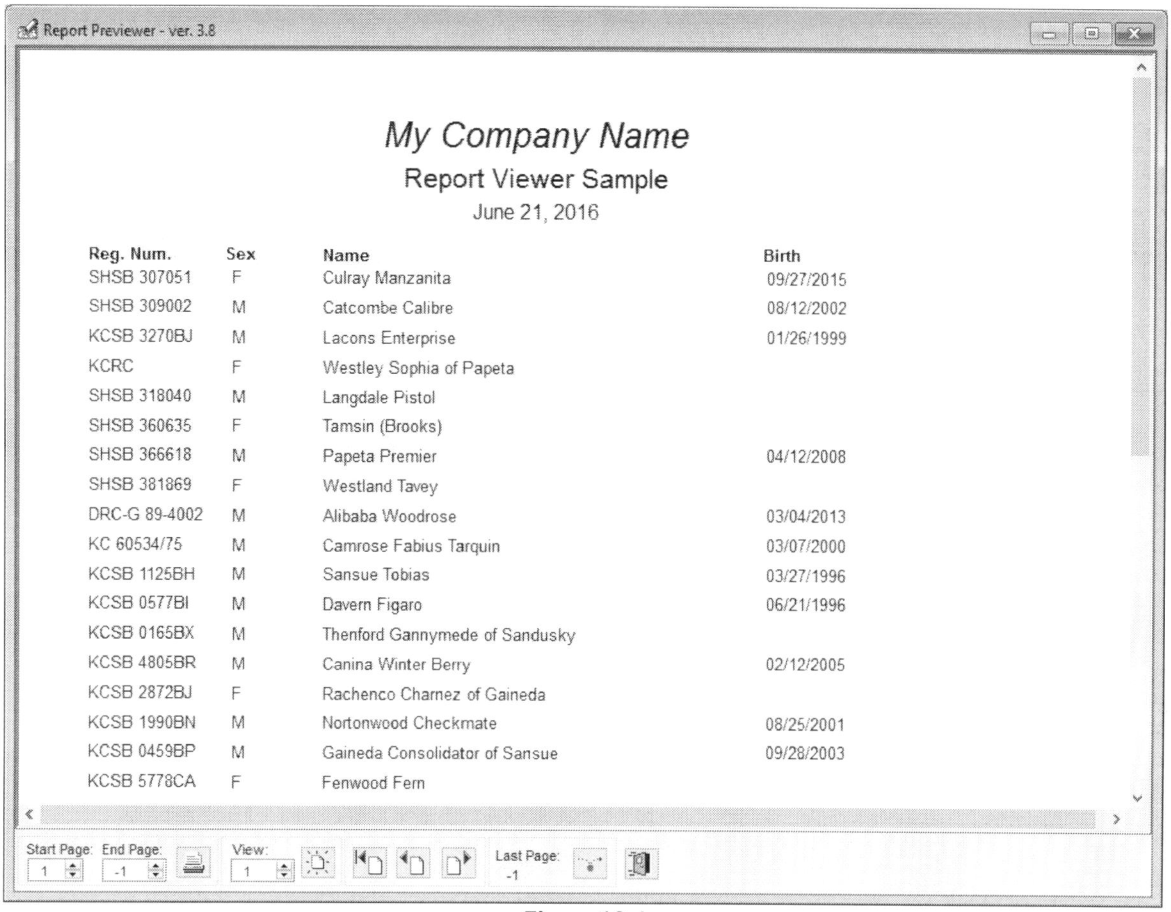

Figure 10-4

However, you can do a lot more with this. For example, by default this form opens as a modeless form. You can pass a parameter that tells it to open modal instead. You can also pass a parameters array to the *reportViewer*, similar to what we did earlier. Part of the primary discussion here involves passing values to the report.

The one difficulty is that this form has no way to obtain input from the user, so how do we allow the user to pass parameters to the report, modifying the way the report is generated?

Since Preview.wfm is meant to be a "general purpose" type report viewer, it is a bad idea to modify it directly. So instead, you would want to create your own front-end that allows the user to select the options for the report.

We will take a look at doing this, using a program to call a dialog that asks for the date range for the birthdates of the dogs. Then we will see how to get this information to work with the Preview form and your report.

The GetDates Form

For starters, you will need a form that allows the user to enter the date range. You could use the form in the dUFLP called "GetDates.wfm", but that form uses some outdated techniques (storing the values to the *_app* object, and so on). Instead, let's create a dialog that we can use for getting the date values from the user.

Some of these instructions are going to be fairly terse, assuming that you are somewhat familiar with the Form Designer, and can find the properties, events and methods of objects in the Inspector, and so on.

To start, click on the "Forms" tab of the Navigator, and double-click the "[New Form]" icon.

Set the following properties:

metric	6
mdi	false
autoCenter	true
showTaskBarButton	false
text	Date Range

Save the form (Ctrl+S) as "GetDates.wfm". Yes, this is the same name as the form in the dUFLP, but since we're not using that one here, there should not be any problems.

Go to the Methods tab of the Inspector, and find *readModal*. Click the tool button. Enter the following code:

```
function form_readModal
   class::Init()
return FORM::readModal()
```

Do the same for the *Open* method:

```
function form_open
   class::Init()
return FORM::open()
```

The code that is used to set up the starting date, beginning on the first day of the year, can be a problem if your date format is not "MM/DD/YYYY". To make that code able to be useful for any date format (which changes based on language drivers, and country settings), add the following complete function (starting with the *function* statement and ending with the *return* statement):

```
function Init
   // Code that is fired when the form is opened:

   // Set the default start date:
   private nYear, cDateFormat
   // save the date format:
   cDateFormat = set("date")
   // set the date to MM/DD/YYYY format:
   set date MDY
   // get the current year
   nYear = year( date() ) // year of current date
   // start date is January 1, current year
   form.dStart = ctod( "01/01/"+nYear )
   // now we want to re-set the date format:
   set date &cDateFormat.
   // end date is the current date
   form.dEnd = date()
return
```

This is still a simple form of what might be needed, since it is possible to modify the character that is displayed between the parts of the date (SET MARK), and so on. However, this will work for this situation.

Next we will add some controls to the form:

Drag a Text control from the Component Palette to the form. Change the *text* to "Select Date Range". Set these properties:

anchor	2 - Top
alignHorizontal	1 - Center
fontSize	14
colorNormal	Blue/BtnFace
borderStyle	1 - Raised

If necessary modify the *height* by dragging the bottom edge of the text control up and down.

Drag a textLabel control to the form. Change the following properties:

text	Start Date

Drag another textLabel control to the form, and place it to the right of the current one:

text	End Date

Drag a spinbox control to the form, and place it under the first textLabel control. Set the following properties:

name	StartDateSpinbox
value - type	Date
width	103 *// or something close to that*

Place a second spinbox under the second textLabel, and set the following properties:

name	EndDateSpinbox
value - type	Date
width	103 *// or something close to that*

Drag a pushbutton to the form and place it under the other controls. Set the following properties:

name	OKButton
text	OK
upBitMap	RESOURCE #20

Drag a second pushbutton to the form and place it to the right of the first. Set the following properties:

name	CancelButton
text	Cancel
upBitMap	RESOURCE #28

With all this in place, we're nearly done, really. Try lining the controls up a bit, moving things so that they look good to you, and resize the form appropriately. The form should look something like:

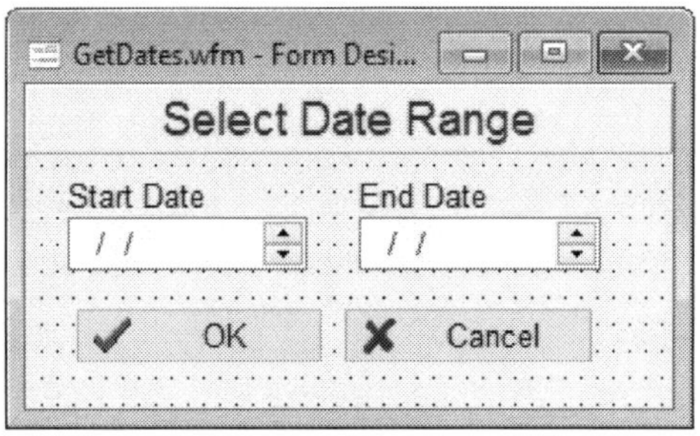

Figure 10-5

We need to modify the code for the Init method so we set the default values for the two spinboxes. To do this, with the form still in the Form Designer, press the F12 button (this brings up the Source Code Editor), and go to the Init method. Add the following just before the "return" statement:

```
// Set default values for Spinbox controls:
form.StartDateSpinbox.value := form.dStart
form.EndDateSpinbox.value := form.dEnd
```

Next we need to tell dBASE what to do when the user clicks the "OK" button, and what to do when they click the "Cancel" button. In both cases, we are going to set the form's custom properties of dStart and dEnd.

Click on the "OK" button, and in the Inspector go to the *onClick* event. Click the tool button. Add the following code:

```
function OKBUTTON_onClick
   // set the custom properties to the values
   // in the spinboxes:
   form.dStart := form.StartDateSpinbox.value
   form.dEnd   := form.EndDateSpinbox.value
   // close the form:
   form.close(true)
return
```

We need to create something very similar for the Cancel button's *onClick* event handler code:

```
function CANCELBUTTON_onClick
   // Cancel button, we need to set the form's
   // custom properties to empty values:
   form.dStart := {}
   form.dEnd   := {}
   // close the form:
   form.close(false)
return
```

Save the form, and exit the Form Designer (Ctrl+W). What we have just done is to create a fairly generic form to obtain a date range, allowing the user to enter a start and end date. What we do with these values is the next thing to deal with. However, just to get a feel for how this works, go to the Command Window, and type the following:

```
set procedure to GetDates.wfm
oForm = new GetDatesForm()
oForm.readModal()
// enter a date range ... click "OK"
? oForm.dStart
? oForm.dEnd
```

We could of course add some error checking to make sure that the start and end dates were valid (start date being less than or equal to the end date, and so on), but let's not make things more complex than necessary for this exercise.

The next thing that we need to do is to create a program that will call the dialog, and when the dialog is closed determine if there are values and what to do from there. (For example, if there are no values selected, either because the user blanked them out and clicked "OK" or because the user clicked the "Cancel" button, we would not want to create a filter for the report ...)

The Program

To create a program, go to the Navigator, click on "Programs", and then double click the "[New Program]" icon. Enter the following code:

```
/*
   GetReport.prg
   This program will open the GetDates dialog form,
   and then based on what the user does, create a filter
   to be used with a report. The report will be displayed
   in the :dUFLP:Preview.wfm form.
*/
private oForm, dStart, dEnd, cFilter

// open the dialog:
set procedure to GetDates.wfm additive
oForm = new GetDatesForm()

// check the value returned by the form:
if oForm.readModal()
   // when the user closes the form:
   dStart = oForm.dStart
   dEnd = oForm.dEnd
   // create the filter string:
   cFilter = ""
   // if we have a start date:
   if not empty( dStart )
      cFilter := [Born =>']+dStart+[']
   endif // not empty( dStart )

   // if we have an end date:
   if not empty( dEnd )
      // if we already have something in the filter:
      if not empty( cFilter )
         cFilter += [ and ]
      endif // not empty( cFilter )
      cFilter += [Born <= ']+dEnd+[']
   endif // not empty( dEnd )
   // for testing:
   ? "Filter = " + cFilter
```

```
endif // oForm.readModal()

// clean up memory:
oForm.release()
close procedure GetDates.wfm
```

Now you need to save this, so press Ctrl+W to save and exit, name the program "GetReport.prg". Try running it. If you have any errors compare the program carefully against the code above. It is likely you may have accidentally dropped a character, misspelled a command or word, or something of that nature when typing it in. If the program runs properly, the dialog will open, you can enter dates, and in the Command Window you will see output that looks like:

```
Filter = Born =>'01/01/2016' and Born <= '06/21/2016'
```

So far, so good. However, ultimately we want this to affect the Preview form, and the report used by the Preview form.

Modify the Existing Report

For this exercise, we need a report, but we want to keep the original as it was, so that if you review this chapter of the book, the original report still works. To make a copy of the first report, go to the Command Window and type:

```
copy file ViewerSample.rep to PreviewSample1.rep
```

When the new report file appears in the Navigator (you may need to click on the "Reports" tab ...), you will want to open the report in the Source Code Editor (right click on it, select "Open in Source Editor"). Highlight the code we added in the report – the new bootstrap code, and delete it all (really!) – go down to the comment statement that begins with "** END HEADER" and back up a line – we need these comments.

We're going to do this a different way, and the custom bootstrap code from earlier would cause some issues.

We should also do one more thing, and that is to change the *className* of the report. Press Ctrl+R (Find/Replace), and in the "Find what" entryfield enter "ViewerSample" (without the quotes). In the "Replace with" entryfield enter "PreviewSample1" (also without the quotes), and then click "Replace All", and "Close" (in that order). Press Ctrl+W to save the report and exit the editor.

The next thing we are going to do is bring the report into the Report Designer, and override the report's *render* method. This method will look to see if there is a parameter array, and if so, it will evaluate it and set the filter for the report.

Since we are not adding code (at least not at this time) to change the sort order, this will actually be a little simpler than the code we just removed from the beginning of the report.

Right click on the report, and select "Design Report". Go to the Inspector, and find the *render* method. Click the tool button. Enter the following code:

```
function form_render()
   // this command ensures the report's render method
   // is available ...
   set procedure to program(1)
   // The "runonce" property checks to make sure
   // that the render event code based on the params
   // array is only called once - when the report is
   // first loaded ... ReportViewers call this when
   // rendering each page, which could cause problems,
   // depending on your code.
   if type( "this.runOnce" ) # "L"
      this.runOnce = true
      if type( "this.ReportViewer" ) == "O"
         // we are being called from a ReportViewer
         // check to see if the ReportViewer's form has
         // a params array:
         if type( "this.ReportViewer.form.params" ) == "O"
            // set params array:
            this.params = this.ReportViewer.form.params
         endif // params array
      endif // type( this.reportViewer ...)

      // if we have a params array, we need to set the
      // filter for the report:
      if type( "this.params" ) == "O" and ;
         this.params.isKey( "filter" )
         // assign the filter property of the
         // rowset being used for the report:
         this.streamSource1.rowset.filter := ;
            this.params[ "filter" ]
      endif // type( "this.params" )
   endif // this.runOnce
return PREVIEWSAMPLE1REPORT::render()
```

This code checks to see if we have already run this code (every time you navigate from page to page in a *reportViewer*, the report is re-rendered, so we don't want to run it more than once), and if we have not, then we look for a *params* array associated with a *reportViewer*. If one exists, we look for the "filter" element of the array, and set it to the report's rowset.

Save the report and exit the Report Designer (Ctrl+W).

We now need to modify the program we started working on, to call the Preview form and pass it the parameters array necessary.

Click on the "Programs" tab of the Navigator, select the "GetReport.prg" program, and right click, selecting the "Open in Source Editor" option.

Go to the two lines that start with the comment "// for testing:" and the one after it, and delete them. We need to add code from here (it is important to note that the associative array key values are case sensitive, so be sure to type "filter" in lower case):

```
// create an associative array:
aParams = new AssocArray()
// add the filter to it:
```

```
aParams["filter"] = cFilter
// Next, we need to set up the Preview form:
set procedure to :dUFLP:Preview.wfm additive
oPreview = new PreviewForm()
// set the params array:
oPreview.params = aParams
// set the Modal property:
oPreview.bModal = true
// set the report filename:
oPreview.Viewer.fileName := "PreviewSample1.rep"
// open it:
oPreview.readModal()
// cleanup - once the Preview form closes:
oPreview.release()
close procedure :dUFLP:Preview.wfm
```

This code now creates the associative array used by the report, and opens an instance of the preview form, sets the appropriate properties, and runs the form. When the user closes the form, we release it, and clean up memory.

Running the program, you should see the GetDates form come up, and then when you close that, the report, with it attempting to set a filter on the data. If you end up with a report that has no data, take a look at the birthdates that are reported – the chances are your filter is outside the range of data in the table.

This is all well and good, but there are other ways to do these things, as you might expect.

A Slightly Simpler, or At Least Different, Way

The use of the associative array is all well and good, but there is another means of using Preview.wfm with your reports and parameters, and it might well be a little more straightforward. However, this requires dBASE Plus 2.5 or later.

To copy the previous report go to the Command Window, and type:

```
copy file PreviewSample1.rep to PreviewSample2.rep
```

Open the new report in the Source Coded Editor. First, you will want to change the name of the class by pressing Ctrl+R and entering "Sample1" in the first entryfield, and "Sample2" in the second (we're just changing the number), and then clicking the "Replace All" button. Then click the "Close" button.

Find in the early code for the report (toward the top) these lines:

```
with (this)
   render = class::FORM_RENDER
endwith
```

and delete them. They are not necessary for the next exercise. Finally, go to the end of the report, and remove the whole code for the overridden *render* method, starting at the line that begins with the word "function", and ending at the line that begins with the word "return".

Save the changes and exit the Source Code Editor (Ctrl+W).

We need to make a copy of the program we've been working with, and then make some changes there. In the Command Window, type:

```
copy file GetReport.prg to GetReport2.prg
```

Click on the "Programs" tab of the Navigator, and right click on the new program, selecting "Open in Source Editor".

Find these lines below and delete them:

```
// create an associative array:
aParams = new AssocArray()
// add the filter to it:
aParams["filter"] = cFilter
```

We need to replace them with some different code. Insert this code where those four lines used to be:

```
// we need to create an instance of the report:
set procedure to PreviewSample2.rep
private rRep
rRep = new PreviewSample2Report()
// now we have this reference, we need to set the filter
// on the rowset:
rRep.streamSource1.rowset.filter := cFilter
```

Notice that we are directly modifying the report from here. This report is in memory, but has not been rendered yet. We have an object reference (variable) named "rRep". This is important, because we can pass the object reference directly to the *reportViewer* in the Preview form. To do this, we need to modify the code that calls the form:

```
// Next, we need to set up the Preview form:
set procedure to :dUFLP:Preview.wfm additive
oPreview = new PreviewForm()
// set the Modal property:
oPreview.bModal = true
// set the reportViewer ref property to point to the
// report object:
oPreview.Viewer.ref := rRep
```

Notice that the code that sets the *params* property has been removed, and also note the last line above – rather than setting the *filename* for the report, we can set the *ref* property instead. This allows us to directly modify the report in code if we want to, and then pass that object reference to the previewer form!

Other Options with Preview.wfm

We haven't really explored all of the options with Preview.wfm. For example, by default, it closes after the user prints a report. What if your user wanted to keep it open? There is a custom property that can be set:

```
oPreview.bClose := false // don't close when done printing
```

Also note that you can use a Command Line type interface with the Preview form, if you would rather not use the code as shown to create an object reference. This can be done like:

```
do :dUFLP:Preview.wfm with rRep, true, "", false
```

In this example, we are passing four parameters – the object reference for the report (if you wanted to use this with the earlier version, passing a *params* array, you would instead use the name of the report file, "PreviewSample1.rep"); telling it to open modal (as a dialog); no *params* array (that's what the two sets of quotes are for – an empty parameter); and the last parameter shown (*false*) tells the Preview form to not close when done printing.

There is a fifth parameter that will display an HTML button, but the dBASE report engine does not generate really good HTML, so the default is for that button to not display. If you add the fifth parameter (or set the property bShowHTML to *true* when you create an instance of the Preview form), the pushbutton will appear.

There is a lot of detail in the comments at the top of the form file for Preview, to view them, you could go to the Command Window and type:

```
modify command :dUFLP:Preview.wfm
```

This will open the form up in the Source Code Editor – it is not a good idea to modify the code, but we'll leave that to you. Anyway, the examples of usage and such are defined in the comments at the top, so if you have forgotten how to use it, you can always take a look.

Cleanup

Create a new report (in the Navigator, click on the .Reports. tab, double-click on the "[New Report]" icon). Select the "File" menu, select "Set Custom Report Class", and in the dialog, click the "Clear Custom Report" button, then click "OK". This clears out the custom report setting in the Plus.ini file, so that the next report you create is not based on this one. Close that report without making any changes.

Make sure the database is closed by going to the Command Window and typing:

```
close databases
```

This will also ensure that you don't end up creating tables in the wrong location, etc.

Source Code

The following is a listing of the sample code in the folders we have been working with. If you downloaded the files from my website the structure will be different (see below). You may use the code contained in these folders for your own applications if you desire, with the caveat that credit be given appropriately.

From working on this chapter:

```
C:\dBASEReports\Chapter 10\GetDates.wfm
C:\dBASEReports\Chapter 10\GetReport.prg
C:\dBASEReports\Chapter 10\GetReport2.prg
C:\dBASEReports\Chapter 10\PreviewSample1.rep
C:\dBASEReports\Chapter 10\PreviewSample2.rep
C:\dBASEReports\Chapter 10\ReportViewer.wfm
C:\dBASEReports\Chapter 10\ViewerSample.rep
```

Downloaded version – same files but with this path:

```
C:\ReportsBookSourceCode\Chapter 10\filename
```

Summary

Giving your users the chance to view their reports before printing them is something many of them will appreciate. Sometimes just seeing the report is enough, and there is no need to print it, sometimes the user may spot something that needs to be changed before printing the report, and so on. Hopefully this chapter has given you some strong insight into using the *reportViewer* object in dBASE, whether or not you wish to use the form that is in the dUFLP called Preview.wfm.

We're moving beyond the basics in the next chapter, so buckle your seatbelts! Multiple table reports and a whole lot more ...

Part II: Multiple Tables, Groups and Summary Calculations

This part of the book focuses on working with Multiple Tables, Grouping data, and with creating calculations that summarize the data – both for groups and for report totals. While these subjects are all related, one does not need multiple tables to create grouped reports, nor does one need multiple tables or grouped reports to create totals for a report. The chapters here will help show this.

Chapter 11: Multiple Tables, and Grouped Reports

One of the most important aspects of working with a database is being able to work with multiple tables to store data. This has many purposes, including avoiding replicating data that isn't necessary (why store a customer record in each invoice, when it makes more sense to store it in a single record in a single table and perform a lookup?). This is called data normalization, and we're not going to get into a discussion why it is a good thing to do *(this is discussed in The dBASE Book)* – it would take too long.

When it comes to reports this can sometimes make things a bit more complex for a developer. The more normalized a database is, the more complex the code is to generate a report. In some cases, this can be handled through the use of a data module, but in others you may find it easier to work with a SQL join (which effectively creates a single rowset combining the data from any and all tables in the join); or perhaps a temporary table. We will take a look at all of these options.

In addition, you will most likely, when working with multiple tables in a report, need to work with grouped reports and perhaps even sub-groups in the report.

We will examine totals, sums and other aggregate functions in the next chapter, but those do go hand-in-hand with grouped reports (totaling up the line items in an invoice, or what have you).

A Place for Our Work

As we work through the chapter we will be needing a place for the files we create, so please create a folder for this chapter:

```
C:\dBASEReports\Chapter 11
```

And in the Navigator, be sure to navigate to this folder.

Grouped Reports

We have done a small amount with grouped reports in earlier chapters, but we are going to spend some time really looking into how they work in this chapter.

A report that is "grouped" means that the data uses a field (or possibly multiple fields) to group the data in some fashion. A group is defined by the contents of the field or fields. If you were to write your own code to group data for processing you would need to store the value of the field (for the example) in a variable, and then process the data one row at a time – this might look something like the following:

```
q = new query()
q.sql := "select * from mytable"
q.active := true
q.rowset.indexName := "some index"
q.rowset.first()
```

```
cBreak = q.rowset.fields["ControlField"].value
// display a group header perhaps?
do while not q.rowset.endOfSet
   if q.rowset.fields["ControlField"]value # cBreak // not equal
      // do some code to handle the break, such as displaying totals
      // change the break value:
      cBreak := q.rowset.fields["ControlField"].value
      // display a group header if we're not at the end
      // of the rowset, or whatever else ...
   endif
   // do whatever processing for the current row that was needed
   q.rowset.next()
enddo
```

This is basically what is happening in the Report Engine, although I am sure that if we were able to delve into the actual C++ code it would be more complex (including determining if a group header exists, doing some "look ahead" type code, and more). The code above is based on some processing I have done in one of my applications.

Luckily we don't have to do all that code for our reports *(although that example might be useful for other purposes)*.

The important thing to note is that when the field or fields used to define the group change, we have to do *something*, otherwise this is not a grouped report.

A grouped report can be done using a single table, and as noted when working with multiple tables a grouped report is almost always how the report is defined. In Chapter 7 (Calculated Fields) we created a grouped report using two tables in a parent/child relationship. Later in the chapter we created a report (Group_PartialField.rep) that grouped the dogs by the first three letters of their registration number, but there was no parent table involved – hence we did this grouped report with a single table.

If you were to bring the report "Group_PartialField.rep" from the Chapter 7 folder into the Report Designer, in the Inspector window, looking at "group1", you would see something like:

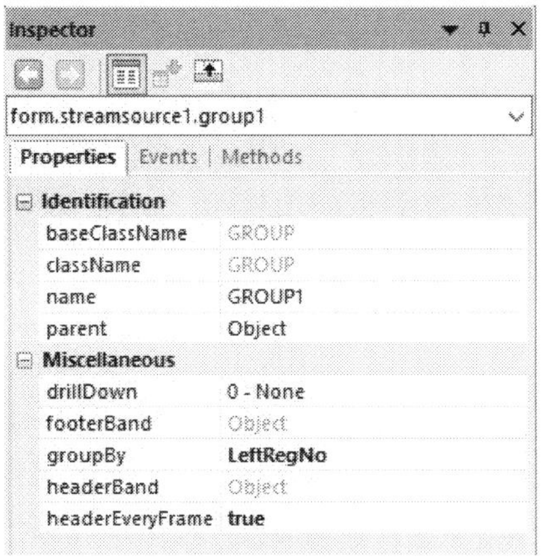

Figure 11-1

There are not a lot of properties that we can modify. Note that while in theory you can change the *name* of the group, I have found that the Report Designer and Report Engine do not handle this well. It is safer to leave the default names for most of the report specific objects.

The most important property shown is the *groupBy* property – this tells dBASE how to work with the data. The other property we have modified is the *headerEveryFrame* property. The default for this is *false*, we changed it to *true*. This allows us to show the group *headerBand* every time we change to a new *streamFrame* – for this report *(and most reports)*, that means for each page. From this point we can drill down to the *footerBand* or the *headerBand* objects.

We will ignore the *drillDown* property – that is aimed at web reports, which we are not working with for this chapter.

There are no events for the group, and most of the methods for the group are aggregate calculations, which we will examine in more depth in the next chapter.

As the primary focus of this chapter is to work with multiple tables, let us move on. Exit the Report Designer, if it asks about saving changes, click the "No" button, as any changes you may have made would not be anything necessary.

In Chapter 7 we also created a grouped report (as mentioned above) that we will want to examine again, that works with more than one table, and with a data module. As a reminder, you don't have to do this with a data module, although it is suggested that you do so.

Change the working folder in the Navigator back to the Chapter 7 folder. Open the "BaseGroup" report in the Report Designer.

You should see something like:

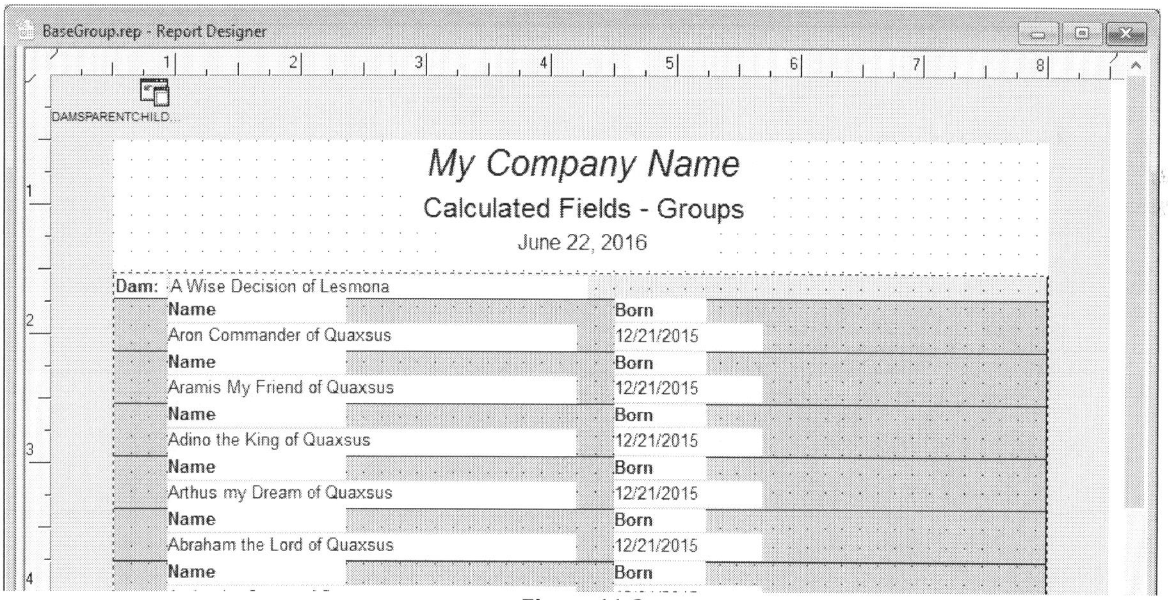

Figure 11-2

You should see something like the image shown above (Figure 11-2). Rather than showing query objects for two different tables, there is a single data module object on the design surface (in the upper left corner).

The important things to note with this report are:

- The report's primary rowset is the parent rowset (Dams1), and the *group* is grouped by a field in the parent rowset (DAM).
- The group *headerBand* object displays data from the parent rowset.
- The *detailBand* displays data from the child rowset (Dogs1).

This is a typical parent/child report. However, there are other types of reports that work with multiple tables. The rest of this chapter will examine some of these.

Exit the report designer without saving changes, so we can start looking at a new report.

Change your working folder to Chapter 11.

An Invoice Report

Invoice reports, if the invoice application is designed properly, will typically work with at least three tables, if not more.

At the absolute basics, an invoice system will have:

- The Invoice table itself, which will contain a key field, a link to the customer, and perhaps some data about the specific invoice (date, some notes, shipping data, perhaps payment information ...).
- A Customer table which has a key field and the fields necessary for the customer data, depending on what the needs of the company are, but typically address, contact information, and more. (And some systems break this down to an address table linked to the customer, a contact table linked to the customer ...) There of course could be lookups for states, country codes, and more.
- A Line-item table – this may either contain links to the inventory, or in some systems it may be simpler to copy data from the inventory to the line-item, and quite importantly a link to the Invoice. This will typically note the number of items sold, the price for each item (which of course in a complex system may vary based on special offers, and so on ...).
- Inventory – the full inventory of everything the company sells.

As you might imagine, this can get to be quite complex. For our purposes we are going to assume that details about the individual items sold are stored in the line-item table, and that the customer data is self-contained (meaning there are no sub-tables linked into it).

We will be using an Orders table, a Customers table, an OrderItems table, and a Parts table. These tables are in the dBASESamples database that ships with dBASE Plus.

A data module has been designed using these tables, called Invoice.dmd. To work with it, go to the Command Window, and type the following:

```
copy file "..\Tables\Invoice.dmd" to Invoice.dmd
```

Open this in the Data Module Designer (double-click it in the Navigator). It should look like:

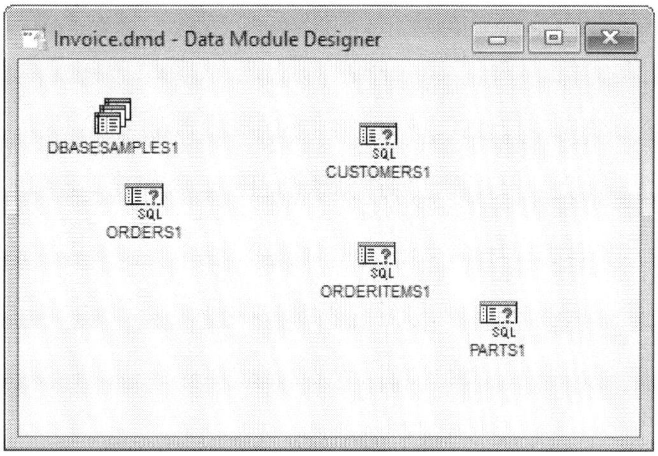

Figure 11-3

This doesn't look all that interesting, and does not show the relationships, despite my having laid it out as closely as I can *(the Data Module Designer is not as graphic as the older dQuery program)*.

The Orders table (the first one) is the parent table for both the Customers and the OrderItems tables. The OrderItems table is the parent for the Parts table (this is the inventory of all items a customer may order).

While a customer may have multiple invoices, it actually works for the Orders table to be the parent here. If you need to look at invoices for all the customers, you could set up a different data module where the data was sorted differently or modify the table layout with the Customers table as the parent of the Orders table, and so on, but for the purposes of creating invoices, and for printing an invoice, we need to do this in this fashion.

We have the data, and we have a data design. Now please note as I've said in this and earlier chapters, while a data module is not required, it can make life easier – we can use this data module on a form, and the same data module on a report, without having to layout the tables each time. That's the power of using a data module – reusability!

Close the Data Module Designer.

Start the Report Designer with a new report, and if your custom report does not come up (it probably won't if you cleared it out at the end of the previous chapter), then go to the File Menu, and bring up the Custom Report dialog, select "MyCompanyReport.crp" and so on as we have done in the past.

The first thing you'll want to do is to change the SecondaryTitleText control to read "Invoice". Save the report by pressing Ctrl+S naming the report "Invoice" *(make sure you are saving this in the Chapter 11 folder)*.

Now we're ready to get in and start working with the invoice. Go to the Navigator window, and click on the "Data Module" tab, then select the file "Invoice.dmd" and drag it to the report design surface.

Notice that when the data module is placed onto the design surface, that the number of detailBands has suddenly increased to the number of rows in the OrderItems table. Click the "Report" tab of the Component Palette, and drag a "Group" object to the design surface. You should automatically see a group *headerband* (light green) with some default text on it. We will change that as we go. The next thing to do, however, is to modify the group object.

In the Inspector find the "group1" object (using the combobox at the top) and make sure it has focus. Click on the *groupBy* property, and in the combobox that appears, select "OrderID". You should now see the report grouped like this:

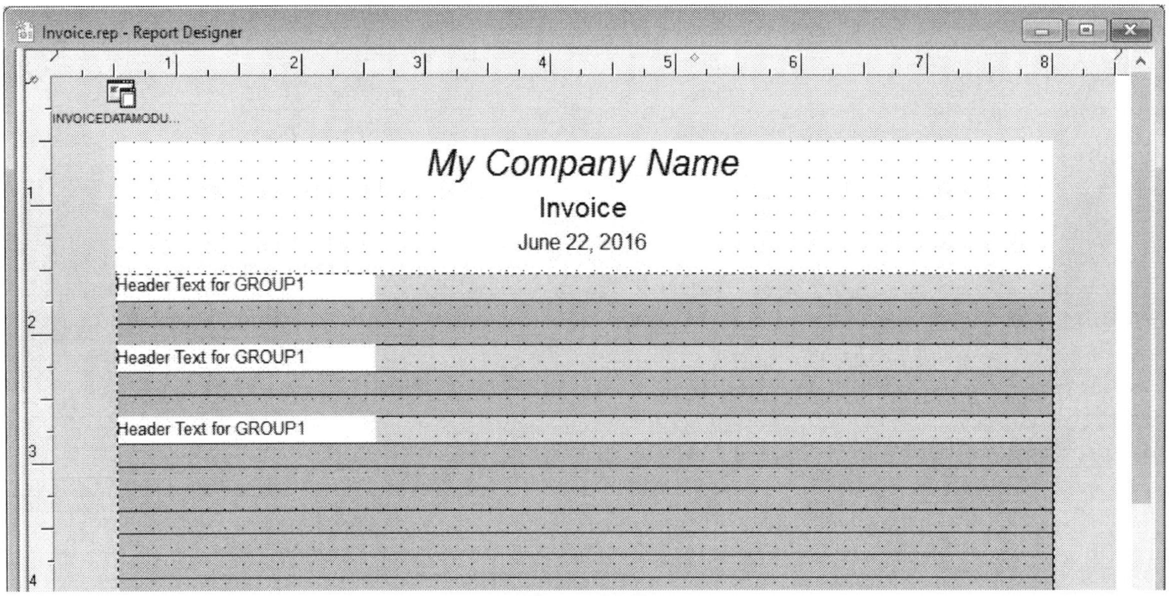

Figure 11-5

This shows multiple invoices, with a different number of line-items for each. This is correct.

Normally an invoice report shows a single invoice on a page. How do we force this? Select the *headerBand* object in the Inspector, and click the Inspect ("I") button. This will show the headerBand's properties.

Click the *beginNewFrame* property and note it defaults to *false*. If you change this to *true* (double-click, or select *true* in the combobox), you should now see only the first invoice on the design surface.

The next thing we will want to do is work on the group *headerBand* for this report – this will contain information we want to appear at the top of the invoice – typically information about the invoice such as Invoice Number, Invoice Date, and customer data.

The *headerBand* is not really tall enough for all that. Change the height in the Inspector, for now, to say, 2 inches. This will give us some room to work and place important information on the report. We can change this again later.

This should give a report design surface that looks something like:

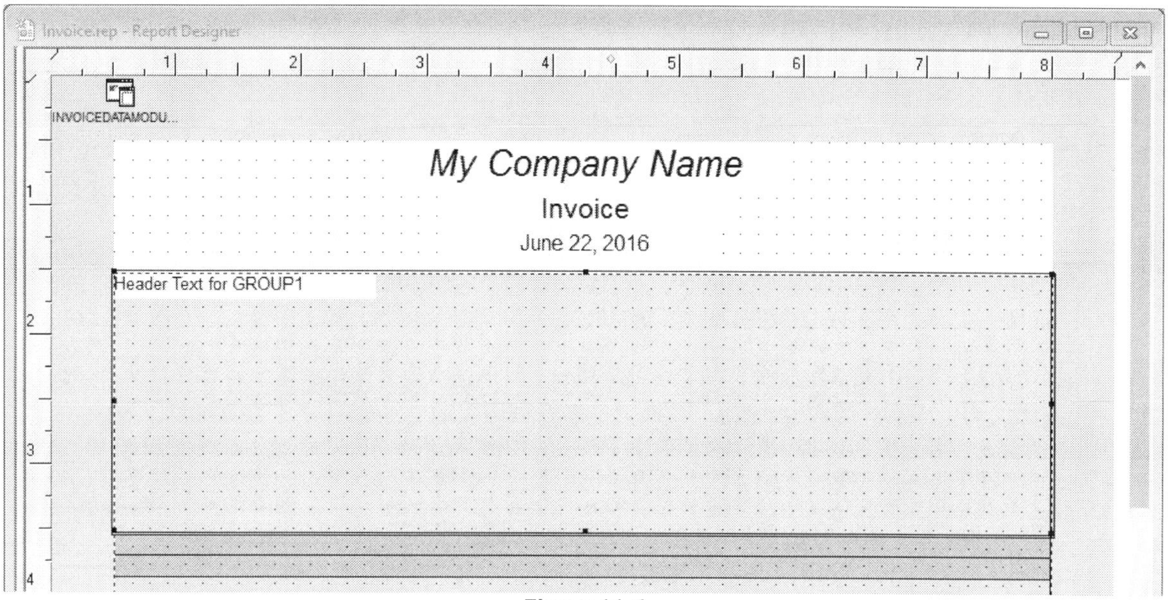

Figure 11-6

Next, delete the default text, and let's start adding our own details to the report.

Drag an instance of "DataHeadingText" to the design surface (from the "Custom" tab of the Component Palette). Move the control as necessary to the top of the band, change the *text* to "Invoice:".

Next drag an instance of "DataText" to the design surface next to the heading text, and change the text by going to the Inspector, and clicking on the *text* property. Click the "Type" (T) button, and select "Codeblock", then the tool button, and enter the following in the dialog:

```
this.form.invoicedatamodule1.orders1.rowset.fields["orderid"].value
```

Yes, this is a bit lengthy, but it is important to have the full path like that.

This should now show the order id, which we can use as an Invoice Number, as the table does not actually have a field for that – this value is unique and for our purposes will suffice as an Invoice Number. You might want to boldface the text for the invoice number and the heading, because these are rather important pieces of information. To do that, click on the first field and, holding the Ctrl key down, click the other text control, and in the Inspector find the *fontBold* property. Change this to *true*, and you are set.

You will also want to place the Invoice Date on the report, probably on the same line as the Invoice Number. Do the same thing that we did before, although you may not need this to be bold. Make sure the fieldname for the date is "OrderDate".

The next thing you will want to do is put the Customer's data in here. *(If you are not sure of the names of the fields, open the table and look at them ...)* This is the exact same process we've just done, but you may not always want to place a heading for each field for the customer – and we will also take a look at the second address line, because this does not always have data. So start laying out the customer data in a way that makes sense to you (and recall some of what we have done in earlier chapters – for example, for the City/State and Zip, you may want to place just a single text control on the report, and use the text control's *canRender* event to handle it). You should end up with something similar to what is shown below (in Figure 11-7).

The codeblock for the Company name should be entered in the dialog as:

```
this.form.invoicedatamodule1.customers1.rowset.fields["company"].value
```

You can use this to set the other fields (replacing "company" with the correct field name).

It is important to note that for everything to work properly, the data heading text and data text for the phone number must be placed on the report after the Company name and before placing the Customer name line on the design surface – this places it in proper "z-order" sequence. If you did not do that, there are ways to fix it – one is to simply delete the text and start over, but you can also close the Report Designer, open it in the Source Code Editor, and cut and paste the text to where it should be. This is a bit tricky getting it into the right place, so if you think about your design first, and place the controls on the surface in the correct sequence to start, it will save some trouble.

Your report should now look *something* like the image shown below. You should be using calculated fields for the name and city/state/zip fields, in the example there is placeholder text in the *text* properties of the fields. When the report renders the text will change to what is defined in the *canRender* event for these fields.

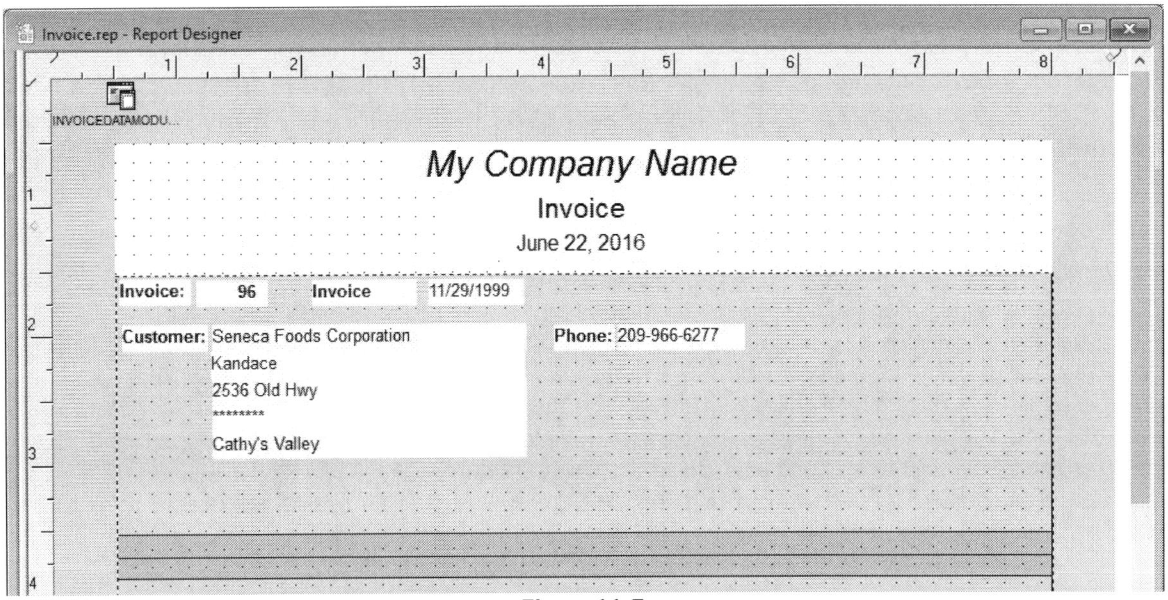

Figure 11-7

If you look at this, you will see several asterisks in the text for the second address line. That tells us that this field is empty, but gives us something we can see rather than just a blank bit of white space on the design surface. However, for the report having a blank line does not look great. We need to deal with suppressing the blank line. We briefly looked at this in Chapter 9 (Labels), and will look at this again in a later chapter, but it is important.

Click on the address 2 text control, and in the Inspector, find *suppressIfBlank*. Set this to *true*.

We're not quite done with the *headerBand*, but we'll come back to it.

Next we need to place details in the *detailBand* – the items in the OrderItems table for this particular invoice. We will lay out the line items in a tabular fashion (in columns).

We would typically want for the line item to include fields like the number of items ordered, the item number, the description of the item, the price of the item, and perhaps the "Extended Price". There is no "Extended Price" field, however – but we'll come back to that. We will not concern ourselves with column headings, and again will come back to that. So, we need to simply lay out the fields in the *detailBand* in columns.

Using the DataText control for the four fields needed (Quantity, PartID, Description (from the Parts table) and Price) you will need the following for your codeblocks:

```
this.form.invoicedatamodule1.orderitems1.rowset.fields["quantity"].value
this.form.invoicedatamodule1.orderitems1.rowset.fields["partid"].value
this.form.invoicedatamodule1.parts1.rowset.fields["description"].value
this.form.invoicedatamodule1.orderitems1.rowset.fields["price"].value
```

This works exactly the same as elsewhere in the report, however it should be noted that it is helpful if you name the controls. The more controls on a report, the more useful the names are, so you can see what you're looking at if/when you look at the source code. If the only names of controls on a report are "datatext1", "datatext2", etc., it becomes difficult when working in the source code to access the correct item.

For the Quantity field, set the *picture* property to "999" (without the quotes), set the *alignHorizontal* property to "2 - Right" for all of the numeric values – this ensures they line up correctly.

Drag another instance of the DataText control to the *detailband* on the right of the other controls, and name it "ExtendedPrice". Click the "Events" tab of the inspector, and click on *canRender*. Click the tool button, and in the Source Code Editor, enter the following:

```
function EXTENDEDPRICE_canRender
   f = form.streamSource1.rowset.fields
   this.text := f["Quantity"].value * f["Price"].value
return true
```

At the moment your report should look something like:

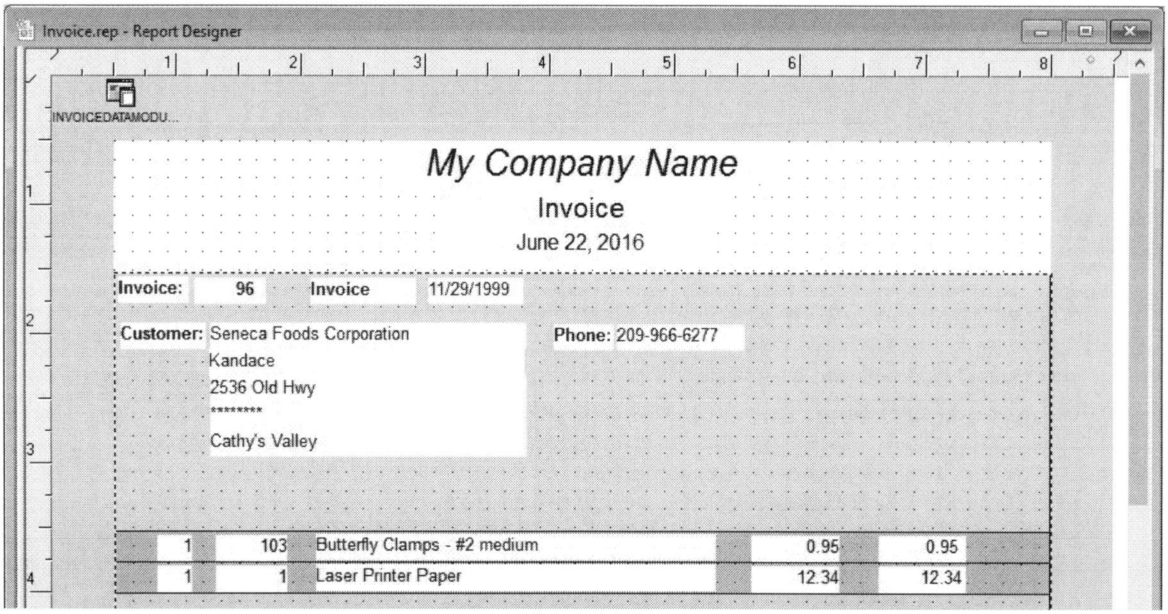

Figure 11-8

The next thing we need to look at is setting column headings for the *detailBand*. For some reports we might consider putting these on the *pageTemplate*, except that the report would look rather odd with the items in the group *headerBand* between the column headings and the data.

Another option would be to place the column headings on the group *headerBand*. We will need to set the *height* of the group *headerBand* to one that will give us room for these controls.

Place a DataHeadingText control on the group *headerBand* control above the first text control (Quantity). Make these changes to properties:

text	"Quantity Sold" (with a space)
alignHorizontal	1 – Center
alignVertical	2 – Bottom
fontBold	true
variableHeight	true (so that this takes two lines)

We want to do something similar for the other controls, coming up with something that looks similar to the image below (Figure 11-9). The first two need to be centered (*alignHorizontal*), the others can be left with the text on the left.

Move the controls you just added around, use the alignment tools (hint: "align bottom" for all of them so that they line up). You might move them up a bit so they are closer to the customer information as well. Then set the group headerBand's *height* to a value smaller than it really needs, such as 1", and may should see the *headerBand* collapse to a height just big enough to display everything.

You could define the *height* to whatever you specifically wanted it to be, but sometimes it is easier to let dBASE handle this. The report should look something like:

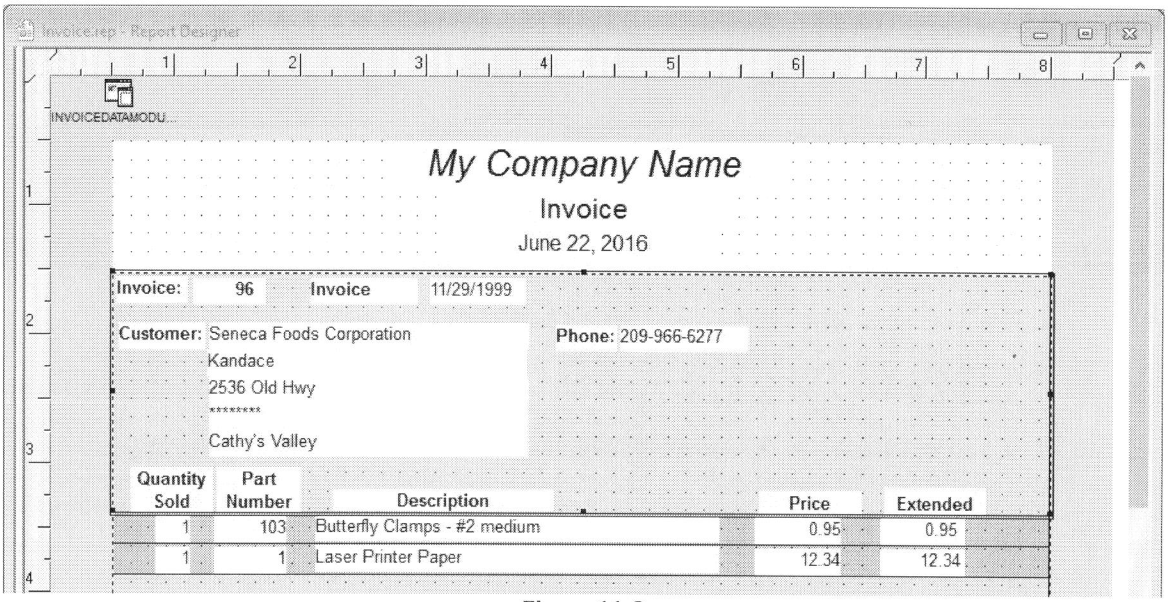

Figure 11-9

The last part of the report really needs to be done in the *group footerBand*, which if you examine the report does not actually appear to be there. That is because the default *height* is 0.

Go to the Inspector's combobox, find the *group* ("group1") and both the *footerBand* and the *headerBand*. Select the *footerBand*, and this will now appear in the Inspector. Set the *height* to 2" for now (type the number in the inspector). There should be a large blue area on the screen under the detailBands.

Typical items for an invoice might include a total of the extended price column, any discount being offered the customer, shipping and handling charges, taxes (if any – for this example we're not dealing with it), and an invoice total. You might include other details such as payment information, and so on.

The first thing we need to do is get a total of the extended price column. This seems like it should be straightforward, but since the extended price is a calculation of its own, it may not be.

Because we're working with multiple tables, we cannot use the "Add Groups and Summaries" dialog to have dBASE automatically insert the appropriate calculation. This is because the controlling rowset for this report is Orders, but we need a total on the Extended Price field which is part of the OrderItems data. The dialog for this will not see the child table.

Yet another reason – this is a field that doesn't exist in the rowset (it is a virtual field), so even if the controlling rowset were the OrderItems rowset, this field doesn't exist and we couldn't use it.

We're going to have to re-think the Extended Price column. The difficulty with the way this works now is that this is not really a field in the table, but it is also not really a virtual field – it is simply a calculated field created in the *canRender* event of a *text* control. This makes the data hard to work with. We could deal with this in the report, but it may actually be a better idea to make the following change in the datamodule.

(Why didn't we do it that way to start with? A couple reasons – I realized the problem as I was writing the chapter, and this is often the way these things are done – a developer has to change something in mid-stream – it is good practice!)

Exit the Report Designer (Save and Exit with Ctrl+W). Click on the Data Modules tab of the Navigator, and right-click the Invoice.dmd file. Select "Open in Source Editor". This will open the data module in the Source Code Editor, so we can modify it. Find the OrderItems query in the source code. Modify the code by adding the statement in bold (the onOpen statement):

```
this.ORDERITEMS1 = new QUERY(this)
   with (this.ORDERITEMS1)
      onOpen = class::OrderItems_OnOpen
      left = 179.0
      top = 103.0
      database = form.dbasesamples1
      sql = "select * from ORDERITEMS.DBF"
      active = true
   endwith
```

And then go to the end of the code, and insert the following *before* the statement "endclass":

```
function OrderItems_onOpen
   // create a calculated field as a virtual field
   // in the Line Items rowset.
   local f
   f = new field()
   f.fieldName = "Extended"
   // when the field object's beforeGetValue() event
   // is executed, "this.parent" is the fields array
   f.beforeGetValue = {||this.parent["Quantity"].value *;
                         this.parent["Price"].value }
   // add the field to the fields array:
   this.rowset.fields.add( f )
return
```

When the data module is executed it runs the code associated with the OrderItems query object, which in this case fires the *onOpen* event handler. This event handler creates a calculated field called "Extended", which is treated in forms and reports as an actual field, even though it is a virtual field. The calculation is as given – we multiply the quantity by the price and we get our extended price for the line item.

Save and exit (Ctrl+W) from the Source Code Editor, and let's move on.

We need to go back to the Report Designer for the Invoice Report. Click on the "Reports" tab of the Navigator, and select the Invoice report. Bring this up in the Report Designer.

The next thing we need to do is remove the *canRender* event for the Extended Price text control. To do that, click on the control in the *detailBand*, and in the Inspector, click the "Events" tab. Note the reference to this code. Click the Tool button. This puts you in the source code, with the cursor in the code itself (below the "function" statement). Go to the "Method" menu, and select "Delete Method". This removes the code, and the reference in the Inspector as well as in the constructor code.

Now we need to change the text to a Codeblock, so go back to the "Properties" tab, find the *text* property, and set the Type to a codeblock, click the tool button and enter this:

```
this.form.invoicedatamodule1.orderitems1.rowset.fields["extended"].value
```

Whew. That was a bit more work than normal. However, what this means is if we need this field in another report or a form, it is already done!

The difficulty as noted elsewhere is that the controlling rowset for this report is not the OrderItem's rowset, but rather the Orders' rowset. What this means is that we cannot use the aggregate functions that are built in to the dBASE reports and instead we need to do this in code.

What we need to do is to create a running total that is used in the report. Each time the Extended Price is rendered, we need to add to the total. We can then use that running total in the group *footerBand*.

We will take another look at Running Totals in another chapter, but for the moment, we need one here. Click on the Extended Price text control in the *detailBand* of the report. We are going to use the *onRender* event of this control – an event that fires *after* the text control has rendered – to create our running total. Click on the tool button for this event, and in the Source Code Editor enter the following:

```
function EXTENDEDPRICE_onRender()
   // see if the running total exists, and
   // if not, create it:
   if type( "form.RT_SubTotal" ) == "U"
      form.RT_SubTotal = 0
   endif
   // now we add to it:
   f = form.InvoiceDatamodule1.OrderItems1.rowset.fields
   form.RT_SubTotal += f["Extended"].value
return
```

What this does is check to see if the custom property of the report (referenced as *form*) exists, and if not, create it – and initialize it (give it a starting value) to zero. Then we take the current value in the OrderItems table and add it to the running total property.

Now that we have the running total, we need to display it.

Place a "DataHeadingText" control on the *footerBand*, setting the text to "Subtotal:" and so on – move it under the Price column.

Place a "DataText" control under the Extended Price column on the group *footerBand*. Change the text to a placeholder such as "Subtotal", and set the *alignHorizontal* property to "2 – Right" so that we get things to line up with the value above it. Set the *name* property to "Subtotal". Next go to the "Events" tab in the Inspector, and click the tool button for the *canRender* event. Enter the following code:

```
function SUBTOTAL_canRender
   // set the text to the form's custom property RT_SubTotal:
   this.text := form.RT_SubTotal
return true
```

We will leave the subtotal value as-is for the moment, but eventually we will want to reset it – this is always a good idea for running totals.

We need to look at other items that might affect the total for the Invoice.

We will add a Shipping and Handling fee, for our purposes we will call it 2.5% of the value of the subtotal. This will be added to the Subtotal for the Invoice Total. Add a "DataHeadingText" control, set the text to "Shipping and Handling:", *fontBold* should be *true*, line it up with the Subtotal text above it. Add a "DataText" control, set the *name* property to "Shipping", *alignHorizontal* to "2" (for right). Click the "Events" tab in the Inspector, find *canRender* and click the tool button. Enter the following code:

```
function SHIPPING_canRender()
   this.text := form.RT_SubTotal * 0.25 // 2.5%
return true
```

> **NOTE**
> This is actually cheating, as the fee would likely be based on weight and other factors – however, the tables we are working with do not include details we might want to use such as the weight of the items sold. We also do not have a discount field, income tax information, and we are not tracking how the payment was made. A properly functional invoicing system would be more robust.

As our Orders table does not have any of the other values (Discount, Sales Tax ...) discussed earlier, we are going straight to the Invoice Total.

Add a "DataHeadingText" control, and set the text to "Total:". Add a "DataText" control and set the *text* property to simply "Total", you might want to set the *fontBold* property to *true*, and set the *alignHorizontal* property to the right (2). Set the *name* property to "InvoiceTotal".

Next go to the "Events" tab of the Inspector, and click the tool button for the *canRender* event. Enter the following code:

```
function INVOICETOTAL_canRender()
   local nTotal
   // get the Subtotal -- from the line items:
   nTotal = form.RT_SubTotal

   // add the shipping and handling fees:
   nTotal += ( form.RT_SubTotal * 0.25 )

   // set the text to the total:
   this.text := nTotal
return true
```

Set the footerBand's height to something like 0.5" which will reduce it to more manageable. Spend a few minutes lining things up, make them look good.

You should have something that looks something like:

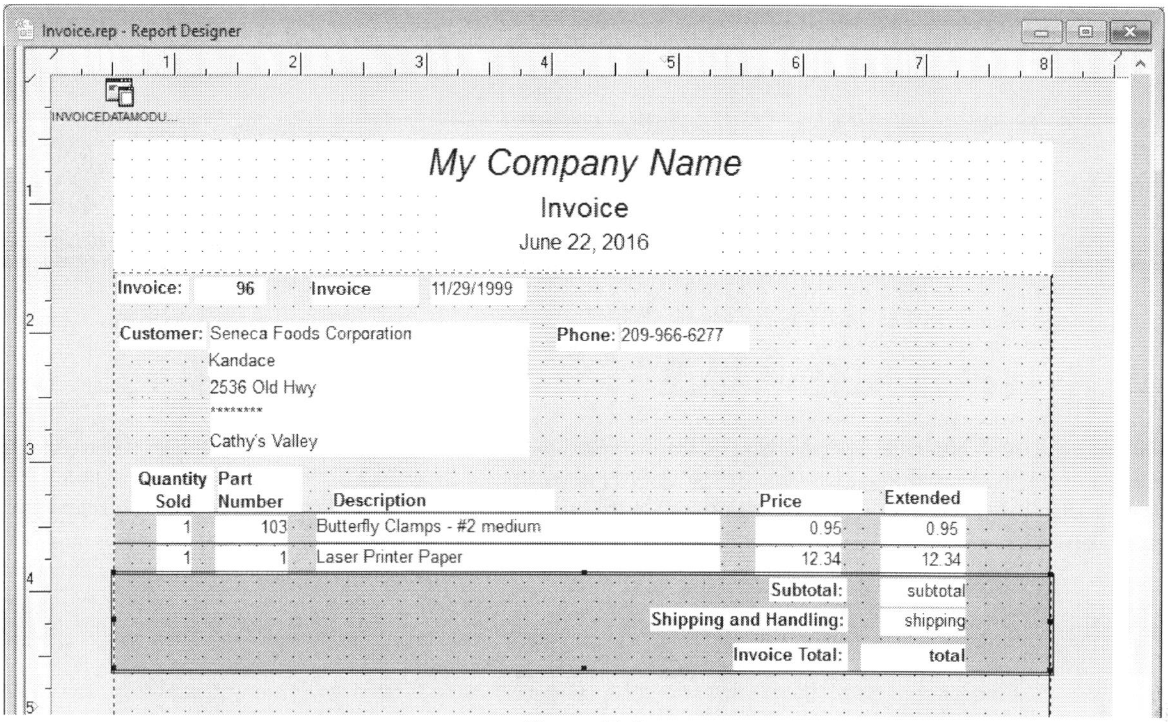

Figure 11-1

There is one more thing that needs to be done. We have the running total for the "Extended" column of the report. One problem, although for an invoice this is not as much of a problem as it would be for other situations – the running total has a value in it. What happens if you navigate to the next Order ID/Invoice number? The amount shown for the first invoice (13.29) would be added to for the second invoice which should have a subtotal of 33.13, but it would show a subtotal of 58.03!

When the *footerBand* is done rendering (using the *onRender* event), we can set the value of the running total back to zero, and all should be well.

If you ran the report, open the report back in the Report Designer, click on the blue surface of the *footerBand*, and in the Inspector find the *onRender* event, click the tool button to bring up the Source Code Editor. Type the following:

```
function FOOTERBAND_onRender
   // Zero out the running total we're using:
   this.parent.parent.parent.RT_SubTotal := 0
return
```

NOTE

For some reason the *footerBand* does not understand a reference to "form", so you must traverse the object path back up:

this = the group *footerBand*
parent = *group*
parent = *streamSource;*
parent = *form* (report)

Now if you were to run the report and page through it, you should get correct subtotals and totals.

One last thing, we can make this more professional looking by adding a line at the bottom of the group's *headerBand*, and at the top of the group's *footerBand*. This puts lines below the headings and above the totals. If the report is not in the designer open it back up in the designer.

Set the *height* of the *headerBand* to 2", and place a line control on the band. Move it so that the line is below the headings – right under them. Set the *left* property to 0, set the *right* property to 7.5 (the width of the *streamFrame*). Make sure the *top* and *bottom* properties are identical. Now set the *headerBand height* property back to 1".

Repeat for the *footerBand*, but placing the control above the subtotal (you may find that you need to move the controls on this band down just a little – holding the Ctrl key, click on all of them, and use the down-arrow key on your keyboard to nudge them all down a little bit).

When you run this, you should see:

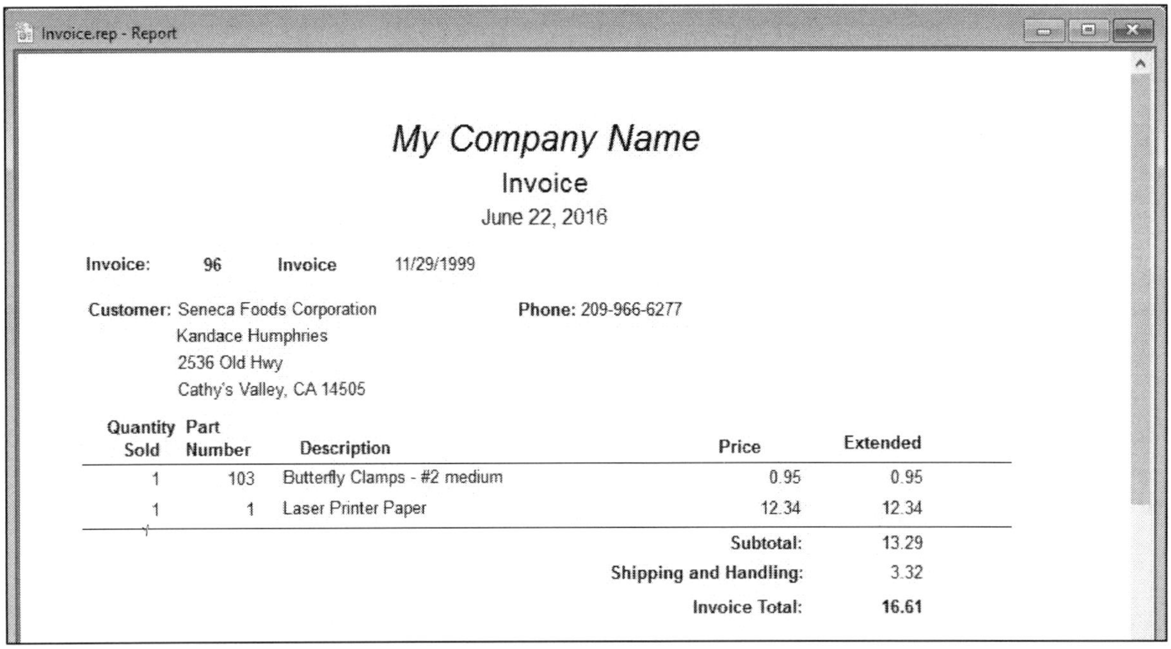

Figure 11-8

We will look at enhancing reports in a later chapter. This is enough to get you started, though.

Now the big problem with this is that you need to be able to get just a specific invoice. We will discuss this in detail in a later chapter, showing examples of selecting a specific row and generating a report. However, just to give a feel for what can be done, we will do something from the Command Window with this report. Close the report, and type the following in the Command Window:

```
set procedure to Invoice.rep
r = new InvoiceReport()
```

Now we can modify any properties of the report we want to. For the moment, what we might want to do is limit the report to a specific invoice, such as invoice number 20.

The controlling table is the Orders table, so the form.streamSource1.rowset property should be pointing to that table. The field we need to filter the data on is the OrderID, so try:

```
r.streamSource1.rowset.filter=[OrderID=20]
```

And then render the report:

```
r.render()
```

You should see Invoice 20 and only Invoice 20 – if you try to navigate the report using the PgUp and PgDn keys on the keyboard, you won't go anywhere.

Close the report.

We learned a lot of different things in the process of creating this report. There are some examples of things we'll cover in more detail later, but also examples of things we covered in earlier chapters, such as calculated fields, some work with tabular *and* form style reports – in this case the *detailBand* was tabular, and the group *headerBand* and group *footerBand* were both form style. We learned about using a data module and how useful the reusable code aspects of that is, and we worked with multiple tables – one in a one-to-one relationship (one customer per invoice) and the other a one-to-many (more than one line-item per invoice).

Subgroups

We have looked at grouped reports in several places in the book so far. However, what if you need to have groups within groups? For example, what if you wanted to show the dogs from the various litters grouped by dams, and then by sires so that all offspring of a specific sire were shown? This will take a little work with the tables we have.

Create a new report in the usual way. Click on the Secondary Title (the one that reads "Purpose of Report"), and then again to place it into edit mode. Change the text to read "Subgroup Report".

Press Ctrl+S to save the report, and name it "Subgroup".

Go to the Navigator and click on the "Tables" tab. Make sure you have selected the "DBASEReports" database, and select the "Dogs" table. Place this on the report design surface. Click on the "DOGS1" query. Bring up the Inspector if it's not already available, and make sure you are on the "Properties" tab. Select the *rowset* property, and click the inspect ("I") button. Click on the *indexName* property, and in the combobox, select "D_S_BORN" – this index tag will sort the data by Dam, then by Sire, and finally by the date the dog was born.

Go to the Component Palette, and click the "Report" tab. Select the "Group" object, and drag it to the report.

For the moment we will use the registration number of the dam, but later we will change this. Click on the "Custom" tab of the Component Palette, and place a "DataHeadingText" control on the group *headerBand* (the green band). Next click on the default text provided by dBASE (the one that says 'Header Text for Group1") and delete it. Move the new text control to the left.

Change the text to read "Dam:", and resize it a little. To the right of this place a "DataText" control, and change the *text* property Type (in the Inspector) to "Codeblock". Click the tool button and enter:

```
this.form.dogs1.rowset.fields["rno_dam"].value
```

This should show the registration number for the dams. The first dam in the table has an empty registration number - you will see asterisks to represent the field.

Next we want to set the group's *groupBy* property. Select "group1" in the Inspector's combobox, and find the *groupBy* property. Click on this and select "RNO_DAM" from the list. You may not see any change in the report, that's okay.

Now let's add a second group. We do this the same way we did before - by selecting the "Report" tab on the Component Palette, and select the "Group" object, dragging it to the design surface.

Note that dBASE automatically places this inside the first group - the group2 *headerBand* shows up below the group1 *headerBand*. We need to do the same thing we did before with the group *headerBand*, but this time we will be using the dog's sire.

We will use the registration number of the sire, but later we will change this. Click on the "Custom" tab of the Component Palette., and place a "DataHeadingText" control on the group *headerBand* (the second green band). Next click on the default text provided by dBASE (the one that says "Header Text for Group2") and delete it. Move the new text control to the left, but not all the way to the left, make it obvious this is a subgroup by indenting it a little.

Change the text to read "Sire:", and resize it a little. To the right of this place a "DataText" control, and change the *text* property Type to "Codeblock". Click the tool button and in the dialog enter:

```
this.form.dogs1.rowset.fields["rno_sire"].value
```

This should show the registration number for the sires. However if the first sire in the table has an empty registration number you will see asterisks instead.

Next we want to set the group's *groupBy* property. Select "group2" in the Inspector's combobox, and find the *groupBy* property. Click on this and select "RNO_SIRE" from the list. You may not see any change in the report, that's okay.

Now we need to add a couple of fields to the *detailBand*. Let's place the date the dog was born first, and then the name. That's all we really need for this example.

To do this (it should start feeling like "second nature", as it were), go to the "Custom" tab of the Component Palette, and select a "DataColHeadingText" control, and place it on the report. Change the text to "Born". Place another "DataColHeadingText" to the right of this one, and change the text to "Name". Line these up.

Next place a "DataText" control under the first heading ("Born"), and line things up a little. Set the *text* property's type to "Codeblock", click the tool button and in the dialog enter:

```
this.form.dogs1.rowset.fields["born"].value
```

To the right of this, place another "DataText" control under the "Name" heading, and line things up a little. Set the *text* property's type to "Codeblock", click the tool button and enter:

```
this.form.dogs1.rowset.fields["name"].value
```

Your report should look something like the following in the designer:

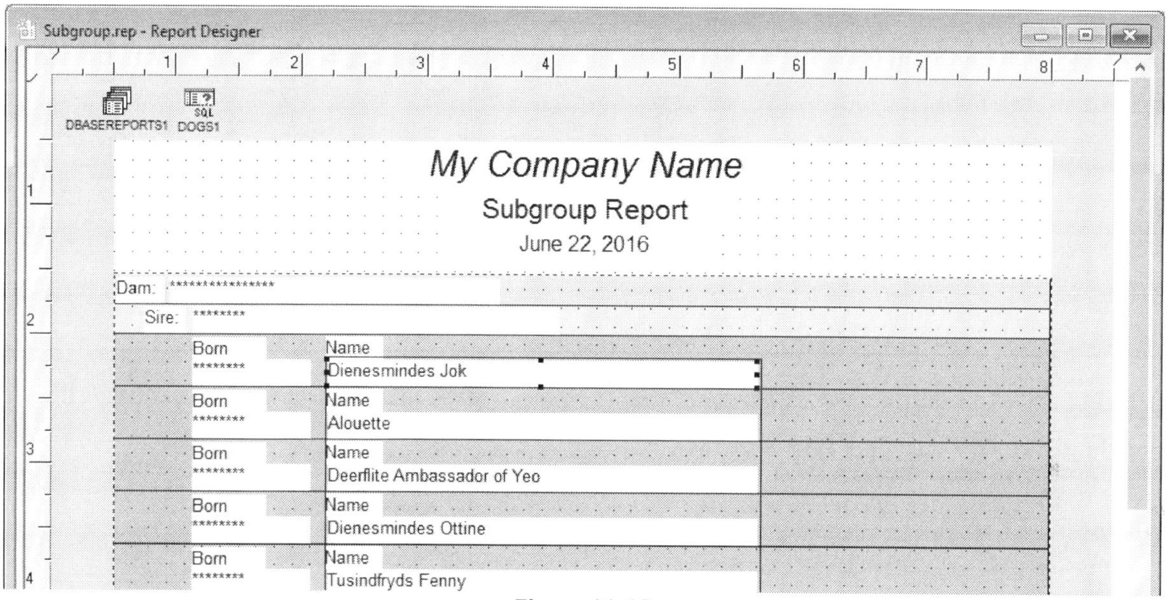

Figure 11-12

In this table there are quite a few dogs that have empty values for their dam and sire registration numbers, and possibly empty birth dates, and they will tend to be grouped together. There isn't much that can be done about this. If you run the report and click through it for several pages (I had to go to page 19 to get the screen below), you will eventually find records with Dams and Sires listed:

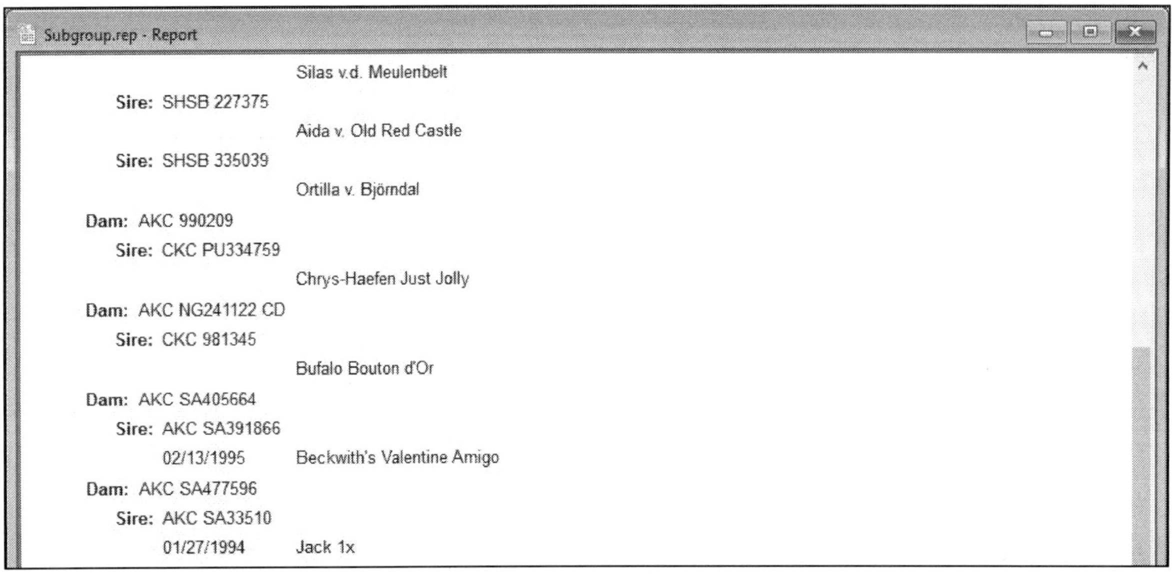

Figure 11-13

The problem with the empty values is that they look wrong, or to be more accurate, someone reading such a report might conclude there is a problem with the report, when it is actually reporting the data accurately. In addition, the registration numbers are not as useful as the names of the dams and sires. There are several things we can do to fix this.

If you ran the report, click on the "Design Report" tool button in the toolbar at the top of the screen, if the report is still in the Designer, leave it there and follow along.

We discussed Lookups in an earlier chapter. This is what we will do to get the names of the dams. There are several ways to do this. For our purposes we will bring the Dams table to the report and use a *lookupRowset* to get the value we need. To do this, go to the Navigator, you should still be on the "Tables" tab. If not, click on that tab. Select the "Dams" table and drag it to the design surface.

For a lookup to work properly, we need to have the field we are looking for as the first field. However, the Dams table actually has a record number field first, which gets in the way of our needs. So make sure that the "DAMS1" query has focus, and find the *sql* property. Note that the default value is:

```
select * from dams.dbf
```

This tells us that it is selecting all of the fields in the table. However, we really are interested specifically in the DAM and NAME fields – we want to look up the registration number (the DAM) field and return the NAME. So change this statement to read:

```
select dam, name from dams.dbf order by dam
```

Next give the "Dogs1" query focus, and in the Inspector's combobox find "fields" (click on it). Select the "RNO_DAM" field, and click the "Inspect" button. Click on the *lookupRowset* property, and select "dams1".

Now again, this may not look like anything has changed, because again the first dam listed is empty. Having the report display "Dam:". when the field is empty is a bit confusing. We can do something about this, however. Click on the DataText control on the first group *headerBand*, and then go to the Inspector window. Select the "Events" tab, and select *canRender*. Click on the Tool button, and dBASE will insert into the report:

```
function DATATEXT1_canRender()
return true
```

Fill in the following code. This will look at the value in the field to see if it is empty, and if so, it will change the text to "Unknown", otherwise it will put the appropriate text into the control.

```
function DATATEXT1_canRender()
   local f
   f = form.streamSource1.rowset.fields
   if empty( f["RNO_DAM"].value )
      this.text := "Unknown"
   else
      this.text := f["RNO_DAM"].value
   endif
return true
```

This is still not as useful as we might like, because it will only display the name of the Dam when the name changes. So the next thing we want to do is modify the group just a little. Find "group1" in the inspector (use the combobox), and then when selected, note that there is a property: *headerEveryFrame.* This will ensure that for each page the header is displayed – change this so it is *true.*

If you run the report, it will take several pages (up to 20 or 21) before you start to see something other than "Unknown" for the Dam. This is because there are a lot of blank values **or** ones that do not have matches in the other table. What is more odd is that you may still get some "Unknown" values – this is most likely because the registration code for the dam in the dogs table does not match anything in the dams table, or the dam's registration number is indeed blank. If we wanted to make this more useful, we could modify this text even more, by doing another modification to the *canRender* event for the control. Add the items in boldface below:

```
function DATATEXT1_canRender()
   local f
   f = form.streamSource1.rowset.fields
   if empty( f["RNO_DAM"].value )
      this.text := "Unknown"
   else
      this.text := f["RNO_DAM"].value.rightTrim()
   endif
   // perform a reverse lookup on the registration number:
   cRegNo = f["RNO_DAM"].lookupRowset.fields[1].value
   if not empty( cRegNo )
      this.text += " ("+cRegNo.rightTrim()+")"
   endif
return true
```

When run, this code will first trim the name that is returned (if one is returned) for the dam, and then it performs a reverse lookup to get the actual value stored in the

RNO_DAM field. If this is not empty, we will add the registration number to the end of the text displayed.

With a small amount of checking, I have found that at least some of the Sires' registration numbers (RNO_SIRE) are contained in the REG_NO field. We can take advantage of that and list the names of at least some of the sires, rather than their registration number (or in combination with their registration number).

This means doing another *lookupRowset*, with similar code as shown above. To do this, we need to place another copy of the Dogs table onto the report! Go to the Navigator, and select the "Dogs" table and drag it to the design surface. You should now see a query object with "DOGS2" as the name. We need to modify the *sql* property for this query in a similar fashion to what we did with the "DAMS1" query – make sure it has focus, and in the Inspector, find the *sql* property. Change it to:

```
select rno_sire, name from dogs order by rno_sire
```

Next we need to select the "DOGS1" query, and in the Inspector find the fields list. Select RNO_SIRE from the fields list, and click the Inspect ("I") button. Select the *lookupRowset* property, and select "dogs2" from the combobox. This will, as before, not look like much, if anything, has changed, because many of the first rows have empty RNO_SIRE fields.

Next we need to add code to the *canRender* event for the sire, in the group2 *headerBand*, similar to what we did before – only making appropriate changes. Click on the text control in this *headerBand*, then in the Inspector click the "Events" tab, and select the *canRender* event. Click the "Tool" button and enter the code below:

```
function DATATEXT1_canRender1()
   local f, cRegNo
   f = form.streamSource1.rowset.fields
   if empty( f["RNO_SIRE"].value )
      this.text := "Unknown"
   else
      this.text := f["RNO_SIRE"].value.rightTrim()
   endif
   // perform a "reverse lookup" to get the registration number
   cRegNo = f["RNO_SIRE"].lookupRowset.fields[1].value
   if not empty( cRegNo )
      this.text += " ("+cRegNo.rightTrim()+")"
   endif
return true
```

One more thing that we should do is to ensure that each Sire is listed at the top of the page, like we are doing with the dams. Otherwise the person reading such a report might have to flip through the pages a lot, which is frustrating, if nothing else. Find the "group2" object in the Inspector's combobox, and select it. Select the "Properties" tab if necessary, and change the *headerEveryFrame* property to *true.*

Now if you run the report, the first pages will show "Unknown" for the Dam and Sire, but after a while you will start seeing names, and registration numbers. Around page 19 in my copy of the report is where I start seeing the Sires listed, and around page 22 I start seeing dams other than "Unknown" showing up, as shown in these screen captures:

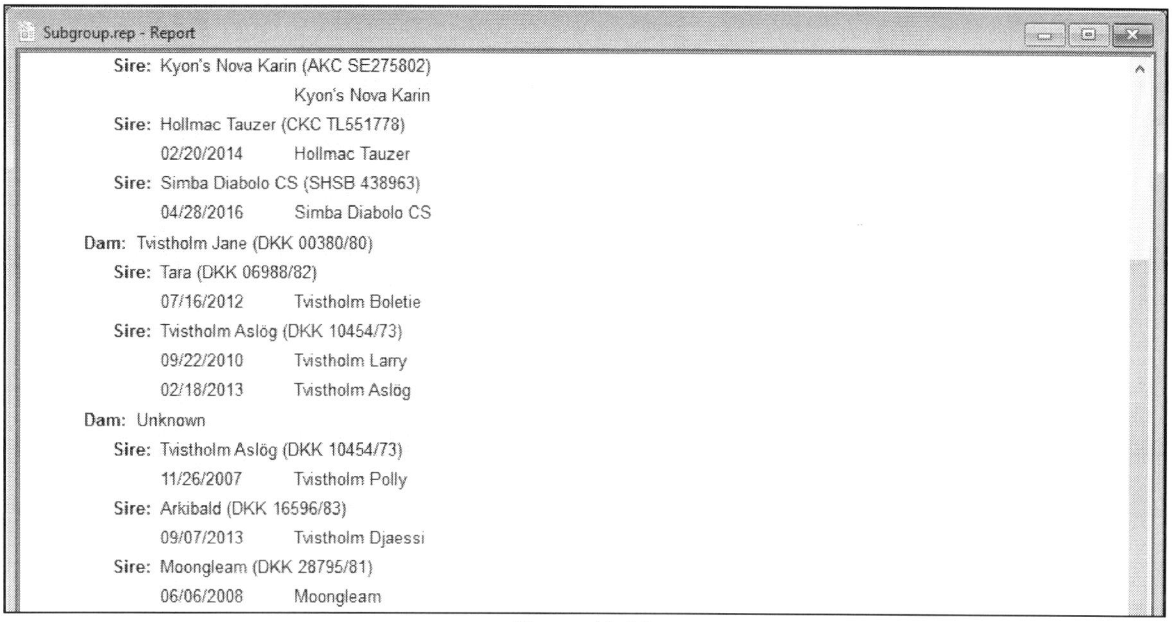

Figure 11-14

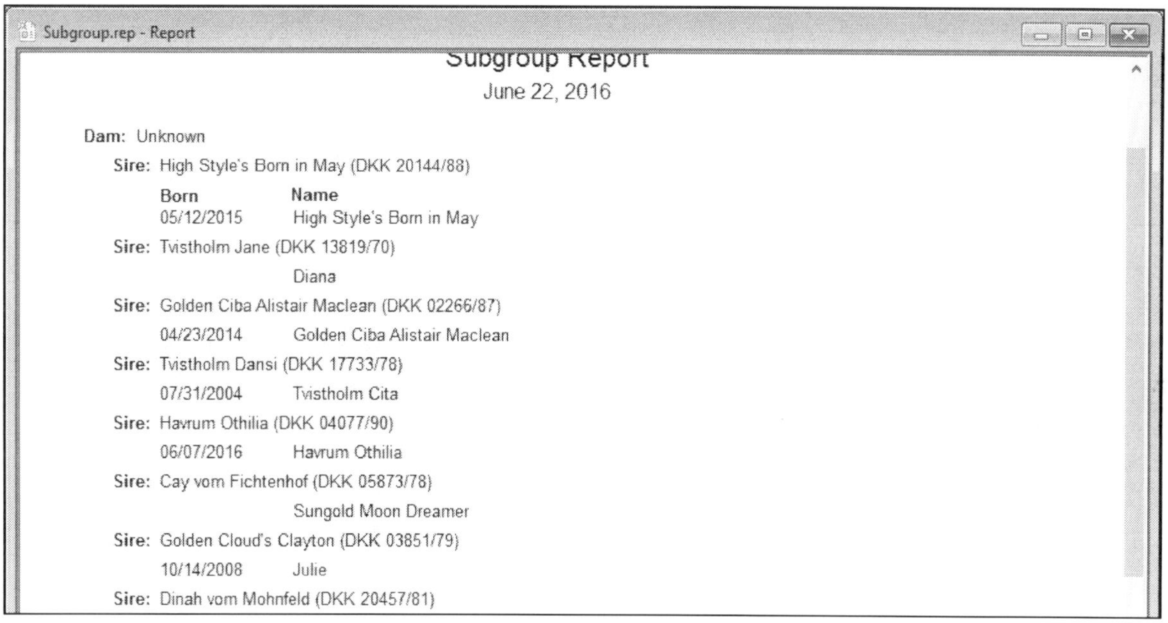

Figure 11-15

It is possible to create subgrouped reports on multiple tables, as well as single tables as we did here. We might have been able to do something similar to this report based on the first report in this chapter, for example.

How many groups can you have on a report? I honestly don't know what the limit, if any, is. One developer told me he has a report that has eight groups nested in it, so the report engine can work at least that deep.

One thing to remember is that the groups depend heavily on how the data is sorted. In this example, the data is sorted by the Dam, the Sire, and then the date of birth. We could have added another group on the birth date to group those with the same birthdate together and get the litters grouped. There are other things we could have done, but for now hopefully this is enough to give you an idea of this capability.

Close the report window.

SQL Joins

Multiple tables can be used for reports in quite a few different ways. I have to thank Frank Polan who also helped me with editing the first edition of this book, as he came up with an example of a SQL join that gives us the same results as the first report in this chapter.

What is a SQL join? It is a way of pulling data from more than one table and creating what can be described as a "virtual rowset" or "virtual table". Many times in dBASE a SQL join is not editable – which can be frustrating for a user, but for a report this is not an issue most of the time as most reports only read the data from the tables anyway.

What advantage is there to using a SQL join over using some other means of creating a parent/child relationship, for example, like we did in the first report in this chapter? Mostly there is the potential of a faster access to the data. There are many ways to join tables, the example we are using performs a "left outer" join. I am no expert on these, and cannot tell you the reason to do it this way versus a "right inner" join – my brain starts to melt when I get into these (I know there's a perfectly logical reason for them).

This topic is being discussed here simply to show that if you are comfortable with SQL joins, you can actually use them for your reports.

The SQL join that Frank created at my request creates a parent/child relationship very much like the one we did earlier, which uses the rowset object's *masterRowset* and *masterFields* properties:

```
select dams.dam, dams.name, dogs.name, dogs.born, dogs.rno_dam from
"dams.dbf" dams left outer join "dogs.dbf" dogs on dams.dam =
dogs.rno_dam order by dams.name, dogs.name
```

We will quickly create a report that uses this, and then move on to the next topic.

Create a new report in the usual manner (make sure you're using the custom report). Change the Secondary Title object to read "SQL Join Example". Press Ctrl+S to save it, and name this report "SQLJoin.rep".

For this example, we're going to set up the data objects "the hard way" (we've been doing this more simply in the past by dragging tables or data modules to the design surface). If you go to the Component Palette there is a "Data Access" tab – select this. We need a database object to start, so drag a Database from the Component Palette to the design surface. If you go to the Inspector window now, the database object ("DATABASE1") has focus. We need to change a couple of properties. Click on the *dataBaseName* property. If you click on the down-arrow button, you should see a list of all available databases. Select "DBASEREPORTS". Now select the *active* property and change it to *true* (which you can do by double-clicking on the value, or by selecting "true" from the drop-down). This is all that is needed for the database object.

Now we need a Query object. Go back to the Component Palette and find the Query object, then drag this to the design surface. This will be named "QUERY1". Go to the Inspector, as we need to change some properties for this object. First note that the *database* property is already set to "form.database1" – which for our needs is correct. We need to set the *sql* property for this. This needs to be the statement shown at the beginning of this section of the chapter. While it is displayed as three lines above, it is really one statement, and should be entered as such. It is easier to do this by clicking on the tool button for the *sql* property, and entering the statement in the dialog that appears:

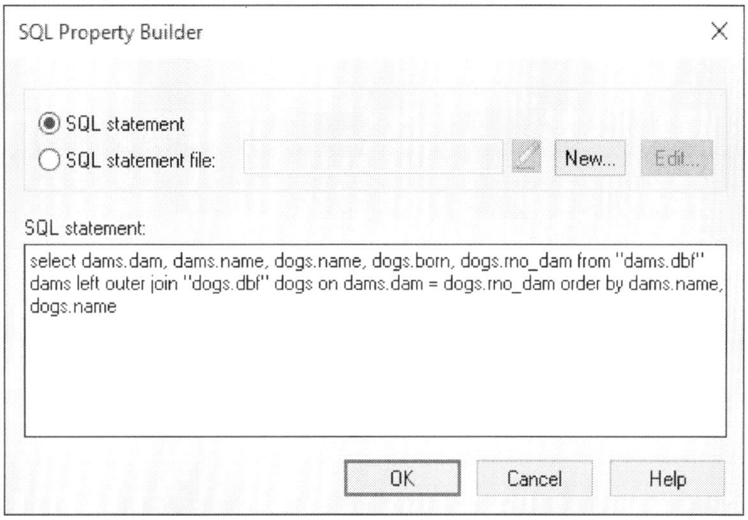

Figure 11-16

Notice that while the statement wraps in the dialog it is one statement. Once you have this entered, click the "OK" button. Obviously dBASE can't show the full statement in the Inspector, but you can view this at any time by clicking on the tool button of the *sql* property of the query.

We need to set one last property – the *active* property – we need the query to be active, so set this to *true*. Now the report shows all the detailBands needed for each row in the virtual table created by this join.

Indeed, if you view the Field Palette, you will see just the fields that were selected, and it shows as "Query1".

We can now create the same sort of grouped report that we did for the first report. Let's place a *group* onto the report (select the "Report" tab of the Component Palette and place it on the report). While the *group* object has focus in the Inspector (if it doesn't, select "group1" from the drop-down list), select the *groupBy* property and set it to "dam", and set the *headerEveryFrame* property to *true*.

The following will seem very familiar, but here we go. Go to the Component Palette and select the "Custom" tab, select a "DataHeadingText" control and place it on the group *headerBand*. Delete the text that says "Header Text for Group 1". Change the text of the "DataHeadingText" to "Dam:", and set the *fontBold* property to *true*.

Next select from the Component Palette a "DataText" control, and place it on the *headerBand* to the right of the heading text. In the Inspector set the *text* property to type "Codeblock", click the tool button and enter:

```
this.form.query1.rowset.fields["name"].value
```

How do we know if we should use "name" or "name_1"? This may not be obvious, but if, in a sql select statement there are two fields with the same name, how can you tell them apart? dBASE has to make a decision, and for the purpose of working with these the first field of the same name does not have a number, the second one is given a number 1, with the underscore separator (hence we get "name_1"), and if there were a third, it would be given the number 2, in the same way, and so on. If you look at the sql statement, the first "name" field is from the dams table (it is defined as "dams.name" in the statement).

To continue this report, in the *detailBand* we will place the name and date of birth fields. Select a "DataColHeadingText" control, and place it on the *detailBand* and change the text to "Name". Repeat this, changing the text to "Born".

Select a "DataText" control and place it under the "Name" heading. Set the *text* property's type to "Codeblock", click the tool button and enter:

```
this.form.query1.rowset.fields["name_1"].value
```

Repeat for the second column, and set the text in the codeblock editor to:

```
this.form.query1.rowset.fields["born"].value
```

You will want to work on lining the text controls up a little, widen the name text, and so on, so that your report looks good. When run, this report should similar to:

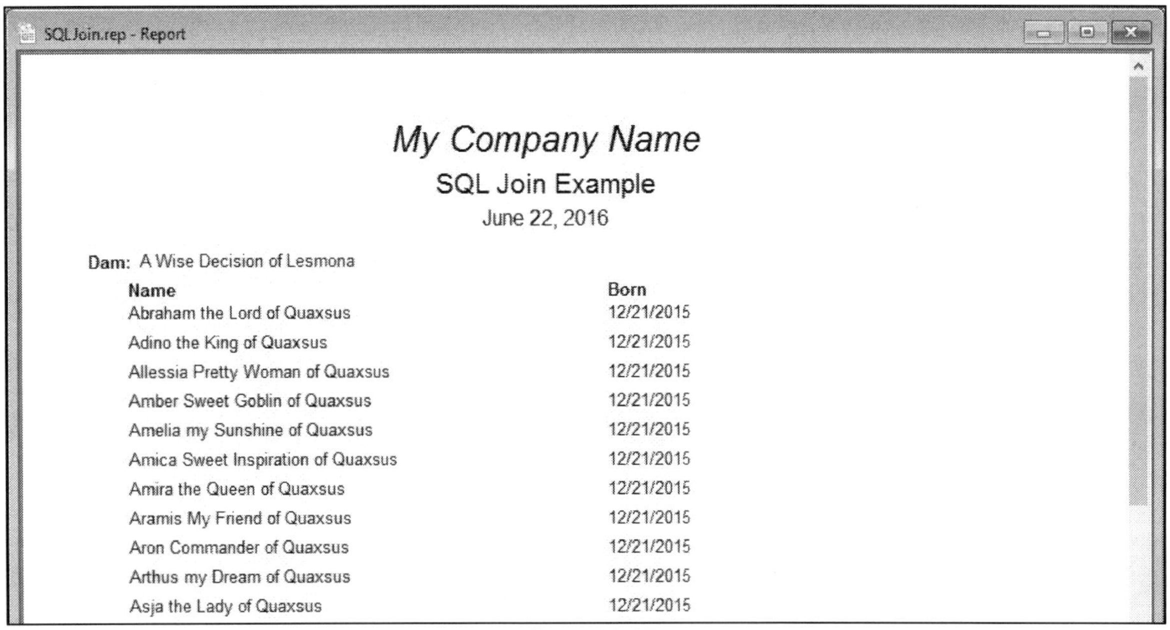

Figure 11-17

Break Across Pages

One thing you will see if you look at this report, is that when a break goes across pages, it is sometimes hard to tell if the header is for a "new" instance of the Dam (in this case) or if it is a continuation of the data for that Dam. One thing that we can do is to check to see if this is a continuation from the previous page, and alert the person reading the report that this is a continuation.

In the Command Window type the following:

```
copy file SQLJoin.rep to Continued.rep
```

Right click on the new report in the Navigator, select "Open in Source Code Editor", and change the following code:

```
local r
r = new ContinuedReport()
r.render()

class ContinuedReport of MyCompanyReportCReport from :MyReports:MyCompanyReport.crp
```

Open the report in the Report Designer. Click on the group1 *headerBand* (the green band at the top of the report), and in the Inspector select the "Events" tab. Find the *preRender* event handler, click the tool button, and enter the following code:

```
function HEADERBAND_preRender()
   // check to see if custom property exists, if not create it:
   if type( "this.BreakField" ) == "U"
      this.BreakField = "XXX" // value not in table
   endif
   // this = headerBand
   // parent = group1
   // parent = streamSource1
   f = this.parent.parent.rowset.fields
   this.DataText1.text := f["Name"].value.rightTrim()
   if this.BreakField == f["Name"].value.rightTrim()
      // add extra text: the word
      // "(Continued ...)" in italics
      this.DataText1.text += " <i>(Continued ...)</i>"
   endif
return
```

This code will check to see if a custom property of the *headerBand* object ("BreakField") exists, and if not, create it with a dummy value. Then it will compare the value agains the current field. If they match we will add the word "(Continued ...)" in italics *(using HTML tags – discussed in a later chapter in a little more detail)*.

When you have this code, we also need to use the *onRender* event for the *headerBand* to set the value of the custom field:

```
function HEADERBAND_onRender()
   f = this.parent.parent.rowset.fields
   this.BreakField = f["Dam"].value.rightTrim()
return
```

Run the code, and you should see on the first page that at the bottom, the group is not complete. If you then go to the top of the second page, you should see:

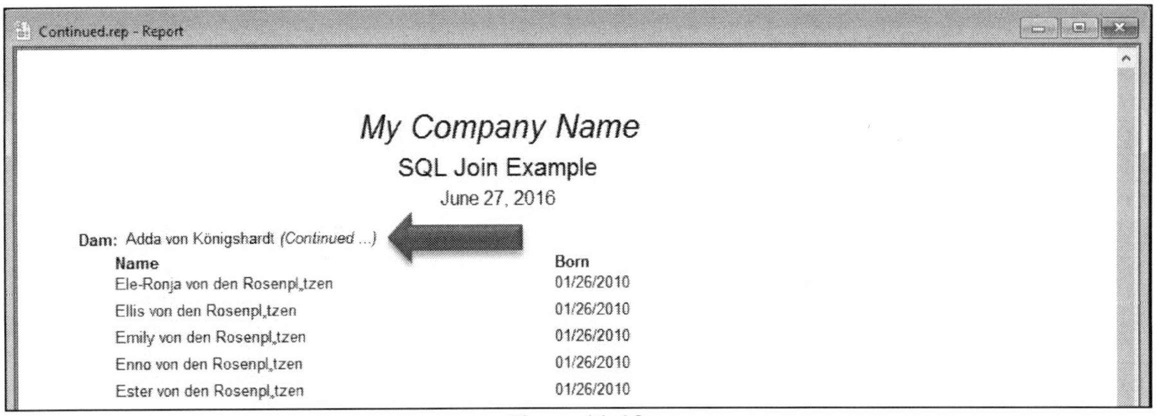

Figure 11-18

There is of course more that can be done. We will look at page breaks for reports in a later chapter of this book. The idea for this came from a discussion with Mervyn Bick when he was helping me figure out an issue with a different report.

Duplicate Values

If you look at the report shown in Figure 11-18, you will see that the date "born" for several of the dogs are identical – this of course in the dog breeding world would assume the same litter. One thing that we can do, that is only briefly discussed in Chapter 2, is tell dBASE that when there are duplicate values, to only show the first one.

Open this report back in the Report Designer, click on the text control that shows the birth date. In the Inspector find the *suppressIfDuplicate* property, and change the setting to *true*. You may see an immediate effect, but even if you do not, when you run the report again, you should see it:

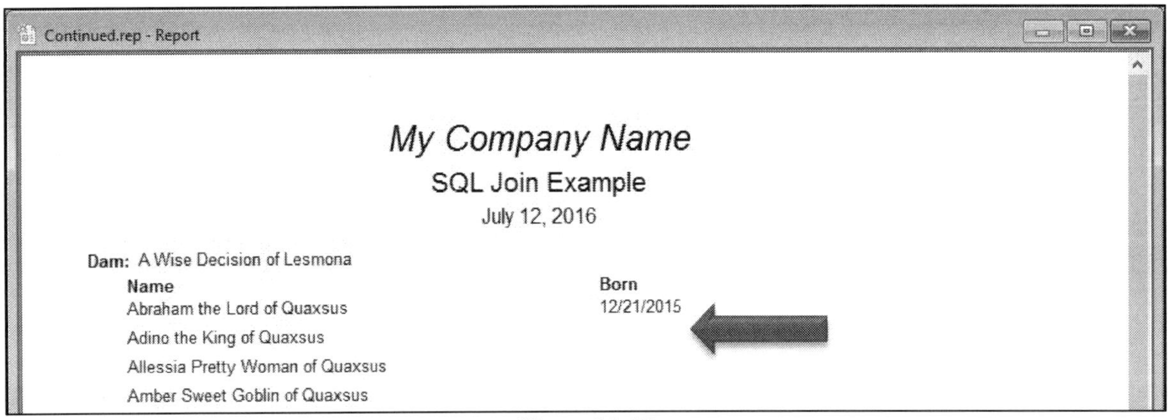

Figure 11-19

Temporary Tables

There are times when working with reports that you have a fairly complex set of tables, and in order to generate a report it seems like it would be easier to work with a single table or "flat file" (although with SQL Joins, or the ability with the data objects in dBASE, and/or the Data Module Designer, you can create reports from a complex set of related tables – sometimes the logic boggles the mind). There are many ways to do this, we'll take a look at a couple. Michael Nuwer explains this well in his tutorial (which use data modules heavily throughout):

> Using a data module has the advantage of reusability. Any methods, calculated fields, lookup fields, etc. that are created for a form can be reused in a report.
>
> The disadvantage of using a data module with a report is that the Report Designer doesn't handle parent-child-grandchild relations very well. Additionally, the Report Designer doesn't handle interleaved data very well, where a Parent table has two Children. For example, an accounting application might store charges in one table and payments in a separate table. To print a Customer statement we need to merge or interleave the charges and payments by date.
>
> An alternative to the data module approach is to use a single SQL query that joins all the tables. ... One disadvantage of an SQL query is that you lose the ability to use your dBASE indexes. In particular, those indexes that use multiple fields or functions cannot be used.

Building Your Own

This is a technique I've used for some applications because it is how my mind works. What is required is a program that does several things – the basics are that it empties out a table specifically designed for a report, and then it loops through the data and adds records as needed, filling in appropriate data.

An example would be to create yet another report similar to what we did at both the beginning of this chapter, and in the SQL Join section. However, rather than use either of those techniques, we will create a new table for the purposes of the report, and then in a program we will populate the table with data from the two tables as necessary. The idea is to see how this can be done, so you can apply it to your own applications if/when needed.

To get started, we need to determine what fields we need for the report.

We have the name of the DAM, and we need the name of each of those born of the dam, and the birth date. This is fairly simple, really.

The table would be structured like this (this is by looking at the table structures of the two tables we need to pull data from):

DamName	Character	60
ChildName	Character	60
Birthdate	Date	8

For some reports this of course could get much more complex *(indeed, the cases that I need to do this for contain many fields pulled from several tables ...)*.

Once you know what the data should look like, there are several approaches you might want to take for handling the report. If your application is used only by one person (or only on a single computer), you could create a table that has the same name all the time for the purpose of the report, and never have any problems – you would simply empty the table before doing anything else. However, if your application is one that might be used by several people on a network and the tables are on the network, you might find that two or more people might want to generate a report using your report table at the same time. This could get awkward. There are at least two ways to deal with this:

- Create a table with the structure you need, and copy the table to a temporary file each time for the report, and erase it when the report is done.
- Create the table needed for the report "on the fly" — in code and erase it when the report is done.

We will assume for our report that there may be multiple users, but we will use the first technique shown - the second has a lot of difficulties behind it, and it is easier to work with the first. The technique below ensures a unique table name, which means that the user should not experience any problems with someone else using the same table at the same time.

In the "dBASEReports" database, there is a table called "ReportTemplate". (In the Navigator click on the "Tables" tab.) Take a quick look at this in the table designer by right clicking on it and selecting "Design Table". You should see:

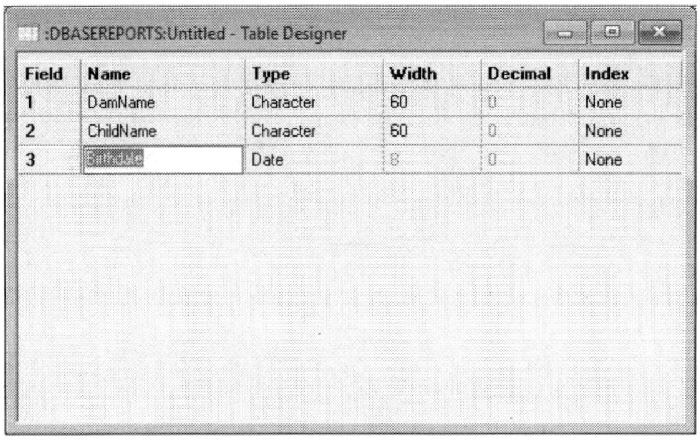

Figure 11-20

Exit the table designer without modifying the table.

To create this program click on the "Programs" tab of the Navigator, and double-click on the "[New Program]" icon. This will bring up the Source Code Editor - enter the code below. Save this as "TempTableReport1.prg".

```
// Create a temporary table for a report
clear

// set up a database object:
local oData
oData = new database()
oData.databaseName := "DBASEREPORTS"
oData.active := true

/*
   ************************************************************
   If you are using dBASE Plus 8 or later, we do not need the
   code below for the BDE Alias to obtain the path to the
   folder referenced by the alias. Instead we can use the
   Database Alias created back in Chapter 3 ...
   ************************************************************
```

```
*/
nVersion = __version__
if nVersion < 8

   // set up a BDE Alias object briefly so we can
   // get the path to the folder with the tables -
   // this is necessary for the FUNIQUE() function
   // to work properly.
   set procedure to :dUFLP:BDEAlias.cc
   local oBDE, cPath
   // create an instance of the object:
   oBDE = new BDEAlias()
   // get the path to the folder:
   cPath = oBDE.databaseDir( "DBASEREPORTS" )
   // clean up memory:
   release object oBDE
   oBDE := null
   close procedure :dUFLP:BDEAlias.cc

else  // current versions of dBASE

   // in 'current' versions of dBASE, using the User BDE Alias,
   // the path is stored in the PLUS.INI file, so we need to read
   // the data from there ... we'll use the INI.cc file in the
   // dUFLP instead:
   set procedure to :dUFLP:INI.cc
   local oINI, cPath
   // instance of the INI object with the path to the
   // file from the app object in dBASE
   oINI = new ini( _app.iniFile )
   // find the value we need:
   cPath = oINI.GetValue( "dBASEReports", "Options" )
   // remove "PATH:" from beginning
   cPath = right( cPath, len( cPath ) - 5 )
   // cleanup
   release object oINI
   oINI := null
   close procedure :dUFLP:INI.cc
endif

// The path returned does not include a trailing
// backslash character:
cPath += "\"

// The FUNIQUE function is used to create a unique
// filename, using wildcards for the characters you
// need. For example, here we.re going to call the
// file: "REPnnnnn.dbf" where the first three letters
// are "REP", the "nnnnn" will be randomly created
// by the function, and the file extension is specified
// as ".dbf". What we need to do is make sure that the
// filename as returned by FUNIQUE does not exist:
local cFile
do while true // infinite loop
   // create a filename:
   cFile = funique( cPath+"REP?????.dbf" )
   // if the table does not exist, exit the loop
```

```
      if not oData.tableExists( cFile )
         exit
      endif
   enddo

   // if we're here we have a unique filename.
   // we must create the table. To do this we will
   // build the command as a character string, and
   // then use the database object to create the table:
   local cTable
   // get just the table name from the path/file string:
   cTable = right( cFile, len( cFile ) - rat( "\", cFile ) )

   // and remove the ".dbf" at the end, because
   // the CREATE TABLE command will create a file
   // called "dbf" if that's there, which is not
   // what we want:
   cTable = left( cTable, at( ".", cTable ) -1 )

   // tell the data object to copy the template table
   // to the temporary table name:
   oData.copyTable( "ReportTemplate", cTable )

   // now we have the temporary table, we can put
   // data into it. This requires setting up
   // the query objects for the tables:
   local qDams, qDogs, qTemp
   qDams = new query()
   qDams.database := oData
   qDams.sql := "select * from dams"
   qDams.active := true
   qDams.rowset.indexName := "NAME"

   qDogs = new query()
   qDogs.database := oData
   qDogs.sql := "select * from dogs"
   qDogs.active := true
   qDogs.rowset.indexName := "DAM"
   qDogs.rowset.masterRowset := qDams.rowset
   qDogs.rowset.masterFields := "DAM"

   qTemp = new query()
   qTemp.database := oData
   qTemp.sql := "select * from "+cTable
   qTemp.active := true

   // now that we have the query objects set,
   // we need to loop through the data, and
   // add rows to the temporary table:
   qDams.rowset.first()
   do while not qDams.rowset.endOfSet
      // output so we know *something* is happening:
      ?
      ? qDams.rowset.fields["NAME"].value

      // inner loop for the child rowset - dogs:
      qDogs.rowset.first()
```

```
   do while not qDogs.rowset.endOfSet
      // output:
      ? " "+qDogs.rowset.fields["NAME"].value

      // for each row in the DOGS table we need
      // a row in the temp table:
      qTemp.rowset.beginAppend()
      // name of the dam:
      qTemp.rowset.fields["DamName"].value := ;
              qDams.rowset.fields["NAME"].value
      // name of the child/dog:
      qTemp.rowset.fields["ChildName"].value := ;
              qDogs.rowset.fields["NAME"].value
      // birthdate of the dog:
      qTemp.rowset.fields["BirthDate"].value := ;
              qDogs.rowset.fields["BORN"].value
      // make sure we save this!
      qTemp.rowset.save()
      // next row in the Dogs table:
      qDogs.rowset.next()
   enddo

   // next row in the Dams table:
   qDams.rowset.next()
enddo

// output:
?
? "** Done building temporary table!"

// we're done building the temporary table!
// code will be added here to generate
// and display the report ...

// cleanup -- we want to delete the temporary table,
// but to do that we must remove references to it:
qTemp.active := false
release object qTemp
qTemp = null
// delete the table:
//oData.dropTable( cTable )

// remove references to the other tables:
qDogs.active := false
release object qDogs
qDogs = null
qDams.active := false
release object qDams
qDams = null

// and finally get rid of the database object:
oData.active := false
release object oData
oData = null
```

> **NOTE**
> If you downloaded the source code and tables for the book, this program should be there (in the Chapter 11 folder) as "TempTableReport1.prg". Rather than typing it up, you could just use the existing version.

That was a lot of typing. If you read the comments, this should be pretty self-explanatory. The output that is shown in the Command Window is just so that you know in the loop where the processing is, and when it is complete. In a fully functioning application it would be better to display a message type form that shows the user what is happening, possibly with a progress bar on it, and so on. Our focus is on reports, however, so we're not going to do the message form here.

Note that the command to erase the table has been commented out – this is because we need an instance of the table to create the report that will use it. The code that is necessary to run and display the report has not been placed in the code above, either. We will come back to all of this after we've created our report.

To run this program, double-click on the file name in the Navigator, or in the Command Window, type:

```
do TempTableReport1
```

This will create a temporary table with the data combined from the two tables – again, the file will be named something *like* "Rep47039.dbf" – you should note the table name as you will need it when creating the report.

Next we need to create the report. Much of this will be quite familiar at this point, but there will be some special changes added to the report for everything to work properly.

Create a new report, and making sure we're using the usual custom report. Change the secondary heading text control to read "Temporary Table Report". Save the report as "TemporaryTable".

We're going to manually place a database object and a query object on the report designer surface from the Component Palette and set the properties by hand. Go to the Component Palette, select the "Data Access" tab, and find the "Database" object. Place it on the design surface. Select the *databaseName* property in the Inspector window, and in the drop down list, find "DBASEREPORTS" and select it. Set the *active* property to *true*.

Next go back to the Component Palette, and select the "Query" object, placing it on the design surface. This next part is tricky, because we need the temporary table to design the report, but ultimately we want to be able to change the table name each time the report is run.

Set the *sql* property to:

```
select * from Rep47039.dbf
```

Be sure to use your table's name instead of "Rep47039.dbf" –the numbers are randomly generated, the name of the file will be different each time.

> **NOTE**
> We are using the temporary table because it has data in it. We could use the Template table, but because it does not have data we cannot see the results of the report in the designer to make sure the report acts correctly and displays the data we want to see.

Press the Enter key, or this string will not be saved in the Inspector.

Set the *active* property to *true*. The report should now show lots of detailBands, because there is quite a bit of data.

For this report we need a group for the Dam names, so go to the Component Palette, select the "Report" tab, and select a *group* object and place it on the design surface. In the Inspector window, the group has focus, set the *groupBy* property to "DamName", and then set the *headerEveryFrame* property to *true*.

Go back to the Component Palette, select the "Custom" tab, and place a "DataHeadingText" control on the group *headerBand* (the green band). Delete the default text that reads "Header Text for Group 1" (click on it and use the Del key ...). Move the heading text control to the left (in the Inspector you can set the *top* and *left* properties to 0, or you can use the mouse to move it ...). Change the text to: "Dam:".

Next place a "DataText" control on the band to the right of the heading text and line it up a bit. You will want to make it wider as well. As we've done before, we need to change the *text* property to a type of "Codeblock", use the tool button and enter this in the dialog:

```
this.form.query1.rowset.fields["damname"].value
```

And again as we've done before, we want to set up the *detailBand* by doing the following:

Select a "DataColHeadingText" control and place it on the *detailBand*, and then place another to the right of it. Change the text of the first one to "Name", and the text of the second to "Birth Date".

Select two "DataText" controls, and place these under the column headings. Set the *text* property of the first to a codeblock, use the tool button and in the dialog enter:

```
this.form.query1.rowset.fields["childname"].value
```

For the second "DataText" control also set the *text* property to a codeblock, use the tool button and enter:

```
this.form.query1.rowset.fields["birthdate"].value
```

You will want to widen the name field, and shift the birthdate controls over to the right. This report should look something like:

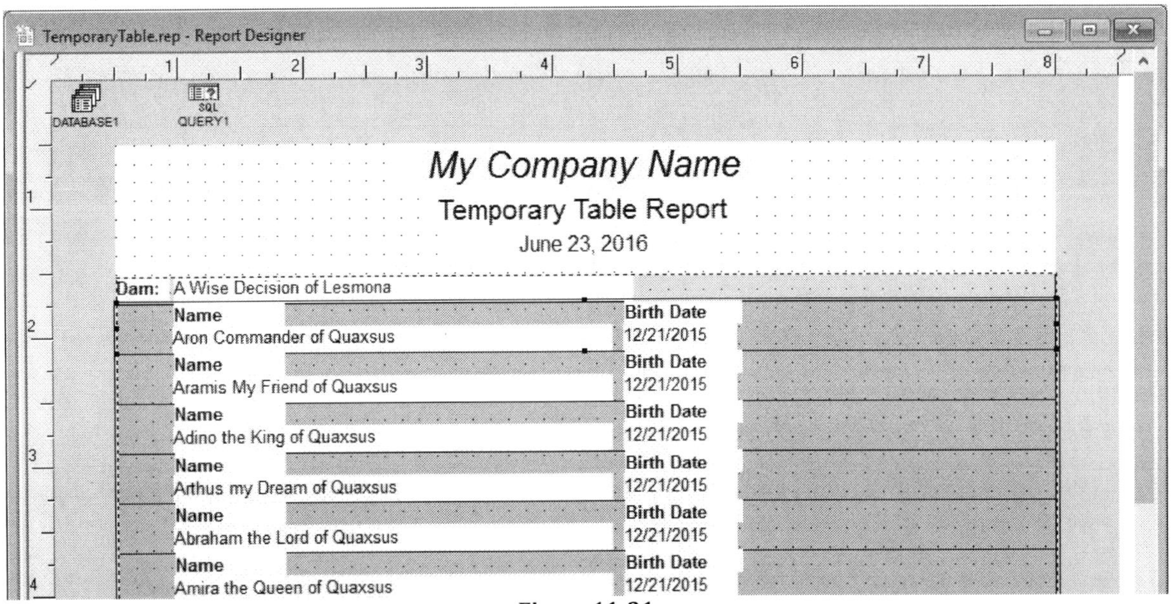

Figure 11-21

When you run this the column headings will show properly, and the report will look very much like others we have done. The one difficulty is that the table this is based on may not exist by that name, ever again – remember this is a temporary table. What do we have to do to solve this?

Well, there are a couple of things. In the report itself, as the ReportTemplate table should always exist, we need to modify the Query object's *sql* property to point to this table. That way, if it becomes necessary to bring the report back into the designer, you will not get an error. To do this, give the query object ("QUERY1") focus (either by clicking on it, or by selecting it in the Inspector window's combobox/drop-down). Select the *sql* property, and change it to:

```
select * from ReportTemplate
```

The display changes rather dramatically, as the table is empty.

Save this and exit the Report Designer. We need to now modify that program we created earlier.

In the Navigator, select the "Programs" tab, and then select the program "TempTableReport1". Right-click and select "Open in Source Editor". Find the comments in the code that look like:

```
// we're done building the temporary table!
// code will be added here to generate
// and display the report ...
```

Let's save this under a new filename before we go too far – this will be the final version, but by saving it under a new name we keep the original in case we wanted to do something with it. To do that, click on the "File" menu and select "Save As ...". Change the filename to: "TempTableReport2.prg".

What we need to do is modify the Query object's SQL property. However, before we do that we should create an instance of the report. So, add the following code after the comments shown above:

```
set procedure to TemporaryTable.rep additive
local oRep
oRep = new TemporaryTableReport()

// we have an instance of the report, now
// let's change the Query1 object's SQL property:
oRep.Query1.sql := "select * from "+cTable

// at this point, if we render this, the temporary
// table will be deleted, perhaps before we want it
// to. Instead, we will use the Preview form from
// the dUFLP (as shown in the previous chapter):
set procedure to :dUFLP:Preview.wfm additive
oPF = new PreviewForm()
oPF.Viewer.ref := oRep
oPF.bModal = true
oPF.readModal()

// when this screen is closed, then we can
// move on and do our cleanup:
oPF.release()
close procedure :dUFLP:Preview.wfm
oRep.release()
```

And finally, we can uncomment (remove the comment marker characters "//") from the statement that deletes the temporary table itself:

```
// delete the table:
oData.dropTable( cTable )
```

Save the program and exit the Source Code Editor (Ctrl+W works well for this).

Before running this program, go to the Navigator, and click on the "Tables" tab. See if you have any tables that appear with the letters "Rep" followed by some numbers (you should have one). If so, click on them (one at a time) and press the Del key. You'll be asked to confirm deletion, but this way you have cleaned up your temporary tables.

Now run the program, and you should see something like:

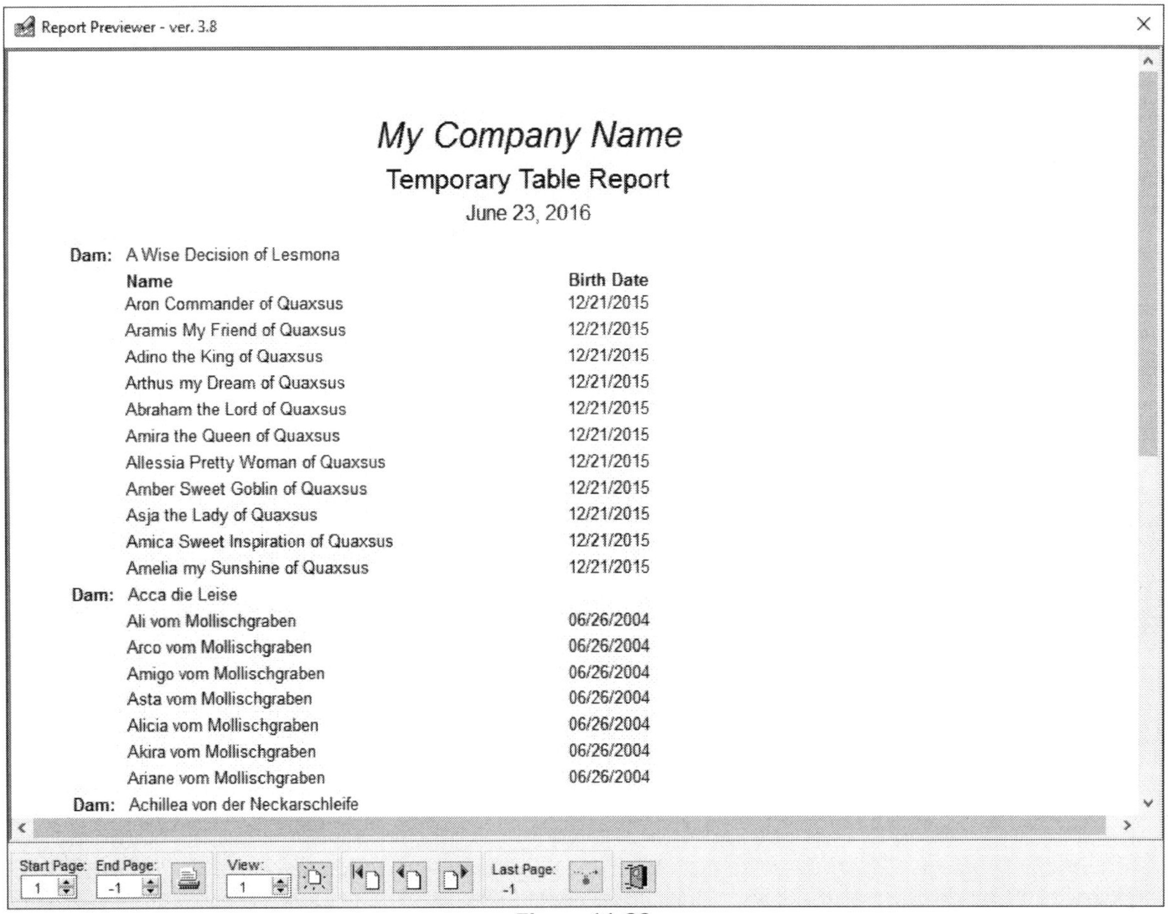

Figure 11-22

You can print this (it's fairly lengthy), or you can just close the preview window. When you close this screen, your code will delete the temporary table that it created, and do the other "cleanup" shown, and then it will be done.

Other Methods

It is possible to create reports with multiple tables in other ways, including Todd Kreuter's TmpQuery.cc, which is in the dUFLP – this creates the temporary query for the report for you. Michael Nuwer's report tutorial discusses this in session VIII, if you wish to examine it.

Cleanup

Create a new report (in the Navigator, click on the .Reports. tab, double-click on the "[New Report]" icon). Select the "File" menu, select "Set Custom Report Class", and in the dialog, click the "Clear Custom Report" button, then click "OK". This clears out the custom report setting in the Plus.ini file, so that the next report you create is not based on this one. Close that report without making any changes.

Make sure the database is closed by going to the Command Window and typing:

```
close databases
```

This will also ensure that you don't end up creating tables in the wrong location, etc.

Source Code

The following is a listing of the sample code in the folders we have been working with. If you downloaded the files from my website the structure will be different (see below). You may use the code contained in these folders for your own applications if you desire, with the caveat that credit be given appropriately.

From working on this chapter:

```
C:\dBASEReports\Chapter 11\Continued.rep
C:\dBASEReports\Chapter 11\Invoice.dmd
C:\dBASEReports\Chapter 11\Invoice.rep
C:\dBASEReports\Chapter 11\SQLJoin.rep
C:\dBASEReports\Chapter 11\Subgroup.rep
C:\dBASEReports\Chapter 11\TemporaryTable.rep
C:\dBASEReports\Chapter 11\TempTableReport1.prg
C:\dBASEReports\Chapter 11\TempTableReport2.prg
```

And a table in the dBASEReports database: ReportTemplate.dbf

Downloaded version – same files but with this path:

```
C:\ReportsBookSourceCode\Chapter 11\filename
```

Summary

Multiple tables can give a programmer or application developer a headache, especially when it comes to reports. Hopefully this chapter has given you a good start at working with them. This chapter does not cover everything that might be needed or possible by a developer.

There have been questions on the dBASE newsgroups about having two separate page layouts, one for one table, and another for another, and having dBASE go back and forth between them, and a variety of other issues of that nature. Some things the Report Designer and Report Engine were not designed to handle, and you may need multiple reports for them.

The next chapter will expand on what we've done here, looking at totals and accumulated values that can be used in *group footerBands*, report *footerBands*, running totals, and more.

Chapter 12: Counting, Accumulating and Running Totals

dBASE has built into the Report Designer and Report Engine the ability to perform some basic mathematical functions that we might need for our reports, such as counting values, averaging values, and getting totals of some fields. These can be done for a group and/or for the whole report.

There are times that we might need to do more, however, or do things that are not as simple and straightforward as the built-in functionality.

In this chapter we will take a look at using both the built-in calculations, but also how to expand our abilities by creating running totals, and more.

A Place for Our Work

As we work through the chapter we will be needing a place for the files we create, so please create a folder for this chapter:

```
C:\dBASEReports\Chapter 12
```

And in the Navigator, be sure to navigate to this folder.

Aggregate Summaries

The aggregate calculations or summaries in dBASE's reporting engine are calculations designed to act on a group of records – either by groups (grouped reports as we did in the previous chapter), or for the whole report. The options for the built-in calculations are:

agAverage()	calculate the average value of a numeric field
agCount()	count the number of records
agMax()	find the largest value in a numeric field
agMin()	find the smallest value in a numeric field
agStandardDeviation()	calculate the standard deviation of a numeric field
agSum()	total a numeric field
agVariance()	calculate the variance of a numeric field

Of course, the usefulness of each of these depends on the data, and the purpose of your report. For example, if you are displaying within a group of records, only text fields, then anything that works on a numeric value is not going to be all that useful.

How do you use these? I find that in order to place these calculations onto a report, it is often easier to use the built-in dialog in dBASE, because the syntax for them is fairly complex.

One difficulty was touched on briefly in the previous chapter, in the Invoice report – when using multiple tables for a report the aggregate summary calculations only seem to work with the parent table. What I mean by this is if the report has a group on a

Customer record, so that the *detailBand* shows just the child records in the OrderItems table, in the group's *footerBand* you cannot total the extended price (for example), because the extended price is not in the parent table. This is why we used a running total for the subtotal as shown in that report.

The aggregate functions are really only useful when grouping in a single table or for use with the parent table. They can be very useful in those particular situations.

Copy the SQL Join example from the previous chapter by going to the Command Window in dBASE, and typing:

```
copy file "..\Chapter 11\SQLJoin.rep" to AgSum.rep
```

Open the report in the Source Code Editor (right click, select Open in Source Editor), and modify the report class name:

```
local r
r = new AGSumReport()
r.render()

class AGSumReport of MyCompanyReportCReport from :MyReports:MyCompanyReport.crp
```

Save and exit the Source Code Editor (Ctrl+W). This ensures that dBASE does not confuse these two reports in memory.

Bring this report into the Report Designer.

In order to work with the aggregate summaries we need to work with the group's *footerBand*. However, if we do this correctly, the *footerBand* will be set up for us, and we will only need to modify things a little bit as we go.

To place an aggregate summary calculation on the design surface, we should go to the "Layout" menu, and select "Add Groups and Summaries ...". This will bring up the dialog we've examined in the past - we need to click on "Summaries" which will allow us to select the option we need. We want a count of the offspring of the specific Dam, so to get this information, select the "Name_1" field, and in the combobox at the bottom (left) of the screen, select "Count". Click the button with the ">" symbol on it, and you should see this:

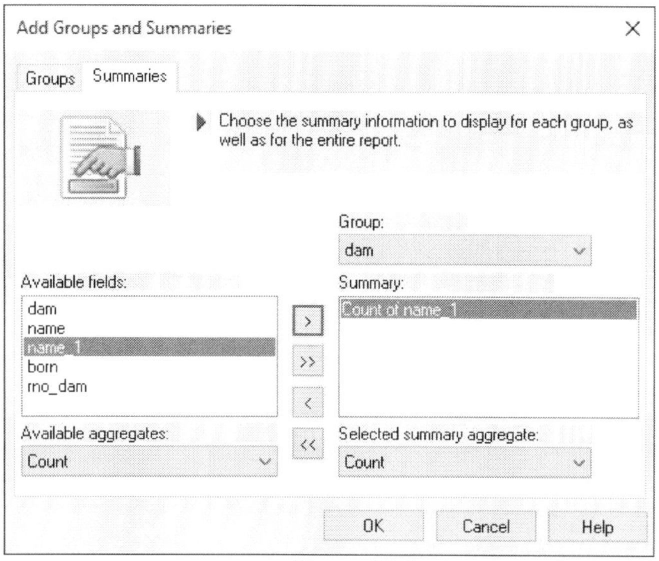

Figure 12-1

Click "OK", and the report should now show a *footerBand*, with two text controls on it:

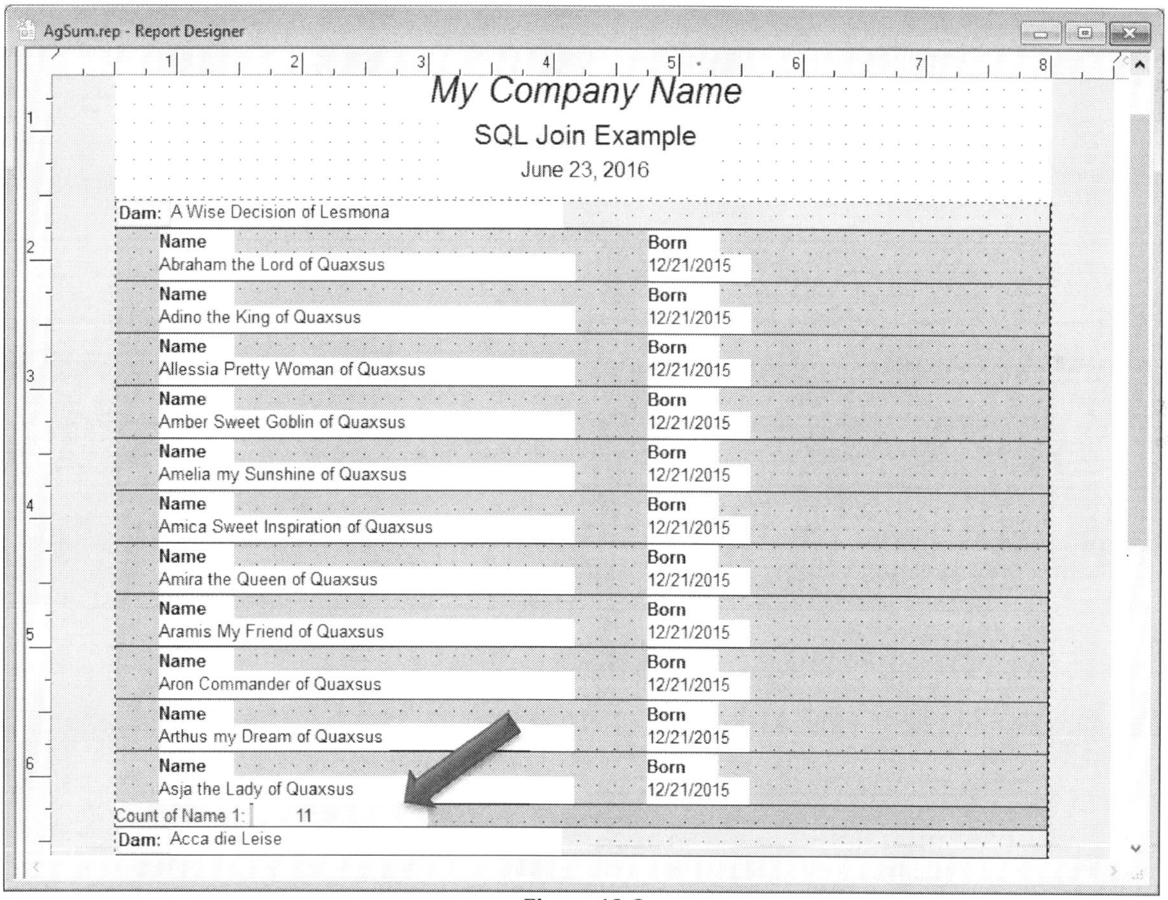

Figure 12-2

(I had to scroll down a little in the designer to show this ...) Just above the second Dam name you should see "Count of Name_1" and the number 11. The *footerBand* is a bluish-purple color, and the text itself is blue. While the *footerBand* color is only shown in the Report Designer, we probably want to change the color of the text. We could force

the use of our custom controls, but for now the important thing is to get used to working with these calculations.

Click on the first control, then hold the mouse down and click on the second. In the Inspector select the *colorNormal* property, and set the color to: "BtnText/BtnFace" (which is what the other text controls are using for this property). Click on any control on the screen to take focus off these two controls, then click on the first text control to give it focus. We want to change the text to something more useful than "Count of Name_1" – click again to place the control into edit mode, and delete the text there, changing it to:

Total Children:

Next go to the Inspector and set the *fontBold* property to *true*. You might want to shift these two controls a bit to the right, to show that they are part of this group, and not a new Dam name, or something.

Before we run the report, we should look at what the *text* property for the calculation shows us. Click on the text that shows the number of children, and then go to the Inspector. Find the *text* property. If you examine it (it will take some scrolling) you will see:

```
{||this.parent.parent.agCount({||this.parent.rowset.fields["name_1"].value})}
```

The calculation is the "agCount" function, and notice that it's being told what field to count.

If you run the report it should now look like:

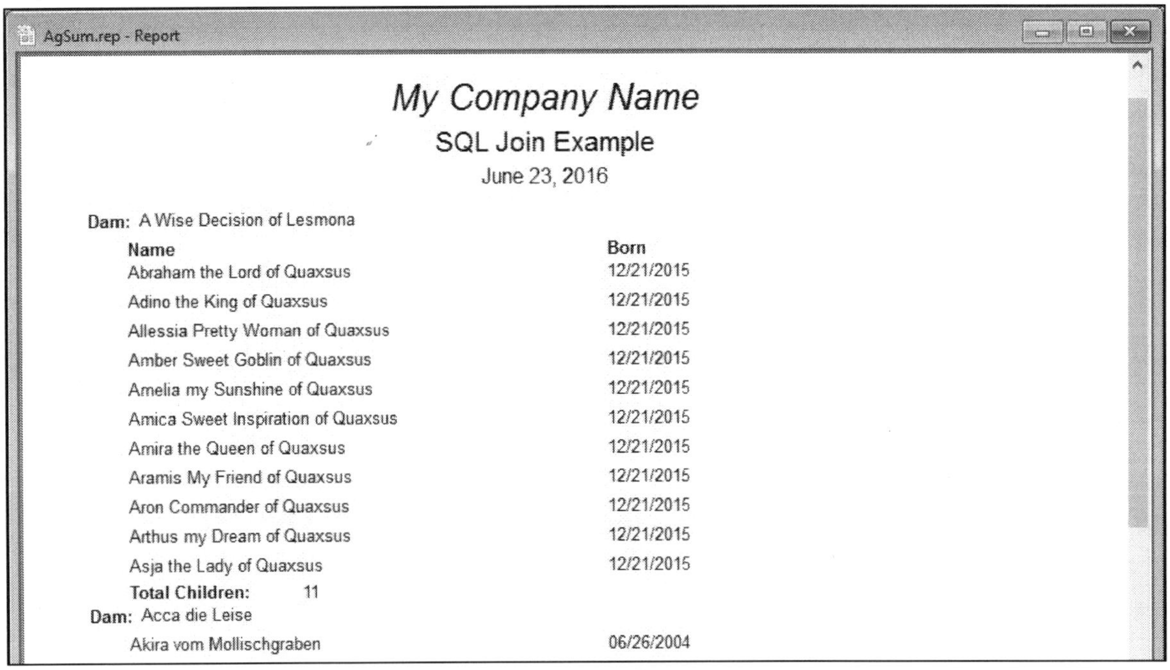

Figure 12-3

We could spend a lot of time working on cleaning this up a bit, and so on, but let's move on. We've added a count, and because of the data that we have, that's all we really can do. If we had a numeric value we could do totals, averages, and more.

However, we can add more totals for the whole report – adding totals at the end of the report in a similar fashion to what we just did. To do that, we need to first return to the Report Designer (the simplest is to use the "Design Report" tool button in the dBASE toolbar).

Because the Report Designer tends to show all data, it is sometimes a good idea for a report where you are working on the *reportGroup's footerBand* to do the following:

1. Right click anywhere on the Report Design surface.
2. Select "Report Designer Properties".
3. In the dialog that appears, find the section titled "Rowset display", and select "One row".
4. Click "OK".

Note that the Report Designer is now showing one record only. This is useful, because we want to add the *reportGroup's footerBand* with totals, and to work on this would normally require us to scroll through the report to the last page (using the PgDn key), which for a large amount of data can take some time. This is a lot faster!

Now we want to go to the "Layout" menu, and select the "Add Groups and Summaries ..." dialog again.

Click on the "Summaries" tab, and do the following:

1. On the left, select:
    a. Name
    b. "Count"
2. On the right, select (at the top):
    a. <Grand Summary>

So that the dialog looks like:

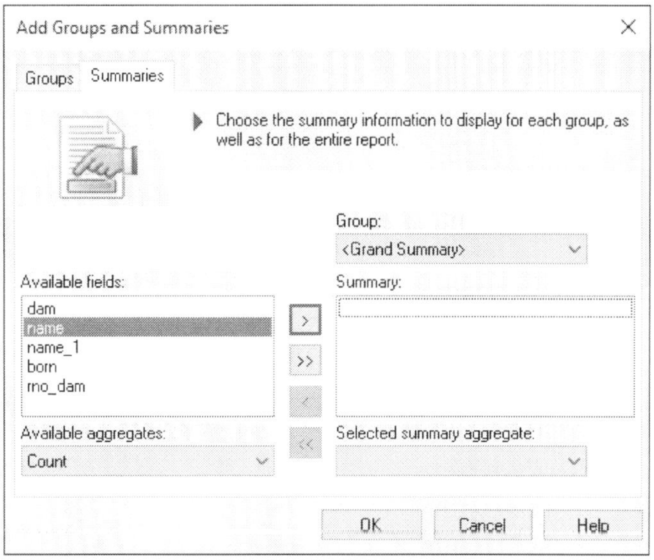

Figure 12-4

Click the ">" button, to add this to the list.

However, note that we are not done – we want to add another calculation:

- On the left, select:
    a. Name_1
    b. "Count"
- On the right, select (at the top):
    a. <Grand Summary>
- Click the ">" button, to add this to the list:

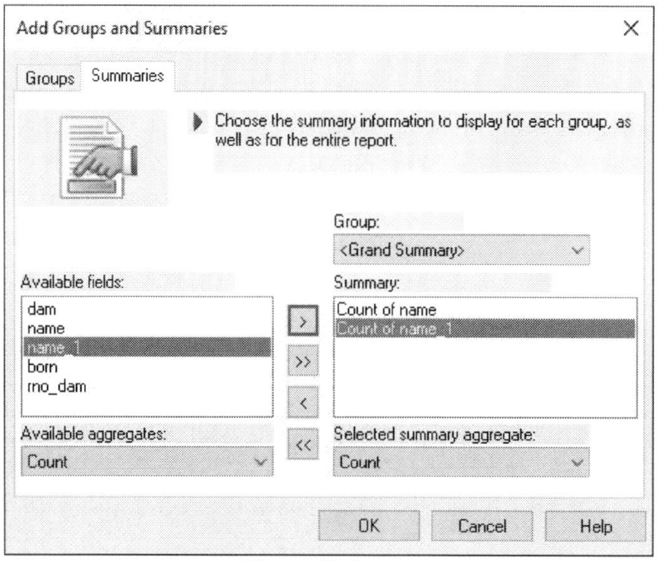

Figure 12-5

Now click "OK". One odd thing is that dBASE places all the different controls on top of each other, so we really need to deal with fixing this.

Select the two controls "on top" – the one that says "Grand summary: Count of Name_1" and the text control to the right that says "1" (click on the first, hold the Ctrl key and click on the second), and use the down arrow to nudge them down the page so that you can see all the text.

You should see two different totals, although at the moment they appear to be the same, since we're only showing one record.

First things first, let's set the colors of all four of these controls – select all four (as we did above), and in the Inspector, set the *colorNormal* property to: "BtnText/BtnFace" (don't enter the quotes). Again, this is the same color as the other controls. Click on some other control to take focus off this selection of text objects.

We want to change the text for the labels from something more useful than the default text created by the Report Designer. Click on the text that says "Grand summary: Count of Name", and then click again to place it in edit mode, and change the text to: "Report Total - Number of Dams:". Next click on the text control that says "Grand summary: Count of Name_1", click a second time to place it into edit mode, and change the text to: "Report Total - Number of Children:".

Select these two controls as we did before, and set the *fontBold* property to *true* in the Inspector. You may find you need to widen the second control a little, and perhaps move the two controls that have the actual totals in them to the right a little to make room.

To make all this look a bit better, you might want to set these same two controls with so that the text is lined up on the right. Click on both if necessary (if they don't currently have focus), and set the *alignHorizontal* property to "2 – Right" in the Inspector, then go to the toolbar and find the "Align Right" button, and select that. Click on the two totals (the numeric values) and line them up on the left by selecting the "Align Left" button. Your report should look something like:

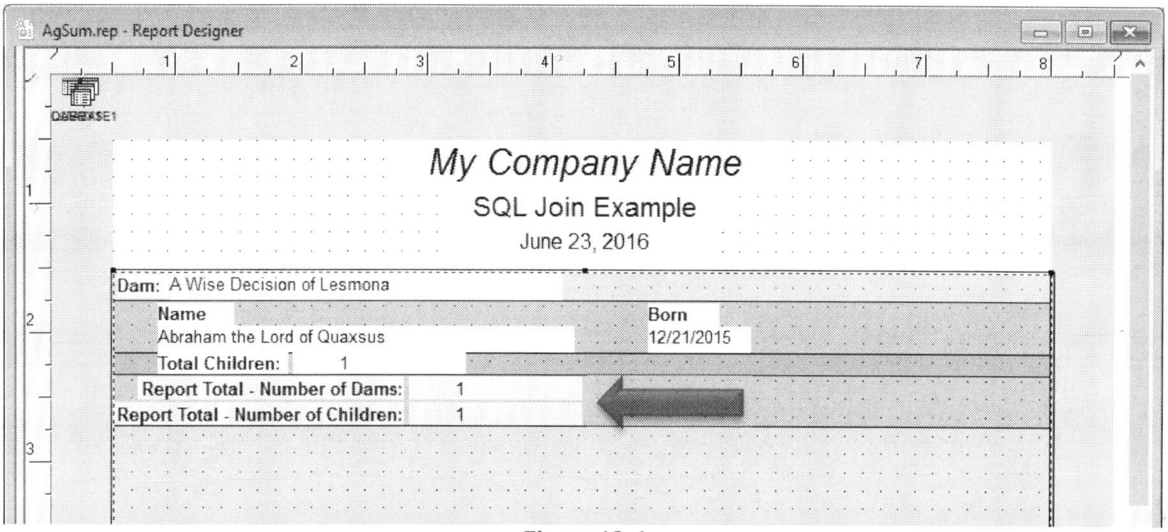

Figure 12-6

We could add lines and so on to make this look even better, but our focus right now is learning how all this works. Click on just the first numeric field (click on some other control to take focus off the two selected controls if they are still selected, then click back on just the first one) – the count of the number of Dams, and go to the *text* property in the inspector. You should see text like:

```
{||this.parent.parent.agCount({||this.parent.STREAMSOURCE1.rowset.fields["name"].value})}
```

When you run the report, you will not see these totals until you get to the last page of the report. As noted, with a lot of data, that's quite a bit of scrolling, but if you were to run this, and use the PgDn key to get to the last page of the report, it should look like:

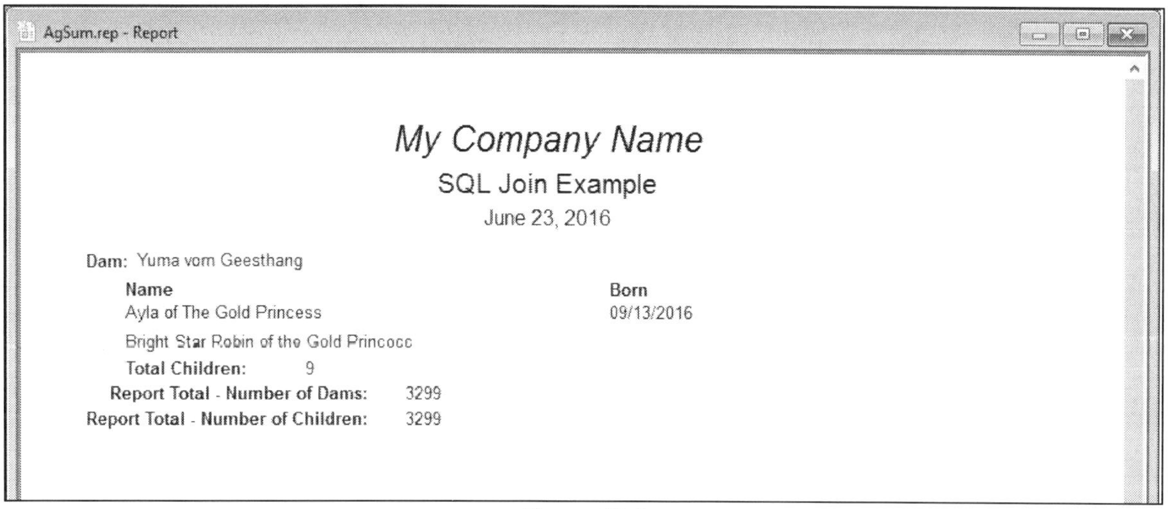

Figure 12-8

Now you will see that the number of Dams and the number of Children is the same – why is that? Well, even though we only *displayed* the Dams once for each group, there are actually 3299 records here, and that's what we told it to count. That's not all that useful, is it? We really want just the number of unique Dams in the final totals. This is because of the fact that we used the SQL Join to create our virtual table.

In order to get that, we are going to have to look at working with running totals. These take a bit more work, but can often provide more useful information than you are going to get with the built-in functions in dBASE.

Running Totals

Running totals are ones that are generated as the report is running, and can be set/reset as needed. To use them we have to define exactly what we want/need them to do.

In some cases, a running total is used to accumulate a value for the whole report (which is what we need to do for our report), and in others, it might be rendered and then reset to zero in each group *footerBand*, and so on. Much depends on what you need for your report. The great thing is that this is completely under your control.

We need to start a total of the number of Dams in the report, so each time the text in the group *headerBand* is rendered, we want to add to the total. When we get to the reportGroup's *footerBand*, we want to display the value. There's no need to set it back to zero, because it will only be rendered once, at the end of the report. One problem with this sort of running total – if, in a *reportViewer* screen you navigate backward, the total may be calculated incorrectly, as the controls are rendered multiple times, producing invalid results. When the report is sent to the printer, it should be fine, however, as the report will render each control only once.

In the Command Window, type the following to copy the report we've been working on:

```
copy file Agsum.rep to RunningTotal.rep
```

Open the new report in the Source Code Editor and change the text that is bold:

```
local r
r = new RunningTotalReport()
r.render()

class RunningTotalReport of MYCOMPANYREPORTCREPORT from :MyReports:MyCompanyReport.crp
```

Press Ctrl+W to save and exit the Source Code Editor.

Open the report into the Report Designer. Click on the total for the "Number of Dams". In the Inspector, select the *text* property, click on the "Type" ("T") button, and select "Numeric". This should set the value to zero, and remove the codeblock. Next we're going to set our focus on the group *headerBand*, and the text there. Select the text that shows the name of the Dam, and go to the Inspector again. You need to click on the "Events" tab, and select *onRender*, and click on the tool button. This will bring up the Source Code Editor, and some default code. We need to set this to the following:

```
function DATATEXT1_onRender()
   // add to Running Total for Dam if we have not already
   // printed the Dam name
   f = form.streamSource1.rowset.fields
   if form.DamName # f["Name"].value
      form.RT_DamCount++
      form.DamName := f["Name"].value
   endif
return
```

Notice that we have not created a custom report property (yet) called "RT_DamCount". We will be adding the necessary code shortly.

This code is more complex than it looks like it ought to be, but this is because we have the report set to render the Dam name at the top of a new page if the group gets split across pages (the group *headerBand*'s *beginNewFrame* is *true*), and because of this, if the Dam name is printed twice, it gets counted twice. By adding code to check for this, we can avoid that particular problem. In this case we check the *text* property of the control to see if it is the same as the current row, and if not, we have a different name and increment the value of the counter, then we set the *text* to the field in the current row. If we do not do this last assignment, the next record could end up incrementing the value again when we didn't want it to. The one confusing thing that you will see is that while some names print more than once, there are only a certain number of *unique* Dam names, and that is all that this will count.

We need to make sure this counter is instantiated properly. To do that, go back to the Inspector, and using the combobox at the top, find "form" (the first item in the combobox list). Click on the "Methods" tab, and select the *render* method. We are going to override this method, and insert our own code, but notice that the Report Designer assumes you still want to call the original code (which we do). Change the code to the following:

```
function form_render()
   // set counter to a value of zero:
   form.RT_DamCount = 0
   // create control for break in DataText1_onRender:
   form.DamName = "XXX" // a value not in the table
return RUNNINGTOTALREPORT::render()
```

When the report is rendered, this counter will be created, and then as we go through the report, the value will be incremented, adding one the first time a new name is rendered.

There is one more difficulty for this total – if the user is viewing the report (as we are) in a reportViewer screen and clicks on the "Previous Page" button in the Toolbar, and then comes back to the last page, the total will have been re-accumulated for all pages of the report, which will give an incorrect value. The simplest solution is to use the text control's *onRender* event, and re-set the total. We do this by clicking on the text for the total number of Dams, and selecting the *onRender* event, then clicking the tool button. Enter the following code:

```
function TEXT2_onRender()
   // reset the counter value to zero:
   form.RT_DamCount := 0
return
```

Finally, we need to tell the text control what to display. Since the running total is not a field in a table, the simplest thing to do is use the *canRender* event for that control. Click on the text that now shows "0.00" for the total number of Dams, and in the Inspector go to the "Events" tab, and find the *canRender* event. Click the tool button. Set the code to:

```
function TEXT2_canRender()
   // display the counter for the running total:
   this.text := int( form.RT_DamCount )
return true
```

We used the integer function (int()) for the value, because otherwise dBASE would display the value with two decimals – or whatever the setting is in your installation of dBASE for the number of decimals (see SET DECIMAL in the online help for dBASE), and this is really just an integer value.

Save the report, and when you run it again, and page down to the last page of the report, the totals should now look like:

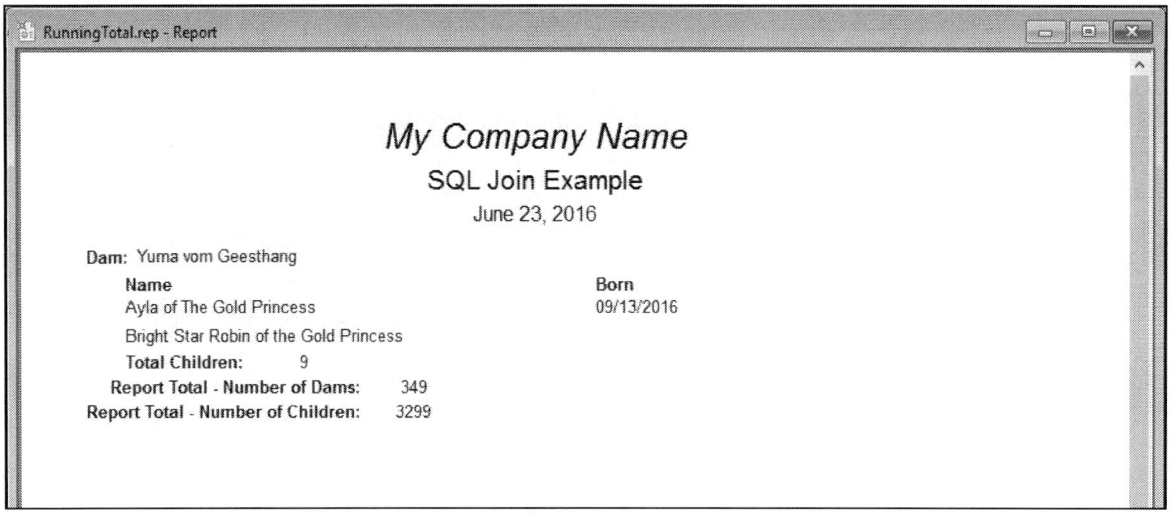

Figure 12-9

The total of 349 is much more reasonable than 3299, which we had before *(and indeed is the number of distinct Dam names in the Dams table)*.

There are, of course, many different things you might want to do with counters and sums.

Conditional Counters (and Sums)

Often you will find that you need to total or accumulate values based on specific conditions. This next example is going to use a combination of things we've done in the past. We want to show the sex of the dogs, and total the number of males and the number of females, based on the sex field. We also want to do this in each group, so we're going to add a field to the report we've been working with, and then add to the *group footerBand* two new counters.

Before we move on, copy the report by typing the following in the Command Window:

```
copy file RunningTotal.rep to Conditional.rep
```

Open the new report in the Source Code Editor, and make the changes in bold in the code at the top of the report:

```
local r
r = new CONDITIONALREPORT()
r.render()

class CONDITIONALREPORT of MYCOMPANYREPORTCREPORT from :MyReports:MyCompanyReport.crp
```

Also, at the end of the report, there is a statement that needs to be modified (press Ctrl+End to take you to the bottom of the source code) – just before the "endclass" statement:

```
return CONDITIONALREPORT::render()
```

Leave this in the Source Code Editor for the moment.

For the conditional counters to work we need to modify the SQL Select statement for the query. If you recall, this is the SQL Join that we did in the previous chapter, and it limits the fields selected for the report.

Change the query to (add the item in bold):

```
this.QUERY1 = new QUERY(this)
   with (this.QUERY1)
      database = form.form.database1
      sql = 'select dams.dam, dams.name, dogs.name, dogs.born,
dogs.sex, dogs.rno_dam from "dams.dbf" dams left outer join "dogs.dbf"
dogs on dams.dam = dogs.rno_dam order by dams.name, dogs.name'
      active = true
   endwith
```

(Add the new field "dogs.sex" and a comma into the sql statement.)

Save the report and exit the Source Code Editor (Ctrl+W).

The next thing to do is to open the report back in the Report Designer. Add a "DataColHeadingText" control to the *detailBand* to the right of the "Born" heading, and set the text to "Sex". You should set the *top* property to the same as the other heading text controls. Then add a "DataText" control under this. Set the *top* and *left* properties appropriately so it lines up with the other controls.

We then want to set the *canRender* event for this text control to morph the data from the letters "M" or "F" to the words "Male" or "Female" – this is something we did back in Chapter 7, but we'll repeat it here. Find the *canRender* event on the Inspector window, and click the Tool button – in the Source Code Editor fill in the code below:

```
function DATATEXT3_canRender()
   // morph the text to "Male" or "Female" ...
   f = form.streamSource1.rowset.fields
   if f["Sex"].value == "M"
      this.text := "Male"
   elseif f["Sex"].value == "F"
      this.text := "Female"
   else
```

```
      this.text := "Unknown"
   endif
return true
```

Remember that this will not be evaluated at the moment, but if you were to save/exit the Report Designer and bring the report back into the designer, you would see the text change appropriately.

With this text set, the next thing we need to do is set up the counters needed. For this to work properly, we need to make sure that when the *group headerBand* has rendered, which will initialize the counters - setting them to zero or setting them back to zero, before we start accumulating values. This is useful for grouped reports to ensure that we always start at the beginning. To do this, click on the *group headerBand* (the green band that shows the Dam name - in this case, click on the green area, not the text controls). The Inspector should show:

```
form.streamSource1.group1.headerBand
```

Click on the *onRender* event, and the tool button. Enter the following code:

```
function HEADERBAND_onRender()
   // initialize counters,
   // parent = group
   // parent = streamSource1
   // parent = form/report
   this.parent.parent.parent.nMales = 0
   this.parent.parent.parent.nFemales = 0
return
```

We assigned these totals as custom properties of the report, because it's easier to find them when we need them. We could have assigned them as custom properties of the *group*, or the *headerBand*, or even the *footerBand*, but that can get confusing.

Next we need to create code that will do the actual accumulating of totals. In this case, we will use the text control that displays the text's *onRender* event, although we could use the detailBand's *onRender* event just as well, and it would accomplish the same thing.

Select the text that currently says "DataText" on the *detailBand*. In the Inspector, find the *onRender* event, click the Tool button, and enter the following code:

```
function DATATEXT3_onRender()
   // accumulate totals for this group:
   f = form.streamSource1.rowset.fields
   if f["Sex"].value == "M"
      form.nMales++
   elseif f["Sex"].value == "F"
      form.nFemales++
   endif
return
```

We could have just assumed in the code shown that either the sex is "M" or "F", but some of the records in the Dogs table have an empty field for Sex. The code above checks to see if the value is either an "M" or an "F". We could also have added a counter for "Unknown", but let's keep it at least a little bit more simple than that.

Finally we need to add text controls onto the *group footerBand*, and then tell the Report Engine how to assign the text to them.

For this to work, set the *height* of the group footerBand larger (if using a metric of Inches, in the Inspector set the height to 1 and press Enter – this will give lots of room – we'll set this back to zero later).

Place a "DataHeadingText" control onto the *footerBand*, and set the text to: "Males:" (without the quotes). To the right of this place a "DataText" control, and change the *name* property to "MalesText".

We need to repeat this for "Females" – change the "DataHeadingText" control's *text* to "Females:" and the Data Text control's *name* to "FemalesText".

Take a moment and try to line things up a little to deal with the appearance of the report.

Setting the text for the totals to show the values could be done in a couple of ways – the first is to use the *canRender* event for each of the text controls, but you could also use the footerBand's *preRender* event and set both of them at the same time. This is what we'll do here – it's a little less work (although for a more complex report, it could be a lot less work ...). Click on the *footerBand* itself to give it focus, and in the Inspector find the *preRender* event – click the tool button, and enter the following:

```
function FOOTERBAND_preRender()
   // set text for the totals:
   // parent = group
   // parent = streamSource1
   // parent = form/report
   this.MalesText.text := this.parent.parent.parent.nMales
   this.FemalesText.text := this.parent.parent.parent.nFemales
return
```

While you are in the Inspector window, set the *height* property of the *footerBand* back to zero (0).

In the designer you should have a report that looks something like:

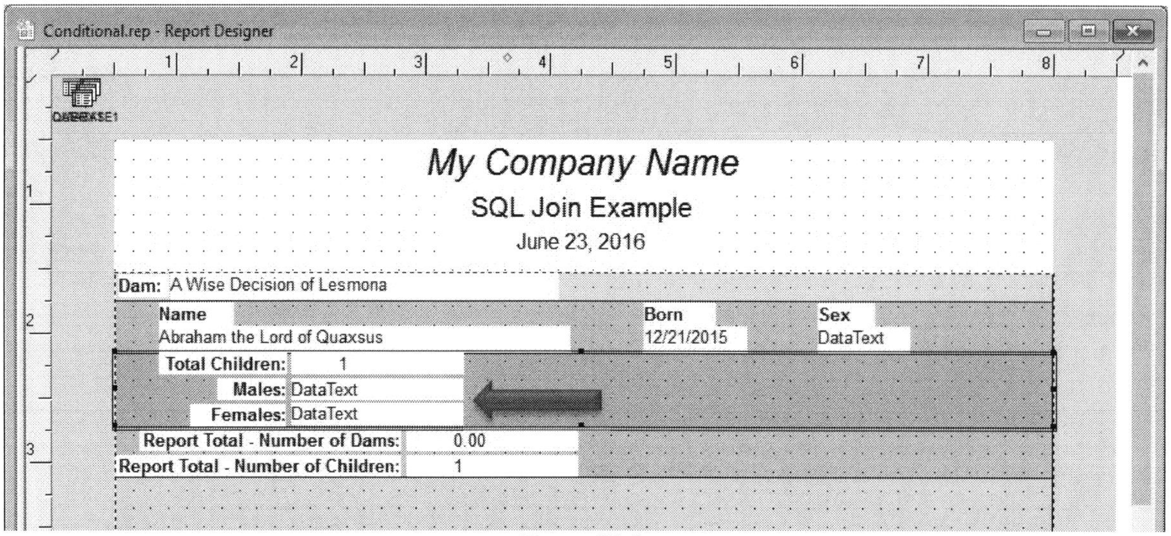

Figure 12-9

Remember that the heading text that should be bold will be bold when the report is rendered, and the next time we bring the report into the Report Designer, and that the calculated fields *may* update properly in the same way. To see this, run the report, which should look something like:

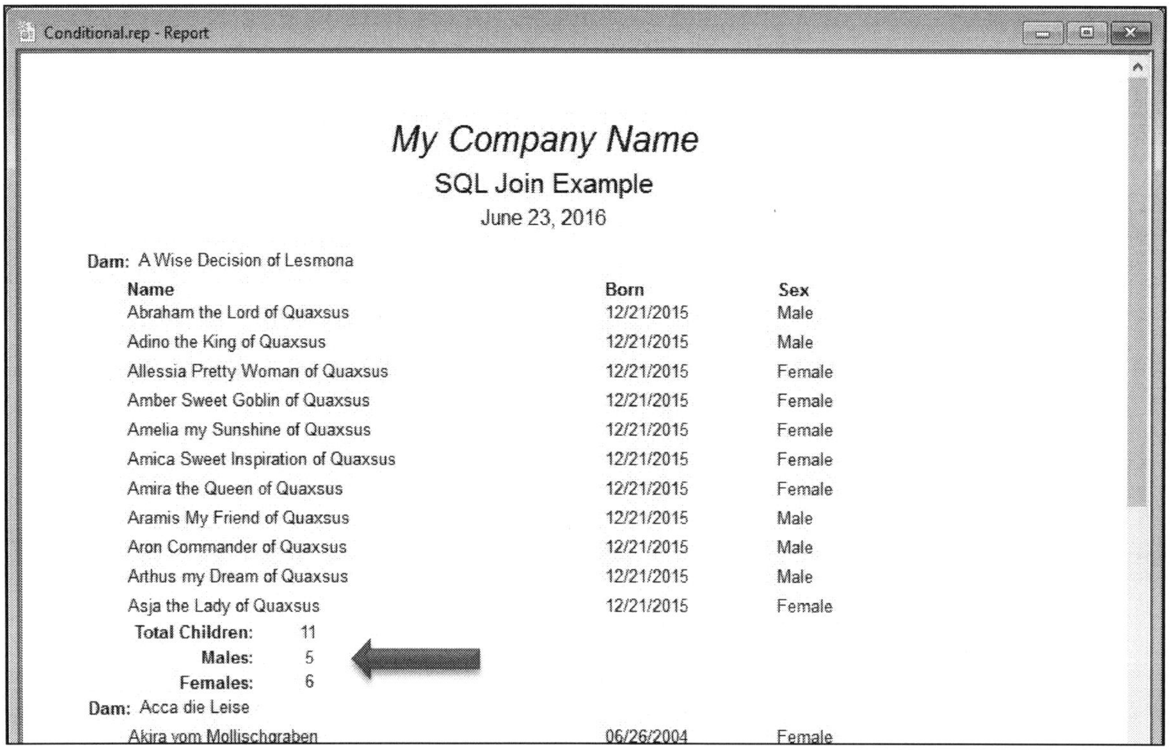

Figure 12-10

When you are done close this window.

Page Totals

The last thing we will look at in this chapter is working with page totals. It is sometimes desirable, particularly when generating a report with a lot of data, to show totals at the bottom of individual pages. These are a subset of running totals. We will continue with a copy of this report, but this will require making some layout modifications to allow for room at the bottom of the report page for any totals we might wish to display.

Before starting, close any open windows in dBASE, and in the Command Window, type the following:

```
copy file Conditional.rep to PageTotals.rep
```

We need to modify, as usual, the references to the report name in the source code, so open this in the source code editor, and rather than doing these one statement at a time, let's use the find and replace dialog. Press Ctrl+R, and in the "Find what:" entryfield, type "conditional" and in the "Replace with:" entryfield, type "PAGETOTALS", click the "Replace All" button, and then click "X" (close button) in the title bar. Press Ctrl+W to save changes and close the Source Code Editor.

Now bring the report back to the Report Designer. Once it is there, we need to change the height of the *streamFrame* – the yellow part of the report area. We are going to want to add room for a row of text controls, and perhaps a line to separate them from the detail part of the report.

The simplest way to do this is to go to the bottom of the report in the Designer surface using the scrollbar on the right. Then click on the *streamFrame*, and change the height by shortening it (resize with the mouse). If your metrics are set to Inches, the *height* of the *streamFrame* should be around 8.38" or so when done.

Go to the Component Palette, and select the "Standard" tab, then select a line, and drag it to the *pageTemplate* area below the *streamFrame*. Again, assuming a metric of Inches for the report, if you set the *left* property to 0, and the *right* property to 7.5, the line will go from the left of the report to the right. You can of course modify this as you feel looks best for your own report. Make sure the *top* and *bottom* properties are identical, or there will be some oddities in the way the line is drawn when the report is rendered.

Next select the "Custom" tab of the Component Palette, and place a "DataHeadingText" control on the pageTemplate, on the left, under the line, and change the text to "Page Totals:". Set the *fontBold* property to *true*, and adjust the text control as necessary.

We're going to add totals for the number of Dams, and the number of male and female offspring on each page of the report. To do this, we need several new text controls, so follow along carefully:

Place a "DataHeadingText" control to the right of the "Page Totals:" control. Change the *text* to "# of Dams:". Place a "DataText" control to the right of this, and change the *name* property to "PT_DamsText" (PT stands for "Page Total").

> **NOTE**
> It is very easy here to accidentally move the *pageTemplate* around, as you are placing text onto it, and trying to move it around with the mouse. If you do move the *pageTemplate*, just go to the Inspector, put focus on the *pageTemplate* if it isn't, and set the margins (*marginLeft*, etc.) to 0.5.

Place another "DataHeadingText" control to the right of the "PT_Dams" text control we just created, and change the *text* to "Male Offspring:". You will want to widen this control so that the text displays in one line, and perhaps shorten the height as this is not automatic. Place a "DataText" control to the right of this, and change the *name* property to "PT_MalesText".

Repeat the above one more time, but change the "DataHeadingText" *text* to "Female Offspring:", and the *name* of the "DataText" control to "PT_FemalesText".

The bottom of the report should look something like:

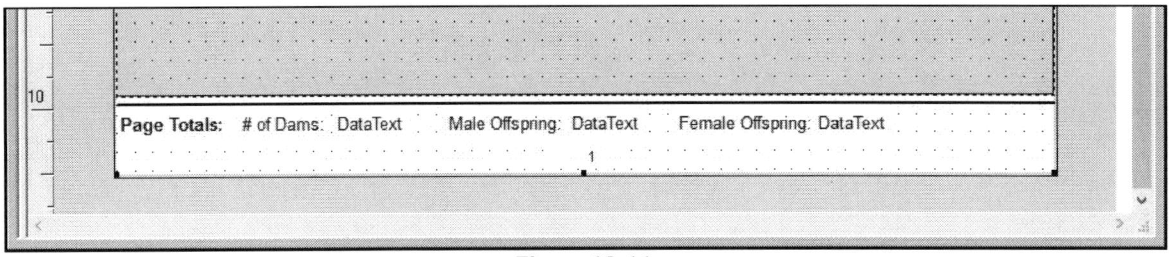

Figure 12-11

Before doing anything else with the text controls, we need to initialize the counters with a value of zero (0) so that they are set up when the report starts. We could do this in several places, including the query object's *onOpen* event, but let's stick with the report, and override the report's *render* method. To do this, go to the Inspector, and find "form" at the top of the combobox (at the top of the Inspector window). Click on the "Methods" tab, and select the *render* method. Click the tool button. Note that we already have code:

```
function form_render()
   // set counter to a value of zero:
   form.RT_DamCount = 0
   // create control for break in DataText1_onRender:
   form.DamName = "XXX" // a value not in the table
return PAGETOTALSREPORT::render()
```

We want to modify the code to include the new totals:

```
function form_render()
   // set counters to a value of zero:
   form.RT_DamCount = 0
   form.PT_Dams = 0
   form.PT_Males = 0
   form.PT_Females = 0
   // create control for break in DataText1_onRender:
   form.DamName = "XXX" // a value not in the table
return PAGETOTALSREPORT::render()
```

Next we need to accumulate the totals appropriately, however these will be done in two different places. We only want to accumulate the number of Dams when the Dam is displayed, so we must do this in the text control for the name that we set up for the Running Total earlier in this chapter. Go to the *group headerBand* at the top of the report, and select the Dam name text (the one that displays the actual name), and in the Inspector, find the *onRender* event. Click the tool button, and you should see the code that is already there. Add the two lines shown in bold just before the "return" statement:

```
function DATATEXT1_onRender()
   // add to Running Total for Dam if we have not already
   // printed the Dam name
   f = form.streamSource1.rowset.fields
   if form.DamName # f["Name"].value
      form.RT_DamCount++
      form.DamName := f["Name"].value
   endif
   // accumulate Page Total:
   form.PT_Dams++
return
```

And the last bit of accumulating values for the counters goes to the text control that displays the sex of the dogs' *canRender* event – add the code in bold:

```
function DATATEXT3_canRender()
   // morph the text to "Male" or "Female" ...
   f = form.streamSource1.rowset.fields
   if f["Sex"].value == "M"
      this.text := "Male"
      form.PT_Males++
   elseif f["Sex"].value == "F"
      this.text := "Female"
      form.PT_Females++
   else
      this.text := "Unknown"
   endif
return true
```

Now there are only two things left to do – the first is to tell the Report Engine to place the appropriate values into the *text* properties of the three text controls that are to display the values, and then we need to reset these once the report is done rendering the page.

In order to set the *text* properties we will do it in one place. You will need to scroll back down to the bottom of the report in the designer, and click on the first "DataText" control ("PT_DamsText"). In the Inspector, select the *canRender* event. Click the tool button, and enter the following text:

```
function PT_DAMSTEXT_canRender()
   // set text for this and other page totals:
   this.text := int( form.PT_Dams )
   this.parent.PT_MalesText.text := int( form.PT_Males )
   this.parent.PT_FemalesText.text := int( form.PT_Females )
return true
```

Notice that we set the *text* property for all three text controls. By setting the *name* property to something meaningful for these controls it makes it easier to read the code and see what we are doing. We could have used the *canRender* event for each text control to set the *text* property individually, and in some cases you might want to do just that, but for this example it is simpler to do it at once time.

The *parent* reference here is to the *pageTemplate* which is the parent of the text controls we need to manipulate, and we are using the *int()* function as mentioned earlier to make sure we display an integer value, rather than a value with decimals, which is unnecessary.

Finally we need to reset the page totals when the page renders. Once more go to the Inspector, and find the "form" at the top of the combobox. When this has focus, select the *onPage* event. Click the tool button, and enter the following:

```
function form_onPage()
   // reset page totals when this page has finished rendering:
   this.PT_Dams := 0
   this.PT_Males := 0
   this.PT_Females := 0
return
```

At this point we should be done. Save your work (Ctrl+S). If you run the report and scroll to the bottom of the first page, you should see:

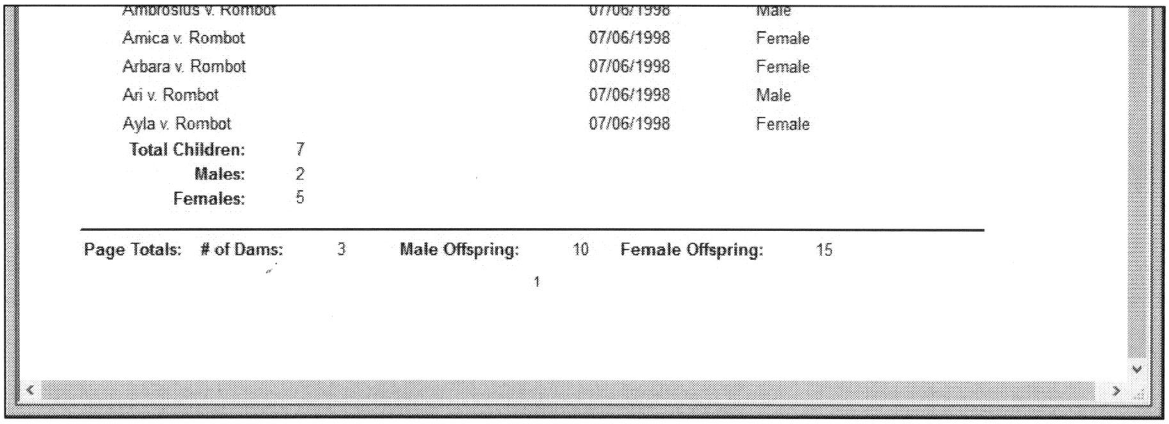

Figure 12-12

and if you go to the next page (PgDn or use the 'Next Page' button in the toolbar) and look at the bottom of the page you should see:

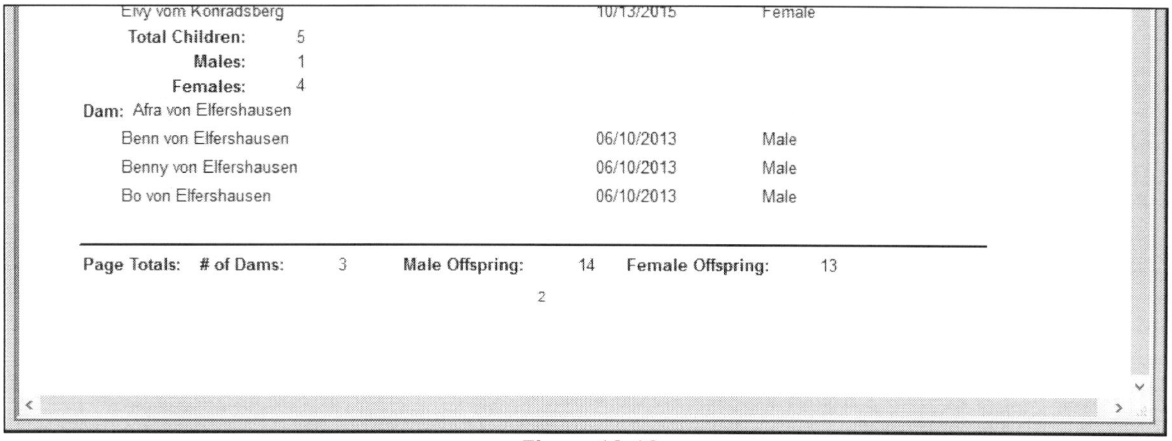

Figure 12-13

And as you go through the report, these totals will be different from one page to another.

Some Notes

The report we copied and worked on through this chapter is not the cleanest looking report. If you scroll through the pages you will see things like totals for a group at the top of a page, but nothing to indicate what group these totals belong to, and that sort of thing. The next chapter will discuss forcing page breaks, a topic that would help a lot with some of these issues.

Aggregate Calculations with Calculated Fields?

In an earlier chapter we discussed using calculated fields as a means to an end. Is it possible to use the aggregate summary calculations built in to dBASE with these calculated fields? The answer is a resounding "Yes!". The reason? Because of the way calculated fields work in dBASE, they tend to act as if they were real fields in the table. So if you used the methods of adding a field object or using the SQL Select to create a calculated field, then as far as dBASE is concerned these are actual fields in the table for the purpose of generating a report, and the aggregate calculations will work fine on them.

Cleanup

Create a new report (in the Navigator, click on the .Reports. tab, double-click on the "[New Report]" icon). Select the "File" menu, select "Set Custom Report Class", and in the dialog, click the "Clear Custom Report" button, then click "OK". This clears out the custom report setting in the Plus.ini file, so that the next report you create is not based on this one.

In this chapter we also set the Report Designer to display only one row of data. We need to set that back to the default. Right click on the report and find "Report Designer Properties" – select that. In the "Rowset Display" box, change the radiobutton selection to "All Rows" and click "OK".

Close that report without making any changes.

Make sure the database is closed by going to the Command Window and typing:

```
close databases
```

This will also ensure that you don't end up creating tables in the wrong location, etc.

Source Code

The following is a listing of the sample code in the folders we have been working with. If you downloaded the files from my website the structure will be different (see below). You may use the code contained in these folders for your own applications if you desire, with the caveat that credit be given appropriately.

From working on this chapter:

```
C:\dBASEReports\Chapter 12\AGSum.rep
C:\dBASEReports\Chapter 12\Conditional.rep
C:\dBASEReports\Chapter 12\PageTotals.rep
C:\dBASEReports\Chapter 12\RunningTotal.rep
```

Downloaded version – same files but with this path:

```
C:\ReportsBookSourceCode\Chapter 12\filename
```

Summary

This chapter delved into using the aggregate summaries in dBASE, creating running totals, page totals and more. The goal is to get you used to the idea that if you can think of a need for it, the chances are that you can do it. Some of what you need to do, because it's not automatic (in other words, something build into the Report Designer or Report Engine) may need a bit of work, using a combination of events and/or methods of the report, but by using these you can get just about any totals that you might need. We did not delve into each of the different aggregate calculations built into the Report Engine, but by using the *agCount()* calculation, hopefully you can see how these work, and how you might use them in your own reports.

The next chapters will get into enhancing the appearance of a report, something that most of us can use some help with.

NOTES:

Part III: Modify Report Appearance

This section of the book will focus heavily on various means of modifying the way your report looks, including hiding parts of the report when it is displayed or printed; setting page breaks; and enhancing the appearance of your reports (making it look fancier, more professional, etc.).

Chapter 13: Hiding Report Elements

One of the more powerful aspects of the dBASE reporting tools is that they are completely object-oriented. This enables us to change any property of the report before the report prints, and thereby change how the report functions. I have found that with several of my reports and labels that I didn't have to have multiple copies of the same report with minor changes to them like I used to in earlier versions of dBASE, using Crystal Reports™. I can have a single report, and before I render it, I can change just about anything – as long as I know how to get to the specific control or property I need to change.

A simple example of this flexibility is setting a filter or a range. You might have a form that gets a parameter from the user. When the print button is clicked you might run code similar to this:

```
oReport = new myReport()
oReport.streamSource1.rowset.setRange( someVar )
oReport.render()
```

This code creates a new instance of the report class, sets the range, then it renders the report. In this chapter we are going to look at hiding particular elements of a report in order to modify its appearance.

A Place for Our Work

As we work through the chapter we will be needing a place for the files we create, so please create a folder for this chapter:

```
C:\dBASEReports\Chapter 13
```

And in the Navigator, be sure to navigate to this folder.

Detail and Summary Reports

Developers often find that their clients or users want a report that prints all the details and another one that prints just the summaries. The dBASE reporting tools make this type of thing rather easy. Essentially, a *summaries only* report is a report with an invisible *detailBand* (and if you have headings in the group *headerBand* that refer to items in the detailBand, these too need to be made invisible).

The example we will use for this is based on one of the reports we created in Chapter 11. In the Command Window:

```
copy file "..\Chapter 11\SQLJoin.rep" to DetailSummary.rep
```

Open this report file in the Source Code Editor, and change the lines at the beginning to:

```
local r
r = new DetailSummaryReport()
r.render()

class DetailSummaryReport of MyCompanyReportCReport from :MyReports:MyCompanyReport.crp
```

then save and exit the Source Code Editor (Ctrl+W). This will ensure we have a unique object name and that the report will function properly. Open the report in the Report Designer.

Before we do anything else, we are going to move the column headings to the group *headerBand*. Why? Well, this way they will appear above the details in the *detailBand* each time we change groups, which can be useful. This is also to show some of the technique we wish to use for the detail versus summary report.

To do this, we need to change the *height* of the group *headerBand* temporarily, so it is large enough for us to manipulate text controls. Click on the green *headerBand*, and in the Inspector set the *height* to 1".

Place a "DataHeadingText" control above the "Name" in the *detailBand*, and change the *text* to "Name" (without the quotes). Do the same for the "Born" column. Line them up with the headings in the *detailBand*, then move them to just below the text at the top of the *headerBand*. Before doing anything else, with both of these controls selected, go to the Inspector and set the *suppressIfBlank* property to *true*. This should look something like:

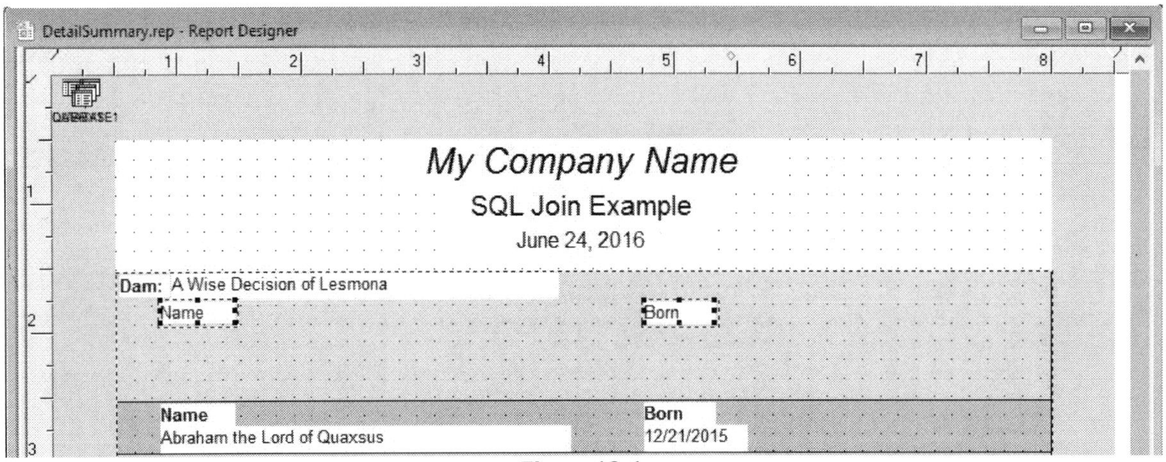

Figure 13-1

Next click back on the *headerBand*, and in the Inspector, set the *height* to zero (0).

Finally, delete the heading controls on the *detailBand*, and move the name and date text controls up to the top of the *detailBand* itself.

This should now look like:

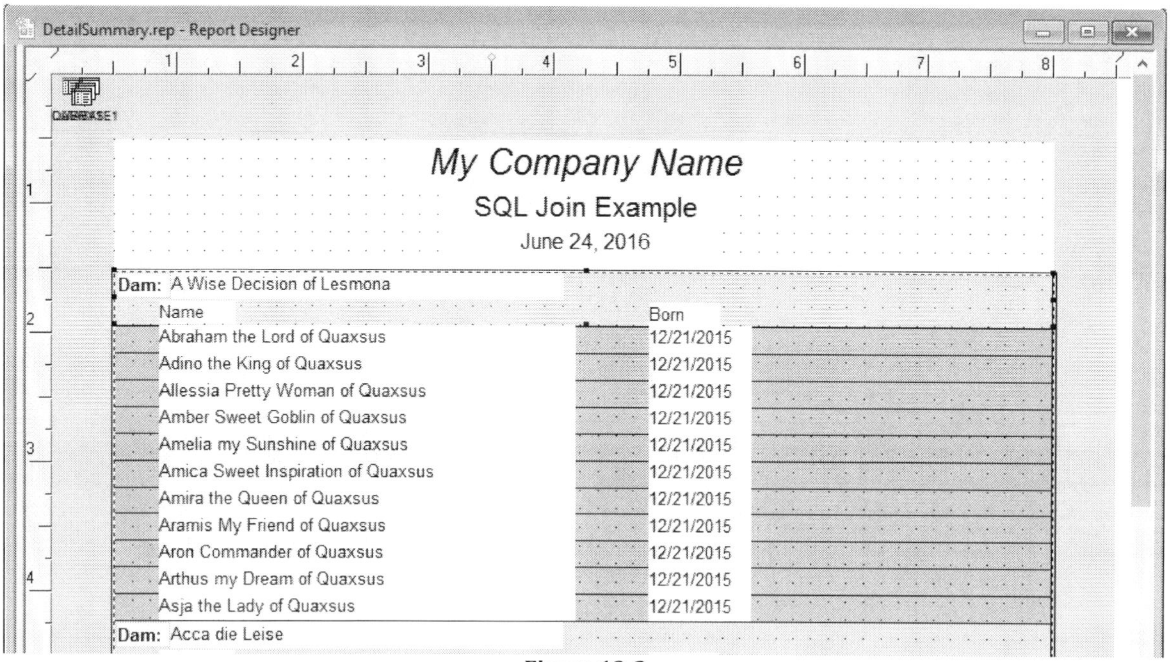

Figure 13-2

Remember that when the report is run, the headings will change to boldface.

We need set up a program that asks the user if they wish to view the report in detail or summary mode, and change the report programmatically as needed. To do this, save your work and exit the Report Designer (Ctrl+W).

Next click on the "Programs" tab of the Navigator, and double-click the "[New Program]" icon, and enter the following code:

```
set procedure to DetailSummary.rep additive
local oRep, nAns

// create an instance of the report:
oRep = new DetailSummaryReport()

// ask the user what they want to do:
nAns = msgbox( "Do you want to show a Summary only?",;
               "Please Confirm", 36 )

if nAns == 6 // Yes
   // Summary only:
   oRep.streamSource1.detailBand.visible := false
   // get the column headings:
   oRep.streamSource1.group1.headerBand.DataHeadingText2.visible := false
   oRep.streamSource1.group1.headerBand.DataHeadingText3.visible := false
   oRep.pageTemplate1.SecondaryTitleText1.text := "Summary Report"
else // user selected No button
   // Detail report:
   oRep.pageTemplate1.SecondaryTitleText1.text := "Detail Report"
endif
```

```
   // render the report:
   oRep.render()
```

It should be noted that if you have changed the names of any of the Text Controls, you need to check the report itself and make sure you are referring to the correct controls. One handy thing here is that if you need to, you can have the Report Designer open at the same time as the Source Code Editor, and you can go back and forth between them – this would allow you to click on the text controls and make sure the control names (such as "DataHeadingText2") are correct in the program.

Save the program as "DetailSummary.prg" (press Ctrl+S to save).

Be careful when typing this code to get the syntax correct. Looking at the code, what does it do? When this program is run, an instance of the report will be created, and then the user will be asked if they wish to show a summary – with a dBASE dialog that will show either a Yes or No option. If they select "Yes", then the report will set the *detailBand* and the heading text controls to invisible (and because we set the *suppressIfBlank* property to *true* earlier, the space reserved for these in the *headerBand* will not be used, and the *headerBand* will compress in height ...), and change the text in the "SecondaryTitleText" control on the *pageTemplate*. If the user selects "No", the only thing necessary is to change the "SecondaryTitleText" control on the *pageTemplate*.

If you run this once and select "Yes" for the Summary report, the report should look something like:

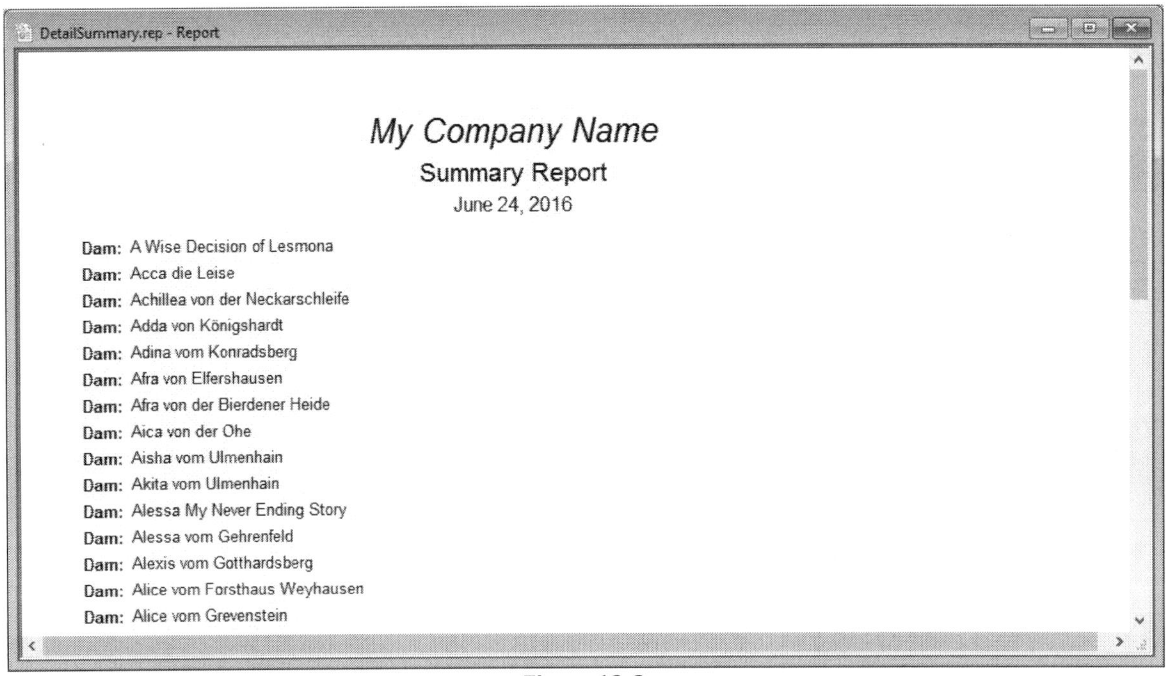

Figure 13-3

and if you close this and run the program again, this time selecting "No" for the summary report, you should see something similar to:

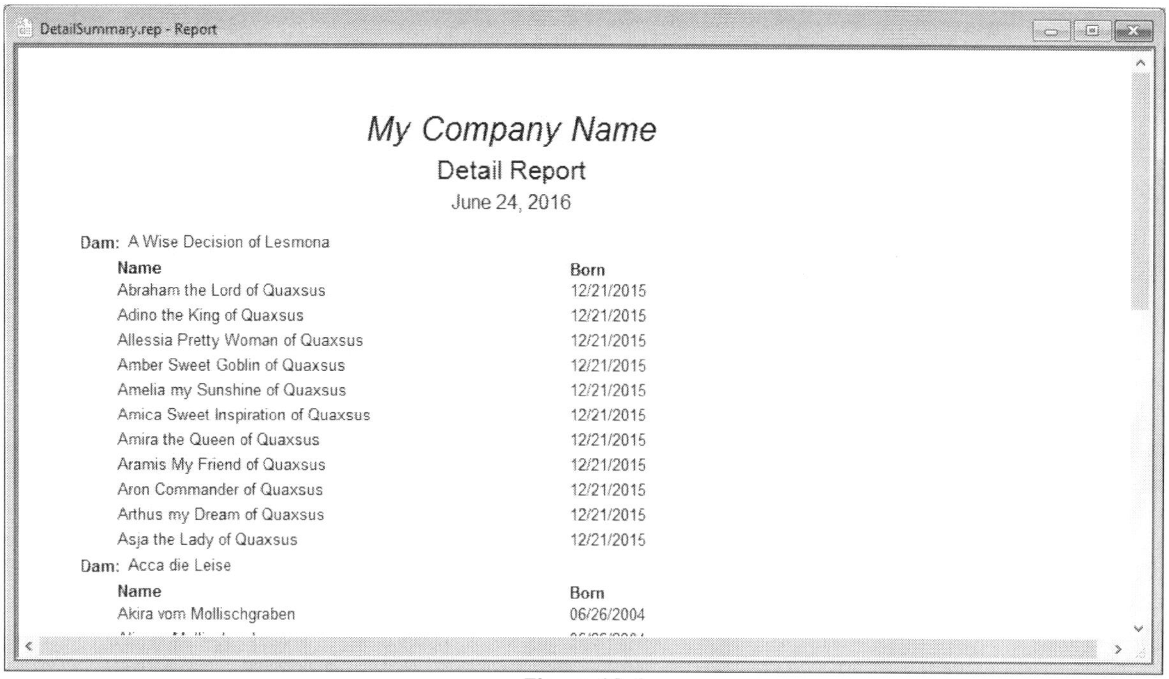

Figure 13-4

This is a very useful thing to know how to do, because as noted at the beginning of the chapter, you do not need to create multiple reports for this kind of situation – a single report can do the job just as well.

It should be mentioned that we could have set this report so that we didn't really need a separate program to change the settings. We could have overridden the report's *render* method, passed a parameter to the report (Detail or Summary), and kept everything encapsulated in the report itself.

This same concept can be used in a variety of ways – the ability to show/hide the *detailBand* could be also used to show/hide headerBands, or whatever you might need. In Michael Nuwer's report tutorial he gives an example of hiding unwanted headerbands in a report where the *detailBand* is empty, and therefore there is no need to show the *headerBand* either. We won't get into that here, but if you think about it, based on what we've done so far, you might see more uses for this kind of control.

Hiding / Displaying Individual Controls

We have already actually dealt with some of this kind of functionality, but this seems like a good place to really discuss the topic in some detail.

It is possible to tell dBASE to conditionally display individual controls only if they have data, or only in some circumstances. When we worked with labels in Chapter 9, we dealt with empty text controls, and having dBASE shift controls *under* the empty ones up. The example there dealt with addresses, where you might have two or three address lines for someone, and in many cases only the first one has any data in it.

Suppressing blank data is not *quite* as straightforward as it might seem. The following information is from the old Knowledgebase article I wrote many years ago on reports:

Reports evaluate in what is called "z-order" (just like forms do); which means that the sequence that objects are defined in the source code file (.REP or .LAB for labels) can be important for certain aspects of a report.

What often happens when creating a report is that you get everything lined up and laid out exactly as you want, and then you add a field or text control somewhere to the report. This last object does not necessarily appear in the correct z-order, and this can cause your report to render differently than you might expect.

There is no layout option to change the z-order for reports as there is in the form designer, so any changes must be done by hand in your source code. (Cut/paste the necessary blocks of constructor code ...)

When creating a report that needs to have blank lines suppressed, follow these rules and you should be ok:

- Make sure, particularly within a specific band, that all of your controls are in the correct z-order. This will require that you open the source for your report and possibly move things around.
- *suppressIfBlank* – must be set to *true* for the control. This (*suppressIfBlank* property) must be set for each control on each "line" of the report that you want to suppress.
- The *variableHeight* property must be set to *false* for the control.
- The *fixed* property must be set to its default value of *false* for the control.

Example: For mailing labels you might have two address lines – but in many cases the second one may be blank. Make sure all of your controls are in the proper z-order, and then check that the second address line (and any subsequent lines such as the city/state/zipcode line) has *suppressIfBlank* set to *true* and *variableHeight* set to *false*.

I asked one of the developers at Borland (Charles Overbeck) who worked on the Report Engine *(when the product was called Visual dBASE 7)* about this, and he explained it this way:

> "The height that will be suppressed if a text control is blank is determined entirely by its *height* property. So if you have a *variableHeight* item with a *height* of 0, and it is suppressed when blank, nothing will change. However, if your *variableHeight* item had a *height* of 200 twips, then other controls would be moved up 200 twips.
>
> Because it's more likely that a *variableHeight* item will have a very small (or even 0) *height* property, it may seem that *suppressIfBlank* works differently on *variableHeight* items, but it is really a function of the value of the *height* property."

Problem: Memos and large character fields, to print properly, must have their *variableHeight* set to *true*. At this point in time the only solution seems to be to print the memo before (z-order) any text that may need to be variable/suppressed.

We have discussed the *canRender* event for controls – by default this returns a value of *true*, which tells dBASE to render the control. However, if the *canRender* event is set to return a value of *false*, we can suppress the control. Combine this with the *suppressIfBlank* property as noted above, and your report can look very clean indeed.

Duplicate Values

This was mentioned in an earlier chapter, but it bears mentioning again. In the report we just looked at, you will see the dates that the dogs were born. You will also note that they are grouped together in litters. It is not always desirable to see the same value over and over like this. What you can do is to click on the text control that displays the value in question, and use the *suppressIfDuplicate* property. Setting this to *true* will only display the date for the first row, and any duplicates will not display. As soon as a different date appears, that will be displayed.

Cleanup

Create a new report (in the Navigator, click on the .Reports. tab, double-click on the "[New Report]" icon). Select the "File" menu, select "Set Custom Report Class", and in the dialog, click the "Clear Custom Report" button, then click "OK". This clears out the custom report setting in the Plus.ini file, so that the next report you create is not based on this one. Close that report without making any changes.

Make sure the database is closed by going to the Command Window and typing:

```
close databases
```

This will also ensure that you don't end up creating tables in the wrong location, etc.

Source Code

The following is a listing of the sample code in the folders we have been working with. If you downloaded the files from my website the structure will be different (see below). You may use the code contained in these folders for your own applications if you desire, with the caveat that credit be given appropriately.

From working on this chapter:

```
C:\dBASEReports\Chapter 13\DetailSummary.prg
C:\dBASEReports\Chapter 13\DetailSummary.rep
```

Downloaded version – same files but with this path:

```
C:\ReportsBookSourceCode\Chapter 13\filename
```

Summary

We looked at modifying a report based on input from the user, changing whether specific parts of the report are displayed, and explained in a bit more detail how and why the *suppressIfBlank* property works for controls on the report. By working with this kind of functionality you can save yourself a lot of work – in earlier versions of dBASE you literally had to have multiple copies of the same report that had these changes in them – now you can use the same report for more than one type of report, and save a lot of time and effort.

The next chapter will take a look at forcing page breaks in a report. There are often very good reasons to break the data up, but this is not always a simple "change this property" situation, which is why a whole chapter is dedicated to it.

Chapter 14: Setting Page Breaks

As a developer you will find there are times that you need to force a page break in a report. The two primary reasons to force page breaks are:

- To force a new page when data changes.
- To keep report bands together on a page.

There are different ways to handle these issues, including a method of the *streamSource* object called *beginNewFrame()*. If you assume that a frame is a *streamFrame* object, and that in most reports the *streamFrame* defines the whole page (we'll look at examples where this is not strictly speaking true in later chapters), then telling dBASE to begin a new frame makes sense.

We can force a page break by calling this method, and the next record will be evaluated and sent to the next *streamFrame*. We'll create an example report that does just that shortly.

Combining this method (*beginNewFrame()*) with some other functionality can enhance our ability to control the report. For example, you can determine the amount of space remaining on the page with the *renderOffset* property (this property belongs to the group *headerBand*, *group footerBand* and the *detailBand* of the report). The *renderOffset* property returns the distance from the top of the *streamFrame* to the bottom of the band that it belongs to. This measurement, when subtracted from the *height* of the *streamFrame*, is the distance to the bottom of the printable page.

If you know this, you can determine if you need to force a page break. However, we want to start with the most simple method of forcing page breaks – the group headerBand's *beginNewFrame* property.

A Place for Our Work

As we work through the chapter we will be needing a place for the files we create, so please create a folder for this chapter:

```
C:\dBASEReports\Chapter 14
```

And in the Navigator, be sure to navigate to this folder.

Page Break When a Group Changes

Our first example is going to use the simplest method of forcing a page break – this is used in a grouped report, to force a break each time the value used to group the report changes.

To do this, we need to copy one of the reports we created in an earlier chapter. In the Command Window:

```
copy file "..\Chapter 11\SQLJoin.rep" to PageBreak1.rep
```

Open this report file in the Source Code Editor, and change the lines at the beginning to:

```
local r
r = new PageBreak1Report()
r.render()

class PageBreak1Report of MyCompanyReportCReport from :MyReports:MyCompanyReport.crp
```

Save and exit the Source Code Editor (Ctrl+W), and open the report in the Report Designer.

If you look at this, the report is grouped by the Dam names, what if we want a page break each time the name of the Dam changes? As it turns out this is quite simple to do. If you click on the green *headerBand* region in the Designer, and then click on the Inspector window to give it focus, make sure you are looking at the "Properties" page of the Inspector, and notice the property called *beginNewFrame.* This defaults to *false*. However, if you set this to true, notice your report changes dramatically. The second Dam name is not appearing in the report, because you have just told the Report Engine that it should place each new Dam name on its own page. Run the report, and page down through it and you will see that this is exactly what is happening.

This is a rather simple version of what can be done to force page breaks, but if it is not necessary to do this in a more complex fashion, why do so? That said, the next example is more complicated.

Page Break When a Group Changes – Programming the Break

For this example we will start with a brand new report. Go to the "Reports" page of the Navigator, and double-click on the "[New Report]" icon to create a new report. If the report does not show our standard custom report definitions, then go to the "File" menu, and select the "Set Custom Report Class ..." option, and as we've done previously, select the "MyCompanyReport.crp" file. Click "OK" and we now have our custom report.

Click on the "SecondaryTitleText" control (the one that says "Purpose of Report") and change the *text* to "Page Break Example 2" (without the quotes). Press Ctrl+S and save the report, giving it a name of "PageBreak2".

We need a table for this report, so bring the Navigator to the front (click on it, or go to the "Windows" menu and select "Navigator"), and click on the "Tables" tab. If the "DBASEREPORTS" database is not showing, select it from the combobox, and find the "Litters" table. Click on this and drag it to the Report Designer surface.

Click on the "LITTERS1" query object on the Report Designer surface, and in the Inspector find the *rowset* property. Click the "I" (Inspect) button, and find the *indexName* property. Select "LIT_DATE" from the list, so that the data will be sorted by Litter Date.

Next we want to back up to the query object and add a calculated field – this will be the month of the litter date – as the data only shows litters for a specific year, we do not need to worry about the year for this report, but we are going to group the data by the month. Click on the left arrow button at the top of the Inspector window (if you hold the mouse over it, the speedTip should say something like "Back to form.LITTERS1"). Click the "Events" tab and find the *onOpen* event. Click the tool button. In the Source Code Editor, enter the following:

```
function LITTERS1_onOpen()
   local f
   // create a new field object
   f = new field()
   f.fieldName := "LitterMonth"
   // add to the fields array
   this.rowset.fields.add( f )
   // set the value
   f.beforeGetValue := {|| month( this.parent["lit_date"].value) }
return
```

Because this field does not *currently* exist (the query's *onOpen* event has not fired yet), we should save our work and close the report with Ctrl+W, and the open the report back in the designer again. By doing this, when you look at the Field Palette, you should see "LitterMonth" in the list of fields.

Before we start adding fields to the *detailBand*, let's do one more thing – we're going to add lookups for the Dam and Sire – because the values stored in this table are numeric keys, rather than the names of the Dams and Sires – this can be useful, but it's easier to see the actual names.

To do this, put focus on the LITTERS1 query object, and in the Inspector select *rowset* and click the "I" button, then select *fields* and click the "I" button, then select "Dam" and click the "I" button. We have just "drilled down" to the field object for the Dam field. Click on the *lookupSQL* property, and type:

```
select Reg_No, Name from Dogs
```

Make sure you press the Enter key before leaving this. Do the same for the "Sire" field. This will return the names of the dogs based on their registration number, which is the value in the "Dam" and "Sire" fields in the Litters table.

Go to the Component Palette and place a "DataColHeadingText" control onto the *detailBand*, and change the *text* to "Dam". Repeat to the right of the first heading and change the *text* to "Sire", and finally to the right of that, place one more of these and change the *text* to "Litter Date". You may need to widen this one so the text fits.

Next select a "DataText" control from the Component Palette and move it under the first column heading. You will need to widen this, but that can be experimented with after we give it the text to display. Select the *text* property in the Inspector, and change the Type to "Codeblock" (click the "T" button). Click the tool button and enter in the dialog:

```
form.streamSource1.rowset.fields["DAM"].value
```

You will see asterisks for many of these for the moment, because they are empty. We will deal with that later. Next do the same for the Sire – place a "DataText" control under the heading, and set the *text* to a codeblock. Then enter a codeblock like that above, but using the "SIRE" field. Again you will see asterisks for many of these *(because they are empty)*. Do not despair, this is correct.

And lastly add a third "DataText" control under the last column heading, set the *text* to a codeblock and enter a codeblock as above, but using the field name of "LIT_DATE". Once you do that, you will see dates appear *(some are quite a way back in time)*.

We need to limit the number of records to ones that have useful information in them. To do this, go back to the "LITTERS1" query object, and select the *rowset* property, and then the Inspect ("I") button. Find the *filter* property and enter:

```
lit_date=>'01/01/2014' AND lit_date=<'12/31/2014'
```

This will limit the litter dates to the year 2014. As soon as you press the Enter key (assuming you typed this correctly), the data will now show values for most of the Dams and Sires and you should see that the dates are all in the year 2014.

What we need to do is to force this report to break each time the *month* changes. How do we do this? The simplest way of doing this would be to add a group on the "LitterMonth" (calculated) field that we added earlier, and then as we did in the previous report, set the headerBand's *beginNewFrame* property. However, the goal here is to show that there are more ways to do this, and you might need the more complex means for your own reports at some point.

The data is sorted by month, and we have the calculated field. What we need to do is first set a custom property of the report called "CurrentMonth". We can do this anywhere, but when initializing a value that will be used throughout a report, I tend to use the overridden *render* method of the report – this is a useful place to do any setup for the report, because the code must fire before the report is rendered. In this case we want to set a starting value of the number 1 for the first month, or January. In the Inspector, find the "form" object (at the top of the combobox list), and select the "Methods" page. Find the *render* method, and click the tool button. Enter the following:

```
function form_render()
   // overridden render method
   // setup report - in this case a custom
   // property that will be used to cause
   // a break in the report:
   form.CurrentMonth = 1
return PAGEBREAK2REPORT::render()
```

The next thing we need to do is create some code that will navigate to the next row in the rowset, compare the month in that record with the current month, and if they are not the same, force a new page. We will do this in the detailBand's *onRender* event – which means that the code will fire once the current record has been rendered, and the rowset moved to the next row. It is vital in code like this that you return to where you were, so examine the code carefully.

We need to compare the value of the LitterMonth field of the current record to the form's CurrentMonth (custom) property that we created in the overridden *render* method, and if they are not the same we want to first set the CurrentMonth to the new value, then force a page break, and of course move the record pointer back to where it was before we moved it (otherwise we would skip every other record in the table!). Sound complicated? Well, it's only a little complex, and if you carefully enter the code as shown below carefully it will hopefully make more sense. To do this, click on the detailBand on the design surface, and in the Inspector find the *onRender* event. Click the tool button, and enter the code below:

```
function DETAILBAND_onRender()
   local oStream, nMonth
   oStream = this.parent

   // move row to next row:
   oStream.rowset.next()

   // check to see if values match, and also
   // make sure we're not moving outside of the
   // rowset:
   nMonth = oStream.rowset.fields["LitterMonth"].value

   // oStream.parent = form - the form reference doesn't work here
   if nMonth # oStream.parent.CurrentMonth and;
      not oStream.rowset.endOfSet
      // reset the custom property:
      oStream.parent.CurrentMonth := nMonth
      // force the page break:
      oStream.beginNewFrame()
   endif

   // move the row pointer back to where it was:
   oStream.rowset.next(-1)
return
```

Once you are done with this, you will not see an obvious change in the report. You will need to run it, so you should try running the report. Navigate to the second page. It should look something like:

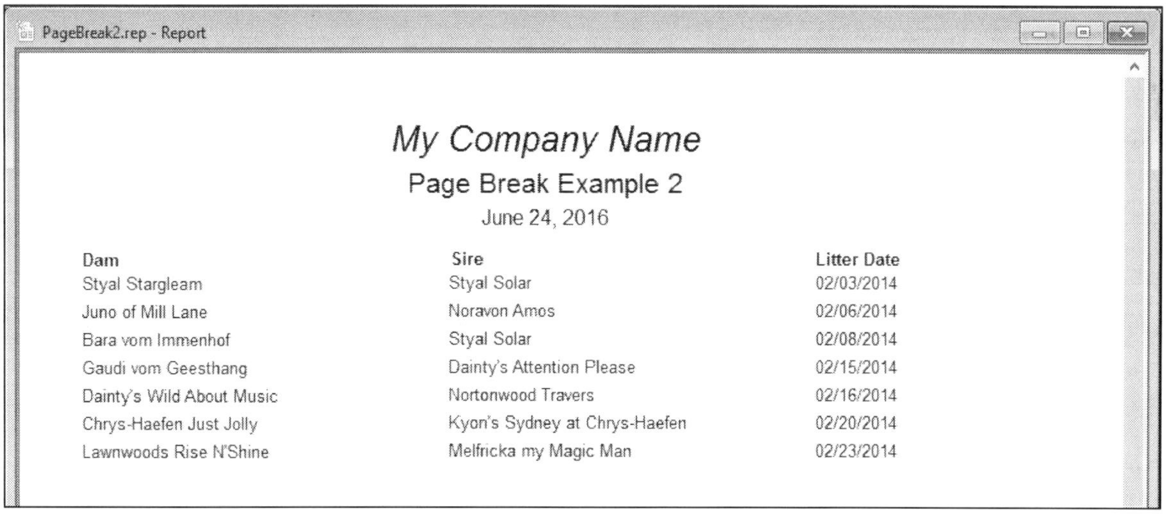

Figure 14-1

If you press PgDn (or use the Next Page button in the toolbar), you will see that each month starts on a new page.

Use a Page Break to Keep a Group Together

This is the most complex of the options we will examine here. There are actually two ways to do this, we will actually do one of them, and I will explain the other.

The problem that often occurs when running a report that has a group with a *group headerBand* that has information that is important in it, is that sometimes the *headerBand* ends up at the bottom of a page (or *streamFrame*) and there is not enough room to display the *detailBand* (or bands) that should go with it. This means you have an orphan *headerBand* sitting there with nothing under it (or only 1 or 2 records) until you go to the next page, and does not look all that great.

dBASE has built in to the report everything you need to make sure that it works the way you want, but it is not a simple task. The basic logic goes like this:

When we render the *footerBand* for a group, we want to see how much space is left at the bottom of the page. We do this by using the *height* of the *streamFrame* and the footerBand's *renderOffset* properties to determine how much space is left (subtract the *renderOffset* from the streamframe's *height*). We then check to see how much space is *needed*, and if there is not enough room, we call the streamSource's *beginNewFrame()* method, which will force the report to go to a new page (or frame).

In this example we are going to use an existing report, and modify it a little. Going back to Chapter 7 again, we want the "BaseGroup" report we worked on, which uses the "DamsParentChild" data module as well. Copy these two files over to the Chapter 14 folder and rename the report "BaseGroup.rep" to "PageBreak3.rep". Open the report in the Source Code Editor, and change the lines shown below (matching the bold text):

```
local r
r = new PageBreak3Report()
r.render()

class PageBreak3Report of MYCOMPANYREPORTCREPORT from :MyReports:MyCompanyReport.crp
```

Save this and exit the Source Code Editor (Ctrl+W). If you run this, you should see that at the bottom of Page 1 the group is not complete – if you go to the top of Page 2, the names continue for this Dam. What we want to do is keep the group together. It is important to note that if the group is larger than a single page this will not keep the group from appearing, and it will have to break across multiple pages.

If you ran the report, close the preview window and open the report in the Report Designer. When you do, change the subtitle text at the top of the report to "Page Break Example 3".

We are going to have to make several other changes, one of which we did in the previous chapter - moving the column heading controls off the *detailBand* and onto the group *headerBand*. Place two "DataHeadingText" controls on the group *headerBand* under the Dam name text controls, and directly above the column heading text controls on the detailBand. Line them up, and change the *text* properties appropriately. Delete the "DataColHeadingText" controls on the *detailBand*, and move the text controls there to the top of the *detailBand*.

The different bands in a report default to having the *expandable* property set to *true*. What this means is that the *height* can expand as needed, but will never get smaller than a specifically defined *height*, if there is one (if the *height* is zero, the band could conceivably be invisible if you set the controls to not render). The problem with setting this is that you also have to specify a valid *height* to include any text controls on the band, or the band will not necessarily display everything. For example, right now the *headerBand* has a *height* of zero – if we set the *expandable* property to *false*, the height of the band would reduce to zero, and would therefore not display.

For our purposes, we need the group *headerBand* to have enough room for the text controls that are on it. A small amount of math will help us determine what the *height* of the band should be. Click on the "Name" column heading. Note that the *height* of this control is 0.21 (if using a metric of Inches). Also note that the *top* is something like: 0.21 (this will vary depending on how your report is laid out – use the value that appears in the Inspector). To determine how tall the *headerBand* must be, we add the *top* of this control to the *height* of this control – which gives us a value of 0.42. Click on the *headerBand*, and in the Inspector set the *height* to 0.42 (or the value you calculated based on your controls). Remember this value – write it down, as we will need this later. Next we need to set the *expandable* property to *false* for the *headerBand*.

Now click on the *detailBand*, and determine the height needed by checking the *top* and *height* properties of the text controls on the band. Since we have only one row of text, this should be pretty basic. If you had a *detailBand* that needed more room, you would need to determine the *top* and *height* of the item at the bottom of the band. Add the *top* and *height* together (in my report this is a *top* of 0.00 and a *height* of 0.21 – giving a total of 0.21). Click on the *detailBand* and set the height to that value. Then set the *expandable* property of the *detailBand* to *false*.

If the *height* of the bands change or are changeable, or worse, have a *height* of zero, the calculations we need to do shortly could be off – if the height changes we can't plan for it, and the Report Engine will not be able to accurately gauge the space we need.

Notice that there does not appear to be a *footerBand* for the group. That's okay – it is actually there, with a *height* of zero (0). In the Inspector find the group, and then the *footerBand* under that (in the combobox). Select this, and find the *onRender* event. Click the tool button for this event, and enter the following code (which is heavily commented – please read the comments as you enter the code, hopefully it will help you understand what is happening):

```
function FOOTERBAND_onRender()
   local oStream, oChild
   local nChildCount, nSpaceRemaining, nSpaceNeeded
   // create reference shortcuts:
   oStream = this.parent.parent
   oChild = this.parent.parent.parent.damsParentChildDatamodule1.dogs1
   // set a bookmark on the current parent row:
   oStream.bookMark = oStream.rowset.bookMark()
   // skip to the NEXT parent row:
   oStream.rowset.next()
   // count the number of child records
   nChildCount = oChild.rowset.count()
   // return the row pointer in the parent to the
   // previous position:
   oStream.rowset.goto( oStream.bookMark )
```

```
      // determine the amount of space remaining on the page:
      nSpaceRemaining = this.streamFrame.height - this.renderOffSet
      // determine amount of space needed:
      // 0.42 is height of group headerBand
      // 0.21 is the height of the detailBand, and we need to
      // multiply that by the number of child records
      nSpaceNeeded = 0.42 + ( nChildCount * 0.21 )
      // determine if there is enough space to print the next
      // group:
      if nSpaceRemaining < nSpaceNeeded // no, there is not ...
         // force a page break:
         oStream.beginNewFrame()
      endif
   return
```

Special thanks to Mervyn Bick for discovering some unnecessary code that was causing this to fail, and helping me out with it.

Note that if we also had a *footerBand* that had text on it we would want to add the *height* of that band to the calculation for nSpaceNeeded shown in the code above.

That's a lot of typing, but a lot of that is comments to help explain it.

When you run the report, you should see that it really does make sure that each group has room on the page to print, and that the group *headerBand* is kept with the detailBands.

The one issue, as can be seen below (Figure 14-2) is that it can leave a lot of white space at the bottom of a page if the group is large but won't fit on the bottom of that page:

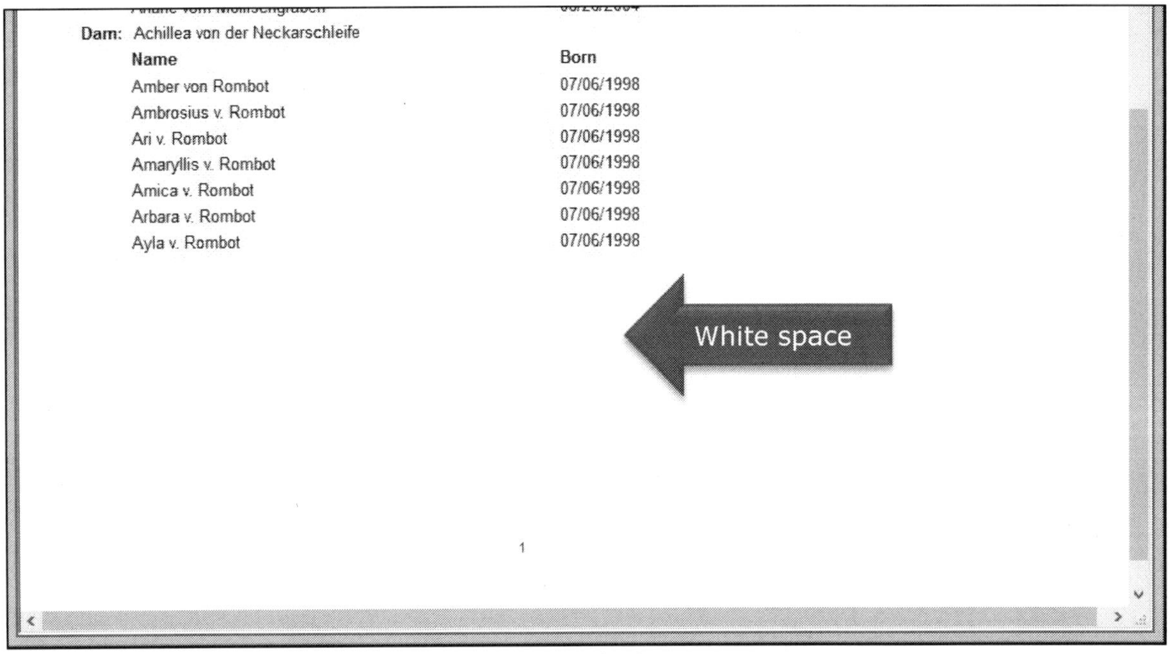

Figure 14-2

In Chapter 11, we looked at simply adding text to the header that says something like "(Continued)", which would not leave so much white space. Depending on the layout of the report, this version (above) could actually make a reader wonder what was going on.

Orphaned Records

One issue with finding ways to break the data is the concern with orphaned records. Mervyn Bick points out if you only display one or two child records at the bottom of the page, and then the rest of a group on the next page, it looks a bit odd. In Word there is a setting for "Widow/Orphan control" – and if turned on, quite literally ensures that if a paragraph is at the bottom of the page, you don't show just two lines – you move the paragraph to a new page.

It is possible to take existing code as shown in the previous report and enhance it just a little to do something similar, but in this case it would deal with the number of child rows in the current group.

To see this, copy the previous report – in the Command Window:

```
copy file PageBreak3.rep to PageBreak4.rep
```

Open the report in the Source Code Editor, and change the code at the beginning of the report to:

```
local r
r = new PAGEBREAK4REPORT()
r.render()

class PAGEBREAK4REPORT of MYCOMPANYREPORTCREPORT from :MyReports:MyCompanyReport.crp
```

Scroll down to the code for the footerBand's *onRender* event handler, and we're going to make some changes:

```
    // multiply that by the number of child records we want
    // to allow as a minimum at the bottom of the page:
    nSpaceNeeded = 0.42 + ( 3 * 0.21 )
```

Note that we removed "nChildCount" and replaced it with "3" here – this allows us to specify the number of records are a minimum at the bottom of the page. Save this and exit the Source Code Editor.

Open the report in the designer, change the secondary title text so the number 3 is changed to a 4. Find the group ("group1" in the Inspector) and set the *headerEveryFrame* property to *true*.

We're going to add the code we used in Chapter 11 to the header so that if a group is continued to a new page we add text that shows it. To do this, click on the *group headerBand* itself (the green bar), find the *preRender* event handler in the Inspector, click the tool button, and add the following:

```
function HEADERBAND_preRender()
   // check to see if custom property exists, if not create it:
   if type( "this.BreakField" ) == "U"
      this.BreakField = "XXX" // value not in table
   endif
   // this = headerBand
```

```
      // parent = group1
      // parent = streamSource1
      f = this.parent.parent.rowset.fields
      this.DataText1.text := f["Name"].value.rightTrim()
      if this.BreakField == f["Name"].value.rightTrim()
         // add extra text: the word
         // "(Continued ...)" in italics
         this.DataText1.text += " <i>(Continued ...)</i>"
      endif
   return
```

And then find the same *headerBand* and in the Inspector set the *onRender* event code to:

```
   function HEADERBAND_onRender()
      f = this.parent.parent.rowset.fields
      this.BreakField = f["Name"].value.rightTrim()
   return
```

(for a full explanation of this code, go back to Chapter 11 ...)

Try running the report. Click the "Next Page" button in the toolbar so that you see Page 3 – scroll to the bottom, and see that there is a bit of white space, although not a lot. At the top of page 4 you will see the header and records that would have started at the bottom of page 3.

Other Enhancements

Mervyn Bick and I worked a bit on this and one version of the report he sent me adds a bit of space when the date changes within a group – the idea being to break the data up just a little. In order to do this he sets another break variable similar to what we used above for the "(Continued ...)" text but uses the detailBand's *onRender* and *preRender* event handlers – when the value changes (in the *preRender* event handler, he sets the *top* property of the controls on the detailBand to a value of "0.09" which moves the controls down a little giving some blank space, and in the detailBand's *onRender* event handler he sets the *top* property back to 0. That's a quick summary, and there is a little more going on, but if you are interested, you should be able to tinker and get it to work.

A Different Method

I was told this method over the phone by someone, and have not tried it myself – it's a bit tricky in that what it does is actually change the *height* of the *streamFrame* if there is not enough room to print the group *headerBand* with at least one record under it.

The concept is that in the *canRender* event of the group *headerBand*, you check the *height* in a similar fashion as above, by checking the *renderOffset* and the streamFrame's *height* – and if there is not enough room to display the *headerBand*, you change the streamFrame's *height* property to the current *renderOffset*. In the group's *onRender* event, you set the streamFrame's *height* property back to what it was before you changed it.

What this does is force the Report Engine to evaluate the positioning, notice that the *streamFrame* does not have room for the group *headerBand*, and move that to the next frame (or page), and then by resetting the *height* of the *streamFrame*, you're ready to try again as you get close to the bottom of the page.

Cleanup

Create a new report (in the Navigator, click on the .Reports. tab, double-click on the "[New Report]" icon). Select the "File" menu, select "Set Custom Report Class", and in the dialog, click the "Clear Custom Report" button, then click "OK". This clears out the custom report setting in the Plus.ini file, so that the next report you create is not based on this one. Close that report without making any changes.

Make sure the database is closed by going to the Command Window and typing:

```
close databases
```

This will also ensure that you don't end up creating tables in the wrong location, etc.

Source Code

The following is a listing of the sample code in the folders we have been working with. If you downloaded the files from my website the structure will be different (see below). You may use the code contained in these folders for your own applications if you desire, with the caveat that credit be given appropriately.

From working on this chapter:

```
C:\dBASEReports\Chapter 14\DamsParentChild.dmd
C:\dBASEReports\Chapter 14\PageBreak1.rep
C:\dBASEReports\Chapter 14\PageBreak2.rep
C:\dBASEReports\Chapter 14\PageBreak3.rep
C:\dBASEReports\Chapter 14\PageBreak4.rep
```

Downloaded version – same files but with this path:

```
C:\ReportsBookSourceCode\Chapter 14\filename
```

Summary

Forcing a page break can be fairly simple, or depending on your needs, it can get a bit more complicated. However, as you can see, just about anything can be done with the Report Designer and the Report Engine of dBASE. Hopefully this has given you an even greater insight into some of what is possible.

It should be noted that examples 2 and 3 are based heavily on Michael Nuwer's Report Tutorial, and while I changed some of the code a little, including where some of it is executed, it works very much like Michael's suggestions. The report "PageBreak3" was using a call to *setRange()* on the child rowset that was throwing everything off, and was completely unnecessary in dBASE Plus 10.3, Mervyn Bick found that and pointed it out to me – I owe Mervyn special thanks for finding that. Sometimes when you have been staring at code for a long time you can't see the problem.

The next chapter will take a look at forcing page breaks in a report. There are often very good reasons to break the data up, but this is not always a simple "change this property" situation, which is why a whole chapter is dedicated to it.

Chapter 15: Enhancing Reports

Reports in dBASE, like with any reporting tool, can look pretty plain, or they can get extremely fancy in layout and design. You, as the developer, have a lot of control over what can be done. So far in this book we have only barely scratched the surface of what can be done to enhance the actual appearance of the controls on the report, to break up reports with a lot of data so that they are more visually interesting, and so on.

As you might imagine, this can take some work, but this chapter is going to look at a variety of things that you can do, and hopefully this will spur your own imagination to other ways of making your reports more interesting.

A Place for Our Work

As we work through the chapter we will be needing a place for the files we create, so please create a folder for this chapter:

```
C:\dBASEReports\Chapter 15
```

And in the Navigator, be sure to navigate to this folder.

Enhancing the Appearance of Text

The text controls in dBASE have many options which we have not really examined. We will take a look at many of these below, and discuss them briefly. We have used a small amount of this functionality, but there is more.

Font Properties

The text control has several font properties that can be used to enhance the appearance of the text. If you examine any report (or form) text control in the Inspector you will see:

Property	Default	Effect
fontBold	false	**Bold**
fontItalic	false	*Italic*
fontName	Arial	Black Chancery
fontSize	10	14 Point
fontStrikeout	false	~~Strikeout~~
fontUnderline	false	Underline

These properties can be changed to enhance the appearance of any report. In our custom classes we set the *fontName* and *fontSize* properties, as well as *fontBold*, but the others are useful as well. You can change individual controls in your reports, and make some fairly dramatic changes to the appearance.

As we have also seen, through the use of custom controls, we can affect the appearance of text controls throughout a report. For example, if you went into the "MyReportControls.cc" file we have the custom classes for this book in and modified the *fontName* property of the "DataText" control, all reports that use that control will display the text with the new font.

Color

The color of text controls can be changed using the *colorNormal* property. This property actually contains two parts – a foreground and a background definition, separated by a slash (/) character. The default *colorNormal* for text controls is: BtnText/BtnFace – these are really Windows color definitions, pulled out of Windows itself, and used more for forms than for reports. However, if you place a text control onto a report, this is the default. What does it mean? BtnText is the default text color, which is black, and BtnFace is the default background color, and while on a form this may be light grey or some other color, for a report this is typically white.

You can define your colors using standard dBASE color definitions – from the old DOS days these colors are:

Color name	Foreground code	Background code
Black	N	N
Dark Blue	B	B
Green	G	G
Cyan	GB or BG	GB or BG
Dark Red	R	R
Purple	RB or BR	RB or BR
Brown	RG or GR	RG or GR
Light Gray	W	W
Dark Gray	N+	N*
Blue	B+	B*
Bright Green	G+	G+
Bright Cyan	GB+ or BG+	GB* or BG*
Red	R+	R*
Magenta	RB+ or BR+	RB* or BR*
Yellow	RG+ or GR+	RG* or GR*
White	W+	W*

These are a bit confusing, especially with the + and * characters (which give a brighter color, + for foreground, * for background).

In order to get black text on a white background, using these colors, you could use:

```
N/W+
```

However, dBASE controls understand the JavaScript standard color names, so you could also use:

```
black/white
```

To reverse the colors:

```
white/black
```

Would give a black background with white text. For more information on colors in dBASE, check the online help, and use the keyword *colorNormal*.

Of course, it should be noted in all of this – if your users' printer does not have the ability to print in color, then setting color values is kind of a moot point. For example, the only printer I use is a laserjet that prints in black toner. I do not have a color printer handy. My reports do not use color because of it. It is possible to print to a PDF so that a report could be printed on a different printer in color by setting the Windows Default printer to the color printer driver, generate the PDF, and then reset the Windows default printer.

Pictures and Functions

The properties of the text control called *picture* and *function* can be used to format numeric values, or character values, or even both. These are quite useful, especially for numeric values. In addition to this, with numeric values you might want to use the *alignHorizontal* property to make sure numbers are lined up on the right. If you are not familiar with the pictures and functions used for formatting, the online help has a lot of information.

If you are using *canRender* to determine the text to display, and you still want to format the controls, you might also want to look at the *transform()* function in dBASE, which allows you to apply a picture (or function).

Border

This was discussed back in Chapter 2, but we haven't done much with it in the book after. Text controls in dBASE have a *borderStyle* property which allows you to define a border for the text control. The default *borderStyle* for a text control is "3 – None", but you can change the *borderStyle* to any of 9 different options. The list (also in the online help for dBASE) is:

Value	Style
0	Default
1	Raised
2	Lowered
3	None
4	Single
5	Double
6	Drop shadow
7	Client
8	Modal
9	Etched in
10	Etched out

These borders use the *frame* of the text control, and can actually cut into the text. The *frame* is a reference to the actual outside edge of the text control – if you click on any text control on a report you will see a black border – this is the *frame*.

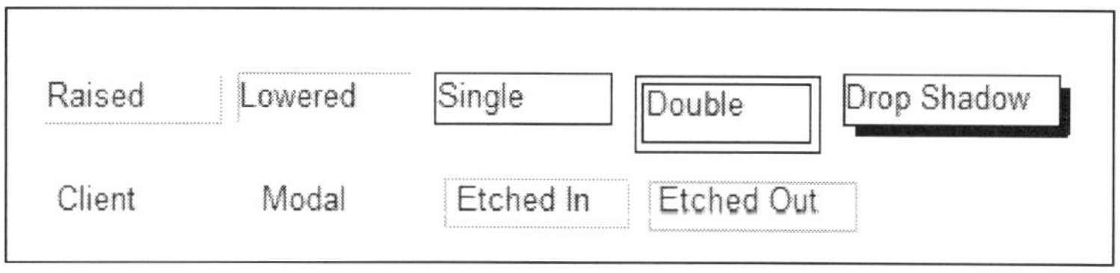

Figure 15-1

Figure 15-1 shows the various settings. The "Double" and "Drop Shadow" settings had to be made larger, and with "Double" I also had to work with the *marginHorizontal* and *marginVertical* settings to pull the text away from the border. The last two look very similar here, but if you view them in the Report Designer you can see a difference.

By adding borders around specific text controls you can grab the eye of the person viewing the report.

HTML

dBASE text controls have access to a subset of HTML – in other words, not *all* HTML tags are recognized, but most of the standard formatting ones are. Why would you want or need to use HTML in your text controls, when the properties of the control already give you a lot of options? You might find that you need to emphasize only some of the text that is displayed, you might want to add a line break at a point you might not normally get one, and so on. Below are some of the HTML tags that can be used in your text controls – it should be noted that most HTML tags require a start and an end tag:

Name	Start Tag	End Tag	Effect
Bold	<b>	</b>	**Boldfaced text**
Italic	<i>	</i>	*Italicized text*
Underline	<u>	</u>	Underlined text
Strikeout	<strike>	</strike>	~~Struck out text~~
Font	<font option>	</font>	Varies
Options for the Font tag: size – 1 to 7, with the default being 3, 1 being smallest color – HTML color options (include JavaScript colors, and Hexadecimal colors which start #) <font size="4" color="red">Some Text</font>			
Break	 		The line break tag does not require an end tag, but in dBASE must be followed by a space. This is a very minor bug in dBASE. It will force a break to a new line.
Paragraph	<p>		The paragraph tag does not require an end tag, but as with the tag, it requires a space after it. This is a minor bug in dBASE. This will, in a report, force a break to a new line. If you output this to an HTML file it will force a break with a blank line after it. A strict interpretation of HTML would require The <p> tag to start a paragraph, and </p> to complete it.

The nice thing is that you can insert these tags into the *text* property of a text control:

```
"<b>Bold This</b> and then <u>underline this</u><br> and start a new line".
```

This is a simple example, but hopefully you get the idea.

Conditional Changes

Of course, some of the power of dBASE comes from the ability to change some of these properties and attributes of the text controls programmatically, and more importantly, when specific conditions are met. You might need in an inventory listing to show all records that have a zero or negative "in stock" amount in red, for example. To do that, you might do something like the following, using the *canRender* event of the text control:

```
function QtyInStock_canRender()
   f = form.streamSource1.rowset.fields
   if f["QtyInStock"].value < 1
      this.colorNormal := "red/white"
   else
      this.colorNormal := "black/white"
   endif
return true
```

Notice that you need to set the *colorNormal* property back to what it was before, otherwise all instances of this text control (in other words, all records after this one) could be the wrong color.

Text vs. TextLabel Controls

You will note that there are two controls that can be used to place text on a report. The Text control and the TextLabel control. Why are there two? One of them, the Text control, has a large quantity of properties and events and has an internal HTML interpreter built into it. The other, the TextLabel control does not have as many properties/events and does not have the internal HTML interpreter built into it.

The Text control has the following properties and events that are not included with the TextLabel control. We have discussed and used some of these, and will come back to some of the others later:

Properties
fixed
leading
marginHorizontal
marginVertical
rotate
suppressIfBlank
suppressIfDuplicate
tracking
trackJustifyThreshold
transparent
variableHeight
verticalJustifyLimit

Events
canRender
onRender

That's quite a bit. Why the difference? The TextLabel control was created as a "lighter" Text control for forms – they take less overhead because each instance of a Text control includes all these properties and events and the HTML interpreter. For reports this isn't as much of an issue, and most developers use the Text control because it *has* these properties and events and the ability to work with HTML. If nothing else, the *canRender* and *onRender* events are rather important to many reports.

Fine Tuning Text Controls

In the previous discussion, we mention quite a few properties of the Text control that we have not discussed in earlier chapters, nor used. This is probably as good a place as any to discuss some of them.

Some properties deal very specifically with the way the text itself is displayed within the confines of the space defined by the text control. What does that mean? When you place a text control onto a report a specific amount of space is reserved around the text to give some padding between the text and the edge of the control. One of these is the *margin*, for example. Let's take a look at these properties briefly. For many developers, it is not necessary to really delve into these, but this book would not be complete if they were not discussed at all.

The *fixed* Property

This property has a logical (*true* or *false*) value, and defaults to *false*. The purpose is to determine if, when attempting to shift text up (see discussions on using *suppressIfBlank* in the previous chapter), this text control is allowed to shift up.

In addition, this will affect what happens if you have a text control with the *variableHeight* property set to *true*, and it is under the control. Assume you have two text controls on the report in the detailBand, Text1 is above Text2. If the *fixed* property of Text2 is false, and the *variableHeight* property of Text1 above it needs more room (we'll discuss *variableHeight* below), then Text2 will shift appropriately down the report. This might affect other objects in the band as well.

If however the *fixed* property is *true* in either case, this control will not shift. In most reports it is a good idea to leave this property at its default value of *false*, however, there might be times when you need a text control to be fixed in place – for example if you are using a pre-printed form – you might need the control to always print at its defined position no matter what other text controls around it are doing.

The *leading* Property

This property controls the amount of space between lines when the text is allowed to wrap. By default this is set to 0, which tells dBASE to use the standard line spacing. However, if you have text wrapping inside a single object (such as a memo field, with the *variableHeight* property set to *true*), you might want to experiment with this property a little to reduce or expand the spacing between lines.

The *marginHorizontal* and *marginVertical* Properties

This is the distance between the text and the *frame* of the object. You might expect the edge of the Text object and the edge of the actual text to be the same, and by default they are – these properties both default to 0. However, if you experiment you can see that you can modify these so that the amount of space between the edge of the Text control and the actual text both horizontally (side to side) and vertically (top to bottom) is larger than 0.

I will leave the application of this to your imagination. One reason for working with these that was shown earlier in this chapter – if you are using the *borderStyle* property, you might want to place a little distance between the border and the text – this would ensure that the text does not touch the border, and therefore is not confused with or by it. This can be more important if you use some of the decorative style fonts which can be quite fancy. This may mean making a text control taller and/or wider than it would normally be.

The *rotate* Property

This property can be used to display text in one of four positions – the default is what you normally see, but you might want to rotate a text control 90 degrees, or 180 degrees *(which would make it upside-down)*, or even 270 degrees. Why would you want to do that? Special labeling for some part of a report, something more fancy (we'll take a look at one idea later) with the company logo, perhaps?

The *suppressIfBlank* Property

We discussed this in the previous chapter, so there's not any real need to get into it here. It should be noted that a text control is considered blank if either the *visible* property is *true* or the *canRender* event returns *false*. In either case, the text control will not display, but the space for it will be reserved on the report unless the *suppressIfBlank* property is *true*.

The *suppressIfDuplicate* Property

This property is useful if you have a report where some values might be repeated, but you only want the value to appear when it is the first instance. The default for this property is *false*, and in most cases should be left that way. An example of when you might want to change this would be in the reports we've done that show the date of a litter of dogs – is it really necessary to show the date for each dog in the same litter? If we set the *suppressIfDuplicate* property to *false*, then the litter date would only appear once (if the report was sorted on that date field).

The *tracking* Property

The *tracking* property is used to specify space between characters. The default is whatever the font specifies. This property allows you to cause extra spacing to occur between the characters *(or remove extra spacing between characters)*. You might use this for special headings or something in a report.

The *trackJustifyThreshold* Property

The name of this property makes it sound like it is related to the *tracking* property, but it's only distantly related. The *trackJustifyThreshold* property is used when the *alignHorizontal* property of a text control is set to "3 – Justify", and is used to specify spacing in order to get words to reach the right margin. The online help describes this better than I can, and it's something you might want to experiment with. As with some of the other properties, this is useful only in certain circumstances – in this case, if the text is wrapping within the text control.

The *variableHeight* Property

This property is used to allow a text control to grow to a larger height if needed, to display text. This is most useful for text controls associated with a memo field in a table. It has an effect on the *detailBand height* – if the detailBand's *expandable* property is *false*, the text may not have enough room to display and will be truncated. If the detailBand's *expandable* property is true, however, the text will expand the *height* of the *detailBand* as needed. This can affect controls beneath it, as discussed above. If you have a control that beneath this one (vertically) on the band that you do not wish to shift, then you should set that control's *fixed* property to *true*.

The *verticalJustifyLimit* Property

This property is very similar to the *trackJustifyThreshold* property, except it affects the amount of space used between lines of a text control when the *alignVertical* property is set to "3 – Justify".

A New Custom Report

Having discussed some of what can be done with text controls beyond what we've *been* doing, let's take a look at doing something that's pretty flashy for a report. For this we are going to create a new custom report – it will have the company name as text down the side of the report.

To do this, we need to create a new Custom report, so go to the Reports tab of the Navigator, and double click the "[New Custom Report]" icon. We need to set the custom report to the "Base.crp" in the folder that has our custom reports. Select the "File" menu, and "Set Custom Report Class ...". Select "Base.crp", and click "OK".

The base custom report has no controls on it by default, so we will want to do something about that.

We're going to place the Company Name down the left side of the report. In order to do this, we need to reduce the *width* of the *streamFrame*. There is no easy way to tell how much room will be needed, so for now, just shift the left of the *streamFrame* toward the right by clicking once on the *streamFrame* (the large yellow part of the report design surface) to give it focus. This will allow you to select the "handle" on the left edge and drag it to the right. You can do this again as needed.

Press Ctrl+S and save this as "MyCompanyVerticalLogo.crp" in the "C:\dBASEReports\Reports" folder that other custom reports are in. You should have something that looks similar to this:

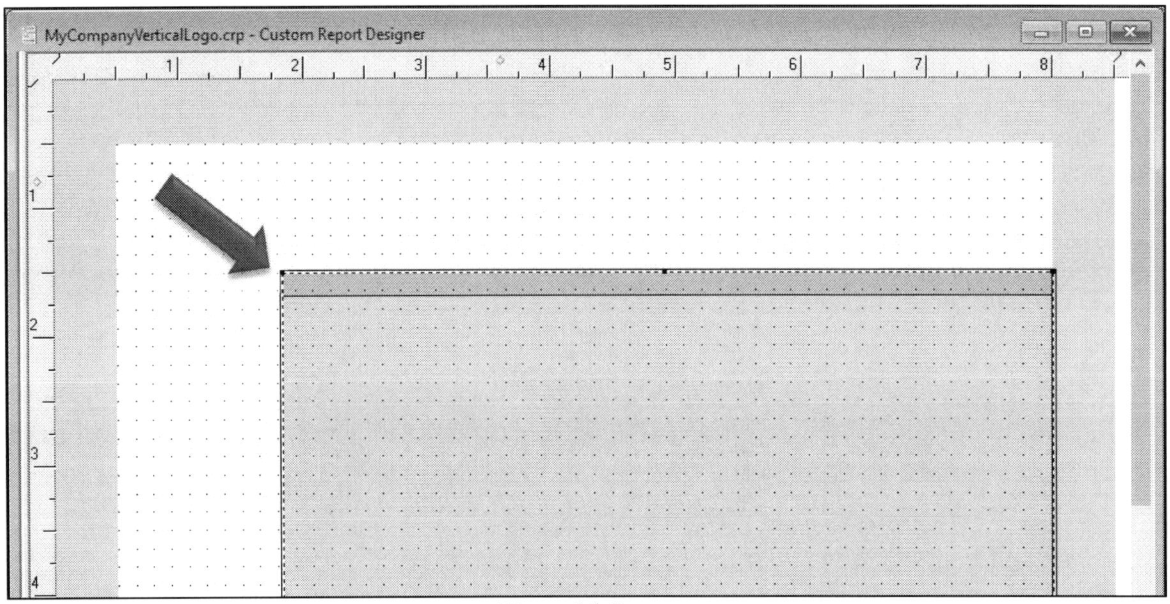

Figure 15-2

Look at the Component Palette – if you do not see a "Custom" tab, go to the Command Window and type:

```
set procedure to :MyReportControls:MyReportControls.cc
```

At this point you will see the "Custom" tab on the Component Palette.

Place a "MainTitleText" control onto the report, but place it over to the left. Notice that it defaults to "My Company Name" – as we've had it appear at the top of other reports. Find the *rotate* property for this control, and select "3 - 270 degrees". Notice the text has been rotated, but it hasn't adjusted its width or height at all. We need to do that. Try adjusting the *height* (and shift the text control) so that it is as tall as the *pageTemplate* – this will mean moving the top and left of the control to the edge of the *pageTemplate*. If you are using a *metric* of Inches for the report, you can actually do this simply by going to the Inspector, and setting the *top* and *left* properties to 0, and the *height* property to 10. This should now look something like:

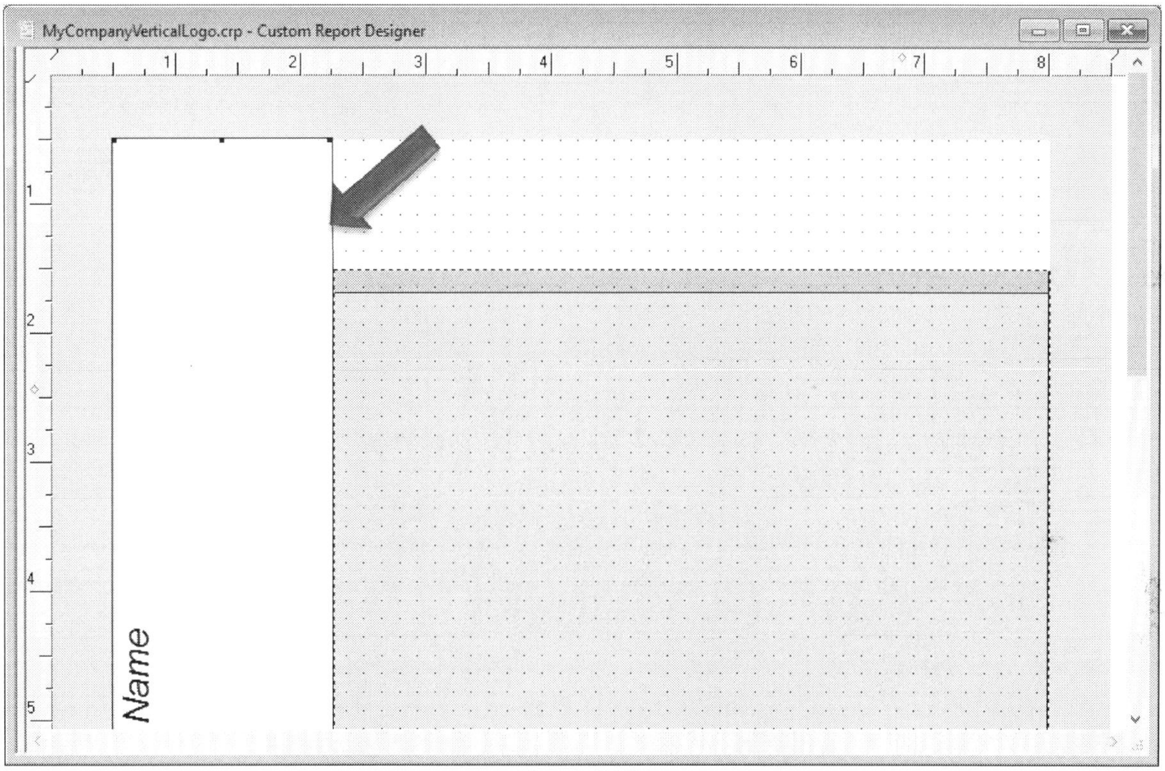

Figure 15-3

The rest of the text is further down the screen than what is shown in Figure 15-3.

Now we need to set the *fontSize* property to something larger. For this example, let's use a *fontSize* of 60. That's pretty big, but take a look at the results:

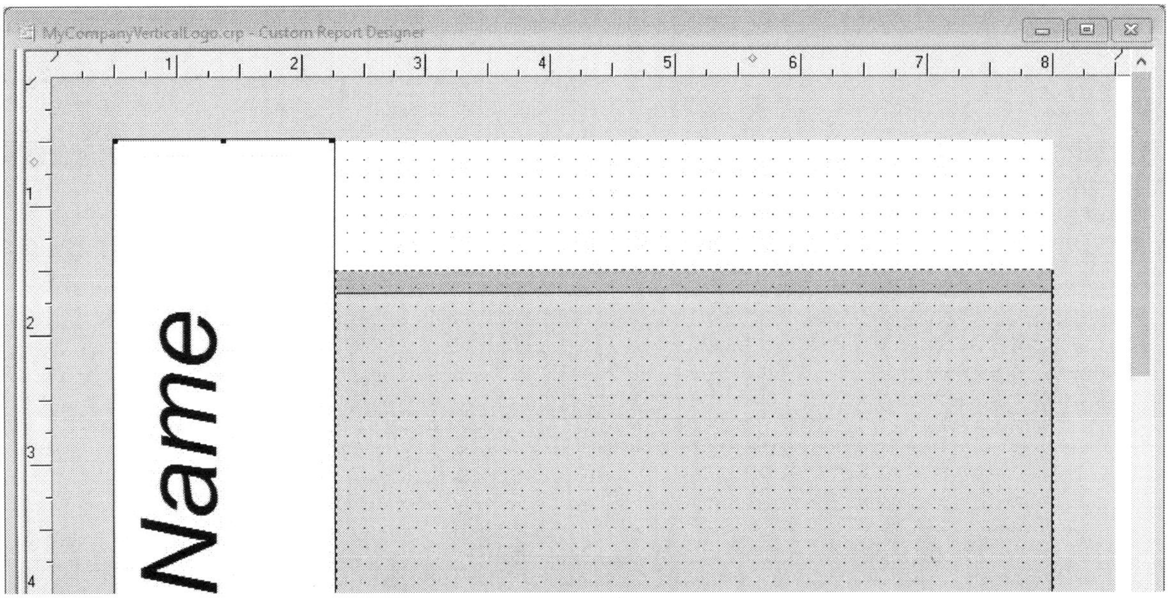

Figure 15-4

NOTE
It is very easy here to accidentally move the *pageTemplate* around, as you are placing text onto it, and trying to move it with the mouse. If you do move the *pageTemplate*, just go to the Inspector, put focus on the *pageTemplate* if it isn't, and set the margins (*marginLeft*, etc.) to 0.5.

The next step is to select a fancier looking font than the default of "Arial". For this example I used a font that is installed on my computer called "Black Chancery" – you will want to use something that is on your computer – not all computers have the same fonts, and I'm not sure this one is installed "standard" with Windows. This is done by clicking on the *fontName* property in the Inspector, and the tool button – it opens a dialog allowing you to select the font you want, and displays the font name in the font selected.

We want the text to fill as much space as we can, so try setting the *fontSize* in the Inspector to a larger value. In the example below it's set to a size of 80:

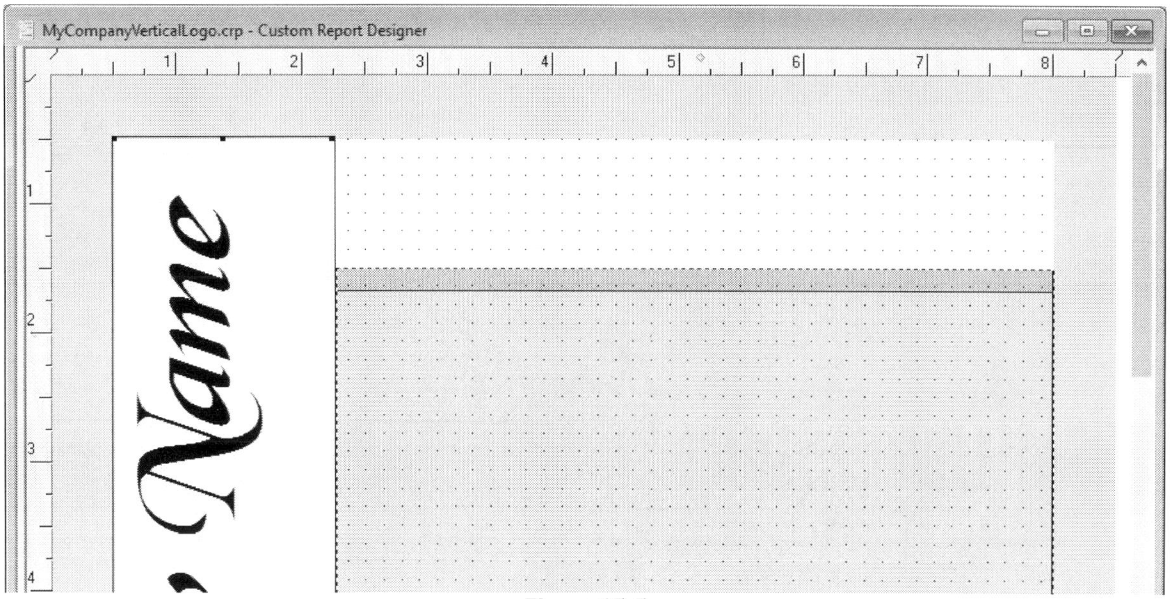

Figure 15-5

Next set the *borderStyle* property to "4 – Single". This will give a single-line border around the company name. If you had a color printer you could set the text to a specific color. Go to the *colorNormal* property in the Inspector and change "BtnText/BtnFace" to read "Lightgrey/white" and press Enter, the color of the control will change to a lighter color:

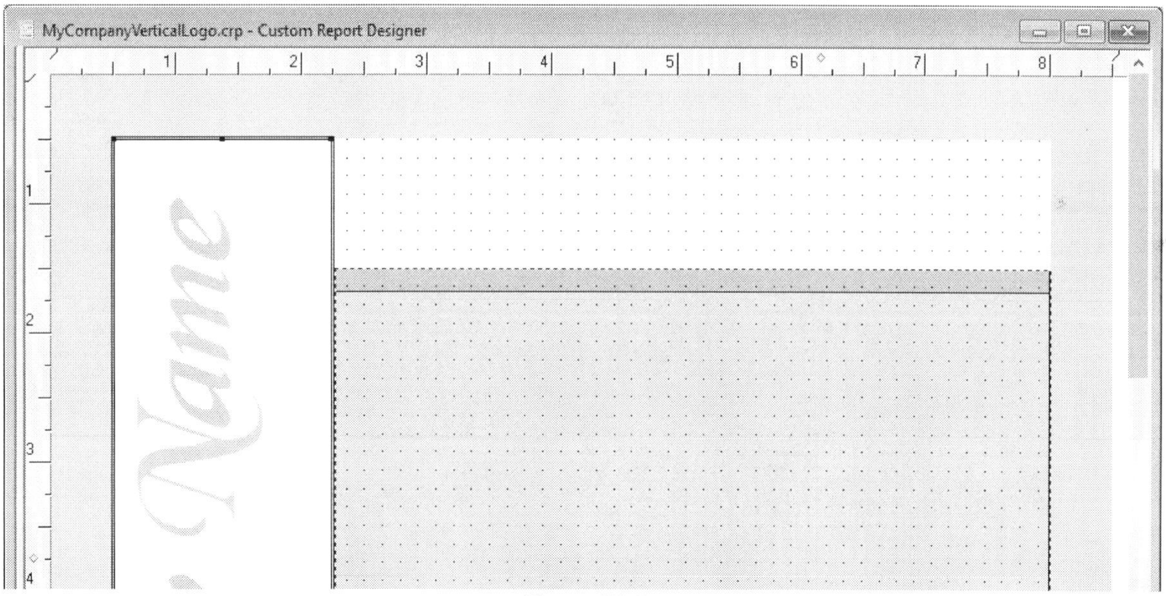

Figure 15-6

If necessary, select the *streamFrame* again, and drag the left side over close to this text control.

We need to add other useful text controls to the custom report class. Place a "SecondaryTitleText" control at the top of the *pageTemplate*, with a "DateText" (not "DataText") below that. Place them close to where you want them, then select both (Ctrl+mouse click), and select the "Layout" menu, select "Align" and "Center Horizontally in Window". There's a lot of blank space at the top of the report now, since the company name is off to the left. You can readjust the top of the *streamFrame* by clicking on it once more, and moving the mouse over the top so that it shows the "resize" arrows, and drag the top up.

You may want to adjust the width of the company name text on the left, make sure you can see the descenders (the bottoms of the letters), and then readjust left side of the *streamFrame* again so it is right up against that control.

The report should now look something like:

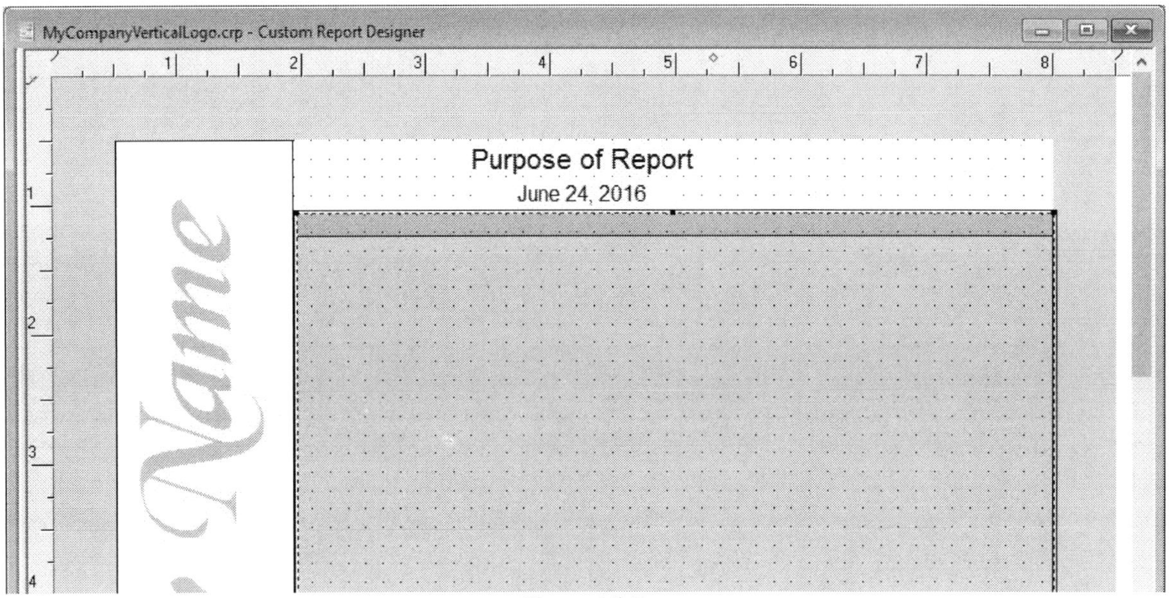

Figure 15-7

You should probably place a page number at the bottom, so scroll down to the bottom of the report. Select the "Paging" tab of the Component Palette and drag a "Pagenumber" text control to under the *streamFrame* (place it on the *pageTemplate*). Readjust the width so you can see the page number. Center the text control on the page ("Layout" menu, "Align" and "Center Horizontally in Window").

Save this custom report and exit the Report Designer (Ctrl+W).

Now that you have this custom report, let's try creating a simple report with it.

In the Navigator window, double click the "[New Report]" icon. We need to select our new custom report, so go to the "File" menu and select "Set Custom Report Class ...", and select "MyCompanyVerticalLogo.crp" from the list. You should see a screen very much like the previous screen shot. Save this in the (Chapter 15 folder) with Ctrl+S as "VerticalLogoSample.rep".

Change the *text* of the SecondaryTitleText to "Vertical Logo Sample". Now go back to the Navigator window and select the "Tables" tab, and if the "DBASEREPORTS" database is not showing, select it in the "Look in:" combobox. Then select the "Dogs" table, and drag this to the design surface. Select the query object's *rowset* in the Inspector, then set the *indexName* property to "NAME".

Place a "DataColHeading" text control (from the "Custom" tab of the Component Palette) onto the *detailBand*, and change the *text* to "Name". Select a "DataText" control and place it under the heading text, widen it by a bit. Then go to the Inspector and set the *text* to a type of Codeblock (use the "T" button), click on the tool button and enter the following in the dialog:

```
this.form.dogs1.rowset.fields["name"].value
```

Adjust the position of these two controls so that they line up and the report looks something like:

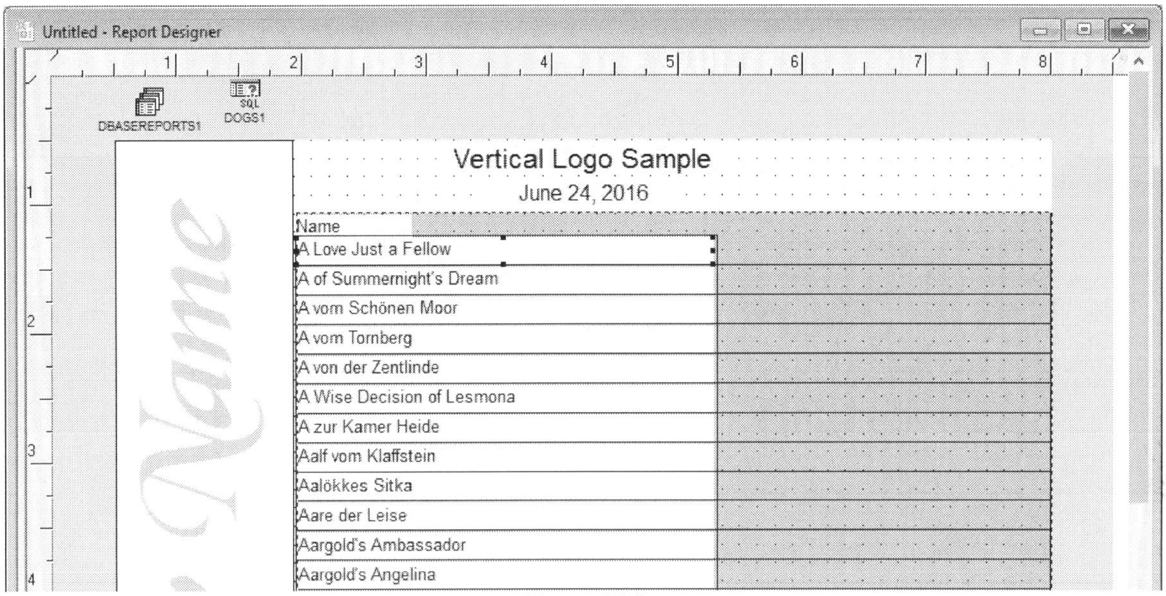

Figure 15-8

Next try running the report. It should look something like:

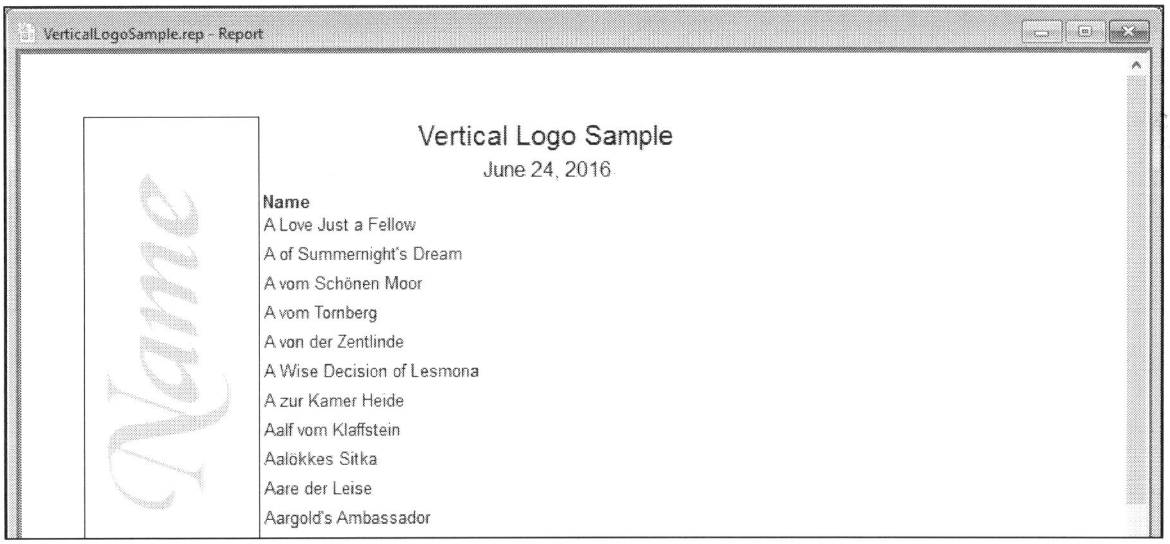

Figure 15-9

That's a lot fancier looking than the reports we've been doing. There are of course other things we could do.

For example, you could put the text behind the *streamFrame*, but you'd probably want to use a lighter shade of grey (you can experiment with the *getColor()* dialog, among other things). You could put a large text control behind the *pageTemplate* that said

"Draft" or "TOP SECRET" if that was what was needed. The only problem with doing something like that is that normally that sort of watermark text is typically at a 45 degree angle across the page, and the *rotate* property of the text control can only rotate to 0, 90, 180 or 270 degrees. At this time I am not sure if there is a way to provide this sort of functionality in a dBASE report unless you tried to work with a background image that contained the text you wanted.

Shapes vs. Rectangles

When working with a report, sometimes you might wish to enhance a part of the report by placing a border around not just a single text control, but perhaps around a group of text controls.

The obvious control to use for this would be a Rectangle object. However, depending on the version of dBASE you are using, there is a bug in dBASE with Rectangle objects and reports. When I wrote the first edition of this book, the Rectangle control tended to print offset (down and to the right) from where they appeared in the designer. This bug seems to have been fixed in current versions.

So why would you use a shape control? The shape control does not appear to have the same bug with printing offset that the rectangle does in older versions. Even better - a shape can have various outlines, you can change the *borderStyle*, and you can set the color of both the inside and the outside of the shape object.

In addition, shape controls have *canRender* and *onRender* events, which the rectangle control does not.

One caveat with using shapes (and rectangles) is that in the z-order of the report this control must be rendered before any controls placed on top of it. If you know you are going to use it in the report before you start designing the report, you can just place it there and then place your text controls on top of it. If, however, you add the shape later, you will need to modify the source code of your report, moving the control's constructor code to a spot before the text controls you wish to display on top of it.

To get a feel for what this looks like we're going to create a new report, but we're going to use the "Base.crp" custom report as the basis because we don't want the text controls that are defined in the report we've been using. Start a new report by double-clicking on the "[New Report]" icon. Select the "File" menu, select "Set Custom Report Class ...", and in the dialog find the file "Base.crp" –x this will be in the same folder as "MyCompanyReport.crp". Click "OK". Now we have the *metric* and some other properties set (margins, and such), but no text controls.

Before doing anything else, save this (press Ctrl+S) as "Shape.rep".

We're going to place some text controls on the *pageTemplate* to give us your company name, address, and so on. Then we'll place a Shape on the report – this is literally so we can see why it is important to place the Shape on the report first. If you have never done this, you will not have seen the problems, and I want to show it to you graphically.

Place a "DataHeadingText" control on the *pageTemplate* in the upper left of the screen. Change the *text* to "My Company Name". Place a "DataText" control under that, and change the *text* to "123 Some Street". Place another under that, and change the *text* to "Some City, ST 99999-1234". You will need to widen these text controls so that they are wide enough for the text. This may mean readjusting the height as well. Place one more "DataText" control under the last one, and change the *text* to "(999) 555-1234".

Spend a little time lining these controls up, so that they look good. Now we want to outline this with a shape. So go to the "Standard" tab of the Component Palette, and place a shape object onto the *pageTemplate*. Notice that this defaults to a circle, and it defaults to white with a black border.

In the Inspector, change the *shapeStyle* property to "1 – Rectangle". Widen this so that it is large enough to cover your text. Doing so, we find that the text is no longer visible – indeed, if you printed the report, the text would also no longer be visible. We need to modify this so that the Shape is first in the z-order, however we can't do this in the designer. Save and exit the Report Designer (Ctrl+W) and open the report in the Source Code Editor. Find this code:

```
this.PAGETEMPLATE1.SHAPE1 = new SHAPE(this.PAGETEMPLATE1)
   with (this.PAGETEMPLATE1.SHAPE1)
      left = 0.0625
      top = 0.0729
      width = 2.1354
      height = 0.8854
      shapeStyle = 1 // Rectangle
      penWidth = 1
      form.SHAPE1 = form.pagetemplate1.shape1
   endwith
```

and move it (highlight it, and cut it with Ctrl+X, then paste it with Ctrl+V) to above this code:

```
this.PAGETEMPLATE1.DATAHEADINGTEXT1 = new DATAHEADINGTEXT(this.PAGETEMPLATE1)
   with (this.PAGETEMPLATE1.DATAHEADINGTEXT1)
      height = 0.2083
      left = 0.1354
      top = 0.1146
      width = 1.5833
      text = "My Company Name"
      form.DATAHEADINGTEXT1 = form.pagetemplate1.dataheadingtext1
   endwith
```

Now that this has been shifted, the shape will be in the correct z-order, and both in the Report Designer and when printed, it will appear correctly behind the text.

Open the report back in the Report Designer. You will most likely need to move both the Shape and the text around a bit, perhaps resizing them so that this looks good. You should have something that looks like:

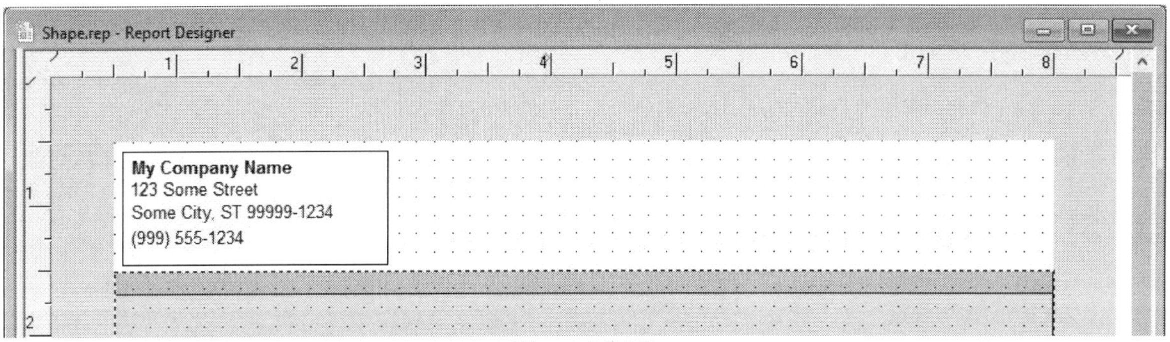

Figure 15-10

This is not all *that* fancy looking, but with a bit of work you could do more. For example, you could experiment with the shape a bit – perhaps using a "Rounded Rectangle" (set the *shapeStyle* to 0) – although that doesn't really look much different. You could play with the colors, the *penStyle* (which allows for dashlines, dotted-lines, and dash-dot lines), the *penWidth* which allows you to change how wide the line is. If the printer this will be printed on can handle colors, for example, you might set the border to red, and the background to a light yellow color by changing the *colorNormal* property to:

red/lightyellow

Of course, the problem with that is that the text controls that are on the shape are still showing a white background. You would need to change the *colorNormal* property of them as well so that the background was the same as the shape – OR you could set the *transparent* property of the text controls to *true* (it defaults to *false*), which tells the text controls to use the background of whatever object is "beneath" them.

Hopefully this will give you some ideas. Of course, the whole bit of having to modify the source code for the report could have been avoided by placing the shape control on the design surface before the text controls – however, this kind of thing happens a lot – you design your report, and the user who is paying you decides that it would look better if ... So the exercise was designed to show how to handle that.

streamFrame Border

It is possible to set the border of the *streamFrame*, which is the area that contains your detailBands. This is done by using the *borderStyle* property just like with the text controls. It outlines the whole *streamFrame*, and can be rather nice looking, particularly if you are using multiple streamFrames on your report (we will discuss that in a later chapter).

Lines

The line object can be used to good effect on a report. We've only briefly looked at them, and we've only used them horizontally – but you can lay out lines in any direction you wish. If you want a line to be vertical it should be noted that shifting it left, right up or down can only be done with the mouse or the Inspector. Normally you can move a line with the keyboard, but that is not the case here.

Otherwise, you can use lines to great effect to break up groups of records for reports, and so on. If you start working with lines, you should experiment with the *width* and *pen* properties, as these can enhance the appearance of your lines as well. The *width* property does exactly what it sounds like – it allows you to change the width (weight) of the line. The *pen* property allows you to change the type of line from a solid line to a series of dashes, or a series of dots, or a combination of dashes and dots.

One option that you should be careful of – the *pageTemplate* has a *gridLineWidth* property – setting this to any value other than zero will place a border around every text control on the report. Unless you have a good reason for setting this, I would leave it at the default of zero.

Images

Images are a very good way to enhance the appearance of your reports. For example, if your company has a logo, you might want to place that onto the report (or a custom report), rather than the "My Company Name" text that we've been using.

The image object also has both *canRender* and *onRender* events, which you can write event handlers for. One thing you might want to do is change an image for the current record based on some condition, for example. Or display an image based on a condition.

A couple of notes about images:

- The *pageTemplate* object has a *background* property that can be used to set a background image, the problem is that this really is only useful if you are intending to output an HTML page from your report – in other words, the Report Engine will not actually print a background image that is set with the *background* property of the *pageTemplate* – the image is not sent to the printer.
- The other note about images that you should be aware of is that with some versions of dBASE some very high resolution images will not print – this is a known bug in dBASE which was addressed in more recent releases.

The pageTemplate

While the *pageTemplate* object has a *colorNormal* property, in older versions of dBASE (2.62 and earlier) it does not appear to have the effect of coloring the *pageTemplate* as you might expect. This has the effect of changing the background color of text objects placed on the report, and that is all.

In current versions of dBASE this has been corrected, and this changes the color of the *pageTemplate*. This is kind of dangerous however – if you have an inkjet printer and a large report, you could wipe out your ink supply quickly. In addition it would only affect the color of the pageTemplate which would leave white space around it to the edge of the paper (based on your report's margins).

Alternating Colors for detailBands

One bit of functionality that is useful for some reports, particularly tabular reports, is the ability to alternate the color of the background of the *detailBand*. This makes it very easy to see the different rows as separate data.

The *detailBand* does *not* have a *colorNormal* property, so how do you do something like this? As you might imagine, this question has come up in the dBASE developer newsgroups, and in answer to the question, several folk have come forward with methods that will handle this. The basic idea is to create a text control that:

- Has no value in the *text* property
- Sets its own *height* and *width* to the appropriate values for the *detailband*
- Determines through a calculation if it should render or not
- Doesn't work well if the *height* of the *detailBand* changes from record to record

This also requires that it be the first control in the *detailBand*, and that the text controls placed on top of this one have their *transparent* property set to *true*, so that the background color is used. There is a custom class for this in the dUFLP (the dBASE Users. Function Library Project) that can be used – and this is what we are going to use for a sample report.

Before creating the report, the following assumes you followed all the instructions back in Chapter 3, and have the dUFLP set up for use. In the Command Window, type:

```
set procedure to :dUFLP:AltBandColor.cc
```

This will make this custom control available in the Report Designer. We need to create a new report, so go to the Navigator window and select the "Reports" tab. Double-click the "[New Report]" icon. If the custom report being used is not the "usual" one, go to the "File" menu and select "Set Custom Report Class ..." and select "MyCompanyReport.crp" for the custom report.

Change the *text* of the SecondaryTitleText control to "Alternate Colored DetailBands". Save this (Ctrl+S) as "AlternateColors.rep".

If you look at the Component Palette, there is a new tab – "dUFLP Report Controls" (if this is not there, the control is probably on the "Custom" tab – what this means is that you missed a step in the setup for the dUFLP). Place an instance of the control "AltBandColorText" onto the *detailBand*. You may need to set the *top* and *left* properties to 0, just to make sure the text control is where it needs to be. Note that the color of the *detailBand* is the color defined for this text control – it may not look like anything happened. We could use a different color, but for now, let's leave it as is.

Next we need a table, so go to the "Tables" tab, and if the "DBASEREPORTS" database is not showing, select that in the "Look in:" combobox, and then select the "Dogs" table. Place this on the report. At this point, depending on the version of dBASE you are using, you may see alternating colors for detailBands already.

Select the "DataHeadingText" control and place an instance onto the report above the *streamFrame* – directly on the *pageTemplate*. Change the *text* to "Name". We want to shift the *streamFrame* down a little so single-click on the *detailBand* part of the report (or select "streamFrame1" in the Inspector) – make sure the Inspector shows "form.pagetemplate1.streamFrame1" in the combobox.

Move the mouse so that the pointer changes to the "size" cursor (usually an up/down arrow) over the top of the *streamFrame* border, and move the *top* of the *streamFrame* down – don't move the *streamFrame* itself, we're just adjusting the top. Then move the DataHeadingText control down to just above the *streamFrame*.

Go to the Component Palette and select the "Custom" tab. Place a "DataText" control on the *detailBand* on top of the "AltBandColorText" control, set the *text* type to "Codeblock", click the tool button and enter this in the dialog:

```
this.form.dogs1.rowset.fields["name"].value
```

Make sure that this text control is at the top of the *detailBand* by setting the *top* property to 0. Line it up with the heading control that is on the pageTemplate. Set the *height* property of the text control to 0.18 (if you are using a metric of Inches – if not, reduce the height, but make sure you can see all of the text). Set the Text control's *transparent* property to *true*. Then set the *height* of the detailBand to the same height as the text. This should look something like:

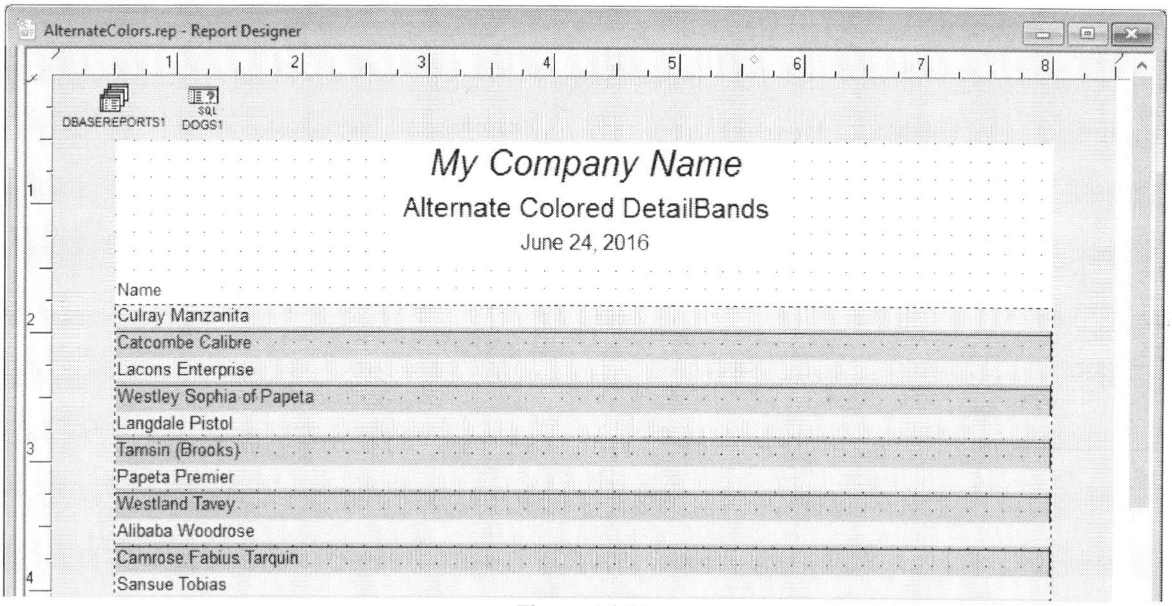

Figure 15-11

This may not look like it is alternating the colors on your screen. The reason is because the code that is executed to determine which band is which color sometimes only executes when the report is in the Report Designer (there is some inconsistency in dBASE here – it is working for this control, but not for the DataHeadingText control ...). To see this, try running the report. You should see something like:

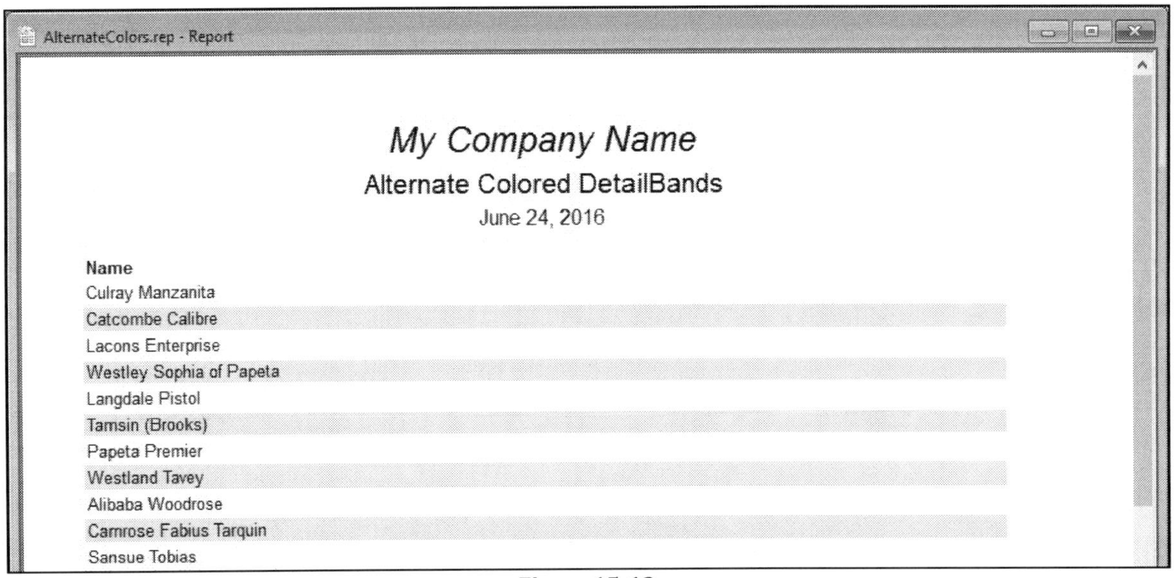

Figure 15-12

If you wanted to change the color for the alternate rows, you can do so in the Inspector by selecting the "AltBandColorText1" control, and changing the *colorNormal* property.

Checkboxes for Logical Fields

There is one more thing we will discuss in this chapter, which is something I find useful, although not all developers will. Logical fields in dBASE tend to be represented in forms (screens) as checkboxes – a box that is empty if the value in the field is not *true*. However, reports do not normally do this, because the checkbox is displayed via a graphic image in the form for dBASE.

It is, however, possible to display an empty box and a box with a check (or an "x") in it depending on the value of the field. This requires the use of yet another custom class, and a bit of extra work, but it can be worth the effort.

The custom class is, like with the alternate band colors, already written, but it takes a little more work to set up than some classes. This one assumes that the font "Wingdings" is available on the computer that is running the report, and that this particular version of the Wingdings font has the characters that we need to display – the empty box, and the box with a checkmark in it. (This could be modified to use graphic images instead, but the class as it stands is designed to be a text control with specific characters displayed.)

Interestingly the tables in the "DBASESamples" database don't seem to include logical fields. In the navigator, make sure that the "DBASEReports" database is selected. In it, you should find a table "LogicalField.dbf". I created it for this purpose – it has some really simple data and only a few records.

Before starting this report, go to the Command Window, and type:

```
set procedure to :dUFLP:RepCntl.cc
```

This will make a few new controls available, but we're really concerned with just one.

Create a new report as we've done in the past. Change the SecondaryTitleText control's *text* property to "Checkbox Text Control", and save the report by pressing Ctrl+S and giving it a name of "CheckboxText.rep".

Go to the Navigator window and select the "Tables" tab, and the "LogicalField" table. Drag this to the design surface. Because the focus of this is the Checkbox Text control, this table only has a couple of fields. In the Inspector find the *rowset* property, click the tool button, find the *indexName* property, change the index to "Name".

Go to the "Component Palette" and select the "Custom" tab. Select the "DataColHeadingText" control and place an instance on the *detailBand*, and change the *text* to "Name". Place another "DataColHeadingText" control to the right of the first, and change the *text* to "Agree?".

Place a "DataText" control under the "Name" heading text. Change the *text* type to "Codeblock", click the tool button and enter the following in the dialog:

```
this.form.logicalfield1.rowset.fields["name"].value
```

Now we have the basics done, let's take a look at the "Agree" field. This is a logical field, but rather than display "true" or "false" in the report, it looks better to use something like a checkbox. So we're going to use a custom class that actually does this for us.

Go to the Component Palette, and select the "dUFLP Report Controls" tab, you should see a checkbox there with the name of it to the right: kmcheckboxtext. Place an instance of this under the "Agree?" heading. This should display a diamond shape with a question mark in it – this is a character in the Wingdings font, and is a place holder for the report.

We need to modify this control a little differently than we normally do. We are going to use the text control's *onOpen* event to assign the field that is to be evaluated to this control. Go to the Inspector and select the "Events" tab. Find the *onOpen* event, and click the tool button. Enter the following:

```
function KMCHECKBOXTEXT1_onOpen()
   this.text = {||this.form.logicalfield1.rowset.fields["agree"].value}
return
```

When the report is first rendered the text property will be assigned this codeblock, and the code that is associated with the custom class will evaluate this field. This report should look something like:

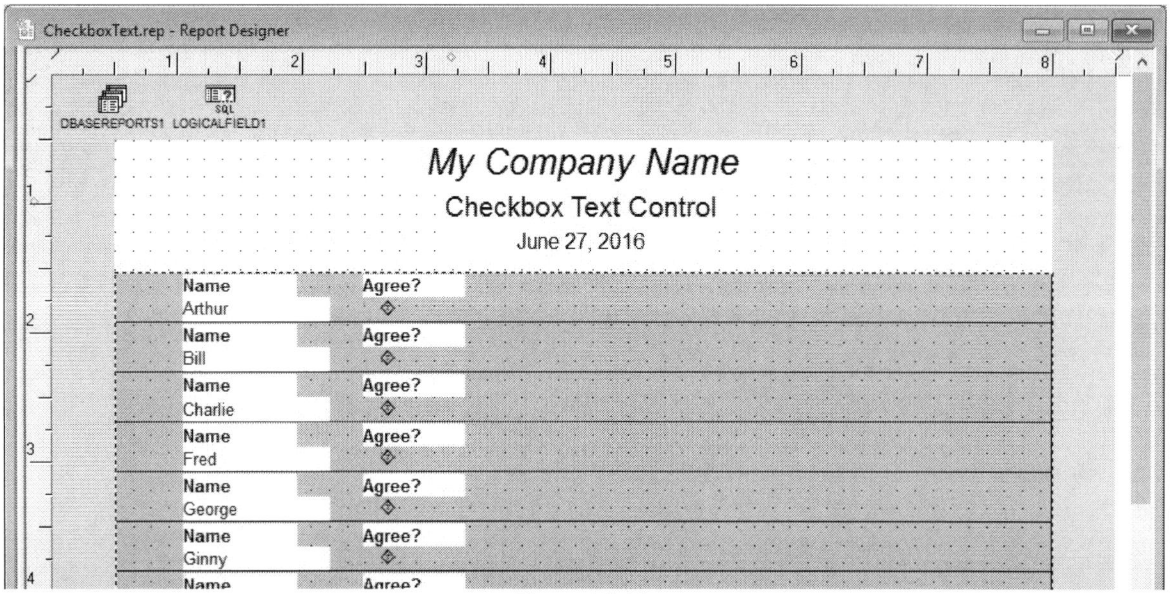

Figure 15-13

As with some of our other reports, this isn't what it will look like when run. If you run this report, you should see something like:

Figure 15-14

What Is Wrong If the Characters Are Not The Same?

It is possible you have a different version of the Wingdings font than I do. There have been at least two of them put out by Microsoft with the operating system. If that is the case, you might need to look at the font and see if you can determine if the characters you need are there at all. In my version of the Wingdings font, the characters being used by this code are:

Number	Character (what it looks like)
180	◈
254	☑
168	☐

If you would rather use a box with an "x" in it when the logical field evaluates to *true*, the character is 253 (☒).

If it turns out that these characters do not match in your copy of this font, you might see if you can find similar characters in other fonts using the Character Map program that is part of Windows (usually it can be found in the Start Menu, under "All apps", "Windows Accessories", but different installations may have this utility in different places – if all else fails, look for: "C:\WINDOWS\SYSTEM32\charmap.exe").

Microsoft ships these fonts with Windows: Wingdings, Wingings2, Wingdings3, and Webdings. In addition, there are a lot of "dingbat" fonts available on the web, some are free of charge.

You can also change the font size if the checkbox control looks too small.

A Note about Fonts

One thing to be concerned about if you use fonts that are not fairly standard, such as Ariel and Times New Roman *(which tend to be installed on everyone's computers)* – you cannot always be sure that some spiffy font you are using is installed on a user's computer. Setting aside legal issues for fonts you may have purchased (check with the people you purchased them from in those cases and make sure distribution is okay), how do you make sure the fonts are available for your users?

Most installers have the ability to install fonts and place them in the appropriate directory for Windows, so that the application can find and use the font. The suggested installer for dBASE is Inno Setup, and there's a section that can be used in the installer to handle fonts. This will be discussed in a later chapter of the book as well.

Cleanup

Create a new report (in the Navigator, click on the .Reports. tab, double-click on the "[New Report]" icon). Select the "File" menu, select "Set Custom Report Class", and in the dialog, click the "Clear Custom Report" button, then click "OK". This clears out the custom report setting in the Plus.ini file, so that the next report you create is not based on this one. Close that report without making any changes.

Make sure the database is closed by going to the Command Window and typing:

```
close databases
```

This will also ensure that you don't end up creating tables in the wrong location, etc.

Source Code

The following is a listing of the sample code in the folders we have been working with. If you downloaded the files from my website the structure will be different (see below). You may use the code contained in these folders for your own applications if you desire, with the caveat that credit be given appropriately.

From working on this chapter:

```
C:\dBASEReports\Chapter 15\AlternateColors.rep
C:\dBASEReports\Chapter 15\CheckboxText.rep
C:\dBASEReports\Chapter 15\Shape.rep
C:\dBASEReports\Chapter 15\VerticalLogoSample.rep
C:\dBASEReprots\Reports\MyCompanyVerticalLogo.crp
```

Downloaded version – same files but with this path:

```
C:\ReportsBookSourceCode\Chapter 15\filename
C:\ReportsBookSourceCode\Reports\filename
```

Summary

Hopefully by reading through this chapter and following along with the exercises you have started thinking about ways you can enhance your own reports, making them look better and more professional. You can do almost anything with the report engine in dBASE, you just have to think about it and try to figure it out. Indeed, in some cases others have gotten there and worked out things that you might want to do (such as the alternating *detailBand* colors), and already set them up so you don't have to do all the work. One idea I flashed on as I was reviewing this chapter, for example – detailBands do not have a *border* or *borderStyle* property. However, using a concept similar to what was done with the alternating colored bands, you could set a border on a text control that had no actual text, but was the same size as the *detailBand*. Or you could just put a shape object on the *detailBand* like we did in the one example. Use your imagination!

The next chapter will start getting much more advanced – multiple columns. This can get pretty involved!

Part IV: Advanced Report Techniques

This part of the book will get into more advanced techniques of using the Report Designer and Report Engine in dBASE, and will also get into programmatic control of reports, and eventually to dealing with generating PDFs and with writing HTML reports. Some of this is not for the faint of heart, because it will delve into coding more than we've done so far in many parts, and some of this will take a lot of patience to learn and use with your own reports. It is also the last main section of this book, albeit a fairly large one.

Chapter 16: Multiple Columns

Early in this book we started talking about reports where the data was laid out in columns, and we named these "Tabular" reports. There were two reasons, the first is that the term "tabular" is a proper definition of what these reports are doing, and secondly, the other was to try to avoid confusion with this chapter of the book.

There are times that you may wish to lay out a report in such a way that the data goes down the page in one column, and then back to the top of the page in another ("snaking" is one term that is sometimes used for this). For example, you will see this in a phone book *(if you can find one these days)* which typically has at two, if not three, columns of names and telephone numbers, listed alphabetically, going down one column, and when reaching the bottom the list continues in the next.

We have already briefly looked at the concepts needed for this in the chapter of this book dealing with Labels. In that chapter we noticed that there were multiple streamFrames – one for each label that was to be printed on a standard sheet of labels.

In order to create a report that uses multiple columns, we simply need to define multiple streamFrames. That sounds easy, but of course it's not really as easy as you might think – or at least part of it is not. The absolute basics are actually quite simple – the layout so that your columns are even is a bit more complicated.

Due to the fact that Custom Reports do not stream all of the objects to a report derived from it, and through experience, I have found that it is better when creating a report that uses multiple streamFrames, to ***not*** start with a Custom Report (that isn't designed for this) to base the report on. *(We'll discuss this again at the end of the chapter.)*

A Place for Our Work

As we work through the chapter we will be needing a place for the files we create, so please create a folder for this chapter:

```
C:\dBASEReports\Chapter 16
```

And in the Navigator, be sure to navigate to this folder.

Starting a Multiple Column Report

The first thing to do is to start a new report in the Report Designer. Depending on whether or not you followed the instructions at the end of the last chapter you worked on, you may need to clear the custom report being used. To do so, go to the "File" menu, and select "Set Custom Report Class ...". Click the "Clear Custom Report Class" button, and then click "OK".

Your report will have reverted to the default report in dBASE, which means you may wish to set some things that were being set automatically with our custom reports. The following properties were being set, and by now you should be able to find and set these pretty easily:

Form
metric 3 - Inches *(or whatever works for you)*

reportGroup headerBand
height 0

reportGroup footerBand
height 0

pageTemplate
marginBottom 0.5
marginLeft 0.5
marginRight 0.5
marginTop 0.5

You might want to save the report now by pressing Ctrl+S and naming this "MultiColumn.rep".

In our custom report, we set the *left* and *width* properties of the *streamFrame*. But for now let's not worry about that – we'll come back to the *streamFrame* in a bit.

If you do not see a "Custom" tab at the top of the Component Palette, you may want to go to the Command Window and type the following:

```
set procedure to :MyReportControls:MyReportControls.cc
```

When you click back on the Report Designer, the Component Palette should now show the "Custom" tab. Click on this, and find the "MainTitleText" control – place an instance on your report at the top of the *pageTemplate*. Find the "SecondaryTitleText" control and place it under the "MainTitleText". Find the "DateText" control and place it under the "SecondaryTitleText" control. Select all three (use Ctrl, hold it down and click on each), then go to the "Layout" menu, and select "Align" and "Center Horizontally in Window". This will get them centered in the report. Click on any part of the report to take focus off the group of controls.

Click on the "SecondaryTitleText" once to give it focus, and again to put it into edit mode and change the *text* to read "Multiple Column Report", without the quotes – readjust the control as necessary.

Scroll down to the bottom of the *pageTemplate*, and let's get that page number in there that we've gotten used to having. If you do not see a "Paging" tab, then go to the Command Window and type the following:

```
set procedure to :ReportControls:Report.cc
```

This will make this component available in the Component Palette when you click back on the Report Designer surface. Now select the "Paging" tab. You should see a single component that shows the number "1". Select this and drag it to the design surface at the bottom of the *pageTemplate*. Adjust the width as necessary. Select the "Layout" menu, and then "Align" and "Center Horizontally in Window".

At this point we have the report ready to go. (Now you can see how useful the Custom Report classes are – normally we don't have to do this each time for a report, because it's already been done.)

In order to define your streamFrames it helps to work out the size of the streamFrames through a calculation.

You do not need advanced math here – this is fairly simple, but there are some considerations. The first thing to note is how wide the printable area is. This is the pageTemplate's width. You can get this information by determining *marginLeft* and *marginRight* properties and adding them (in this case, they should both be 0.5 inch, giving a total of 1 inch when added together), and subtracting that from the *width* of the *pageTemplate*, which is 8.5 inches. This gives a printable area of 7.5 inches.

Next you need to determine how many streamFrames you need for your report. For our example we will use 2, but the following can be used for any number. You need to determine how much space you want *between* the streamFrames as well. For our report we will use 1/4 inch or 0.25. If you have two columns, you need one space area between them. The best way to handle this is to use a calculation along the following lines:

PageTemplate.width	8.5
marginLeft	-0.5
marginRight	-0.5
Subtotal	7.5 inches
(# of columns - 1 (spacer)) * spacer width (0.25): (2 - 1) * 0.25	[=0.25]
Subtotal (space left)	7.25 inches
Divide Subtotal by # of columns	7.25/2 = 3.63 inches per streamFrame

Look at this carefully. It assumes 2 columns, if we had 3 columns, the number of spacers would be 2 – to provide space *between* each column.

The next thing to do is set the first streamFrame's properties. Click on the yellow part of the Report Designer (the *streamFrame*). In the Inspector window, change the *left* property to 0. Change the *width* property to 3.63. You might want to set the *height* property to fill as much of the *pageTemplate* as possible. This will be approximately 8.70 inches for this report.

There are two ways we can place a new *streamFrame* onto the report. The first is to copy the current *streamFrame* using Windows' copy and paste, the other is to drag a *streamFrame* from the Component Palette to the design surface. Both have their advantages. For example, if we use Windows' copy and paste, the properties of the current *streamFrame* are copied as well, so the *height* and *width* will already be set. The disadvantage is that the *streamSource* for the new *streamFrame* may not be set (and if we do not have any data set to use this will not be set anyway). If we place a *streamFrame* onto the report from the Component Palette and we have a *streamSource* for the report set, then this will automatically be set for the new *streamFrame*, but the *height* and *width* properties will not be set.

Click on the *streamFrame* (the yellow section of the report), and press Ctrl+C (or select the "Edit" menu and "Copy"). Note that Windows doesn't tell you that it did anything. Next click on the *pageTemplate* (to give it focus), and press Ctrl+V (or select the "Edit" menu and "Paste"), and you should see a second streamFrame. How can you tell? It's not that easy, is it? Look at the Inspector – you should see "streamFrame2" (you may need to select it in the Inspector's combobox). That's really the only way of knowing at the moment.

At this point we need to move the second *streamFrame* to where it needs to go. The only property we are concerned with is the *left* property. To determine the *left* for this streamFrame, we use the *width* of the first *streamFrame* (3.63) and we add the spacer width (0.25) to it, which gives us:

3.63 +0.25 = 3.88

Set the *left* property of streamFrame2 to 3.88 in the Inspector (press the Enter key after typing the number or it will not be kept), and it will move to the right. The new *streamFrame* will appear as white, but that's okay *(we haven't "hooked" up the two streamFrames so that they know about each other yet)*. You might want to double check that the top and height properties are correct, but they should be.

Adding Data to the Report

We're going to do a very simple report for this, because our streamFrames are not very wide (they could be wider if we made this a *landscape* report).

Go to the Navigator window in dBASE, and select the "Tables" tab. If the "DBASEREPORTS" database is not open, select the "Look in" combobox and select the database. Select the "Dogs" table from the Navigator and drag it to the design surface. While the "DOGS1" query has focus, go to the Inspector and select the *rowset* property, and the tool button. This will drill down to the rowset and select the *indexName* property. Select "Name" for the index tag to use.

Next go to the Component Palette, and select the "Custom" tab. Select the "DataColHeadingText" control and place one on the *detailBand*. Change the *text* property of this control to "Name".

Select the "DataText" control from the Component Palette and place this under the column heading. Change the text Type to "Codeblock", click the tool button and enter the following in the dialog:

```
this.form.dogs1.rowset.fields["name"].value
```

At this point your report should look something like:

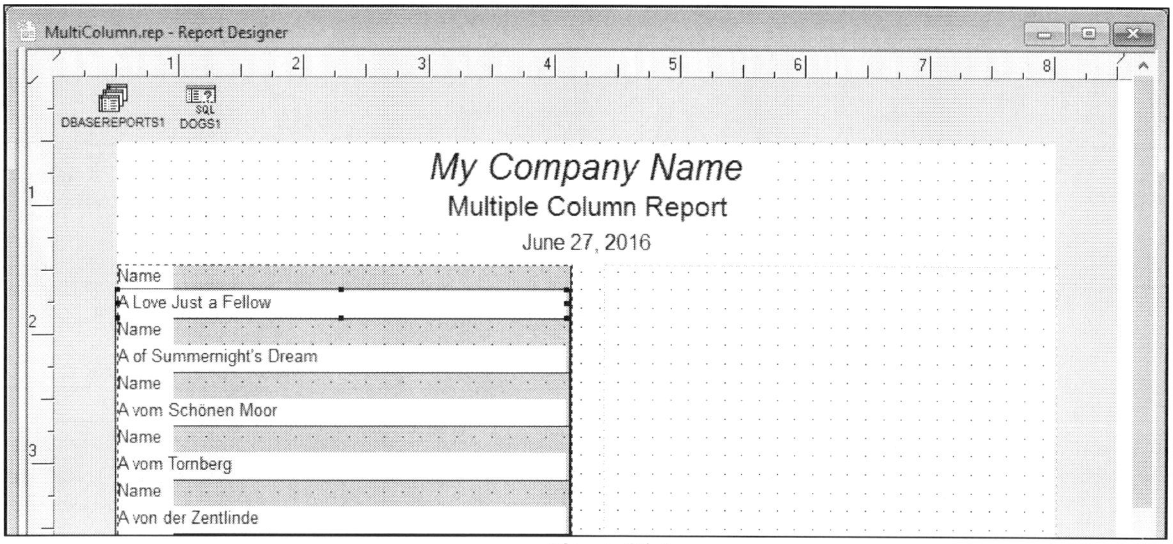

Figure 15-1

The *streamFrame* on the right really only appears as an outline. Why is that? Because we have not set the *streamSource* for that *streamFrame*. In theory we could have a totally unrelated *streamSource* from that used in the first *streamFrame* here, but this would be very problematic, because a report only has one "controlling" *streamSource*, and the first one will be the one that determines navigation in the table(s) and so on.

Click on the second *streamFrame* (which you should be able to do, even though it's just an outline on the Report Designer surface). Find the *streamSource* property. Select "STREAMSOURCE1" from the drop-down that appears in the Inspector, and notice that the *streamFrame* now contains data:

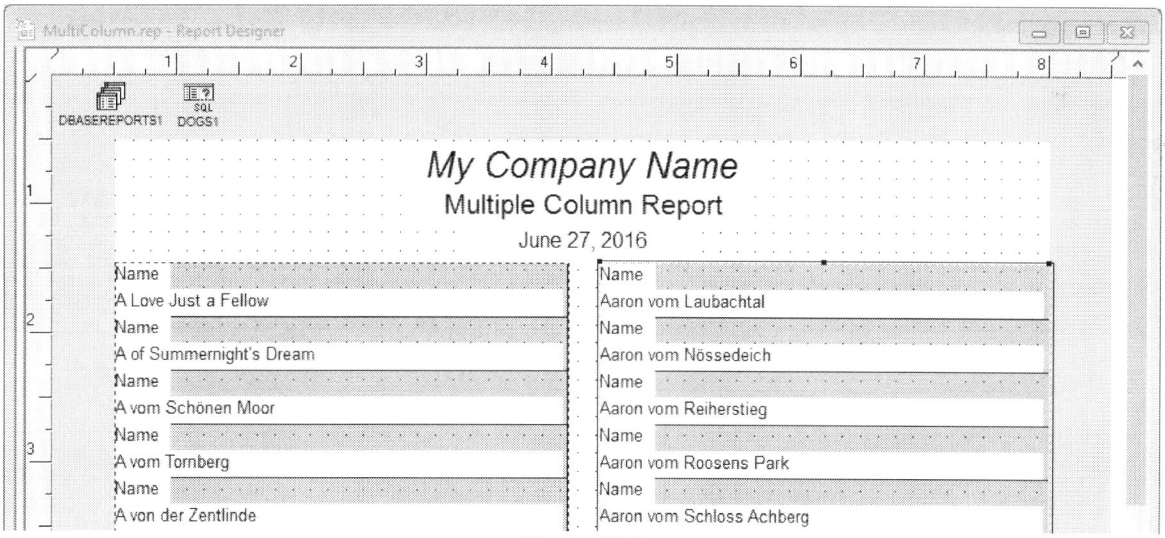

Figure 15-2

And of course when we run the report, the column heading control should appear only at the top of each *streamFrame*. Why is that? If you were to examine the source code for the "DataColHeadingText" control, you would see that we are checking the detailBand's *firstOnFrame* property – the keyword here is "Frame". This is a reference to the *streamFrame*. When you run the report you should see something like:

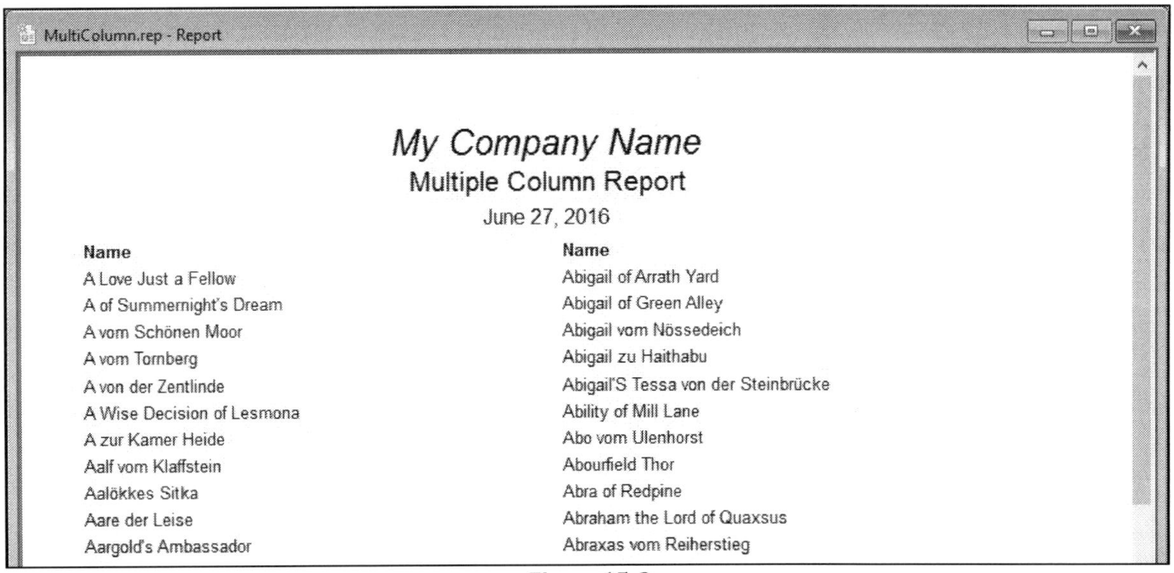

Figure 15-3

If you scroll up and down the page you will see the names are alphabetical, and they "snake" from the bottom of the first column to the top of the next.

Appearance Issues

In an earlier chapter we discussed setting borders on objects and such. This might be a useful place to have a border around the *streamFrame*. It helps break up the page a little, and makes it very obvious that the data is in columns. Another option would be to place a vertical line between the two columns, basically in the middle of the spacer" region that we defined between them. Either way is effective. To place a border on each *streamFrame*, set the *borderStyle* property to the style you want.

For this example I feel it *might* look better with a vertical line between the streamFrames *(this is a matter of aesthetics, and mine may not match yours)*. Open the report in the designer if it is not. On the Component Palette select the "Standard" tab, and find "Line" drag it to the design surface. By default a line is horizontal, so we need to work with the properties. Dragging the line will be tricky, it might be easier to just work with the Inspector.

The top of the *streamFrame* (relative to the *pageTemplate*) is 0.95", so set the same value for the *line*. The *height* of the *streamFrame* is set to 8.70, but we need to take into account that the *top* property is where the *streamFrame* starts on the *pageTemplate* – so add the top to the height, which will give 9.65. Set the *bottom* property of the line to 9.65. Set the line's *left* and *right* properties to 3.74 which will place the line close to center, and try running the report:

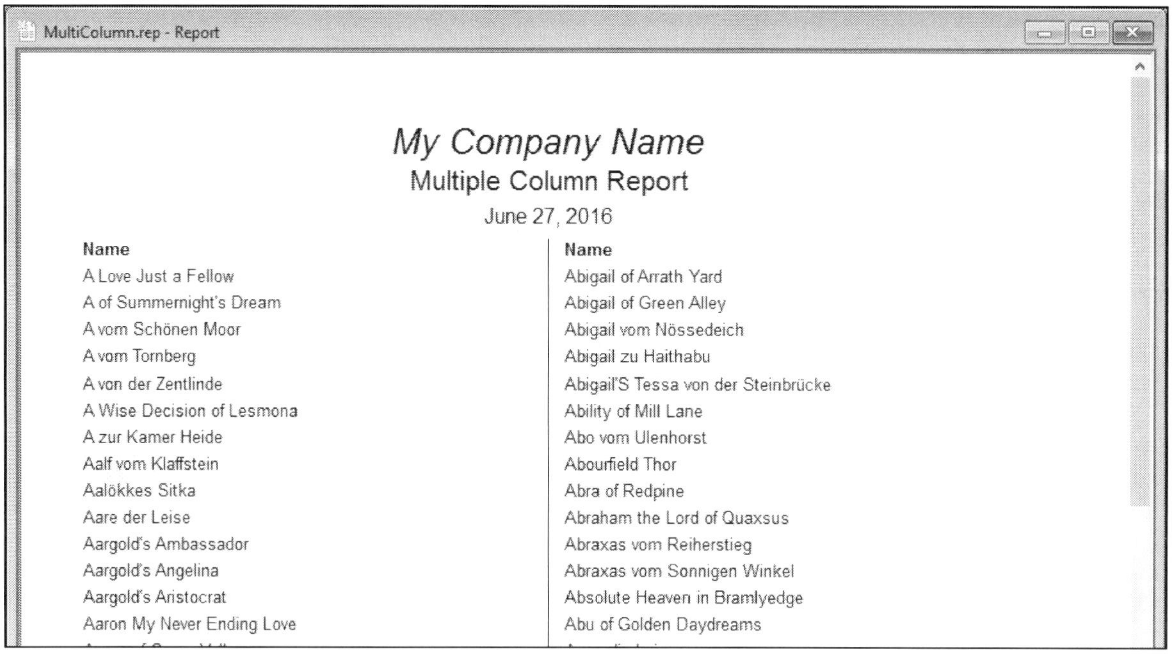

Figure 16-4

As you can see, this breaks things up nicely, and it is quite obvious what is happening. Of course, you may feel that the line is a bit odd, and perhaps would prefer using a border on the streamFrames, or to not do anything at all – the choice is yours!

More Than Two Columns?

Of course you can have more than two columns. A lot depends on the data you are printing, the paper size you are using, you may choose to turn the report to Landscape.

The basic calculation given earlier in this chapter still works you just have to substitute the appropriate values (number of streamFrames, number of spacers, etc.)

What Else Can You Do with Multiple streamFrames?

At this point you are really limited to your needs and imagination. Can you use multiple streamFrames in a horizontal fashion so that you have one *streamFrame* above another? Certainly you can, if that's what you need to do with your report. How about more streamFrames, like with labels? As we discussed in the chapter on labels, a *streamFrame* is how each label is defined, so you could have four streamFrames on the page, for example – the important thing to watch is the z-order of the source code for these streamFrames.

Can you have a custom report that uses multiple streamFrames? Sure you can. Rather than doing the steps we did here, you could do them in a Custom report, and then all you would need to do is make sure that the custom report class was selected, and you can create your report from there. At the beginning of the chapter I recommended against using a Custom Report for multiple streamFrames. What I meant by this is that unless the multiple streamFrames are part of the Custom Report definition (the constructor code), there may be problems trying to define and create a report that has a single streamFrame in the custom class. It's all related to the way that the Report Designer streams out the constructor code for the reports. If you define a Custom Report with multiple streamFrames, and use that to base a report on, you should be fine.

Cleanup

As we did not use a custom report, there is no need to clear out the active custom report.

Make sure the database is closed by going to the Command Window and typing:

```
close databases
```

This will also ensure that you don't end up creating tables in the wrong location, etc.

Source Code

The following is a listing of the sample code in the folders we have been working with. If you downloaded the files from my website the structure will be different (see below). You may use the code contained in these folders for your own applications if you desire, with the caveat that credit be given appropriately.

From working on this chapter:

```
C:\dBASEReports\Chapter 16\MultiColumn.rep
```

Downloaded version – same files but with this path:

```
C:\ReportsBookSourceCode\Chapter 16\filename
```

Summary

This chapter hopefully opens your eyes to some new concepts with the report capabilities of dBASE. Having multiple streamFrames can give you a lot of flexibility for your reports.

The next chapter is going to get more complicated with multiple pageTemplates!

Chapter 17: Multiple *pageTemplates* and Binding Offsets

We've not done a *lot* with the *pageTemplate* as an object. We have defined the page dimensions, and we have set margins (*marginLeft*, etc.). However, while you may not have realized it, you can actually use multiple pageTemplates for a report. The hint is in the property of the *pageTemplate* called *nextPageTemplate*. This may seem obvious, however to a lot of developers it isn't.

Why would you want to have multiple pageTemplates? I can think of at least one reason, and if you really think about it hard you might find more. The first reason that immediately comes to mind *(possibly because I have dealt with this kind of thing in the past)* is a situation where your reports must be offset depending on whether they are even numbered or odd numbered pages, so that when photocopied or printed back-to-back, there is an offset that can be used for binding the report. Word has settings for this which I use for this book.

This type of report might require two different pageTemplates – one for odd numbered pages, and one for even numbered pages. *(This is effectively the way that Word ends up doing it.)* As we will see, there's another way to handle this as well.

For this chapter of the book, we'll create a fairly simple report. The idea is to focus on the multiple *pageTemplate* aspect of the report, not the actual contents of the report itself.

As with the Multiple *streamFrame* report we did in the previous chapter, because Custom Reports do not stream out all the objects in a way that makes it easy to work with, we need to start with a report that is *not* based on a custom report. Once you have something the way you want it, you can make a custom report – if you are in a situation where you need multiple reports with this kind of an offset, this would be useful. We're going to keep things simple and just create one report.

A Place for Our Work

As we work through the chapter we will be needing a place for the files we create, so please create a folder for this chapter:

```
C:\dBASEReports\Chapter 17
```

And in the Navigator, be sure to navigate to this folder.

Starting a Multiple *pageTemplate* Report

The first thing to do of course is to start a new report in the Report Designer. Depending on whether or not you followed the instructions at the end of earlier chapters you worked on, you may need to clear the custom report being used. To do so, go to the "File" menu, and select "Set Custom Report Class ...". Click the "Clear Custom Report Class" button, and then click "OK".

Your report will have reverted to the default report in dBASE, which means you may wish to set some things that were being set automatically with our custom reports. The following properties were being set, and by now you should be able to find and set these pretty easily:

Form
metric 3 - Inches (or whatever works for you)

reportGroup headerBand
height 0

reportGroup footerBand
height 0

pageTemplate
marginBottom 0.5
marginTop 0.5
We will work on the *marginLeft* and *marginRight* properties in a bit.

streamFrame
height 8.70

We will come back to the other *streamFrame* properties later.

You might want to save the report now by pressing Ctrl+S and naming this "MultiPageTemplate.rep".

If you do not see a "Custom" tab at the top of the Component Palette, you may want to go to the Command Window and type the following:

```
set procedure to :MyReportControls:MyReportControls.cc
```

When you click back on the Report Designer, the Component Palette should now show the "Custom" tab. Click on this, and find the "MainTitleText" control – place an instance on your report at the top of the *pageTemplate*. Find the "SecondaryTitleText" control and place it under the "MainTitleText". Find the "DateText" control and place it under the "SecondaryTitleText" control. Select all three (use Ctrl, hold it down and click on each), then go to the "Layout" menu, and select "Align" and "Center Horizontally in Window". This will get them centered in the report. Click on any part of the report to take focus off the group of controls.

Click on the "SecondaryTitleText" once to give it focus, and change the *text* to read "Multiple PageTemplate Report", without the quotes (readjust the width and re-center the control if necessary).

Scroll down to the bottom of the pageTemplate, and let's get that page number in there that we've gotten used to having. If you do not see a "Paging" tab, then go to the Command Window and type the following:

```
set procedure to :ReportControls:Report.cc
```

This will make this component available in the Component Palette when you click back on the Report Designer surface. Now select the "Paging" tab. You should see a single component that shows the number "1". Select this and drag it to the design surface at the bottom of the *pageTemplate*. Adjust the width as necessary. Select the "Layout" menu, and then "Align" and "Center Horizontally in Window".

At this point we have the report ready to go.

Binding Offsets with Two *pageTemplates*

Let's take a look at this concept a bit more clearly. Normally when you print a report, it is printed on one side of the page, and you can take into account any binding easily by setting the *marginLeft* of the *pageTemplate* a little larger if you need to.

However, if you are printing a report in duplex mode *(for printers that will print on both sides of a page)*, or photocopying the report back-to-back and you know the report will have a binding on the left edge (the usual place for this sort of thing), you need to take into account the fact that for even numbered pages, the left and right margins need to be different from the margins on the odd numbered pages.

The default starting page of a report is page 1, which makes it an odd numbered page. It tends to be the first page when viewing the report, and would be on top. Any offset will be on the left side of this piece of paper, to push the page to the right a little, leaving room for the binding.

This is done with the *marginLeft* property of the *pageTemplate*. Our usual (for all reports to this point) *marginLeft* has been 0.5 inches or ½ inch. In many cases this might be enough, but let's assume the need for an extra 1/4 inch – this would mean our *marginLeft* would need to be set to 0.75. To adjust, we would want to subtract the same amount from our *marginRight*.

To see this, go to the pageTemplate in our current report, and set the *marginLeft* to 0.75 and the *marginRight* to 0.25. By doing this, we still have the same amount of printing area that we would if we were not planning for the binding offset.

Now let's set the *streamFrame* so that it takes the amount of space needed (the width of the *pageTemplate*). Click on the *streamFrame*, and set the *left* property to 0, and the *width* property to 7.5.

Before we go any further, let's put some data on the report. This will help view the changes better.

Go to the Navigator window in dBASE, and select the "Tables" tab. If the "DBASEREPORTS" database is not open, select the "Look in" combobox and select the database. Select the "Dogs" table from the Navigator and drag it to the design surface. While the "DOGS1" query has focus, go to the Inspector and select the *rowset* property, and the inspect button. This will drill down to the *rowset* and select the *indexName* property. Select "Name" for the index tag to use.

Next go to the Component Palette, and select the "Custom" tab. Select the "DataColHeadingText" control and place one on the *detailBand*. Change the *text* property to "Name". Select the "DataText" control from the Component Palette and place this under the column heading. Change the *text* Type to "Codeblock", click the tool button and enter this in the dialog:

```
this.form.dogs1.rowset.fields["name"].value
```

The Second *pageTemplate*

The next thing to work is the second *pageTemplate*. However, the Report Designer does not give us a means to add a new *pageTemplate* to a report, and setting up the necessary relationships is not very easy in the Designer either.

This needs to be done in the Source Code Editor. Save your work and exit the Report Designer (Ctrl+W). Then open this report (MultiPageTemplate.rep) in the Source Code Editor.

In the Source Code Editor highlight all the code that begins with:

```
this.PageTemplate1
```

Make sure you include the WITH and ENDWITH statements – if you leave any of this out, these items will not appear on the alternate *pageTemplate*.

In our example, we should start with:

```
this.PAGETEMPLATE1 = new PAGETEMPLATE(this)
   with (this.PAGETEMPLATE1)
      height = 11.0
      width = 8.5
      marginTop = 0.5
      marginLeft = 0.75
      marginBottom = 0.5
      marginRight = 0.25
      gridLineWidth = 0
   endwith
```

and end with:

```
this.PAGETEMPLATE1.PAGENUMBER1 = new PAGENUMBER(this.PAGETEMPLATE1)
   with (this.PAGETEMPLATE1.PAGENUMBER1)
      height = 0.2083
      left = 3.2708
      top = 9.7708
      width = 0.4583
      form.PAGENUMBER1 = form.pagetemplate1.pagenumber1
   endwith
```

Once you have highlighted all of this code, press Ctrl+C to copy it to the Windows clipboard. Move the cursor below the last line you've highlighted and copied, and above this statement:

```
this.STREAMSOURCE1 = new STREAMSOURCE(this)
```

Press Ctrl+V (paste) to paste it from the Windows clipboard. You now have duplicate code.

What you want to do now is find every place in the COPY of the code (don't change the original code) that says "PAGETEMPLATE1" and change it to "PAGETEMPLATE**2**" – in other words:

```
this.PAGETEMPLATE2 = new PAGETEMPLATE(this)
   with (this.PAGETEMPLATE2)
      height = 11.0
      width = 8.5
      marginTop = 0.5
      marginLeft = 0.75
      marginBottom = 0.5
      marginRight = 0.25
      gridLineWidth = 0
   endwith
```

all the way down to:

```
this.PAGETEMPLATE2.PAGENUMBER1 = new PAGENUMBER(this.PAGETEMPLATE2)
   with (this.PAGETEMPLATE2.PAGENUMBER1)
      height = 0.2083
      left = 3.2708
      top = 9.7708
      width = 0.4583
      form.PAGENUMBER1 = form.pagetemplate2.pagenumber1
   endwith
```

In addition, anywhere you have "form.somecontrol1", you should change the number to 2, but only "form.". We have four text controls right now on the pageTemplate, we need to change the references from "form.MainTitle1" to "form.MainTitle2". Otherwise dBASE may get confused and overwrite these custom properties with the wrong reference.

Be careful – the first part of the constructor for these controls has the word "PAGETEMPLATE1" in there twice, so make sure you change it in both places.

Next, go to the constructor for PageTemplate2, and reverse the *marginLeft* and *marginRight* values – these should now look like:

```
this.PAGETEMPLATE2 = new PAGETEMPLATE(this)
   with (this.PAGETEMPLATE2)
      height = 11.0
      width = 8.5
      marginTop = 0.5
      marginLeft = 0.25
      marginBottom = 0.5
      marginRight = 0.75
      gridLineWidth = 0
   endwith
```

We need to modify come code at the end of the report's constructor code.

Go to the code just before the "endclass" statement, you will see:

```
this.form.pagetemplate1.nextPageTemplate = this.form.pagetemplate1
```

This tells the Report Engine that when pageTemplate1 is done rendering, what the next *pageTemplate* is – so it can change templates. In this case, the default is to point back to the first *pageTemplate*.

We need this to point to pageTemplate2! So change the statement to:

```
this.form.pagetemplate1.nextPageTemplate = this.form.pagetemplate2
```

Once you have done this, copy the statement (highlight it, and press Ctrl+C), and then paste a copy of this below this statement (which will require you move the cursor to the next line and press Enter, and move the cursor back up), then change it to:

```
this.form.pagetemplate2.nextPageTemplate = this.form.pagetemplate1
```

We are telling the Report Engine that when done rendering pageTemplate2, we want to go back to pageTemplate1. Basically we are going from one *pageTemplate* to the other, and when done with that one, we go back to the first.

Copy this statement:

```
this.form.pagetemplate1.streamframe1.streamSource = this.form.streamsource1
```

And paste a new copy below it in the code, and change the copy to:

```
this.form.pagetemplate2.streamframe1.streamSource = this.form.streamsource1
```

This sets the *streamSource* for pageTemplate2 to the same as for pageTemplate1. Does this mean that you can have multiple *streamSources* and all that? Well, you could try it, but my understanding of the way the Report Engine handles this is that it will not work because only one *streamSource* is used to control the report.

This whole block of code should now look like:

```
this.firstPageTemplate = this.form.pagetemplate1
this.form.pagetemplate1.nextPageTemplate = this.form.pagetemplate2
this.form.pagetemplate2.nextPageTemplate = this.form.pagetemplate1
this.form.pagetemplate1.streamframe1.streamSource = this.form.streamsource1
this.form.pagetemplate2.streamframe1.streamSource = this.form.streamsource1
this.form.streamsource1.rowset = this.form.dogs1.rowset
```

Save this and exit the Source Code Editor (Ctrl+W).

At this point you can try running the report – if you got everything correct, it will run. If you did not, find the statements that are pointed to you by the error messages, and double-check your work. If the report runs, you should see the first page looking something like:

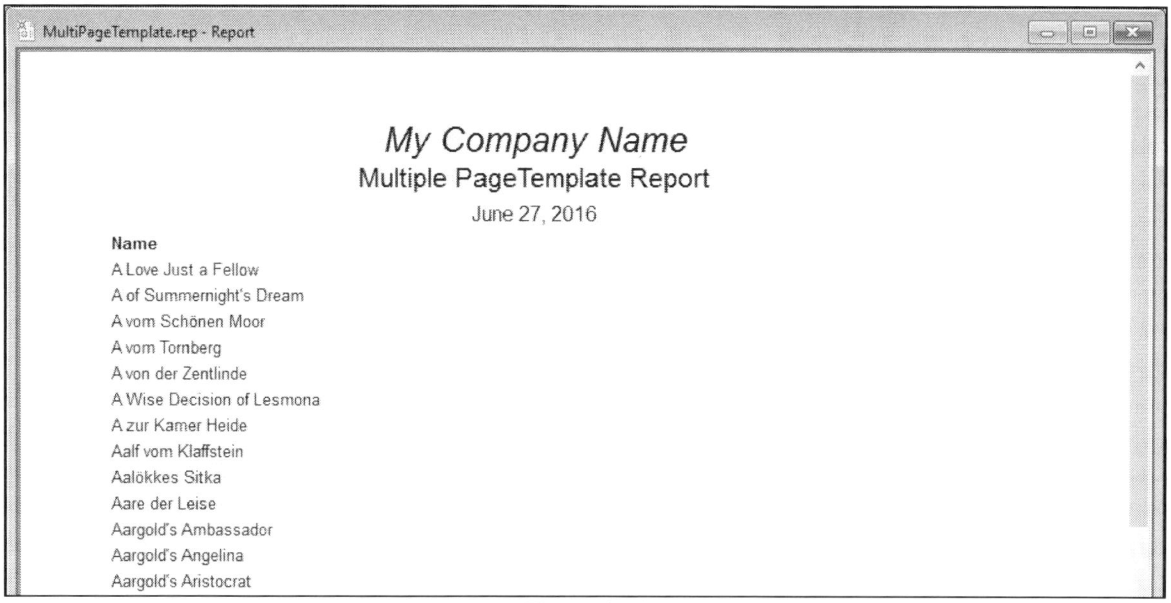

Figure 17-1

This doesn't look *really* different, but compare page 2 (use the PgDn key or the Next Page button in the toolbar):

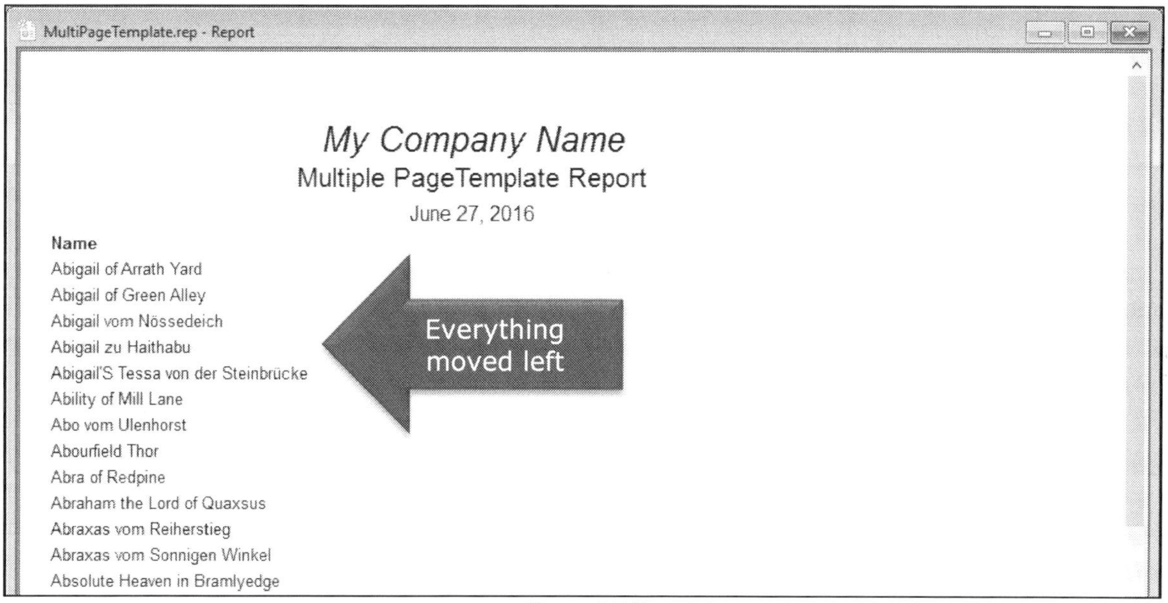

Figure 17-2

Notice that the text is off to the left for this page. If you were to print these and copy them back to back, everything should be fine. This would of course be more obvious if we had text on both sides of the *streamFrame*, or if we set the streamFrame's *borderStyle* property.

Close the preview screen, and bring the report into the Report Designer.

If you click on the *pageTemplate* (the white space) of the design surface, you will see in the Inspector that it tells you that you are on pageTemplate1. Now press the PgDn key, this will take you to the second page of the report in the Report Designer. If you click on the *pageTemplate* here, the Inspector will show you that you are on pageTemplate2.

For some reason the Designer seems to have a display issue with the second *pageTemplate*, in that it is still trying to show pageTemplate1 and the controls *on* pageTemplate1 as well as pageTemplate2. This may look something like:

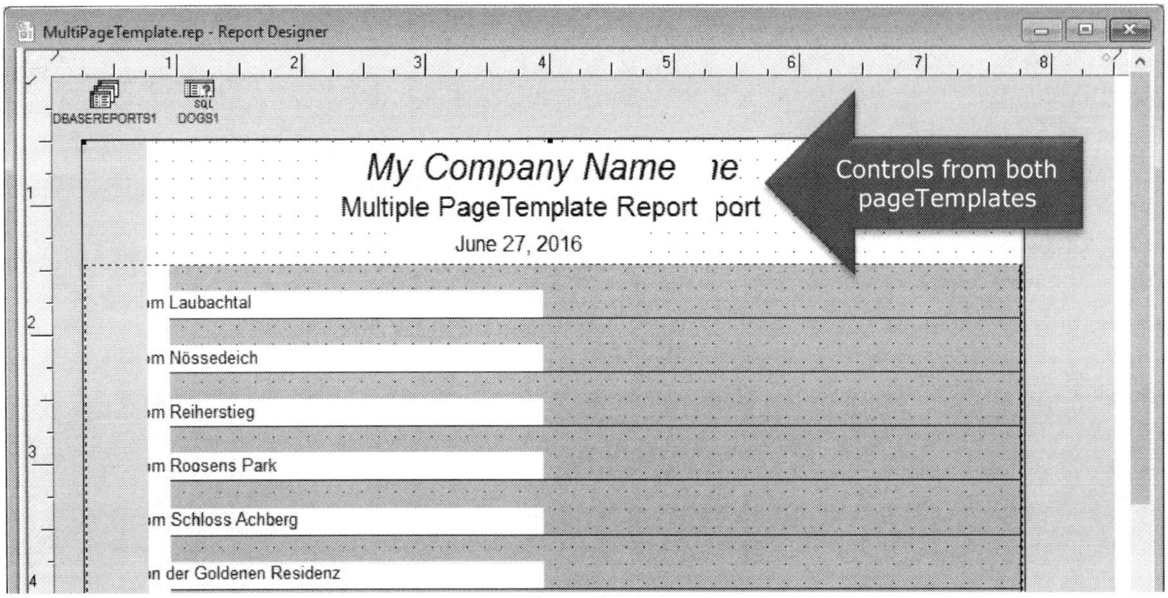

Figure 17-3

If you click on the text controls, only the ones that are on pageTemplate2 will be active, even though you see controls from pageTemplate1 (you can tell if you look at the Inspector's combobox).

You can modify pageTemplate2 here, as noted, changing the text if you wanted, so that the two different pageTemplates had different text, depending on if they were odd or even numbered pages. The biggest advantage to using this technique (as opposed to one you'll see in shortly) is that you can set different page headings and/or page footers, based on whether the page is even or odd numbered, very much like you often find in a book *(like this one)*.

You could take this further and have more pageTemplates, but keeping track of what is what and which *pageTemplate* points to which might become a little tricky.

It is also possible to have the binding edge at the top of a printout – you would instead modify the *marginTop* and *marginBottom* properties, where in this example we worked with the *marginLeft* and *marginRight*.

This was, perhaps, a hard way to do the binding offset, but the purpose was to show how to work with multiple pageTemplates, if you so desired.

Another Way to Handle Binding Offsets

There is a simpler way to do binding offsets using a text object that modifies the pageTemplate's *marginLeft* and *marginRight* properties, without the need of creating a second *pageTemplate*. This can be done as either a custom text class, or by using a regular text control on the report surface. The important thing is to have code similar to the following set up to execute in the text control's *text* property – which is not something we have done before. By doing this as the *text* property, we can force the margins to be evaluated before the page renders. This will seem a little odd, but it has been tested and works.

To see this we are going to create yet another simple report, but this one can actually use a custom report class! So, to get started, create a new report, and when the Report Designer starts, go to the "File" menu, select "Set Custom Report Class ...", and find the "MyCompanyReport.crp" custom report class file. Click "OK" when done, and the report will now inherit the properties we are used to seeing. Save this by pressing Ctrl+S and call it "BindingOffset.rep".

Click on the SecondaryTitleText control and give it focus, and change the *text* to say "Binding Offset Example". The first page of this report is going to be an odd numbered page, and because of that, we want to set the properties for the pageTemplate's margins. Click on the *pageTemplate*, and set the *marginLeft* to 0.75, and set the *marginRight* to 0.25.

Go to the Navigator window in dBASE, and select the "Tables" tab. If the "DBASEREPORTS" database is not open, select the "Look in" combobox and select the database. Select the "Dogs" table from the Navigator and drag it to the design surface. While the "DOGS1" query has focus, go to the Inspector and select the *rowset* property, and the Inspect button. This will drill down to the *rowset* object. Select the *indexName* property. Select "Name' for the index tag to use.

Next go to the Component Palette, and select the "Custom" tab. Select the "DataColHeadingText" control and place one on the *detailBand*. Change the *text* property to "Name". Select the "DataText" control from the Component Palette and place this under the column heading. Change the *text* Type to "Codeblock", click the tool button and enter the following in the dialog:

```
this.form.dogs1.rowset.fields["name"].value
```

Now we have the report set to display some data, let's add a new text control to the *pageTemplate*. Place a "DataText" control to the right of the "DateText" control on the *pageTemplate* itself. Set the *text* property to say "Binding Offset Text".

Press the F12 key, which will bring the Source Code Editor for this report to the front of the windows displayed, and go to the bottom of the code, just before the ENDCLASS statement. Place the cursor there and add this code:

```
function BindingOffsetText
   nPageNo = this.form.reportPage
   if mod( nPageNo, 2 ) == 0 // even number
      form.pageTemplate1.marginLeft := .75
      form.pageTemplate1.marginRight := .25
      cText = "Even number page"
   else
      form.pageTemplate1.marginLeft := .25
      form.pageTemplate1.marginRight := .75
      cText = "Odd number page"
   endif
return ( cText )
```

This code will be executed and change the pageTemplate's *marginLeft* and *marginRight* properties depending on whether the current page is even numbered or odd numbered (divisible by 2 with no remainder, which is what the *mod()* function does – if you need a clear explanation, look in the online help at this function).

The confusing part of this code is that the margins appear to be backward. Since the *pageTemplate* will have already rendered when this code is executed, we need to actually assume that while the current page is even or odd, that we want to set the margins for the *next* page – so when the page is even numbered, we are actually setting the margin for the next page which will be odd numbered (not divisible by 2), providing the correct offset.

We need to force the report engine to execute this code when the text is supposed to be rendered. To do this, we will assign an event handler using the text control's *onOpen* event. Back in the Designer window (click on it to give it focus), click on this control if it does not have focus, and then in the Inspector go to the "Events" tab, and find *onOpen*. Set the Type to "Codeblock" (the other option is "Null"), in the inspector set the text to this codeblock (we are not using the dialog because it doesn't know how to handle the leading semicolon):

```
{; this.text = class::BindingOffsetText }
```

Be sure to press enter after doing this.

We set this here because we want the Report Engine to make sure that this code is executed each time. If we tried setting it in most other places (besides perhaps an overridden *render* method for the Report itself), the Report Designer would have attempted to stream out the current text value when we saved the report, which would destroy the reference to the code we want executed.

Running the report, the odd numbered pages will look like:

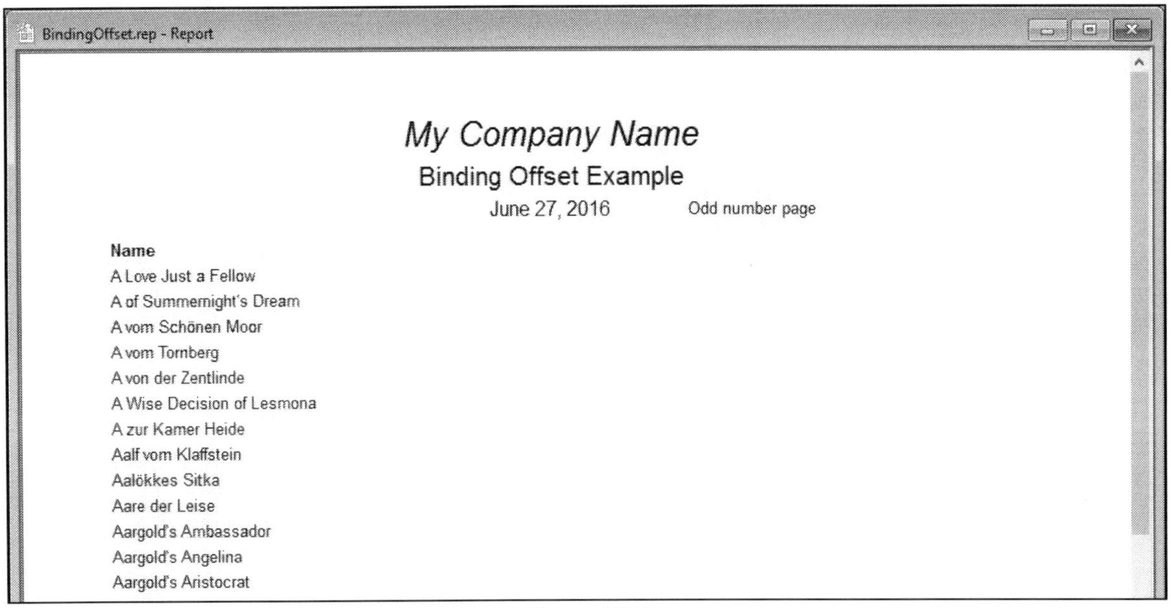

Figure 17-4

And the even numbered pages will look like:

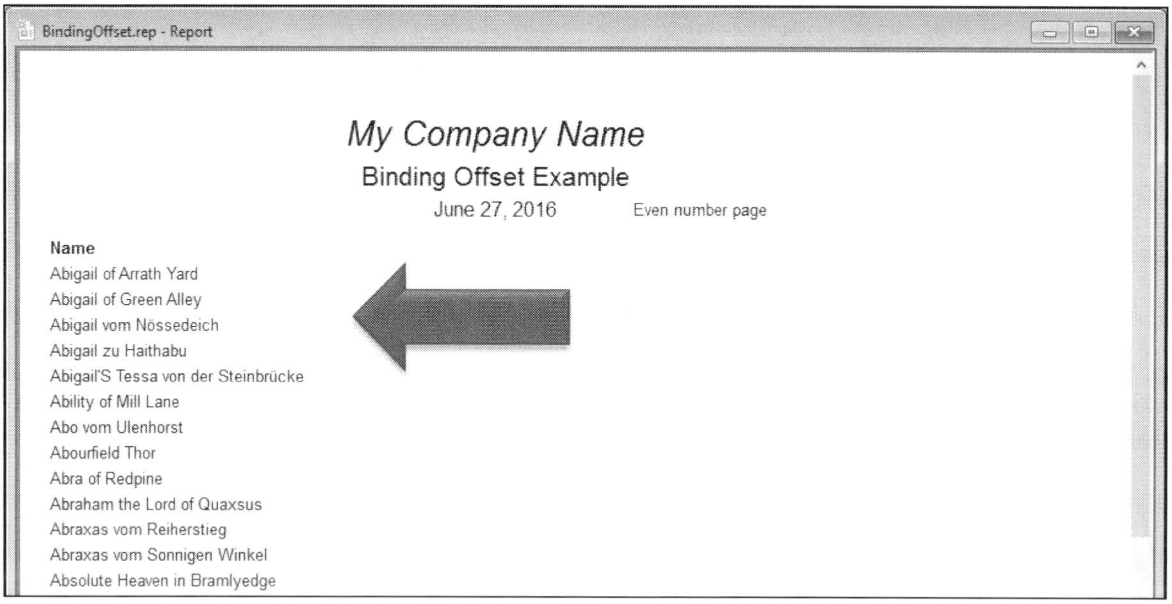

Figure 17-5

The advantage to this control is that you do not need to fiddle with multiple pageTemplates. It does take a bit of work wrapping your head around when and how the code executes, especially since we're actually executing the code from the *text* property, which is not something we've looked at before.

The text can be anything you want it to be, or you could even set the text property to be blank, by setting the cText variable in the code shown to ".". This could be encapsulated into a custom class, and there is a variation of this in the dUFLP, in the file "BINDING.CC".

A Cover Page

Multiple pageTemplates might provide a way to have a cover page for a report that would allow you to do quite a lot that you might not be able to do by using the reportGroup's *headerBand* (something we will discuss in the next chapter).

The theory would be that pageTemplate1 would be the cover page, and working with the code we looked at earlier, pageTemplate2 would be used to define the rest of the report.

```
this.firstPageTemplate = this.form.pagetemplate1
this.form.pagetemplate1.nextPageTemplate = this.form.pagetemplate2
// the big change would be here - the nextPageTemplate for
// pageTemplate2 would point back to pageTemplate2 ...
this.form.pagetemplate2.nextPageTemplate = this.form.pagetemplate2
this.form.pagetemplate1.streamframe1.streamSource = this.form.streamsource1
this.form.pagetemplate2.streamframe1.streamSource = this.form.streamsource1
this.form.streamsource1.rowset = this.form.dogs1.rowset
```

This is just a thought and has not been attempted by this author.

Cleanup

Create a new report (in the Navigator, click on the .Reports. tab, double-click on the "[New Report]" icon). Select the "File" menu, select "Set Custom Report Class", and in the dialog, click the "Clear Custom Report" button, then click "OK". This clears out the custom report setting in the Plus.ini file, so that the next report you create is not based on this one. Close that report without making any changes.

Make sure the database is closed by going to the Command Window and typing:

```
close databases
```

This will also ensure that you don't end up creating tables in the wrong location, etc.

Source Code

The following is a listing of the sample code in the folders we have been working with. If you downloaded the files from my website the structure will be different (see below). You may use the code contained in these folders for your own applications if you desire, with the caveat that credit be given appropriately.

From working on this chapter:

```
C:\dBASEReports\Chapter 17\BindingOffset.rep
C:\dBASEReports\Chapter 17\MultiPageTemplate.rep
```

Downloaded version – same files but with this path:

```
C:\ReportsBookSourceCode\Chapter 17\filename
```

Summary

Multiple pageTemplates definitely are not something that you might need for every report that you do. However, the fact that you *can* do this, and you *can* have more than one *pageTemplate* can lead to some very interesting reports if you are careful.

The next chapter is going to discuss uses for the *reportGroup headerBand* and *footerBand*.

Chapter 18: *reportGroup headerBand* and *footerBand*

In most of the chapters of this book we've ignored the Report's *reportGroup* object. This object is a very specific object for the report itself, as opposed to groups used when rendering the data. The *reportGroup* object can be used for totals and summaries of all the data in the report, and we did use this a little in the chapters on groups and totals, using the reportGroup's *footerBand* object to display report totals.

Otherwise, when creating new reports (Custom or otherwise) we have been setting the *height* of the reportGroup's *headerBand* and *footerBand* to 0 and ignoring them.

The most important thing to note about the two bands associated with the *reportGroup* object is that the reportGroup's *headerBand* object only displays **on the first page** of the report – it is not repeated on subsequent pages; conversely the reportGroup's *footerBand* object only displays **on the last page** of the report – it is also not repeated on other pages of the report.

Why would you need these? Many reports do not. However you might need a cover page or an introduction to the report. We have already seen that the reportGroup's *footerBand* can be used for the totals, and other aggregate calculations (or running totals) for a report. You might want to use this for a summary of the report, you could even have text that combined data using the aggregate calculations.

Let's start with a simple report, and then enhance it by adding some of this functionality.

A Place for Our Work

As we work through the chapter we will be needing a place for the files we create, so please create a folder for this chapter:

```
C:\dBASEReports\Chapter 18
```

And in the Navigator, be sure to navigate to this folder.

A Simple Report

To start with, let's create a new report in the Report Designer, based on our standard "MyCompanyReport" custom report. To do this, double-click the "[New Report]" icon in the dBASE Navigator Window. Select "File" and "Set Custom Report Class ...", and as we've done many times before, find the "MyCompanyReport.crp" file, select it, and click "OK". Our report starts as usual.

Click on the "SecondaryTitleText" control to give it focus, and again to place it in edit mode, and change the *text* property to "reportGroup – headerBand", and save the report (Ctrl+S) as "ReportGroupHeaderBand.rep".

Select the "Tables" tab in the Navigator Window (bring it to focus), and if the "DBASEREPORTS" database is not selected, select it in the "Look in" combobox. Select the "Dogs" table and drag it to the design surface. While the "DOGS1" query has focus, go to the Inspector and select the *rowset* property, and the Inspect button. This will drill down to the rowset and select the *indexName* property. Select "Name" for the index tag to use.

Next go to the Component Palette, and select the "Custom" tab. Select the "DataColHeadingText" control and place it on the *detailBand*. Change the *text* property to "Name". Select another "DataColHeadingText" control and place this to the right of the first on the *detailBand*. Change the *text* property to "Date of Birth" (widen the control if needed). Select one more "DataColHeadingText" control and place it on the right of the *detailBand*. Change the *text* property to "Sex". Spend a moment lining these controls up.

Select the "DataText" control from the Component Palette and place this under the column heading. Change the *text* Type to "Codeblock", click the tool button, and in the dialog enter the following:

```
this.form.dogs1.rowset.fields["name"].value
```

Repeat this for the "BORN" field (change the codeblock to reflect the fieldname), and the "SEX" field, placing the text controls under the appropriate headings. Spend as much time as you need lining these controls up, so that your report looks good. Save your work (Ctrl+S). Your report should look something like:

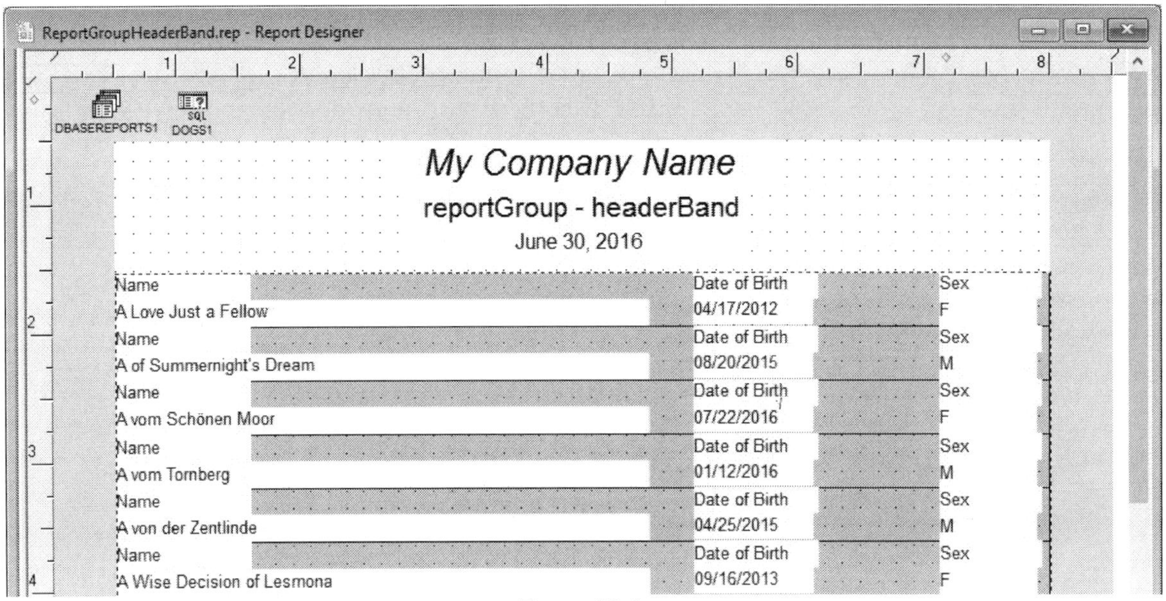

Figure 18-1

Now we need to do something with the reportGroup's *headerBand* object. However, at the moment, this does not appear to exist! If you recall, back in Chapter 3 when we created the Custom Report "MyCompanyReport.crp", which this report is derived from, we set the *height* property of the *reportGroup headerBand* to 0. The simplest way to find the reportGroup's *headerBand* is to go to the Inspector window, and in the combobox at the top, select it. You will see something like:

- reportGroup
    - footerBand
    - headerBand

in the Inspector – select "headerBand". On the design surface you will see an outline where the *headerBand* would be if the *height* were not zero. In the Inspector find the *height* property, and set it to a height of 0.17 (this assumes a report *metric* of "3 – Inches" – this is the default band *height* when the metric is set to inches – if using another metric, set the band's *height* to an appropriate value). This should now appear something like:

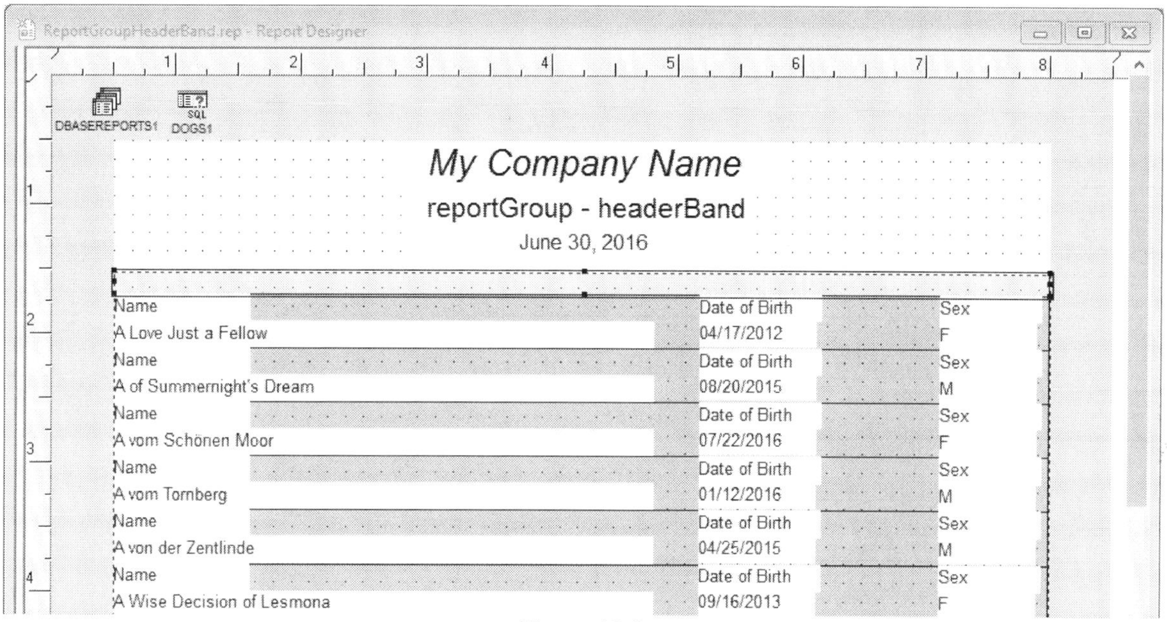

Figure 18-2

To create an introduction to the report we can do this in several ways, but let's start simple at the moment. Place a "DataText" control onto the green *reportGroup headerBand* object, set the *top* and *left* properties to 0, and the *width* to 7.5 (the width of the page). Change the *text* property of this control to the following:

```
This report is a sample showing how the reportGroup's headerBand works
in a dBASE Plus report. We can put whatever we want into the text here,
and we can have multiple objects if we want or need to. We could add
images, shapes, and more. This is however just an example to see how it
works.
```

Notice as you type that the band's *height* does not automatically adjust to the height of the text. Once you move control from this text control, the band *should* adjust itself. If it does not, try going to the Inspector window, find the *headerBand* object for the *reportGroup*, and the *expandable* property – see if it is set to *true* (this is the default value). If the band has not adjusted at this point, try setting the *expandable* property to *false* and then back to *true*. This should force it to readjust at that point.

The problem is that this text looks like it will run into the details of the report. We can solve this simply by adding a line object under the text. Set the height of the reportGroup headerBand to 1 (or an equivalent amount for the metric you are using).

Next, go to the Component Palette, and select the "Standard" tab, select a "Line" object and place it under the text on the *headerBand*. You may need to use the mouse to move this up and down. Make sure in the Inspector that the *top* and *bottom* properties of the line are the same value, or the line will be slightly at an angle when rendered. Set the *left* property to 0, and the *right* property to 7.5 (width of the *detailBand*). Try setting the line object's *width* property to 2, to make it a bit wider than normal. Set the height of the *headerBand* back to .17 (or even 0) at this point.

> **NOTE**
> If you see that the "ColHeadingText" controls on the *detailBand* are overlapping the line a little, you can move them down in the *detailBand*. This is an aesthetic issue, making the report look good – the overlap will actually change the appearance of the line a little. *(Suggestion: Ctrl+click on all six controls, use the down arrow button once to nudge all of them at one time down – that should be enough ...)* Moving all of the controls on the *detailBand* down just a tiny amount won't affect the report much, if at all, and will make it look cleaner.

When you run the report (use the "Run Report" button in the toolbar), you should see something like:

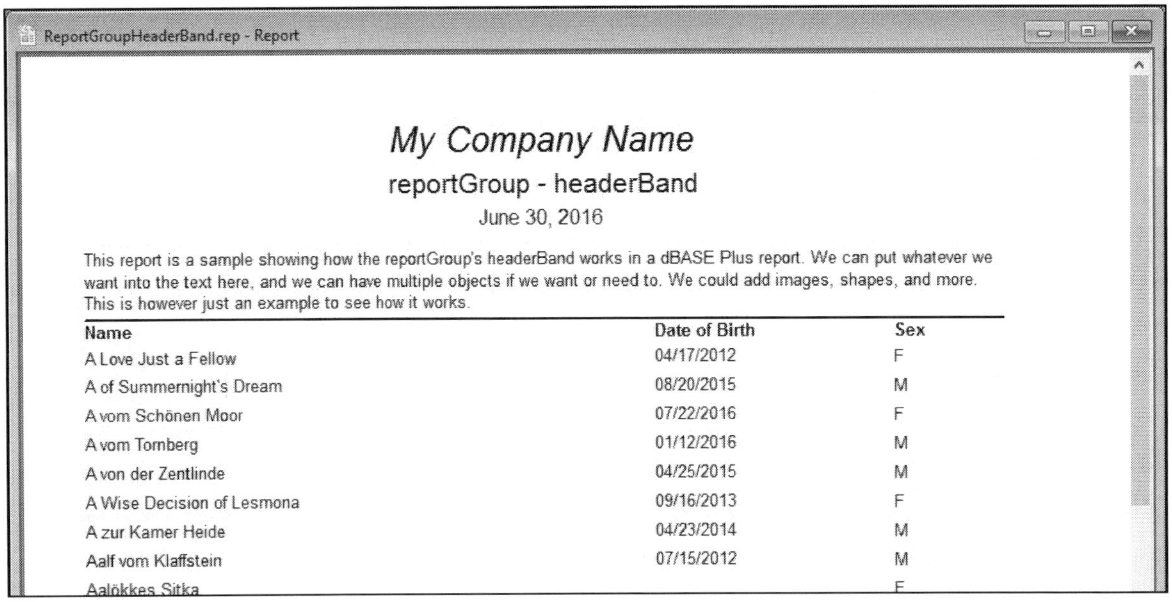

Figure 18-3

If you use the PgDn key (or the "Next Page" button in the toolbar), the second page does not show the reportGroup's *headerBand*, which is how it should be:

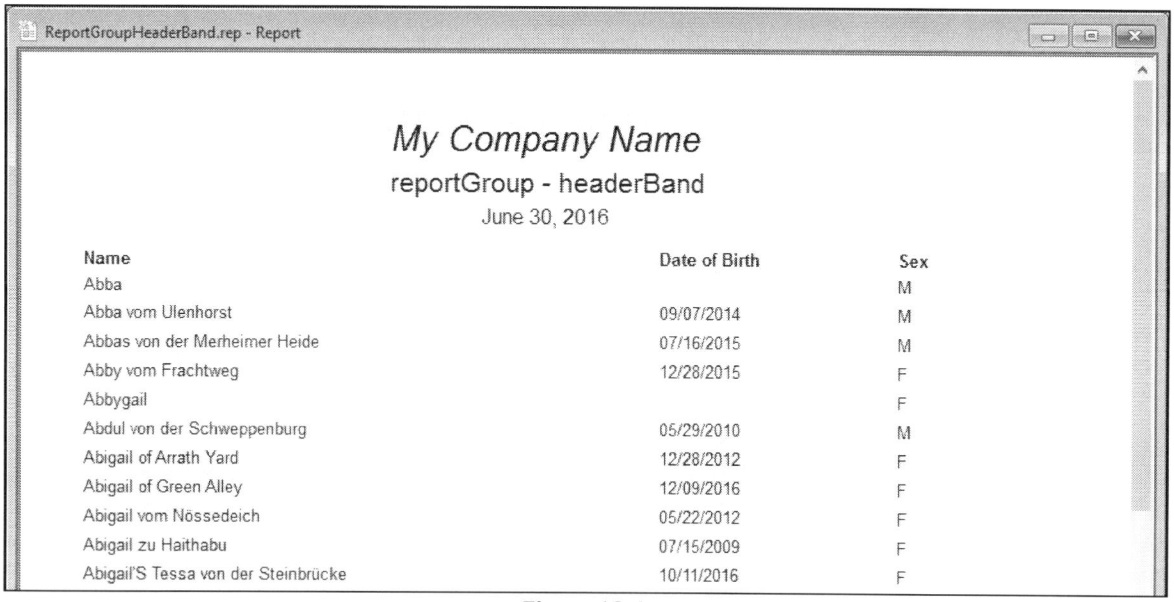
ReportGroupHeaderBand.rep - Report

My Company Name

reportGroup - headerBand

June 30, 2016

Name	Date of Birth	Sex
Abba		M
Abba vom Ulenhorst	09/07/2014	M
Abbas von der Merheimer Heide	07/16/2015	M
Abby vom Frachtweg	12/28/2015	F
Abbygail		F
Abdul von der Schweppenburg	05/29/2010	M
Abigail of Arrath Yard	12/28/2012	F
Abigail of Green Alley	12/09/2016	F
Abigail vom Nössedeich	05/22/2012	F
Abigail zu Haithabu	07/15/2009	F
Abigail'S Tessa von der Steinbrücke	10/11/2016	F

Figure 18-4

Notice that the reportGroup's *headerBand* is part of the *streamFrame*, it does not affect the text at the top of the report, and it prints only within the *streamFrame* area of the report.

Setting the reportGroup's *headerBand* On Its Own Page

What if you wanted the reportGroup's *headerBand* to be on its own page? In other words, you might want a cover page or title page, or report introduction placed on one page, and have the data and main report (the *detailBand*, etc.) start on the next page (page 2). How would you do this?

Bring the report back into the Report Designer. Select the *reportGroup headerBand* either by clicking on the green space in the Designer, or by selecting it in the Inspector window. Select the "Events" tab, and you will see two events – *onRender* and *preRender*. The *onRender* event fires once the *headerBand* has rendered, and before anything in the *detailBand* (and any group headerBands that might exist if you are working with a grouped report) executes or is rendered. Select the *onRender* event and click the tool button. In the Source Code Editor enter the following code:

```
function HEADERBAND_onRender()
   // force a new page once this band renders
   // this = headerBand
   // parent = reportGroup
   // parent = report or form
   this.parent.parent.streamSource1.beginNewFrame()
return
```

(Yes, we could have done this as a codeblock ...) Save this (Ctrl+S) and run the report. Notice that now the reportGroup's *headerBand* is on the first page, and the data in the Dogs table does not start until you go to Page 2 of the report.

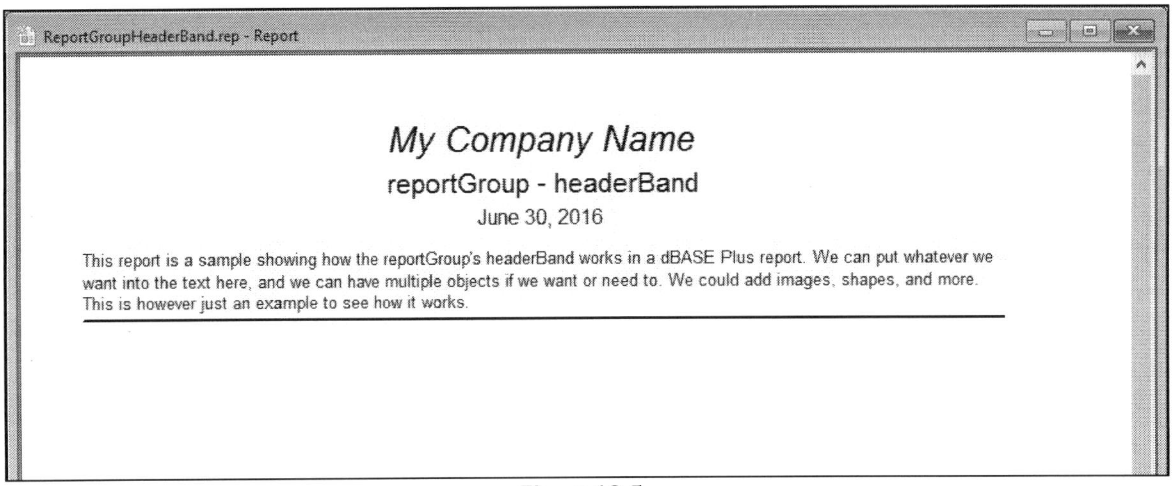

Figure 18-5

However, as you can see, the text that is on the *pageTemplate* still prints. We could turn that off, it's not that hard to do using the *canRender* event of the individual controls – the concept would be to check for report's *reportPage* property, and if the value is 1 (the first page), don't render (return false) the controls.

We could even get fancy, and programmatically change the top of the *streamFrame* object so that it starts higher on the page, taller ... if we are on page 1 doing the same sort of thing as above (remember that when the page changes to 2, you would need to re-set the streamFrame properties you modified). You can add a company logo on the first page only this way, and a lot more. Hopefully this gives you an idea of what can be done, however.

Using the *reportGroup footerBand*

In previous chapters we worked with the *reportGroup footerBand* to do report summaries using the Aggregate calculations. As noted there, since the parent of the *footerBand* is not the same as with a regular group, the path used to get to the data is different than it would be with a regular *group footerBand*. Other than that, these work pretty much the same.

In the Command Window type the following:

```
copy file ReportGroupHeaderband.rep to ReportGroupFooterband.rep
```

Open the new report in the Source Code Editor, and use the Replace dialog (Ctrl+R) to change the className of the report – replace "HEADERBANDREPORT" with "FOOTERBANDREPORT" to avoid any issues with copies of reports in memory. Save changes and exit the editor (Ctrl+W).

Open the report in the Report Designer, change the text of the "SecondaryTitleText" control to "reportGroup – footerBand", and save changes.

In the Inspector find the *reportGroup*, and then the *footerBand*. Change the height temporarily to 1", and then we need to change a Report Designer property so we can actually get to the *footerBand* without a lot of work. Right click on the Report surface and in the menu select "Report Designer Properties", select "One row" under the "Rowset display", and click "OK".

Now you will see a single record, but with the report's *footerBand* available to work with. Similar to the headerBand for this report, place a "DataText" control onto the surface of the report, move it to just below the top of the *footerBand*, to the left (set the left property to zero), then widen it to fill the *footerBand*. Put the control into edit mode (click on the text that is there), and type the following:

```
This report is showing how the reportGroup's footerBand can be used for
a summary on a report. We can place, as with the headerBand anything we
wish to on the surface, including shapes, images, and so on. This is
just an example to show how it works.
```

Add a *line* above the text you just added, similarly to what you did in the headerBand *(make sure the top and bottom properties are the same or the line will attempt to do a diagonal line ...)*.

Set the *height* of the *footerBand* to 0. You should see something similar to:

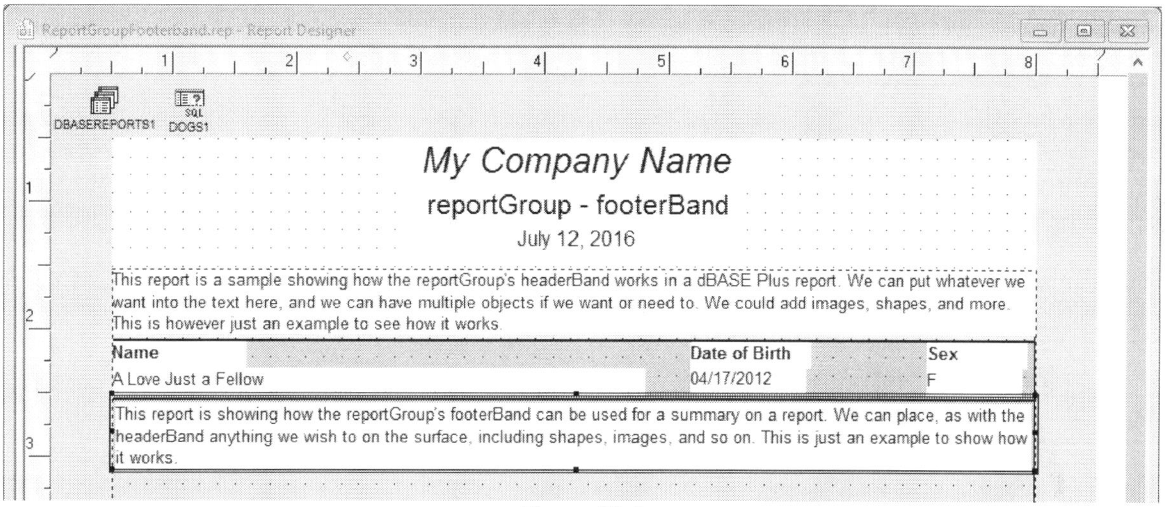

Figure 18-6

It is a good idea to set this so that we are seeing all the rows of the report again, or we might make things confusing the next time we work with the report. Right click on the design surface, select "Report Designer Properties", and select "All rows", click "OK".

If you were to run the report and scroll (PgDn, etc.) to the last page of the report, you should see something like:

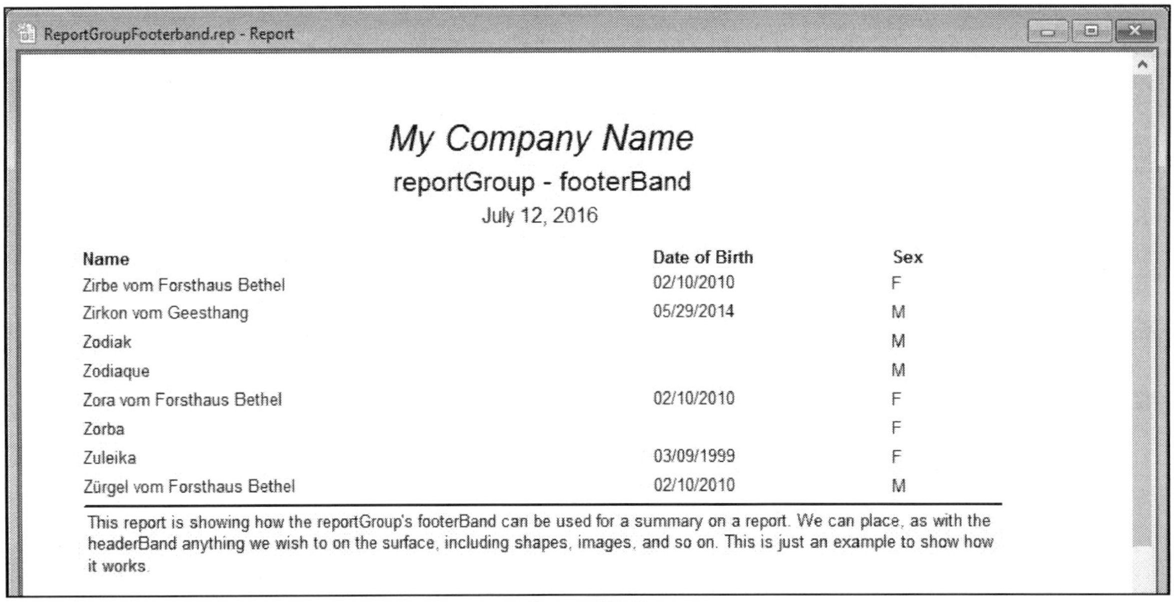

Figure 18-7

As noted at the beginning of the chapter, the *reportGroup footerBand* only prints on the last page of the report. However, if you look at Figure 18-7, it prints under the last data. If the report had *group* footerBands involved, this would *appear* after those as well. It doesn't display on the bottom of the page (which is sort of implied by the term "footer").

We could do something similar to what we did with the reportGroup *headerBand*, the only difference being that it's hard to force a new page for the *footerBand*.

If we wanted the *footerBand* to be on its own page, the *beginNewFrame* property would work in this situation. In the Inspector, find the *reportGroup*, and under that, find the *footerBand*. Find the *beginNewFrame* property and set it to *true*.

If you run the report, and scroll to the last page:

Figure 18-8

It is possible you might encounter a situation where this added a blank page to the report, but you could work with the band's *preRender* event, check to see if the current page was the last page by using the report's *isLastPage* method (which returns a true or false value) and determine if you needed to force a new page break.

Close the window if necessary.

Cleanup

Create a new report (in the Navigator, click on the .Reports. tab, double-click on the "[New Report]" icon). Select the "File" menu, select "Set Custom Report Class", and in the dialog, click the "Clear Custom Report" button, then click "OK". This clears out the custom report setting in the Plus.ini file, so that the next report you create is not based on this one. Close that report without making any changes.

Make sure the database is closed by going to the Command Window and typing:

```
close databases
```

This will also ensure that you don't end up creating tables in the wrong location, etc.

Source Code

The following is a listing of the sample code in the folders we have been working with. If you downloaded the files from my website the structure will be different (see below). You may use the code contained in these folders for your own applications if you desire, with the caveat that credit be given appropriately.

From working on this chapter:

```
C:\dBASEReports\Chapter 18\ReportGroupFooterBand.rep
C:\dBASEReports\Chapter 18\ReportGroupHeaderBand.rep
```

Downloaded version – same files but with this path:

```
C:\ReportsBookSourceCode\Chapter 18\filename
```

Summary

This chapter really only touched on some of what can be done with the *reportGroup header* and *footer* bands, but the idea was to get you thinking about it, and try to experiment a bit to come up with things you can do using these objects. We also looked, in a previous chapter (12) at running totals and using those in various ways, so if you need to go back to that for your report, it's worth a look.

The next chapter is going to discuss grouping your data in more complex ways that we have tended to do in earlier chapters.

NOTES:

Chapter 19: Grouping Data on Partial or Multiple Fields

In earlier chapters we discussed grouping data, so the concept of grouping should be familiar to you. However, there are times when you need to group data on part of a field, or on multiple fields. Both of these cases can be handled in a similar fashion, but we should take a look at how you might accomplish this.

A Place for Our Work

As we work through the chapter we will be needing a place for the files we create, so please create a folder for this chapter:

```
C:\dBASEReports\Chapter 19
```

And in the Navigator, be sure to navigate to this folder.

Grouping on a Partial Field

We covered this topic in Chapter 7 ("Grouping on Part of a Field"). If you need to look at this, go back to that chapter. A quick synopsis is that we created a calculated field that extracted the left three characters of a field in the table, and we used that to group the data. The reason we did this was that the field was completely unique and would have had one *detailBand* for each entry – defeating the purpose of grouped reports. It seems silly to repeat the project here.

Grouping Data by Multiple Fields

This topic is actually quite similar to the concepts used for Partial Fields, and uses the same technique, but the results will be quite different.

Create a new report by double-clicking on the "[New Report]" icon in the dBASE Navigator. Save the report with Ctrl+S and call it "GroupMultiField.rep". Click on the "SecondaryTitleText" control to give it focus and change the *text* property to: "Group On Multiple Fields". Readjust the width and make sure the control is centered properly.

In the Navigator window select the "Tables" tab. Select and drag the "DOGS" table to the design surface of the report. While the "DOGS1" query has focus, go to the Inspector, find the *rowset* property, click the Inspect button. Now find the *indexName* property for the rowset, and select "D_S_BORN" as the index tag to use for this report.

We're now going to create the calculated field that we will use to group the data by. Each dog's record has a registration number for both the Dam and Sire. We want to group on both of these so that we can get the data grouped by the parents of the dogs. While the "DOGS1" query has focus, in the Inspector go to the "Events" tab and select the *onOpen* event. Click the tool button and add the following code:

```
function DOGS1_onOpen()
   local f
   f = new field()
   f.fieldName := "DamSire"
   // this should be a single line:
   f.beforeGetValue := {|| this.parent["RNO_DAM"].value +
this.parent["RNO_SIRE"].value }
   // add to fields array:
   this.rowset.fields.add( f )
return
```

Now, because the calculated field will not exist until we reopen the query, we should close the report in the designer (Ctrl+W) and reopen the report back to the designer. If you look at the "Field Palette" after doing this, you should see "DamSire" in the list of fields for the "Dogs1" table.

Go to the Component Palette and select the "DataColHeadingText" control, placing it on the *detailBand*, indented from the left (we will be adding a group *headerBand* with some text as before). Change the *text* property to "Registration". You may want to widen this, because when it displays in bold text, it will need more room. Now do the same, placing the next control to the right, and changing the *text* property to "Name". Take a moment and line the column heading controls up.

Go back to the Component Palette and select the "DataText" control, and place it under the first column heading text. Change the type of the *text* property to "Codeblock", click the tool button, and in the dialog enter:

```
this.form.dogs1.rowset.fields["reg_no"].value
```

You will need to widen the text control enough so that the registration number does not wrap inside the text control. Select another "DataText" control, and repeat the steps shown above (placing the control under the second heading), but set the *text* property to:

```
this.form.dogs1.rowset.fields["name"].value
```

Go to the Component Palette and click on the "Report" tab. Select the "Group" icon and drag it to the design surface. Go back to the "Custom" page of the Component Palette, and place a "DataHeadingText" control on the *group headerBand* (the green band). Select the text that says "Header Text for Group1" and delete it (press the "Del" key). Move the "Heading Text" control to the left and top of the band, and change the *text* property to "Dam:".

Place a "DataText" control on the *group headerBand* to the right of the heading text. Change the type of the *text* property to "Codeblock", click the tool button, and enter the following in the dialog:

```
this.form.dogs1.rowset.fields["rno_dam"].value
```

(The first group will likely show asterisks in the text, because the field is empty – that's okay, it's supposed to do that! Some of the data has empty values for the rno_dam and rno_sire fields.)

On the same band, add another "DataHeadingText" control to the right of the "DataText", and change the *text* property to "Sire:". Place a "DataText" control on the *group headerBand* to the right of the new heading text. Change the type of the *text* property to "Codeblock", click the tool button and enter the following in the dialog:

```
this.form.dogs1.rowset.fields["rno_sire"].value
```

We need to set the group's *groupBy* property – this is vital to getting the data to be grouped the way we need it. Right now this property is empty. Find the "group1" object in the Inspector, and then the *groupBy* property. Click the down arrow, and find the "DamSire" field, and select this. One more thing for the report itself, let's set the *headerEveryFrame* property to *true*, so that as you scroll through the report the *group headerBand* will appear at the top of each page.

In order to make the report more useful, let's make sure that the data we view has actually got information in the registration number fields for the dams and sires. Otherwise scrolling through the data to see anything meaningful will be frustrating. To do this, we're going to set a filter on the data. Click on the "DOGS1" query object, and find the *rowset* object in the Inspector. Click the Inspect button, and find the *filter* property. Enter the following:

```
rno_dam<>'' and rno_sire<>''
```

(Note: the '' part of the statement above are two single quotes, in other words ' followed by ' with no space between them – they represent an empty character string.)

After typing the string above in the *filter* property be sure to press the Enter key, or the change to the filter will be ignored.

When you run the report, you should see something like the following:

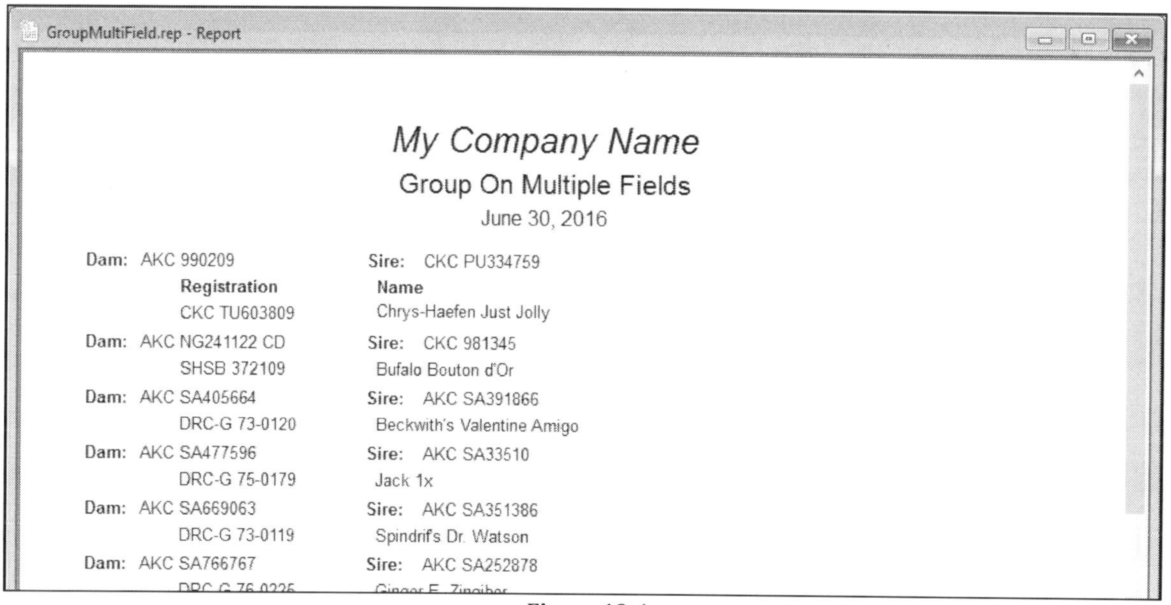

Figure 19-1

If you scroll through the report you should see eventually places where there are multiple dogs for the same dam and sire. For example on page 2 here, you will see the same Dam with different Sires, and a few records down two offspring for the same Dam/Sire:

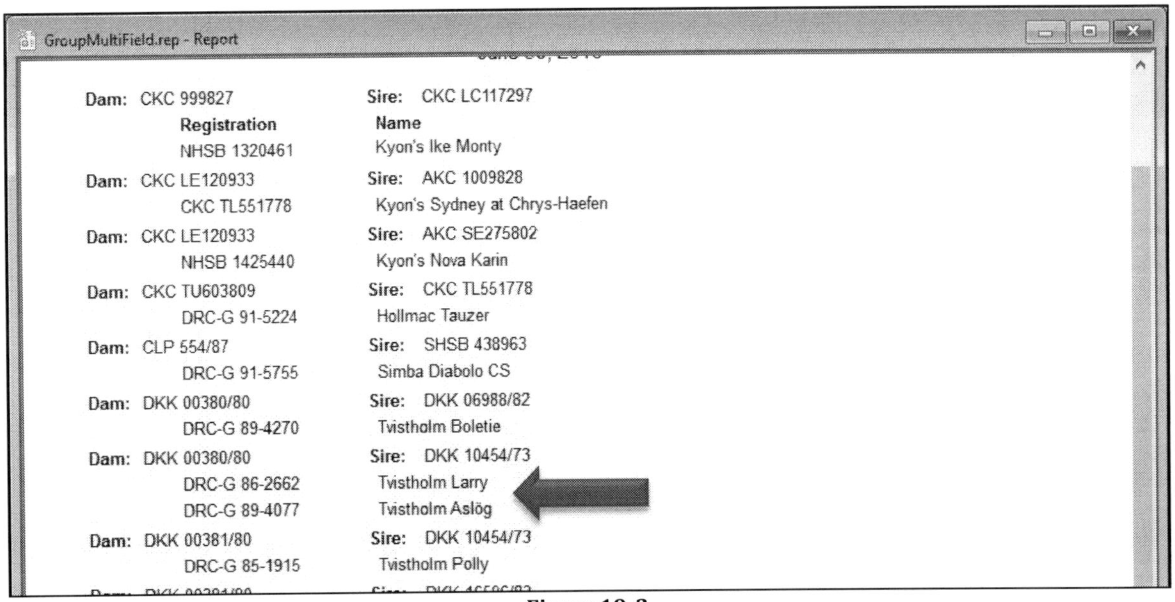

Figure 19-2

Close the report viewer.

Cleanup

Create a new report (in the Navigator, click on the .Reports. tab, double-click on the "[New Report]" icon). Select the "File" menu, select "Set Custom Report Class", and in the dialog, click the "Clear Custom Report" button, then click "OK". This clears out the custom report setting in the Plus.ini file, so that the next report you create is not based on this one. Close that report without making any changes.

Make sure the database is closed by going to the Command Window and typing:

```
close databases
```

This will also ensure that you don't end up creating tables in the wrong location, etc.

Source Code

The following is a listing of the sample code in the folders we have been working with. If you downloaded the files from my website the structure will be different (see below). You may use the code contained in these folders for your own applications if you desire, with the caveat that credit be given appropriately.

From working on this chapter:

```
C:\dBASEReports\Chapter 19\GroupMultiField.rep
```

Downloaded version – same files but with this path:

```
C:\ReportsBookSourceCode\Chapter 19\filename
```

Summary

While grouping on partial or multiple fields seems like it should be a difficult thing, it's not really all that hard to do. The important thing is determining exactly how you want the report to look. For example, the report we did in this chapter could actually have been done with two groups and we wouldn't have needed the calculated field – the first group's *groupBy* could have been on the "RNO_DAM" field, and the second group's *groupBy* field could have been on the "RNO_SIRE" field. As with most reports, a lot depends on the needs of the individual report.

In the next chapter we'll take a look at working with cross-tab reports.

NOTES:

Chapter 20: Cross-Tab Reports

What exactly is a cross-tab or cross tabular report? This is a concept that causes many developers to blink, stutter in confusion, and sometimes walk away from a conversation. I used to think it was similar to turning a table on its side so that the fields acted like rows, and the rows acted like fields, and in a way I was *sort of* correct, but not really.

A cross-tab report is one that summarizes data in a (hopefully) simple way. If you have worked with Excel™ and Pivot Tables, cross-tab reports are very similar to those. An example I found on the web uses data that we have not yet looked at in this book that might help show what is meant by this.

Suppose we have a table that lists household expenses (or for a business, business expenses, but we'll stick with the data I have). This table might have fields for a date, a category, an amount spent, and perhaps a notes field so that you could explain in more detail what the purchase was. To keep things simple, we'll keep the categories as:

Auto Repair/Maintenance
Auto Fuel
Groceries
Household
House Payments
Miscellaneous

A useful cross tabular report would be to show how much was spent each month for each of these categories. The report might include a monthly average for each category, as well as an annual total. In order to do this, you would need to create a new table that was designed to have fields for the category, the month (12 of them), a field for the average, and a field for the total. Then you would need to create a program that filled in the cross tab table, and create a report from it. This chapter is going to walk through the steps of the process, one at a time.

A Place for Our Work

As we work through the chapter we will be needing a place for the files we create, so please create a folder for this chapter:

```
C:\dBASEReports\Chapter 20
```

And in the Navigator, be sure to navigate to this folder.

The Household Table

This table is already in the data you downloaded for the book, and should be in the "DBASEREPORTS" database. Go to the Navigator and select the "Tables" tab. If the "DBASEREPORTS" database is not open, select it in the "Look in" combobox. Click on the "Household" table. The table structure can be viewed by opening the table in the Table Designer (right click on it and select "Design Table").

This table is not 100% realistic for most households – there would most likely be more categories, and more entries, but it is here for an example. Indeed, the data could be broken down to categories and subcategories, and the cross-tab report could use both. In a proper fully normalized database application the category (and subcategory if we had one) would be stored in a separate table (or tables), and a reference to the category (and subcategory) would be stored in the Household table.

There are index tags on the "EntryDate" and "Category" fields. However, that's not all of the index tags. If you go to the "Structure" menu, and select "Manage Indexes", you should see a dialog that shows the two index tags just mentioned, and a third, called "Cat_Unique", which is literally a unique index tag for the Category field. The reason for this will be explained later when we look at the program needed to create the report. (Click the "Close" button to close this dialog.)

Close the table, and if asked about any changes, click "No". This way you will not cause this table to have any differences from what is discussed in the chapter.

If you double-click on the table, you should see something like this:

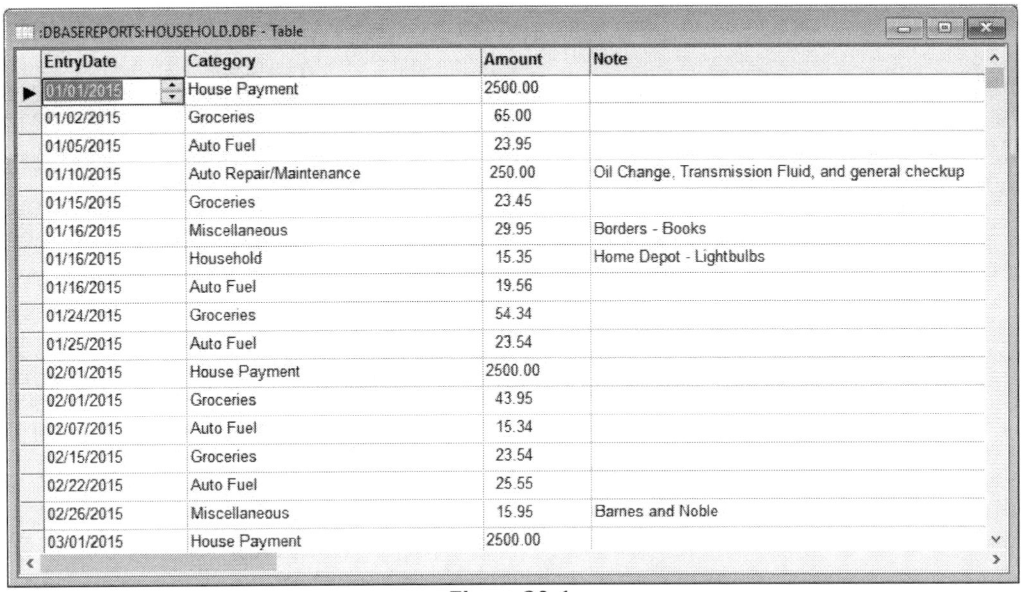
:DBASEREPORTS:HOUSEHOLD.DBF - Table

EntryDate	Category	Amount	Note
01/01/2015	House Payment	2500.00	
01/02/2015	Groceries	65.00	
01/05/2015	Auto Fuel	23.95	
01/10/2015	Auto Repair/Maintenance	250.00	Oil Change, Transmission Fluid, and general checkup
01/15/2015	Groceries	23.45	
01/16/2015	Miscellaneous	29.95	Borders - Books
01/16/2015	Household	15.35	Home Depot - Lightbulbs
01/16/2015	Auto Fuel	19.56	
01/24/2015	Groceries	54.34	
01/25/2015	Auto Fuel	23.54	
02/01/2015	House Payment	2500.00	
02/01/2015	Groceries	43.95	
02/07/2015	Auto Fuel	15.34	
02/15/2015	Groceries	23.54	
02/22/2015	Auto Fuel	25.55	
02/26/2015	Miscellaneous	15.95	Barnes and Noble
03/01/2015	House Payment	2500.00	

Figure 20-1

The data was created specifically for this exercise, and as noted elsewhere is not real. However, it should give us something to work with for the example. One thing to note is that the table would most likely have data for multiple years in it. This one has data for each month of the year 2015, and a few entries for the beginning of the year 2016, so that we can see how to filter the data later.

Close the table, and let's move on.

The Cross-Tab Table

In order to create the report we want, some method of putting the data into an appropriate format is needed. There are many ways to do this, and when I asked around in the dBASE newsgroups I was given many ideas and suggestions. At the end of the chapter we will look at a few other ideas, in case you need something different from what is being discussed here.

For this report, we need to create a new table. We could do this in code, and delete it once the report was done, or we could just create a table that will be used for the report. For this simple example, we will create the table and when we get to the code, the first thing the code will do is make sure the table starts out empty.

The purpose of the report is to provide totals for each month for each category, a monthly average for each category for the year, and a total for each category for the year. To do this, we need quite a few fields.

With the Navigator showing the "Tables" tab, double click on the "[New Table]" icon. This will bring up the Table Designer for a new table.

Add the following fields, with the structure given:

Fieldname	Type	Width	Dec	Index
Category	Character	25		Ascend
Jan	Numeric	9	2	
Feb	Numeric	9	2	
Mar	Numeric	9	2	
Apr	Numeric	9	2	
May	Numeric	9	2	
Jun	Numeric	9	2	
Jul	Numeric	9	2	
Aug	Numeric	9	2	
Sep	Numeric	9	2	
Oct	Numeric	9	2	
Nov	Numeric	9	2	
Dec	Numeric	9	2	
MonAvg	Numeric	9	2	
CatTotal	Numeric	9	2	

Press Ctrl+W to save and exit the Table Designer, and call this "HouseholdCT" (CT for Cross-Tab).

The width for the numeric fields is 2 digits wider than the amount field in the Household table, which is enough room for our totals.

The Program

In order to get the data that is needed for the report, we will need a program that pulls the data for each category for each month, creating appropriate totals, including storing a value of zero if there are no entries for any specific month for any specific category.

The following program is very specific to this data. When I queried dBASE developers I got a couple of programs that were meant to be "generic" – meaning that you told it what fields to total and all of that, and it created a table for the data, to generate the report from. I find that many "generic" programs cannot do all of what might be needed for any specific report *(from personal experience, having attempted to write a few of these)*.

To create a new program, go to the "Programs" tab in the Navigator window, and double click the "[New Program]" icon. This will bring up the Source Code Editor. Type the following. Watch for errors and typos. There are a lot of comments in the code to help understand what the code is doing – while you can leave those out, it's a good idea to have the comments in the code so that you can read the code later and understand what is going on.

```
/*
   HouseholdCrossTab.prg
   Creates data used for HouseholdCT table from the Household
   table, and in the HouseholdExpenses report.
*/
// Set up a database object to point to the data:
local oData
oData = new database()
oData.databaseName := "DBASEREPORTS"
oData.active := true

// Before we do anything else, we should empty
// the table used for the Cross Tab report:
try
   oData.emptyTable( "HouseholdCT" )
catch( exception e )
   // if we have an error emptying the table
   // we should let the user know, and then
   // stop processing. Normally any error
   // at this point will either be a typo
   // in the table name, or the table
   // is in use somewhere and we can't empty it.
   msgbox( e.code+" - "+e.message+chr(13)+;
           "Could not empty table, report cancelled!",;
           "Unexpected error!", 16 )
   // deactivate/release data object:
   oData.active := false
   release object oData
   oData = null
   // return from this program
   return
endtry

// set up data objects for the tables needed
local qHousehold, rHousehold, fHousehold
local qCT, rCT, fCT

// Household table:
qHousehold = new query()
qHousehold.database := oData
qHousehold.sql      := "select * from Household"
qHousehold.active   := true

// create two object shortcuts
rHousehold = qHousehold.rowset
fHousehold = rHousehold.fields

// set first index we need:
rHousehold.indexName := "Cat_Unique"

// Cross Tab table:
qCT = new query()
```

```
qCT.database := oData
qCT.sql      := "select * from HouseholdCT"
qCT.active   := true

// create two object shortcuts
rCT = qCT.rowset
fCT = rCT.fields

// don't allow null values in fields when adding rows:
rCT.autoNullFields := false

// ----------------- Actual Processing -----------------
// The first thing we need to do is get the categories, and
// add rows to the Cross Tab table - one for each category:
local cCat
rHousehold.first() // first row of unique index for Category
do while not rHousehold.endOfSet
   cCat = fHousehold["Category"].value.rightTrim()
   // add a row to the Cross Tab table for each category:
   rCT.beginAppend()
   fCT["Category"].value := cCat
   rCT.save()
   rHousehold.next() // next row
enddo

// Now that we have the Categories in the Cross-Tab table, we need
// to get the totals, averages and all that. However, we also need
// to get the *year* for the report. We could hard-code it into the
// program, but that would require changing the program each time you
// wanted to generate the report, which is not very user-friendly,
// or efficient. Instead, we need a form to allow the user to select
// the year. The following assumes a four digit year (SET CENTURY ON).
set procedure to CT_GetYear.wfm additive
local f, nYear
f = new CT_GetYearForm()
f.YearSB.rangeMin := 2015 // set the "lowest value acceptable"
f.YearSB.rangeMax := year( date() ) // set largest to current year
f.YearSB.value := year( date() ) // set default to current year
f.readModal()

// get the year that was displayed
// in the Spinbox control "YearSB":
nYear = f.YearSB.value

// release and close the form:
f.release()
release object f
f = null
close procedure CT_GetYear.wfm

// set to a different index, otherwise
// we will never see more than the six
// unique records we have in the table.
// We'll be using a combination of
// filter techniques to get the data
// we need.
rHousehold.indexName := "EntryDate"
```

```
// We have the year, we need to move on. We need
// to set a filter - this can be done in many
// ways, but as the book says, let's keep it simple.
// We know the year, we know each year starts at
// January 1, and ends at December 31, we can
// use the filter property for the household rowset.
//
// by using the setRange method of the rowset,
// we take advantage of the index "EntryDate",
// and can limit the data in a very fast way,
// this is faster than using a filter ...
// The date is being converted from a string
// to a date value (CTOD()):
local dStart, dEnd
dStart = ctod( "01/01/"+nYear )
dEnd = ctod( "12/31/"+nYear )

// set the range:
rHousehold.setRange( dStart, dEnd )

// Now this is the tricky part of what we need to do.
// We need to get the totals for each category
// for each month of the year, as well as averages
// for each category and totals for each category.
// As the number of categories could easily change
// from time to time that the report is run, we need
// to be flexible. Since we have the categories stored
// in the CT table, we will loop through that table
// to get the data for each category. Then it gets
// even more interesting.

// For a larger amount of data, or a more complex set
// of calculations, you might consider a progress form
// that would display, showing how far along in the
// table you are. Testing this with the test data,
// the process is fairly fast, and doesn't need a
// progress form.
local cCat, nMonth
rCT.first()
do while not rCT.endOfSet
   // we need to go through the data and get information
   // for each category - totals and such for each month.
   // The first thing to do is get the current Category:
   cCat = fCT["Category"].value.rightTrim()
   // Then we set a filter (on top of the setRange!)
   // on the Household table:
   rHousehold.filter = [Category=']+cCat+[']
   rHousehold.first()
   // next we want to loop through the Household table:
   do while not rHousehold.endOfSet
      // While looping through the data, now filtered for
      // the category in the CrossTab table, we need
      // to accumulate data for the months, and for the
      // total field:
      fCT["CatTotal"].value += fHousehold["Amount"].value
      // For each month it's a little trickier.
```

```
        // The HouseholdCT table has one field before
        // the months, so one relatively simple way to
        // handle this is to get the month of the
        // record in the Household table's EntryDate field,
        // and add one to it, and accumulate the value
        // in the field in HouseholdCT that relates to
        // that number. For example, if we are looking
        // at a month of January, the second field in the
        // HouseholdCT table is "Jan", which is the appropriate
        // field to add the data to:
        nMonth = month( fHousehold["EntryDate"].value )
        fCT[ nMonth+1 ].value += fHousehold["Amount"].value
        // save changes in this record:
        rCT.save()
        // next Household record:
        rHousehold.next()
     enddo
     // before moving on, let's calculate the average and
     // store it in the table - this is the category total
     // (for the year) divided by 12 (12 months in a year):
     fCT["MonAvg"].value := ( fCT["CatTotal"].value / 12 )
     rCT.save() // save this in the record
     // next CrossTab record
     rCT.next()
  enddo

  // Done looping through the Categories
  // and done creating the data we need for
  // the report.

  // Cleanup - deactivate data objects:
  qCT.active := false
  release object qCT
  qCT = null
  qHousehold.active := false
  release object qHousehold
  qHousehold = null
  oData.active := false
  release object oData
  oData = null

  // ********************************************
  // code to call the report should be added here
  // ********************************************
  // -  end of program HouseholdCrossTab.prg
```

Okay, that's a lot of typing, and you really should check it over for typos. Save your work (Ctrl+W) as "HouseholdCrossTab.prg" and exit the Source Code Editor.

Before you attempt to run this, you will need to create the form that is called to get the year for the report. This is a fairly simple form, but follow along.

Create Form to Get Year for Report

Go to the Navigator window, and select the "Forms" tab. Double-click the "[New Form]" icon. In the Form Designer, do the following, using controls from the "Standard" tab.

For the form itself, set the *text* property to "Cross Tab Report - Select Year", and if you wish, set the *icon* to some icon from the Resource that ships with dBASE. While looking at the form in the Inspector, you might want to also set the following properties:

Metric	6 - Pixels
autoCenter	true
maximize	false
minimize	false
mdi	false

Save the form with Ctrl+S and name it "CT_GetYear.wfm".

Place a text control at the top of the form (from the Component Palette), and set the following properties:

anchor	2 - Top
text	Cross Tab Report - Select Year
alignHorizontal	1 - Center
fontSize	12
fontBold	true

Adjust the *height* of this text using the mouse, or the Inspector, so that the text fits.

Place a textLabel control under the first text, and set the following properties:

fontBold	true
text	Year for Report:
alignHorizontal	2 - Right

And adjust the *width* and other position and size properties as needed.

Place a spinbox control to the right of the textLabel you just created. Set the following properties:

picture	9999
rangeRequired	true
name	YearSB

Adjust this so that the textLabel and the spinbox compliment each other on the form. Place a pushbutton under these two controls. Set the following properties:

default	true
upBitmap	RESOURCE #20
name	OKBtn
text	OK

Adjust the size of the pushbutton so it looks good to you. Then click the "Events" tab and select the *onClick* event. Enter the following for the event:

```
{; form.close() }
```

Don't forget to press the Enter key after typing this or the Inspector will forget it.

Adjust the form's size and move controls as needed. The form should look something like this in the Form Designer:

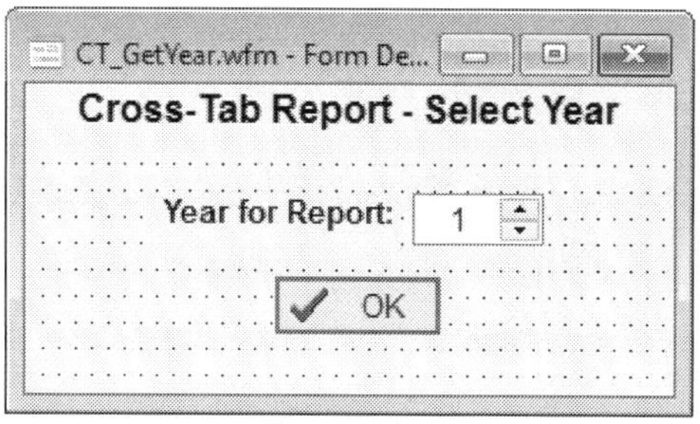

Figure 20-2

Back to the Program

Try running the program, and if an error occurs, try comparing against the code shown in these pages. When run you should see the Get Year form, but it should now look like:

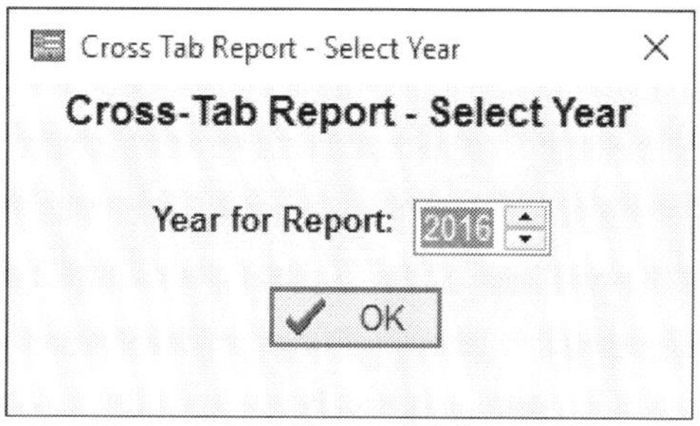

Figure 20-3

If you set the year to 2015, and click the "OK" button the code will run (on my computer pretty quickly), and it will then end. Nothing obvious will have happened because we have not created the report and set the program to display it.

However, if you view the data in the table, you should see something like the following – which is only part of the data, but you should get the idea (go to the Navigator, select the "Tables" tab, and double-click the HouseholdCT table):

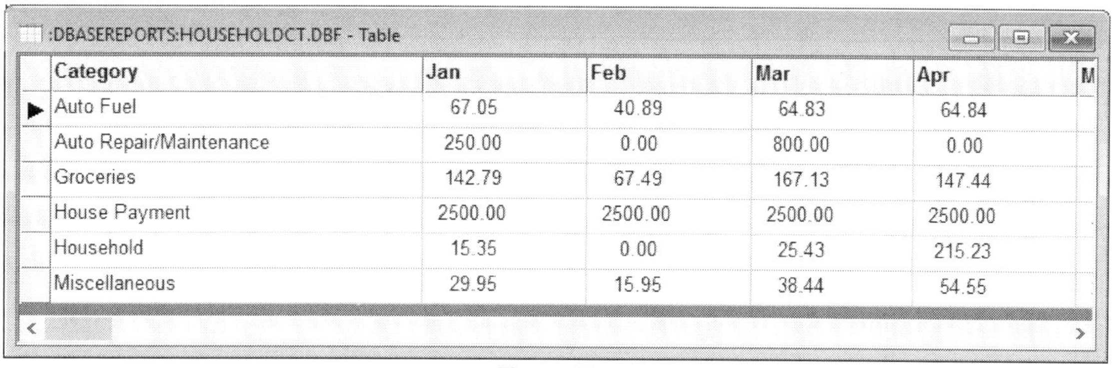

:DBASEREPORTS:HOUSEHOLDCT.DBF - Table

Category	Jan	Feb	Mar	Apr	M
Auto Fuel	67.05	40.89	64.83	64.84	
Auto Repair/Maintenance	250.00	0.00	800.00	0.00	
Groceries	142.79	67.49	167.13	147.44	
House Payment	2500.00	2500.00	2500.00	2500.00	
Household	15.35	0.00	25.43	215.23	
Miscellaneous	29.95	15.95	38.44	54.55	

Figure 20-4

Once done examining the data, close the table.

The last few steps will involve creating the report, and then modifying the program to do what is needed to display the report in a preview screen.

Creating the Cross-Tab Report

This report will be similar to some of the others we have done but we need it to be a landscape report, for starters, so we have room for all the data. Go to the Navigator and select the "Reports" tab, and double click the "[New Report]" icon. In the Report Designer, select the "File" menu, and "Set Custom Report Class ...". Select the "MyCompanyReportLandscape" custom report we created in Chapter 8. Click "OK", and the report options should be set.

Click on the "SecondaryTitleText" control and change the *text* to "Household Expenses". Save the report (Ctrl+S) as "HouseholdCrossTab.rep".

Go the Navigator window and select the "Tables" tab, and drag the "HouseholdCT" table to the design surface. In the Inspector window select the *rowset* object, and click the Inspect button. Now select the *indexName* property and select "Category".

Place "DataColHeadingText" controls on the *detailBand* with the following *text* properties:

Category
January
February
March
April
May
June
July
August
September
October
November
December
Average
Total

> **NOTE**
> One of the odd quirks in the Report Designer is that when placing these controls on the surface, you may find that one (or more) of them start acting up – the text appears to shift, and when you click on it you cannot give the control focus. If this starts happening, save your work, close the report (Ctrl+W) and then reopen the report in the designer. This clears out whatever odd memory conflict or whatever is happening.

Note that as you place these on the *detailBand* that you are going to run out of room – do not panic. Place them where you can for the moment.

Once you have them all placed on the *detailBand*, select them all by holding the Ctrl key and clicking on them with the mouse. If you have problems you can do this for each individual control as well, but it will take longer. Select the *fontSize* property and change it to 8. Change the *height* of the same group of controls to 0.15.

Now you will need to readjust the *width* of these controls. Once you have done that, readjust the heading controls' *top* and *left* – you may have to do this manually for each, but you want them lined up. Remember to leave a bit of room for the Category data, which is wider than the totals we want to display.

> **TRICK**
> Adjusting the width (or height) of the controls can be done either through the Inspector, or you can click on a control, hold the Shift key, and use the left/right or up/down keys to adjust them.

Next you will want to place "DataText" controls under the heading controls, setting the *fontSize* to 8 for each as you place them onto the *detailBand*. Set the *height* to the same as the heading control (0.15 if your metric is set to inches).

Make sure to set the *text* type to "Codeblock" for each of these controls, and then set the text using the following as the example:

```
this.form.householdct1.rowset.fields["category"].value
```

After placing the first DataText control onto the report for the "Category" field and setting the appropriate properties, you should have something that looks like:

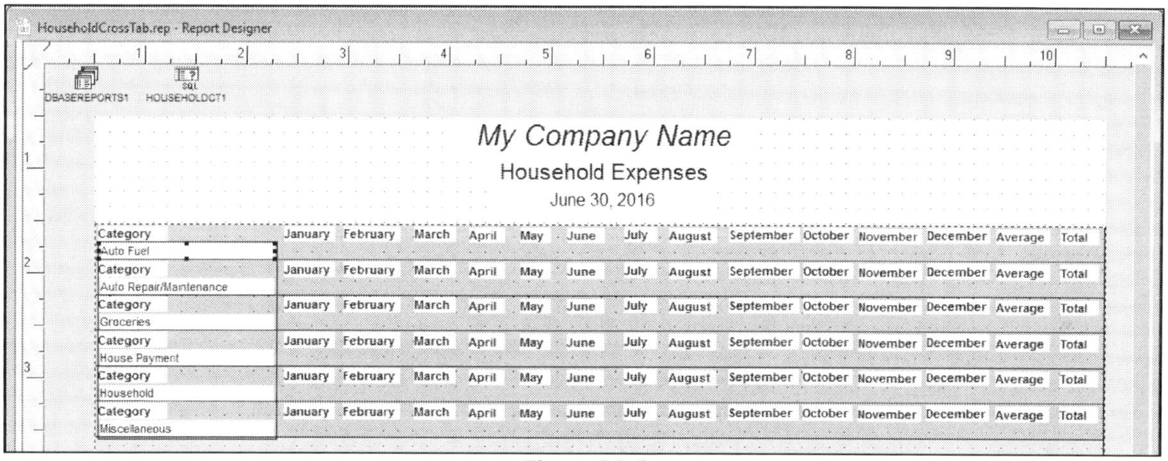

Figure 20-5

For the numeric values, do the same thing we did for the Category, but change the field in the codeblock to the first three letters of the month (Jan, Feb, etc.). Set a *picture* for the numeric value so that it is easier to read. The standard separator for values in the thousands is a comma (,) and using the *picture* property we can set something to display properly with a *picture* of "99,999.99" (without the quotes). Set the *alignHorizontal* property to "2 – Right".

You may want to, rather than setting all the different properties each time, get the DataText object for January set the way you want, and then copy it to the Windows clipboard, then paste it under the February heading. At that point you would need to change the *codeblock* so that it used the "Feb" field, instead of the "Jan" field, and deal with lining the control up on the *detailBand*, but you would not need to set the other properties. Repeat for each field across the *detailBand* that you need.

Remember that the last two fields are called "MonAvg" and "CatTotal". Spend some time lining up the controls and trying to make this look good.

> **NOTE**
> This is where "nudging" controls comes in really handy – using the arrow keys to move them left/right, etc. Suggest setting the *top* property for the DataText controls to 0.15 (if your *metric* is inches).

You should have something that looks similar to:

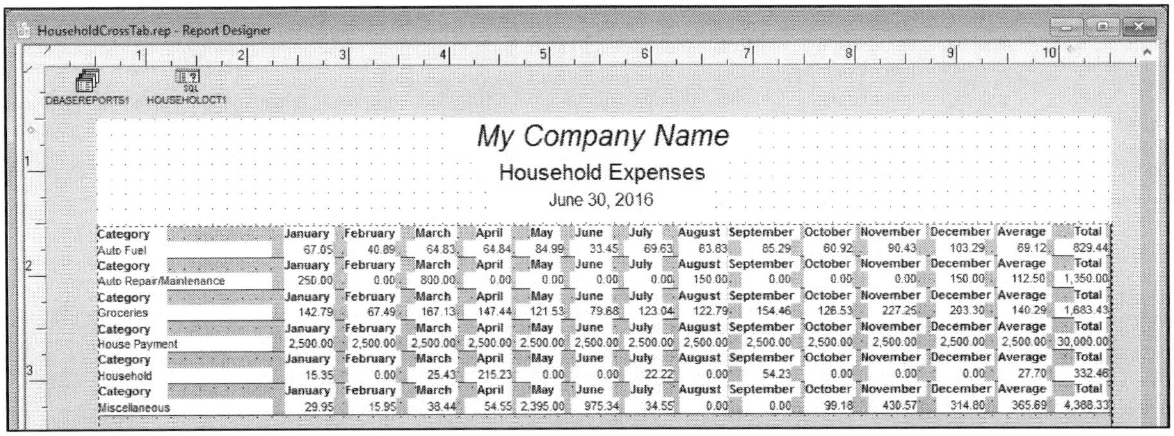

Figure 20-5

The last thing that is needed are column totals – the totals for each month's expenses, and so on. The simplest way is to place the totals on the reportGroup's *footerBand*. Go to the Inspector window, and in the combobox find the *reportGroup* object, and under that you should see the *footerBand* – select it. Change the *height* to something large enough for us to place our controls on – the default is 0.17" for a band, but you might want to temporarily make it larger – say, 0.5" if you are using a *metric* of inches (if not use something that will give some working space) – we can change the height back later if we need to.

Go to the "Standard" tab of the Component Palette and select a line object. Place it on the *reportGroup footerBand* (the purple-blue colored band), and move it toward the top of the band. Set the *left* property of the line to 0, and the *right* property to 10 (again, if using inches – if not make it the width of the *streamFrame*). Make sure the *top* and *bottom* properties are the same, but move it close to the top of the band – try a setting of 0.02, and move it a little at a time to get it just right *(in the example I set the top and bottom properties to 0.04)*. You might want to set the *width* property of the line to 2, just to make it more solid.

Place a "DataHeadingText" control (from the "Custom" tab of the Component Palette) under the line and to the left of the report, and change the *text* property to read "Totals:". Set the *alignHorizontal* property to "2 – Right". Change the *fontSize* property to 8, and the *height* property to the same as the other text controls on the *detailBand*.

Next we want to get the totals for the different columns of the report. The simplest way to do this is to go to the "Layout" menu, and select "Add Groups and Summaries ...". The dialog that comes up is showing the "Groups" tab, we want the "Summaries" tab – click on that. By default the dialog shows "<Grand Summary>" on the right, and if you click on the first column we want to total, "Jan", notice that the dialog shows "Sum" under it. Click the ">" button, to set the Sum Aggregate calculation for the "Jan" column, then repeat for all columns but the "Category" column. Make sure it is a "Grand Summary" and "Sum". The dialog should look something like:

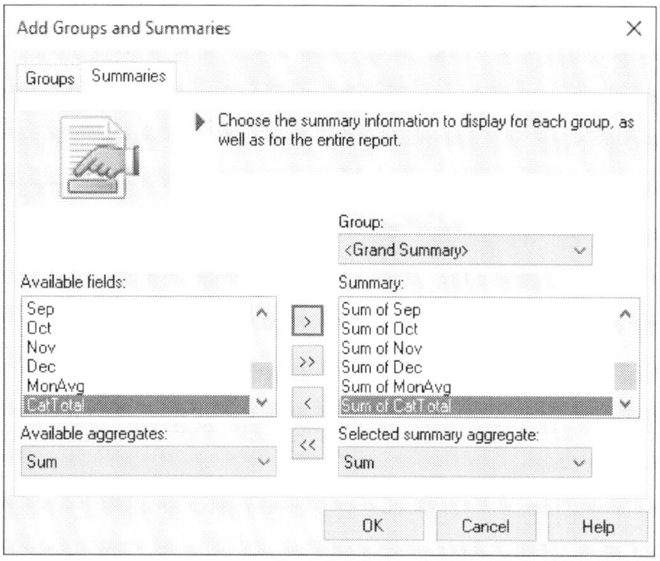

Figure 20-6

Click "OK".

This will place a bunch of controls on the *reportGroup footerBand*. The first thing we will want to do is delete the text-only controls that do not have the calculations in the *text* property, as we do not need them. Click on each control that says "Grand summary" followed by some text, and as you click on it, press the Del key to delete it.

Notice that all of the controls with the calculations in them are placed on top of each other. It's an odd quirk of the way the code that generates the summaries works – the *top* and *left* properties are not adjusted for any other controls that might be on the band. The most recently generated item is on top, which will make this a little easier.

Click on the text control on top, and then look at the *text* property in the Inspector. This should be something like (on a single line of course):

```
{||this.parent.parent.agSum({||this.parent.STREAMSOURCE1.rowset.fields[
"CatTotal"].value})}
```

This tells us which control this is, and that we need to move it to the right on the report, so that it is under the "Total" column on the right. We could change the font and other properties now, but let's get them close to where we want them first. Then we can "fine-tune" the report a bit.

Move the controls so that they are under (or close to it) the columns that they belong to. Select all of these total text controls (Ctrl+mouse click for each), and set these properties:

fontSize	8
picture	99,999.99
colorNormal	BtnText/BtnFace
height	0.15

Reminder: the *colorNormal* for these controls will show the grey background, but when the report is rendered they will appear correctly as white.

Adjust the *width* – you can do this for all the selected controls by using the Shift key and the right or left arrows (hold the shift key and use the left arrow to make the control smaller, the right arrow to make it wider). One trick to getting the controls to line up with the columns above them – as the text controls' *alignHorizontal* property is set to "2 – Right", if you click on one control, then hold the Ctrl button, and the other, then use the alignment buttons in the toolbar – specifically "Align Right", the controls should be pretty close, if not perfectly lined up.

Set the *top* properties so that they are all the same for all the text controls (including the heading control on the left) on this band.

Once you have the text controls lined up, click on the *reportGroup footerBand* itself to give it focus, and set the *height* to zero (0) in the Inspector. The report should look something like this in the designer:

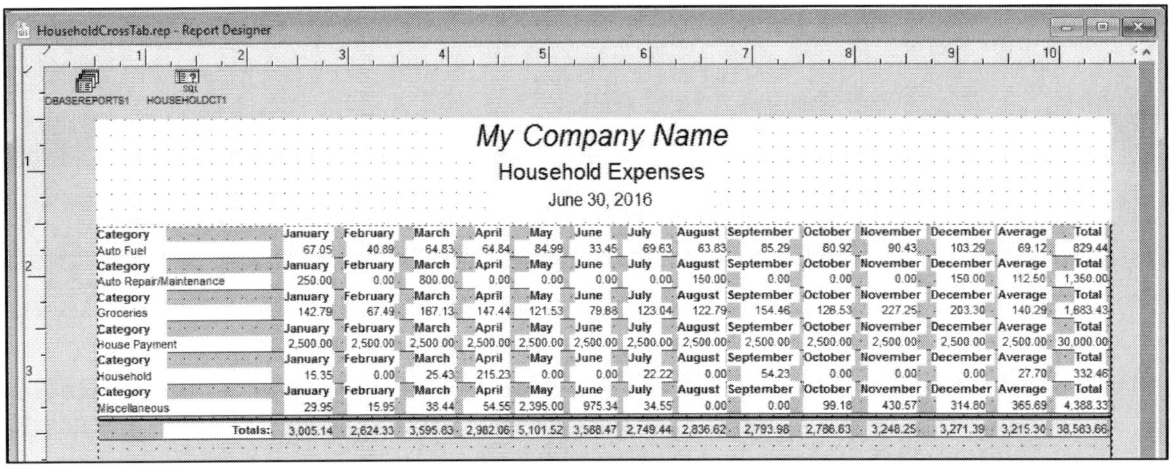

Figure 20-7

If you run the report it should look something like:

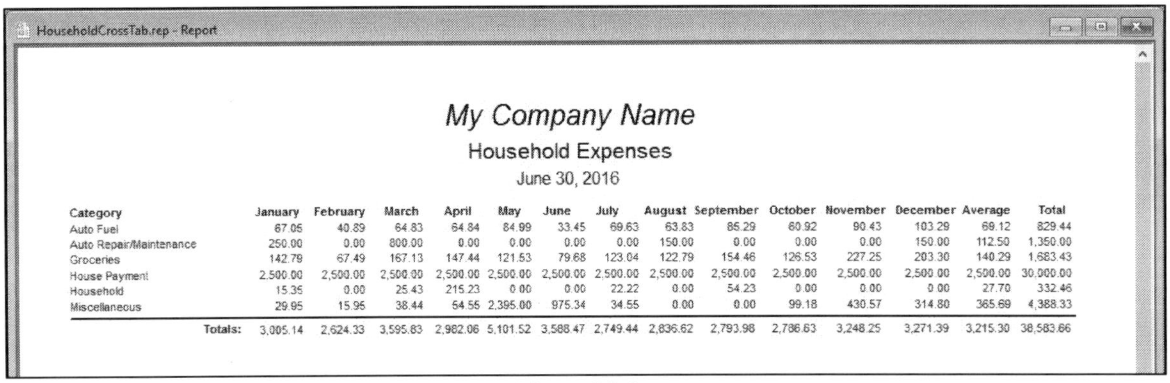

Figure 20-8

Only a little bit more – we need to finish the program. Close the Preview window.

Finishing the Program

In the Navigator window, select "Programs", click on the program named "HouseholdCrossTab.prg", and right click – select "Open in Source Editor". The program will now display – we need to go to the bottom of it, and find the section that reads:

```
// ******************************************
// code to call the report should be added here
// ******************************************
```

We want to add some code here, which will make the report available, and will display it in the dUFLP Preview window –x highlight the comments shown above in the program, and replace them with:

```
// This is the code to generate the report - once
// displayed, the user can print it or not ...:
local oRep
set procedure to HouseholdCrossTab.rep additive
oRep = new HouseholdCrossTabReport()
// display it in a modal preview screen:
do :dUFLP:Preview.wfm with oRep, true // modal
// clean up memory:
oRep.release()
```

Test the program by running it. When asked for the year, select 2015, and click "OK". View the report in the Preview form. This part of the tutorial is now complete. It wasn't easy, but hopefully this has given you an idea how to do your own Cross-Tab style report(s).

Other Methods of Creating Cross-Tab Type Reports

The example created for this chapter of this book is simply one means of creating a Cross-Tab report. There are lots of other ways that this can be done. The following are from suggestions provided by dBASE developers in the dBASE newsgroups:

- Export the data into Excel™ – and use the Pivot object to create a cross tab report. (Robert Bravery and others)
- Using local SQL you can perform union joins and such to create a rowset that will give you the data you would want for a Cross Tab report. (Eric Logan – Eric suggests looking at this website: http://www.onlamp.com/pub/a/onlamp/2003/12/04/crosstabs.html)
- Try working with one of the "generic" cross tab programs that are available. Ashton Tate had one in their Technotes magazine for dBASE IV, and there have been some programs posted in the dBASE newsgroups.

Cleanup

Create a new report (in the Navigator, click on the .Reports. tab, double-click on the "[New Report]" icon). Select the "File" menu, select "Set Custom Report Class", and in the dialog, click the "Clear Custom Report" button, then click "OK". This clears out the custom report setting in the Plus.ini file, so that the next report you create is not based on this one. Close that report without making any changes.

Make sure the database is closed by going to the Command Window and typing:

```
close databases
```

This will also ensure that you don't end up creating tables in the wrong location, etc.

Source Code

The following is a listing of the sample code in the folders we have been working with. If you downloaded the files from my website the structure will be different (see below). You may use the code contained in these folders for your own applications if you desire, with the caveat that credit be given appropriately.

From working on this chapter:

```
C:\dBASEReports\Chapter 20\CT_GetYear.wfm
C:\dBASEReports\Chapter 20\HouseholdCrosstab.rep
C:\dBASEReports\Chapter 20\HouseholdCrosstab.prg
```

Created in the dBASEReports Database Folder: HouseholdCT.dbf

Downloaded version – same files but with this path:

```
C:\ReportsBookSourceCode\Chapter 20\filename
```

Summary

This chapter deals with a complex subject by walking you through a complete process. As noted at the end of the chapter there may be other, possibly better, ways to do Cross-Tab reports – this was my first attempt at creating one based on an example I found on the web. Some database and report tools have options built into them to create Cross-Tab reports without all the work we had to do, and perhaps at some point in the future the developers at dBASE will give us this ability. For now, you at least have a framework to work from for the future.

In the next chapter the really fun stuff begins – using dBASE programming code to modify the way reports work, change the appearance of a report, and much more.

Chapter 21: Programmatic Control of Reports

This chapter is going to deal with a variety of different topics, and may get a bit lengthy. Be prepared to take a break periodically, and possibly skip over some of the material if you would rather not deal with it.

We've seen bits and pieces of how reports (and labels) in dBASE are just programs with a different structure than a form, or even a program (with a .prg extension). This chapter is going to delve into a variety of ways you can alter your reports programmatically, either from within the program, by the use of special custom controls, or from within the report itself.

None of this is super easy, which is why it is in the advanced part of this book, but by the time you are done working with the different techniques shown in this chapter you should be able to do just about anything you might want to do in a report in dBASE.

A Place for Our Work

As we work through the chapter we will be needing a place for the files we create, so please create a folder for this chapter:

```
C:\dBASEReports\Chapter 21
```

And in the Navigator, be sure to navigate to this folder.

A Sample Report

This first report we will work with is specifically designed for the first part of the chapter. This report is not going to use one of the larger tables, but will have enough data to provide several pages so that we can experiment with some options.

Create a new report. Go to the "File" menu and select "Set Custom Report Class ..." and select the "MyCompanyReport.crp" file. Save this (Ctrl+S) as "HouseholdExpenses.rep". Click on the "SecondaryTitleText" control and change the *text* property to: "Household Expenses".

Go to the Navigator window, and select the "Tables" tab. If the "DBASEREPORTS" database is not showing, select it in the "Look in" combobox. Click on the "Household" table, and drag it to the design surface. While the "HOUSEHOLD1" query has focus, select the *rowset* in the Inspector, click the Inspect button. Select the *indexName* property, and select "EntryDate".

Next we want to place some headings on the *detailBand*, using the "DataColHeadingText" control. Go to the Component Palette, and select the "Custom" tab. Select "DataColHeadingText" and place it on the *detailBand* on the left. Change the *text* property to "Entry". Place another "DataColHeadingText" control to the right of the first and change the *text* property to "Category". Repeat and change the *text* property to

"Amount". Repeat one last time (there will be four headings) and change the *text* to "Note".

Now place a "DataText" control under the first heading text. Change the *text* Type to "Codeblock", click the tool button and enter the following in the dialog:

```
this.form.household1.rowset.fields["entrydate"].value
```

Repeat for the other three fields, changing the field name from "entrydate" to "category", "amount" and "note". If the value for the "Amount" field does not appear, make the text control wider. Adjust the width and positioning of the text controls to get things to line up.

Click on the "Amount" "DataText" control, change the *alignHorizontal* property to "2 – Right", and the *picture* property to "9,999.99". You might also want to click on the "DataColHeadingText" control above this and change the *alignHorizontal* property to "2 – Right" as well, so that the heading and the data line up a bit better.

Once you have all that done, it should look something like:

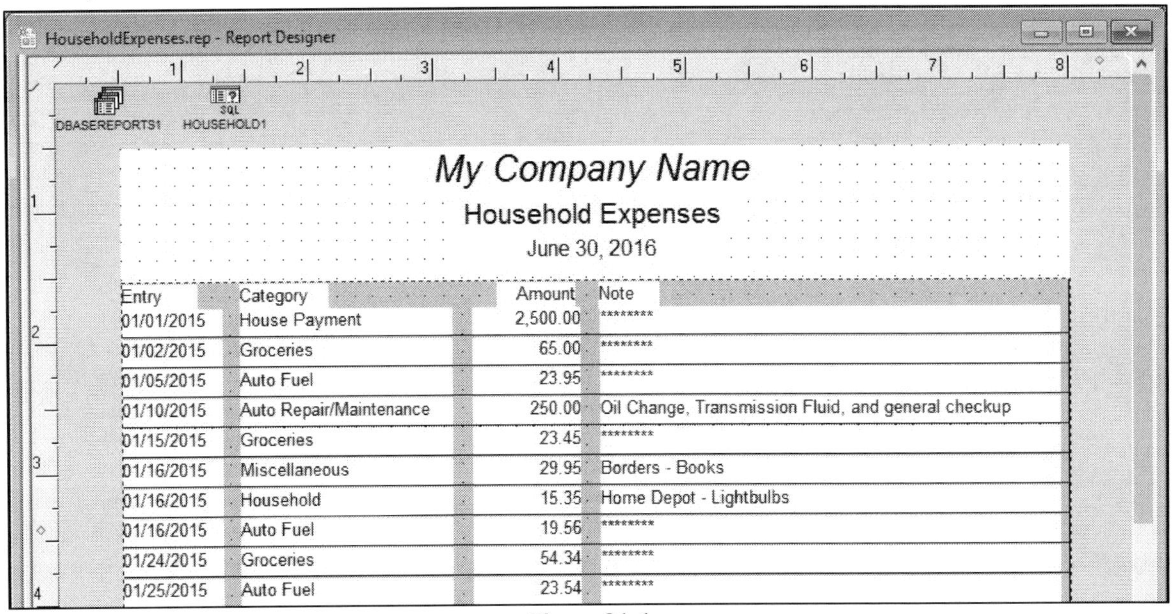

Figure 21-1

Run it to check and see how it looks, but this report will do what we need.

Changing Report and Control Properties Programmatically

We have seen in earlier chapters that we can change properties of a report, or a report's controls, within the report itself using such techniques as the *canRender* event of controls, *preRender* and *onRender* for others, and so on. We have briefly discussed overriding the report's *render* method as well, to control a report (see Chapter 10).

However, did you know that if you need to, you can change properties of both the report and the controls on the report from outside the report? Indeed, you can change the table being used for a report by modifying the query object's (or data module ...) *sql* property, you can change the *text* properties (and other properties) of controls, all from outside of a report.

A simple version of this, which should get you started thinking about the concept, would be to change the "SecondaryTitleText" control's *text* property before rendering a report. In the Command Window, type the following, and we will see how easy it is to change properties of a control on a report before the report is rendered:

```
set procedure to HouseholdExpenses.rep
oRep = new HouseholdExpensesReport()
oRep.pageTemplate1.SecondaryTitleText1.text := "Modified Outside The Report"
oRep.pageTemplate1.SecondaryTitleText1.colorNormal := "blue/white"
oRep.render()
```

This should display the report with the SecondaryTitleText control having different text than what is in the report's constructor code, and the color of the text object is now blue (with a white background, but that is normal). (Close the report preview.)

We could have changed the *width* of the text control as well, so that all the text displayed, or the *fontSize* and made it a bit smaller, or ...

Using your imagination, you can do a *lot* with this capability. If you have a report that is designed properly, you could use it for multiple types of reports, such as setting filters on the data before rendering the report, and based on the filters, setting the properties of text controls to show what the filters are. If you set a range of dates for a report, for example, you could show that in a text control on the *pageTemplate*, and before rendering the report both set the filter *and* change the text control to reflect the begin and end dates used for the filter.

An example of this would be to do the following – in a real application you might request the dates in a fashion similar to what was done in earlier chapters, but for now let's just do this in the Command Window.

```
set procedure to HouseholdExpenses.rep
oRep = new HouseholdExpensesReport()
oRep.Household1.rowset.setRange( {01/01/2015}, {01/31/2015} )
oRep.pageTemplate1.SecondaryTitleText1.text := "Data for January, 2015"
oRep.render()
```

Notice that when the report renders the data is limited to January, 2015, and the SecondaryTitleText control displays the text we assigned.

You can of course get more complex, and if you wanted to, actually change, say, the orientation of the report, and the *pageTemplate* object's margins, the streamFrame's size properties, and more and turn a report from portrait to landscape.

What this boils down to is that by being able to control the report from outside the report's code, meaning that you do not have to hard code everything into the report, your reports can do just about anything!

(If you have not, close the report preview window.)

Page Numbering

This part of the chapter has two sections – they are similar in that they both deal with modifying the display of the page number on a report. They both have very different results.

In most of the reports we've worked with in this book we have used a custom class that ships with dBASE called "PageNumber". This control is in the source code alias "ReportControls" and the custom class file "Report.cc". To view this, go to the Command Window, and type:

```
modify command :ReportControls:Report.cc
```

If you examine the control, what it is doing is simply returning the value of the report object's *reportPage* property. This is important for both of the two following sections of this chapter. Close this file without changing anything, and let's look at the options.

Custom Page Numbers

There are situations where you may wish a report to start the page number at a different number than 1, even though the first page printed is actually the first page of the report. Or, you might wish your report to show other than just a numeric value, something like "Page 1". I am sure you can come up with other scenarios.

Most of this is pretty easy. You can do this in a custom class of your own, or you can put a text control onto a report and set the code there.

Let's do both of these options as Custom Classes in dBASE, because this means they can be reused whenever needed for any report. We will start with the simplest page numbering class, and then look at the more complex one.

To create a new text class, we need to place it in a custom control file (.cc). To keep things simple, let's put these in an existing .cc file. Go to the Command Window and type:

```
modify command :MyReportControls:MyReportControls.cc
```

This will open the custom class file we have been working with in the Source Code Editor, and we can add new controls to the end of this file.

Scroll down to the bottom, past the last *endclass* statement. We're going to add the first page numbering control – type the following:

```
class PageNum( parentObj ) of DataText( parentObj ) custom
   // Class that outputs "Page n" where "n" is the current
   // page number - the value of the report's reportPage
   // property:
   with( this )
      fontSize = 8
      text = class::PageValue
   endwith

   function PageValue
      local cPage
```

```
         cPage = "Page "
         if type( "this.form.reportPage" ) == "N"
            // add page number to end of text
            cPage += this.form.reportPage
         else
            // if this is not used on a report,
            // return word "ERROR"
            cPage := "ERROR"
         endif
      return( cPage )
   endclass
```

This looks like a lot of typing for a relatively simple control. However, this is designed to handle a potential problem – using a control designed for a report on a form. It is always a possibility. Let's examine this briefly.

Note that this control is subclassed from the "DataText" control. This allows us to define the *fontName* (and other properties) for our all of our controls in one place. If you wanted this to have a different *fontName* or completely unique from the definition of the "DataText" control, then we could just define this as a subclass of the default "text" object in dBASE, or even just add the *fontName* property in the code for this class.

The actual work is done in the method "PageValue" – which is executed when dBASE tries to render the *text* of the control. We are creating a variable with the word "Page" followed by a space, and then concatenating the report's *reportPage* value to the end of the string. If the control is placed on a form, we are replacing the text with the word "ERROR".

To see this in action, bring the HouseholdExpenses report we created at the beginning of this chapter into the Report Designer. Because our new custom class is in the file that has all of our other classes, it is automatically loaded and should appear in the Component Palette (it will look like the other text controls). Find "PageNum" and drag it to the top right on the *pageTemplate* of the report. You should see something like:

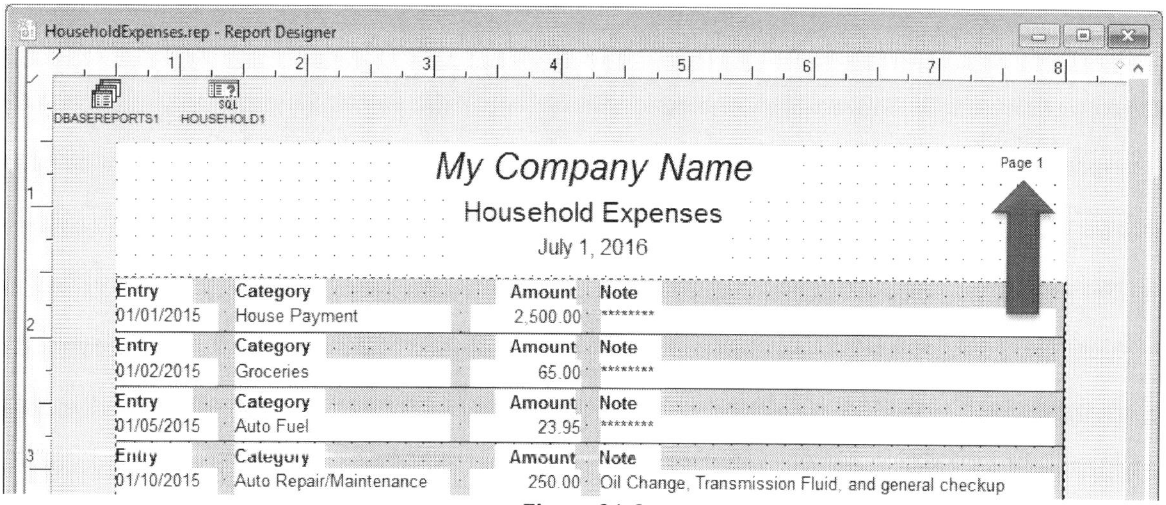

Figure 21-2

When you run the report and go to Page 2, you should see something like:

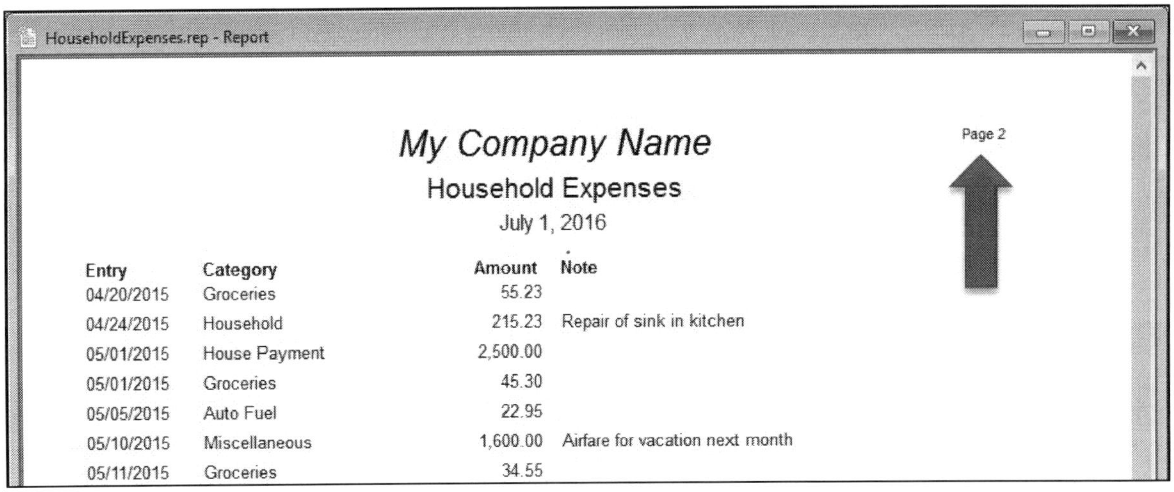

Figure 21-3

And so on. This is a fairly simple control, but by doing this, you can hopefully get a feel for some of the possibilities.

Page Number Offsets

The next control deals with a variation on a theme. This control displays the page number using the report's *reportPage* property, but what if you need your report to begin the page numbers at a number that is not 1 *(possibly because you want to have a cover page on the report; possibly this is one of several reports that are being combined for a project ...)*? This is not the same as starting printing on page 2, which can be done in other ways *(see later in this chapter)*, but most specifically if you want the first page to be numbered 3, and the second page to be numbered 4, and so on throughout the report, basically offsetting the page number by some value (in this example, an offset of 2 – adding 2 to each page number).

We will create another custom class to do what is needed. This class will have a custom property called *pageOffset*, which will be used to determine the number of pages to offset the report's *reportPage* property by. Go to the Command Window and type:

```
modify command :MyReportControls:MyReportControls.cc
```

Go to the end of the file and enter this code:

```
class PageNumOffset( parentObj ) of DataText( parentObj ) custom
   // Page Number Offset class, this offsets the report's
   // reportPage property by some number, so that the first
   // page of the report will be form.reportPage+offsetvalue
   // When using this class, place it on a report, and then
   // in the text control's onOpen event, enter:
   // {; this.pageOffset := 2 }
   // where "2" is the amount you wish to add to the
   // reportPage value to offset the page number.
   with( this )
      fontSize = 8
      text = class::PageValue
   endwith
   this.pageOffset = 0 // default to zero

   function PageValue
```

```
      local nPage
      nPage = 0
      if type( "this.form.reportPage" ) == "N"
         // add page number to end of text
         nPage := this.form.reportPage + this.pageOffset
      else
         // if this is not used on a report,
         // return zero
         nPage := 0
      endif
   return( nPage )
endclass
```

Check your typing and make sure everything is correct. Note that we have some instructions in the comments at the beginning of the class constructor – this is so that we can remember how to use this without having to come back to this chapter of the book later.

Save the file and exit the Source Code Editor (Ctrl+W). Open the HouseholdExpenses report in the Report Designer. For the moment leave the previous PageNum text control where it is. Go to the Component Palette and find the "PageNumOffset" component (on the "Custom" page) and place this under the "PageNum" control. At this point, this control should look like the regular "PageNumber" control that ships with dBASE. However, if we follow the instructions we typed above, we will see that it is indeed different.

Click on the "Events" tab of the Inspector window, and select the *onOpen* event. Enter in the Inspector the following codeblock:

```
{; this.pageOffset := 2}
```

This assigns the value 2 to the text control's custom property *pageOffset*. Save the report and run it (use the "Lightning" button in the toolbar to run the report from the Designer). You should see something like:

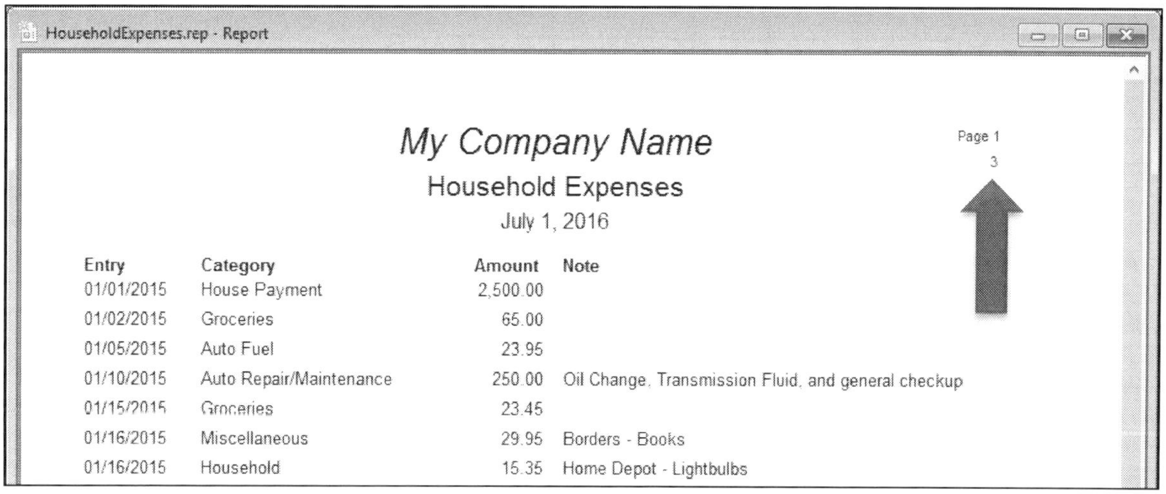

Figure 21-4

Notice that the "PageNum" control shows the *reportPage*, and the "PageNumOffset" control shows the same value plus 2 – which is precisely as it should be. If you go to the second page of the report, you should see "4" and so on.

Close the report preview window, and let's move on.

Page x of y

The last item to look at when discussing page numbers is one that periodically comes up – that is, a report that displays text along the lines of:

Page 1 of 25

The difficulty lies in knowing how many pages there are in your report.

If the height of your *detailBand* never changes, and you are not using group header or footer bands for your reports, you can work out through some calculations the number of pages that are in the report. This would require knowing how tall the *detailBand* is and how tall the *streamFrame* is, as well as the number of records that are being rendered in the report. The calculation would be something along the lines of:

```
(nRecords * detailBandHeight ) / streamFrameHeight
```

This should give you the correct number of pages. You could add in headerBands and footerBands, which would of course complicate the calculation. However, any calculation can be wrong, as there can be complexities in the report including a variable height *detailBand*, header and footer bands, and more.

The custom class we are going to examine and experiment with handles this fairly well, but it is complex and can be slow for large reports.

> **NOTE**
> The original Page X of Y control was created by me, but Mervyn Bick recently went and looked at it, and figured out how to make it run faster for larger reports. That said, since the report must be rendered *(even if it is not seen)* to get the last page number, it may still take a bit to get that value.

Why? The original version of this control rendered the report to a temporary file (rather than to the printer), so that it could determine the last page number. The current version renders the report to a hidden *reportViewer* window which is faster. It then returns the last page number and uses that in the text control for the normal rendering of the report.

The control is contained in the dUFLP, and is called "PageXofY.cc". You can view the source code by going to the Command Window and typing:

```
modify command :dUFLP:PageXofY.cc
```

There is a lot of explanation in the code. In order to use this class, close the Source Code Editor (without changing anything), and in the Command Window type:

```
set procedure to :dUFLP:PageXofY.cc
```

Next open the HouseholdExpenses report in the designer. One *very* important aspect of this class is that it was designed with a *metric* of "0 – Chars". Go to the Inspector and set the *metric* property to "0 – Chars" (if you haven't already). Then go to the

Component Palette, and notice a new tab – "dUFLP Report Controls". Select this, and you will see a single control – "Pagexofy". Drag an instance of this over to under the other two page number controls we added earlier.

> **NOTE**
> If the control's width is very small, widen it. You *should* see "Page 1 of 9999". Sometimes it will not display the "9999" part of the control -widen the text object if needed.

Now the control is on the report, set the report's *metric* back to what you were using previously (example, "3 – Inches").

You should see something like:

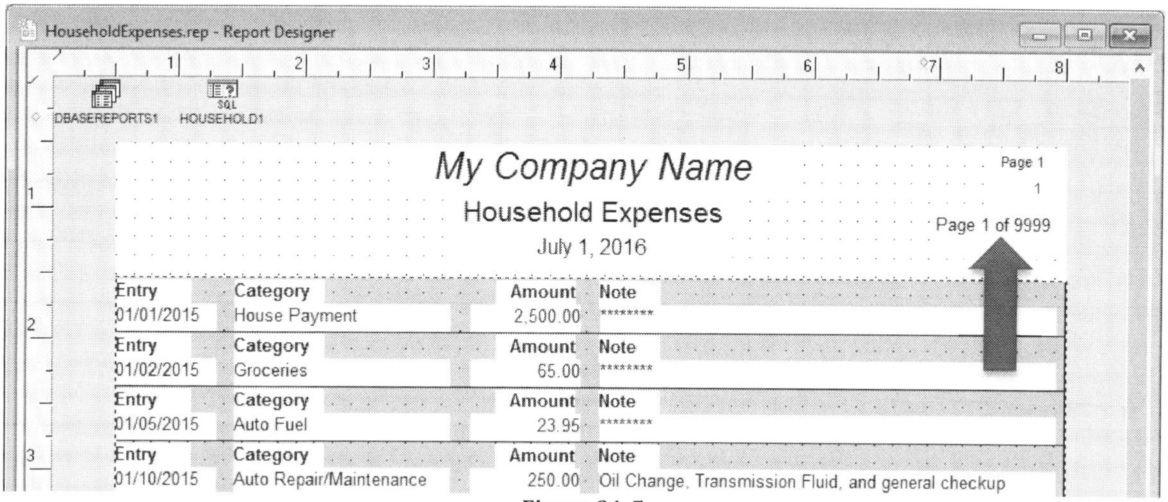

Figure 21-5

When the report is rendered this will change. Try running the report. You will see a "Counting Pages" dialog, even if for only a moment.

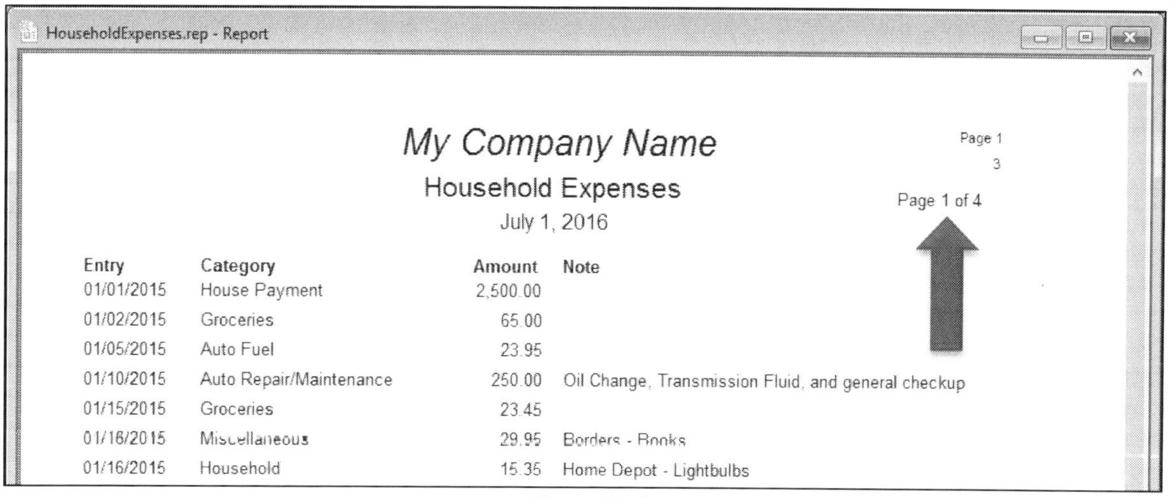

Figure 21-6

It will most likely say something like "Page 1 of 4". As you scroll through the report it will of course update and show "Page 2 of 4" and so on.

> **NOTE**
> There is a problem with the control if you use the "Previous Page" button in the toolbar or the PgUp key – somehow it loses track of the report class. This can be fixed by opening the report file (HouseholdExpenses.rep) in the Source Code Editor, and adding to the source code in the constructor code (after the "CLASS" statement) this command:
>
> ```
> set procedure to program(1)
> ```
>
> This ensures that the report's object references are available when re-rendering the report as needed when paging backward.

Why all this work to render the report, save the page number of the last page, and so on? Why doesn't dBASE know the last page of the report? The reason is that dBASE reports are "live" reports – if your application is a single-user application this may not make much sense, but in a networked application where there may be lots of users, the data could be being updated at the time someone is about to generate a report, and there could be more data in the table(s) (or less if someone is deleting records) used by the report then when the report was first instantiated. This means that it is very hard for us to know what the exact last page of the report will be.

(For what it is worth, there is a wishlist request in the queue for the developers at dBASE to allow the developer to state that they do not wish the report to assume "live" data – this would speed up paging back and forth in a report.)

Close the report preview window.

Different Layouts for the detailBand

The *detailBand* of a report, as seen in various places earlier in this book, can have a different height depending on the controls displayed, and more. Todd Kreuter took this one step further in a report that is part of an article in dBulletin issue 13 (http://www.jpmartel.com/bu13_f.htm – "DBF Definition Utility").

This report has three potential layouts for the *detailBand*, which seems pretty amazing. The way that Todd does this is by using the group headerBand's *preRender* event, and changes the text controls displayed, the text itself, the size of the text controls and more in a case statement. This is not that hard to do, but it does take a lot of patience. Todd explains it to some extent in the article, and of course if you examine the code that is in the article, you will see what he's doing. The following is just a part of the code (included here with his permission):

```
function HeaderBand_preRender()
   ***************************
   *- Purpose: Change text and position of controls
   // depending on header type (field or index)
   local nOffset
   do case
      case this.parent.parent.rowset.fields["GKey"].value = "A"
         with (this.parent.headerBand)
            title1.text = ""
            label1.text = "Type/Version"
            label2.text = "Language"
```

```
            label3.text = "Primary Key"
            label4.text = "Converted"
            label5.text = ""
            label2.left = 105
            label3.left = 210
            label4.left = 315
            label5.left = 360
            label2.width = 80
            line1.right = 355
         endwith
         with (this.parent.parent.detailBand)
            text2.left = 105
            text3.left = 210
            text4.left = 315
            text5.left = 360
            text1.width = 100
            text2.width = 100
            text3.width = 100
         endwith
      case this.parent.parent.rowset.fields["GKey"].value = "B"
         nOffset = this.parent.parent.parent.params["WidthB"]

   *** and the code continues from here ***
```

This continues for two more options ("B" and "C"). As you can see, this is fairly complex, and as noted takes a bit of working out, but once done you can have a pretty slick report with what *appears* to be three different detailBands, but is really only one, but more flexible than normal.

Creating Controls "On the Fly"

There may be times in a report where you need to create text controls on an "as needed" basis. I worked on a project for a client who needed a report that had totals at the end for different categories of data. However, when the report was printed, he had an option to select all categories, or a range of categories which were numbered 1 through "n" (where "n" is the last one in the table). The report could conceivably show all categories, another run of the report where he showed categories 2 through 5, and so on. The big difficulty is that the "n" value could change over time as he added more categories (or perhaps deleted some, finding he no longer needed them). It also seemed a bit odd to have hard-coded totals that showed a value of 0 for categories that were not displayed on the report.

When the report is generated, a lot of processing is done in a program, and part of that is accumulating the totals needed. An array of data is passed as a parameter to the report (see some of what we did in Chapter 10 with overriding the report's *render* method).

The following code is extracted from the report for this client – it is in the overridden *render* method of the report. It creates text controls "as needed" in the reportGroup's *footerBand*. The reason I am showing you this is to give you some idea of what can be done. We will not create our own report for this, because it's a complex thing to do, but you should at least be aware of the possibilities:

```
// totals in reportGroup footerBand:
*******************************************
*** The fun part is that for this to work
*** we will have to create each text control
*** individually, and set it where it needs
*** to go based on the previous control ...
*******************************************
oFB = form.ReportGroup.FooterBand
nTop = 0.10
for i = 1 to form.TypeTotals.size/5
   cText = "oFB.TotalHeading"+i
   &cText. = new text( oFB )
   with( &cText. )
      top = nTop
      left = 0.79
      height = 0.17
      width = 3.25
      text = "** Type "+form.TypeTotals[i,1]+" Totals ("+;
             form.TypeTotals[i,2]+")"
   endwith
   // other totals
   cText = "oFB.TotalCount"+i
   &cText. = new text( oFB )
   with( &cText. )
      top = nTop
      left = 4.79
      height = 0.17
      width = 0.46
      text = form.TypeTotals[i,3]
      picture = .999,999.
      alignHorizontal = 2 // right
   endwith
   cText = "oFB.TotalRevenue"+i
   &cText. = new text( oFB )
   with( &cText. )
      top = nTop
      left = 5.33
      height = 0.17
      width = 1.01
      text = form.TypeTotals[i,4]
      picture = "999,999,999.99"
      alignHorizontal = 2 // right
   endwith
   cText = "oFB.PercentRevenue"+i
   &cText. = new text( oFB )
   with( &cText. )
      top = nTop
      left = 6.55
      height = 0.17
      width = 0.59
      // this is one statement and shouldn't wrap:
      text = ( form.TypeTotals[i,4] /
      form.streamSource1.rowset.fields["TINV"].value ) * 100
      picture = "999.999"
      alignHorizontal = 2 // right
   endwith
   cText = "oFB.TotalCost"+i
```

```
      &cText. = new text( oFB )
      with( &cText. )
         top = nTop
         left = 7.41
         height = 0.17
         width = 1.01
         text = form.TypeTotals[i,5]
         picture = "999,999,999.99"
         alignHorizontal = 2 // right
      endwith
      cText = "oFB.PercentCost"+i
      &cText. = new text( oFB )
      with( &cText. )
         top = nTop
         left = 8.77
         height = 0.17
         width = 0.59
         // this is one statement and shouldn't wrap:
         text = ( form.TypeTotals[i,5] /
         form.streamSource1.rowset.fields["TINV"].value ) * 100
         picture = "999.999"
         alignHorizontal = 2 // right
      endwith
      // some code snipped out to shorten this topic a little
      // increment the top:
      nTop += 0.17 // for new row
   next
   // and deal with the final totals:
   nTop += 0.14
   oFB.text1.top := nTop
   oFB.text3.top := nTop
   oFB.InvTotal.top := nTop
   oFB.InvCost.top := nTop
   oFB.InvProfit.top := nTop
```

If you examine this you can see that it is creating text controls using the "nTop" variable to set the *top* property, so that each set of totals and related information are on the same line, calculations are performed for the text using values passed as part of the array (form.TypeTotals – an array with two dimensions of data – rows and columns), and more. This took a bit of work to get "just right", as you might imagine. Note that outside of the loop, we increment the "nTop" variable a bit more, and display the "final totals" or perhaps "grand totals" would be a better term, which are created in this particular report by using the standard dBASE Aggregate Summary functions.

Using this concept as an example, you could, theoretically, add whatever controls you needed to a report on an "as needed" basis. The flexibility is truly astounding.

Getting Data from another Table

Every once in a while a developer ends up needing to do something really unusual. This may be for a personal project, or it may be for a client. Sometimes the needs of the report are not what one might call "standard". The previous two topics are good examples of this. This section of the chapter is another of those really odd things that I ended up needing to do some time back.

First, a brief explanation: Those who know me in the dBASE community know I have some unusual hobbies – I participate in a medieval re-creation organization (the SCA) – some of the testing I have done with dBASE over the years is using code for applications for this group, and I have in the past been a roleplaying gamer (RPG gaming – D&D, and the various other types of games out there). The application I wish to reference is one I worked on for my gaming for some years. In order to create a "character sheet", I found that with my data normalized and in many different tables, that for the report to work properly I needed to pull the data carefully. My *detailBand* in this report covers the whole *streamFrame*, so it's not set to be flexible in size like you might normally do for most reports. Instead I have places where I needed to display only a maximum of 5 rows of data from a child table, and if there is more data, well, it doesn't get printed on this page (subsequent reports can be generated as needed). *(For those curious, I used shapes heavily for this report to get most of the rectangles…)*

In order to do what I needed, I set up code in a text control's *canRender* event, and in that event handler's code I look at the child table, and fill the text controls that need to be filled. The section in question on the part of the report displayed below is under "Weapons". Note that there are five rows there, but only four have any data. If the character had more than five weapons, only the first five would display here.

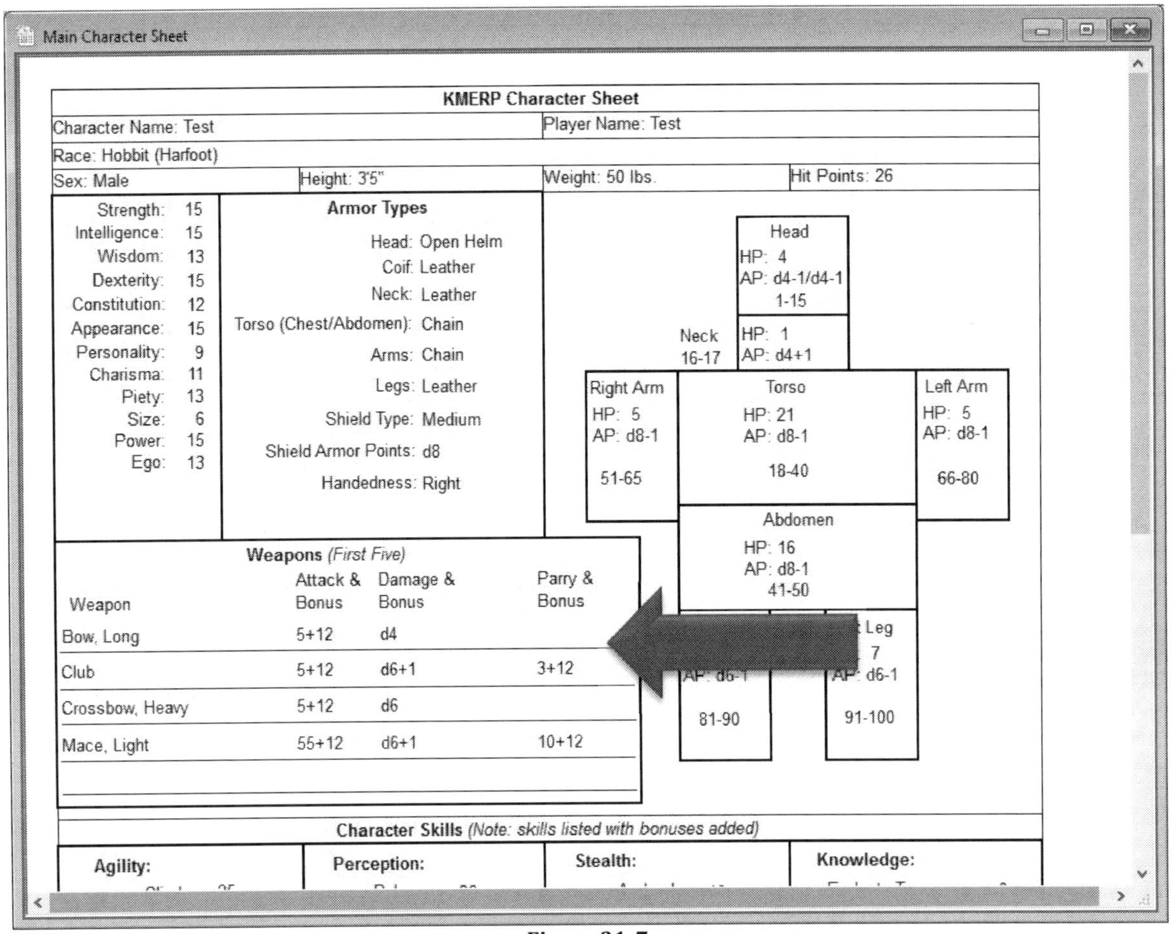

Figure 21-7

While this code could be more concise, it does what is needed. The code is all in the first text control's *canRender* event (the one that on the report shown says "Bow, Long"). The following is an excerpt of that code:

```
function WEAPON1_canRender()
   // This event will set the weapons for page 1 for display
   // purposes
   qWeap = new query()
   qWeap.database := form.KMERP1
   qWeap.sql :=  "select * from CharWeapons"
   qWeap.active := true
   rWeap = qWeap.rowset
   fWeap = rWeap.fields
   f = this.parent.parent.parent.streamSource1.rowset.fields

   nLink = f["LinkField"].value
   rWeap.filter = ":Character Link: = "+nLink
   rWeap.first()
   // Set default text as blank:
   this.text                       = ""
   this.parent.Weapon1Attack.text = ""
   this.parent.Weapon1Damage.text = ""
   this.parent.Weapon1Parry.text  = ""
   this.parent.Weapon2.text        = ""
   this.parent.Weapon2Attack.text = ""
   this.parent.Weapon2Damage.text = ""
   this.parent.Weapon2Parry.text  = ""
   this.parent.Weapon3.text        = ""
   this.parent.Weapon3Attack.text = ""
   this.parent.Weapon3Damage.text = ""
   this.parent.Weapon3Parry.text  = ""
   this.parent.Weapon4.text        = ""
   this.parent.Weapon4Attack.text = ""
   this.parent.Weapon4Damage.text = ""
   this.parent.Weapon4Parry.text  = ""
   this.parent.Weapon5.text        = ""
   this.parent.Weapon5Attack.text = ""
   this.parent.Weapon5Damage.text = ""
   this.parent.Weapon5Parry.text  = ""

   // loop through the character weapon table:
   if rWeap.count() > 0
      this.text = fWeap["Weapon Name"].value.rightTrim()
      this.parent.Weapon1Attack.text = ;
            iif( fWeap["Attack"].value > 0, fWeap["Attack"].value, "" )
      if not empty( f["Attack Bonus"].value ) and;
         not empty( this.parent.Weapon1Attack.text )
         this.parent.Weapon1Attack.text += "+"+f["Attack Bonus"].value
      endif
      this.parent.Weapon1Damage.text = fWeap["Damage"].value.rightTrim()
      if not empty( f["Damage Bonus"].value ) and ;
         not empty( this.parent.Weapon1Damage.text )
         this.parent.Weapon1Damage.text += " ("+f["Damage Bonus"].value.rightTrim()+")"
      endif
      this.parent.Weapon1Parry.text = ;
            iif( fWeap["Parry"].value > 0, fWeap["Parry"].value, "" )
      if not empty( f["Parry Bonus"].value ) AND ;
         not empty( this.parent.Weapon1Parry.text )
         this.parent.Weapon1Parry.text += "+"+f["Parry Bonus"].value
      endif
```

```
      // Try second one
      if rWeap.next() and not rWeap.endOfSet
         this.parent.Weapon2.text = fWeap["Weapon Name"].value.rightTrim()
         this.parent.Weapon2Attack.text = ;
            iif( fWeap["Attack"].value > 0, fWeap["Attack"].value, "" )
         if not empty( f["Attack Bonus"].value ) and;
            not empty( this.parent.Weapon2Attack.text )
            this.parent.Weapon2Attack.text += "+"+f["Attack Bonus"].value
         endif
         this.parent.Weapon2Damage.text = fWeap["Damage"].value.rightTrim()
         if not empty( f["Damage Bonus"].value ) and ;
            not empty( this.parent.Weapon2Damage.text )
            this.parent.Weapon2Damage.text += " ("+f["Damage Bonus"].value.rightTrim()+")"
         endif
         this.parent.Weapon2Parry.text = ;
         iif( fWeap["Parry"].value > 0, fWeap["Parry"].value, "" )
         if not empty( f["Parry Bonus"].value ) AND ;
            not empty( this.parent.Weapon2Parry.text )
            this.parent.Weapon2Parry.text += "+"+f["Parry Bonus"].value
         endif
      endif // 2

   // code repeats for the other three weapons ... at this point
   // if I were still working on this code, I would probably put it
   // into a loop and make the code a bit more succinct.

   qWeap.active := false
   release object qWeap

return true
```

This is yet another example of the fact that dBASE reports are literally just dBASE code, and as such, you can do pretty much anything you want or need to in your reports to get the data *just right.*

Sending a Report to the Printer

It may seem odd, but to this point in the book, we have not spent a lot of effort sending your report to the printer. This is largely because we didn't want to waste a lot of paper printing reports, among other things.

So, how *do* you send your report to the printer?

If the report is in a preview window – the default when you "run" a report in dBASE, you will see in the toolbar a button with a printer on it, and if you hold the mouse over this button, the text will read "Print ..." (the ellipsis or "..." means a dialog is associated with this). Clicking the button will bring up a printer dialog, and you can choose the printer you want, and set other options. This is all pretty standard.

If you use the dUFLP's Preview.wfm, there is a printer button at the bottom of the form that can be used to send the report to the printer, and again you can choose from whatever printer you wish.

However, we haven't really looked at anything else involved in printing a report.

As noted, the default output destination when you run a report in dBASE is to a report preview window. How do you control this? To understand this better, bring the HouseholdExpenses report we created at the beginning of this chapter into the Report Designer.

Go to the Inspector window, with the report having focus (the Inspector will show the word "form" in the combobox – in this case, "form" is the report object). On the "Properties" page of the Inspector you will see a three properties that are of interest to this discussion – *output*, *outputFilename* and *printer*. The last is actually an object, and we will come back to it in a moment.

Click on the *output* property, and notice that you have several options here. These are:

0 - Window
1 - Printer
2 - PrinterFile
3 - Default
4 - HTMLFile
5 - CGI response

Option 0 and 3 are the same – the default is to a Window, or specifically the dBASE preview window. Option 1 is to a printer, which is of interest to this discussion. Option 2 is to a "Printer File" – this is a file that has all kinds of binary stuff in it which can be sent to the printer. I have found that since each printer is different, that unless you know that your client(s) have the exact same printer(s) this is really pretty pointless. Option 4 will be discussed in a later chapter of this book (briefly), and Option 5 is really for full web-based applications, a topic too vast to even try to discuss in this book.

Of course, the *output* property, being a property of the report can be set by you. You can, for example, set the property in the report itself to "1" and the next time you run the report, it will go to the printer. The problem is, how do you know *which* printer it will go to? If you have multiple printer drivers (or multiple printers) installed, dBASE will assume (unless told otherwise) to send the report to the **Windows default printer**.

How do you know what printer that is? One way is to look at the way Windows defines your printers. The dialog shown below is from my installation of Windows 10, found by going to the "Start" menu, and selecting the "Settings" option, followed by "Devices". The list of printers will vary from computer to computer, and of course different operating systems may display this information differently.

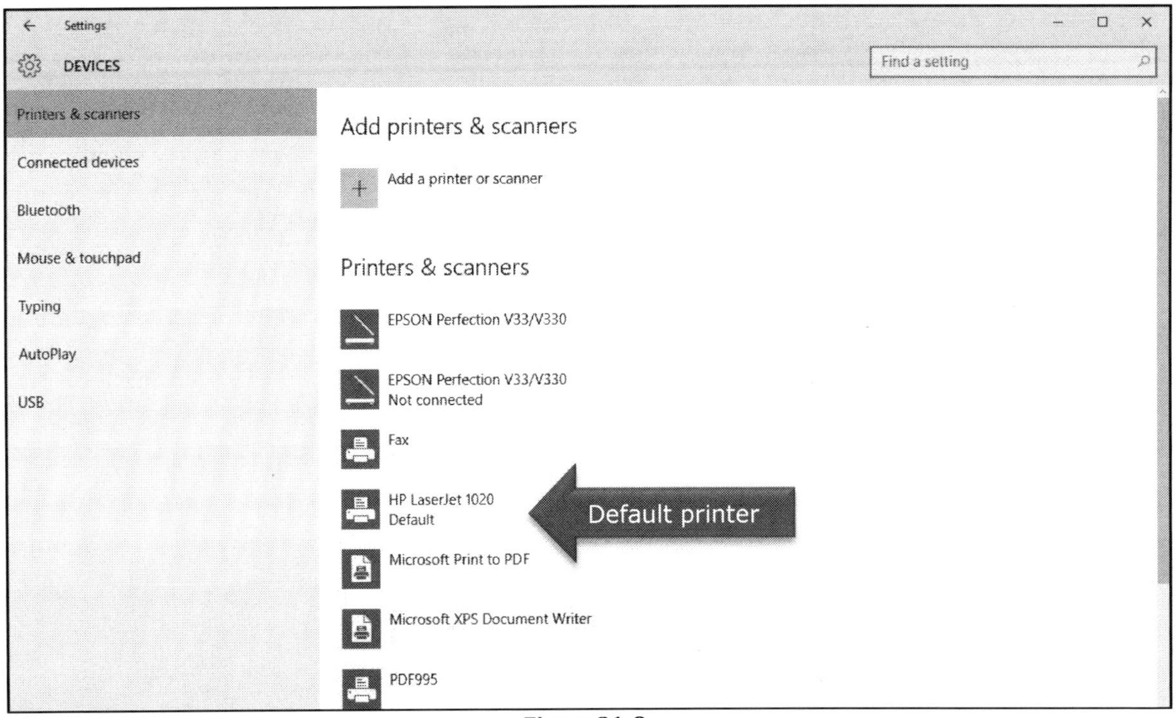

Figure 21-8

The printer that says "Default" is, oddly enough, the default printer in Windows. You can change the default printer in Windows by clicking the printer and clicking the button "Set as Default".

If you know what printer the user wishes to always use for a report, and have installed a printer driver on your pc for that printer – you don't need to physically have that printer, you can actually embed this information into a report. How? If you select the *printer* object in the Inspector, and click the Inspect button, you will see properties of *printerName* and *printerSource*. By selecting the *printerSource* property, and selecting "2 – Specific", then selecting the *printerName* property and clicking the tool button, then selecting a printer from the dialog that appears, you are writing into the source code for the report the printer that will be used for the report.

The problem is, this will be written to the source code for your report (with the printer object that is streamed out by the designer), and it will be in the compiled object used by the dBASE Runtime for a deployed application. If your client or user either gets rid of that printer, or it's no longer available on that computer, or anything of that sort, the report will not print. An error message will be displayed every time they attempt to print the report.

This is not a good solution. Instead there are better ways to handle this. The best solution is to have the user select the printer, using the *choosePrinter()* dialog. However, while there is a *choosePrinter()* function in dBASE, that is not the one that affects reports that use the dBASE Report Engine. The *choosePrinter()* function is really used for other output generated through dBASE's streaming (?, ??, etc.) commands, and such.

Application Default Printer

There are two calls to the printer that can be used for reports. The dBASE application object (_app) has a *printer* object associated with it. As part of that object there is a method called *choosePrinter*. Selecting this will set the _app.printer.printerName property, which can be used by default for all reports in dBASE. So you could have your user select the default printer for the application this way.

In your application you could have a "preferences" option that allows the user to select a default printer, and then issue:

```
_app.printer.choosePrinter()
```

The default for this is to use the "Printer Setup" dialog for Windows, and as noted, the name of the printer is then stored in the application object's *printer* object's *printerName* property. You can query this by typing:

```
? _app.printer.printerName
```

If you get back an empty string, it means nothing was selected. For an application you might want to save the value in that string when the application closes (perhaps in a .INI file for the application, or in the Windows Registry), and then when the application starts, retrieve the information and store it back to _app.printer.printerName.

Selecting the Printer for the Report

That said, you might simply want to call the report's *printer* object's *choosePrinter* method instead. For example, if you were to do the following in the Command Window:

```
set procedure to HouseholdExpenses.rep
oRep = new HouseholdExpensesReport()
oRep.output := 1 // Printer
oRep.printer.choosePrinter()
oRep.render()
```

As soon as you clicked the "OK" button, dBASE would attempt to print to either the printer selected, or the Windows default printer if no printer was selected.

choosePrinter Parameters

The *choosePrinter* method (of both the _app.printer object and the report.printer object) has two parameters. The first is a title that can be displayed in the titlebar of the dialog. If you do not wish to change the title, leave this out.

However, the second parameter can specify which of two printer dialogs to display. More confusing is that there are two defaults.

```
_app.printer.choosePrinter() // will display the Print Setup dialog
```

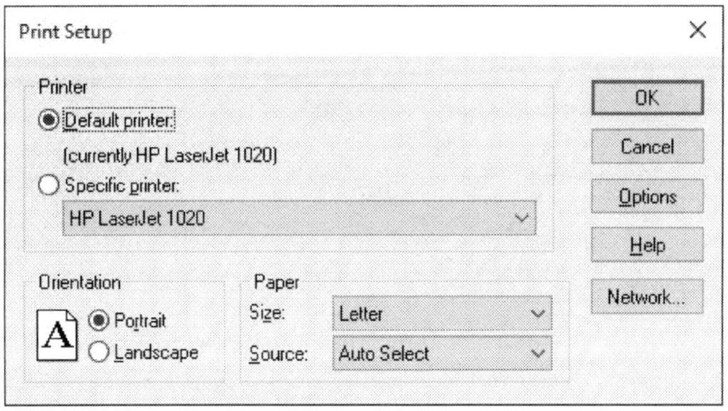

Figure 21-9

```
// call the report's printer's choosePrinter dialog:
set proc to HouseholdExpenses.rep
r = new HouseholdExpensesReport()
r.printer.choosePrinter()
```

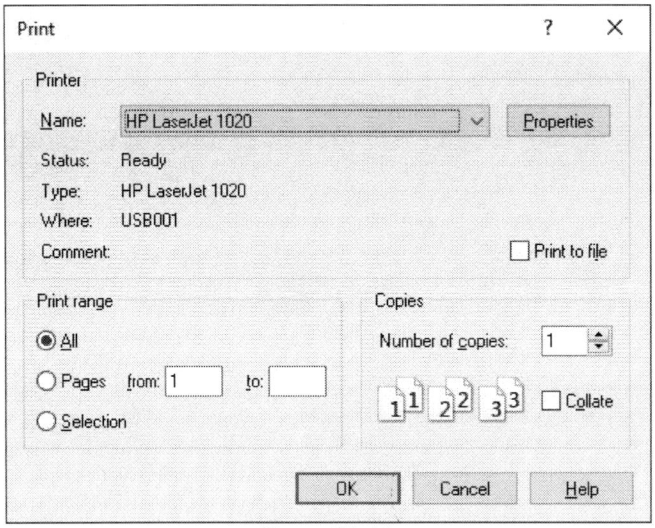

Figure 21-10

If you want to use the "other" dialog from the default, for example, for the _app.printer object:

```
_app.printer.choosePrinter("Print", false)
```

Notice that you have to either enter a character string or two sets of quotes ("") to give an empty string, the first parameter must be there if you wish to use the second one. To use the Print Setup dialog from the report:

```
r.printer.choosePrinter("Print Setup", true)
```

The text you place in the quotes for the title bar can be anything. So you could use:

```
r.printer.choosePrinter("Setup the Printer", true)
```

And the title of the dialog would say "Setup the Printer".

Options – *startPage*, *endPage*, Number of Copies

Did you know it was possible to set the *startPage*, *endPage*, and number of copies for a report, and that the information would be passed on to the *choosePrinter* dialog? If you know that a report needs to only print pages 3 to 5, for example, you could do the following:

```
set procedure to HouseholdExpenses.rep
r = new HouseholdExpensesReport()
r.startPage := 3
r.endPage := 5
r.output := 1 // Printer
r.printer.choosePrinter()
r.render()
```

If there is no page number 5, then the report will stop at the end of page 4 – meaning that the Report Engine will not send a "blank page" to the printer. The default value for the report's *startPage* property is 1, and the default value for the report's *endPage* is -1, which means that it will go to the end of the report.

To set the number of copies, you would use:

```
r.printer.copies := 2
```

The default value for the printer object's *copies* property is 1.

The only thing that is missing is a *collate* option when printing multiple copies – your clients would need to be aware of the fact that if they want their multi-page reports collated they would need to check the option on the Print dialog.

Printing from an Array

The first time someone asked about this concept in the dBASE support groups, I didn't think it was possible. However, as noted all through this chapter, the Report Engine is just dBASE code, and you can do almost anything with it if you put your mind to it.

An array is effectively a virtual table – it has columns and rows to hold data, but when whatever code is using it is done the data contained in the array is gone – very much like virtual fields, and so on.

What can be confusing is that the report engine assumes that you are using a standard *rowset* object assigned to a *streamSource*. So you can trick dBASE by creating a table that has a single row – this allows you to define a *detailBand* on the report, and from there, you can build all the rest of what you need in code. As a matter of fact, you can create the table in your code, and when the report has processed, you can delete it.

Create Report Objects

The code used to demonstrate this is fairly involved in that it will create an array of data from the Dogs table which is what will be used in the report, it will create a temporary table to assign to the *streamSource*, and then it will create the report objects necessary to put the report together and render it.

As usual, there is a lot of commentary in the code itself to help you read it and understand what is happening.

Sample Code

```
/*
   ReportFromArray.prg
   Create a report using an array as the "dataSource".
   This is a little tricky, read the comments carefully
*/
close databases

// Set up the database object:
dData = new database()
dData.databaseName := "DBASEREPORTS"
dData.active       := true

// For this to work we need a simple table with
// one record. This will be connected to the
// streamSource of the report once we build it
// If it exists, delete it:
if file( "TempTable.dbf" )
   erase TempTable.dbf
endif
// This table will be created in the current directory
cCmd = "create table TempTable (CharField char(20))"
&cCmd.
// the table needs a single row so we have one detailBand
// in our report:
use TempTable
append blank
replace CharField with "Some Data"
use

// We need to open the dogs table, pull some data
// from it and load it into an array:
qDogs = new query()
qDogs.database := dData
qDogs.sql      := "select * from dogs"
qDogs.active   := true
qDogs.rowset.indexName := "Name"

// Next we need an array:
aExample = new array( 1,2 ) // start with one row and two columns

// loop through the table and get nMaxRecords records
// for the purpose of our test:
nMaxRecords = 30
nCurrent    = 0

// start at top of table
qDogs.rowset.first()

// make sure we get nMaxRecords and we don't
// go past the endOfSet for the rowset:
do while nCurrent < nMaxRecords and not qDogs.rowset.endOfSet
   nCurrent++ // increment counter

   // if more than one row, grow the array by one row:
   if nCurrent > 1
```

```
      aExample.grow( 1 )
   endif
   // fill in the data
   aExample[nCurrent, 1] = qDogs.rowset.fields["Name"].value.rightTrim()
   aExample[nCurrent, 2] = qDogs.rowset.fields["Born"].value
   // next record:
   qDogs.rowset.next()
enddo // end of loop

// now we have the array, we can close the query:
qDogs.active := false
release object qDogs
qDogs := null
// don't need the database object, either:
dData.active := false
release object dData
dData := null

// we will need a reference to the temporary table:
qTemp = new query()
qTemp.sql    := "select * from TempTable"
qTemp.active := true

// here is where it gets tricky, we're going to create the
// report objects completely in code. To assist I used
// an existing report for the top/left and various other
// properties of some of the controls:
oRep = new report()
oRep.metric := 3 // Inches

// objects on the report:
oPT = new pageTemplate( oRep ) // contained by the report
// set the pageTemplate's margins and size:
oPT.height       := 11.0
oPT.width        := 8.5
oPT.marginTop    := 0.5
oPT.marginLeft   := 0.5
oPT.marginBottom := 0.5
oPT.marginRight  := 0.5

// streamFrame:
oSF = new streamFrame( oPT ) // contained by the pageTemplate
oSF.height = 8.65
oSF.left = 0.0
oSF.top = 1.0
oSF.width = 7.5

// streamSource:
oSS = new streamSource( oRep ) // contained by the report

// text on the pageTemplate for report headings:
oPT.MainTitle = new text( oPT )
oPT.MainTitle.text            := "My Company Name"
oPT.MainTitle.metric          := 3      // Inches
oPT.MainTitle.height          := 0.3646
oPT.MainTitle.width           := 3.0833
oPT.MainTitle.alignHorizontal := 1      // Center
```

```
oPT.MainTitle.fontSize        := 20.0
oPT.MainTitle.fontItalic      := true
oPT.MainTitle.left            := 2.2083
oPT.MainTitle.top             := 0.0

// secondary title:
oPT.SecondaryTitle = new text( oPT )
oPT.SecondaryTitle.text            := "Report From Array"
oPT.SecondaryTitle.height          := 0.2708
oPT.SecondaryTitle.width           := 2.3333
oPT.SecondaryTitle.metric          := 3      // Inches
oPT.SecondaryTitle.alignHorizontal := 1      // Center
oPT.SecondaryTitle.fontSize        := 16.0
oPT.SecondaryTitle.left            := 2.5833
oPT.SecondaryTitle.top             := 0.3854

// date:
oPT.DateText = new text( oPT )
oPT.DateText.text := {||cmonth(date())+" "+day(date())+", "+year(date())}
oPT.DateText.height          := 0.2083
oPT.DateText.width           := 2.1042
oPT.DateText.metric          := 3      // Inches
oPT.DateText.alignHorizontal := 1      // Center
oPT.DateText.fontSize        := 12.0
oPT.DateText.left            := 2.6979
oPT.DateText.top             := 0.6771

// assignments necessary for report to function:
oRep.firstPageTemplate        := oPT
oPT.nextPageTemplate          := oPT
oSF.streamSource              := oSS
oSS.rowset                     := qTemp.rowset // now we have a detailBand

// at this point we have one detailBand and everything else
// will go on that:
oDT = oSS.detailBand
// start with some column heading text:
oDT.NameHeading = new text( oDT )
oDT.NameHeading.text            := "Name"
oDT.NameHeading.fontBold        := true
oDT.NameHeading.fontName        := "Arial"
oDT.NameHeading.fontSize        := 10
oDT.NameHeading.suppressIfBlank := true
oDT.NameHeading.canRender       := {||this.parent.firstOnFrame}
oDT.NameHeading.metric          := 3 // Inches
oDT.NameHeading.height          := 0.2083
oDT.NameHeading.left            := 0.0208
oDT.NameHeading.top             := 0
oDT.NameHeading.width           := 0.5729

// start with some column heading text:
oDT.BornHeading = new text( oDT )
oDT.BornHeading.text            := "Born"
oDT.BornHeading.fontBold        := true
oDT.BornHeading.fontName        := "Arial"
oDT.BornHeading.fontSize        := 10
oDT.BornHeading.suppressIfBlank := true
```

```
oDT.BornHeading.canRender       := {||this.parent.firstOnFrame}
oDT.BornHeading.metric          := 3 // Inches
oDT.BornHeading.height          := 0.2083
oDT.BornHeading.left            := 3.9896
oDT.BornHeading.top             := 0
oDT.BornHeading.width           := 0.6979

// now we build the text controls for the individual rows
// of the array. We will rely heavily on macros here as it
// is the easiest way to do this in a loop:
for i = 1 to aExample.size / 2 // two columns

    // name of the text control (Name field)
    cName = "oDT.text"+i+"_1" // first row would name this text1_1
    // create the text control
    cCmd = cName + " = new text( oDT )"
    &cCmd. // execute macro

    // set properties (note double quotes and brackets for delimiters):
    cCmd = cName+".text = ["+aExample[ i, 1 ]+"]"
    &cCmd.
    cCmd = cName+".width = 3.6979"
    &cCmd.
    cCmd = cName+".top = "+(i*.21) // 0.21" tall
    &cCmd.

    // repeat for second field (Born)
    cName = "oDT.text"+i+"_2" // first row would name this text1_2
    // create the text control
    cCmd = cName + " = new text( oDT )"
    &cCmd. // execute macro

    // set properties (note single and double quotes for delimiters):
    cCmd = cName+".text = '"+aExample[ i, 2 ]+"'"
    &cCmd.
    cCmd = cName+".width = 0.9479"
    &cCmd.
    cCmd = cName+".top = "+(i*.21) // 0.21" tall
    &cCmd.
    cCmd = cName+".left = 4.0"
    &cCmd.

next // element in aExample array

// if all is well, we need to render the report:
oRep.render()

// cleanup:
qTemp.active := false
release object qTemp
qTemp := null

// delete the temporary table:
erase TempTable.dbf
```

Note that if you really want to experiment with this, you can download it with the rest of the sample code for this book.

Caveat: this code is based on code in one of the documents I wrote in the early 2000s for the Knowledgebase, but has been enhanced quite a bit.

Issues

There are some issues with this code. For example, you can't report more than one page of data, as there is only one *detailBand*. The code could probably be modified so that there were new detailBands for each row – it would change the program substantially – as a matter of fact, at that point you might as well be just using a report the "normal" way. With this example, there is only one *detailBand*, which cannot cross pages. In the code, I limited the number of records to 30 for that reason. *(Some experimentation could tell you exactly how many rows you could display ...)*

Report to Text

Reporting to text files can be a little tricky. Text files by their very definition have little or no formatting, fonts will not be streamed out to them, and so on.

There are several ways to approach this if you need to do something along these lines.

Generic/Text Printer Driver

First, much depends on the version of Windows you have, and whether or not this driver is even installed. Windows 10, for example, does not have this driver automatically available to you. Doing some research on the internet, I have found you can *add* this driver to Windows 10 by following these steps:

Click the Start Menu
Click "Settings"
Click "Devices"
Click "Add a printer or scanner"

At this point, Windows will start scanning your computer for possible printers to add to the list of available drivers. After a moment you should see:

"The printer that I want isn't listed"

Click this text. The following dialog will appear:

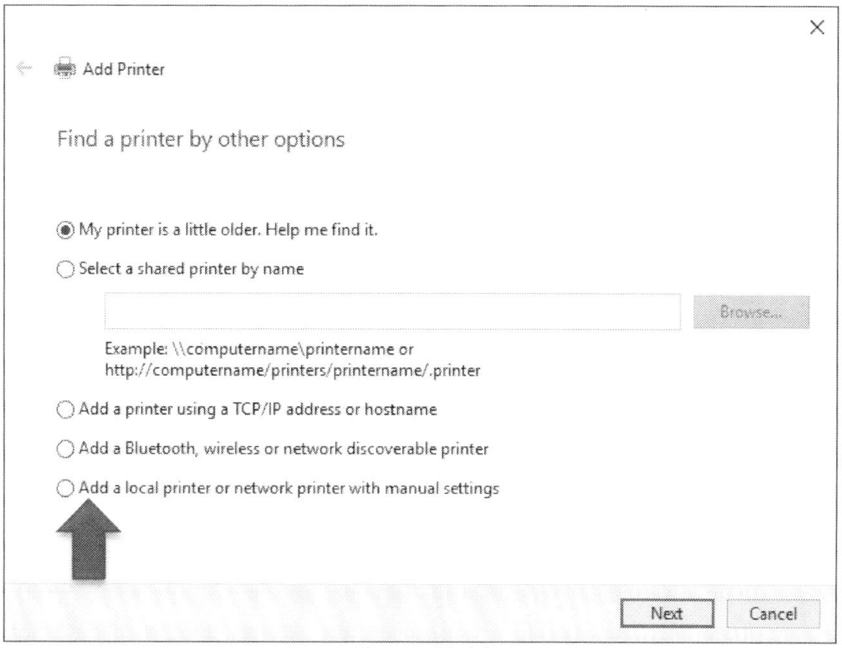

Figure 21-11

Select the last radiobutton "Add a local printer or network printer with manual settings", and click "Next".

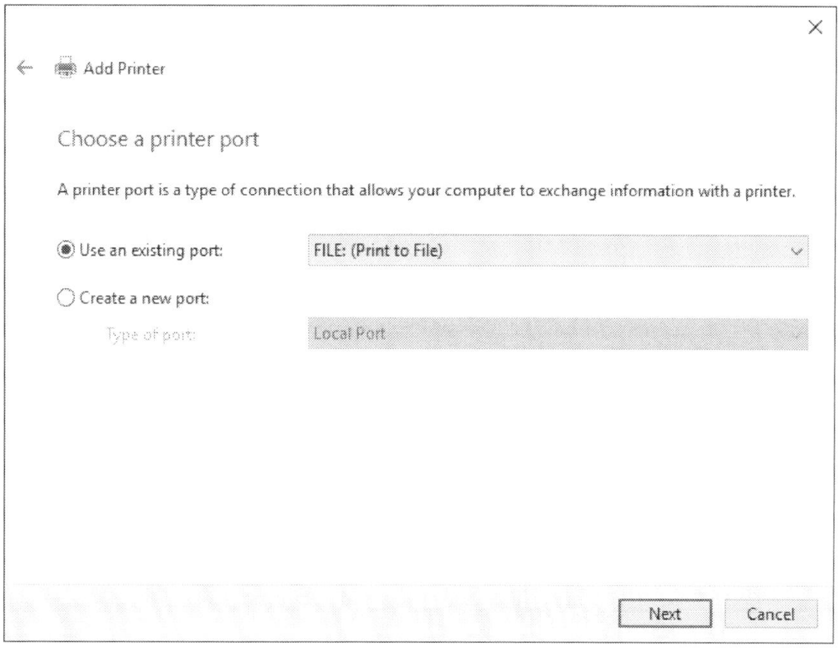

Figure 21-12

The default port will be "LPT1", change it to "File: (Print to File)" as shown in Figure 21-12. Click "Next".

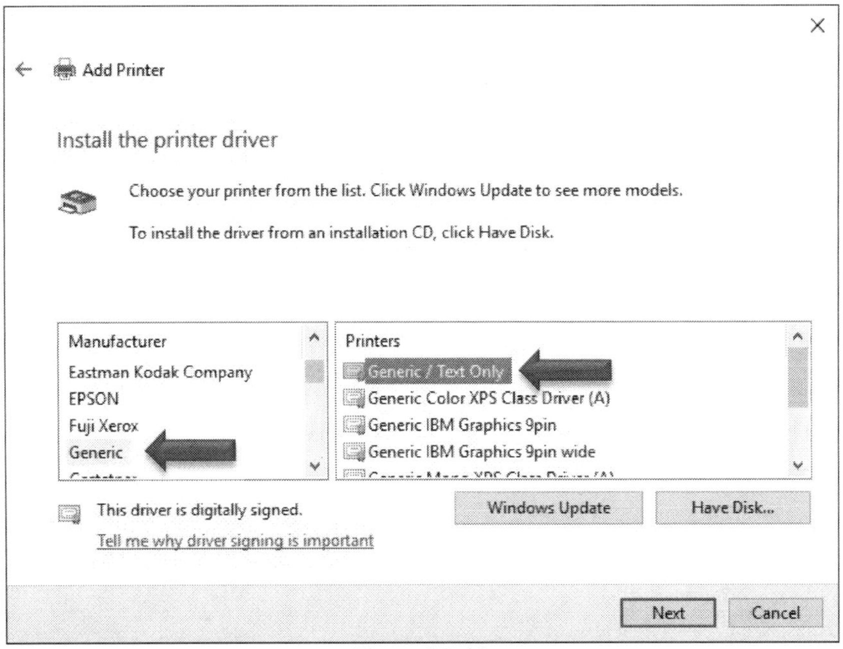

Figure 21-13

Under "Manufacturer" select "Generic", under "Printers" select "Generic / Text Only". Click "Next".

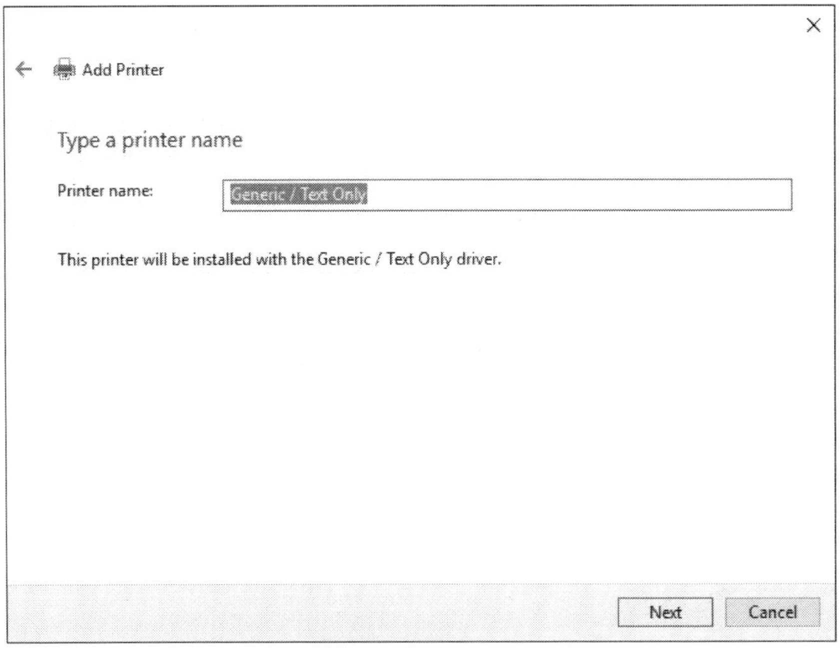

Figure 21-14

It is probably a good idea to leave the "Printer name:" as the default. Click "Next". Briefly you will see a message that Windows is installing the driver, and then the next screen (Figure 21-15) will appear:

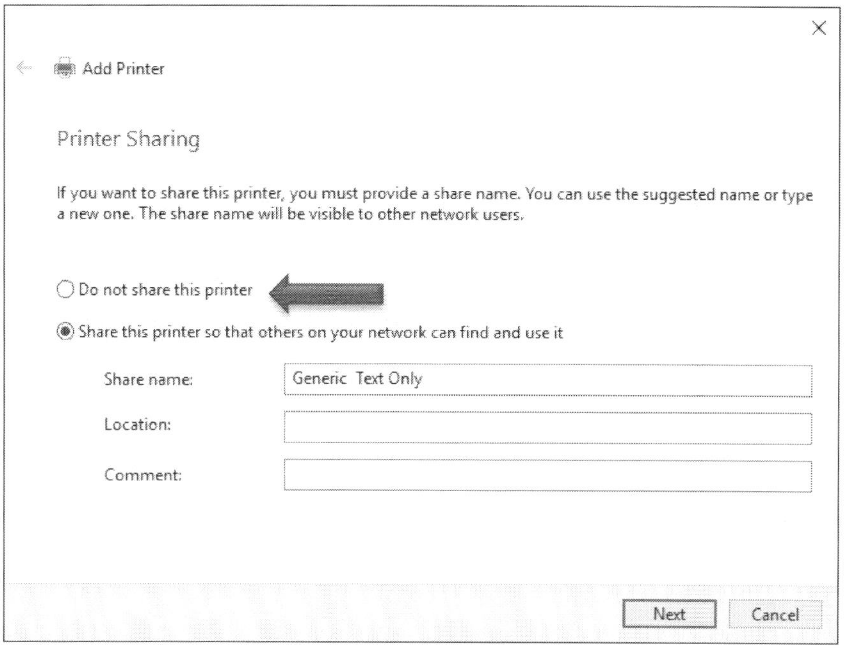

Figure 21-15

If you wish to share this on a network, you can. For now let's just move on. I suggest if you are not going to share it that you click the "Do not share this printer" radiobutton. Click "Next".

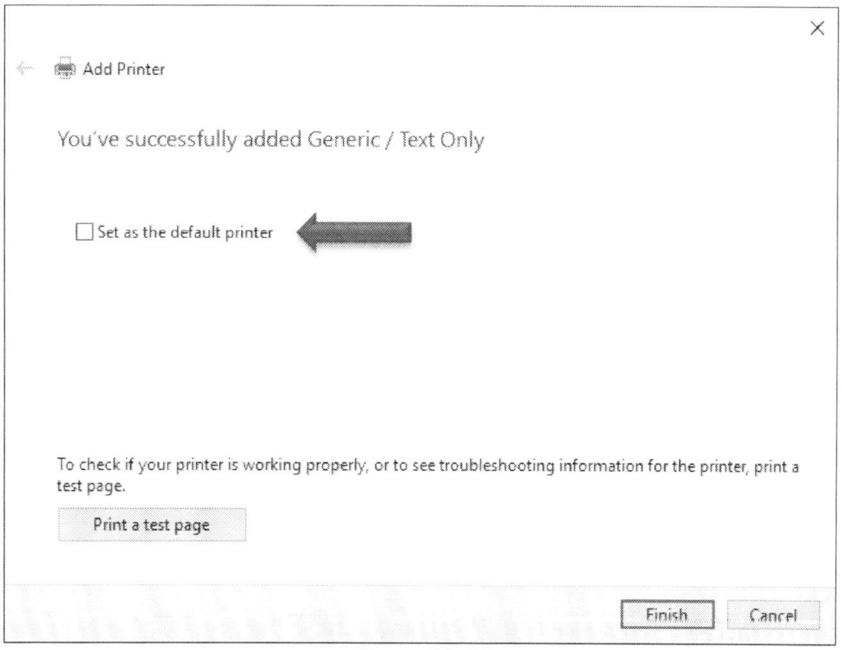

Figure 21-16

Uncheck the "Set as the default printer" checkbox, and then simply click the "Finish" button.

On the "Printers & scanners" page you will now see the "Generic / Text Only" driver.

Print a Report to Text

Having the correct printer driver available, you can now try printing a report *to* that driver. In the Command Window, try the following:

```
set procedure to HouseholdExpenses.rep
r = new HouseholdExpensesReport()
r.output := 1
r.printer.choosePrinter()
```

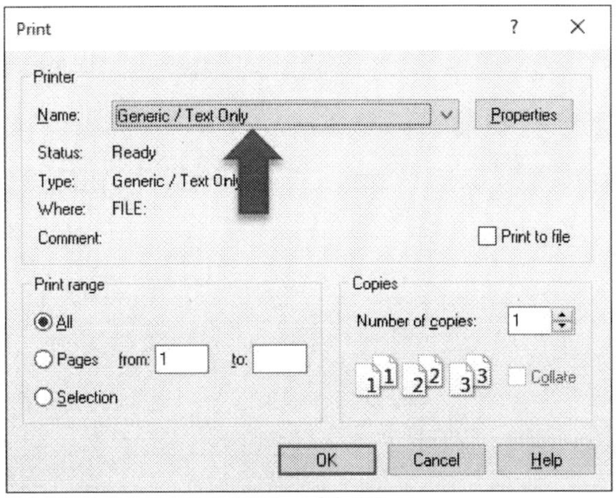

Figure 21-17

```
// the choosePrinter dialog appears as in Figure 21-17
r.render()
```

When the choosePrinter dialog comes up, select the "Generic / Text Only" driver. Click "OK". After you type the last line above, you will be asked for the name of the file. Enter "HouseholdExpenses", and click "Save".

You won't see this file in the dBASE Navigator, because the default file extension is ".prn". You should be able to view it though, by typing in the Command Window:

```
modify command HouseholdExpenses.prn
```

You should see something like:

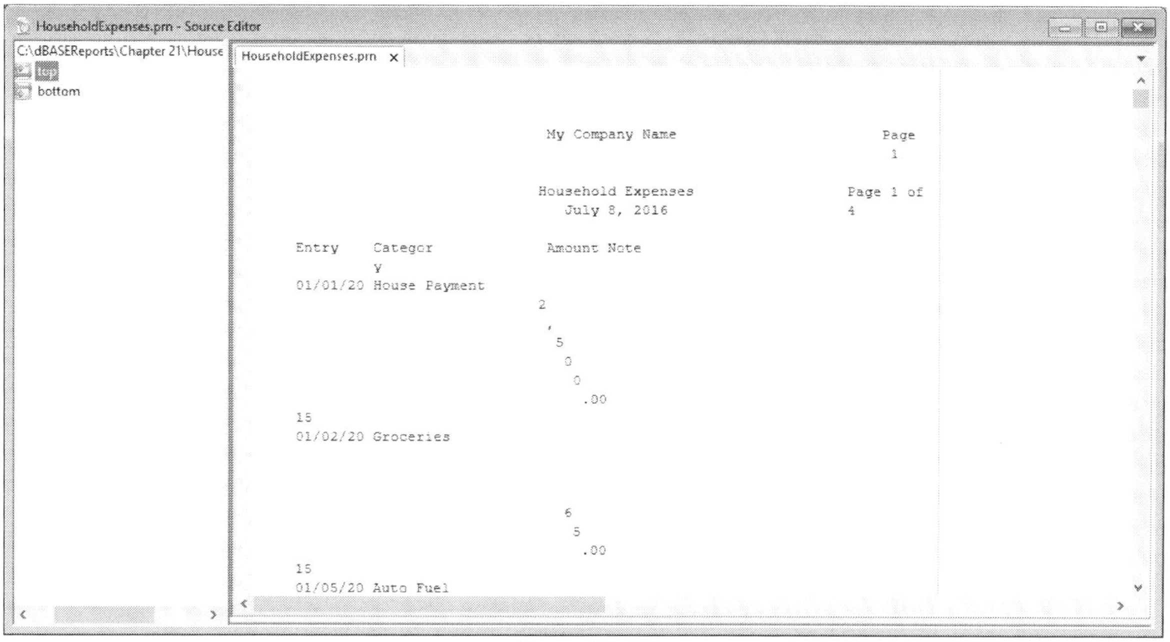

Figure 21-18

This doesn't look all that good, does it? You would need to really spend a lot of effort creating a report that would look good in text, including the width of various controls, and setting the font for your text controls to a "monospaced" font (such as "Courier New"), and so on.

Having gone through all of that, there are other ways we can generate a report to a text file.

Using the File Object

In The dBASE Book there is discussion of using the dBASE file object to read and write text files. But we didn't really deal with creating reports. Like anything, this can get complicated. However, what if we wanted to output a report similar to the Household Expenses report? This can be done, but it will take some effort.

Things to consider:

- There will be no "pages" so having a page number is not very useful.
- How wide do you want to set the report? I recommend 80 characters, but of course you could make it wider.
- Laying things out for a tabular report will require working with spacing issues.

That said, the following program (read the comments carefully) will generate a variation of the Household Expenses report as a standard .txt file:

```
/*
   HouseholdExpensesText.prg
   Generate a version of the Household Expenses report to a text file,
   80 characters wide ...
*/

// Set up the database and query objects:
local dData, qHE, rHE, fHE
```

```
dData = new database()
dData.databaseName := "DBASEREPORTS"
dData.active       := true

qHE = new query()
qHE.database       := dData
qHE.sql            := "select * from Household"
qHE.active         := true

// shortcuts
rHE = qHE.rowset
fHE = rHE.fields

// index:
rHE.indexName := "ENTRYDATE"

// set up information for "report"
nWidth = 80

// set up file object:
fOut = new file()
fOut.create( "HouseholdExpenses.txt", "W" ) // Write access

// output the headings:
// "MainTitle"
cHeading = "My Company Name"
fOut.puts( CenterText( nWidth, cHeading ) )
// "SecondaryHeading"
cHeading = "Household Expenses"
fOut.puts( CenterText( nWidth, cHeading ) )
// Date:
cHeading = cmonth(date())+" "+day(date())+", "+year(date())
fOut.puts( CenterText( nWidth, cHeading ) )
// blank line:
fOut.puts( "" )

// column headings -- tricky, because we need to get everything
// to line up ...

// The Date will take 10 characters (MM/DD/YYYY)
// The Category is defined as 24 characters
// the Amount field is 7.2 (seven digits, 2 decimals)
//    but we want it to look like: 99,999.99 -- so add
//    one more for the comma (width of 8)
// The Note field is maxed out at 254 characters,
//     but most notes are not that long ...
// We should have at least a couple of blank spaces between
// columns. However, the words for the headings are even
// trickier:
cColumnHeadings  = "Entry"
cColumnHeadings += replicate( " ", 7 ) // 10-5 (5) for the field
                                       // and 2 for blank space
cColumnHeadings += "Category"
cColumnHeadings += replicate( " ", 19 ) // 25-8 (17) and 2 for blank

cColumnHeadings += " Amount"
cColumnHeadings += replicate( " ", 4 ) // 9-7 (2) and 2 for blank
```

```
cColumnHeadings += "Note"
// output the headings:
fOut.puts( cColumnHeadings )

// loop through the table and list the data out:
rHE.first() // first row in table
do while not rHE.endOfSet // loop to end of table

   // initialize the text variable:
   cRow = ""

   // EntryDate:
   cRow += fHE["EntryDate"].value

   // blank spaces:
   cRow += "  " // 2 spaces

   // Category -- normally when outputting such
   // a value, I would trim the field. However,
   // in this case, let's just use the "untrimmed"
   // value which will include spaces on the right:
   cRow += fHE["Category"].value

   // blank spaces:
   cRow += "  " // 2 spaces

   // Amount is tricky -- we want it to line
   // up on the right, and we want a picture
   // for it so that we have commas ...
   // we will use the transform() function
   // and a picture:
   cRow += transform( fHE["Amount"].value, "99,999.99" )

   // blank spaces
   cRow += "  " // 2 spaces

   // Note -- we want to truncate this to keep it at
   // 80 characters per line. We are currently using
   // 50 characters, so the most we can use is 30:
   // The other problem is that if the value of the
   // "Note" field is null (empty), we end up wiping out
   // the string here (string+null = null).
   cNote = new string( fHE["Note"].value.rightTrim())
   cRow += left( cNote, 30 )

   // output the row:
   fOut.puts( cRow )

   rHE.next() // next row
enddo // end of loop

// cleanup:
fOut.close()
release object fOut
fOut := null
qHE.active := false
```

```
release object qHE
qHE := null
dData.active := false
release object dData
dData := null

// done!

function CenterText( nWidth, cText )
   // to center text we need to know the width of the
   // report, and the text we want to center:
   local nSpaces
   // subtract the length of the text to be centered
   // from the width we are centering IN, and
   // divide by 2:
   nSpaces = ( nWidth - len( cText ) ) / 2
   // add number of spaces on the left:
   cText = replicate( " ", nSpaces ) + cText
return cText
```

This program when run (which executes very quickly) will generate a text file ("HouseholdExpenses.txt") that looks like this:

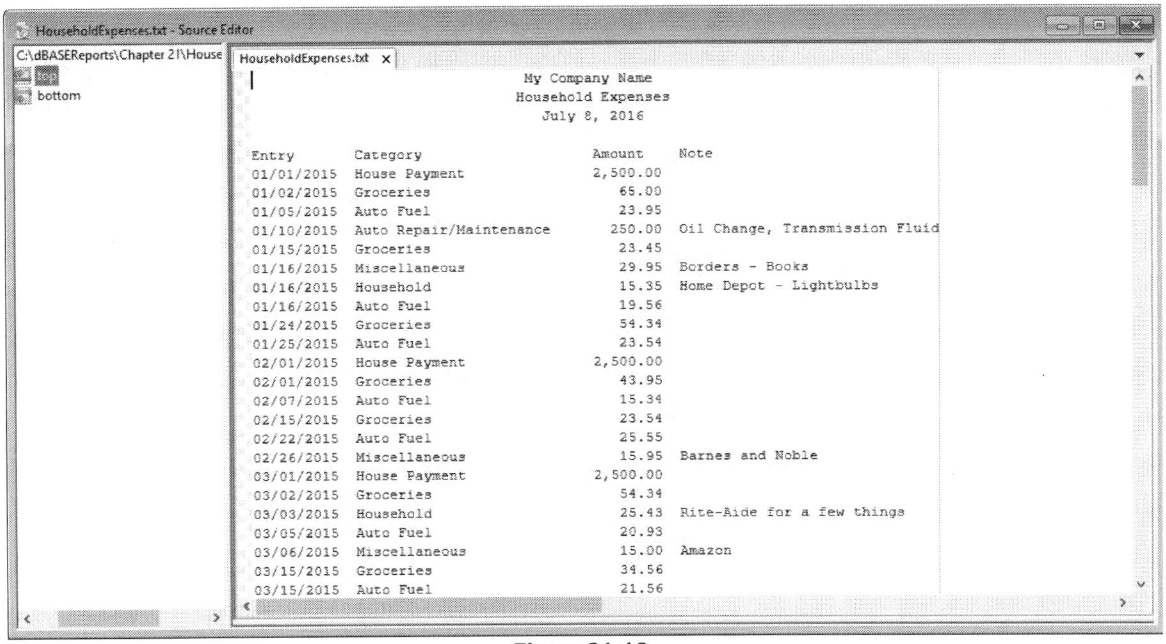


```
                              My Company Name
                             Household Expenses
                                July 8, 2016

Entry        Category                      Amount    Note
01/01/2015   House Payment               2,500.00
01/02/2015   Groceries                      65.00
01/05/2015   Auto Fuel                      23.95
01/10/2015   Auto Repair/Maintenance       250.00    Oil Change, Transmission Fluid
01/15/2015   Groceries                      23.45
01/16/2015   Miscellaneous                  29.95    Borders - Books
01/16/2015   Household                      15.35    Home Depot - Lightbulbs
01/16/2015   Auto Fuel                      19.56
01/24/2015   Groceries                      54.34
01/25/2015   Auto Fuel                      23.54
02/01/2015   House Payment               2,500.00
02/01/2015   Groceries                      43.95
02/07/2015   Auto Fuel                      15.34
02/15/2015   Groceries                      23.54
02/22/2015   Auto Fuel                      25.55
02/26/2015   Miscellaneous                  15.95    Barnes and Noble
03/01/2015   House Payment               2,500.00
03/02/2015   Groceries                      54.34
03/03/2015   Household                      25.43    Rite-Aide for a few things
03/05/2015   Auto Fuel                      20.93
03/06/2015   Miscellaneous                  15.00    Amazon
03/15/2015   Groceries                      34.56
03/15/2015   Auto Fuel                      21.56
```

Figure 21-19

While it is plain text, it comes out looking decent. You could of course widen the report to more than 80 characters, and do a lot of other things with this. This is just an example of what is possible.

Output for Other Applications

The other option for generating output from your data is to output the data in text files that can be read by other software, such as Excel™. The most common file format for data is Comma Separated Values (CSV).

dBASE can output to CSV in several ways. Using the old database manipulation language (XDML), this can be as simple as:

```
use household order ENTRYDATE
copy to HouseholdExpenses.csv delimited
```

If you then examine the file:

```
modify command HouseholdExpenses.csv
```

You should see:

```
20150101,"House Payment",2500.00,
20150102,"Groceries",65.00,
20150105,"Auto Fuel",23.95,
20150110,"Auto Repair/Maintenance",250.00,"Oil Change, Transmission
Fluid, and general checkup"
20150115,"Groceries",23.45,
20150116,"Miscellaneous",29.95,"Borders - Books"
20150116,"Household",15.35,"Home Depot - Lightbulbs"
20150116,"Auto Fuel",19.56,
20150124,"Groceries",54.34,
20150125,"Auto Fuel",23.54,
20150201,"House Payment",2500.00,
20150201,"Groceries",43.95,
20150207,"Auto Fuel",15.34,
20150215,"Groceries",23.54,
```

(This is part of the data), note the "Note" field is wrapping for the fourth row above.

When generating the .CSV file, dBASE creates another file with the same name but an extension of .SCH, which is stands for "Scheme". This defines the fields in the .CSV file, which may be needed by some software. If you open it, this file looks like:

```
[HOUSEHOLDEXPENSES2]
Filetype=Delimited
Delimiter="
Separator=,
CharSet=DBWINWE0
Field1=EntryDate,Date,08,00,00

Field2=Category,Char,25,00,08

Field3=Amount,Float,07,02,33

Field4=Note,Char,254,00,40
```

It is possible to use other file formats with the COPY TO command, check the online help with dBASE ("help copy to").

Other Methods of Exporting Data

In the dUFLP is a "wizard" style program called "ExportData.wfm" – this wizard is designed to assist exporting data in a variety of file formats, which include Excel, CSV, other tables, other database formats, and a lot more. There are some other programs in the dUFLP that can be used for specific file exports.

You can also write code to do a lot of things yourself using techniques shown here and in my other books, but I am a firm believer in the idea that you shouldn't reinvent the wheel.

Programming and Labels

There are a couple of advanced topics that can be discussed regarding labels and programming, but for the most part labels work the same as reports, and all of the techniques discussed in this chapter should also work with labels.

Skipping Labels on a Sheet of Labels

If you work with sheets of labels, there will most likely come a time when you find that they are expensive, and when you print a lot of labels, you often end up with the last sheet having empty labels that were not printed on. You can throw these sheets away, but what if you could tell dBASE to skip to the first available label and start there?

> ⚠ **WARNING**
> Before spending any time on this – if your printer is a laser printer (or your client's printer is a laser printer), the code here is not suggested – the heat from the drum used for a laser printer makes reusing labels a bad idea – often labels will peel off the sheet and stick to the drum, which is very bad for it. Also it is very time consuming and labor intensive to remove the labels and all the adhesive stuck to the drum.

Basically, if you recall from Chapter 9 (Labels), a label is just a *streamFrame* – if your sheet of labels has 30 labels on it, your label definition will have 30 *streamFrames*, one for each label.

It is possible through the use of the *streamSource* object's *beginNewFrame* method and some fancy coding to skip the *streamFrame* (or labels) you need to, to start printing at a specific label. One aspect of the code below that you should be aware of – you only want to do this if you are on the first page of labels. The code below assumes that the first page has some blanks you wish to skip, and that the next page is a full sheet of labels (this is not using a real set of labels – it is just an example – you could substitute the label file and the name of the label's class from the chapter on labels earlier in this book, if you wish).

```
set procedure to MyLabels.lab
rMyLab = new MyLabelsReport()
private p, cEvent, i, nSkipLabels
nSkipLabels = 10 // number of labels to skip

p = rMyLab.pageTemplate1 // shorten references

// Loop through the streamFrames ...
for i = 1 to nSkipLabels
    cEvent = "p.streamFrame"+i+".canRender"
    // the event must be set ONLY for the first page - otherwise
    // we will skip this streamFrame for all pages ...:
    &cEvent. = {; iif( this.parent.parent.reportPage = 1, ;
      this.parent.parent.streamSource1.beginNewFrame(), null ) }
next
rMyLab.render()
```

This is a nifty little trick, but be careful when experimenting with it. One of my editors *(from the first edition of this book)* noted that you can place this code in the actual label file if you wanted to – it would need to be placed in the Source Code above the comment that says:

```
** END HEADER - do not remove this line
```

And add the command "return" just before the comment and after "rMyLab.render()". The one problem with placing this in the label's source code would be that it would be there the next time you ran the labels, which could cause some issues for you.

Filtering Data for Labels

When it comes right down to it – labels are just reports with a different file extension and more streamFrames than most reports have.

Why is that statement so important? Because everything we have discussed in this chapter and in other parts of this book that deal with filtering data for reports, programmatically changing reports, and so on, all apply to labels. You can do all of those things if you need to with your labels, so you could print a range of mailing labels, for example, from one postal code to another, or even if the data had dates in it, you could set a range of dates. All of the discussions that deal with this sort of thing apply to labels. There's no need to really discuss it all again!

Cleanup

Create a new report (in the Navigator, click on the .Reports. tab, double-click on the "[New Report]" icon). Select the "File" menu, select "Set Custom Report Class", and in the dialog, click the "Clear Custom Report" button, then click "OK". This clears out the custom report setting in the Plus.ini file, so that the next report you create is not based on this one. Close that report without making any changes.

Make sure the database is closed by going to the Command Window and typing:

```
close databases
```

This will also ensure that you don't end up creating tables in the wrong location, etc.

Source Code

The following is a listing of the sample code in the folders we have been working with. If you downloaded the files from my website the structure will be different (see below). You may use the code contained in these folders for your own applications if you desire, with the caveat that credit be given appropriately.

From working on this chapter:

```
C:\dBASEReports\Chapter 21\HouseholdExpenses.csv
C:\dBASEReports\Chapter 21\HouseholdExpenses.prn
C:\dBASEReports\Chapter 21\HouseholdExpenses.rep
C:\dBASEReports\Chapter 21\HouseholdExpenses.sch
C:\dBASEReports\Chapter 21\HouseholdExpenses.txt
C:\dBASEReports\Chapter 21\HouseholdExpensesText.prg
C:\dBASEReports\Chapter 21\ReportFromArray.prg
```

Downloaded version – same files but with this path:

```
C:\ReportsBookSourceCode\Chapter 21\filename
```

Summary

A lot of information is covered in this chapter. Some of it may seem like it's repeating information from earlier in the book, but the idea was to expand on that information; and to present some new and interesting ideas that can be used to make your reports more powerful, flexible, and give you some of the control that you may have thought you were missing with dBASE Reports.

The next chapter deals with writing data back to a table from a report. Explanations for why you might need this ability are included in the chapter.

Chapter 22: Writing Data from Reports

Typical reports in dBASE open tables in a "read-only" fashion. This means that there is really no need to write to the tables when generating a report, you are pulling data *out of* the tables but not writing back *to* the tables.

Once in a while an application requires that you write some information back to a table, often if printing is a part (or in some cases the final part) of processing some data. You might want to write the date a record was printed, or set a logical field to *true* to show that the record in question was printed.

Other options might include writing an aggregate summary to a table (for example, in the Dams table you might want to save summaries of the total number of male and female offspring for each Dam, which could be queried somewhere else in the application).

This seems like it's a fairly straight-forward concept when put like this, and it really is fairly easy, particularly if you have done all the other exercises in this book to this point.

We are going to do the first – marking a record as printed. While the sample data for the report we will create is not billing information, we can still do what is needed. The DOGS table has a field called "Printed" and it is a date field. This is what we will use. However, we need to create a sample report to do this.

A Place for Our Work

As we work through the chapter we will be needing a place for the files we create, so please create a folder for this chapter:

```
C:\dBASEReports\Chapter 22
```

And in the Navigator, be sure to navigate to this folder.

Create the Sample Report

Start a new report in the Report Designer. If this is not using the "MyCompanyReports" custom report to base the report on, select the "File" menu, select "Set Custom Report Class ...", find the "MyCompanyReports.crp" file, and so on. Save this by pressing Ctrl+S as "WriteData.rep".

Click on the "SecondaryTitleText" control and change the *text* property to "Write Data From a Report". *(Deal with widening the control, re-centering it, as needed.)*

Go to the Navigator window, and select the "Tables" tab. If the "DBASEREPORTS" database is not displayed, select it in the "Look in" combobox, and drag the "DOGS" table to the design surface of the report. With the "DOGS1" *query* still having focus, go to the Inspector, select the *rowset* object and click the Inspect button. Find the *indexName* property and set the index tag to "NAME".

Go to the Component Palette and drag a "DataColHeadingText" control to the *detailBand*, and change the *text* property to "Name". Repeat and place this next heading to the right of the first (with some space because the Name field is relatively wide), and change the *text* property to "Registration". Like always, spend a moment lining these up.

Next select a "DataText" control and place it under the first heading text. Set the *text* property's type to "Codeblock", click the tool button, and enter the following in the dialog:

```
this.form.dogs1.rowset.fields["name"].value
```

Repeat this previous step for the REG_NO field, changing the field name in the statement above. Widen the controls as needed, and spend a moment lining things up. Your report should be similar to other reports we've done in earlier chapters right now.

Marking Records as Printed

Once we have the report itself, we need to be able to actually write data to the record when the record has been printed. One problem involved here is that by default when you open tables for reports, dBASE sets the query object's *requestLive* property to *false*. The problem? With this property set to *false*, you cannot write to the table. The simple fix is to select the "DOGS1" query object, and in the Inspector select the *requestLive* property – change this to *true*.

This is actually fairly easy, but there are some considerations. For example, when just *viewing* the report, do we want to write to the "Printed" field, or should we wait until we actually print the report? Do we want to only print records that have not previously been printed?

The last can be done by setting a filter on the table (using the rowset object's *filter* property, for example; or one of several other methods of filtering data in dBASE).

How do we know if the record is being *printed* rather than just displayed in a preview window? This is actually rather simple as well – we can check the report object's *output* property – if it is set to "1" we are rendering the report to a printer.

The other part of this is determining which event to use to write to the table. For our purposes, we will use the detailBand's *onRender* event – the rowset's pointer has not yet moved to the next row when this event fires, and the data has been rendered.

Click on the *detailBand* itself in the Report Designer, and go to the Inspector. Select the "Events" tab, and find the *onRender* event. Click the tool button, and in the Source Code Editor enter the following code:

```
function DETAILBAND_onRender()
   // write to the "Printed" field:
   if this.parent.parent.output == 1 // Printer
      this.parent.rowset.beginEdit()
      this.parent.rowset.fields["PRINTED"].value := date()
      this.parent.rowset.save()
   endif
return
```

Save this and exit the Report Designer (Ctrl+W).

Testing the Report

We could send this to the printer to test it, but unless you have a lot of paper to waste, this table is fairly large, and it might take some time.

Run the report and view it. Then close the report preview window. Now go to the Navigator window and if necessary select the "Tables" tab. Double-click on the "DOGS" table and scroll over to view the PRINTED field. Note that it is blank.

How do we test to see if this really works properly? We can comment out some of the code and then test the report, then come back and uncomment the code once we know it works. To do this, click on the "Reports" tab of the Navigator. Select this report (WriteData.rep) and bring it up in the Source Code Editor. Go to the end of the report, and add the double-slashes as shown below before the "if" and "endif" statements:

```
function DETAILBAND_onRender()
   // write to the "Printed" field:
   //if this.parent.parent.output == 1 // Printer
      this.parent.rowset.beginEdit()
      this.parent.rowset.fields["PRINTED"].value := date()
      this.parent.rowset.save()
   //endif
return
```

Save this and exit the Source Code Editor (Ctrl+W).

Now run the report again, and scroll through a few pages of the report. It should be noted that unless we actually render the records in the report, then the *onRender* event of the detailBand will not fire for a record, and because it does not fire, then the code to write to the table is not executed. The reason I mention this is that when we go back and view the data, we will see that some of them will show the PRINTED field as empty and some should have the current date. Close the report preview window.

To see the data in the same sequence it displayed in the report, type the following in the Command Window:

```
use dogs order name
browse
```

Now if you scroll through the data, you will see the PRINTED field is filled in for the first records, but depending on how far through the report you went, not all of the records have values.

When done viewing the data, close the Browse window, and in the Command Window type:

```
use
```

You may wish to reset the data. To do this there are several ways (this is dBASE and the dBASE Language dBL, after all). The simplest is by using a local SQL command:

```
update dogs set printed=null
```

This will go through and update the PRINTED field by replacing what is there by a null value.

To make this a bit more "real", we can set a filter on the "BORN" field, and limit the data in the report to just some of the records. When we then view the report, we will see only some of the records have been marked as "printed".

In the Command Window:

```
update dogs set printed=null
set procedure to WriteData.rep
r = new WriteDataReport()
r.streamSource1.rowset.filter = [born => {01/01/2016} and born <= {12/31/2016}]
r.render()
```

Scroll through the 24 pages of the report and then close the preview window. Then back in the Command Window:

```
use dogs order name
browse
```

Scroll to the right so you can see the "Printed" field, and note that only the records that were displayed in the report were modified.

Before we call this complete, however, the code should be re-set so that the data is only written to if we are printing the report. Open the report in the Source Code Editor, and remove the two sets of slashes we added to comment the "if" and "endif" statements shown above. The code should look like it did when we first entered it. Save your work and exit the Source Code Editor.

It should be noted that for a real application, it is likely if you were using the "PRINTED" field properly you would want to empty the field before opening the report. The ability to write back to the table for this is limited based on how you envision using it.

Cleanup

Create a new report (in the Navigator, click on the .Reports. tab, double-click on the "[New Report]" icon). Select the "File" menu, select "Set Custom Report Class", and in the dialog, click the "Clear Custom Report" button, then click "OK". This clears out the custom report setting in the Plus.ini file, so that the next report you create is not based on this one. Close that report without making any changes.

Make sure the database is closed by going to the Command Window and typing:

```
close databases
```

This will also ensure that you don't end up creating tables in the wrong location, etc.

Source Code

The following is a listing of the sample code in the folders we have been working with. If you downloaded the files from my website the structure will be different (see below). You may use the code contained in these folders for your own applications if you desire, with the caveat that credit be given appropriately.

From working on this chapter:

```
C:\dBASEReports\Chapter 22\WriteData.rep
```

Downloaded version – same files but with this path:

```
C:\ReportsBookSourceCode\Chapter 22\filename
```

Summary

While you may not need to write data to a table from a report very often, it is possible, and not that hard to do, as shown here. The important thing is remembering the *requestLive* property of the query object needs to be set to *true*.

The next chapter will briefly look at different methods of generating an HTML report from dBASE. This is becoming very important in today's world.

NOTES:

Chapter 23: Writing to HTML

With the whole world seemingly moving everything to the internet, the ability to write reports to HTML is a big deal these days. I want to note right up front that this chapter is *not* about creating web applications using dBASE. This topic is potentially huge, and could easily require a whole book *(and yes, I have considered it – no, I don't think I am ready to tackle the subject – there are other developers who are better equipped for that if they were so inclined)*. A full web application includes all the interaction with data over the web, allowing queries, user updates, etc., and we won't be discussing that here. This chapter is about creating HTML *reports* – outputting HTML from the Report Designer, and also another method of creating an HTML report.

A Place for Our Work

As we work through the chapter we will be needing a place for the files we create, so please create a folder for this chapter:

```
C:\dBASEReports\Chapter 23
```

And in the Navigator, be sure to navigate to this folder.

Using the Report Designer to Create an HTML Report

The dBASE Report Designer and Report Engine were designed with some limited HTML capabilities. However, there are some problems in the way dBASE generates HTML which we will examine.

The simplest thing to do is see how dBASE generates an HTML report from a normal report. In the Navigator, make sure you are in the folder for Chapter 23 (create it if necessary), and in the Command Window, type:

```
copy file "..\Chapter 21\HouseholdExpenses.rep" to "HouseholdExpenses.rep"
```

Open this in the Report Designer. First, let's get rid of the page number controls in the upper right – we don't need them here, and the last one might cause some problems. Simply select them (Ctrl+click) and press the Del key to delete these three controls.

Save the report and exit the Report Designer. We could set properties of the report to output directly to HTML, but we can also do this either from a program or from the Command Window in dBASE. In the Command Window type the following:

```
set procedure to HouseholdExpenses.rep additive
r = new HouseholdExpensesReport()
r.output := 4 // HTML File
r.outputFilename := "HouseholdExpenses.htm"
r.render()
```

dBASE should create a new HTML file called "HouseholdExpenses.htm". To see it, in dBASE click on the "Other" tab of the Navigator window. If you do not see the file, go to the "View" menu and select "Refresh" (this updates the list of files in the folder the Navigator is pointed to). Double-click the file "HouseholdExpenses.htm". This should open the file in your default web browser (whatever is set as the default in Windows). For me this is Netscape™. You should see something similar to the following:

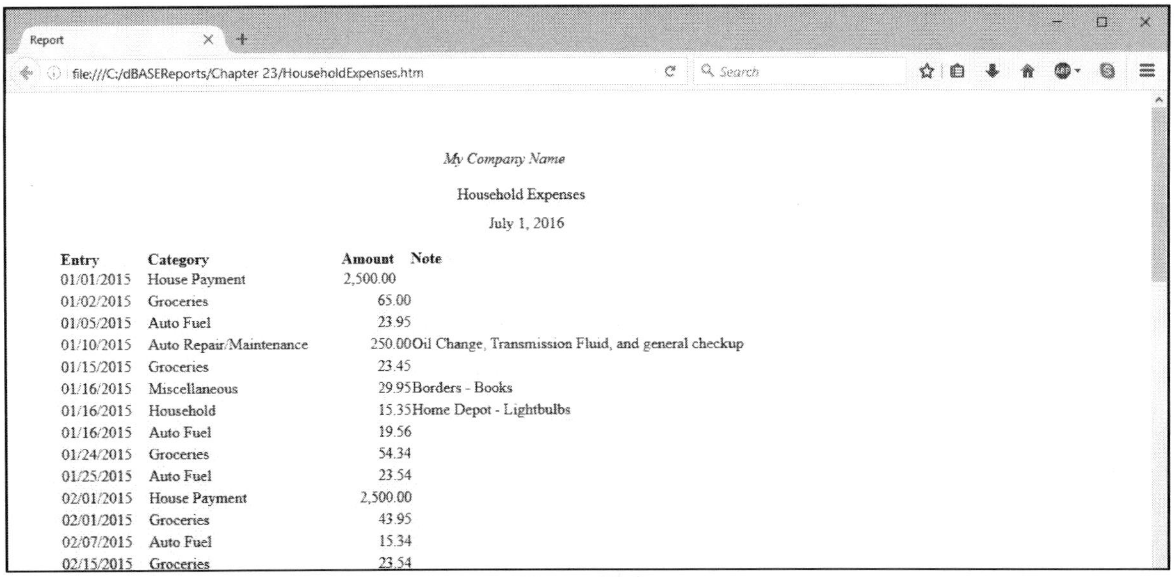

Figure 23-1

This doesn't look like it does in either the Report Designer, or when we previewed the report, does it? The problem here is that dBASE is trying to output this as best it can, but it's trying to do it with some older internet technologies, and it has some calculations built in for spacing and sizing of things that don't quite work correctly. While I have hopes that the dBASE R&D team will eventually revisit this, there are much better ways to handle generating HTML from dBASE, and rather than spend a lot of time here trying to fix this report (we could work on using standard HTML tags to define font names, sizes and attributes ...).

Close the web browser.

Drilldown Reports

One thing that the dBASE Report engine can do that takes a lot more work to try to create manually, is what is called a "Drilldown" report. This kind of report works with grouped reports, by allowing you to see group headings on one page, and then click a link to see details. This only works for HTML reports, however, because the *reportViewer* object is not interactive.

To see this, we need a grouped report. In the Command Window type the following:

```
copy file "..\Chapter 11\SubGroup.rep" to Drilldown.rep
```

Open this report in the Source Code Editor, press Ctrl+R (to open the Replace dialog), and replace "SubGroup" with "DrillDown" (use "Replace All") and then close the dialog.

Open this report in the Report Designer, in the Inspector find "group1", and note the *drilldown* property. This property has several options, dealing with how headers and footers are repeated. The default is "0 – None".

Select "2 – Drilldown, Repeat Header". Notice that the report now shows only the headers for "group1". When you run the report (below) the headers will repeat in the detail region, which make it easier to read the report.

Repeat the same setting on "group2", changing the *drilldown* property to "2 – Drilldown, Repeat Header".

If you were to simply run the report right now, the report would look very much like what we see in the Report Designer. However, if you changed the report to output to HTML as we did earlier, we will see something different.

Save the report, and in the Command Window:

```
set procedure to Drilldown.rep additive
r = new DrilldownReport()
r.output := 4 // HTML File
r.outputFilename := "Drilldown.htm"
r.render()
```

When this completes (dBASE will show it generating over 300 "pages"), find "Drilldown.htm" and open it in the browser. You should see something like:

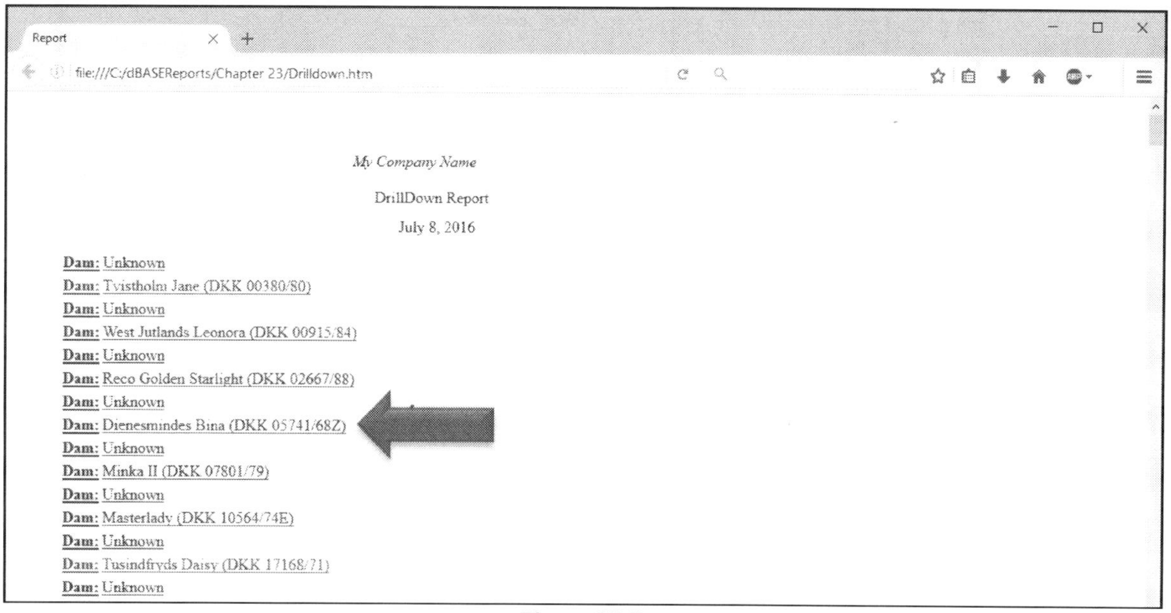

Figure 23-2

If you click on one of the links (such as "Dienesmindes Bina", you will see something like:

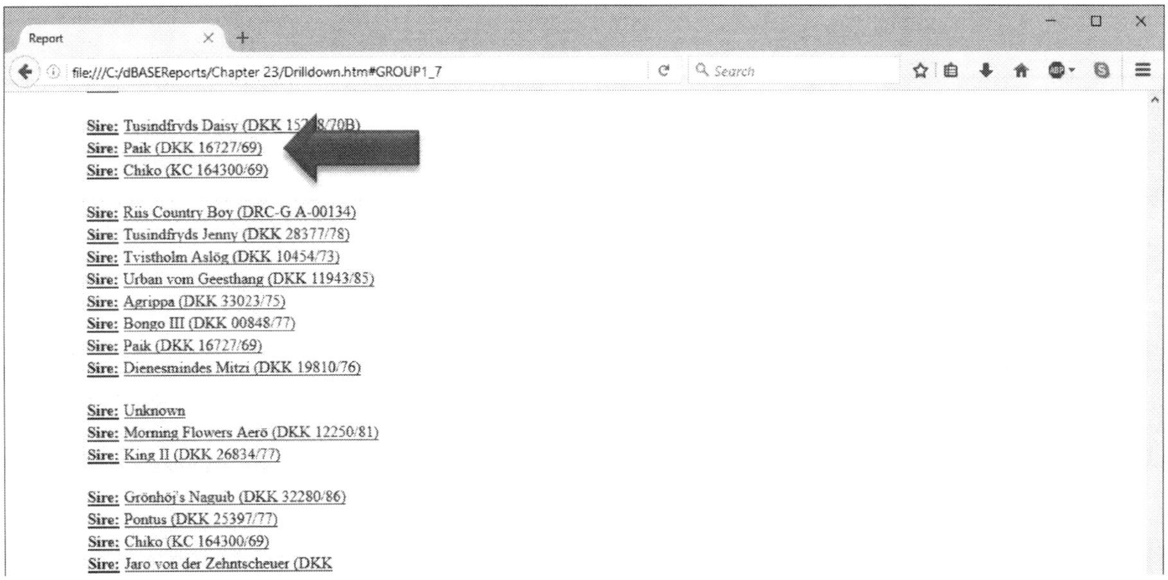

Figure 23-3

If you then click on one of the Sires, such as "Paik" (second one on the page above), you should see something like:

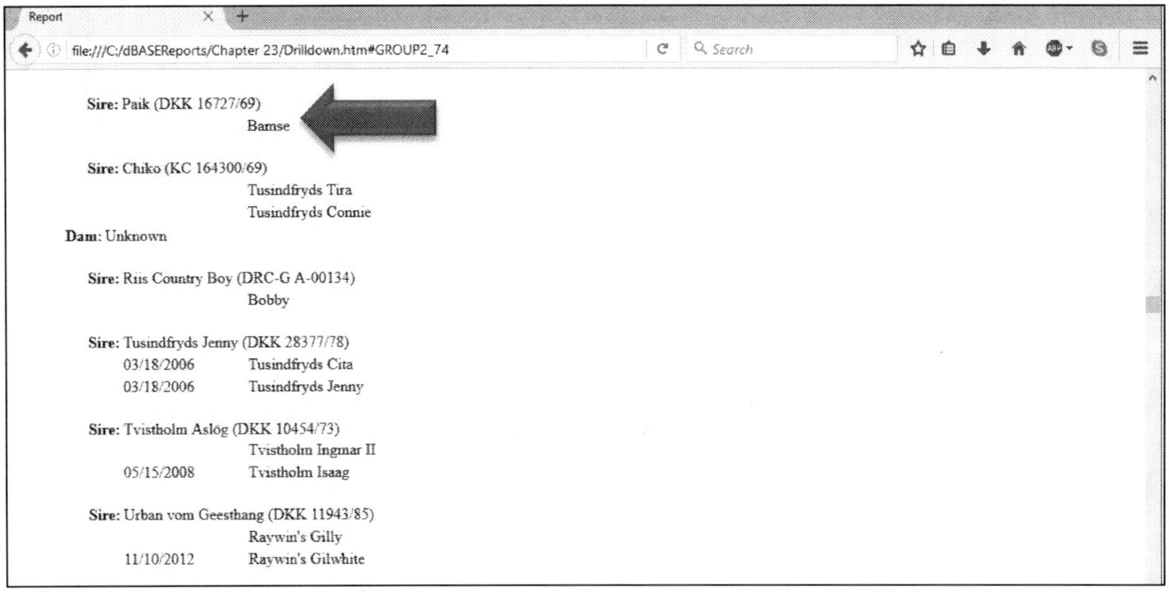

Figure 23-4

If you scroll up you should see somewhere above this the heading for the Dam we selected as well.

While the report doesn't look all that good (we could have worked with the *text* controls and set various properties ...), you can see how the *drillDown* option works.

Close the web browser, and let's take a look at an alternative means of generating an HTML report that is fast, efficient, and gives you a lot of control.

Using a Program to Generate HTML

Over the years I have attempted to automate a lot of things in dBASE to see how things work. If you examine what is in the dUFLP you will see some of my attempts – some work well, some were interesting experiments. One of those experiments is a custom class called "HTMLCLAS.CC". I don't suggest we use this here, but you might want to look it over at some point. It could be used to generate a lot of HTML tags, often using the string object that is built into dBASE, which has a lot of methods for HTML built in.

Instead, you might want to create a custom class file of your own that had a set of methods that could be called to generate parts of an HTML file, without having to re-write them all for each report you might wish to generate as HTML.

Some HTML Basics

HTML is the web standard for displaying information. It is a set of tags which start with an angle bracket (<) and end with an angle bracket (>), used to define parts of the HTML document, and to determine how to format and control the information that is displayed. Most HTML tags actually are composed of two parts – a start tag and an end tag.

An HTML file typically has two major sections – a Header, and a Body. For *good* HTML you should always begin an HTML file with a specific tag and end it with another. For readability your code should be indented (similar to below). The following is an example of a very basic HTML file:

```
<html>
   <head>
      <title>A Title for the Title Bar of the Browser</title>
   </head>
   <body>
      The main part of the HTML document here - between the
      body tags is what is displayed in the browser.
   </body>
</html>
```

As noted, this is pretty basic. There are a lot of tags, and any good reference on HTML will define them. I will try to explain the tags that are used in this chapter, but I recommend a book, or using some of the web references that are available to learn more about HTML. In order to supplement what is being done here, I will also use some style options that are part of yet another web standard called CSS or Cascading Style Sheets *(consider CSS as a version of the way that inherited code works with Object-Oriented Programming – a change in a class will cascade down to any part of the HTML page that uses that class – the same thing occurs with CSS – a modification in the style sheet automatically affects any items derived from that class)*. Some of these options can be used as options for tags, but you can also store a lot in a CSS file. We won't get into all the permutations and options – it is a complex area. If you are familiar with CSS and HTML you should have little problem with the following. If you aren't, watch what you type carefully – one typo (a missing quote for example) can cause some weird effects.

A Basic HTML Output Class

I have found that the easiest way to create an HTML page from dBASE tables is to use the file object in dBASE. It is fast, it is efficient, and you don't have to know a lot about low-level file handling to use this. I have also found that a basic custom class can save a lot of work in the long run (like many things in programming, creating a useful tool may take some time in the beginning, but in the long run is worth the effort).

We're going to create a basic class that we can then modify as needed, either adding new methods, or modifying the existing ones.

To do this, go to the Command Window, and type:

```
create file MyHTML.cc
```

The class itself is not going to be subclassed from anything – it will be a generic dBASE object. In the Source Code Editor type:

```
/*
   MyHTML.cc
   A custom class for generating an HTML Report or file from
   dBASE Plus.
*/

class MyHTML
   // spacing at the beginning of the lines
   // should insert the same spacing in the
   // output file.

   // custom properties for indentation:
   this.cTab = "   " // three spaces
   this.cTab2 = this.cTab+this.cTab
   this.cTab3 = this.cTab2+this.cTab
   this.cTab4 = this.cTab3+this.cTab
   this.cTab5 = this.cTab4+this.cTab

   function Header( cTitle )
      local cText
      cText  = cTab+[<head>]+chr(13)
      cText += cTab2+[<title>]+cTitle+[</title>]+chr(13)
      cText += cTab+[</head>]+chr(13)
   return cText
endclass
```

Note that this is just the beginning of what we will need for our report. One thing I have found is that it is a good idea to test things as you create them, which is what we will do. Save this and exit the Source Code Editor (Ctrl+W).

We only have one method – "Header" – this method has a parameter called "cTitle". We will want to pass a character string to this to display in the title bar of our browser. The addition of the "chr(13)" to the end of each line simply ensures that when the text we are creating is placed in the output file, each line will, as shown in the method, appear on its own line. We'll see this in a moment.

In order to test our work so far, we need a program that we will use (and update as well as our custom class) as we go.

In the Command Window type:

```
create file MyHTMLReport.prg
```

This will again open the Source Code Editor. Type the following:

```
/*
   MyHTMLReport.prg
   A program to generate an HTML Report of the Household Expenses
   table.
*/
// open the custom class file with our HTML code in it:
set procedure to MyHTML.cc additive
oHTML = new MyHTML()

// we will add data objects and such here later
// Create the file object we need:
oRep = new file()
oRep.create( "HouseholdExpenses2.htm" )

// start with the HTML tag:
oRep.puts( [<html>] )

// Output the HTML Header section:
oRep.puts( oHTML.Header( "Household Expenses Report" ) )

// put the body tag in manually for now:
oRep.puts( oHTML.cTab+[<body>] )

// any headings on the report itself should go here
// the "body of the report" will go here ...
// ending body tag:
oRep.puts( oHTML.cTab+[</body>] )

// end with the closing HTML tag:
oRep.puts( [</html>] )

// close the file
oRep.close()

// release the file object
release object oRep
oRep = null
```

There are a places in the code as shown that say "will go here" or "should go here" – we'll come back to it all. For the moment, check your work, save the program and run it (Ctrl+W will save and exit, and double-clicking the program in the Navigator will run it, or use the "Run Program" button in the toolbar).

It won't look like anything has happened. This is normal. If you go to the Navigator window, and click on the "Other" tab, then select "View" and "Refresh" you should see the new file "HouseholdExpenses2.htm" – if you double click this, a browser window will open with what appears to be a blank page. However, if you look at the *titlebar* or *tab* on the browser window, you should see "Household Expenses Report".

If you close the browser window that just came up, you can open the file in the Source Code Editor by right clicking on it and selecting "Open in Source Editor". You should see something like:

```
<html>
   <head>
      <title>Household Expenses Report</title>
   </head>

   <body>
   </body>
</html>
```

This is what it should look like. Since there is nothing between the <body> and </body> tags, there is nothing to display in the actual page.

Report Headings

Just like we did for standard dBASE Reports, we might want to create some basic report headings. If we were getting completely into CSS, we might even define them in a CSS file, but let's keep it simple.

Open the MyHTML.cc file in the Source Code Editor, and let's add some methods.

The first one will be the MainHeader – very similar to the "MainHeaderText" control we created back in Chapter 4 of this book. We want to be able to generate a heading that is of a good size, and so on. We can also set this up like the Header method we created earlier for HTML to accept a parameter, and change the text as needed or use a default value. Before the ENDCLASS statement, add the following code:

```
function MainHeader( cHeader )
   local cText
   // The combinations of this.cTab (and so on) and chr(13)
   // help with indentation of the HTML for readability,
   // and making sure each statement is on its own line.

   // center it:
   cText = this.cTab2+[<center>]+chr(13)

   // Font: Arial, 20pt, italic:
   cText += this.cTab3+;
            [<span style="font-family: Arial; ]+;
             [font-size: 20pt; ]+;
             [font-style: italic;">]+chr(13)

   // if a value is passed don't use the
   // default:
   if not empty( cHeader )
      cText += this.cTab4+;
               cHeader+chr(13)
   else
      cText += this.cTab4+;
               "My Company Name"+chr(13)
   endif
   cText += this.cTab3+[</span>]+chr(13)
   cText += this.cTab2+[</center>]+chr(13)
```

```
   return cText
```

This method uses the "style" option for a "span" tag in HTML. This allows us to apply our own styles. As with the custom class we defined previously, if we do not specify a different text, this will display the words "My Company Name".

Before testing this, let's add two more methods to the class – after the "return" statement shown above, and before the "endclass" statement in the file, add the following:

```
function SecondaryHeader( cHeader )
   local cText
   // center it:
   cText = this.cTab2+[<center>]+chr(13)

   // Font: Arial, 16pt:
   cText += this.cTab3+;
            [<span style="font-family: Arial; ]+;
            [font-size: 16pt;">]+chr(13)

   // if a value is passed don't use the
   // default:
   if not empty( cHeader )
      cText += this.cTab4+;
               cHeader+chr(13)
   else
      cText += this.cTab4+;
               "Purpose of Report"+chr(13)
   endif
   cText += this.cTab3+[</span>]+chr(13)
   cText += this.cTab2+[</center>]+chr(13)
return cText

function DateText
   local cText
   // center it:
   cText = this.cTab2+[<center>]+chr(13)

   // Font: Arial, 12pt:
   cText += this.cTab3+;
            [<span style="font-family: Arial; ]+;
            [font-size: 12pt;">]+chr(13)

   // build the date:
   cText += this.cTab4
   cText += "Date: "+cmonth(date())+" "+day(date())+", "+year(date())
   cText += chr(13)
   cText += this.cTab3+[</span>]+chr(13)
   cText += this.cTab2+[</center>]+chr(13)
return cText
```

If you examine the code, the "SecondaryHeader" method is largely a copy of the "MainText" method, but we are not using italic, and the font size is 16 point, instead of 20. If we do not pass a parameter, the text displayed will be "Purpose of Report". The "DateText" method returns the same text as the custom class by the same name in our report classes.

To test all three of these together, modify the program MyHTMLReport.prg in the Source Code Editor, and add the program statements shown in boldface below – find the comment shown and add these commands:

```
// any headings on the report itself should go here
oRep.puts( oHTML.MainHeader() )
oRep.puts( oHTML.SecondaryHeader( "Household Expenses" ) )
oRep.puts( oHTML.DateText() )
```

If we wanted to change the text that displays as "My Company Name", we could add it in the call to the "MainHeader" as we did in the "SecondaryHeader" above. There are no parameters for the "DateText" method, but we do need the open and close parentheses.

If you run this program, and then double-click (in the Navigator) the HTM file that we generated it should look something like:

Figure 23-5

Since this is HTML we could experiment with font colors and more. For our purposes, this is fine for now. Close your web browser.

The next part deals with getting the data into the HTML report. This is of course going to be more complex. The basics of what we will do is to loop through the data, and as we do, build a set of tags for an HTML table (which is not the same thing as a database table – it is a way of laying out information).

I have found that for testing purposes, when using an HTML table, it is useful to set a border, even if when you are done the border is removed. This makes it easier to see where things are in relationship to each other.

We could try defining methods of the custom class for your HTML table and HTML table elements (rows and data cells), but for now let's not. While hopefully you can see how useful a full set of custom classes would be, it takes a lot of work, so we're going to do most of it in the program itself.

Open the program "HouseholdExpenses.prg" in the Source Code Editor, and let's look at code we need to add or modify.

At the beginning of the program we need to create some data objects, so let's start there.

```
// we will add data objects and such here later
oData = new database()
oData.databaseName := "DBASEREPORTS"
```

```
oData.active       := true
oHE = new query() // "HE" = Household Expenses
oHE.database := oData
oHE.sql      := "select * from Household"
oHE.active   := true

// some shortcuts to the rowset and fields array:
rHE = oHE.rowset
fHE = rHE.fields

// index:
rHE.indexName := "EntryDate"

// go to the first row of the table:
rHE.first()
```

Save your work by pressing Ctrl+S (this is just a "safety" thing – I tend to automatically hit Ctrl+S every so often).

Next we want to add the code that creates the HTML table, loops through the data, and outputs the HTML tags necessary to display it properly. This will get a bit complex, so follow along carefully. Add the following after comment at the top:

```
// the "body of the report" will go here ...
oRep.puts( oHTML.cTab2+[<p>] ) // add a blank line into the report

// center the report in the browser window:
oRep.puts( oHTML.cTab2+[<center>] )

// output the beginning of the HTML table:
oRep.puts( oHTML.cTab3+[<table border="1">] )

// add some column headings:
oRep.puts( oHTML.cTab4+[<tr align="left" style="font-family:Arial; font-size: 10pt;">] )
oRep.puts( oHTML.cTab5+[<th>Date</th>] )
oRep.puts( oHTML.cTab5+[<th>Category</th>] )
oRep.puts( oHTML.cTab5+[<th align="right">Amount</th>] )
oRep.puts( oHTML.cTab5+[<th>Note</th>] )
oRep.puts( oHTML.cTab4+[</tr>] )

// we need to loop through the table here:
do while not rHE.endOfSet
   // we start with a table row tag (this is one statement):
   oRep.puts( oHTML.cTab4+[<tr valign="top" style="font-family:Arial; font-
size: 10pt;">] )
   // here's where we put the data that is to be
   // displayed for the report - this is with the table data tags:
   oRep.puts( oHTML.cTab5+[<td>]+fHE["EntryDate"].value+[</td>] )
   oRep.puts( oHTML.cTab5+[<td>]+fHE["Category"].value+[</td>] )
   // right align the Amount, and format it:
   oRep.puts( oHTML.cTab5+[<td align="right">]+;
              transform( fHE["Amount"].value, "9,999.99" )+;
              [</td>] )
   oRep.puts( oHTML.cTab5+[<td>]+fHE["Note"].value+[</td>] )

   // and we end with an end table row tag:
   oRep.puts( oHTML.cTab4+[</tr>] )
```

```
      // next row in data table:
      rHE.next()
   enddo // done looping through the table

   // end of the HTML table tag:
   oRep.puts( oHTML.cTab3+[</table>] )
   // turn off the centering
   oRep.puts( oHTML.cTab2+[</center>] )

   // you could add something as a footer here
   // if you wished ...
```

And at the end of the program:

```
   // clean up memory by closing the data objects:
   oHE.active := false
   release object oHE
   oHE = null

   oData.active := false
   release object oData
   oData = null
   // done!
```

Check your work, that's a bit of typing. Once you have checked your work, try running the program. Notice that it runs very quickly!

Try looking at the report by going to the "Other" tab of the Navigator, and double-clicking the report file "HouseholdExpenses2.htm". This should look something like:

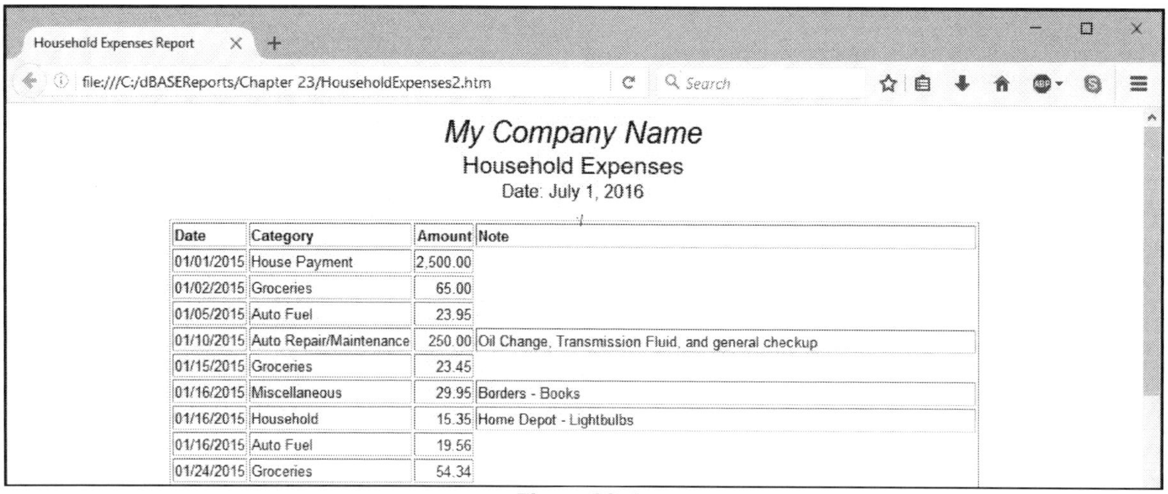

Date	Category	Amount	Note
01/01/2015	House Payment	2,500.00	
01/02/2015	Groceries	65.00	
01/05/2015	Auto Fuel	23.95	
01/10/2015	Auto Repair/Maintenance	250.00	Oil Change, Transmission Fluid, and general checkup
01/15/2015	Groceries	23.45	
01/16/2015	Miscellaneous	29.95	Borders - Books
01/16/2015	Household	15.35	Home Depot - Lightbulbs
01/16/2015	Auto Fuel	19.56	
01/24/2015	Groceries	54.34	

Figure 23-6

You could leave the borders on the table. If you want to remove them, however, you will see that some of the text is very close – the columns are right next to each other. One solution is to insert a blank column between each column with data in it. You have to be careful doing this – there are two places we define table rows, one for the column headings, and another for the data. This is how I would do it (modify the code as shown):

```
// add some column headings:
oRep.puts( oHTML.cTab4+[<tr align="left" style="font-family:Arial; font-size: 10pt;">] )
oRep.puts( oHTML.cTab5+[<th>Date</th>] )
oRep.puts( oHTML.cTab5+[<th>   </th>] )
oRep.puts( oHTML.cTab5+[<th>Category</th>] )
oRep.puts( oHTML.cTab5+[<th>   </th>] )
oRep.puts( oHTML.cTab5+[<th align="right">Amount</th>] )
oRep.puts( oHTML.cTab5+[<th>   </th>] )
oRep.puts( oHTML.cTab5+[<th>Note</th>] )
oRep.puts( oHTML.cTab4+[</tr>] )
```

The HTML element " " is what is called an *entity* and it serves a special purpose – to display some specific character or characters. In this case, we are displaying what is called a "non-breaking space" (NBSP) – or in this case three of them. This will give us three spaces between columns, which will open things up a little in the report. We need to also add something for the data itself:

```
// we start with a table row tag:
oRep.puts( oHTML.cTab4+[<tr valign="top" style="font-family:Arial; font-size: 10pt;">] )
// here's where we put the data that is to be
// displayed for the report - this is with the table data tags:
oRep.puts( oHTML.cTab5+[<td>]+fHE["EntryDate"].value+[</td>] )
oRep.puts( oHTML.cTab5+[<td>   </td>] )
oRep.puts( oHTML.cTab5+[<td>]+fHE["Category"].value+[</td>] )
oRep.puts( oHTML.cTab5+[<td>   </td>] )
// right align the Amount, and format it:
oRep.puts( oHTML.cTab5+[<td align="right">]+;
           transform( fHE["Amount"].value, "9,999.99" )+;
           [</td>] )
oRep.puts( oHTML.cTab5+[<td>   </td>] )
oRep.puts( oHTML.cTab5+[<td>]+fHE["Note"].value+[</td>] )
```

Save this code and re-run the program. You should see something like:

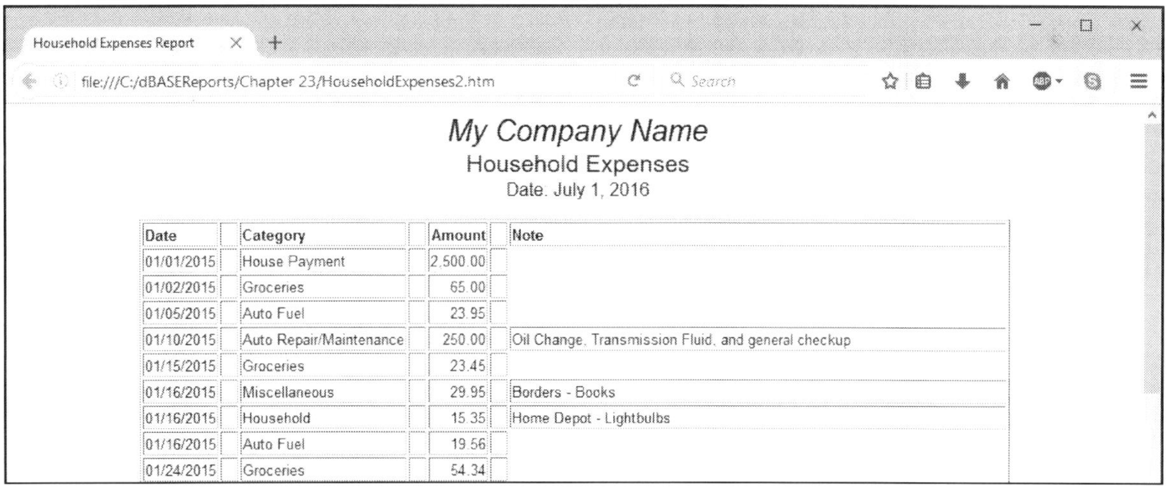

Figure 23-7

This does look a bit odd – the new columns we added give us blank squares in the table. The solution is to remove the border – this is done in one place:

```
// output the beginning of the HTML table:
oRep.puts( oHTML.cTab3+[<table>] )
```

By removing the "border=..." part of the tag, no border will display, and if you run this report again, you should see:

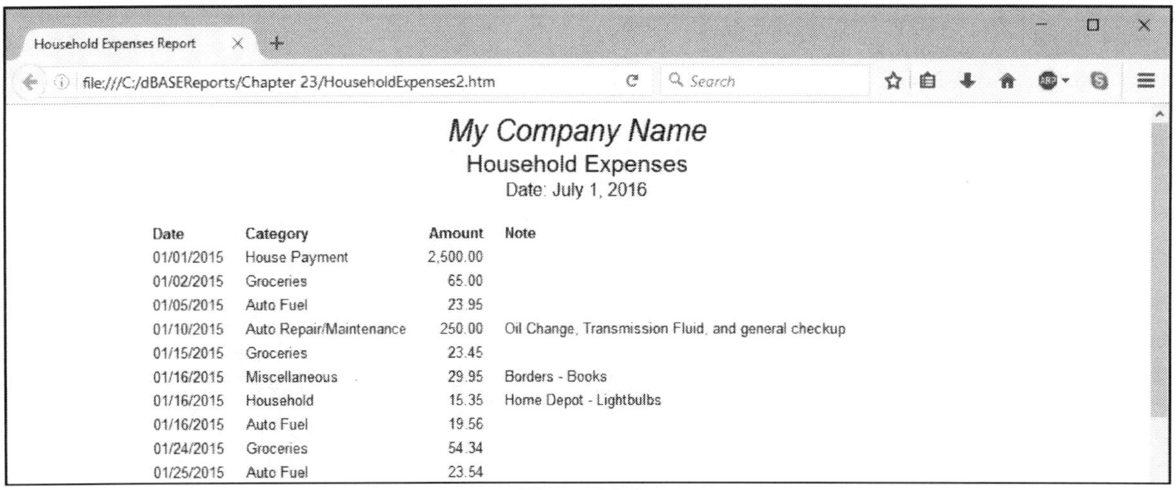

Figure 23-8

The idea here was to give you an idea of what can be done. Using a combination of HTML and CSS (and we barely scratched the surface on both of these), as well as your dBL programming knowledge, you can do a *lot* with creating some good looking reports. We could have modified the code here to display alternating colored rows in the (HTML) table, for example, with very little effort. We could easily add totals as another example. With a bit more work this report could be broken into multiple "pages", with HTML hyperlinks to move back and forth between pages.

What always amazes me as a programmer is just how fast this sort of thing is – if you had a huge table with thousands of records it would not run much slower than what we just did, even if you added totals, and a lot more.

Now that your appetite has been whetted for HTML type reports, if you need to do them, you have a good jumping off place.

NOTE

The HTML Table tags were not really discussed in much detail above, here is a list of what were used:

Begin Tag	End Tag	Definition
<table>	</table>	Table begin/end
<tr>	</tr>	Table row begin/end
<th>	</th>	Table header *(default to bold, centered)*
<td>	</td>	Table data

Those are the actual tags, there are, if you look at the code in the program we built for this chapter, options to modify things such as alignment, and in the table rows font properties were set, and so on.

Cleanup

Create a new report (in the Navigator, click on the .Reports. tab, double-click on the "[New Report]" icon). Select the "File" menu, select "Set Custom Report Class", and in the dialog, click the "Clear Custom Report" button, then click "OK". This clears out the custom report setting in the Plus.ini file, so that the next report you create is not based on this one. Close that report without making any changes.

Make sure the database is closed by going to the Command Window and typing:

```
close databases
```

This will also ensure that you don't end up creating tables in the wrong location, etc.

Source Code

The following is a listing of the sample code in the folders we have been working with. If you downloaded the files from my website the structure will be different (see below). You may use the code contained in these folders for your own applications if you desire, with the caveat that credit be given appropriately.

From working on this chapter:

```
C:\dBASEReports\Chapter 23\Drilldown.htm
C:\dBASEReports\Chapter 23\Drilldown.rep
C:\dBASEReports\Chapter 23\HouseholdExpenses.htm
C:\dBASEReports\Chapter 23\HouseholdExpenses.rep
C:\dBASEReports\Chapter 23\HouseholdExpenses2.htm
C:\dBASEReports\Chapter 23\MyHTML.cc
C:\dBASEReports\Chapter 23\MyHTMLReport.prg
C:\dBASEReports\Chapter 23\trans.gif
```

This last is generated when you create an HTML report from dBASE and is used for spacing ...

Downloaded version – same files but with this path:

```
C:\ReportsBookSourceCode\Chapter 23\filename
```

Summary

While dBASE's Report Engine *can* do HTML reports, as we've seen, you are probably better off coding your own. This will require some work at the beginning of the process, but frankly it will be easier in the long run. You should familiarize yourself with HTML and CSS techniques, which will greatly enhance your abilities to generate simple code that looks really good. We barely touched on either of these. To learn more about HTML and CSS check out your local book store, and also some of the online websites, such as the W3C schools:

```
http://www.w3schools.com
```

This site has a lot of good reference material, and of course just going to a search engine and asking for "HTML Tutorial" or "CSS Tutorial" will likely give you many places you can learn more about these subjects.

For an example of a website that shows some possibilities of what can be done using dBL to generate HTML web pages and reports, visit:

```
http://heralds.westkingdom.org/Awards
```

This site works with a list of over 15,000 entries and growing, and every web page on it is generated by dBL code (this is one of my "strange hobby" things ...), and another example that is even more complex:

```
http://history.westkingdom.org/who.htm
```

Click on any of the letters and a listing of a variety of types of data show up.

The next chapter is going to go over a few topics that are asked about in the newsgroups periodically, and may include some tools that you will find useful.

Chapter 24: Miscellaneous Report Topics

The point of this chapter, which is the last of this book (not counting the appendix), is to cover some issues or topics that don't really fit into the other chapters of this book. You may find answers to some pressing need of your own here.

The Report *title* Property

We didn't discuss this earlier, because it seems a bit odd to have a *title* property for a report as it doesn't display on the report itself. The primary purpose of the *title* property is to display specific text in the report preview window when you run a report without setting the *output* property to something other than the default.

An example would be with the Household Expenses Report we created for Chapter 21 and worked with again in Chapter 23. Using the Navigator make sure you are in the Chapter 23 folder. If you were to go to the Command Window in dBASE and type:

```
set procedure to HouseholdExpenses.rep additive
oRep = new HouseholdExpensesReport()
oRep.render()
```

The title bar of the preview window displays the name of the report file with the word "Report" after it:

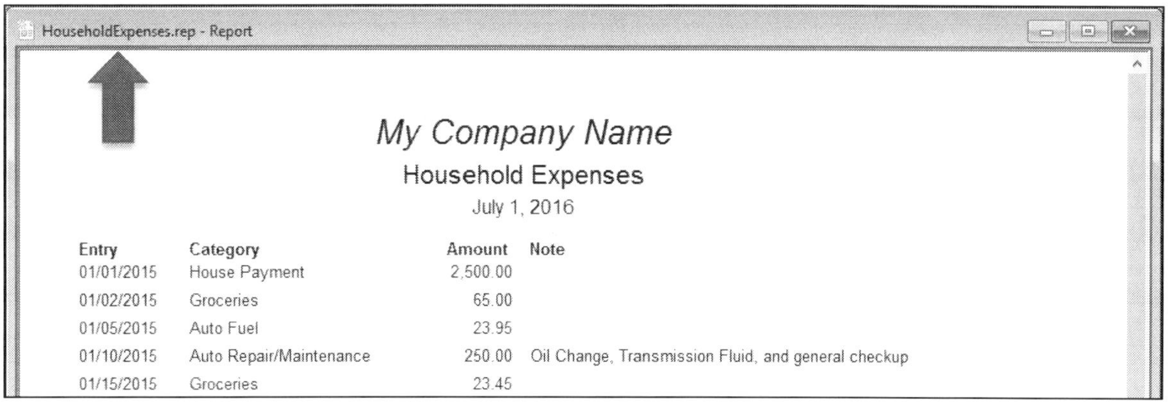

Figure 24-1

On the other hand, if you opted to use the *title* property as in the commands shown below:

```
set procedure to HouseholdExpenses.rep additive
oRep = new HouseholdExpensesReport()
oRep.title := "Household Expenses Report"
oRep.render()
```

The title bar actually displays whatever text you put inside the quotes:

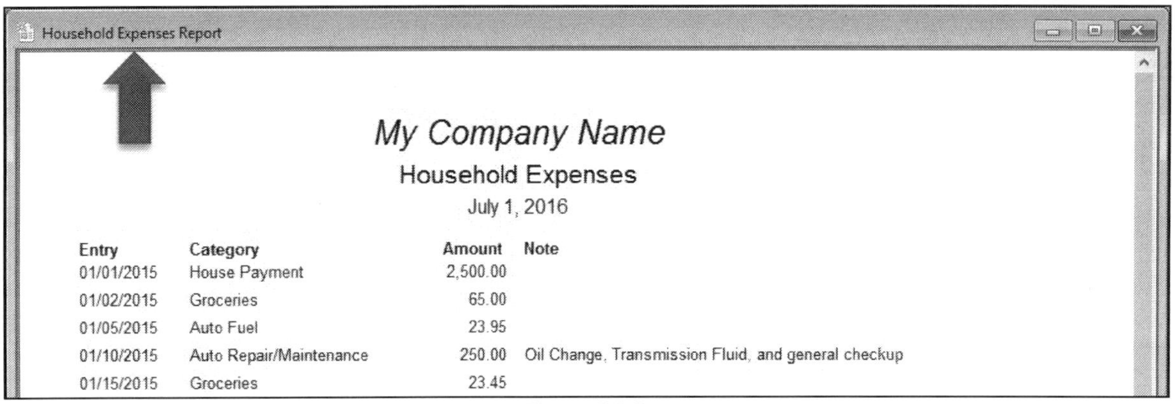

My Company Name

Household Expenses

July 1, 2016

Entry	Category	Amount	Note
01/01/2015	House Payment	2,500.00	
01/02/2015	Groceries	65.00	
01/05/2015	Auto Fuel	23.95	
01/10/2015	Auto Repair/Maintenance	250.00	Oil Change, Transmission Fluid, and general checkup
01/15/2015	Groceries	23.45	

Figure 24-2

Like all report properties, the *title* property of the report can be set in the Report Designer (or added to the code of your report) and it will always be displayed as written.

The Preview form in the dUFLP also checks for the *title* on a report, placing the text in the title bar of the Preview form, if you set one.

This property has at least one other use, which we will discuss later in this chapter when we examine writing reports to PDF files.

Barcodes

Barcodes are useful for applications that track inventory, for some bulk mailing applications, and more. The problem is that dBASE itself does not automatically generate barcodes. The reason? Well, at least in the Windows world of applications, a barcode is simply another font. There are a lot of fonts available with a lot of special purposes (we looked at using a couple in earlier chapters).

If you go online and use Google or some other search engine, and the keyword "barcode", you will find a ton of information about barcodes.

The big question is, how do you use them in dBASE itself?

Writing Barcodes

Writing barcodes is fairly simple. You need (as noted above) a barcode font for the specific type of barcode you need to generate, and it needs to be installed in a way that Windows (and/or your application) can find and use it. If you search the web for "3of9" as a font (you might use in Google, for example the keywords "3 of 9, font", again you will find a lot of possible solutions, including some free versions of a font you can use. I visited one such site:

```
https://www.barcodesinc.com/free-barcode-font/
```

which has a free download of a file called "free3of9.zip".

Open the .zip file when you download it, and double click one of the two files named "fre3of9x.ttf" or "free3of9.ttf". You will be shown a strange looking screen that is simply an attempt to show the font. However at the top of the screen, Windows gives an "Install" button. Click that. The font will now be available for you to use.

You might try creating a sample report, and placing a text control on the report. Set the text control's *fontName* property to the one you just installed (in the case of the one I downloaded from above, it appears in the font dialog as "Free 3 of 9", although the displayed text is a barcode), and set the *fontSize* property fairly large so you can see what you are doing. Then set the *text* of the object to something like:

```
*123456789*
```

The asterisks are the standard delimiters for a barcode – a barcode reader will understand that these are the start and end of the barcode. The text above, when changed to the barcode font in question, should look like:

(This is at a fontsize of 36!)

There are some details in the text file that comes with the font that you may want to read. For example, Word has an autocorrect setting that converts text that starts and ends with asterisks to bold automatically, which I had to turn off for this.

Reading Barcodes

In order to read barcodes into the computer, typically a dBASE application would require a barcode reader that acts as if it were reading into the keyboard. These devices are all different, and the only suggestion I can make here is that if your application requires reading barcodes, that you work with your client and obtain a barcode reader device they intend to use (same make/model), and work with it to make sure it will scan the code it needs to, that your code interacts correctly with it.

Special Fonts and Your Application

I mentioned in at least a couple of the earlier chapters of this book (and the previous section of this chapter) using special fonts for some situations.

I will discuss deploying fonts to your clients later, which obviously would be important.

I want to mention one issue – copyright. If you go out on the web and find a bunch of fonts, some of them are called "freeware", which means that you can use them with no issues, no one is making money off the font, etc. However, some are called "shareware", meaning you should pay for the use of the font if you use it. You can also purchase fonts either singly or in packages. In the case of the shareware or purchased fonts, there is a concern about copyright and your rights when you use those fonts. Some developers allow you, once you have purchased a font, to freely distribute it. Some do not. You should check with these developers – they may require a "per seat" license, for example – where they get a certain amount of money per computer the font is installed on.

Output to PDF

dBASE does not have a native ability to generate PDF files. While this seems like it would be a useful thing, and indeed it has been requested by developers, until or unless this capability is added to dBASE, you will need to use some other means of writing to PDF files.

However, do not despair, this is not as difficult as it might seem. Printing a report to a PDF is really as simple as using a special printer driver that does all the work. You can purchase from Adobe the full Acrobat™ software, but this is not exactly cheap. The reader is free, but the software from Adobe is not.

Again, do not despair. There are plenty of software packages on the market that you can purchase that are not expensive, and will do the job well.

One difficulty is communicating with the printer driver from your dBASE application. You will need to check the documentation for the software to see how that works. Some are easier to work with than others.

For my own applications I have found PDF995 to be an excellent Shareware software package. Shareware is a means of trying a software package before you purchase it. Many Shareware packages are not expensive, but this one surprised me – it's only $10, and it works like a charm, is fast, efficient and does everything I've needed. You can download and try this software at:

```
http://www.pdf995.com
```

Note that this is not a paid advertisement – I am not making any money off this. I just like the software a lot. I am not trying to force anyone to go out and purchase this software, if you are not interested, then you might move on to the next chapter of the book.

Communicating with PDF995 from dBASE

Most of what you need to print to PDF995 is to modify the PDF995.ini file. To do this, I use the INI.CC custom class in the dUFLP. The following code is extracted from a program I use fairly regularly to send reports to PDF995:

```
// see if PDF995 is installed:
/*
   ------------------------------------------------------------------
   IsDir() -- Jim Sare/Ken Mayer -- works on network
   drives and local drives ...   -- updated from FileEx.cc, this
   should work on Windows Vista and Windows 7 where write permissions
   can be a problem -- the older version that this replaces
   had some issues ...

   Usage: IsDir( "some path" )
   Returns: Logical
*/
#ifndef IsDir
    #define isDir(cDir) ( new array().dir( cDir+"\*.", "D" ) > 0 )
#endif

private oReg, nError, hOut, cNewPath, aFiles, oINI, fMessage, aParams, r
private lDone, oFile

if not isdir( "C:\Program Files (x86)\PDF995" )
   msgbox( "PDF995 is not installed, cannot generate PDF Files for Award List.",;
           "PDF995 error", 16 )
   return
else
   cPDF995Path = "C:\Program Files (x86)\PDF995"
```

```
endif

// we need to modify PDF995.ini to handle the path:
set procedure to :dUFLP:ini.cc addi
oINI = new ini( cPDF995Path+"\res\pdf995.ini" )

// save current settings:
cOutPutFolder = oINI.getValue( "Parameters", "Output Folder" )
cInitialDir   = oINI.getValue( "Parameters", "Initial Dir" )
cOutputFile   = oINI.getValue( "Parameters", "Output File" )
// new settings:
oINI.setValue( "Parameters", "Output Folder", cNewPath )
oINI.setValue( "Parameters", "Initial Dir", cNewPath )
oINI.setValue( "Parameters", "Output File", "SAMEASDOCUMENT" )
oINI.flush()

// open report file:
set procedure to AwardList.rep addi

// ================ West Kingdom Reports ===================
// Parameters array:
aParams = new AssocArray()
aParams["OP"] = false
aParams["Region"] = "West"

r = new Alpha2Report()
r.output                 := 1 // Printer
r.printer.printerSource := 2 // Specific
r.printer.printerName   := "PDF995"
r.printer.resolution    := 4 // High
r.params = aParams // use params array
// This needs to change -- it's used for filename:
r.title := "WestAwardList"
// Actually do it
r.render()
```

For a large report, this sometimes takes a bit after the report has been rendered for PDF995 to complete the process. I add some code to test to see if the file exists where it should end up (PDF995 creates the file somewhere else, and then moves it to the "final" location), and I also check to see if it is a minimal size:

```
lDone = false
do while not lDone

   if not file( hOut.cPath+"WestAwardList.pdf" )

      sleep 5 // wait 5 seconds
      loop
   else // file exists, but is it big enough? If it's not
        // at least 120K it's not ...

      nSize = oFile.size( hOut.cPath+"WestAwardList.pdf" ) / 1024

      if int( nSize ) < 120
         sleep 5
         loop
```

```
      else
         lDone = true
      endif
   endif

   if lDone
      exit
   endif
enddo
```

When everything is done (this is an extract from a much larger program), I reset the PDF995.ini file and perform any other cleanup I need to:

```
// reset PDF995.ini file:
// Reset settings:
oINI.setValue( "Parameters", "Output Folder", cOutputFolder )
oINI.setValue( "Parameters", "Initial Dir", cInitialDir )
oINI.setValue( "Parameters", "Output File", cOutputFile )
oINI.flush()
oINI.release()
close procedure :dUFLP:ini.cc

// cleanup
close procedure awardlist.rep
close procedure message2.wfm
fMessage.release()
r.release()
```

The code looks fairly complex at first. The first thing it does is make sure PDF995 is installed on the users' computer by checking for the folder that contains the software using a default location – if you install PDF995 anywhere else, this code would need to be modified. If the software is not installed, then it cancels the rest of the processing for the program.

If it is installed the program changes the default settings for PDF995, which normally asks the user for the location of the PDF file and a filename, to bypass that step, and defines the folder the output should go. Note that it saves the current settings before changing them. It creates a parameter array for the report (this is something discussed in earlier chapters of this book), creates an instance of the report, and sets some report properties to send the output to the PDF995 printer driver. Before rendering the report, notice that the *title* property of the report is set – this is used to name the PDF file that is created. In this example, the file will be called "WestAwardList.pdf" because the *title* property is "WestAwardList".

The next bit of code is to ensure that the file is of a specific size or larger before calling it done. This is to avoid some potential issues later – if the report is not complete and you tried to email it or upload it to an internet server, you might not get the whole report.

Finally we reset the PDF995.ini file to its previous state. This code has been working great for many years with a specific application of my own and generating several PDFs one after the next.

Creating Forms

Normally a dBASE developer thinks of "Forms" as screens or windows in dBASE. When discussing reports, however, a form is something that might be printed as a "pre-printed" form for a customer – or even something where some data is filled in and printed, and a customer must fill in (and perhaps sign), or whatever.

We could spend a bit of time discussing creating these, but really what this sort of thing boils down to is using the controls as we discussed back in Chapter 14. The shape object, using border properties (*borderStyle*) for some objects, creating line objects, combined with text, and even images, can give you some really fancy pre-printed forms. Use of the *fixed* property to ensure some controls (such as lines, rectangles, etc.) don't move can help a lot.

Printing to Pre-Printed Forms

Some clients may have pre-printed Invoice or other forms that you will need to print your reports to. It seems like this should be a difficult task, but really what it boils down to is careful planning and effort on your part.

I had to create a report that printed on a client's pre-printed Invoice forms, which were among other things in three different colors (one for the client, two for filing). The process I found worked well for me was to simply use a ruler that matched the *metric* property of the report (if the metric property is set to Inches, use a ruler that gives you values in inches), and design the report, placing the text controls where they need to be, either on the *pageTemplate*, the *detailBand*, or wherever necessary, using measurements you have taken from the form.

However, that is seldom enough, and you will want to do some trial-and-error printing. If you do not have lots of copies of the pre-printed forms (my client gave me only one), then best thing to do is print on plain paper, and hold the form up either in front of, or behind, the test print. Check to make sure everything lines up. If it doesn't (and it probably won't the first time), do some minor changes, move things as needed, etc.

What this process really boils down to is a lot of patience and trial-and-error. There is no hard and fast rule for doing this that I can give. In my particular case, in the program that generates the report I added a call to the dBASE *msgbox()* function telling the user to make sure the printer had enough copies of the form (they can print lots of invoices at one time) and when the *choosePrinter()* dialog comes up to click the "Collate" checkbox (for multiple copies of the invoice, that was important); the code sets the report's printer object's *copies* property to 3 among other things (there is code elsewhere to select which invoices to print and all that); and when the printing is done it reminds the user through another call to the *msgbox()* to remove the invoice forms from the printer's paper tray (otherwise the next report printed would be on those forms).

Tractor Feed Printers

John Creed wrote an article for dBulletin on this exact topic, but I thought I'd summarize the basics of what needs to be done. If you need more information, please check out dBulletin, issue 16, the article is titled "Custom Tractor-Feed Printers in Windows" (http://www.jpmartel.com/bu16_b.htm).

A "Tractor Feed" printer is typically (although not always) a dot-matrix printer. The one thing these are great for is unusual sized paper and forms. While some laser and inkjet printers can handle them, these are great for some situations.

The basics for using a tractor-feed printer, and using custom sized paper (if you are using standard 8.5" by 11" paper, for example, this is not something you should have to worry about), are:

- The end-user's (client, etc.) computer must have a new printer set up – this can be using a printer driver that is already installed, but you must very specifically set up a new printer.
- Give it a unique name.
- Set the custom paper size.

This seems simple enough. Of course, different operating systems (different versions of Windows) handle this differently, and upgrading from an older version of Windows to a newer one will not generally bring custom printer settings across – so if your client upgrades, then this will need to be done again. Indeed if this is on a multi-user (networked for example) system, then each computer would need to have the same process repeated.

Your report or program that sends the report to the printer might require that you set the report object's *output* to "1" (for "Printer"), the *printerSource* to "2" (for "Specific"), and the *printerName* property needs to be set to the unique name mentioned above. While you could hardcode this in the report by setting these properties, you could also let the user select the printer using the *choosePrinter()* method as well, but you would want to make sure the instructions for the user were very clear.

Deploying Reports and Associated Files

The following assumes you are using Project files to deploy applications. More details on these can be found in The dBASE Book.

When you work with custom reports and custom controls for reports, it becomes really important to be sure to include *everything* necessary for your reports to run properly in the Project File. For example, most of the reports created in the various chapters of this book rely on at least one Custom Report. The Project Explorer in dBASE does not automatically include these files. We also used various custom classes, and again the Project Explorer will not automatically find these files.

When we worked on our reports, most of them used:

- MyCompanyReport.crp
- base.crp

While it wasn't obvious that "base.crp" was used, the other custom reports were all derived from that one. When you deploy your application you would need to include both of these files in the Project as well as any reports derived from them.

In addition, our reports used:

- MyReportControls.cc
- PageNumber.cc

And again your Project would need to include these. If you used any custom controls from the dUFLP, you would need to include those in the Project as well.

If your reports used any graphics (that weren't included in a table, such as the Fish table), you would need to deploy those as well.

Fonts

Fonts are not as easy to deploy, because the Project Explorer in dBASE doesn't know how to work with them without a lot of work. When I work with Inno Setup to deploy applications, I don't rely on the Project Explorer to communicate with it.

You have to include the truetype or other font file you need to install in the [Files] section:

```
[Files]
; This is one statement and should not wrap inside Inno Setup
Source: "C:\Windows\Fonts\Blackcha.TTF"; DestDir: "{fonts}";
FontInstall: "Black Chancery Medium"; Flags: onlyifdoesntexist
uninsneveruninstall
```

You need to include the file path for the Source or Inno Setup will assume the folder your application is in. There is more information in the help for Inno Setup as well (including a flag for non-TrueType fonts).

One thing to keep in mind when you deploy fonts to your clients is that if the font is on their machine, they can use it for other things, which may violate any licensing agreements you have with the creator of the font.

Using the Windows API through dBASE

In the dUFLP is a file called FontSetter.cc – this small custom class file has methods that allow adding a font to the Windows Registry and removing it, as needed. The biggest advantage to this is that you could deploy a font with your application and just place it in the same folder as the main program files, or in some related folder. In your startup code you could register the font, and then when the application closed you could unregister it, thus making the font available for only your application. This is something definitely worth checking out if you are concerned about copyright issues for fonts, or if you just don't want the font installed to the main Windows fonts folder.

Cleanup

Create a new report (in the Navigator, click on the .Reports. tab, double-click on the "[New Report]" icon). Select the "File" menu, select "Set Custom Report Class", and in the dialog, click the "Clear Custom Report" button, then click "OK". This clears out the custom report setting in the Plus.ini file, so that the next report you create is not based on this one. Close that report without making any changes.

Make sure the database is closed by going to the Command Window and typing:

```
close databases
```

This will also ensure that you don't end up creating tables in the wrong location, etc.

Summary

This chapter, as noted in the introduction to it, was meant to give you at least a bit of discussion about some topics that come up fairly regularly in the dBASE newsgroups but were not covered elsewhere in this book.

As you have hopefully seen by working your way through this book, the Report Engine (and Report Designer) are capable of a lot of things. Hopefully this book covers most of what you need to know, or at least given you enough knowledge to puzzle out how to do what you need to do.

Appendix

With all the coverage of the Report Designer and the Report Engine in dBASE, I thought it only fair to mention that there are other ways to do reports from dBASE. In most cases these are other software packages, but take a look. I am not going to go into any depth at all here on how to actually use these, but thought they should at least be mentioned.

The dUFLP

Discussed in several places in this book, the dUFLP (dBASE Users' Function Library Project) was created by this author so long ago that I couldn't give a date (the late 80s?). It was at a time when there was no such library of freeware code, and I was collecting useful bits from everywhere I could find it – books, other developers who posted code, from various technical articles put out by Ashton-Tate, Borland, and so on. It is a freeware library of code, maintained by yours truly, updated periodically with new code and improvements to existing code. If you want to try something that you have seen done the odds are there is something in this library that can help you accomplish what you need. It can be downloaded from here:

```
http://www.goldenstag.net/dbase/#duflp
```

Be sure to read the setup instructions (this is also discussed in Chapter 3 of this book).

Streaming Output

The dBASE Language (dBL) has embedded in it a fairly robust, but hard to use *(as there is no visual frontend)* output tool called "Streaming Output". This is the use of the ?, ?? and ??? commands, with some *style* options, to output text to the printer or a text file. This is all done by hand, and frankly there are some problems with it – mostly the complexity of the code necessary to generate a good looking report.

Streaming in this fashion is really "old school", but if you look in the online help for dBASE under "PRINTJOB", or "?" you will find the beginning of what can be done.

To get you started, a simple bit of code (this has been tested – it outputs to the Command Window):

```
open database dbasereports
set database to dbasereports
use dogs order name
PRINTJOB
   bodystyle = "Arial, 9, Swiss"
   scan
      ? name at 5 style bodystyle
      ?? born at 40 style bodystyle
   endscan
ENDPRINTJOB
use
close databases
```

In order to actually send this to the printer you would need to take some additional steps.

If you are interested in some examples, take a look at this old dBASE Advisor article I wrote (November, 1995):

```
http://www.goldenstag.net/dbase/dBASEAdvisor/dBASEAdvisor_1995_11.pdf
```

I am pretty sure I wrote some other articles about this, but sadly over the years I have gotten rid of old CDs from conferences and don't wish to spend hours going through conference notes (which oddly I still have) to find the articles.

I wanted to mention it here in an attempt to be thorough, but frankly it is not highly recommended.

QR3 – by Ronnie MacGregor

If you spend much time in the dBASE newsgroups, you will have seen the name of this author. He's a friendly person, easy to talk to, and an excellent coder. He wrote "QR3" as a means of generating dBASE reports, using the Report Engine, but not using the dBASE Report Designer.

There is an article on using this in dBulletin issue 9 by Bob Rimmington – the title is a bit misleading because the Ronnie later changed the name of it. The title of the article is User Report Generator (URG), and there is another article in dBulletin, issue 18 titled Quick Reports 3 by Ronnie himself on using this program.
This article can be gotten at any of the websites that mirror the dBulletin, and of course from the original. The article on QR3 can be found here:

```
http://www.jpmartel.com/bu18_d.htm
```

You can download QR3 from the article itself, so there's no need for another URL here.

List & Label

At the German dBASE Developer's Conference DBKON 2002, List & Label was introduced. Unfortunately, the only article I can find on this is in German, by Lutz Conrad, in dBulletin, the article is titled: Reporting mit dBASE Alternativen zum internen Reportgenerator, and is in dBulletin issue 20:

```
http://www.jpmartel.com/bu20_d.htm
```

This appears to also have been written in dBASE itself, and maybe at some point someone can translate the article so that those of us who do not read German can learn how to use it. It has some capabilities from what I can figure out that the dBASE Report Engine does not, including the ability to print to PDF.

Crystal Reports

When dBASE 5.0 for Windows was first introduced, an arrangement had been made by the developers of Crystal Reports to include a version that worked with the dBASE QBE files ("Query By Example"), and with dBASE tables directly. This version worked fine with dBASE 5.0 for Windows and with Visual dBASE versions 5.5 through 5.7. However, when developers moved from the 16-bit versions of dBASE to the 32-bit, Crystal Reports did not come across. There were multiple reasons for this, including a change of ownership of Crystal Reports (which was purchased I believe by Seagate at the time), and the fact that the R&D team at Borland was creating a new Report Engine for Visual dBASE 7.0.

Note that Crystal Reports is a commercial software package, and so you would want to deal with any issues involved in deploying an application of your own that used it, including any fees that would be owed the corporation that owns and developers Crystal Reports (now SAP from the looks of things). You can find out more about the software directly from SAP at:

```
https://www.sapstore.com/solutions/99013/SAP-Crystal-Reports-
2013?countryCode=US&url_id=text-ww-sapstore-microsoft-shell-cr
```

What this meant is that those who really liked working with Crystal Reports were sort of left out in the cold. Current versions of Crystal Reports do not have the direct interaction with dBASE tables and more importantly with data modules (the 32-bit version of the QBE file).

That said, there are developers working with Crystal Reports in its current incarnation with dBASE. There is an article in dBulletin issue 14, by Michael Kusch (translated by Jason Walker) that discusses using Crystal Reports 7 with dBASE through the use of the Crystal Reports ActiveX control:

```
http://www.jpmartel.com/bu14_a.htm
```

This article has not been updated for the most recent versions of Crystal Reports, but it should help if you are interested in working with Crystal Reports.

Using dQuery to Create Reports

Let's cut this really short – I left the heading in because it was in the first edition of the book. However, please note that dQuery no longer ships with dBASE. There used to be a separate product that you could purchase from dBASE, LLC called dQuery™, but it is no longer integrated into dBASE itself *(looking at products sold by dBASE, I don't see this anymore)*. There is no need to get into a lengthy discussion of working with this and your dBASE applications at this time.

NOTES:

Index

_

/

A

B

C

D

E

F

G

H

I

J

L

M

N

U

V

W

X

Z

Made in United States
Orlando, FL
04 November 2026

90206098R00234